THE INSIDERS'® GUIDE TO

NORTH CAROLINA'S Outer Banks

D1069685

———— ❋♡❋ ————

This book is dedicated to the
sweet memory of

Cameron Miller McOwen
July 1997 - May 1998

We at Insiders' Publishing are richer
because he chose to be among us for this
short time. We will never forget his
strong spirit and laughing eyes.

——————————

THE INSIDERS' GUIDE TO

NORTH CAROLINA'S Outer Banks

by
Catherine Kozak
and
Mary Ellen Riddle

Insiders' Publishing
105 Budleigh St.
P.O. Box 2057
Manteo, NC 27954
(252) 473-6100
www.insiders.com

Sales and Marketing:
Falcon Publishing, Inc.
P.O. Box 1718
Helena, MT 59624
(800) 582-2665
www.falconguide.com

•

19th EDITION
1st printing

•

Publications from The Insiders' Guide®
series are available at special discounts for
bulk purchases for sales promotions,
premiums or fundraisings. Special editions,
including personalized covers, can be
created in large quantities for special
needs. For more information, please write
to Karen Bachman, Insiders' Publishing,
P.O. Box 2057, Manteo, NC 27954, or call
(800) 765-2665 Ext. 241.

ISBN 1-57380-068-6

Insiders' Publishing

Publisher/Editor-in-Chief
Beth P. Storie

Advertising Director/
General Manager
Michael McOwen

Creative Services Director
Giles MacMillan

Art Director
David Haynes

Managing Editor
Dave McCarter

Project Editor
Bridget Millsaps

Project Artist
David Todd

Project Manager
Georgia Beach

Insiders' Publishing
An imprint of Falcon Publishing Inc.
A Landmark Communications company.

Preface

The Outer Banks is not conveniently located. Two-, three-, four-hour drives are expected and routine to the residents who live here. Our work force is geared to seasons and tourism, and sometimes it's hard to make a good living. Shopping is limited; services, though far more complete than in recent history, are patchworked. Those of us who live here shrug and smile — it's a trade-off that is heavily weighted toward the good life. We're blessed, and we know it.

On NASA aerial maps, our strand of sand may look like the continent's afterthought, but our land was the welcome mat to the first English-speaking settlers in the country. The Outer Banks is stranded farther away from its main coast than any other barrier islands in the world. Although the shore has very slowly over the centuries crept west, it still stubbornly and mysteriously maintains its crooked post miles out into the Atlantic. Buffeted century after century by storms — many escorted by the nearby mighty Gulf Stream — the geology of these narrow, low-slung islands is unique in its steadfast adaptability. Its inhabitants have been no less resilient. When you step foot on these sandy shores, you will join a legion of steely adventurers, renegade thinkers and rugged survivors who have been captivated by the unbidden forces of nature.

Welcome to the land of beginnings! Feast your senses on wide beaches, whispering sea oats and undulating dunes — a land where the pace of life is geared to the unceasing sand-sharpened breezes and wild winds. From the gifts and punishment of the glorious and untamed waters of these indomitable islands have sprung heroes, pioneers, pirates and inventors. Tales of courage and creativity, bloody battles and savage shipwrecks, resourcefulness and compassion: All are part of the mystique of the Outer Banks.

Here, the first English colonists set up camp. Blackbeard and his band of buccaneers anchored sloops along the shallow sounds. Wilbur and Orville Wright also flew the world's first airplane, buoyed by stiff winter winds and brazen determination.

From remote national wildlife refuges, sheltered seashores and protected maritime forests to upscale resort communities, these strips of shifting sand offer both peaceful retreat and awesome adventure. Windsurf or Jet Ski. Surf fish or stroll the endless beaches. Charter a deep-sea fishing boat and fight an ocean giant. Grab the binoculars, and watch birds. Soar from the East Coast's highest sand dune in a hang glider. Catch some waves, and surf some of the best swells on the Atlantic Seaboard as the breakers barrel toward the beach. It's all here for the choosing, and boredom is not an option.

Only in the last 15 years or so have these ribbons of sand confronted the rapid-fire development that other coastal areas saw years earlier. One of only four states in the nation that forbids hard structures like seawalls, which can cause severe narrowing of beaches, North Carolina learned the tough lessons of coastal management by watching the mistakes of other ocean states. To a large extent, the Outer Banks owes its still healthy, wide beaches to the luck of its relatively late bloom. Isolated geographically by fences of water, the barrier islands were accessible only by boat until the 1930s, when the first major bridges from the mainland were constructed. Once travel improved, word of the Outer Banks' lovely weather and beautiful beaches spread, and vacationers and transplants poured in a steady stream over the shallow sounds, fishing rods and bathing suits ready.

Life on the Outer Banks has changed dramatically since then, but much of the beauty and color remains unsullied. Native families, many descendents of shipwreck survivors, still make their livings through commercial fishing. Much of the seafood we are so famous for here is caught locally by fifth-generation watermen. A visitor to Colington, Wanchese, Hatteras Island or Ocracoke will mingle among people who speak with the distinctive Outer Banks brogue, an accent carried over by English settlers and sustained by centuries of isolation.

Four lighthouses (Currituck's red brick beacon, the inland light at Bodie Island, Cape Hatteras's famous candy-striped tower and the squat, whitewashed watchdog on Ocracoke Island), once sentinels for sailors traversing the shipwreck-strewn Graveyard of the Atlantic, dot these storm-swept shores.

Wild horses roam the northernmost protected refuges, descendants, some believe, of Spanish mustangs that swam ashore from shipwrecks more than three centuries ago. Waterfowl abound throughout these islands and the peninsula, attracting bird-watchers, hunters and long-lens photographers. The East Coast's best fishing also awaits anglers on the decks of offshore charter boats, atop numerous piers and bridges, and off miles of ocean and sound shores.

There are plenty of biking and in-line skating paths along flat roadways, and horses can be rented for leisurely strolls along the ocean and dirt roads through the island marshlands.

Painters, sculptors and other artisans open their galleries to browsers in almost every local village. Musicians, comedians and poets provide evening entertainment in a variety of cafes and nightclubs. The entire family can cuddle up under the stars at Roanoke Island's Waterside Theater and watch the acclaimed historical production *The Lost Colony*, the longest-running outdoor summer theater drama in the nation.

Despite its rise as a favorite resort destination, the Outer Banks continues to be a kickback kind of place. You don't have to dress up here. Shorts and sandals are the accepted garb in even the finest locales. Shrimp and crab, dozens of species of fresh-caught fish, often hauled in that very day by Outer Banks fishermen, are available at nearly every one of the slew of restaurants that serves tourists and locals alike.

While you're trekking the dunes, frolicking in the pristine waters or enjoying the Carolina blue skies and eye-popping sunsets, don't forget that the magic of these freak-of-nature overgrown sand bars has inspired some of the most dramatic moments in American history. Remember that you are walking the sands of some of the most dynamic barrier islands on earth.

Some things have stayed the same since Sir Walter Raleigh's party first laid eyes on Roanoke Island more than 400 years ago. These barrier beaches still startle visitors as well as natives with their rugged beauty and capricious topography. The fragile landscape remains at the mercy of the sea, furious with storm one season, calm and glittering the next.

Summer isn't the only time to enjoy the Outer Banks, although the season from Memorial Day through Labor Day is by far the most packed with people and things to do. Fall offers fabulous fishing and windsurfing; spring brings bird-watching and bicycling. And winter is deliciously devoid of almost everyone.

Spend a little time here, and you'll understand why many of us came back to stay — or never left. We hope this book helps you find exactly what you want in your visit to our vibrant barrier beaches.

About the Authors

Catherine Kozak

A suburban girl raised a half-hour from New York City, Catherine was bewitched early on by the din and edgy vibrancy of Manhattan. Countless jaunts from her sleepy Jersey suburb into one of the wackiest, most wretched and wonderfully wild metropolises in the world gave her a keen insight into the virtue of contrasts. After ricocheting from coast to coast and points in between for 20 years since leaving the Northeast, a fortuitous soft landing on the Outer Banks more than three years ago has convinced Catherine that dynamic places take very different forms.

She's found these barrier islands, so tenuously anchored in the glorious, cranky Atlantic, most suitably robust. On the Outer Banks, weather is king; the waters enforce the laws of the land. From her first wind-whipped, salty moment on the wide-open beaches here, Catherine was entranced by the rough-hewn spirit of its people and landscape.

A staff writer for *The Virginian-Pilot's* North Carolina bureau in Nags Head, Catherine took the life-experience route before finally securing a degree in journalism from State University of New York at New Paltz in 1990. After the math requirement spooked her away from her initial career choice in wildlife management in the late '70s, Catherine left school and ventured across the country, the first of many road trips that fostered her delight in regional America.

A subsequent five-year roost on the beautiful central California coast primed her passionate regard for spectacular bodies of water. She moved to the Outer Banks in 1995 and the allure of the Atlantic swallowed her whole. Before relocating to these magical barrier islands, Catherine covered state politics in Albany, New York, as an intern at the *Legislative Gazette*. She most recently lived in Saugerties, New York, where she freelanced for daily and weekly newspapers and regional newsletters. As a member of the team for the *Kingston Daily Freeman* that reported on the Woodstock '94 music festival, she won the New York Newspaper Publishers Association distinguished local reporting award of excellence.

After moving to the Outer Banks, she freelanced for various publications, including *The Virginian-Pilot* and its free weekly tabloid *The Coast*, where she now works. To Catherine, there is no better job than writing about people, places and events. Although her duties have included banding pelicans, conversing with renowned scientists and meeting numerous celebrated personalities, the most rewarding part of her job is mingling with the everyday folk that make the Outer Banks so special.

Catherine lives with her partner, Drew, and her children Jake, 17, and twins Casey and Dylan, 9, in a canalfront house that is visited nightly by pastel sunsets, shimmering moon glow and glittering stars. She loves to read, collect books and haunt libraries, and she refuses to get cable television.

Mary Ellen Riddle

Mary Ellen Riddle was born and raised in the northeastern United States, then moved to North Carolina in 1973 to attend art school at East Carolina University. She earned an undergraduate degree in fine art and has spent her career working in media as a writer, photographer, illustrator and radio newscaster.

Mary Ellen currently writes a weekly art review column featuring profiles, show reviews and educational issues for *The Virginian-Pilot's* weekly tabloid, *The Coast*. She is the art editor for the *North Beach Sun*. She's a feature writer for the national publication *The Sportfishing Report*. Mary Ellen is a practicing fine art black-and-white photographer. A wall mural she painted of flora and fauna indigenous to North Carolina is on permanent display at the Museum of Natural History in Raleigh.

As a supporter of the arts, it is Mary Ellen's goal to put the Outer Banks on the map as a bonafide cultural arts community. In her literary focus on the arts, she avoids conventional art critiques and rather looks to nurture the creative spark we all possess.

Mary Ellen loves to read and collect books.

She has seven brothers and sisters and two children. Despite having grown up traveling back and forth to New York City with her father, she enjoys the small-town feel of her island home. She occasionally longs for the fast pace of the city but is content to reside on Roanoke Island, home to clean air, nearby beaches, quiet evenings and neighborhood get-togethers.

Mary Ellen looks forward to creating time for making art and creative writing. Parenting is her biggest challenge and greatest joy.

Acknowledgments

Mary Ellen Riddle

I am grateful to the many people who supplied me with information to include in The Insiders' Guide® to North Carolina's Outer Banks. Each kernel of data played a valuable role in the construction of a usable and up-to-date manual. Special thanks goes to Richard Hess, who always has time for my multiple calls and questions on real estate. I am especially grateful for his knowledge and ability to correctly analyze a mercurial field. Joe Malat is my fishing expert. His congenial nature and willingness to share a broad base of knowledge always is helpful. Sharon Miller in Ocracoke always fills in the gaps when it comes to life and changes on that sandy haven. Gee Gee Rossell helps bring Hatteras Island to life with her poignant observances of island life. Thanks to Steve Brumfield for his insights into the nature of an island economy and to Lane DeGregory for sharing information on the Hatteras digs.

Special thanks to John Harper, who supplies sustenance, child care, Diet Cokes, Mint Milanos . . . the essentials. Thanks to my editor Bridget Millsaps, whose insights were necessary and helpful, and to managing editor Dave McCarter, whose keen eye gives the book a final stamp of approval. My co-author Cate is a friend in a very special category . . . a lifer! We are bonded by our walk through fire. I thank my son Christopher and daughter Zoe, who bring me joy. Warm regards to The GG's: my dear friends Linda Ritchie Crassons, Dawn Enochs and Chris Kidder, who form a humorous and strong alliance against the pesky little annoyances of life.

Catherine Kozak

When you take on a project this big, it's good to think about farm families and fishermen and women in labor — you work as hard as you have to until the work is done. Through many a long night and weekend researching, fact-checking and writing this book, I've stifled a whine, gritted my teeth and pushed on after checking in with the big picture. The truth is, authoring the 19th edition of this book has been a wonderful stretch. I've learned more about the home that I've adopted, the characters that people these quirky, down-to-earth (sand?) islands and, frankly, myself, than I could've predicted.

Corny though it might sound, I really must first thank the hundreds of hard-working folk I phoned, people who put aside what they were doing, often at most inconvenient times, to be helpful. Most people I talked to were patient and respectful: I'm working, she's working, seemed to be the general attitude. I admire the spunk and dedication of our labor force on these isolated islands, and this experience has made me proud to be one of its many interlocking links.

Next, thank you to Beth Storie for again having confidence in my abilities and allowing me to take on this challenge. And to Dave, I am grateful for your straightforwardness and respect as an editor. Not to forget Bridget — your cheeriness made the job much easier during the rough spots. Special thanks go to Lane DeGregory, my colleague and friend who did such fine work on the 17th edition of this book, making my job on the 18th and 19th much easier. Your shoes were tough to fill, and your faith in me meant a lot. And to Mary Ellen, my patient co-author: We've weathered a lot, individually and together, in the these last years while writing this book. Your friendship has been invaluable through the thick of it all. You've been a strong shoulder to cry on and a wonderful companion to giggle and gossip with — when we had time. Much gratitude also goes to my colleagues at The Virginian-Pilot: to Drew, for scouting for the photographs I needed without complaining and for feeding me valuable tid-

bits; to Rob, who let me work around book deadlines without once trying to make me feel guilty; and to Paul and Susan for listening.

My family deserves much appreciation. Thank you to my parents for teaching me perseverance and for tolerating my unavoidable neglect. You taught me the virtue of hard work, honesty and self-respect, and that's served me well in this past year. And to my brothers Steve, Gary and Kevin: What's better — an Emmy, CD recordings, a book or a house? Let's ask Mom and Dad. Thanks for your support, despite my doubts (and yours). But most important, thank you to Jake, Casey and Dylan, my children, who put up with my absence and did their best to learn to wait.

And finally, to Drew, the man of my dreams. You've taught me so much about this area we call home . Through all of the long weekends and nights that I've worked on this book, your love has held me steady. You've supported me and boosted me up through thick and thin. My deep love and appreciation are for you, my dearest friend and closest companion.

Table of Contents

Directory of Maps

Distances To The Outer Banks

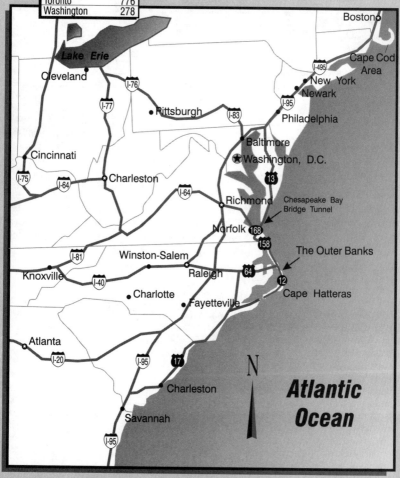

The Outer Banks

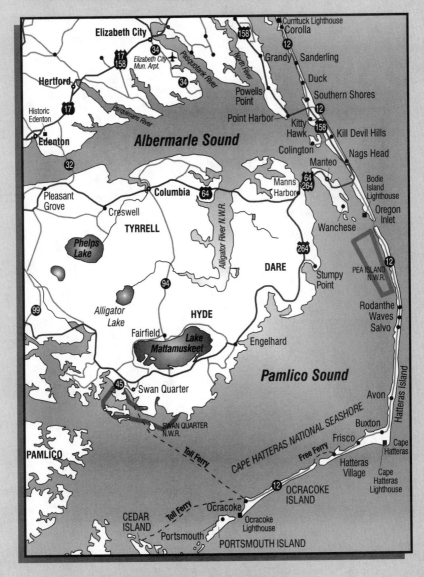

Northern Beaches

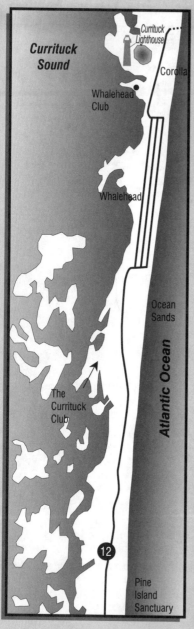

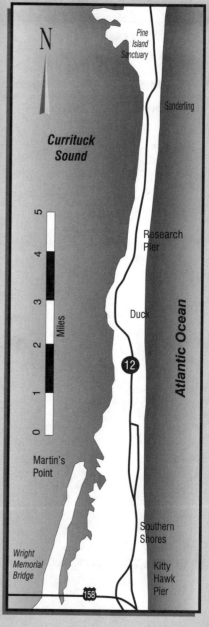

Kitty Hawk & Southern Shores

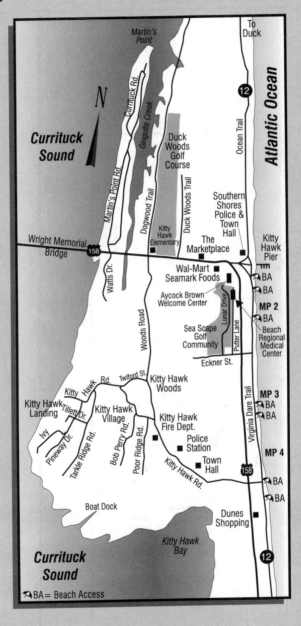

Kill Devil Hills

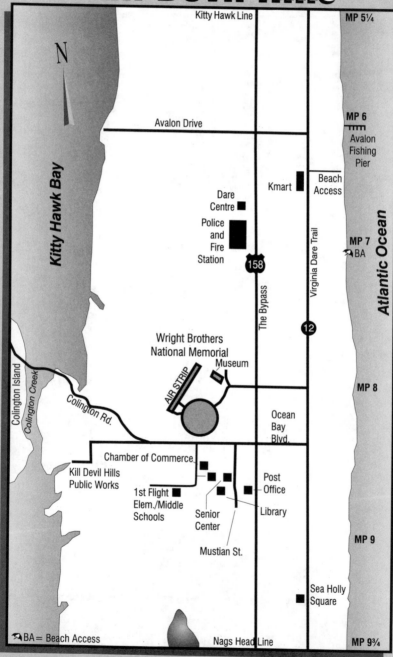

Kitty Hawk Line

MP 5¼

N

Avalon Drive

MP 6

Avalon Fishing Pier

Kitty Hawk Bay

Kmart

Beach Access

Dare Centre

Police and Fire Station

MP 7
⌂BA

158

The Bypass

Virginia Dare Trail

Atlantic Ocean

12

Wright Brothers National Memorial

Museum

MP 8

AIR STRIP

Colington Island

Colington Creek

Colington Rd.

Ocean Bay Blvd.

Chamber of Commerce

Kill Devil Hills Public Works

1st Flight Elem./Middle Schools

Senior Center

Post Office

Library

Mustian St.

MP 9

Sea Holly Square

⌂BA= Beach Access

Nags Head Line

MP 9¾

Wright Brothers National Memorial

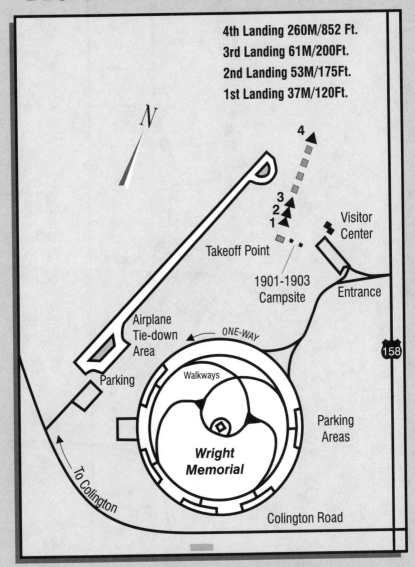

4th Landing 260M/852 Ft.
3rd Landing 61M/200Ft.
2nd Landing 53M/175Ft.
1st Landing 37M/120Ft.

N

4

3
2
1

Visitor
Center

Takeoff Point

1901-1903
Campsite

Entrance

Airplane
Tie-down
Area

ONE-WAY

Parking

Walkways

158

*Wright
Memorial*

Parking
Areas

To Collington

Colington Road

Nags Head

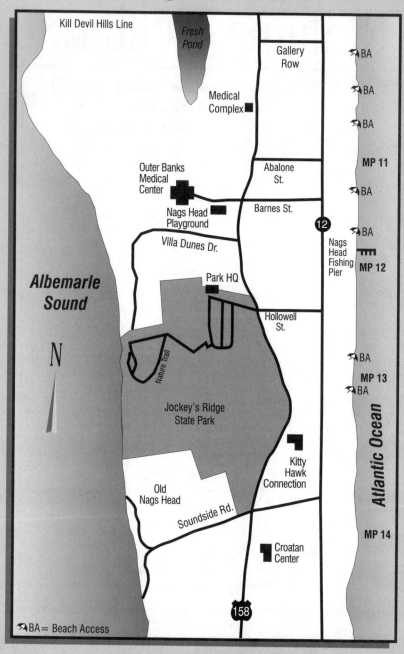

Kill Devil Hills Line

Fresh Pond

Gallery Row

Medical Complex ■

Outer Banks Medical Center

Nags Head Playground

Villa Dunes Dr.

Abalone St.

Barnes St.

Albemarle Sound

N

Park HQ

Nature Trail

Hollowell St.

Jockey's Ridge State Park

Kitty Hawk Connection

Old Nags Head

Soundside Rd.

Croatan Center

MP 11

BA

BA

12

Nags Head Fishing Pier **MP 12**

MP 13
BA

BA

Atlantic Ocean

MP 14

158

BA = Beach Access

Nags Head (Cont.)

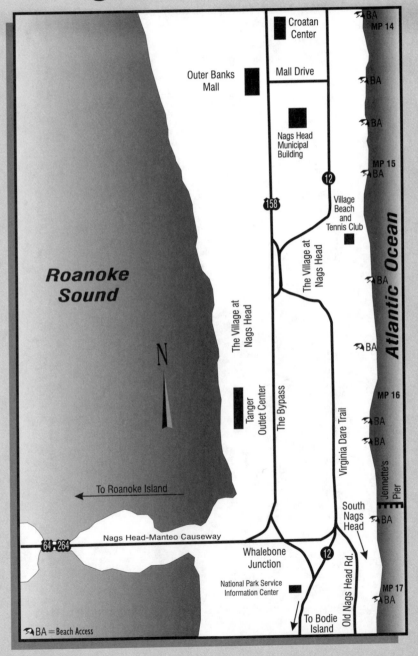

Roanoke Island

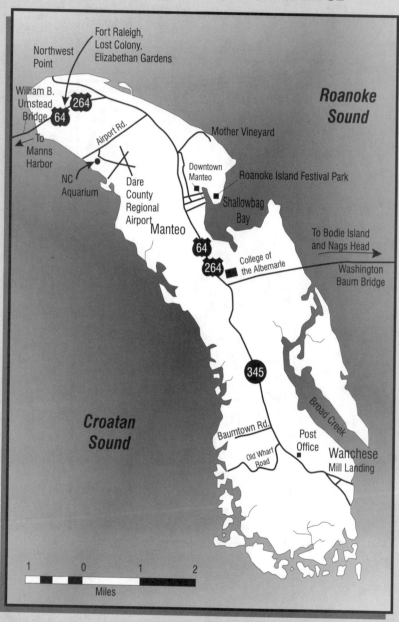

Northwest Point

Fort Raleigh, Lost Colony, Elizabethan Gardens

William B. Umstead Bridge

To Manns Harbor

264

64

Airport Rd.

Mother Vineyard

NC Aquarium

Dare County Regional Airport

Downtown Manteo

Roanoke Island Festival Park

Manteo

Shallowbag Bay

64

264

College of the Albemarle

Roanoke Sound

To Bodie Island and Nags Head

Washington Baum Bridge

345

Broad Creek

Croatan Sound

Baumtown Rd.

Old Wharf Road

Post Office

Wanchese

Mill Landing

1 0 1 2

Miles

Fort Raleigh
National Historic Site

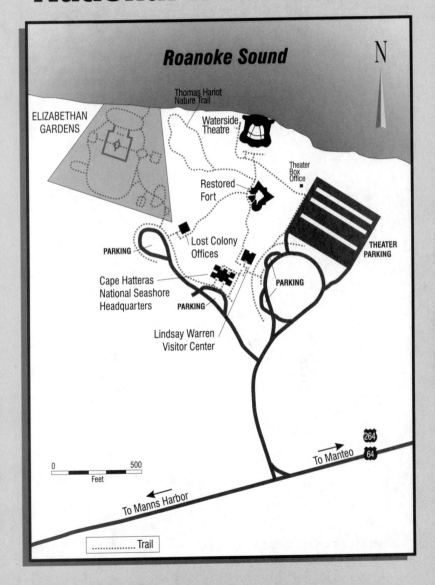

Downtown Manteo

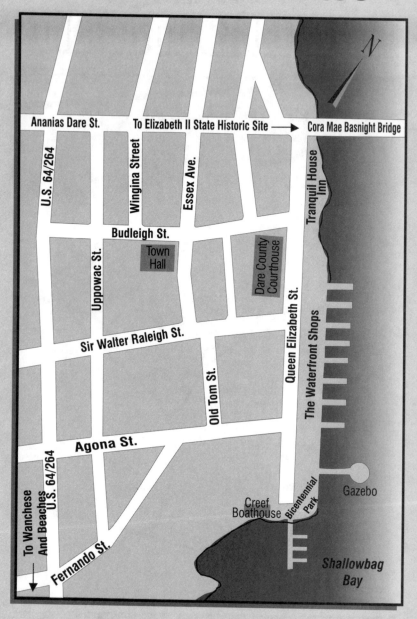

Roanoke Island Festival Park

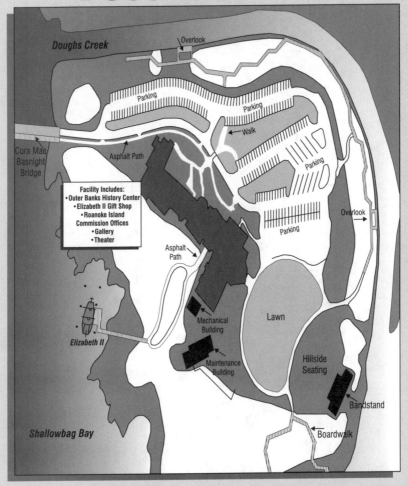

Bodie Island

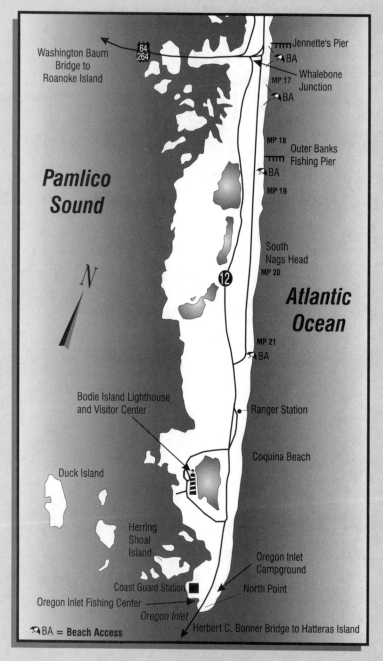

Washington Baum Bridge to Roanoke Island

64 264

Jennette's Pier

BA

Whalebone Junction

MP 17

BA

Pamlico Sound

MP 18

Outer Banks Fishing Pier

BA

MP 19

South Nags Head

MP 20

N

12

Atlantic Ocean

MP 21

BA

Bodie Island Lighthouse and Visitor Center

Ranger Station

Coquina Beach

Duck Island

Herring Shoal Island

Oregon Inlet Campground

Coast Guard Station

North Point

Oregon Inlet Fishing Center

Oregon Inlet

Herbert C. Bonner Bridge to Hatteras Island

BA = **Beach Access**

Northern Hatteras Island:
Pea Island National Wildlife Refuge

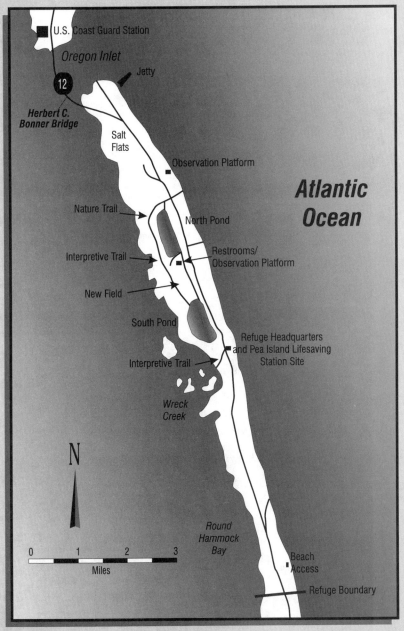

U.S. Coast Guard Station

Oregon Inlet

Jetty

12

Herbert C. Bonner Bridge

Salt Flats

Observation Platform

Atlantic Ocean

Nature Trail

North Pond

Interpretive Trail

Restrooms/ Observation Platform

New Field

South Pond

Refuge Headquarters and Pea Island Lifesaving Station Site

Interpretive Trail

Wreck Creek

N

Round Hammock Bay

Beach Access

0   1   2   3
Miles

Refuge Boundary

Hatteras Island (South)

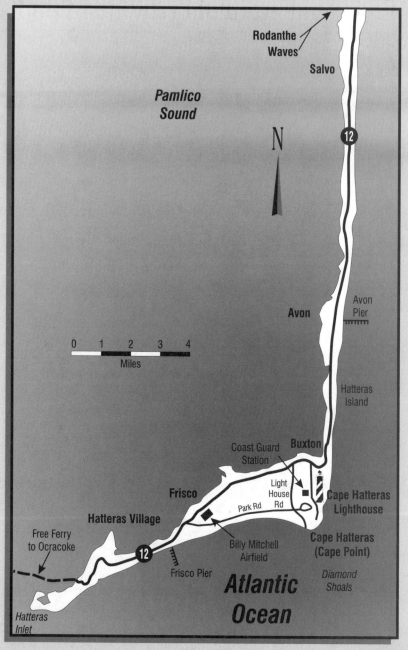

Cape Hatteras Area

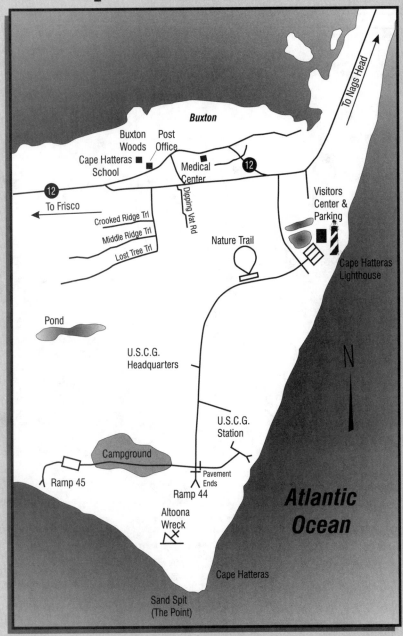

Buxton

Buxton Woods
Post Office
Cape Hatteras School
Medical Center
12

12
To Frisco
Visitors Center & Parking

Dipping Vat Rd

Crooked Ridge Trl
Middle Ridge Trl
Lost Tree Trl

Nature Trail

Cape Hatteras Lighthouse

To Nags Head

Pond

U.S.C.G. Headquarters

N

Campground
U.S.C.G. Station

Ramp 45
Pavement Ends
Ramp 44

Altoona Wreck

Atlantic Ocean

Cape Hatteras

Sand Spit (The Point)

Hatteras Village

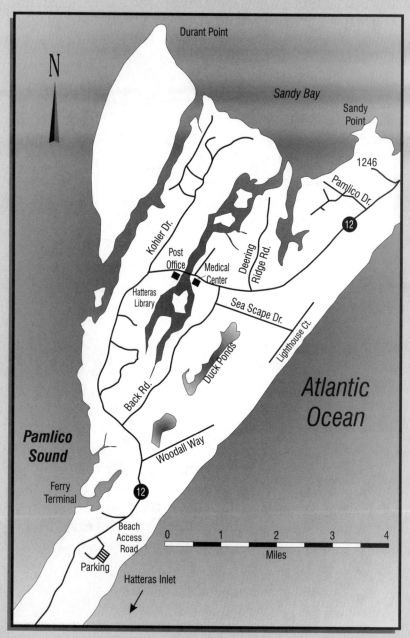

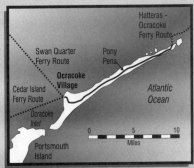

Ocracoke Island

Hatteras -
Ocracoke
Ferry Route

Swan Quarter
Ferry Route

Pony
Pens

Ocracoke
Village

Cedar Island
Ferry Route

Atlantic
Ocean

Ocracoke
Inlet

Portsmouth
Island

0   5   10
Miles

Ocracoke Village

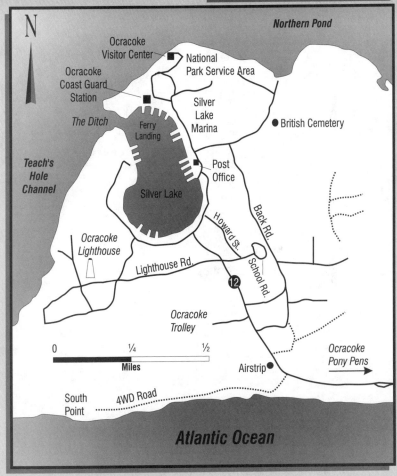

N

Northern Pond

Ocracoke
Visitor Center

National
Park Service Area

Ocracoke
Coast Guard
Station

Silver
Lake
Marina

The Ditch

● British Cemetery

Ferry
Landing

Teach's
Hole
Channel

Post
Office

Silver Lake

Ocracoke
Lighthouse

Howard St.

Back Rd.

Lighthouse Rd.

School Rd.

12

Ocracoke
Trolley

0   ¼   ½
Miles

Ocracoke
Pony Pens

Airstrip ●

South
Point

4WD Road

Atlantic Ocean

Count the steps as you make your way to the top of Cape Hatteras Lighthouse.

How to Use This Book

Continuing the 19-year tradition of *The Insiders' Guide® to North Carolina's Outer Banks*, we've updated, revised and added to our extensive collection of favorite restaurants, shops, attractions, events, getaways and much more.

Most information in our guide is arranged geographically from north to south. Besides introducing you to the area's fascinating history and hidden treasures, we provide practical information on medical services, camping, real estate, vacation rentals, ferry schedules, fishing sites and other areas of interest. New for the 19th edition are chapters on area Media outlets and Worship options, and we've added even more relocation information with chapters on Retirement and Education and Child Care. We've designed *The Insiders' Guide® to North Carolina's Outer Banks* as a

handy reference for all aspects of life here. Keep it in hand, and let us accompany and guide you along every step of your Outer Banks journey. Or have a copy ready to lend to visiting relatives and friends.

After beginning with chapters on our storied history and the various ways to get to and around the Banks, we provide colorful overviews about each area along these barrier islands, from the sand-trail villages of Carova to the windswept shores of Ocracoke Island. Comprehensive chapters tailored to meet your personal needs follow. You'll find Accommodations, Real Estate, Arts and Culture, Annual Events, Kidstuff, Recreation and more — there are more than 25 information-packed chapters. If you're looking for a cozy dinner spot, browse through our Restaurants chapter. If you want to spend the afternoon in search of

a special souvenir, turn to Shopping. If you've always wanted to try scuba diving, parasailing or surfing, all the information you'll need is waiting in Watersports.

We've arranged this book so you can read it bit by bit, turning to those particular pages that pique your interest while breezing by those that don't. But please go back and thumb through any parts you may have skipped at first. We bet you'll learn something and maybe even discover some new favorite spots or pastimes along the way. Be sure to note the passel of excellent maps tucked in here at the book's beginning as well.

The Outer Banks and the rest of northeastern North Carolina are in the process of changing area codes. As of autumn 1998, the area code for our part of the state will be 252, not the old familiar 919. Until September, either area code may be used. We have included the new 252 code with all the local phone numbers listed in this guide.

Finally, feel free to mark up this guide. Jot down your own discoveries, observations and experiences, and let us know about them. We'd love to hear any suggestions or comments you have that will help us improve our effort to make the most of your time on the Outer Banks. Reach us online at our website (www.insiders.com) or write to us in care of:

The Insiders' Guide® to the Outer Banks
P.O. Box 2057
Manteo, NC 27954

Former President George Bush was on hand in May 1998 for
the rededication of the Wright Brothers monument.

About 18,000 years ago, sea levels were almost 400 feet lower than they are today, and North Carolina's coastline was 50 to 75 miles east of its present-day location.

History

The Outer Banks, tenuous bands of sand that lie less than 40 miles inside the Gulf Stream and, in places, more than 20 miles from the North Carolina mainland, are a geological wonder. These barrier islands are accessible only by bridges, boats and planes. Their remoteness, fragility and continual exposure to sea and storms give the islands and inlets a constantly changing aspect. Born in swirling seas and abandoned by retreating mother earth, the Outer Banks' dreamy genesis reminds one of Hilton's paradisal Shangri-La.

In the Beginning . . .

About 18,000 years ago, when continental glaciers trapped much of the world's ocean water, sea levels were almost 400 feet lower than they are today. North Carolina's coastline was 50 to 75 miles east of its present-day location. And the principal rivers of the region (the Neuse, the Tar, the Currituck and the Chowan) flowed across the continental shelf and cascaded over its front slope into the Atlantic Ocean.

When the sinking sea reached its lowest level and winds began carrying sediment from the west, a high ridge of sand dunes formed on the easternmost edge of the mainland. Glaciers began to melt. The sea level began to rise. And the land's vast forests and marshes began a slow retreat away from the rising waters. In their wake, they left huge river deltas rich in materials. Those materials ultimately formed the Outer Banks.

Sea levels continued to rise over the next few thousand years, but the newly formed barrier islands that paralleled Carolina's coast weren't covered by the higher tides. Instead, an unusual combination of winds, waves and weather enabled the Outer Banks to maintain its elevation above the ocean and to migrate as a unit.

Today, the islands' eastern edges still move backward in response to rising waters. On the west side, they build up, narrowing the wide series of brackish bodies of water called sounds that separate the barrier islands from the mainland.

Ocean levels rise about a foot every 100 years. The shoreline moves westerly at a rate of 50 to 200 feet per century along most of North Carolina's coast. On parts of Hatteras Island, the Atlantic eats 14 feet of beach each year.

Geologists refer to the Outer Banks and similar land forms as "barrier islands" because they block the high-energy ocean waves and storm surges, protecting the coastal mainland. Barrier islands are common to many parts of the world, and many have similar features, yet no two of them are alike. Winds, weather and waves give each its own personality. Inlets from the sounds to sea are ever shifting, opening new channels to the ocean one century, closing off primary passageways the next. And folks who venture from one area of the Outer Banks to another soon will realize even along this small stretch of sand that there is a vast variety of topography, flora and temperatures (see our Natural Wonders chapter). An examination of the 16th-century paintings, drawings and maps created by explorer Gov. John White reveal this same diversity, but they also act as valuable documentation suggesting what the land was like and, when compared to today's geological maps, its transformation since the time when the first English explorers arrived here.

Early Explorers

Jutting far into the ocean near the warm waters of the Gulf Stream, the Outer Banks was the first North American land reached by English explorers. A group of colonists dispatched by Sir Walter Raleigh set up the first English settlement on North American soil in

1587. But Native Americans inhabited these barrier islands long before white men and women arrived.

Historians say humans have been living in North Carolina for more than 10,000 years. Three thousand years ago, people traveled throughout the Outer Banks hunting, fishing and feeding off the forest. The Carolina Algonkian culture, a confederation of 75,000 people divided into distinct tribes, spread across 6,000 square miles of northeastern North Carolina.

Archaeologists believe that as many as 5,000 Native Americans could have inhabited the southern end of Hatteras Island from 1000 to 1700 A.D. These Native Americans formed the only island kingdom of the Algonkians. Isolation afforded these people protection and the sole use of the island's seemingly limitless resources. The Croatan lived comfortably for more than 800 years in the protection of the Buxton Woods Maritime Forest at Cape Hatteras. Contact with Europeans proved fateful, however. Disease, famine and cultural demise had eliminated all traces of the Carolina Algonkians by the 1770s.

Early ventures to America's Atlantic seaboard proved difficult for European explorers because of the high winds, seething surf and shifting sandbars. In 1524 Giovanni de Verrazzano, an Italian in the service of France, plied the waters off the Outer Banks in an unsuccessful search for the Northwest Passage. Verrazzano thought the barrier islands looked like an isthmus and the sounds behind them, an endless sea. According to historian David Stick, the explorer reported to the French king that these silvery salt waters must certainly be the "Oriental sea ... which is the one without doubt which goes about the extremity of India, China and Cathay." This explorer's misconception, that the Atlantic and Pacific oceans were separated by only the skinny strip of sand we now call the Outer Banks, was held by some Europeans for more than 150 years.

About 60 years after Verrazzano's visit, two English boats arrived along the Outer Banks, searching for a navigable inlet and a place to anchor away from the ocean. The captains, Philip Amadas and Arthur Barlowe, had been dispatched by Sir Walter Raleigh to explore the New World's coast. They were hoping to find a suitable site for an English settlement.

The explorers finally found an entrance through the islands above Cape Hatteras, probably at the present-day Ginguite Creek north of Kitty Hawk. They sailed south through the sounds until arriving at Roanoke Island. There, they disembarked, met the natives and marvelled at the abundant wildlife and cedar trees. Their expedition had been successful, and they reported to Raleigh on the riches they had found and kindness with which the Native Americans had received them.

During the next three years, at least 40 English ships visited the Outer Banks, more than 100 English soldiers spent almost a year on Roanoke Island, and Great Britain began to gain a foothold on the continent, much to the dismay of Spanish sailors and fortune-seekers.

Lost Colonists

In May of 1587 three English ships commanded by naturalist John White set sail for the Outer Banks with Sir Walter Raleigh's (thus Queen Elizabeth's) blessing and backing. Earlier explorers had dubbed the land "Virginia," in honor of the virgin queen Elizabeth. The expedition, which included women and children for the first time, arrived at Roanoke Island on July 22. Colonists worked quickly to repair the cottages and military quarters left by the earlier British inhabitants. They fixed up a fort the soldiers had abandoned on the north end of the island and made plans for a permanent settlement. Less than a month later, the first English child was born on American soil. Virginia Dare, granddaughter of Gov. John White, was born on August 18, a date still celebrated with feasts and festivities at *The Lost Colony*.

One week after his granddaughter was baptized, John White left her and 110 other colonists on the Outer Banks while he returned to England for food, supplies and additional recruits for the Roanoke Island colony. A war with Spain, meanwhile, had broken out. So when White was again ready to set sail for the Outer Banks the following spring, his queen refused to let any large ships leave England, except to engage in battles. White did not get back to the American settlement until 1590. By then, it had disappeared.

The houses were gone, destroyed and deserted. White's own sea chests had been dug from their shallow hiding places in the sand, broken open, their contents raided. His daughter, granddaughter and all the other English colonists had vanished — leaving no trace except for two cryptic carvings in the bark of Roanoke Island trees. "CRO" was scratched into the trunk of one tree near the bank of the Roanoke Sound. "CROATOAN" was etched into another, near the deteriorating fort. White thought these mysterious messages meant the settlers had fled south to live with the friendly Croatan Indians on Hatteras Island.

The abandoned settlement site showed no signs of a struggle, no blood, bodies or even bones. Some say the colonists were killed by natives or carried away in a skirmish. Others think they were lost at sea, trying to sail home to England. Still others believe they skirted west across the sounds and began to explore the Carolina mainland. Or perhaps they headed to other areas of the Outer Banks, their footsteps scattered in the blowing sands. . . .

Historians have debated the "Lost Colony's" fate for more than 400 years. Archaeologists continue to dig on Roanoke Island's eastern edges. Scholars from across the country gather to discuss the strange disappearance and even have established a special research office on the subject at East Carolina University in Greenville. Archaeologist David S. Phelps, director of East Carolina University's Coastal Archeology Office, has been digging on the Outer Banks for more than a decade.

Erosion from Hurricane Emily in 1993 unearthed remnants of a Croatan Indian civilization in Buxton. Phelps' team has uncovered artifacts that could prove that some members of Sir Walter Raleigh's "Lost Colony" migrated south to Hatteras Island from the Fort Raleigh area. The discovery of lead bullets, fragments of European pottery and brass and copper coins indicate a mingling of the Croatan and English cultures.

Each summer, for more than a half-century, actors have recreated the unsolved mystery in America's longest running outdoor drama, *The Lost Colony*, held at the settlement site in Waterside Theatre (see our Attractions chapter).

Shipping and Settlement Into the 1700s

A century passed before English explorers again attempted to establish settlements along the Outer Banks. Throughout this time, however, European ships continued to explore the Atlantic seaboard, searching for gold and conquerable land. Scores of these sailing vessels wrecked in storms and on dangerous shoals east of the barrier islands. Spanish mustangs, some say, swam ashore from the sinking ships on which they were being transported overseas. Descendants of these wild stallions roam in the Currituck National Wildlife Refuge. Others are corralled in a National Park Service pen on Ocracoke Island.

Although the Outer Banks beaches had few permanent people until the early 1700s, small colonies sprouted up across the Virginia coast and what is now the Carolina coast during the late 1600s. The barrier islands blocked deep-draft ships from sailing into safe harbors, where they needed to anchor and unload supplies for mainland settlers. Smaller vessels, fit for navigating the shallow sounds, transported goods from the Outer Banks to the mainland. People passed through these strips of sand long before they settled here.

Ocracoke Inlet, between Ocracoke and Portsmouth islands, was the busiest North Carolina waterway during much of the Colonial period. The inlet was a vital yet delicate link in the trade network, and it was deeper than most other area egresses. Navigational improvements to the inlet began as early as 1715 when the British government made it an official port of entry. Pilot houses were set up at Ocracoke to dock the small transport boats and temporarily house goods headed inland. Commer-

The Wright Flyer

History repeated itself recently on the Outer Banks of North Carolina. Not too far from the site where Wilbur and Orville Wright built a glider in 1902 that was the predecessor of their famous powered flying machine, seven youths, dubbed the "All Hands On 1902 Wright Glider Club," operating under the sponsorship of the First Flight Rotary Club, constructed a replica of the flying machine. While the children's creation did not lead to worldwide fame, they got a taste of completing a dream from start to finish and won first place in the Kitty Hawk Cup competition in the middle school category. Winners receive cups and plaques sponsored by Global TransPark, an Eastern North Carolina industrial air complex.

The competition, in its second year in 1998, calls for kids to plan and carry out projects that focus on aviation and is open to high- school and middle-school students statewide. It operates under the auspices of the First Flight Centennial Commission, which was organized to formulate plans for the 100th anniversary commemoration of first flight and to promote awareness of what aviation has done for North Carolina, and vice versa. Thanks to prior planning by the Wright Brothers, it took the youths, ranging in age from 13- to 15-years-old, only four months to

— continued on next page

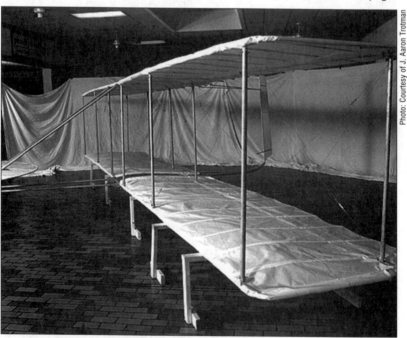

Photo: Courtesy of J. Aaron Trotman

A replica of the Wright Brothers' 1902 glider recently
was built by seven Outer Banks youths.

complete the machine that — when it is not on loan — is publicly displayed at the Outer Banks Mall in Nags Head.

The Wright glider project was the brainstorm of Nags Head artist Glenn Eure. He worked closely with First Flight Middle School art teacher Bill Johnson and several other community members to teach the children how to read blueprints, use tools, sew cloth for wings and complete the "flyable" machine. Unlike the original glider, the replica was built with modern, lightweight materials. Heavy cotton canvas was replaced by hang-gliding cloth, and aviation aluminum and cable replaced more cumbersome wire and wood. Twenty sheets of blueprints made from the original glider guided them.

The replica was displayed recently in Raleigh on the Capital grounds as part of a state travel and tourism show. The glider's departure from the Outer Banks echoed the Wright brothers experience 94 years ago when five men from the Kill Devil Life Saving Station were on hand to assist the brothers in their experiment. It was only fitting for Eure to enlist the help of eight lifeguards from Beach Lifeguard Service to lift the contraption into an 18-wheeler. After reaching the state capitol, the plane was reassembled under a tent, ready to be viewed by Governor Jim Hunt. Though the new glider has not been flown, it very nearly "took flight" while there. The children waited anxiously for Governor Hunt's arrival. There were about 40 other exhibits for him to view, but the kids couldn't wait any longer because they had to start the journey back to the Outer Banks. The plane was disassembled and left with Eure. Not long after the van's departure, word spread that the Governor was on his way. Eure quickly reassembled the plane. Dark clouds formed overhead and the wind started to rip as a storm rolled in. The tent was flapping furiously. Eure feared the plane would be blown aloft if the tent was not held in place. He sat at the center pole and grasped the rod. For over an hour he held tight with whitened knuckles. Obviously it was his intention to keep the flyer aground — a very different goal than that of the Wrights nearly 100 years ago. The storm finally passed and the Governor appeared and praised the invention and the dedication of the youth glider club.

The Wright glider replica is making its own kind of history. It will be on display at the Norfolk International Airport from April to September of 1998. It then returns home to the Outer Banks Mall on U.S. Highway 158 in Nags Head. For more information on the Kitty Hawk Cup Competition write to: First Flight Centennial Commission, 109 East Jones Street, Suite 246-C, Raleigh, NC 27601; or call (919) 715-0209.

---

cial traffic increased along this Outer Banks waterway for many years.

Countless inlets from the sea to sound have formed and closed since the barrier islands first formed. More than two dozen inlets appear in the historical record and on maps dating from 1585. Yet only six inlets currently are open between Morehead City and the Virginia border. Studies of geographic formations and soil deposits indicate that, at some point in time, inlets have covered nearly 50 percent of the Outer Banks. Attempts to harness the inlets have proven costly and, for the most part, have been doomed to failure. Even today, recreational and commercial watermen continue to fight environmentalists for the rights and federal funding to build $97 million jetties in an effort to stabilize

Oregon Inlet, which separates Nags Head and Bodie Island from Hatteras Island.

The first land the British government granted in North Carolina was what is now Colington Island, a small spit of earth surrounded by the Currituck, Albemarle and Roanoke sounds, between Kill Devil Hills and the mainland. Sir John Colleton, for whom the island is named, set up a plantation on the island's sloping sand hills in 1664. His agents planted corn, built barns and houses and carried cattle across by boat to graze on the scrubby marsh grasses. According to historians, this was the beginning of the barrier islands' first permanent English settlement.

Over the next several decades, stockmen and farmers set up small grazing stocks and gardens on the sheltered sound side of the Outer Banks. Runaways, outlaws and entrepreneurs also arrived in small numbers, stealing away in the isolated forests, living off the fresh fish and abundant waterfowl and running high-priced hunting parties through the intricate bogs and creeks. Inhabitants also engaged in salvaging: When a shipwrecked vessel floated onto the shore, local residents made quick work of wielding the wood off the boat, loosening sails from the masts and scavenging anything of value that was left on board. If victims were still struggling ashore, the locals helped them, even setting up makeshift hospitals in their humble homes.

The inaccessibility of the barrier islands and wealth of goods that passed through the ports made the Outer Banks a prime target for plundering pirates. The most infamous of all high seas henchmen was Edward Teach, better known as Blackbeard, a rum-drinking Englishman whose raucous crew set up shop on the south end of Ocracoke Island. After waylaying countless ships and stealing valuable cargo for more than two years, Blackbeard finally was beheaded by a British naval captain in 1718, in a slough off his beloved Ocracoke.

Settlement and sparse development continued through the early 1700s, and by 1722 almost all of the Outer Banks was secured in private ownership. Large tracts of land, often in parcels with 2,000 acres or more, were deeded to noblemen, investors and cattle ranchers. Some New England whalers also relocated to the barrier islands after British noblemen encouraged such industry. Whales were sliced open and their blubber, oil and bones sold and shipped overseas. The huge marine mammals were harpooned offshore from boats or merely harvested on the sand after dying and drifting into the shallow surf.

Although small settlements and scores of fish camps were scattered from Hatteras Village almost to the Virginia line, Ocracoke and the next island south, Portsmouth, continued to be the most bustling areas of the Outer Banks through the middle of the 18th century. British officials enlisted government-paid pilots to operate transfer stations at Ocracoke Inlet, between the two islands, and carry goods across the sounds to the mainland. A small town of sorts sprang up, as the people finally had found some steady occupation and were assured of regular wages.

In 1757 the barrier islands' first tavern opened amidst a sparse string of wooden warehouses and cottages on Portsmouth Island. About 11 years later, a minister made the first recorded religious visit to the Outer Banks when he baptized 27 children in the sea just south of the tavern. Today, a Methodist church and a few National Park Service-supervised cottages are all that remain on Portsmouth Island (see our Daytrippin' chapter).

War and Statehood

As much of a hindrance as the string of barrier islands and their surrounding shoals and sounds had been to shipping, the Outer Banks proved equally invaluable as a strategic outpost during the Revolutionary War.

Only local pilots in small sailing sloops could successfully navigate the shifting sands and often unruly inlets that provided the sole passageway between the Atlantic Ocean and North Carolina mainland. So, big British warships could not anchor close enough to sabotage most Carolina ports. Colonial crafts, instead, ferried much-needed supplies through Ocracoke Inlet, up inland rivers and small waterways, to the new American strongholds in New England.

By the spring of 1776, however, British troops began threatening the pilots at Ocracoke, even boarding some of their small sloops and demanding to be taken inland, where they could better wage war. Colonial leaders then hired independent armed companies to defend

Every year on August 18th, *The Lost Colony* outdoor drama commemorates the birth of Virginia Dare by including a real infant in the christening scene.

the inlets. They abandoned these small forces by autumn of the following year. British boats, however, continued to beleaguer the Outer Banks. Ships landed along Currituck's islands, so sailors could steal cattle and sheep. The redcoats anchored off Nags Head, going inland for fresh water and whatever supplies they could pilfer. They raided fishing villages, plundered small sailboats and came ashore beneath the cloak of darkness. Ocracoke Inlet, especially, suffered under their persistent attacks.

In November 1779, North Carolina legislators formed an Ocracoke Militia Company, hiring 25 local men as soldiers to defend their island's independence. This newly armed force was issued regular pay and rations. Its members successfully saved the inlet and American supplies until fighting finally stopped in 1783, six years after the United States declared its independence.

About 1,000 permanent residents made their homes on the Outer Banks by the time North Carolina became a sovereign state under the 1789 Constitution. Most of these people sailed down from the Tidewater area of Virginia or across from the Carolina mainland. These hearty folk lived in two-story wooden structures with an outdoor kitchen and privy. They dug gardens in the maritime forests, built crude fish camps on the ocean and erected rough-hewn hunting blinds along the waterfowl-rich marshlands. After frequent storms crashed along their coasts, the residents continued to find profit in the shipwrecks strewn along nearby shoals and shores.

Lighthouses Along the Graveyard of the Atlantic

More than a dozen ships a day were carrying cargo and crew along Outer Banks waterways by the dawn of the 19th century. Schooners and sloops, sailboats and new steamers all journeyed around the sounds and across the oceans, often dangerously close to the coast in search of the ever-shifting and shoaling inlets.

At that time, waterways were the country's primary highways, and North Carolina's barrier islands were the Grand Central Station of most eastern routes.

Hurricanes and nor'easters, which still threaten Outer Banks locals, took many boats by surprise, ending their voyages and hundreds of lives. Statesman Alexander Hamilton dubbed the ocean off the barrier islands "The Graveyard of the Atlantic" because its shoals became the burying grounds for so many ships. Close to 1,000 vessels have been lost along North Carolina's craggy coast. In an attempt to help seamen navigate the treacherous shoals, the federal government authorized the Banks' first lighthouses in 1794: one at Cape Hatteras in the fishing village of Buxton and the other in the Ocracoke harbor, on a half-mile-long, 60-mile-wide pile of oyster shells dubbed "Shell Castle Island." Shell Castle Lighthouse first illuminated the Atlantic in 1798. The Cape Hatteras beacon took a little longer to erect. It was finally finished in 1802. Two subsequent structures have sat on the same Buxton spot, but the Shell Castle beacon has long since succumbed to the sea.

Ship captains complained that the early lighthouses were unreliable and too dim. Vessels continued to smash into the shoals. So in 1823 the federal government financed a 65-foot-high lighthouse on Ocracoke Island. The squat structure was whitewashed, with a glass tower set slightly askew on its top. It is the oldest lighthouse still standing in North Carolina.

Officials raised the Cape Hatteras tower to 150 feet in 1854. Five years later, they built two new Outer Banks beacons, at Cape Lookout and on Bodie Island. Both of those lighthouses were improved and rebuilt in later years.

On December 16, 1870, the third lighthouse at Cape Hatteras was illuminated. Standing 208 feet tall and using a multifaceted lens to refract its whale-oil beam across miles of sea, this spiral-striped structure is the tallest brick lighthouse in the world. It's open for tours about six months of the year, but tides and hurricanes are threatening to erode its foundation and send this tall tower tumbling into the sea.

Currituck Beach's red-brick beacon was the last major lighthouse to be built on the barrier island beaches. A 150-foot tower that also is open for tours, this lighthouse was completed in 1875. It watches over the Whalehead Club, near the western shores of Corolla. It is the only unpainted lighthouse on the Outer

Statuary at the Wright Brothers National Memorial in Kill Devil Hills reminds visitors of the momentous first flight that Outer Banks history proudly claims.

Banks and the only one held in private ownership. All other Banks beacons are owned by the National Park Service and operated by the U.S. Coast Guard.

Summer Settlements

In the early 1800s mainland farmers and wealthy families along Carolina's coast suffered each summer from the malady of malaria. They thought this feverous condition was caused by poisonous vapors escaping from the swamps on hot, humid afternoons. Physicians recommended escaping to the seaside for brisk breezes and salt air.

Nags Head was established as a resort destination primarily by a Perquimans County planter who bought 200 acres of ocean-to-sound land for 50¢ an acre in the early 1830s. Eight years later the Outer Banks' first hotel sprang from the sand near the sound, near

what is now Jockey's Ridge State Park. Guests arrived at Nags Head Hotel from across the sounds on steamships, disembarked at a long, low boardwalk behind the 200-room hotel and spent weeks enjoying the beaches and the hotel's formal dining room, ballroom, tavern, bowling alleys and casino.

In 1851 workers enlarged the hotel and added a mile-long track of rails so mule-pulled carts could ease vacationers' journeys to the ocean. The hotel burned down and was rebuilt; later, it was buried by sand. Jockey's Ridge dune, the East Coast's tallest, swallowed the two-story structure bit by bit. Hotel clerks offered discounts during the final years for fellows who didn't mind digging their way into their rooms. But some bachelors complained that chickens rather than chicks were following them home at night through the dark tunnels of sand.

Wealthier visitors who wanted to stay the whole summer built their own vacation cottages on the barrier islands' central plains and eventually on the ocean. Some fathers carried their entire households — cows, pigs, sheep and all — across the sounds on small sailing sloops to spend the season at Nags Head. By 1849 a local visitor remarked that between 500 and 600 visitors were bathing daily at the barrier island beach.

Meanwhile, locals lived in small wooden houses in the woods, selling fresh fish and vegetables to the new tourists, thereby earning unexpected extra income each summer.

Civil War Skirmishes

Outer Banks inlets again proved important military targets after the War Between the States erupted in 1861. Union and Confederate troops stationed armed ships at Hatteras and Ocracoke inlets and set up early encampments. North Carolina crews, who joined their Southern neighbors and seceded from the United States, captured boats filled with fruit, mahogany, salt, molasses and coffee along the enigmatic inlets. Forts, too, were built along the barrier islands, although erosion and storms have long since erased all traces of such structures. Fort Oregon was constructed on the south side of Oregon Inlet; Fort Ocracoke on Beacon Island, inside Ocracoke Inlet. Fort Hatteras and Fort Clark were across from each other at Hatteras Inlet, by then the primary passageway between the ocean and sounds. Approximately 580 men defended those two forts. Seven cannons were mounted inside, aimed across the inlet from one fort to the other in a cross-fire position so that the entire waterway could be covered from within the high walls.

By the fall of 1861, however, federal forces had overtaken Hatteras Inlet and controlled most of the Outer Banks and lower sounds. Confederate troops still ruled Roanoke Island and the upper sounds. They built three small fortresses on the north end of their stronghold to reinforce their position

and to block all access through Croatan Sound.

Union troops also were amassing. In January 1862 Gen. Ambrose Burnside led an 80-boat flotilla from Newport News to North Carolina's Outer Banks. Water was so scarce on this trip that some soldiers resorted to drinking vinegar out of sheer thirst. Others died of typhoid before the battle even began. But on February 7 more than 11,500 members of the federal army amassed for a Roanoke Island attack (an overlook at Northwest Point on the northern end of the island commemorates this site today). At least 7,500 men raided the shores at Ashby's Harbor that night, near Roanoke Island's present-day Skyco. About 1,050 Confederate soldiers fought to maintain their foothold.

After hours of battle around what is now the Nags Head-Manteo Causeway, the rebel troops finally were forced to surrender. Union troops captured an estimated 2,675 of these Southerners. Federal forces held Roanoke Island, and most of the Outer Banks, for the rest of the Civil War.

A Settlement for Freed Slaves

After Roanoke Island fell to Union troops, Union leaders had to decide what to do with the slaves from the former Confederate camp. Gen. Benjamin F. Butler at Fortress Monroe set a precedent by declaring slaves as contraband, successfully using the notion against the rebels. Word spread of this action, and black women and children began flocking to Union camps where they were allowed to settle peacefully. Once word reached the underground network of servants, abolitionists and free blacks, the number of freedom-seeking folk migrating to Dare and Currituck counties increased. At the outbreak of the Civil War, only a few hundred slaves lived along the Outer Banks. But two months after falling to Union troops, Roanoke Island was

The *Elizabeth II* is the state ship of North Carolina.

filled with more than 1,000 runaway and recently freed slaves. Inhabitants of the colony worked as porters for Union officers and soldiers and as cooks, teamsters and woodcutters. The federal government offered these African-American men $8 per month plus rations and clothing to build a fort, Fort Burnside, on the north end of Roanoke Island. Women and children, who made up three-fourths of the population of blacks on the island at that time, collected only $4 a month, including clothing and ration benefits.

By June 1863, officials had established an official Freedmen's Colony on Roanoke Island, west of where the Elizabethan Inn now stands. The government granted all unclaimed lands to the former slaves and outfitted them with a steam mill, sawmill, grist mill, circular saws and other necessary tools. About 3,000 African Americans lived here in a village with more than 600 houses, a school, store, small church and hospital.

Union forces began accepting African-American troops soon after they established the settlement. By the end of July, more than 100 members of the Freedmen's Colony formed the nation's first African-American army regiment. The new colony would have survived were it not for the government's decision to return all lands to the original landowners after the war was over. The Freedmen's Colony was abandoned in 1866. Federal officials quickly transported many of the former slaves off the Outer Banks. Others remained on Roanoke Island to work the waters and the land.

Brave Men and Britches Buoys

After the war, normal life resumed on the barrier islands. Commerce commenced again along the ocean, increasing quickly with steamers now outnumbering sailboats and onetime warships joining private shipping companies. Storms, too, continued to wrack the shores and seamen, sometimes even sinking iron battleships into oblivion.

Seven U.S. Lifesaving Stations were established on the Outer Banks in 1874 in an attempt to help save sailors' lives, if not salvage some of the ships. The stations included: Jones's Hill near the Currituck Beach lighthouse; Caffrey's Inlet north of Duck; Kitty Hawk Beach south of the present pier; Nag's (sic) Head within current town boundaries; Bodie's (sic) Island south of Oregon Inlet; Chicamacomico, which is still open to visitors in Rodanthe and conducts simulated rescue drills each summer; and Little Kinnakeet, on the west side of N.C. 12 in Avon, which is being renovated by the National Park Service as part of a historic preservation project.

During their first season of employment, lifesaving station keepers were paid $200 per year to supervise six surfmen from December through March. Lifesavers lived in the sparse wooden stations, often sleeping six to a room, and kept constant watch over the Atlantic from inside elevated towers that poked out of the stations' roofs. The men walked the beach 24 hours a day. Two from each station would leave at the same time, one heading north, the other south. After 3 to 6 miles, they'd meet a surfman from the neighboring station, also walking either north or south, and exchange tokens to prove they had completed their patrol.

Stations were operated mostly by long-time Outer Bankers. Good swimmers and sea captains who knew the wild waters, these men risked their lives (and many perished) trying to pull others from the ocean. During the winter of 1877-78, more than 188 shipwreck victims and surfmen died within a 30-mile stretch of beach on the northern Outer Banks. That summer, Congress authorized 11 additional lifesaving stations, including ones for Wash Woods and Penny's Hill in Carova, Kill Devil Hills, Hatteras and Pea Island (which had an all-African-American crew). The Lifesaving Service also added a seventh surfman to each station. Crews were then employed from September through April. Rescue techniques advanced with new equipment and the surfmen's experience in ocean survival.

Before motorized rescue craft were available, lifesaving teams had to row deep-hulled wooden boats, often through overhead waves. If they made it through the seething seas to shipwrecks, they sometimes couldn't carry all of the sailors back to shore in one trip. As a result, they devised a pulley system to haul men off the sinking vessels. Dubbed a "Britches Buoy," the device consisted of a pair of short pants sewn around a life preserver ring and hung on a thick rope by wide suspenders; the rope was wound around a handle crank mounted to a wooden cart on shore. Shipwreck victims struggled into the britches, usually with the assistance of surfmen in the rescue boat, and gave an "all-clear" tug on the rope. With the buoy sewn into the seams around their waists, these sailors didn't sink. Even in the highest seas, they could keep their heads above water while lifesaving crews back on shore reeled them safely onto the sand.

Surfmen at Outer Banks lifesaving stations saved thousands of lives during hurricanes and hellacious northeast blows. In 1915 the Lifesaving Service became part of the U.S. Coast Guard. Coast Guardsmen continue to aid barrier island boaters with a variety of state-of-the-art rescue craft stationed at modern Oregon Inlet and Hatteras Island stations.

Historic Happenings, Modern Influences

Government jobs of lifesavers, lighthouse keepers and postmasters employed increasing numbers of Outer Banks residents at the dawn of the 20th century. Other locals continued to profit from summer tourists. But most remained poor fishermen, farmers, stockmen, store clerks, hunters and hunting guides.

In 1902, however, the barrier islands recorded another first when Thomas Edison's former chief chemist began experimenting with wireless telegraphy. Radio pioneer Reginald Fessenden transmitted the first musical notes to be received by signal from near Buxton on Hatteras Island to Roanoke Island. He wrote to his patent attorney that the resulting sounds were "very loud and plain, i.e., as loud as in an ordinary telephone."

In 1900 Ohio bicycle shop owners Wilbur and Orville Wright arrived by boat at Kitty Hawk, looking for reliable winds. Three years later, on December 17, 1903, the Wright brothers soared over Kill Devil Hills sand dunes in the world's first airplane. Only a handful of local Bankers looked on in amazement as the flyer stayed aloft for 59 seconds, flying 852 feet. The site is now marked with a stone monument in a National Park set along the original runway. A replica of the historic airplane, hangar and brothers' shack are on display at the Wright Brothers Memorial (see our Attractions chapter).

In the 1930s, bridges linking the Outer Banks to the mainland brought thousands more tourists and profound changes to the islands. Visitors now could drive to popular summer resorts at Nags Head rather than rely on steamships. Hotels, rental cottages and restaurants sprang up to accommodate the influx.

Post-Depression era politics promulgated the Civilian Conservation Corps (CCC), which set up six camps along the barrier islands. Throughout the '30s, these government workers performed millions of dollars worth of dune construction and shoreline stabilization. The dunes you see along the east side of N.C. 12 did not grow that tall naturally. CCC workers planted much of the grass and scrubby shrubbery to help stave off erosion along the ocean.

Although it was mostly waged continents away, World War II spread all the way across the ocean to the Outer Banks' doorstep. German U-boats lurked in near-shore shipping lanes, exacting heavy losses to Allied vessels. At least 60 boats fell victim to the submarines, though the Germans experienced losses of their own: The first U-boat sunk by Americans lies in an Atlantic grave off the coast of Bodie Island. Longtime barrier island residents recount having to pull their shades and extinguish all lights each night during the war so ships and submarines could not easily discern the shoreline.

Talk of the country's first national seashore began in the 1930s. By 1953, when the Cape Hatteras National Seashore finally was established under the auspices of the National Park Service, it stretched from Nags Head through Ocracoke Island.

Today, the Outer Banks are some of the most popular yet pristine beach resorts on the Atlantic coast. Fewer than 30,000 people make the barrier islands their permanent home. But more than 300,000 visit our sandy shores each summer weekend. Please see our Area Overviews chapter for a modern portrait of our Outer Banks communities.

Getting Here, Getting Around

It's really a breeze to get to the Outer Banks, and there are many ways to do so. But just to be neighborly — an Outer Banks trait — we've outlined the routes to our haven by land, sea and air. Once you're here, before you complain that there's no public bus transportation, wiggle your toes in the sand and remember that you've left behind city conveniences to commune with Mother Nature.

Few folks who visit here from points north, south, east and west leave untouched by the elements. At vacations' end, you may drive, fly or sail away from the Outer Banks, but we can guarantee there's always a little bit of the wind, sand and sea that escapes with you. These stowaways can cause hypnotic trances to occur while you're landlocked elsewhere. Dreamy states may overtake you without notice. There is only one antidote. Come back.

Most folks come to the Outer Banks on four wheels and usually have no problem arriving, finding their way around and returning home. We've divided the chapter into a "Getting Here" section followed by a "Getting Around" section. We initially guide you here by car then share more adventurous transportation options. Following are suggested approaches from the west and north. For information on a southerly entrance to the Outer Banks, see our Ferries section in this chapter.

Getting Here

By Land

Arriving From the West

If you approach from western North Carolina or from the southern United States along interstates 85 or 95 you'll take U.S. Highway 64 E. to reach Roanoke Island, which is connected to Nags Head by the Washington Baum Bridge.

U.S. 64 will take you through Williamston, Jamesville, Plymouth, Creswell, Columbia (home of Pocosin Arts on Water and Main streets, a thriving cultural arts center and gallery), over the Alligator River, through East Lake and Manns Harbor to Roanoke Island, home of *The Lost Colony* (see our History and Attractions chapters).

As you enter the Alligator River National Wildlife Refuge, U.S. 64 is lined with canals and creeks. The reflection of trees and the sun sparkling on the water create dazzling views. It is a sparse area with few stops between Plymouth and the Outer Banks, so fuel up before you leave either Williamston (approximately 1 hour and 45 minutes from Manteo) or Plymouth, especially if you're traveling at night. If you have to pull off the road, do so carefully and choose a wide shoulder, if possible. Canals alternate sides of the road, and it's safer to pull off on the side without the canal.

Along this route watch for deer, black bears, red wolves and a wide variety of birds. You'll spot an occasional blue heron wading in the roadside creeks. The state adorns the byways with an abundance of colorful poppies. It's very tempting to pick the lush beauties, but please leave them in place for the next traveler to enjoy.

Continuing east on U.S. 64, you'll cross the William B. Umstead Bridge or as locals call it, the Manns Harbor Bridge, that takes you to Roanoke Island. The Roanoke Island Visitor Center at Fort Raleigh is the first information center from this direction (see our informational box for more specifics). In a few minutes you'll pass through quaint Manteo on Roanoke Island. Once through Manteo, you can turn right to go to the fishing village of Wanchese at the junction of U.S. 64 and N.C. Highway 345 (referred to by locals as Midway). Or veer left, still on U.S. 64, to head toward Nags Head, Cape Hatteras and the Outer Banks beaches. Overhead signs make it very difficult to get lost. If you do, just blame it on the scenery.

The Cape Hatteras turnoff will be on your right just about a mile from the eastern terminus of the Washington Baum Bridge. At this intersection, referred to as Whalebone Junction, you can bear left onto U.S. Highway 158 in Nags Head or go straight to connect with the Beach Road, which will take you north from Nags Head through Kitty Hawk. (Note that South Nags Head is accessed in this area via Old Nags Head Road.) A right turn at Whalebone Junction puts you on N.C. Highway 12 toward Bodie Island and the Oregon Inlet Fishing Center. After crossing the Herbert

C. Bonner Bridge onto Hatteras Island, N.C. 12 will take you through Rodanthe, Waves, Salvo, Avon, Buxton, Frisco and Hatteras Village. A ferry in Hatteras Village will take you to Ocracoke Island.

Arriving From the North

Backtrack to Williamston for a minute for an alternate route to the Outer Banks. Traveling on U.S. 64, you may choose to turn in Williamston at the U.S. Highway 17 junction that will take you to Elizabeth City. If you follow signs to Nags Head and Manteo from there, you'll arrive on the beach from the north. U.S. 17 is also the route most Virginians follow.

Folks traveling from points north can pick up I-64 E. in Virginia Beach or Norfolk. From Richmond and points northwest, follow I-64 E. to I-664 E., and take the Monitor-Merrimac Bridge-Tunnel to cross the James River. I-64 continues near Suffolk.

From I-64, Exit 290 B takes you down Battlefield Boulevard in Chesapeake to Va. Highway 168. Follow Va. 168 E. to U.S. 158 E. At this junction, you will be about an hour from the Wright Memorial Bridge that crosses the Currituck Sound to the Outer Banks. Travel at your leisure on U.S. 158, for the road from Chesapeake to the Wright Memorial Bridge is dotted with antiques shops, thrift stores and vegetable and fruit stands. You'll pass a delicious Thai restaurant in Powell's Point and a 1950s-style diner in Grandy.

Northern travelers can take U.S. 17 S. to Deep Creek instead of taking I-64. U.S. 17 follows the Intracoastal Waterway through the Great Dismal Swamp before intersecting N.C. Highway 343 near South Mills. Follow N.C. 343 to Camden, and then pick up U.S. 158 to the Outer Banks.

It doesn't matter which way you arrive.

INSIDERS' TIP

Locals avoid grocery shopping on crowded summer weekends and shop for several weeks worth of food at a time. Early morning and late evenings are the least-crowded times.

A four-wheel-drive vehicle is necessary for a day at Oregon Inlet.

Those who love it here believe that eventually all roads lead to the Outer Banks.

When approaching the Wright Memorial Bridge, bear in mind that peak travel times are from noon to 6 PM on Saturday and Sunday in the summer season (Memorial Day to Labor Day), and delays are possible. Travel advisories are posted at the bridge on a flashing sign for your convenience.

After crossing the Wright Memorial Bridge, you will be in Kitty Hawk. Well-marked signs lead you to your destinations. Turn left on N.C. 12 to head to Southern Shores, Duck, Corolla and Carova, or continue on U.S. 158 through Kitty Hawk and toward Kill Devil Hills, Nags Head, Roanoke Island and Hatteras Island. At the junction, the Aycock Brown Visitor Center is on the right. Stop here for a wealth of vacation information. The Outer Banks Chamber of Commerce, on Ocean Bay Boulevard in Kill Devil Hills (if you're approaching from the north, turn right toward Colington at the stop light), is another great information stop. About 8 miles from the welcome center, you'll have to decide whether to get in the left lane and take the road to Hatteras or get in the right lane to go to Roanoke Island. To the right is Manteo, and to the left is the Cape Hatteras National Seashore, taking you to Hatteras and Ocracoke islands.

By Air

Airports and Airstrips

Dare County Regional Airport
Airport Rd., Roanoke Island
• **(252) 473-2600**

If you own your own plane or would like to fly to the Outer Banks, contact this airport. They have two lighted runways. The longer runway measures 4,300 feet, the shorter is 3,300 feet. Jet-A and 100 low-lead fuel is available as well as unleaded auto fuel. This airport has a VOR (Voice Omni Radio) and nondirectional beacon approach. Operating hours are 8 AM to 7 PM daily. Car rental service is available. Weather observations are called in on the hour. There are no scheduled shuttles to the Norfolk Airport, but two airway services, Outer Banks Airways, (252) 441-7677, and SouthEast Air, (252) 473-3222, run shuttles to Norfolk out of this airport (see subsequent listings).

First Flight Airstrip
Wright Brothers National Memorial, U.S. Hwy. 158, MP 8, Kill Devil Hills
• **(252) 441-4460**

At First Flight your stay is limited to 24 hours. This is an unattended strip, and you need to land and take off in daylight hours since there are no lights. No reservations are necessary, and there is a sign-in book on the premises. No fuel is available. The runway is 3,000 feet.

Billy Mitchell Airstrip
N.C. Hwy. 12, Frisco • (252) 995-3646

Planes arriving on Hatteras Island use this unattended airstrip on national park land. Since the strip is not attended, the above phone number supplies an automated weather observation report for the area. There are no lights or fuel here. The runway is approximately 3,000 feet long. There is a parking lot.

Norfolk International Airport
Off Norview Ave., Norfolk , Va.
• **(757) 857-3351**

Norfolk International is a full-service airport that's open 24 hours a day. Some Outer Banks airway companies run chartered shuttles from the Norfolk airport to the Outer Banks. The airport itself does not have scheduled shuttles, so you'll need to use one of the companies mentioned in this section to arrive here by air. NIA offers air service on AirTran, American, Continental, Delta, Northwest, TWA, United, USAirways and five other commuter airlines. For main passenger information call the above number. Jet-A and 100LL fuel are available.

Air Service

Outer Banks Airways
1714 Bay View Dr., Manteo
• **(252) 441-7677**

Outer Banks Airways offers charter service from Norfolk International Airport to First Flight Airstrip in Kill Devil Hills, Dare County Regional Airport on Roanoke Island and to a private airstrip on Pine Island in Duck. The latter two airstrips are unlighted, and landings and takeoffs are restricted to daylight. The Kitty Hawk Aero Tours component of this company also offers sightseeing air tours. Advance reservations are required (see our Attractions chapter).

SouthEast Air
Dare County Regional Airport, 408 Airport Rd., Manteo • (252) 473-3222, (888) 289-8202

SouthEast Air is an on-demand charter service that flies single- and twin-engine and cabin-class aircraft to most East Coast destinations including New York City, Philadelphia, Washington, Norfolk, Raleigh, Charlotte and Myrtle Beach. On arrival, passengers can choose from any of the Outer Banks airstrips for landing. SouthEast Air flies out of the Dare County Regional Airport and also offers air tours, aerial photography and flight instruction. Call for current price information.

Island Flying Service
N.C. Hwy. 12, Frisco • (252) 995-6671

Call Island Flying Service for short flights from Hatteras Island to Ocracoke or sightseeing tours that include the Cape Hatteras Lighthouse. This flying service uses the Billy Mitchell Airstrip in Frisco.

INSIDERS' TIP

If you're out for the night and plan to drink alcohol, play it safe and call one of our 24-hour taxi services for a ride to and from your destination.

Pelican Airways
(252) 928-1661

Pelican Airways offers short hops from Hatteras to Ocracoke Island and sightseeing tours. It also provides air taxi service and flights to major airports. Please call for reservations and additional information.

By Water

A great way to recapture some of the excitement early settlers must have felt as they approached the Outer Banks by water is to do it yourself. Discuss the journey with a local sailor or captain first — a good rule of thumb to follow when navigating unfamiliar waters. Also, pick up a copy of the *Mid-Atlantic Waterway Guide*; it provides the most detailed information available about the area's waterways.

From The North

From points north, you'll begin at the Intracoastal Waterway in the Hampton Roads, Virginia, area. If the weather is fair, it takes a full day to travel down the ICW to the Outer Banks. The open waters of the Albemarle Sound can be quite choppy, even dangerous, so beware.

There are two ICW routes to the Outer Banks. One is from Great Bridge, Virginia, across the Currituck Sound to Coinjock, North

Carolina, the North River and the Albemarle Sound. An alternate route from Hampton Roads takes you to Deep Creek, Virginia, through the Great Dismal Swamp to Lake Drummond in North Carolina, through South Mills to the Pasquotank River, where "the ditch" (the ICW) joins the Albemarle Sound. Follow charts across Albemarle Sound to the Alligator River, then follow either the Croatan Sound or the Roanoke Sound to the town of Manteo. It's about 80 nautical miles from Hampton Roads to Manteo.

The Waterfront Marina in Manteo, (252) 473-3320, provides public docking facilities. The marina supplies power and water at each slip and charges rates on a per-foot basis. In Manteo, you'll find a lovely boardwalk and a small town full of friendly locals and interesting sights. Shops, restaurants and entertainment are all in easy walking distance, as are several lovely inns if you want a break from your berth. (See the Area Overviews and Attractions chapters for details.)

Another docking option is Pirate's Cove Marina on the Roanoke Sound between Manteo and Nags Head, (252) 473-3906. Open year round, Pirate's Cove accommodates pleasure boats as long as 75 feet. Showers and laundry facilities are included with slip rentals. The on-site ships store and restaurant are open to the public. Check out the great view from the restaurant and bar,

Hurricane Mo's. Tennis and pool facilities are available for a nominal fee. Personalized service is this marina's specialty. Offshore and inshore fishing charters are the most popular form of recreation here (see our Fishing chapter). From Pirate's Cove, Oregon Inlet and the Atlantic Ocean are just a short ride away.

Still another option is Salty Dawg Marina in Manteo, (252) 473-3405. This top-notch facility sports 55 slips, all with power and water, and a modern, air-conditioned bathhouse. Salty Dawg offers commercial towing of boats on the water. They are just minutes from downtown Manteo, and provide a courtesy car. The marina is open year round, seven days a week. It's a good idea to call for reservations on holidays. For information on other marinas, please see our Fishing chapter and the Boating section of our Watersports chapter.

From The South

Arrival by boat from the south begins by crossing the Core Sound to pick up the ICW near Beaufort, North Carolina. Cross the Pamlico Sound to the mouth of the Neuse River. Cross the Neuse to Belhaven, where the canal resumes to the northeast.

Ferries

Landlubbers can also enjoy an Outer Banks arrival by boat thanks to the North Carolina Ferry System. If coming from North Carolina, follow U.S. 70 E. from New Bern to Havelock and pick up N.C. Highway 101; follow to N.C. Highway 306, and then take the ferry to Bayview near historic Bath. Follow N.C. Highway 99 to Belhaven, where you pick up Highway 264 to Swan Quarter. Choose an overland course along N.C. Highway 94 across Lake Mattamuskeet, then U.S. 64 to Manteo — or select another ferry from Swan Quarter to Ocracoke Island. It sounds complicated, but signs will guide you.

An alternate route follows U.S. 70 through Havelock to Beaufort. U.S. 70 continues from Beaufort to Harkers Island, following the Core Sound to N.C. 12, where you pick up the Cedar Island Ferry to Ocracoke Island. The voyage across the Pamlico Sound is well worth the two hours it takes to arrive in Ocracoke. Cross Ocracoke Island from south to north, and pick up the Hatteras Island Ferry to the upper Outer Banks.

Ferry passage is a good way to reduce your driving time if you're heading to the southern portion of the Outer Banks. It also gives you a chance to stretch and move around while still making progress. Unless you have your own boat or plane, it's the only way to reach picturesque Ocracoke Island. The ferries transport cars to the island, although we suggest biking or walking as the best ways to get around Ocracoke.

Following is information on the Outer Banks ferry services. You can get more information by writing to Director, Ferry Division, Morehead City, NC 28557, or by calling (800) BY FERRY. Truckers: For information about weight and size limitations, call the specific location. Toll-free numbers are good east of the Mississippi only.

Hatteras Inlet (Ocracoke) Ferry

This free, state-run service links the islands of Hatteras and Ocracoke. The 40-minute crossing carries you from Hatteras Village past Hatteras Inlet across the Pamlico Sound. The ferries accommodate 30 vehicles including cars and large camping vehicles and are run frequently in the summer to avoid excessive delays. The Hatteras Ferry does not require reservations, as do the Cedar Island and Swan Quarter ferries to and from Ocracoke Village. There are public restrooms at the Hatteras Island dock, and heads are on board. The information number for Hatteras is (800) 368-8949, or (252) 986-2353.

Summer Schedule

Leave Hatteras	Leave Ocracoke
5 AM	5 AM
6 AM	6 AM
7 AM	7 AM
7:30 AM	8 AM
Then every 30 minutes until . . .	
7 PM	7 PM
8 PM	8 PM
9 PM	9 PM
10 PM	10 PM
11 PM	11 PM
Midnight	Midnight

Winter Schedule

November 1 through April 30, ferries leave Hatteras and Ocracoke every hour on the hour from 5 AM to midnight. Additional departures may be scheduled as needed.

Swan Quarter and Cedar Island

To avoid possible delay in boarding the Ocracoke-Cedar Island Toll Ferry and the Ocracoke-Swan Quarter Toll Ferry, reservations are recommended. These may be made in person at the departure terminal or by telephone. To make reservations for departures from Ocracoke, call (800) 345-1665 or (252) 928-3841; from Cedar Island, call (800) 856-0343 or (252) 225-3551; and from Swan Quarter, call (800) 773-1094 or (252) 926-1111. Office hours are usually 6 AM to 6 PM, but the office stays open later during the summer.

Reservations may be made up to 30 days in advance of departure date and are not transferable. These reservations must be claimed at least 30 minutes prior to departure time. The name of the driver and the vehicle license number are required when making reservations. Information on tolls and vehicle weight limits follows the ferry information.

Ocracoke-Swan Quarter Toll Ferry

This two-hour ferry ride, which can accommodate 28 cars, connects Ocracoke with Swan Quarter in Hyde County on the mainland. You'll go through Swan Quarter National Wildlife Refuge and connect with U.S. Highway 264 with its gracious old cedars lining the way.

Year-round Schedule

Leave Ocracoke	Leave Swan Quarter
6:30 AM	*7 AM
12:30 PM	9:30 AM
*4 PM	4 PM

*Additional departures: Memorial Day through Labor Day. One-way fares and rates are listed at the end of this section.

Ocracoke-Cedar Island Toll Ferry

Though it takes two-and-a-half hours, this is a popular path for those going south from Ocracoke. The alternative is to drive back to Nags Head and get on U.S. 64/264 or to take the ferry to Swan Quarter. This ferry, which can carry 50 cars, leaves Ocracoke Village and takes you across the Pamlico Sound to Cedar Island. From Cedar Island, those going south can take U.S. 70 to Morehead City. Take a good book and a basket of snacks. Relax and enjoy the view from the ferry.

Summer Schedule

Leave Cedar Is.	Leave Ocracoke
7 AM	7 AM
8:15 AM	---
9:30 AM	9:30 AM
---	*10 AM
---	10:45 AM
Noon	Noon
*1 PM	---
1:45 PM	---
3 PM	3 PM
---	4:30 PM
6 PM	---
8:30 PM	8:30 PM

*Additional departures: Memorial Day through Labor Day.

Spring and Fall Schedules

Leave Cedar Is.	Leave Ocracoke
7 AM	7 AM
9:30 AM	9:30 AM
Noon	Noon
3 PM	3 PM
6 PM	6 PM
8:30 PM	8:30 PM

Winter Schedule

Leave Cedar Is.	Leave Ocracoke
7 AM	7 AM
10 AM	10 AM
1 PM	1 PM
4 PM	4 PM

Toll Ferry One-Way Fares

- Pedestrians, $1
- Bicycles and Riders, $2
- Single vehicles or combinations 20 feet or less in length, and motorcycles (minimum fare for licensed vehicle), $10

Photo: Courtesy of Jeanne Reilly

Don't pass up a chance to explore our area canals by boat.

• Vehicles or combinations from 20 to 40 feet in length, $20

• All vehicles or combinations 40 to 55 feet in length having a maximum width of 8 feet and height of 13 feet, 6 inches, $30

Vehicle Gross Load Limits

The following weight limits apply for all crossings:

• Any axle, 13,000 pounds
• Two axles (single vehicle), 24,000 pounds
• Three or more axles, 36,000 pounds (single or combination vehicle)

Getting Around

By Auto

We've gotten you here; now let's get you around.

Let's get the traffic report out of the way first. As residents of a resort community, we have to deal with radical changes in the number of travelers on our roads during the summer. Traffic more than triples during June, July and August, offering a great contrast to the less-traveled highways of fall and winter, but we know that visitors enrich our economy, and we welcome you, traffic and all. Besides, if you're used to big-city traffic, you'll find the summer traffic tolerable. Naturally, roads can get congested during a hurricane evacuation, but county authorities do a good job with advance warnings (see the Beach Information and Safety chapter for more). Bear in mind the following traffic tips, and you should experience smooth sailing.

The northern route up N.C. 12 toward Duck and Corolla can get a bit bogged down on summer weekends, especially during lunch and dinner hours. Just remember to allow an extra half-hour or so when traveling to the northern Outer Banks on summer weekends. You may want to call the various municipalities or radio stations to see when traffic is heaviest during holidays. And if you have to travel during high traffic hours, don't panic.

Welcome and Visitors Centers

Aycock Brown Visitor Center at Kitty Hawk
U.S. Hwy. 158, MP 1½, Kitty Hawk • (252) 261-4644

Information is abundant at the Aycock Brown Visitor Center at Kitty Hawk, which appears like a lifesaving station at the end of a long journey to rescue weary travelers and first-time visitors to the Outer Banks. Named for a locally legendary 1950s photographer, this building sits a mile east of the Dare County base of the Wright Memorial Bridge. It is one of three such welcome centers that the Dare County Tourist Bureau operates.

Resources include area maps, tide charts, ferry schedules and brochures. Free community newspapers such as *The Coast*, published by *The Virginian-Pilot*, and the *North Beach Sun* offer feature stories that highlight the local area. The welcome center is staffed with Insiders who can answer all your questions.

The center is open from 9 AM to 5 PM, with extended hours during the spring, summer and fall months. The building and the public restrooms are handicapped-accessible, and the picnic area is a welcome sight for those who have been riding a long time. Contact the Dare County Tourist Bureau at (800) 446-6262 for more information.

Outer Banks Chamber of Commerce Welcome Center
Colington Rd. and Mustian St., Kill Devil Hills • (252) 441-8144

On the south side of Colington Road, near the corner of U.S. 158 at Milepost 8, a wooden building with a covered porch houses the Chamber of Commerce's Welcome Center in Kill Devil Hills. This center overflows with free information that's helpful to both visitors and permanent residents. It's a clearinghouse for written and telephone inquiries, and the friendly staff can give information on activities, accommodations and annual events.

The mailing address is P.O. Box 1757, Kill Devil Hills, NC 27948. The center is open year round from 9 AM to 5 PM Monday through Friday.

Dare County Tourist Bureau
U.S. Hwy. 64, Manteo • (252) 473-2138, (800) 446-6262

With the state's first drive-up information window and a new sprawling headquarters on the main road through Manteo, the Dare County Tourist Bureau is equipped to help visitors and residents find almost any Outer Banks information. The bureau has a large collection of brochures, maps and promotional materials about area offerings, and the staff can answer most questions quickly. You'll also be able to access data on demographics and business opportunities on the Outer Banks.

Tourist Bureau offices are open year round Monday through Friday from 8:30 AM to 5 PM. For specific information and a free detailed vacation guide, write to Dare County Tourist Bureau, P.O. Box 399, Manteo, NC 27954.

Roanoke Island Visitor Center at Fort Raleigh
U.S. Hwy. 64, Roanoke Island • (252) 473-6373

This information center is on the north end of Roanoke Island across from Fort Raleigh National Historic Site in the rest area. It also is operated by the Dare County Tourist Bureau. It's open daily 9 AM until 5 PM from Memorial Day through September. From October through Thanksgiving, it is open Friday, Saturday and Sunday from 9 AM

— continued on next page

until 5 PM. It closes during December, January and February and reopens in the spring around Easter time.

Nags Head Visitor Center at Whalebone
Whalebone Jct., Nags Head • (252) 441-6644

Operated by the Dare County Tourist Bureau, this wooden welcome center sits just south of the Whalebone Junction intersection on N.C. 12. It's open daily 9 AM until 5 PM from Memorial Day through September. From October through Thanksgiving, it is open Friday, Saturday and Sunday from 9 AM until 5 PM. It closes during December, January and February and reopens in the spring around Easter time. The staff can answer all kinds of questions about southern destinations along the Outer Banks. These restrooms are also some of the few you'll find on this remote stretch of N.C. 12. The wooden structure also serves as a hunter contact station.

Pea Island Visitors Center
N.C. Hwy. 12, Pea Island • (252) 987-2394

The Pea Island Visitors Center offers information, free public restrooms and paved parking. Wildlife and waterfowl exhibits enhance the public building. There are plenty of nature-related gifts to choose from and an excellent assortment of wildlife books for all ages. In summer the center is open daily from 9 AM to 4 PM. Off-season you can visit Thursday through Sunday from 9 AM to 4 PM. It's closed Christmas Day. This also is an exciting stop for birders. A nature trail winds through the refuge, which is a haven for a wide variety of seasonal and year-round species. Pick up a free nature trail map at the center.

Hatteras Island Visitors Center
Off N.C. Hwy. 12, Buxton • (252) 995-4474

About 300 yards south of Old Lighthouse Road, past the Texaco station and Sharky's eatery, a large wooden sign welcomes visitors to the Cape Hatteras National Seashore and Hatteras Island Visitors Center. Turn left if you're heading south, toward the split-rail fence, and follow the winding road past turtle ponds and marshes.

If you turn left at the four-way intersection, you'll head toward the Cape Hatteras Lighthouse and the National Park Service Visitors Center. Turn right, and you'll wind up at the Cape Point campground and the off-road vehicle ramps as well as a picnic area and nature trail. Surf fishing, sunbathing, swimming, surfing and four-wheel driving are allowed along most areas of the beach here year round. Go straight through the intersection and you'll discover an all-day, free parking lot that accommodates large vehicles like RV's, campers and buses.

The visitors center is near the lighthouse, past a newly expanded parking area. It's in the former house of the assistant lighthouse keepers, which was built in 1854. This two-story, wooden frame home was renovated in 1986 and is adjacent to the smaller keepers quarters. It houses an extensive museum of lifesaving artifacts and lighthouse memorabilia. Free exhibits include information on shipping, wars and Outer Banks heroes.

A small bookstore in the keepers quarters at the visitors center sells literature on lifesaving stations, lighthouses and Hatteras Island history. Clean restrooms also are available here. Volunteers offer a range of summer interpretive programs on the visitors center's wide, covered front porch. Activities change seasonally, with fall and spring programs also conducted. Call ahead for a schedule, or pick one up at the information desk inside.

The visitors center is open from 9 AM to 5 PM daily from September through mid-

— continued on next page

Photo: Courtesy of Jeanne Reilly

New and old, the Wright Memorial Bridge provides the
final link to the Outer Banks from the North.

June and from 9 AM to 6 PM from mid-June through Labor Day. It's closed Christmas Day. Hours are subject to change in the off-season.

Ocracoke Island Visitors Center

Near the Cedar Island and Swan Quarter Ferry Slips, Ocracoke Island • (252) 928-4531

This seasonal visitors center at the southern end of N.C. 12 is a clearinghouse of information about Ocracoke Island. It's run by the National Park Service across from Silver Lake. If you're arriving on the island from the Hatteras ferry, stay on the main road until you reach the T-intersection at Silver Lake. Turn right and continue around the lake, counterclockwise, until you see the low brown building on your right. Free parking is available at the visitors center.

Inside, there's an information desk, helpful staff, a small book shop and exhibits about Ocracoke. You can pick up maps of the winding back roads that make great bicycle paths, and arrange to use the Park Services docks.

The visitors center is open March 1 through December 31 from 9 AM to 5 PM. Rangers offer a variety of free summer programs through the center, including beach and sound hikes, pirate plays, bird-watching, night hikes and history lectures. Check at the front desk for changing weekly schedules. Restrooms are open to the public in season.

Waiting isn't so bad. Roadside swaying grasses and incredible sunsets help. Beware of the gorgeous cloud formations, as they can be very distracting to the driver. Snacks can be a lifesaver, especially if you have children; however, after the first few miles there are plenty of places to stop for food, drinks and shopping along this route.

While we have a few congested spots to deal with from time to time, we have a simple road layout that makes it almost impossible to get lost. These barrier islands, including Roanoke Island to the west, have only three major roadways. U.S. 158 crosses the Wright Memorial Bridge into Kitty Hawk and winds through the center of the Banks to Whalebone Junction in Nags Head. This five-lane highway (the center lane is for turning vehicles only) also is called the Bypass or Croatan Highway. In this book, we will refer to it as the Bypass or U.S. 158.

N.C. Highway 12 runs along the beach, parallel to U.S. 158. A two-lane road, it stretches from the southern border of the Currituck National Wildlife Refuge in Corolla to the ferry docks at the southern tip of Hatteras Island. N.C. 12 picks up again on Ocracoke, spanning the length of the tiny island, ending in its picturesque village. N.C. 12 also is called Ocean Trail in Corolla, Duck

Road in Duck, Ocean Boulevard in Southern Shores and Virginia Dare Trail or the Beach Road from Kitty Hawk through Nags Head. In this book, we will refer to it as N.C. 12 (or occasionally as the Beach Road, when talking about that stretch from Kitty Hawk through Nags Head).

On Roanoke Island, U.S. 64/264 also is called U.S. 64 or Main Highway. This stoplight-filled road begins at the Nags Head-Manteo Causeway, runs across the Washington Baum Bridge, through Manteo, across the William B. Umstead Bridge and through Manns Harbor on the mainland.

U.S. 158 and N.C. 12 run primarily north and south. Smaller connector streets link seaside rental cottages to year-round neighborhoods west of the Bypass. And most locals are friendly, patient, helpful folk who will be glad to point you in the right direction.

If you truly want to relax and spend your vacation days island-style, kick off your shoes and travel on foot. You can walk for miles down the beaches, collecting shells and wading, stopping at various beach accesses that will take you back to the Beach Road (N.C. 12). There are plenty of restaurants and fishing piers that run the length of the Outer Banks, so you're usually not far

Relax and enjoy the 40-minute ride on the Hatteras-Ocracoke Ferry.

from food and drink. Most spots welcome casual diners. When walking the Beach Road, watch out for vehicles with the mirrors that stick out — the road is narrow. This road is not the best choice for bicycles as a result. You can easily explore Manteo on foot, and biking is a safe alternative in that town.

By Bike

The Outer Banks boasts several bike paths. Running the length of Roanoke Island is an asphalt path dotted with benches. The path has awakened the athlete in many lo-cals, young and old, who are now seen walking, riding bikes and in-line skating regularly. It's a wide, safe path that we are grateful to have. In South Nags Head a wide concrete path runs the length of Old Oregon Inlet Road down to N.C. 12, accommodating those headed toward the Cape Hatteras National Seashore. The town of Kill Devil Hills sports a scenic asphalt route off Colington Road, running down National Park Service property past the rear of the Wright Brothers National Memorial. Duck has a bike trail on the east side of the road running from the village's southern boundary to the Greenleaf Gallery. It picks up again on the northern end of the

INSIDERS' TIP

Check out our Recreation chapter for fun "getting around" opportunities including dolphin tours and more extensive watersport activities.

village at Ship's Watch development and continues through Sanderling. It is projected that a new addition to the trail will run through the village on the east side, and a new trail on the west side will be constructed running from the Currituck County line through the village and the entire Duck community. The bike path that runs through Southern Shores along N.C. 12 does not allow in-line skating. Call each township for specific bike path restrictions.

If you're going to enjoy these paths or bike anywhere else on the Outer Banks, please wear a helmet. You can rent bikes at several rental services, and many accommodations offer bikes and helmets as a courtesy (see our Recreation chapter). Watch out for the sand that blows on the road. This can get in your eyes as you pass the dunes and can be slippery when applying brakes. Follow the normal rules of the road that apply to cars, stopping at lights and stop signs and yielding to pedestrians. There is a lot of foot traffic near the beach, so whether you're on a bike or in a car, watch out for that rolling beach ball, which is usually followed by a child.

Taxis, Limos and Tours

As we stated in our introduction, there is no public transportation system here, but there are plenty of alternatives available.

Bayside Cab
(252) 480-1300

Bayside is on U.S. Hwy. 158 at Milepost 6, and offers point-to-point service 24 hours a day.

Beach Cab
(252) 441-2500

The familiar sky blue taxis of Beach Cab offer 24-hour service and Norfolk International Airport pickups.

Buxton Under The Sun
(252) 995-6047

This business offers 24-hour service, four-wheel drive rentals and shuttle service to Norfolk International Airport. They offer drop-off and pick-up service to surf fishing destinations.

The Connection
(252) 473-2777

The Connection is a shuttle service that operates between Norfolk and the Outer Banks. It offers door-to-door shared-ride and private service. The vehicles are full-size, air-conditioned passenger vans that can accommodate groups, families, bicycles, surfboards, sailboards, etc. Child safety seats are provided free upon request. Discounts are available for reservations made in advance, for shared rides and for parties of two or more. Service is on demand, so reservations are recommended.

Historically Speaking's Outer Banks Tours
(252) 473-5783

Historically Speaking offers year-round step-on tour guiding and receptive tour services (lodging, meals, attractions) for bus groups, conferences and conventions, complete with commentary on the natural and cultural history of Roanoke Island and the Outer Banks. Call for your personalized tour consultation. Step-on guides are CPR-certified. Fun-filled itineraries are individually designed. Private evening programs offer traditional Outer Banks music and sea song singalongs, and there are costumed living history performances of Elizabethan music and culture from the time of Sir Walter Raleigh's Roanoke colonies (see our Attractions chapter).

Island Limo
(252) 441-LIMO, (800) 828-LIMO

If it's a stretch limo you want, Island Limo has a selection to suit your every need. Island Limo also provides a daily shuttle to and from Norfolk International Airport from Memorial Day to Labor Day and offers airport service via private sedan year round. You can also take advantage of its four-wheel drive off-road excursions to Hatteras Island, Oregon Inlet and Carova Beach.

Island Taxi
(252) 441-7000

Island Taxi provides 24-hour cab service and transportation to the Norfolk airport. Corolla callers should dial 453-4108, while Duck callers dial 261-3027.

Outer Banks Transit
(252) 441-7090

OBT provides scheduled trips to the airport and other Norfolk destinations. Package deliveries and pickups are also accommodated.

Car Rentals

Car rentals are available at the Dare County Regional Airport on Roanoke Island off Airport Road, (252) 473-2600, daily from 8 AM to 7 PM. You can also rent a car at: B & R Rent-A-Car at R.D. Sawyer Motor Company, U.S. 64, Manteo, (252) 473-2141; and Outer Banks Chrysler/Plymouth/Dodge/Jeep, U.S. 158, MP 5, Kill Devil Hills, (252) 441-1146. For four-wheel-drive rentals, call Buxton Under The Sun, (252) 995-6047.

We have more than just good looks and a nice personality on the Outer Banks: We have history. We have drama. We have lots of good stories to tell.

Area Overviews

Even with planes and bridges, the Outer Banks still is a remote land where sounds divide the mainstay of inland jobs from the pursuit of the outland dream. Goods and services have increased dramatically since the days of virtual isolation from the rest of the world, but the pulse of life on these barrier islands is still set by wind and water.

The Outer Banks has a beautifully rugged National Seashore that accounts for much of our well-preserved beaches. The sounds and ocean here are clean and the weather is temperate. We have more than just good looks and a nice personality, though: We have history. We have drama. We have lots of good stories to tell. Once you leave the mainland and arrive on these barrier islands, you will want to hear it all.

If you started at the Virginia line at Carova and traveled south on N.C. Highway 12, you'd drive about 100 miles before the road ends at Cape Hatteras. Hop on the free ferry to Ocracoke Island, where you can drive another 14 miles on the same road to reach Ocracoke Village. Within the breadth of that stretch you can witness the incredible diversity of the Outer Banks. "The sunsets here are the prettiest I have ever seen," Orville Wright wrote his sister in 1900. "The clouds light up with all colors, in the background, with deep clouds of various shapes fringed with gold before. The moon rises in much the same style, and lights up this pile of sand almost like day." Whether it's the sunrise or the sunset, or what goes on in between, the Outer Banks still offers the most extraordinary of what life has to offer.

In this chapter we offer overviews of the areas that make up the Outer Banks, taking you on a north-to-south tour of Corolla and Currituck's Beaches, Duck and Sanderling, Southern Shores, Kitty Hawk, Kill Devil Hills, Nags Head, Roanoke Island, Hatteras Island and Ocracoke Island.

Corolla and Currituck's Beaches

Fewer than 15 years ago, Currituck County's Outer Banks beaches were the barrier islands' outback. Seeming to stretch infinitely from north of Duck to the Virginia border, wide windswept expanses of sandy terrain lay virtually untouched except by winds, blue herons and wild horses (see our Close-up in the Attractions chapter). While other island communities on the Outer Banks became boomtowns in the late 1970s, the northern beaches remained undiscovered.

But their time has come. From these barren dunes harboring a few fishing shacks and a handful of private homes, thousands of upscale houses, including 5,000-square-foot mansions, have sprung up on miles of recently paved subdivision roads. A family-owned convenience store that supplied the only local goods for fewer than 100 permanent residents has been overshadowed by a modern grocery chain store. A 124-year-old lighthouse has become more important as a landmark for tourists than a guide for sailors. A large rustic lifesaving station has been renovated and expanded into an exclusive convention center, hotel and restaurant. The northern beaches' first chain hotel has been approved for construction in 1999. Dozens of eateries offer a variety of cuisine, and three quality resort shopping plazas are available to fulfill almost every desire of the 15,000 or more visitors that flock to the northernmost Outer Banks in the summertime.

In a span of 10 short years, the permanent population of the Corolla-area beaches grew from 171 residents in 1985 to 620 residents in 1995; meanwhile, the seasonal population skyrocketed from 4,271 to 19,370 in the same period. Within that decade, 70 permanent houses and 563 seasonal rental houses expanded to 255 permanent homes and 2,039 seasonal houses.

The tiny community where everyone knew everyone else has undergone enormous change in its transformation into a favorite travel destination, but development has been tasteful and aesthetically pleasing.

From Fishing Village to Vacation Destination

The remoteness of Currituck's Outer Banks kept these spectacular sea oat-strewn dunes isolated long after the barrier island's southern beaches had grown in leaps and bounds. The lack of a permanent population and the accompanying services put a built-in damper on tourism and growth. In 1972, coastal officials called Currituck County's 23 miles of beaches "the longest undeveloped strip of coastal land on the Eastern Seaboard." One telephone, which only allowed outgoing calls, served the entire area. The spit island was not even connected to line-distributed electricity until the 1950s. Families placed weekly food orders with the postmaster, who ran a tiny general store in his house. The few visitors to Corolla traveled on a sandy lane or the beach at low tide.

Winston-Salem developer Earl Slick saw possibilities in the vast stretches of untouched beach and soundfront, and in 1973 he changed the face of the northern Outer Banks. For $2 million, he and his Coastland Corporation purchased 636 acres just north of the Dare County line from Texas oil tycoon Walter B. Davis.

Slick proceeded two years later to erect a wooden guardhouse at the southern tip of his property, barring all but residents or landowners from entering Currituck beaches. Impassioned protests, which at times came to blows, eventually put the matter in the hands of the North Carolina Supreme Court. Finally, on November 1, 1984, the state took over the road that stretched from the Dare County line north. As security guards watched, bulldozers toppled the guard post, opening free passage

www.insiders.com

See this and many other
Insiders' Guide® destinations
online — in their entirety.

Visit us today!

all the way to Corolla and clearing a path for widespread development.

Despite its relative isolation before Slick's arrival, the northern beaches have always had their own unique history and allure. After the Civil War, Currituck Beach was the largest community on the Outer Banks between Kitty Hawk and Virginia. Fishing families lived in small wooden houses near the sound. The area's reputation as "Sportman's Paradise" had its genesis at this time, when hunters discovered the plentiful waterfowl nesting near or overflying the Currituck Sound.

In 1874, the U.S. government put Currituck's beaches on the map by building the Currituck Beach Lifesaving Station and the Currituck Beach lighthouse. The lifesaving station, one of the Outer Banks' original seven outposts, was first named Jones Hill, then Whaleshead and finally, Currituck Beach. The 150-foot-tall red-brick beacon lifesaving station, the last major lighthouse built on North Carolina's barrier islands, cost $178,000 to construct.

The tiny fishing community was officially named Corolla the following year, when the federal government installed a modest post office down the road a bit from the lighthouse. Three names were rejected before a local teacher suggested to postal officials to call the village after the inner petals of a flower, the corolla (pronounced "cuh-RAHL-uh" by locals). The square little post office is still in use today, the only one on the Outer Banks operating north of Kitty Hawk.

Throughout the early 1900s, Currituck County's barrier islands grew in popularity as a retreat for recreational hunters who flocked to the dense marshlands each fall for the annual waterfowl migration. You can still spot crudely built duck blinds along the swampy shores. Elaborate hunt clubs erected by Northerners in the 1910s and 1920s have been turned into resort community clubhouses, real-estate offices and county-owned estates. The Whalehead Club, the largest and most magnificent of all the Outer Banks hunting lodges, is being restored with tourism tax profits. This Currituck County facility is open for tours daily

Photo: Courtesy of Bob Reardon

Catch a sunrise before catching some waves on the Outer Banks.

throughout the summer season and will some-day house a wildlife museum. (See our Attractions chapter.)

Putting aside its appeal as premier hunting and fishing grounds, Corolla was unsentimentally regarded as little more than a wasteland of sand. Until about 25 years ago, Currituck County was even known to give tracts of barrier island land away with purchase of mainland tracts.

Getting to Currituck County's Outer Banks

In the 1950s, Virginia and North Carolina officials began talking about building a road from Sandbridge, in Virginia Beach, to Corolla, which would traverse a long spit of solid sand and the state line. That route, however, was never started. Today, only property owners with special permits can get through a metal gate at the North Carolina border and arrive in Corolla from the north.

The rest of the populace must drive up N.C. 12 from the south to get to Currituck's beaches. Turn onto N.C. 12 at its junction with U.S. 158 in Kitty Hawk, 1.5 miles east of the Wright Memorial Bridge's eastern terminus; then, travel through Southern Shores,

Duck and Sanderling, and you'll hit the county line. Although it's only about 10 miles from Kitty Hawk to the Currituck County border, and another 12 miles to the end of the road at Carova, the trip can take up to an hour or more on certain days during the peak season.

Once you pass through Duck, you'll notice the roadside starts opening up and the terrain looks sparser and wilder. Watch your speed limits, because police are on the lookout for speeders who forget themselves on the straight two-lane road when traffic is light.

By the year 2001, state officials are planning to start construction of a two-lane 4.8-mile bridge spanning the Currituck Sound from Aydlett to Corolla. The proposed project, which is still in the early planning stages and has not yet been approved, would cut about 40 miles off the trip from U.S 158 in Currituck County to N.C. 12 in Corolla.

Corolla Today

By the time its first upscale strip shopping center had unfurled its colorful window displays in the early 1990s, Corolla residents had been enjoying home mail delivery for several years. They had their first spanking-new bank built shortly before then. By 1995, Corolla had its first hotel, the Inn at Corolla Light (see Accommodations). That same year, the county issued more than 100 building permits for new stores and houses. Growth has continued at a steady pace, making Corolla a construction boomtown.

In the past decade, developers and individuals have built more than 1,500 homes between the Dare County line and the Virginia border. At least 100 businesses have opened their doors. Planning officials have approved development of thousands of new structures. The Currituck Club, one of Corolla's newest subdivisions, opened in July 1996. The community boasts an 18-hole, 6800-yard championship golf course, designed by world-renowned golf course architect Rees Jones (see our Golf chapter). The 3.7 miles of soundside property will eventually include 600 patio homes, single-family homes and condominiums situated on half-acre lots, and it will have beach oceanfront access. (See our Real Estate chapter for more information.)

Most visitors to Currituck's beaches tend to rent the huge homes that straddle the undulating sand dunes. The average Corolla house sleeps 10 to 15 people, includes 3,332 square feet of living space and is available for weekly rentals. Many of the contained communities also offer exercise facilities, racket or golf clubs, indoor and outdoor swimming pools, boardwalk beach accesses and hot tubs. (See our Accommodations chapter.)

Retail stores scattered throughout this upscale area sell items ranging from handmade hammocks to custom-designed jewelry. Restaurants appeal to all tastes from raw or steamed seafood to elegant European dining. And watersports — personal watercraft, windsurfing, sailing and more — are available from early spring through fall (see our Shopping, Restaurants and Watersports chapters for details).

Although the streets and sidewalks often overflow during the summer tourism season, the permanent population of Currituck County's Outer Banks is still small, estimated at about 500 people. A county satellite office keeps them connected with Currituck's services, but children who live in Corolla year round travel more than two hours by bus to attend Dare County schools — the closest ones to their resort community.

Currituck National Wildlife Refuge

A few miles north of the Currituck Beach Lighthouse, the multistory mansions become more sparse and the paved two-lane highway dead-ends at a sand hill. Here, wildlife sanctuaries provide a safe haven for endangered piping plover, feral boar and other wildlife. A 4-foot-tall fence stretching a mile from sound to sea marks the southern barrier of this 1,800-acre sanctuary, where the remaining herd of Corolla's wild horses still range (see the Close-up in our Attractions chapter). People can walk through the fence, however, and four-wheel drive vehicles can cross through a cattle gate.

Once Corolla's most popular tourist attraction, the wild horses no longer roam freely in the populated village, but the Corolla Wild Horse Fund is headquartered at the lighthouse, where gift items and membership information are available.

Isolated Outposts North of the Road's End

There is no real route from Corolla to the Virginia border. Still, a few hundred homes line this expanse of sand. On summer afternoons, more than a thousand four-wheel-drive vehicles create their own paths on the beach as they drive into and around a community called Carova — where North Carolina meets Virginia. Note that even Carova's name is a melding of both states.

In May 1998, a new ordinance requiring permits to drive ATV's to Carova went into effect. Call the county satellite office at (252)453-8555 for more information.

About 300 permanent residents reside along these remote beaches, and new homes go up every year. Residents negotiate tides and beach not only in off-road and four-wheel-drive vehicles, but also in regular cars with big deflated tires. Bicyclists sometimes manage at dead low-tide to scoot around the fence into Sandbridge, Virginia, which natives in pre-fence days did routinely.

Despite being relatively protected from civilization, the area is patrolled by county, state

Drive onto the Point at Hatteras Inlet for a day of fishing and lazing in the sun.

and federal officers. An unpaved road behind the dune line into Carova is now overgrown and impassable, but several bike and hiking trails are used frequently. Most residents and visitors to Swan Beach, Carova, North Swan Beach and the Seagull subdivisions drive on the beach above the water line or on well-tread tracks on the softer sand.

If you don't have a four-wheel-drive automobile, you probably shouldn't risk the tricky business of driving on the beach. Local guides will be glad to show you around in off-road vehicles. Corolla Outback Adventures rents open-air, low-to-the-ground four-wheelers (see our Recreation chapter). Watch out for tree stumps, though. An ancient forest that historians say grew along the sound more than 800 years ago still thrusts its sea-withered trunks through the waves at an area known as Wash Woods.

If you travel off-road in this area, you'll soon see a giant sand dune near the sound. Lewark's Hill, which some people call Penny's Hill, is the tallest dune on Currituck's beaches. From the top, hikers can spot a string of marsh islands in the sound, including Monkey Island, a waterfowl rookery and site of a dilapidated hunting lodge.

Whether you're staying in one of Currituck Beach's exclusive rental homes or camping somewhere on the southern Outer Banks, Co-rolla and Carova are well worth exploring. Once that new bridge is built, the still-isolated northern barrier island beaches are bound to boom even more.

Duck and Sanderling

A sleepy seaside village spanning the Outer Banks' skinniest strip of sand, Duck woke up to tourism in the early 1980s. Since then, it's burgeoned into a weeklong and day-trip destination all its own. Somewhere between elite and quaint, Duck's accessibility and diversity have made it one of the fastest growing resort communities on the Outer Banks.

The two-lane highway through the center of town teems with tourists throughout the summer. More year-round locals are moving here every month. And restaurants and retail shops are opening by the dozens each May.

Duck is a classy town edged with a rustic, seafarer vibe. Within its waterfront boutiques, art galleries and eclectic eateries, visitors will find authentic Outer Banks offerings. Duck's young development is obvious: It has none of the cragginess of its older, weatherbeaten neighbors like Kitty Hawk. Vacationers who choose to stay here are generally a bit more affluent than those who select the central beaches or Hatteras Island. Most stay in rental cottages that are nicely tucked into shady, tree-lined niches. A bed and breakfast inn accommodates nightly guests, but no hotels or fast-food joints have sprung from these sandy shores.

Along the sound, Duck resembles a historic New England port town. The brilliant white spire of the Duck Methodist Church rises above the gnarled live oaks and wind-bent hickory groves. Weathered clapboard buildings of simple, single-gable construction are linked by wide wooden boardwalks spanning swampy wetlands. These shops, which look like clusters of quaint, colorful cottages, carry everything from kaleidoscopes to locally designed kids' clothing.

There's no place better to watch the tangerine sun sink into the sound than from the sea oat-lined decks of Duck's soundfront stores and restaurants.

Eel Pots and a Growing Economy

Like most barrier island beach communities, Duck was a small fishing village during its early existence. Families lived in rough-hewn wooden houses set atop two-foot blocks that kept the floors above the level to which the sea or sound had been known to rise during storms. With more trees and thicker underbrush here than in other areas of the Outer Banks, many Duck residents farmed small garden plots to supplement their seafood and waterfowl diets. Hogs, cows and chickens were raised in the woods

Watermen worked from dawn until dark, netting fish from the beach with long-haul seines, taking dories out in the sound to set pound nets, and trapping crabs with wooden crates. Whole crews of women, men and children toiled together for days mending heavy cotton fishing nets, sometimes garnering up to 25 cents an hour for their trouble. During the Great Depression, children, and sometimes grownups, made a decent living catching "peelers" — blue crabs that shed their shells. Crab shedding businesses, still a major fishing enterprise on the Outer Banks, first cropped up in Duck. Peelers are harvested on the full moons in May, June and July every year. Eel

pots also were prevalent along the shallow shores and shoals. Made of thin wood and more rounded than the crab pots, these contraptions' contents gave local fishermen an item to export. They packed the long, snake-like creatures in salt, stored them in barrels and trucked them along the sand trails to Hampton Roads markets, where eel were once eaten in abundance.

The first post office opened in Duck in 1909, when postmaster Lloyd Toler gave the community its charming moniker in honor of the area's abundant waterfowl. The facility was abandoned by 1950. Year-round residents today have to travel to Kitty Hawk for their mail. Elementary school children go there to attend school as well.

Little changed in Duck until the late 1970s. Single-family homes were sparsely scattered throughout the thick shrubbery, and small wooden boats bobbed from tree trunks turned into pilings.

Tourism took over about 1980, when small shops began lining up along the two-lane road through town and larger houses sprang from the beach areas. Barrier Island Station, among the biggest and most popular timeshare resorts on the Outer Banks, opened one of Duck's first full-service restaurants and now includes an indoor and outdoor pool, tennis courts, a communal hot tub and live evening entertainment on a covered waterfront deck.

In 1990, you had your choice of five restaurants between Kitty Hawk and Corolla. Today more than 25 locally owned establishments offer breakfast, lunch and dinner: a coffeehouse, a pizza parlor, an upscale deli with unusual homemade salads, scads of sandwich shops, bistros and a marvelous wine bar and cafe. Shopping runs the gamut of galleries, boutiques and colorful shops offering offbeat wares, crafts created by local artisans and quality sea-themed souvenirs (see our Restaurants and Shopping chapters for more details).

Recreational offerings abound here too and are being added to every season. You can learn to windsurf, rent a sailboat or a trimaran, or let a captain take you on a sunset cruise. Speed across the sound on a Jet Ski, paddle around a marsh island in a canoe or kayak, or bounce about the waves on an inflatable banana boat.

No matter what your tastes in food, fashion or fun, you will find something to enjoy in the now-bustling village of Duck.

Getting to Duck

To get to Duck if you're coming to the Outer Banks from the north, turn left onto N.C. 12 at its junction with U.S. 158 in Kitty Hawk, 1.5 miles from the Wright Memorial Bridge's terminus. Travel through the flattop homes of Southern Shores, and wind around the dunes on the two-lane highway. On good days, Duck is a 10-minute drive from Kitty Hawk. In heavy summer traffic, bottlenecks form in the village, causing backups that last for miles and, sometimes, more than 30 minutes.

N.C. 12 curves through the center of Duck. All the commercial development is along this road, confined to the highway by zoning ordinances, landscaped with lovely local foliage. Drive slowly — even us locals are astounded by the fetching sights around every bend.

The sea is quite close to Duck, as is the sound, so many rental homes provide the rare opportunity for viewing both bodies of water from upstairs open-air decks. Wild beans, peas and cattails cover the marshy yards, most of which are at least partially wooded, with the houses tucked between the trees.

True to its name, Duck is home and passageway for a variety of nesting and migrating shore birds and waterfowl. Streets are named after these feathered creatures, which often come to call. Loons, cormorants, gannet and flocks of terns and gulls soak up the sun's warmth near the water's edge. You can sometimes see swans and mallards swimming in the sound at sunrise.

On the northern edge of Duck, a U.S. Army Corps of Engineers research facility occupies the site of a former Navy bombing range. Military weapons recovery crews have dug up thousands of unexploded ordnances around here, and an 1,800-foot-long pier now provides scientists with an important opportunity to track subsurface currents, study the effects of jetties and beach nourishment projects and chart the movements of the slender strips of sand. (Turn to our Attractions chapter for more information.)

Beyond the pier, heading north toward Corolla, the Duck Volunteer Fire Department, the Dare County Sheriff's Office northern beach station and the Duck Recycling Center offer free local services.

Sanderling

About 5 miles north of Duck, through an open wilderness area, Sanderling is the northernmost community on Dare County's beaches — an isolated, exclusive, upscale enclave with 300 acres stretching from sound to sea.

The community itself was initiated in 1978, setting a precedent for excellence among vacation destinations. These neighborhoods, barely visible from the road, approach land planning sensitively, preserving as much natural vegetation as possible and always aiming for architectural excellence. They are well worth searching out.

In 1985, the Sanderling Inn and Restaurant opened in the restored Caffey's Inlet Lifesaving Station, built in 1874. With cedar-shake siding, natural wood interiors and English country antiques, it has the appearance of turn-of-the-century Nags Head resorts and the ambiance of a European escape. It's large and airy, with wide porches that provide plenty of room for conversation, drinks and soaking in the sunrise in wooden rocking chairs. (See our Accommodations and Restaurants chapters for details.)

North of Sanderling, Palmer's Island Club is a 35-acre development with 15 oceanfront one-acre lots and at least eight estates ranging from 6,000 to 10,000 square feet each. The homes are engineered to withstand 120

INSIDERS' TIP

Corolla public beach access is available only at the Whalehead Beach subdivision. Public restrooms with handicapped access can be found at the northern end of the Pine Island subdivision on the oceanfront.

mph winds. Signature architectural embellishments are scaled to match the grandeur of the natural environment.

Southern Shores

Stretching from sound to sea, Southern Shores is heralded as one of the most beautiful, well-thought-out developments on the Outer Banks. Interwoven with canals, maritime hardwood forests, dunes and private beaches, its scenic beauty is hard to match. Real estate agents call Southern Shores property one of the best Outer Banks values for long-term investment.

Southern Shores is south of Duck and north of Kitty Hawk. You can enter this community via N.C. 12, South Dogwood Trail, which runs alongside Kitty Hawk School, or by Juniper Trail, which runs perpendicular to the Marketplace shopping center.

Yesteryear and Today

Southern Shores was the first planned community on the northern Outer Banks and a pioneer for underground utilities. The visionary Frank Stick, developer, artist, outdoorsman and self-trained ichthyologist, bought the land comprising Southern Shores in 1947 for $30,000. Today it is worth more than $430 million.

Stick worked eight years developing the northern Outer Banks community, and his careful development is evident throughout the town today. He had his hands full designing and building cottages and homes, supervising the platting of lots and the installation of roads. A master illustrator, who studied under the distinguished Howard Pyle, Stick later shared the task of developing the virgin land with his son, David. Much like a watercolor from the era in which the senior Stick thrived, Southern Shores was developed to resemble a *Wind in the Willows* paradise.

Home to cardinals, finches, mocking birds, Canadian grosbeaks, woodpeckers, quails, raccoons, deer and squirrels, this idyllic place with seas of white dogwoods blooming in spring speaks to the Sticks' love and dedication for preserving the natural habitat. Perhaps nowhere else on the Outer Banks better illustrates the harmonious coexistence of human development and nature.

The small oceanside community consists of approximately 4 square miles and lies alongside N.C. 12 as it stretches through the northern Outer Banks. As you drive through the town along this winding, two-lane road, you'll see open skies, dunes with low scrub vegetation, vacation homes including old-style cottages with the vintage flattops, intermittent with large, expensive beach homes. If you turn off the highway away from the ocean onto one of the side roads, the landscape changes dramatically. Here you'll find neighborhoods and subdivisions of year-round homes, green lawns, hardwood trees draped with Spanish moss, dogwoods and a sprawling golf course.

A Haven of Solitude

Comprised of mostly single-family homes, Southern Shores is predominantly a residential town uncluttered by the commercial aspects of other Outer Banks areas, making it the perfect place to seek solitude. Residents enjoy canoeing or kayaking in the canal system designed by the younger Stick, a local historian and published author. Though not the painter his father was, David's artistic talent was in full swing when he created these panoramic lagoons that connect interior properties to Jean Guite Bay and Currituck Sound.

The community includes two private marinas, soundside picnic and bathing areas and ocean beach accesses situated every 600 feet. The accesses are available only to residents and vacationers staying in the area, affording every beachgoer enough elbow room to comfortably spread a blanket or throw a Frisbee. A soundside wading beach on N. Dogwood Trail is a favorite spot for families because the shallow sound water is a safer place for children to swim than the ocean. In the summer, the picnic area has toilet facilities on site. Paved and unpaved bike trails meander through the town. Anyone can use the facilities, but to park you must belong to the civic association or get a town sticker. In either case, you have to be a property owner or guest to park in Southern Shores.

The golf course at Duck Woods Country Club winds its way through a residential neighborhood of Southern Shores, offering outstanding play in a pristine setting among tall pines, dogwoods and other foliage. The 18-hole course is the oldest on the Outer Banks and accepts public play year round (see our Golf chapter).

The 40 original families who inhabited Southern Shores formed the town's first civic association. The Southern Shores Civic Association acts like a parks and recreation department. It owns, operates and maintains the marinas, playgrounds, beach accesses and crossovers for residents, property owners and guests. Membership dues cover costs, but most of the physical upkeep is done by volunteers in the community.

Today the population has expanded to 1,800 year-round residents, with retirees accounting for a large percentage of the population. The occupations of working residents vary greatly including landscapers, teachers and attorneys. The town hall is on a small hill off N.C. 158 on Skyline Road.

It's been 51 years since Stick first purchased Southern Shores, but due to slowly exposed development, there still is real estate available. Raw land on the oceanfront or soundfront is hard to come by these days, but those wanting to purchase property can obtain homes or land in the beach zone, dunes or woods. Due to careful planning, Southern Shores has land reserved for a future civic center and several plots to be developed for other town needs.

The nearest retail establishment, The Marketplace, includes a movie theater, a Food Lion and a multitude of smaller shops (see our Shopping chapter). This complex sits at the edge of Southern Shores, just east of the base of the Wright Memorial Bridge. However, the shops, restaurants and services of Kitty Hawk and Duck are only minutes away.

Incorporated in 1979, Southern Shores is but a year from celebrating its 20th anniversary. While growth has occurred in the development over the last 51 years, the developers' spirit of conservation is felt with every bike ride, every sunset and every tour of the waterways that weave together flora, fauna and humankind. The town continues to be environmentally conscious and is the first Outer Banks community to offer curbside recycling.

Kitty Hawk

If you're coming to the Outer Banks from Virginia, the first town you'll reach is Kitty Hawk. This beach municipality begins at the eastern end of the Wright Memorial Bridge over the Currituck Sound and stretches sound-to-sea for about 4 miles. Within its town limits are a maritime forest, fishing pier, golf course, condominiums and a historic, secluded village where Wilbur and Orville Wright stayed while conducting experiments on their famed flying machines.

Southern Shores forms the northern boundary of Kitty Hawk; Kill Devil Hills is to the south. Milepost makers give travelers hints about where they are. Most rental cottages, shops, restaurants, attractions and resorts in this area can be located by green milepost markers along U.S. 158 (Insiders call this the Bypass) and N.C. 12 (Insiders call this the Beach Road). The first milepost marker is in Kitty Hawk where the highway splits near the Aycock Brown Welcome Center.

What's In a Name?

With its name bonded to aviation history, and its positioning as one of the gateways to the reputed wide, undeveloped beaches of the Outer Banks, Kitty Hawk might not be what you expect — at least at first glance. Much of the 4 miles of beachfront here is narrower and appears more developed than any other place on the barrier islands. Even though Wilbur and Orville Wright certainly disembarked and

camped for short times in the village of Kitty Hawk, they didn't fly here. Their experiments and successful flights were accomplished a few miles down the road in Kill Devil Hills.

Now that we've got that straight, enjoy Kitty Hawk for what it is: an economical place to stay offering lots of family-oriented activities, a fishing pier, some great eateries, convenient shopping and all the fun you could want on a clean beach. Plus, tucked away within the borders of Kitty Hawk's 12 square miles are some of the loveliest and most exclusive communities in the central beach area.

Keep in mind that when you just feel like taking a ride, the Beach Road through Kitty Hawk is one of the few stretches on the entire Outer Banks where you can see the ocean right out your car window. As you cruise south along the beach, you'll start noticing some weatherbeaten houses perched tenuously on the shoreline. At high tide and in stormy weather, waves crash under the house pilings and wash out truckloads of sand. The ocean plays chicken every year with these tired beach

cottages, and just about every year a cottage cries uncle and collapses into the pounding surf. After every "big blow," local gossip (we love to talk weather here) inevitably comes around to an update on the Kitty Hawk cottages. You've likely gotten a good view of one of them on The Weather Channel, which, to the tourist bureau's chagrin, seems to delight in showing the wreckage of a particular Kitty Hawk beach house clinging pitifully to the sands during a storm. Once they're gone, they're gone, as federal coastal management law now forbids building closer than 60 feet from a coastline's first line of vegetation. A couple more were lost to nor'easters in the winter of 1997-98.

By one popular version, Kitty Hawk owes its colorful name to a derivation of local Indians' references to goose hunting season as "killy honker" or "killy honk." Eighteenth-century documents record this northern beach community as "Chickahauk." Other theories say the name evolved from "skeeter hawk," mosquito hawks that were prolific in the area, or from ospreys or similar raptors preying on the area's kitty wren.

The History of
"A Hospitable People"

Primarily a fishing and farming community from the late 18th century through the early 1900s, Kitty Hawk Village grew up along the wide bay that juts into the barrier islands along Albemarle Sound. By 1790, a builder, merchant, shoemaker, minister, planter and mariner all owned deeds to the sandy, sloping marshlands that now comprise Kitty Hawk. The community received additional goods from ships and ferries arriving from Elizabeth City and Norfolk.

In 1874, one of the Outer Banks' seven original lifesaving stations was built on the beach at Kitty Hawk. A U.S. Weather Bureau opened there the following year and remained in service until 1904. This weather station provided the Wright brothers with information about local wind patterns, which was the impetus for the Ohio bicycle shop owners to test their wings at Kill Devil Hill.

The first families of Kitty Hawk were named Twiford, Baum, Etheridge, Perry and Hill. These hearty folk were self-sufficient, building their own boats, fishing, farming and raising livestock on the open range. Many descendants of these early inhabitants still live on the west side of Kitty Hawk. A drive along winding Kitty Hawk Road, which begins just north of the 7-Eleven, will lead you to other streets with such names as Elijah Baum Road, Herbert Perry Road and Moore Shore Road. Along the latter is a monument that designates the spot where Orville and Wilbur Wright assembled their plane before successfully completing their historic flight a few miles away in 1903.

"I assure you, you will find a hospitable people when you come among us," Kitty Hawk Lifesaving Station Capt. Billy Tate wrote to Wilbur Wright in 1900. Tate described the local terrain as "nearly any type of ground you could wish . . . a stretch of sandy land 1 mile by 5 with a bare hill in the center 80 feet high, not a tree or a bush anywhere to break the wind current." The winds, he wrote, were "always steady, generally from 10 to 20 miles velocity per hour. If you decide to try your machine here and come, I will take pleasure in doing all I can for your convenience and success and pleasure."

Wilbur arrived at Kitty Hawk in September of that year. He traveled by rail from Dayton, Ohio, to Elizabeth City, where he boarded *The Curlicue* bound for the Outer Banks. The boat trip took two days in hurricane winds. Wilbur stayed with the Tates until Orville arrived, and then the two set up camp in Kitty Hawk Village.

Members of the Kitty Hawk Beach Lifesaving Station crew assisted the brothers with their early experiments. Even though many of the first flights were conducted near Kill Devil Hills, the Wright's first Outer Banks visit — and their letters carrying a Kitty Hawk postmark — etched this town's name in the annals of history around the world. It's not surprising that many visitors think the Wright Brothers National Monument is in Kitty Hawk, instead of 3 miles south atop Kill Devil Hill.

The first post office in Kitty Hawk opened November 11, 1878. A second one was established in 1905 to serve the western section of the community. In 1993 the biggest post office facility on the Outer Banks was built on the eastern side of U.S. 158 in Kitty Hawk.

Residents of this town floated their own $7,000 bond in 1924 to build a school. Housed in a single building, the grammar and high

INSIDERS' TIP

Enticing as Jockey's Ridge is on summer's day, don't visit this amazing dune in the blazing heat — you'll burn your feet and feel like you're in the Sahara within minutes. Wait till the sun is lower in the sky, and bring drinks and sunglasses. Glasses are particularly handy to keep the sand out of your eyes when the wind is stiff. Of course if the breeze is stiff enough, hang gliders will brave the heat, but they wear socks or tennis shoes.

school served fewer than 100 students until a Dare County high school consolidated Outer Banks children at a single facility in Manteo. Today, Kitty Hawk still has its own elementary school. Middle-school students travel by bus to Kill Devil Hills to attend First Flight Middle School, and high-school students still ride to Manteo, almost an hour's commute with stops each way for some.

The Transition to Vacation Destination

Unlike Nags Head, which has been a thriving summer resort since before the Civil War, Kitty Hawk didn't become a vacation destination until about 65 years ago. A group of Elizabeth City businessmen bought 7 miles of beach north of Kitty Hawk Village in the late 1920s and formed the Wright Memorial Bridge Company. By 1930, they had built a 3-mile wooden span across the Currituck Sound from Point Harbor to the Outer Banks. Now, travelers could finally arrive at the barrier island beaches by car from the mainland. Kitty Hawk land became popular — and a lot more pricey. Summer visitors streamed across the new bridge, paying $1 per car for the privilege.

With the sudden boom in tourism, development shifted from the protected soundside hammocks to the open, windswept beaches. Small wooden cottages sprung from behind dunes on the oceanfront. As the beach eroded over the years, wind and water had its way with many of the beachfront homes. Since 1993, more than a half-dozen houses have been swept away during hurricanes and nor'easters, providing newfound ocean frontage for the neighbor cottage across the street.

Even the original Kitty Hawk Lifesaving Station had to be jacked up and moved to a more protected site on the west side of the Beach Road to prevent tides from carrying it to a watery grave as well. The station is now a private residence, but travelers can still recognize the original Outer Banks gabled architecture of this historic structure.

In the western reaches of this community, the maritime forest of Kitty Hawk Woods winds for miles over tall ridges and blackwater swamps. Here, primarily year-round residents make their homes on private plots and in newly subdivided developments. Some lots are a lot larger here than in other central beach communities. The twisting vines, dripping Spanish moss and abundant tall trees also offer a seclusion and shelter from the storms not found in the expansive, open oceanfront areas. On summer days, locals often ride horses around the shady lanes of old Kitty Hawk Village, reminiscent of days before bridges.

Although you'll find some businesses tucked back in the trees of Kitty Hawk Village, at the western end of Kitty Hawk Road near the sound, most of this town's commercial outposts are along the Bypass and the Beach Road. The Outer Banks' only Wal-Mart is in Shoreside Centre near the end of the Wright Memorial Bridge. And Regional Medical Center at MP 1½ offers a full range of emergency and outpatient services.

If you're headed for the beach, you'll find a public bathhouse at MP 4½. The public is also welcome to use the Dare County boat launch at the end of Bob Perry Road, where locals and visitors can set sail during a hot summer day and watch the dolphins frolic in Kitty Hawk Bay.

From water-skiing to fishing, Kitty Hawk presents exceptional recreational possibilities. With all the water fun rounded out with delicious regional food establishments, convenient shopping and medical services, along with history and natural beauty, it's obvious why Kitty Hawk is a favorite beach retreat for young families, retirees and college students.

Kill Devil Hills and Colington Island

Even among all the other romantic and striking names of Outer Banks communities, Kill Devil Hills swirls a little longer in the imagination before rolling off the tongue. The sand dune where the Wright Brothers revolutionized transportation, Kill Devil Hill, legend has it, was named after the wretched-tasting kill-devil rum that may have been washed up in barrels from shipwrecks in early Colonial days. Another tale has the three hills named after a rogue called Devil Ike who blamed the theft of

Photo: Courtesy of Bob Reardon

Set aside a day (or night) for fishing from one of the many piers in the area.

shipwrecked cargo on the devil, whom he claimed to have chased to the hills and killed. Other local lore tells of a Banker who, atop one of the dunes, tried to kill the devil he had traded his soul to for a bag of gold.

The Outer Banks' first incorporated town, Kill Devil Hills is bookended nicely by Kitty Hawk and Nags Head. Spanning the barrier island from sound to sea, this beach community is the geographic and population center of Dare County, with about 5,000 permanent residents. Hundreds of thousands of tourists also visit this bustling beach town each summer. Indeed, the intersection of Ocean Bay Boulevard and Colington Road — where the Wright Memorial, a beach bathhouse, the post office, the town municipal center, the county chamber of commerce, the library and the entrance to the only road to Colington Island are grouped — is the busiest junction in the county.

Despite the trend toward bigger and more exclusive resort homes and amenities elsewhere on the Outer Banks, Kill Devil Hills remains attached to its place in history as a family-oriented beach for visitors and a centrally located town of moderately priced housing for the permanent population. Kite flying, sea kayaking, windsurfing, sunbathing, air flight tours, shopping, restaurants, motels, churches and schools combine to make this town a top choice for many, as it has been for more than a half-century.

Condominiums and franchise hotels dot the 5 miles of once-barren dunes. More than 41 miles of paved roads have replaced sandy pathways. Fast-food signs have sprung up along the five-lane U.S. Highway 158, forming the Outer Banks' commercial hub.

Building Bridges to the Tourist Trade

Kill Devil Hills is the only town on the beach that has streetlights along the Bypass, and it's the only place on the Outer Banks where you can get just about everything. Unlike Nags Head, which has been a resort destination since the mid-1800s, Kill Devil Hills' population did not really begin to grow until new bridges were constructed from the mainland across the sounds in the early 1930s. Kitty Hawk and Nags Head both had docks for steamer ships bringing passengers from Elizabeth City and Norfolk. Kill Devil Hills was seldom visited until cars could more easily reach the Outer Banks.

The federal government built a lifesaving station in Kill Devil Hills in 1879. At the time

Wilbur and Orville Wright arrived from Ohio to test their famed flying machine at the turn of the century, the few permanent residents living along the barren central beaches were mainly lifesavers, fishermen and salvagers. Even on December 17, 1903, when the Wrights made their first historic flight on windswept flatland below Kill Devil Hill, only a handful of local people watched in awe as the airplane finally soared under its own power.

Schoolchildren and their parents going back and forth to First Flight Elementary and First Flight Middle schools are treated to the sight of the Wright Brothers Memorial every day, looming under its varied sun- or moon-drenched shadows. Motorists can spy it from the Bypass or Colington Road. Recently, a 2-mile bike path was constructed on the outskirts of the landmark, and now in-line skaters, bikers and joggers exercise in range of the spell of history.

In the summer of 1952, U.S. Representative Lindsay C. Warren, D-N.C., was vacationing at the Croatan Inn on the Outer Banks. One night, historians say, Warren met Kill Devil Hills Coast Guard Capt. William Lewark on the hotel's sprawling deck. The men looked around them at the four dozen wooden "beach box" houses that had sprung from the sand over the past 20 years. Warren warned of over-expansion. He told Lewark that his seaside village ought to be zoned. He told the captain to create a town. So Lewark drafted a petition, called on his neighbors and convinced 90 of the area's 93 voters to support incorporation. On March 6, 1953, the General Assembly officially recognized Kill Devil Hills as the first town on Outer Banks beaches.

The new town almost died in infancy though. On May 4, 1955, the day that Emily Long Mustian, the town's first elected mayor, was scheduled to take office, the new town ceased to be a town. Fed up with taxes that had jumped to 30¢ from 10¢ per $100 of property value since incorporation, citizens passed a referendum repealing the town charter.

Kill Devil Hills was reborn, however. On February 29, 1956, the North Carolina Supreme Court ruled that the petition by which the referendum had been conducted was invalid and reversed the repeal vote. In the mid-1950s, when Kill Devil Hills' founders began planning their incorporated community, they worked from a town hall on a site that now houses Four Flags Restaurant on the Beach Road. Newly elected officials struggled to provide fire and police protection while residents balked at climbing taxes.

Residents of neighboring communities began looking for similar services but worried that the municipality might expand to encompass them. A 1955 newspaper report said that Kill Devil Hills commissioners refused to let their "new" 1925 fire truck respond to a call in neighboring Nags Head because the blaze was outside town limits. Nags Head was incorporated six years later.

Developers, meanwhile, aimed at selling prime properties in the newly incorporated town of Kill Devil Hills. Lots in Avalon, one of the Outer Banks' first subdivisions, used to be sold by developers who sat at card tables under beach umbrellas at the piers, hawking the plots for $250 each. Most of the property purchasers had their permanent homes in Hampton Roads. Today, those lots list at more than $25,000, but they're still some of the cheapest land in Dare County.

By the 1970s, business was booming in Kill Devil Hills — both with summer cottage rentals, motel traffic and year-round residents. The Outer Banks' first fast food restaurant, McDonald's, opened in 1978. The next year, Pizza Hut set up shop on a nearby Bypass lot. The rest of what locals call "French Fry Alley" developed in the late '70s and early '80s. As developers began stacking condominiums on the beaches as fast as they could, county commissioners hastily enacted a 35-foot building height moratorium to prevent spoiling the eye-appeal of the barrier beaches.

In 1986, commissioners financed streetlights for the town's 5 miles of highway, giving their municipality a special glow at night. By the end of the '80s, Kill Devil Hills employees had moved into a new complex on Veterans Drive, and the town had gotten its first large-scale shopping center. Complete with a full-size Food Lion, The Dare Centre completed the town's self-sufficiency in late 1989.

By the time the town turned 40 four years later, about 98 percent of Kill Devil Hills' private property already had been platted. Some

residents began looking for ways to retain their small-town feeling while becoming increasingly citified. Others expressed amazement at the ways in which their community was developing: adding a new soccer field for children, creating adult recreation programs and welcoming new retail shops each summer.

Colington Island

In 1633, Colington Island became the first land in Carolina to be deeded to an individual. Today this 2-mile-long, 2.5-mile-wide island, although developing rapidly, is one of the last of the Outer Banks communities to experience growth.

The east end of Colington Island lies a mile west of the Wright Brothers memorial, linked by a bridge over Colington Creek, which separates the island from Kill Devil Hills and the Dare County beaches. Colington's other borders are surrounded by open water. Kitty Hawk Bay is to the north and Buzzard Bay is to the south. The mouths of four sounds (Currituck, Albemarle, Croatan and Roanoke) converge on the west side of this family community.

Colington, named after its first proprietor Sir John Colleton, was originally tilled to grow grapes for a winery shortly after settlers in 1664 founded the first Outer Banks community. The grapes, along with crops of tobacco, fruits and vegetables, all eventually failed after three successive hurricanes. But by the early 1800s, a thriving fishing community sprung up on what was now two halves of the island: Great Colenton and Little Colenton, cleaved in 1769 by the Dividing Creek. Fishing, crabbing and hunting sustained islanders for generation after generation. Eventually, often years behind the rest of the barrier islands, Colington natives got paved roads, telephones and electric service.

Now, they have tourism. Just like the four-or five-generation families that live here, Colington Island has its own unique Outer Banks' identity. High, uneven dunes meet dank, brackish swamplands. Thick groves of pine, dogwood, live oak, beech and holly drip Spanish moss over expanses of sandy shoreline. Thin creeks widen to unexpected harbors and bays. In the summer months, soft-shell crab holding pens illuminate strips of scrubby yard along the sounds at night, the naked lights bulbs glaring out of the darkness like a Reno casino. Advertisements for waterfront property in pricey new subdivisions are posted not far from where trailers and campgrounds line the twisting road. Mansions are barely evident perched on their sandy shelves overlooking Colington Road, the most heavily traveled secondary road in Dare County.

Since Colington Harbour, the island's first subdivision, was built in 1965, at least four other subdivisions have been constructed along canals, marshlands, soundfronts and in woodlands throughout Colington Island. After a year of weighing benefits and risks, newcomers and natives last year hammered out a reasonable zoning plan. Several restaurants, a storage garage and a go-cart track mingling with crab shedders and fish houses along the road illustrate the conflict and challenges this sheltered community faced over dramatic change. With new development being approved every year, residents have accepted that growth is inevitable. The future face of Colington will be determined by the strength of the zoning plan and the people who molded it.

Nags Head

Home of the Outer Banks' first resort, the community of Nags Head is south of Kill Devil Hills and north of Oregon Inlet. It stretches from the Atlantic Ocean to the Roanoke Sound and has remained a popular vacation destination for more than 150 years.

The booming summer scene was once anchored by cottages towering over the shallow sound, elaborate hotels facing the mainland and calm-water canoeing, crabbing and conversation. This relaxed style of soundside vacationing has long since been overrun with shifting sands and varying values.

Nags Head Woods, an ancient maritime forest, and Jockey's Ridge, the East Coast's highest sand dune, are the jewels within the borders of our old-timer of the Outer Banks' resort areas. People seem to prefer the powerful ocean to the tranquil sound tides today, and most visitors only see the sound when they're crossing it by bridge or if they're boating or windsurfing. But for nearly a century, the sound was the place to see and be seen. The beach was merely a midday diversion, and Nags Head was the center of Outer Banks tourism.

Nags Head History and the Story Behind the Name

The primary resort destination on these barrier islands for more than a century, Nags Head has been the official name of the area since at least 1738 when it first appeared on maps. Historians say the beach town got its name from the free-range horses that once roamed throughout the islands. The much more colorful legend we Insiders prefer is that Nags Head was derived from a custom locals used to lure ships to the shores with clever trickery. Securing a lantern from a Banker pony's neck, residents would drive the horse up and down the beach, the light swinging with the same motion as a sailboat. The unsuspecting offshore vessel would then steer toward the light and proceed to get grounded, often wrecked, on the shoals. The locals would then promptly ransack what was left of the hapless ship.

In the early 1830s, a Perquimans County planter explored the then-deserted Outer Banks "with the view of finding a suitable place to build a summer residence where he and his family could escape the poisonous miasma vapors and the attendant fevers," wrote author and historian David Stick in *The Outer Banks of North Carolina*. "He explored the beach and the sound shore and picked his house site overlooking the latter, near the tallest of the sand hills." The planter paid $100 to an unknown Banker for the 200 acres and built the first summer house on the Outer Banks in Nags Head.

In 1838, the Outer Banks' first hotel was built in Nags Head midway between the sound and the sea. A two-story structure, the grand guesthouse had accommodations for 200 travelers, an elaborate ballroom, a bowling alley, covered porches and a 5-foot-wide pier that extended from the hotel's front a half-mile into the sound.

The 1850 census showed that 576 people, including 30 slaves, lived year round in Nags Head, but hundreds more came each summer. By that time the soundside community had become a well-known watering hole for the families of mainland farmers, bankers and lawyers.

Elizabeth City doctor William Gaskins Pool was the first person to build a home on the seaside in 1866, according to a 19th-century journal kept by Outer Banks resident Edward R. Outlaw Jr. On September 14, 1866, Pool purchased 50 acres "at or near Nags Head, bordering on the ocean, for $30" and constructed his one-story cottage 300 feet from the breakers. "But over there by themselves, his family was very lonely," Outlaw writes in his book, *Old Nag's Head*.

Seeing that the Pools could survive beside the sea, more people began building their houses on the eastern edges of Nags Head. By the early 1900s, homeowners were erecting their cottages on logs so they could roll them back from encroaching tides. Some of the houses moved three or four times during residents' lifetimes. Along skinny strips of sand, after big storms, you can still see house movers jacking up rental homes and sliding them away from the sea.

Today, hotels, restaurants, piers, go-carts and rambling residences line Nags Head's oceanfront. Primarily private cottages remain secluded on the sound and along the quiet, exclusively residential community of South Nags Head. A Scottish links-style golf course beckons travelers to tee off on some of the area's most challenging fairways.

Nags Head became an incorporated town in 1961. As it did more than a century ago, this beach area continues to attract anglers and surfers, nature lovers and shoppers, families and fun-seeking adventurers. A half-century ago, Newman's Shell Shop opened as the first store on the beach. Charter boat captains Sam and Omie Tillett opened a restaurant at Whalebone Junction more than 50 years ago to serve breakfast to their fishing parties. The one-story wooden eatery across from Jennette's Pier still bears their names — and still serves some of the best she-crab soup around.

Hang-gliding enthusiasts, both aspiring and experienced, come here from across the East Coast to soar from atop the Atlantic's tallest inland sand dune, Jockey's Ridge. The best kite flying and sunset views are also found atop this natural phenomenon. Hikers, strollers and nature lovers delight in the wooded wonderment of the Nags Head Woods Preserve, where diverse flora and fauna can be enjoyed in stunning silence. (Turn to our Natural Wonders chapter for details.) Simply watching dolphins leaping in the sound is the best entertainment available, a treat even those of us who live here never tire of. Artists from all around display their work in a variety of mediums in shops and studios along Gallery Row. The Carolinian, one of the Outer Banks' oldest still-operating hotels, offers nightly comedy shows in a large downstairs nightclub throughout the summer.

The barrier islands' only amusement park, Dowdy's, has a Ferris wheel, bumper cars and merry-go-round near MP 11. The Outer Banks' only enclosed mall is on the Bypass at MP 17. A bike path winds along the Beach Road from Whalebone Junction through South Nags Head.

Although the old Casino has long-since closed across from Jockey's Ridge, nightspots including Kelly's Tavern and George's Junction continue to offer live entertainment most summer nights.

Hotels and good restaurants abound in Nags Head. Rental cottages range from simple to spectacular — in corresponding price ranges. Nags Head has tennis courts, personal watercraft rental outfits, surf shops, movie theaters, miniature golf courses, in-line skate rental stores and even the area's only bowling alley.

Since it's centrally located on the Outer Banks, Nags Head is a favorite destination of people who want to take daytrips to Hatteras Island and Corolla. If you don't want to get in the car again once you've arrived at your vacation destination, you can get everything you want within walking distance of most Nags Head hotels and cottages.

Whether you're looking to escape the bustle of the beach by taking a quiet canoe ride through the Nature Conservancy's Nags Head Woods Ecological Preserve or dance the night away at a tropical tavern, this Outer Banks beach town remains one of the area's most popular resorts.

Roanoke Island

Nestled between the Outer Banks and the North Carolina mainland, Roanoke Island is one of the most historic places in America. People sometimes confuse our island's history with that of Jamestown, Virginia, where the first "permanent" English colony thrived in the early 17th century. The confusion between the two revolves around the word permanent. Roanoke Island is the very place to which Sir Walter Raleigh dispatched an expedition of Englishmen who were the first Europeans to step foot in the New World in 1584. It is the same island where the first established English colony in America disappeared in a cloud of mystery (see our History chapter); hence the lack of "permanence." Despite having a slippery foothold on history, the Lost Colony has left a permanent hunger in the minds of the curious. Theories concerning their fate abound, as our History chapter outlines, but until archeologists dig up some real proof, we'll continue to ponder the fate of Virginia Dare and her clan, an unexplained disappearance that began tearing at the heart of her father, Governor John White, five centuries ago (see our History chapter).

For those who appreciate concrete links to the past, relics exist that have been retrieved from the waters surrounding Roanoke Island — artifacts that hold hidden, centuries-old secrets. Many local folk and archaeologists alike have combed the island for treasures from the Native American culture, earliest English settlements and Civil War times (read our History chapter for more information on these Roanoke Island highlights). Old English coins,

a powder horn, a vial of quicksilver, weapons, bottles, iron fragments, pottery and arrowheads have been discovered here. Some of these remnants can be seen at Fort Raleigh National Historic Site on the north end of the island (see our Attractions chapter), while others found their way into personal collections. Roanoke Island native Hubby Bliven opened The Roanoke Heritage Gallery and Museum on the island mostly with artifacts he's been collecting since his youth. Archaeologists continue to search today for clues to the bygone era. Speculation exists that an ongoing dig occurring on Hatteras Island could uncover some indication that the Roanoke colony left the island with friendly Croatan Indians and relocated on Hatteras.

Today, you can gaze from the grand bridges that connect this tiny island, measuring 3 miles wide and 12 miles long, to the rest of the world, and with a little imagination, its history comes alive. Bordered by the Roanoke and Croatan sounds and threaded throughout by canals, creeks, bay and marsh, the natural geography inspires romantic visions in visitors and locals alike.

You can't help but be a nature lover if you live on Roanoke Island. Early mornings and late afternoons in the spring, summer and fall, find marsh rabbits nibbling roadside grasses for long stretches. Red-winged black birds looking much like holiday ornaments, adorn the bushes scattered alongside the road. They really stand out in the winter when the leaves have left trees barren. Scan the creeks in the warm months, just before entering Roanoke Island from the west, and you can see turtles lined like soldiers on half sunken logs and along the banks. Crossing the Washington Baum Bridge from the east, we regularly spot osprey flying overhead, clutching dangling snakes or fish in their claws. (Try not to remove your eyes from the road too long, and definitely do not stop on the bridge!) Of course, a wide variety of fish, such as spot, croaker, pigfish, sea mullet, sheepshead and stripers, inhabit the surrounding waters. Boats and recreational water vehicles of all sorts share the sounds and bays in fair weather. Crabbers, windsurfers, sailors, Jet Skiers, small fishing crafts and big charter vessels cross paths on a daily basis.

By land, you can experience a walk back into time at the new Roanoke Island Festival Park, at the *Elizabeth II* State Historic Site in Manteo. The park features a soundside nature path, the Thomas Hariot Trail, named after the 16th century author, who, after having explored the area, wrote the first book about the New World written in Elizabethan English. Hariot studied the Native Americans and made a survey of the natural resources. Only six copies are said to exist today of his literary treatise. A 20th-century Hariot (also known as a costumed interpreter) wanders the trail that hugs Roanoke Sound and offers insight into the natural surroundings.

Getting Here

Roanoke Island is west of Nags Head and due east of Williamston, North Carolina. It certainly is easier and quicker to get here now than it was centuries or even decades ago due to the construction of several bridges. While you won't have to forge a path through reeds like our ancestors, you still can reach the island by water. Roadsters can choose from at least four routes; all are scenic. Some are more remote than others, or you can choose to fly a small plane into the Dare County Regional Airport on the north end of the island. Believe it or not, it's not unusual to see folks ride in on bicycles. For specific directions see our Getting Here, Getting Around chapter.

Island Economy and Tourism

At the heart of Roanoke Island is the desire/conflict to preserve a small-town feeling while finding ways to make a living. Islanders mostly work in tourist- and service-oriented businesses, at fishing-related jobs, as writers and artists, in local government and the public school system. (Manteo is also the corporate headquarters for The Insiders' Guide Inc. publishing company.)

With the fluctuating financial climate in mind, it's fortunate we have history we can market. Our Attractions chapter describes our top sites such as The Elizabethan Gardens, The North Carolina Aquarium, Fort Raleigh National Historic Site, The Outer Banks History Center, The Elizabeth II State Historic Site, Roanoke Island Festival Park, The Roanoke Heritage Gallery and Museum and The Lost Colony.

An interesting place to read up on Roanoke Island lore and view old photographs and maps is at the Outer Banks History Center, on what used to be known as Ice Plant Island. This island is now referred to as Roanoke Island Festival Park (see our Arts & Culture chapter).

Don't overlook the main branch of the Dare County Library on Highway 64, just across from Manteo Elementary School, as a source for more island information. Check out their North Carolina Reference section. You'll discover a good many books there are written by Insiders. For overall Outer Banks information, such as maps, brochures and other local data, stop in at the Dare County Tourist Bureau, beside the 7-Eleven on U.S. 64. The staff is friendly and helpful, and there's even a convenient drive-through window if you find it's too hard to get the kids and paraphernalia out of the car.

Inside information also can be had by talking with some of our old-timers. Conversation with lifelong locals is bound to reveal a body of knowledge that would give the Outer Banks History Center a run for its money. There are plenty of boat captains that run fishing charters out of Outer Banks marinas who can fill your ear with tales. Stories by natives bring to life the days when islanders drove horses and buggies through the mud to catch a movie downtown and how it felt to venture offshore to fish for the first time. You'll hear tales of pregnant women who delivered their babies with the help of a midwife at the local doctor's house and spent time recuperating there. Pick up a copy of *Memories of Manteo and Roanoke Island, N.C.*, by Suzanne Tate as told by Cora Mae Basnight, if you're unable to make a personal connection. This oral history, from the mouth of a native and the mother of the current Senator Pro Tem of the North Carolina Senate, Marc Basnight, is a delightful book accented by interesting photographs. Ms. Basnight, according to Tate's book, holds the record for playing the same role longer than any actress in American Theater. Her role as Agona, a Native American squaw, in *The Lost Colony* is legendary.

Lots of exciting tales revolve around *The Lost Colony*, the historic outdoor drama that outlines the story of the first English settlement and its disappearance. Pulitzer Prize-winning playwright Paul Green brought this production to Manteo in 1937, and it has played a major role in the lives of local folk ever since (see our Arts and Culture chapter). In 1997, the production held its 60th anniversary, and thespians and theater-folk from the world over returned to the island to reminisce and celebrate the occasion.

Generations of families grew up acting in the annual play. From representing the infant, Virginia Dare, to playing the role of Gov. John White or Chief Manteo, many a Roanoke Island resident nurtured a love of history through the play and a love of theater as a result. And Andy Griffith, who played Sir Walter Raleigh in his first acting stint, is a Roanoke Island resident.

William S. Powell's *Paradise Preserved* is the definitive source where you can study the history of the Roanoke Island Historical Association, perpetuators of the historic play. Powell offers an exciting account of the creative endeavors of Mrs. Mabel Evans Jones, the author and producer of local pageants on Roanoke Island that predate Green's play. Evans, the former Superintendent of Schools in Dare County, ran a summer arts camp on the island back in the early 1920s. As it is with the archeologist, the more you dig, the more you're likely to uncover concerning Roanoke Island's roots and tales of the people who have called the island home.

Yesteryear and Today

Prior to the settling of Manteo in the 1860s, islanders had established two sparsely populated residential settlements on Roanoke Island called the Upper End and the Lower End. The Upper End referred to the north end of Roanoke Island, and the lower end described the area that is now called Wanchese. About 100 years later, a third settlement was formed by former slaves and has been referred to as California. Manteo and the village of Wanchese were named after two Native Americans who befriended the early English explorers.

California

When the black residents of the island's north end were forced to relocate in the 1930s, they settled in a section of Manteo west of U.S. 64. Between Shallowbag Bay and Croatan Sound, south of the Dare County Regional Airport, California referred to land that stretched from Bowserstown Road to Burnside Road. At the turn of the century, the tract was

bought by 11 black men and divided among them. Nobody is sure why the area was named California, but its history includes an account of children tacking a hand-painted sign to a tree in a fig orchard on the west side of the community, christening it such.

California history shines with memories of blacks and whites ignoring Jim Crow laws to pass back and forth between communities via White Cross Way, also called Bay Street, to help one another. The isolation of Roanoke Island may have helped islanders weather the postwar civil rights conflict without mayhem. Skin color did not prevent neighbors from delivering baskets of fruits and vegetables to anyone in need.

Today, most of Dare County's minority population still lives in what was once the California community, half of which lies in the town of Manteo and just outside the town limits in Dare County.

More on Manteo

Manteo became Dare County's seat in 1870 and was incorporated as a town in 1899. Islanders soon erected the first courthouse and established a post office. The white-columned brick courthouse that stands in downtown Manteo today was built in 1904 to replace the original wooden structure. One of the earliest private homes built on the Upper End in the 1780s, was the Etheridge home, also referred to as Drinkwater's Folley. It was moved in the 1930s from a wooded area between Heritage Point and the Elizabethan Gardens to its present location at U.S. 64 at the Morrison Grove turnoff. Another private home that bears note is the Colonial-style dwelling built in Manteo in 1872 that later became the Tranquil House, whose rooms entertained Thomas Edison and radio pioneer Reginald Fessenden. The Tranquil House also did a tour of duty as a barracks during World War II. The original Tranquil House is gone now, but the name lives on at a different location. Today there's a new Tranquil House Inn, which operates as a bed and breakfast in downtown Manteo on The Waterfront.

In the late 1800s Roanoke Island acted as a valuable port. Large boats from Old Dominion Streamline of Norfolk, Virginia, made daily stops on the westside end of the island at Skyco (between Manteo and Wanchese), while Manteo's Shallowbag Bay was a busy port for smaller boats. In 1906, Shallowbag Bay was dredged, allowing access to larger boats such as the river steamer Trenton. For nearly 20 years, mail, freight and passengers arrived daily on this vessel.

As new infrastructure tied the island to other areas, Roanoke Island became less remote and things began to change. In 1928 the Washington Baum Bridge was completed, linking Roanoke Island to the Outer Banks beaches. Two years later the Wright Memorial Bridge was constructed to tie those beaches to Currituck from the north. New roads were built from Elizabeth City and Manteo, and as the automobile became more popular, boat usage declined somewhat.

Fire has ravaged the Manteo waterfront five times since 1920. Oil that was brought to the island by barge was stored in tanks on the waterfront. The presence of all that oil caused great problems when the town caught fire. All that was available to put the early fires out was an old-fashioned bucket brigade, with volunteers forming a line and handing buckets of water from one person to another. During the course of these five fires, various sections of town were destroyed, including the old Hotel Roanoke. The only mercantile building to survive all the fires is the little white building on Budleigh Street that now operates as E.R. Midgett Insurance. Adequate fire-fighting equipment, a modern water system and brick were introduced to the town when rebuilding began in the 1930s.

Manteo continues to be the hub for Dare County's business. From 1983 through 1987, major renovations took place in the town as part of America's Quadricentennial. Fifteen-hundred live oaks and crepe myrtles were planted on the island's main corridor along U.S. 64. Buildings and streets were restored, bringing new glory to the town.

On July 13, 1984, Manteo entertained Princess Anne of England, North Carolina Gov. James B. Hunt Jr. and newsman Walter Cronkite as part of America's 400th Anniversary Celebration. A memorial stone on the waterfront commemorates the event.

Manteo today does a good job reflecting its history. The downtown Manteo Waterfront complex featuring shops, restaurants and private residences is built in Old World-style architecture. You can sit at outdoor picnic tables or benches along the docks or in one of the window-lined restaurants and view the Elizabeth II (see our Attractions chapter), which is berthed across the bay from the Manteo waterfront at Roanoke Island Festival Park. Reminders of our Native American and English heritages are evident in many of the town's street names including: Ananias Dare, Wingina, Sir Walter Raleigh, Queen Elizabeth, Essex and Uppowac. Traveling these byways threading through historic Manteo are a number of structures worth noting.

In Manteo proper on Budleigh Street, you'll find the English Tudor-style Ye Olde Pioneer Theatre, the oldest family-operated movie theater in the United States, which is celebrating its 64th year in 1998 (see our Attractions chapter). You can actually get a bag of popcorn here for 50¢, and that's after paying only $3 to get in. The town hall, on Budleigh Street has an interesting history as the former site of the Roanoke Island Academy. Two teachers taught grades 4 through 11 there, and the auditorium doubled as a moviehouse before the new theater was built. The Theodore S. Meekins house on Sir Walter Raleigh Street that now operates as the White Doe Inn (see our Accommodations chapter) is one of Manteo's most elegant buildings. The basic structure of the house was built before 1900. Featuring long porches, rounded glass in the turret windows, the white, three-storied inn is listed in the National Register of Historic Places. A reference for historic Manteo sites is *The Manteo Walking Tour*, available at the Manteo branch of

INSIDERS' TIP

Don't pull off the road anywhere on the Outer Banks unless it's a paved area. Many cars get stuck in the soft sand here and have to get towed out.

the Dare County Library on Highway 64. They have two copies of this guide booklet. One copy is on permanent file in the North Carolina section, but a second copy can be checked out of the library. While the pamphlet is not completely accurate, we mention it because it is the only reference that lists historic Manteo structures.

There are approximately 800 registered voters in Manteo, and the small town has a population of 1,081. It continues to grow as it annexes outlying properties, and as far as new building, Manteo proper — the historic downtown area — is fairly well-developed with only a few select lots left. People are drawn to the charm and the quaintness and the small town atmosphere here. A recent police survey showing no serious crime to speak of in the town also reflects its desirability. If there is any significant future growth to Manteo, which is currently home to five churches and four schools, expansion would be to the south, but that's very indefinite.

Wanchese

Wanchese, on the southern end of the island, has a more isolated feel than Manteo. For years it's operated as a fishing port. The village reflects a lifestyle that's a tad different than its northern island neighbor. Drive the streets and you'll see wooden houses, built in some cases 80 to 100 years ago, that have been lovingly maintained. In many backyards you still find boats in various sizes and states of repair, linking their owners with the ever-important sea.

Many old seagoing vessels fill Wanchese Harbor, living out their last days in a place decades of men have used as a regular point of departure. While time will always bring change in the fishing industry — change in species, seafood quantities, boat styles and government regulations — in Wanchese today, you can track living threads that were established long ago when men thrived in the industry and navigated solely by the stars. Still living today are at least three or four generations of anglers, men and women alike, from families who have at one time or another called Wanchese home. The Tilletts, the Baums and the Etheridges, names you'll notice a lot on the Outer Banks, are just a few. Some have crossed over from commercial fishing to become sport fishermen, and many work as boat builders.

Today, as many as 50 fishing trawlers from up and down the East Coast use Wanchese Harbor, as do hundreds of smaller commercial and sport-fishing boats. The village features several seafood companies that ship fish all over the country. Most seafood caught in Dare County goes through Wanchese, and an estimated 27.5 million dollars worth or 39 million pounds was landed in the county in 1995 (this is the latest figure available on record). Boats fish North Carolina's offshore and inshore waters and also depart Wanchese Harbor to fish off New England in the winter. On the east side of the harbor is the state-owned Wanchese Seafood Industrial Park where seafood and marine-related industries are based (see our Attractions chapter). The park features boat-maintenance facilities, seafood plants, boat builders and state fisheries operations.

Wanchese has 852 registered voters out of an estimated 1,875 people living in the small fishing community. An average of only three to four homes and/or buildable lots comes available annually. There is plenty of undeveloped land in Wanchese that is buildable, but it is privately owned.

Boat Building

A section on Roanoke Island would be incomplete without a nod to a very special livelihood shared by native islanders. Boat building was and continues to be a major part of Roanoke Island living. From the small bateau put together in a backyard shed to the 72-foot yachts constructed at major boat-building operations, Manteo and Wanchese share in this rich heritage.

Winters of the past would find many fishermen holed up in shops crafting juniper vessels that would take them farther from home than many had ever imagined. The *Sharpie* and the *Shallowbag Shad Boat* were designed and built in Manteo. Near where the Elizabeth II Boathouse is now located on the Manteo waterfront, George and Benjamin Creef operated the Manteo Machine Shop and Railways in the 19th century. The shop was built in 1884, and boats were hauled out of the water and serviced there. It was at this location that "Uncle Wash" Creef built the first shad boat, now documented as one of the most important fishing vessels of its time because its design allowed it to effectively work nets and carry weight and still ride well in the water.

Boats are still built on Roanoke Island today — huge, sleek vessels painted in light hues and buffed to a sun-splintering shine. Each spring, these brand-new 50-foot-plus boats emerge from private building barns and are tugged slowly down the highway to Wanchese to be put in the water for the first time. On board the boat, the happy construction crew carefully lifts power lines as their vessel moves down the road, invariably delaying traffic. Smiles wreath the faces of the crew: After six to eight months of hammering, sanding and painting they are ready to christen the fruit of their labor. It is a tense time, too, for no one really relaxes until everyone sees that the boat sits and moves "just right" in the water. You can hear the admirers exclaim "pretty work" as the vessel begins her maiden voyage. The crowd always includes family members and friends who wouldn't miss the celebration.

Hatteras Island

The sea is a strong tonic that humans sometimes crave at the expense of security. Nowhere is this desire more obvious than in the people who live on the little stretch of sand that juts precariously out into the Atlantic Ocean just off North Carolina's coast. Hatteras Island residents accept the stresses of living with a seasonal economy dependent on good weather, their share of storm damage and cultural isolation while carving out solid lives in the shifting sand. The decision to live on the threshold of land and sea forges an intimate relationship with nature. Like passionate lovers, each contributes joys and sorrows that cannot easily be put asunder. Why live in an ever-changing environment? Because blood is thicker than water. And locals know it's really Mother Nature's wind, sea and salt that courses through every Hatteras islander's veins.

Hatteras Island is south of Nags Head and north of Ocracoke Island. Hatteras Island measures 60 miles from Ocracoke Inlet to Hatteras Inlet. It consists of seven small towns. Running north to south they are Rodanthe, Waves, Salvo, Avon, Buxton, Frisco and Hatteras Village. You can enter the island from the north by car via N.C. 12 by crossing the Herbert C. Bonner Bridge or south by ferry via Ocracoke Island. As with our other townships and islands, you can also reach the area by air — setting down on a small airstrip in Frisco — or by boat. (See our Getting Here, Getting Around chapter for airfield and ferry information and our Fishing chapter for marina information.)

The interior of the Currituck Beach Lighthouse in Corolla is a photographer's dream.

Nags Head Woods offers a cool reprieve from the sun-drenched beaches.

Photo: Courtesy of Mary Ellen Riddle

Island Living, Economy and Tourism

Overall, Hatteras' residents live and work supported mostly by tourism, fishing, real estate, teaching and government employment. Because of the seasonal economy, weather-related economic setbacks and lack of corporations and industries that hire mass amounts of people, it's not unusual for residents to have more than one job. Cleaning cottages on the side provides extra money, and you may find that your waiter during the summer months is a professional from another trade altogether.

Necessity also provokes creativity, and many locals sell their carvings or paintings in local shops and galleries. One thing remains clear about most barrier island residents: They choose to be here.

Families thrive despite typical small-town inconveniences. They pattern their living styles accordingly. You won't find a Kmart on the island, but mail-order companies get their share of business. There's no movie theater on the island, but the stands are packed at the Cape Hatteras High School basketball games (even folks with no kids attend). The Cape Hatteras team, appropriately called the Hurricanes, made it to the state playoffs in 1997 and '98. Part of their success has been attributed to the fact that the players grew up playing basketball together and have a strong rapport with their hometown coach. With a school that has only 95 to 100 male high school students to choose from (it's the smallest school in its state athletic classification), the fervor generated at home and away games is award-winning in and of itself. Word has it that the away games have their share of Hatteras fans in the stands, which says a lot coming from islanders whose ancestors had to be pried from their homes during hurricane evacuations.

It only has been in the last three or four years that Hatteras residents have left the island in large numbers during a county-mandated evacuation. We have national footage of damages to other areas from Hurricane Hugo and Andrew to thank for it. Weather plays a regular role in Hatteras life. When the island is evacuated during a hurricane warning, it's not unusual for the locals to lose a week's worth of income. This creates great financial hardship for businesses.

Even smaller storms cause delays when the roads flood. A recent nor'easter found parts of N.C. 12 under water during high tide for four days. It's not uncommon to find a pair of boots left by the front and back door of a islander's home. Residents even sometimes leave a day early to get to the Norfolk International Airport on time, avoiding last-minute delays from flooded roadways. When the Herbert C. Bonner Bridge, which spans Oregon Inlet, was hit and damaged by an unwieldy dredge during a storm in October 1990, islanders who worked on the mainland or needed to leave had to travel off Hatteras by boat or ferry. Long days ensued, as travel time greatly multiplied. Nature and islanders are so entwined, it's hard to tell where the sea mist ends and the foggy breath of life begins.

Despite the imposing tone Mother Nature can cast over the barrier island, (the county has a great evacuation policy that has visitors leaving the island in plenty of time) visitors flock here annually to enjoy its beauty and seclusion. Today there are enough conveniences, restaurants and diversions within reach to entertain even sophisticated vacationers. The Cape Hatteras School, with help from the local arts council, brings in cultural events for the residents. There are also several noteworthy art galleries on the island (see our Arts and Culture chapter).

Avon has its very own Food Lion and Ace Hardware. There is a new county-funded community center in Buxton, the Fessenden Center, that has meeting rooms, a gymnasium with a basketball court and a softball field. Ground has been broken on a county-run reverse-osmosis water plant in Buxton, which will improve service and quality and could affect the real estate industry as a result. Deeper wells will tap into a saltwater aquifer that lies below the fresh water source currently in use. The water will be desalinated at the plant. Costs for water may rise, but there will be more of it. Currently residents self-impose water conservation. Short showers, recycled pool water, gardens planted with vegetation that requires little watering and low flow shower heads and toilets have become part of the norm.

History tells us, though, that even without these modern additions, folks would still come to relax Hatteras style, to do a little crabbing, clamming, fishing, beach walking, bird-watching or chatting with the old fishermen who relax at the docks. Many a modern day adult vacationer has been coming to the Outer Banks since childhood. In fact, generations of families can call Hatteras Island their summer home.

The island has obvious drawing cards, the sea and unique landscape. Both natural and artificial recreational activities abound. Some of the best windsurfing and surfing in North America can be done in the waters along Hatteras Island (see our Recreation, Attractions and Watersports chapters). Surfers from all over the East Coast come to Hatteras Island to surf the breakers, especially during strong nor'easters. Surfers look forward to hurricane season from June through November, when big northern swells push the waves to 8 feet and sometimes higher. National surfing championships are held in Buxton (see our Annual Events chapter).

Hatteras Island is famous as an East Coast fishing hotspot. Moving through the ocean about 40 miles offshore are the Gulf Stream, a shelf current and the Deep Western Boundary Current, all of which cross near the Continental Shelf's edge. The influence of this convergence is both positive and negative. These crossing currents spawned Diamond Shoals, creating the groundwork for danger but also supplying a rich habitat for game fish (see our Natural Wonders and Fishing chapters).

While the watery Graveyard of the Atlantic gives Hatteras a bad rap, with shipwrecks lining almost the entire length of the underwater coastline, a wide variety of species of fish travel up the Gulf Stream supporting a more positive billing: "The Billfish Capital of the World." World-

Photo: Courtesy of J. Aaron Trotman

Ocracoke Inlet Lighthouse continues to emit one long flash every few seconds from a half-hour before sunset to a half-hour after sunrise.

record fish have been caught both offshore and in the surf at Cape Hatteras Point, where red drum come to feed. Much of the tip of Hatteras is lined with marinas where recreational charter boats take visitors to the inshore and offshore waters (see our Fishing chapter). Full-service tackle shops, staffed with knowledgeable folks, speckle the barrier island.

North of Rodanthe and just south of Oregon Inlet is the Pea Island National Wildlife Refuge, and a unique maritime forest lies farther south in Buxton (see our Attractions and Natural Wonders chapter for descriptions of both).

There are three National Park Service campgrounds on Hatteras Island (at Oregon Inlet, Frisco and Cape Point) offering more laid-back and less expensive camping than the rest of the Outer Banks camping facilities. Several private campgrounds also are established in the island communities (see our Camping chapter).

If Mother Nature hasn't sold you on Hatteras Island's perks, check out our Recreation chapter for those artificial amusements that can be enjoyed by the whole family.

Yesteryear and Today

Thousands of years ago, Native Americans settled on Hatteras Island and called it Croatan. Originally marked Cape S. John on 16th-century maps, the island's history is filled with diverse tales of Civil War battles, fabulous fishing stories, shipwrecks and life-saving efforts (see our History and Fishing chapters).

The residents of this 33-mile-long barrier island, who could only reach the outside world by boat until the Bonner Bridge was built to span Oregon Inlet in 1963, were a people so isolated that their speech today still maintains the direct flavor of their ancestors. Need was the driving force behind livelihood

---

INSIDERS' TIP

Listen carefully to the native Ocracoke dialect. Linguists are fascinated by Ocracokers' distinctive speech. If you're feeling "quamish" (pronounced qualm-ish) down Ocracoke way, chances are you are suffering from an upset stomach.

choices. Everyone fished for food, and seafood was traded on the mainland for provisions and corn. Windmills, a profusion of which dotted the landscape, provided the power to turn corn into flour. Commercial fishermen harvested whale oil, turtles, oysters and even seaweed. And the island was once covered with roving livestock gobbling up protective vegetation.

The village of Kinnakeet, now Avon, was the heart of a thriving shipbuilding industry. Materials were gathered from the oak and cedar forests on the sound side of the island. The islanders built their homes there, in the woody hammocks, seeking safety from high waters and winds. Timbers also were used to fashion clipper ships. It was a base for a large fleet of small schooners. Many of these were used to harvest oysters.

The Cape Hatteras Lighthouse in Buxton has towered over the island's low-lying terrain since 1870. Rising 208 feet, it is the tallest brick lighthouse in the nation (see our History and Attractions chapters). Tours are offered all summer. Within reach of the light shed by the tower are the treacherous and ever-changing Diamond Shoals. The shoals have claimed hundreds of vessels, and lifesaving teams, at one time riding horse-drawn carts through the sand, saved thousands of seafarers' lives off these shores. Today, modern equipment aids in navigation, and the Cape Hatteras Light still operates, but the power of the sea, shuffling weather patterns and changing inlets still cause captains to traverse the waters with care.

Much of Hatteras Island is undeveloped National Park Service property. But scattered north to south along the coast are the seven villages, hugging what is loosely termed "Highway 12," a thin strip of blacktop often covered with sand and water. More often than not, it seems the children of Hatteras' oldtimers stay or return to carry on family traditions in these villages. This may be why the flavor of the area has not changed too drastically over the years despite the influx of vacationers and outsiders looking for summer homes. Most of the people who move here are seeking just what the island presents: the domination of nature coupled with the feel of a small community.

There are more than 5,000 year-round residents living on Hatteras Island with a total of 2,569 registered voters. With the blink of an eye, you can drive past these tiny villages, ending up in circular Hatteras Village at the island's tip. This is where you pick up the ferry to Ocracoke Island. The majority of churchgoers attend Methodist or Assembly of God services, but there is also a relatively new Catholic church in Buxton.

While 75 percent of Hatteras Island is National Park land, lots and homes are available for purchase, and each village has a mix of low to upper income choices. The addition of a reverse-osmosis water plant on the north end of the island breathed new life into the Rodanthe, Waves and Salvo communities in the spring of 1996, allowing many additional parcels to be built upon. Formerly using electric-generated water pumps, the residents are now able to maintain a steady water flow even when storms knock out the power. Utility lines have been upgraded over the last few years, so power outages are not as frequent. Cape Hatteras has plenty of real estate available, but their infrastructure, including their school, would have to be expanded to accommodate new residents.

Islanders are looking for a boost in the economy once North Carolina's highway plan is complete. U.S. 64 from Raleigh to the Outer Banks is scheduled to be completely four-laned, or well into the process of becoming so, by the year 2000. A new bridge, also part of the highway package, is scheduled to be constructed from Manns Harbor to Wanchese. These upgrades will cut travel time for vacationers coming to the island from the west.

As our visitors come and go annually, the wind and sea claim and deposit coastline, birds and fish rendezvous in our wetlands and coastal waters and as residents board up windows or open their doors to sunny skies each year, what remains unchanged is the desire to be a part of the flow, Hatteras style.

Ocracoke Island

Insiders generally see Ocracoke as a tourist hotspot during the warm months and romantic hideaway during the off season, but

The Outer Banks landscape is dotted with historic
reminders such as the Cape Hatteras Lighthouse.

they grab any chance they have to visit, regardless of the calendar. There's just no place like this quaint island with its pristine beaches and homey atmosphere. Maybe the coziness comes from the fact that the island is "hugged" from all sides by water. The land is but a slender strip of sand, geographically much like the other Outer Banks islands. At its widest the 16-mile-long island is only about 2 miles across, narrowing in some spots to a half-mile, where sound and sea are both visible from the two-lane road.

After disembarking from the Hatteras ferry, you are released onto N.C. 12 toward the village. Sea oats and dunes line the left side of the road. The right side of the road is lined with marshlands grasses, and exquisite creeks meander toward the sound. Occasionally you'll see some old fishing skiffs tied up on the creeks, giving you the first hint of human life on Ocracoke Island. The drive through this beauty (we've gotten some fantastic photos of the creeks) alone makes the journey to Ocracoke worthwhile. The northern beaches are sparsely populated, while the surf along the southern beaches is usually lined with four-wheel-drive vehicles and anglers, especially in the fall when fishing is best.

Despite our enthusiasm for the drive, it's not easy to discuss all that makes Ocracoke

Island so special. The obvious is that it's beautiful, off the beaten track and much of it is protected as a National Seashore and therefore undeveloped. But there's so much history embedded in this land and soaked in the people that it's hard to find words to express that which is almost vaporous. You can absorb the unspoken by quietly walking the beaches and backroads of the village. Breathe deeply of the salty air that has filled the lungs of its inhabitants for centuries, and be prepared for a lifelong affair with this southern isle.

Getting Here

Access to Hyde County's Ocracoke Island is limited to sea and air. A free 45-minute ferry ride across the waters of Pamlico Sound transports islanders and visitors to the north end of Ocracoke from Hatteras Island. Once you hit land, it's a 12-mile drive past undeveloped marshlands and dunes to the village. Two toll ferries connect the island with the mainland. The Cedar Island and Swansboro ferries, each a two-and-a-half-hour ride, arrive and depart from the heart of downtown Ocracoke on the southern end of the island. A small airfield allows private planes to land near the heart of the island (see our Getting Here, Getting Around chapter).

Warm hospitality, salty ocean breezes and over 13 miles of pristine national seashore await you on Ocracoke Island. Visit Blackbeard's stomping grounds, see the rare Banker ponies and enjoy the king of peaceful vacation that you con only find in one place–the treasure of the outer banks.

Ocracoke Island

NORTH CAROLINA
252-928-6711

Island Economy and Tourism

Vacationers flock to Ocracoke during the warm months to partake of her natural beauty and savor her history. Once a simple fishing village where islanders primarily lived off the sea and her bounty, Ocracoke today operates as a vacation resort about nine months out of the year. Tourism and traffic have changed the pace of this traditional fishing village, but the influx of visitors is necessary to maintain a healthy economy.

While many Ocracokers work at tourist-related businesses, year-round residents also are employed by the National Park Service, in the local school, in the building industry or as commercial and recreational fishermen.

Ocracoke Island offers a variety of sightseeing options that radiate from a core village atmosphere. You can ride bikes all over the quaint island, and the village is small enough to be seen on foot. Park the car and

walk around the heart of the town that surrounds Silver Lake. Wander around on the back roads:

Specialty shops, galleries and old island cottages are just waiting to be discovered. Casually elegant restaurants and come-as-you-are eateries offer several opportunities for a meal, and friendly natives will make recommendations and point you in the right direction (we outline almost a dozen tasty spots in our Restaurant chapter).

Sailboats moor in the protected cove of Silver Lake, and charter and fishing boats fill the downtown docks. Year round half- and full-day fishing excursions are offered. All accommodations — bed and breakfast inns, a few hotels, rental cottages and private campgrounds — are close to the activity of the island. (See our Shopping, Fishing and Accommodations chapters for details.)

On the oceanside about halfway to the village, you'll see tents and camping trailers dotting the dunes. This popular National Park Service campground is open from late spring to early fall and requires advance reservations (see our Camping chapter). Our Attractions chapter outlines the island's historic hotspots in detail. Make sure you take in the British Cemetery (see our Annual Events chapter) and the stately Ocracoke Inlet Lighthouse. Come January, the flow of visitors subsides, and islanders take a break from long, seven-day work weeks. Off-season tourists still can find available accommodations. Only Howard's Pub, a local eatery, stays open through the winter with any consistency.

Yesteryear and Today

It is said that when the first English explorers arrived at Ocracoke, the island was attached to Hatteras Island and jointly bore the name of Croatan. Ancient maps indicate that Ocracoke may once have been connected to its southern neighbor, Portsmouth Island, and together the islands were called Wokokon.

Names are great history trackers, and while folks entertain many stories as to how Ocracoke was named, two theories hold most popular. One is that the name descended from Wokokon, not a far stretch from the island's current moniker. The Wokokons, a tribe of Native Americans, journeyed to Ocracoke to feast on seafood, historians say. In 1657, a survey map showed the island as Wococock. A more fanciful story surrounds the legend of Blackbeard the pirate. It is said that on the morning of his demise, Blackbeard's assassin impatiently awaited the dawn and the coming of his enemy, looking ashore to the island and yelling "O Crow Cock Crow! O Crow Cock!" The legendary Blackbeard, or Edward Teach, is only a small part of Ocracoke history. And while there are several shops and a museum dedicated to his legend, some Ocracokers today don't care to place importance on the 18th-century villain. His fleet included four boats and 400 crewmen, and by the mid 1700s he'd plundered at least 25 ships (see our Attractions chapter).

During Blackbeard's era it became clear to the colonists of North Carolina that there was a need to improve trade and navigation along the coast. The Colonial assembly passed an act in 1715 to establish the Ocracoke Island as a port and to maintain pilots and their assistants who helped guide ships safely from sea to shore at "Ocacock Inlett."

It was not until 1730 that they pilots actually came. Their numbers increased over the years, and 33 years later these "squatters" were given 20 acres of land for themselves and their families. By November 1779 the Ocracoke Militia Company was established to protect the inlet (see our History chapter).

Ocracoke was initially owned by several inhabitants. Three successions of absentee owners followed. The fourth owner, William Howard, bought the island in 1759 and at his death deeded all his land to his son, Wallace Howard. Land was sold by both Howards to various families on the island. Descendants of the Howards reside on the island today. A family graveyard is near Village Craftsmen on Howard street. The craft and gift shop is run by Philip Howard.

In 1770 Ocracoke was annexed to Carteret County and remained there until it was moved to Hyde County in 1845. By the year 1850, there were 536 residents on Ocracoke Island. Thirty-six of them were employed as pilots.

Ocracoke history is filled with stories of shipwrecks and lost lives. The islanders worked to rescue stranded sea travelers and ships and housed and fed those who survived. Crabs and a wide variety of seafood kept their bellies full. While the island inhabitants were forced to witness the ocean's wrath as she smashed ships and stole human life, as if in repayment she provided for them, though sometimes in the most unlikely way. Wrecked ships tossed up a variety of goods, including lumber, shoes, clothing and bananas. But these luxuries were small in contrast to the toll the sea took as the churning waters swallowed not only sailors, but also women and children. The year 1823 saw the construction of the Ocracoke Inlet Lighthouse. The white brick structure has stood steady in Ocracoke village for 174 years, guiding sailors to safety (see our Attractions chapter). Several lifesaving stations were also built on the island in the late 1800s and early 1900s. In 1940 a Coast Guard station was erected. Coast Guardsmen continue to watch over Ocracoke waters today, but the island lost eight Coast Guard families within the last few years when federal budget cuts forced a closing of the island's Coast Guard building. Service is still provided around the clock by a rotating group of 10 men, but the families were relocated to Hatteras Island. Modern technology has helped diminish the number of wrecks these days. When accidents do occur, they usually involve offshore fishing vessels caught in foul weather.

The dredging of Cockle Creek and creation of Silver Lake Harbor in 1931 played a role in Ocracoke's development as a sizeable fishing industry. Access to the village was improved and fairly large boats now could safely enter and dock at the village. In 1953, most of the island became part of the Cape Hatteras National Seashore, with the exception of the village. The first hard surfaced road was constructed four years later connecting the village to a spot near Hatteras Inlet. These changes came during a decline in the fishing industry.

Though tourism now replaces fishing as Ocracoke's main source of income, islanders continue to ply the sea for food and fun. Two fish houses operate throughout the year, and a variety of species including Spanish and king mackerel, bluefish, red drum, cobia, amberjack, tuna and billfish are caught in sound, inlet and ocean waters.

Gas and water shortages in the '70s and '80s saw a decline in the boating traffic in Ocracoke waters. Fishing activity decreased with the increase of regulations. The days of visitors hauling home a cooler chock-full of trout are now replaced by excursions yielding a much smaller haul due to regulations. But with a recent upgrade of the local plant, water is no longer a serious problem, and boaters are returning to the island in larger numbers. Many local businesses now operate their own electrical generators, helping eliminate power surges and brownouts. During the summer months, traffic clogs the harbor area as vehicles and bicycles take to the narrow roads, but the villagers are working closely with the North Carolina Department of Transportation to find ways to eliminate this problem.

The year-round population of Ocracoke has not changed dramatically since 1850. Today between 600 and 700 people call Ocracoke Island home. Public school children, grades K-12, attend classes at the Ocracoke School. And community concerns are aired at the Ocracoke Community Center where the Ocracoke Civic and Business Association meets. Welcomed progress to the barrier island includes the addition of several vegetable stands, and today the once-isolated community supports two grocery stores and a True Value Hardware Store.

The real estate market is busy on Ocracoke Island. A recent revaluation has brought about tax increases of 200 to 300 percent for some property owners. There is a fair amount of vacant land available on the island, mostly inland. It's rare to find a waterfront lot for sale, and only one to two canalfront lots sell per year. Regardless, the island's beauty and isolation will always be a major drawing card for visitors and locals alike.

On the eastern flyway of migrating land and water birds, Ocracoke is a birder's paradise with brown pelicans flying in formation over the waves, sandpipers leaving thin footprints in the sand with their tenuous steps, herons gracing the salt marsh and warblers, grosbeaks, cardinals and willets dotting the trees. Live oaks lend majesty and a sense of strength to the fragile isle.

Famous for its legendary wild ponies, Ocracoke has 180 fenced-in acres set aside for the small herd to roam, and visitors to the island can see a group of them at a special lookout midway down N.C. 12. The National Park Service rotates four ponies at a time from the range to a pen to let folks get a close-up view (see our Attractions chapter).

To learn more about Ocracoke Island, we suggest you pick up a copy of *Ocracokers* by Alton Ballance. He speaks beautifully of the history of his home, giving words to the vaporous atmosphere and salty spirit of the islanders like no one else has. All proceeds from this literary gem go to the Ocracoke School.

Restaurants

Like critters from their winter dens, restaurateurs emerge en masse from their cold-weather haunts around March and return to work just about the time those wicked northeasters are no longer a threat. It's a busy time on the Outer Banks, with owners unshuttering buildings, sprucing interiors, hiring staff and tweaking menus. The restaurant business on these barrier beaches ebbs and flows according to the weather, and everyone knows it's life or death, business-wise, in the summer. People who run eateries aim to please — and mostly, they do. Whether you're treating yourself to a delectable dinner while on vacation or just trying to find a quick, satisfying supper for your hungry family after a long day on the beach, you'll likely find what you want and need on the Outer Banks. Dining out is one of the most enjoyable activities you can do frequently, easily and oftentimes, inexpensively. The Outer Banks has a wide array of restaurants from which to choose, offering food to please every palate and price ranges to suit any pocketbook. There are upscale cafes with European ambiance and unusual culinary creations and down-home fish houses where your meal may be caught only a few feet from your table.

International fare, as well, has made its way to these isolated islands with Mexican, Thai, Italian, Chinese, French and even Caribbean-style eateries springing from the sand in recent years. Ethnic cooking also has crept into even the most traditional restaurants, and many chefs have revised their menus for the summer season to reflect a wider variety of healthful alternatives and even vegetarian offerings.

Competition keeps increasing too. Besides the dozen or more restaurants that changed owners or managers over the winter, every year several more open in time for the summer season.

Increasingly, restaurants are opening earlier in the spring and staying open longer into the fall each year. The shoulder seasons have become popular times to dine out because the off-season offers the same friendly service and great food with less crowds. Most eateries now open by March and don't close their kitchens until after Thanksgiving. Many even have decided to serve their full line of selections year round.

Although seafood has always been a mainstay for barrier island cooks and their customers, chefs schooled at culinary institutes around the world are making their way into Outer Banks restaurants and are changing the way we all eat out. Besides the traditional fried flounder, steamed shrimp and you-pick-'em blue crabs, which will never be removed from many area menus, bistros now serve poached salmon over beds of just-made saffron linguine; cafes coddle discriminating diners with everything from roasted duck breasts drizzled with raspberry cassias sauce to chick pea and black bean hummus dip with pita chips; and many eateries pride themselves as much on the food's artistic presentation as on serving the freshest, highest quality ingredients available.

Wine, too, is rapidly becoming one of our restaurants' biggest drawing cards. Several Outer Banks eateries host wine-tasting weekends in the off-season, and many have decided to serve 12 or more types of wine by the glass for those who want to sample several kinds. Wine-by-the-bottle lists expand each season, and restaurants along the northern beaches sometimes offer 50 or more varieties of the world's finest wines.

Most Outer Banks restaurants serve beer and wine, at least for dinner; however, those in Corolla and on Colington, Roanoke, Hatteras and Ocracoke islands are forbidden by law to offer mixed drinks. Some establishments allow brown bagging, however, whereby you can bring in your own liquor. Call ahead to make sure it's OK. And ask if they provide setups.

Dinner isn't the only meal to eat out, of course. A variety of bakeries, diners and even seafood restaurants now serve big breakfasts and weekend brunches. Most places are open for lunch throughout the summer, and some even serve bathing suit-clad customers just off the beach. The majority of restaurants, however, still require you to wear shirts and shoes. Many cooks will package any meal to go, though, and some eateries even have started delivering, with menus offering much more than just pizza that can be dropped off at your door.

If you're eating an evening meal out, feel free to dress as comfortably as you desire. Even most of the expensive, elite establishments welcome sun dresses, sandals and shorts. Some restaurant managers say everything from evening gowns and suits to jeans and T-shirts are acceptable at their linen-cloaked tables.

Reservations aren't taken at many restaurants. Others, however, suggest or even require them. The Blue Point in Duck, Ocean Boulevard in Kitty Hawk and Colington Cafe on Colington Island all get so booked up in the summer that you usually have to call at least three days ahead to secure a table. The fare at these fabulous places, however, is well worth the wait.

If sticking to a budget is a concern, you can have homestyle meals from tuna steaks to North Carolina barbecue for less than $8 in many Outer Banks family-style restaurants. Western Sizzlin', Golden Corral and, of course, fast-food eateries from McDonald's to Wendy's all also offer their standard fare here. For this chapter, we haven't included any chain restaurants; we think you already know what to expect from those spots.

Price Code

For your convenience, we've included a pricing guide with each restaurant listing to give you a general idea of what to expect when the tab comes. The costs are based on entrees for two people, excluding appetizers, dessert or alcoholic beverages. Many area eateries also have senior-citizen discounts and children's menus to help families cut costs. Most entrees include at least one vegetable or salad and some type of bread. Prices vary, obviously, if you select the most or least expensive items on the menu; this guide is a generalization hitting the mid-range prices of restaurants' most popular meals. Here's our breakdown:

$	$25 and lower
$$	$25 to $45
$$$	$45 to $75
$$$$	$75 and higher

Price ranges do not reflect North Carolina's 6 percent sales tax or the gratuity, which should be 15 percent to 20 percent for good service. Some restaurants offer early evening dining discounts to encourage patrons to avoid peak dining hours. Most have at least two or three daily specials that change depending on the availability of food and the whims of the chef.

Seafood is, and probably always will be, one of the biggest draws for Outer Banks diners. Caught in the sounds, inshore ocean and as far out as the Gulf Stream by local watermen, much of the fish served here lived or swam near the barrier islands and often makes it to your plate less than two days after being landed. Some restaurants, how-

INSIDERS' TIP

Even though there is a coastal Carolina seafood focus at most Outer Banks eateries, almost all establishments serve at least one, and usually more, vegetarian choices. Almost all restaurants are willing to meet your needs and make a meatless entree, if possible.

ever, are importing increasingly more fish from foreign countries. Ask your waiter where the seafood came from if you're fishing for Outer Banks-only food. If you want someone else to clean and cook your catch, Nags Head Pier Restaurant will gladly prepare your own "fish of the day" for you.

Raw bars always are great bets for relatively cheap, yet succulent, seafood. Oysters, clams, crab legs and shrimp are served on the shell or slightly steamed, and some places even include vegetables. Soft-shell crabs also are an Outer Banks speciality worth raving about, served from Easter through early July. Don't be put off by the spidery legs hanging off these crustaceans. Just consume the entire creature, shell and all — it's a whole lot quicker and easier than having to pick the meat out of hard shells once the crabs stop molting later in the summer.

If you're into picking your own crabs, however, you'll probably want to spread out some newspaper at your cottage or find an outdoor picnic table to absorb the mess. You can buy the locally caught blue crabs already steamed, or you can cook them yourself in a big kettle. You can catch your own crabs in area sounds, inlets and bays by dangling a chicken neck from a long string and letting the shellfish wrap its claws around the meat. Just be careful when you're taking it off the line to drop it in your bucket before it latches onto your finger. Always steam crabs while they're still alive, and don't eat the gray lungs or yellow mustard-like substance inside.

Restaurants in this chapter are arranged from north to south from Corolla through Ocracoke. Seasons and days of the week each place is open are included with each profile. Unless otherwise noted, these eateries accept at least MasterCard and Visa, and many accept other major credit cards as well.

We've also added some primarily carry-out and outdoor dining establishments that offer quick, cheap eats, cool ice-cream concoctions and perfect items to pack for a picnic or offshore fishing excursion.

Whatever you're hungering for, you'll find it here.

Corolla

Corolla Pizza & Deli
$ • Austin Complex, N.C. Hwy. 12, Corolla • (252) 453-8592

This take-out-only deli serves subs, sandwiches, Philly cheese steaks and pizza by the pie or slice for lunch and dinner. Each pizza is made to order on hand-tossed dough. Regular red sauce and gourmet white pizzas, including the ever-popular chicken pesto pizza, are available. During the summer season, Corolla Pizza offers free delivery. You can walk in or call ahead to have your order waiting. Corolla Pizza is open seven days a week in summer. Call for off-season hours.

Nicoletta's Italian Cafe
$$$ • Corolla Light Village Shops, N.C. Hwy. 12, Corolla • (252) 453-4004

Since this small Italian cafe opened six years ago near the red brick Currituck Beach Lighthouse, it has earned a fine reputation for a wide variety of well-prepared foods. This classy little bistro features tables covered in white linen and each adorned with a single, long-stemmed red rose. Waiters whisk about in crisp black and white uniforms. A thick burgundy floral carpet cushions their steps, while Frank Sinatra tunes often echo softly in the background.

Nicoletta's menu features a variety of fresh seafood, veal, chicken, pastas and salads. Special appetizers and dinner selections change each evening, and there's an abundance of authentic Italian dishes from which to choose, all with wonderful homemade sauces that seduce the palate.

A select wine list is available, and homemade desserts change weekly. A cup of espresso or cappuccino is a great way to end the evening. Reservations are highly recommended; a separate room is available for private parties. Dress is casual, and children are welcome (there's even a special menu to suit younger appetites). Nicoletta's is open seven days a week in summer. Call for off-season schedules.

Horseshoe Cafe
$$ • Corolla Light Village Shops, N.C. Hwy. 12, Corolla • (252) 453-8463

Six years ago, Horseshoe Cafe brought

Southwestern cuisine to the northern Outer Banks. Here you'll find homemade crab cakes seasoned lightly with chili powder for that Tex-Mex flair. Vegetarian chili also is a stand-out. There's also plenty of good seafood, steaks, chicken and barbecue on the menu. All the desserts are homemade, from Key lime pie to sopapillas drizzled with honey. Choose from a variety of flavored coffee, mocha cappuccino and even hazelnut espresso to top off your meal.

The decor here fits the theme. Bull horns, wool rugs, cacti and, of course, horseshoes line the walls. A Mexican tile bar offers a cool place to sit a spell and sip one of 25 kinds of beer served. The wine list is extensive too.

Horseshoe Cafe serves breakfast, lunch and dinner seven days a week in summer. Sandwiches are available for a light supper along with the full entree offerings. A children's menu offers smaller portions and prices, and the wait staff even provides crayons to keep your tykes entertained. Reservations are suggested.

Smokey's Restaurant

$ • Monteray Plaza, N.C. Hwy. 12, Corolla • (252) 453-4050

This down-home restaurant opened in 1991 and is the only one on the northern banks to have survived under one owner. Its specialties include North Carolina barbecue, pork ribs, fried chicken, fresh tuna steaks, crab cakes, fried and steamed shrimp and fried clams. They offer all the trimmings from coleslaw and baked beans to onion rings. We especially recommend the fried sweet potato sticks for an unusual side dish; they're a nice alternative to the usual french fries and complement any meal. Appetizers range from "The Corolla Burst," a super colossal onion served in the shape of a flower, to jalapeno poppers to Buffalo wings. Sandwiches and salads also are available throughout the day.

Smokey's offers a children's menu and will package most of its items for take-out. Desserts, wine and beer also are available. This restaurant is open for lunch and dinner

March through December. In season, it serves seven days a week; call for off-season hours.

Miriam's

$$ • Monteray Plaza, N.C. Hwy. 12, Corolla • (252) 453-2571

Owner/chef Ann Runnels has had a great response since she opened this New American cuisine restaurant in July 1996. Diners love Miriam's comfortable and casual ambiance—contemporary geometric decor and classy white walls, but people keep coming back for the creative cooking. Talk about mouthwatering: Try the seafood Napoleon, with layers of shrimp, scallops, crab, smoked salmon and puff pastry, finished with a roasted red pepper cream coulis. Or how about brown sugar and mustard-marinated sliced pork? It's sliced pork tenderloin served with braised red cabbage slaw and cheddar-scallion mashed potatoes. A different pasta dish is available every night, and one or two specials are offered daily. The specials are usually centered around the freshest fish available that day. Filet mignon, chicken and seafood dishes can also be selected off Miriam's delectable menu items.

A children's menu is available. There's also a full beer and wine menu. Make sure you save room for one of their desserts, which are all made in-house and are as fresh and sinful as you could ask for. Try the warm apple and blueberry oatmeal-crusted cobbler with whipped cream. Our other favorites include warm chocolate mint cake with raspberry sauce and bananas Foster cooked in brown sugar and rum, encased in phyllo dough. Miriam's is a nonsmoking restaurant open daily for dinner only May though December. Reservations are encouraged.

Weeping Radish Brew Pub

$ • Monteray Plaza, N.C. Hwy. 12, Corolla • (252) 453-6638

If you want a light meal and a mug of some of the best local microbrew beer, check out this little pub at the northern end of the Outer Banks. Like it's big sister, the Weeping Radish Brewery and Bavarian Restaurant in Manteo (see our entry in this chapter), this

HORSESHOE CAFE

COROLLA, N.C.

Seafood  Steaks

•

SOUTHWESTERN CUISINE

•

Friendly Service

**Breakfast Lunch Dinner
Beer & Wine**

Corolla Light Shops
453-8463
Reservations Suggested

Try our
hot salsa
now bottled
to go

pub serves Weeping Radish beers on tap. The Fest, Corolla Gold and Black Radish brews are always available, and the others vary depending on what's being brewed at the brewery in Manteo. For the teetotalers, there's a lip-smacking Weeping Radish root beer. There is also a limited pub menu with sandwiches, hot dogs, German sausages, burgers and a chef's choice that changes daily. The pub is open from 11:30 AM to 5 PM in the off-season. It stays open to 11 PM in the summer months.

Steamer's Restaurant & Raw Bar
$$ • TimBuck II, N.C. Hwy. 12, Corolla
• (252) 453-3344

This 50-seat restaurant and raw bar serves lunch and dinner year round. Lobster, shrimp, oysters, clams and mussels are available as well as lamb, veal, grilled beef, chicken and even sandwiches. Diners will enjoy the waterside view from this upscale but casual restaurant that boasts 28-foot vaulted ceilings. If you have to wait for a table, you can wear a "patron pager" and stroll through TimBuck II until you're beeped. Steamer's also offers desserts and appetizers as well as microbrewery beers, wine and Black and Tans (that hearty, layered combination of Guinness and Bass Ale) to complement the fresh, local seafood.

Steamer's Shellfish To Go
$ • TimBuck II, N.C. Hwy. 12, Corolla
• (252) 453-3305

The most innovative idea to hit the beach in a long time, Steamer's Shellfish To Go is Corolla's version of the popular New England-style clam bake. Housed in a separate location next to Steamer's restaurant, it's a gourmet seafood market that offers full take-out of the best the Outer Banks has to offer presented in a refreshingly different fashion. Steamer's bills it as a service that provides the perfect night in. Steamer's Shellfish To Go features a full steam bar, gourmet dinner entrees to go and an extensive selection of wines and microbrews. Choose a mix-and-match pick of six of the microbrews to take home. Fresh local fish is also prepared for take-out. Or — here's the real fun part — your selection can be packed in its own steamer pot with fresh vegetables and taken home to steam yourself. The steamer pots are cans that contain layers of seafood, Red Bliss potatoes, onions and corn. You go home, add a cup of water and place it on your stove to cook. Thirty-five minutes later — presto! — you have a gourmet meal. Other offerings include soups, salads, seafood pasta salad, ribs, rib-eyes, side orders of fettuccine Alfredo and fresh Gulf Stream fish and plenty more. Shellfish To Go is open seasonally from 11 AM to 9 PM.

Planet Corolla
$ • TimBuck II, N.C. Hwy. 12, Corolla
• (252) 453-4644

Formerly The Mane Street Eatery, this festive restaurant serves a wonderful variety of fresh food at family prices. Colorful linen tablecloths under glass tops and brightly-painted walls sets the tone for an enjoyable meal of Southern and international fare. Some examples include chicken breast stuffed with Monterey Jack cheese and baked in white wine and tarragon sauce, or Delmonico steak cooked on the grill and served with vegetables and your choice of a starch. A wide variety of steak, chicken, seafood and pasta round out the menu. A different pasta is offered every day, along with the fresh fish catch of the day. The Outer Banks' favorite — crab cakes — is also included as one of the offerings here.

A kid's menu is available too. If you're looking for a cool drink, try a specialty frozen daiquiri or pina colada made with wine (remember, no liquor is served in Corolla eateries). Some flavors to choose from include raspberry, peach or mango. A good selection of microbrews and wine served by the glass or the bottle are also offered. For a topper, try a homemade dessert like New York-style cheesecake or blueberry Key lime pie. Planet Corolla also offers live music in the style of James Taylor and Jimmy Buffet most nights from Memorial Day through Labor Day. (See our Nightlife chapter.) The eatery serves lunch and dinner six days a week in the summer. In the off season, only lunch is served. Planet Corolla is open year round. Call ahead for carry-out items. Reservations aren't accepted.

Neptune's Grill & Arcade
$, no credit cards • TimBuck II, N.C. Hwy. 12, Corolla • (252) 453-8645

A locals' favorite, this casual grill offers quarter-pound burgers, Philly cheese steaks, North Carolina barbecue, fried oysters, salads and veggie burgers and a variety of sandwiches to eat-in, carry-out or have delivered. French fries, cheese fries, frozen candy bars and cookies also are available, as are beer and wine.

This is a low-key burger joint where you can sit at booths or tables. It features the only pool table north of Duck; pinball and Foosball offer added family entertainment. Neptune's Grill is open for lunch and dinner year round. Bring the kids — there's a special children's menu. In summer, Neptune's serves food seven days a week; call for off-season hours. See our Nightlife chapter for after-hours offerings.

Leo's Deli & Baked Goods
$ • TimBuck II, N.C. Hwy. 12, Corolla • (252) 453-6777

Reubens, pastrami sandwiches, deli creations and potato, pasta, tuna and Greek salads all are prepared here daily year round for eat-in or carry-out. Leo's also has a huge array of ice cream, doughnuts, bagels, bread, croissants, cookies, pies and cakes, and serves espresso and cappuccino. This combination deli-bakery serves beer and wine and is open for breakfast, lunch and dinner. Hours vary in the off-season. Outdoor tables are provided if you want to soak up some sun during summer.

Sorrel Pacific Cuisine
$$ • TimBuck II, N.C. Hwy. 12, Corolla • (252) 453-6979

The only eatery in Corolla with a soundside view, this lovely restaurant with the lovely name offers fresh seafood and continental and American fare with an exotic twist. Sorrel is both a herb and the name used to describe a chestnut-colored horse with white markings — perhaps like one of Corolla's famous wild horses. Pacific cuisine, of course, is food that is flavored with Hawaiian, Chinese, Thai or Japanese spices. The decor — a blend of green, black and blue colors and Japanese rice paper screens shown off by lots of big windows — is cozy and doesn't overdo the Pacific theme.

For lunch, standard fare such as burgers, fish or shrimp-salad sandwiches are often served with a side dish of pineapple tossed with mango and coconut. Dinner offerings at Sorrel Pacific include such entrees as coconut-flavored shrimp, steak with roasted vegetables and mashed potatoes, tuna sushi rolled with rice and seaweed and fresh spring rolls. Fresh fish is prepared with delightful and palate-surprising Pacific flavorings. Vegetarian fare is also available, and there is a children's menu. Diners can choose a beverage from an extensive list of domestic and imported beers and wines. Specialty frozen drinks made with wine and all natural ingredients are very popular here.

Enjoy a drink in the enclosed windowed bar overlooking the sound, or sit outside on the patio for your meal or just a refreshing drink. Steamed shrimp and steamed crab legs are available at the bar.

As it embarks on its forth season, Sorrel Pacific Cuisine is offering extended brunch hours in the summer. Call for the schedule. Brunch, which is mostly standard American cuisine, is available Sunday from 10 AM to 2:30 PM. In the off-season, only dinner is served. In the summer, dinner is available nightly, and lunch will be offered on varying days. Sorrel Pacific closes for a few months in the winter, so call for off-season hours.

Grouper's Grille & Wine Bar
$$$ • TimBuck II, N.C. Hwy. 12, Corolla • (252) 453-4077

Tucked between handmade hammocks and quaint gift shops at this upscale shopping village, Grouper's opened in 1996 and visitors

---

INSIDERS' TIP

With the *Outer Banks Recipes from the Blue Point Bar & Grill* you can experiment at home with some of the superb recipes that make the Duck restaurant a barrier island favorite. Pick up a copy for $19.95 at the Blue Point or at its sister in Kitty Hawk, Ocean Boulevard.

have been singing its praises ever since. This restaurant provides an array of enticing offerings in an atmosphere of understated elegance — and is well worth the 35-minute drive from Nags Head.

Angus beef, free-range chicken, fresh local seafood and vegetarian entrees are made all the more mouthwatering with unusual spices and sauces. The menu changes seasonally so that only the freshest available ingredients are used. Local seafood is served with an international twist. Pasta, chicken, lean-generation pork and beef are all prepared with flair.

Each meal begins with fresh-baked bread. Huge appetizers include such temptations as Grouper's crab cakes, with mounds of jumbo lump crabmeat; seared tuna loin sashimi; chardonnay-steamed little neck clams; Moulard duck spring rolls; goat cheese and smoked chicken-stuffed empanadas; or fresh mozzarella and vine ripe tomatoes drizzled with a roasted red pepper puree. Organic salad greens are prepared with an assortment of delicious in-house dressings. Grouper's extensive wine list boasts more than 100 varieties by the bottle and a large by-the-glass selection. A generous number of domestic, imported and microbrewed beers round out the drink choices. Don't forget dessert. It's made on the premises, and the selections are beyond sinful.

The atmosphere here is as delightful as the dinners, with open post-and-beam wooden ceilings, butter-colored tablecloths set with flickering candles and large windows surrounding the dining room. Upscale but casual, the eatery makes diners comfortable in suit and tie or in blue jeans. Grouper's is open for lunch and dinner from March through November. Reservations are recommended.

Duck

Sanderling Inn Restaurant
$$$ • N.C. Hwy 12, Sanderling • (252) 449-0654

The restored lifesaving station at the Sanderling Resort just north of Duck houses one of the Outer Banks' most acclaimed restaurants. Multiple dining rooms enhanced with rich woods and brass offer peeks at the glistening sound through expansive windows. Here, progressive Southern regional cuisine is served for breakfast, lunch and dinner. A three-course, $15.95 Sunday brunch, available from 11:45 AM to 1:30 PM, is the best on the beach.

Start the morning off with Chef Glen Aurand's delectable menu, which has included malted Belgian waffles with fried apples and warm maple syrup or orange cinnamon French toast. For lunch, try such delicacies as the grilled fish of the day or a seafood platter featuring mussels, clams and shrimp. Other mouthwatering offerings include the oyster Po' Boy sandwich, cold poached salmon or classic shrimp. In the interest of serving only the freshest food, the menu changes frequently according to the season.

Dinner entrees include baked salmon Rockefeller, stuffed with spinach and oysters, and crab cakes made with all backfin meat. Seasonal, regional seafood is the menu's main focus, but beef, pork and poultry also are offered. Save room for the delectable desserts. The Sanderling has a full bar that includes a wide range of wines from around the world. A children's menu is available, and reservations are strongly encouraged. All three meals are served seven days a week throughout the year. The chef is always ready to accommodate any special dietary needs.

Duck News Cafe
$$ • N.C. Hwy. 12, Duck • (252) 261-6117

For a spectacular view of the sun setting over Currituck Sound, sample a dinner selection at this northern Duck restaurant. Selections nightly include Italian entrees, shrimp served three ways, crab imperial, marinated locally caught tuna, slow-roasted prime rib and aged beef tenderloin. Chicken with special sauces, soft-shell crabs in-season, crab cakes, clam chowder and Caesar salads are other options.

Key lime pie, brownies à la mode and a Lady Godiva ice cream drowned in chocolate liqueur all are delightful desserts. The full bar has four types of beer on tap. This casual, family-oriented restaurant (there's a children's menu) sits across from the Sanderling Inn. Reservations are recommended. Dinner is served from early spring through fall.

Cravings Coffee Shoppe
$ • Duck Common Shopping Center, N.C. Hwy. 12, Duck • (252) 261-0655

This delightful eatery is the perfect place to pop by for a quick breakfast before hitting the beach or to indulge yourself in a delectable dessert and coffee after dinner. You can eat inside, on an open-air deck or take the tasty treats home with you. Table service is not available; you order and pick up your food from the counter.

Order a fresh New York-style bagel with one of six flavored cream cheeses. Homemade pastries, breads and muffins also are baked each day. The ice cream is homemade as well. Out-of-town newspapers are also available each morning if you miss browsing through big city dailies such as The Washington Post and The Wall Street Journal.

For lunch, try an Italian sandwich on just-baked bread. Of course, every type of coffee drink you can concoct is available, from four types of brewed coffee that change daily to espresso, cappuccino, mocha drinks and other fancy combinations. You can also buy gourmet coffee beans, gift baskets and other items at a small shop inside Cravings. Cravings is open year round. In summer the eatery serves into the evening; it's open weekends only in winter.

Barrier Island Restaurant
$$ • N.C. Hwy. 12, Duck • (252) 261-3901

The first restaurant to open in Duck, Barrier Island Restaurant is on the Currituck Sound, with a large waterfront deck out back with both covered and open-air portions that offer great views of the sunset and sparkling water. Ospreys, ducks and windsurfers testing their sails on the Currituck Sound afford constant entertainment during the day. At night, live music is offered throughout the summer (see our Nightlife chapter).

Outer Banks seafood is a speciality, along with pasta, steaks, crab cakes, lobster and chicken. A light-fare menu, including homemade pizza and sandwiches, is available in the tavern late into the night. Appetizers, desserts and separate selections for children are also on the menu. The restaurant serves lunch and dinner year round; a weekend breakfast buffet is available.

The Village Wine Shop & Red Sky Cafe
$ • Village Square Shops, N.C. Hwy. 12, Duck • (252) 261-8646

This innovative cafe boasts the only wine bar on the beach and some of the best bread you'll enjoy anywhere. All bread and pizza are made on the premises in a wood-fired oven, and a wide variety of wines are available to sip by the glass. Along with the aromas emanating from the local organic herbs used in the food, the smell of the bread cooking is enough to get you salivating.

Owner/chef Tom Hix can whip up an impressively eclectic range in gourmet food: Mexican, French, Italian, Greek, Indian and Californian. The thin-crusted pizza with sun-dried tomatoes, pesto and fresh mozzarella cheese is out of this world. This is not ordinary pizza: This is heaven. It's the cafe's huge and unusually creative subs and sandwiches that pack the most punch, however. Our favorite is the Mt. Olympus, made with tomato, spinach, feta cheese, basil and marinated olives with pesto on French bread. Other inviting combos include Gavilanian Gobbler: smoked turkey, smoked Gouda, tomato, bacon, lettuce, red onion with Red Sky sauce on wheat bread; or Continental Divide: roast beef, bacon, monterey jack, coleslaw and red onion with barbecue sauce on sourdough bread. All sandwiches are reasonably priced and filling. Compared with vegetarian slim pickings at most eateries, the range of interesting vegetarian sandwiches — and meat lovers would swoon too — is wonderful.

For dinner, try a quesadilla or one of the four or five main courses that change nightly. Fresh Outer Banks seafood and pasta dishes are just two possibilities. Hix will be experimenting with a tapas-style menu in 1998, which will give diners a taste of the cafe's numerous specialties. An excellent selection of wine from all over the world can be purchased by the bottle or by the glass, and three microbrew beers are available on tap.

Interesting items can be found for sale on shelves lining this airy, very pleasant shop with wine racks, gourmet coffee and organic food products. The Village Wine Shop & Red Sky Cafe is open daily year round for lunch and dinner.

Diners can choose from an abundance of eateries serving delectable dishes and offering impressive wine lists.

Elizabeth's Cafe & Winery

$$$ • Scarborough Faire, N.C. Hwy. 12, Duck • (252) 261-6145

Well known across the East Coast for its wine and wonderful food, Elizabeth's has earned international acclaim from *The Wine Spectator* magazine for consecutive years since 1991. For the past five years, this cafe was one of a handful in North Carolina to win Best of the Award of Excellence. In 1996 Elizabeth's was one of only 245 restaurants in the nation to win the honor. Owner Leonard Logan recently added a walk-in wine cellar and retail sales area and expanded the restaurant to accommodate handicapped patrons and to provide more room between tables.

Elizabeth's is a delight from ambiance to entrees. It's warm and casual inside, with a fireplace that's usually lit on chilly evenings. Service always is excellent, and the owner will personally select a vintage wine to comple-

ment any meal. Winemakers from around the world are featured here during special dinners held in August.

Besides the regular menu offerings, which include country French and California eclectic foods that change continually, prix-fixe dinners (seven-course meals and accompanying wines) are available every night in the summer. All the dishes are made with fresh ingredients, from seafood and steaks to unusual pastas. A new wine bar with cold appetizers, cheeses and croissants serves dining delights all afternoon and into the evening. A pastry chef also creates different desserts daily: Elizabeth's Craving is sinfully delicious.

This cafe is very popular, so reservations are highly recommended. On some summer weekends the owner has had to turn away as many as 500 potential diners. Besides all the fine wines, the restaurant also serves French beer by the glass, poured from wine-bottle-size containers. See our Nightlife chapter for more of Elizabeth's delights. The restaurant is open on weekends for dinner year round and for lunch and dinner seven days a week in-season.

Fishbones Raw Bar & Restaurant
$$ • Scarborough Lane Shoppes, N.C. Hwy. 12, Duck • (252) 261-6991

Specializing in locally caught seafood, this raw bar and grill opened in the summer of 1995 and won the Outer Banks chowder cook-off with an original recipe during its first year in business.

Midday items include sandwiches, crab cakes, fried seafood and creamy soups such as tomato conch and, of course, chowder. Dinner entrees offer such Caribbean cuisine favorites as calypso eggplant and coconut shrimp, in addition to pastas with fresh clam sauce, lobster tails, crab legs and more than a dozen raw bar selections. The hot crab dip, barbecue shrimp and conch fritters all are outstanding appetizers. This is a casual place with a full bar, five types of beer on tap, 50 bottled beers from all over the world, a wine list and several microbrews from which to choose. Desserts also are available.

Fishbones serves lunch and dinner seven days a week year round, and specials change daily for both meals. Carry-out is available on all menu items. Reservations are not accepted.

The Afterdeck Bar & Grille
$ • Osprey Landing Shops, N.C. Hwy. 12, Duck • (252) 261-7133

Formerly the Osprey Gourmet, the Afterdeck boasts one of the best views of the Currituck Sound in Duck. Indeed, you can even see ducks paddling lazily in the sound through the windows of the large porch here. You can also sit outside on the deck and watch the variety of shorebirds that stop by for a dip or a snack in the shallow sound. Plan on eating dinner on the deck while the sun puts on a show as it sinks into the shimmering water.

Owner/chef Mary Beth Johnston was schooled at the L'Academie de Cuisine in Bethesda, Maryland — and the food shows off her creative flair. Offering contemporary cross-cultural cuisine with an emphasis on fresh seafood and lighter fare, the Afterdeck features such delights as outrageous crab-

cake sandwiches, steamed shrimp, lemon-pepper chicken salad, baby-back ribs, fresh fish, Black Angus burgers and homemade salads. Dinner specials are offered nightly, and twice weekly diners will be treated to acoustic guitar entertainment between 6 PM and 9 PM.

Don't forget all the homemade, delectable desserts. Especially popular are the vanilla bean crème brûlée, butter pecan chocolate chip bread pudding and pecan turtle brownies. A full children's menu is available, along with sundaes, shakes and sodas. There is also a fantastic selection of imported beer and wine, including wonderful British lagers. The Afterdeck is open from 10 AM through 10 PM daily in the summer. In the fall and spring, hours are from 10 AM until sunset daily. The eatery is closed December, January and February.

The Blue Point Bar & Grill
$$$ • The Waterfront Shops, N.C. Hwy. 12, Duck • (252) 261-8090

This waterfront bistro is one of our favorite places to dine on the Outer Banks. It's been open for lunch and dinner since 1989 and consistently receives rave reviews from magazines such as Southern Living and Gourmet as well as admiring local audiences. Here, regional Southern cooking brings a cosmopolitan flair to the area. A 1950s-style interior with black-and-white checkered floors, red upholstery and lots of chrome provides an upbeat, bustling atmosphere. An enclosed porch not only overlooks the sound, it actually overhangs it. There's also a small bar facing the aromatic kitchen where you can watch your appetizers being prepared while sipping a cocktail as you wait for a table.

The Blue Point's menu is contemporary Southern cuisine and changes seasonally. Starters range from scallops to tuna cakes, each artistically arranged and flavored with the freshest combination of seasonings. Try the duck confit, slow-cooked meat on jalapeno corn bread with tamarind barbecue sauce. Entrees range from jumbo lump crab cakes served with rice and black beans and Currituck corn on the cob, homemade soups, unusual seafood dishes, steaks, salads and perfect pastas. Desserts, like the bourbon pecan pie or the key lime pie, are divine.

If you're into creative cooking that's sure to tantalize every taste bud — and awaken some

you might not even have realized you had — this restaurant is a must-stop on the Outer Banks. It's open for lunch and dinner year round, and reservations are highly recommended. In January, February and March, The Blue Point closes Mondays and Tuesdays. The eatery is also closed the first three weeks in December, but the rest of the year it's open seven days a week. Good thing — we're addicted!

Roadside Bar & Grill
$$ • N.C. Hwy. 12, Duck • (252) 261-5729

Occupying a renovated 1932 cottage, this 4-year-old restaurant is warm and homey, with hardwood floors inside and a patio dotted with umbrella-shaded tables out front. In the summer, live jazz and blues music is performed here three nights a week (see our Nightlife chapter).

A casual, fine-dining establishment, Roadside offers 8-ounce burgers and crab cakes for lunch. The clam chowder is chock-full of shellfish, and a raw bar serving all sorts of shrimp, oysters and clam combinations is open all afternoon.

For dinner you can choose from fresh salads with mangos and other exotic fruits, loads of locally caught seafood, just-sliced steaks, whole lobsters and poultry platters. Other specials change daily for lunch and dinner. Homemade desserts include chocolate bread pudding with Jack Daniels caramel sauce and steaming slices of Mom's Apple Pie. The full

bar has a nice selection of microbrewed beers. The restaurant is open year round seven days a week. Reservations are not accepted.

Duck Deli
$ • N.C. Hwy. 12, Duck • (252) 261-3354

This casual deli on the east side of the highway opened 11 years ago primarily to serve locals lunch. Since then, it's expanded to offer breakfast, lunch and dinner seven days a week, 11 months of the year (the eatery closes during January).

Barbecue pork, beef, chicken and ribs are the specialities here. Sandwiches, Philly cheese steaks and subs are served all day, as are side salads, garden burgers and coleslaw. A full breakfast menu includes everything from eggs and pancakes to omelettes. For dessert, you can get sweet on cherry and peach cobblers, homemade brownies or a frozen yogurt bar with plenty of toppings. Beer is served at Duck Deli, and everything is available to eat in or take-out. Duck Deli is also the home of the booming Outer Banks business Carolina Blue Smoked Wildfish Co., whose gourmet food products are sold all over the country.

Herron's Deli and Restaurant
$ • N.C. Hwy. 12, Duck • (252) 261-3224

With a full menu available for carry-out or to eat in, this casual deli serves breakfast and lunch seven days a week all year and adds

dinner hours in the summer. Booths and tables are available indoors, and picnic tables offer outdoor dining. Hot and cold Italian subs, cheese steaks, cheeseburgers and crab cakes are among the most popular items in the afternoon and evening. We recommend the soups, from chili specials to she-crab bisque and Hatteras-style chowder.

A big breakfast menu features French toast, sausage gravy, omelettes, eggs and homemade biscuits. Desserts range from cakes and brownies to homemade strawberry pie. Beer and wine also are available.

Swan Cove
$$$ • N.C. Hwy. 12, Duck
• (252) 255-0500

This elegant establishment opened in 1995 and has gained a reputation as one of the finer establishments in Duck. Unbelievable views are available from the soundfront dining room, where tablecloths and cut flowers grace each table and crystal glasses sparkle during sunset hours. There's a separate lounge with a full bar and an extensive wine list upstairs.

The menu changes frequently to incorporate new offerings. Swan Cove uses all local produce, seafood and fresh herbs and specialize in low-fat, light cooking. Entrees include duck, pastas, French-cut pork chops, three kinds of Outer Banks fish, seafood bouilla-baisse over saffron fettuccine, tenderloin steaks and fresh salads. Warm rolls and garden vegetables come with each dinner.

A great bet for starters: Shrimp stuffed with Gouda, wrapped in bacon and served with smoky barbecue sauce. For dessert, try choosing between a chocolate layer cake, peanut butter pie and seasonal fresh fruits drizzled with fabulous sauces.

Swan Cove is open seven days a week in-season, serving lunch and dinner; dinner only is served in spring and early fall. There is a children's menu. Reservations are suggested.

Southern Shores

Southern Bean
$, no credit cards • The Marketplace,
U.S. Hwy. 158, MP 1, Southern Shores
• (252) 261-JAVA

Opened in September 1995, this gourmet coffee shop caters to folk looking for healthy light meals in addition to a great cup of brew. Southern Bean serves breakfast and lunch year round and adds dinner hours in the summer. Three types of just-brewed coffee always are simmering here, filling the air with tantalizing aromas.

This comfortable place serves every type of speciality coffee drink imaginable, from espresso and cappuccino to iced lattes —

even in decaf varieties. More than 30 flavors of freshly roasted coffee beans are sold by the pound here. You can eat inside at Southern Bean, sip a warm blend at an outdoor table or order your drinks and food to go. All menu items are either vegetarian or seafood, and sandwiches range from hummus to peanut butter-and-honey; try the bean bagel topped with sun-dried tomatoes, pesto, red onion slices, cream cheese and sprouts. Muffins, croissants, cinnamon rolls and other bakery items also are available. No sandwich costs more than $5. This is also one of the few places on the Outer Banks where you can get fresh-squeezed juices and a wide variety of fruit smoothies.

Southern Bean is open seven days a week year round.

Kitty Hawk

Kitty Hawk Pier Restaurant
$, no credit cards • N.C. Hwy. 12, MP 1, Kitty Hawk • (252) 261-3151

One of the most popular breakfast places on the beach, this ultra-casual restaurant, which opened in 1954, is somewhere you'll feel comfortable just rolling out of bed and rolling into. Pancakes, eggs, sausage, French toast, omelettes, biscuits, hash browns, grits, sausage, bacon and anything else you could desire for a filling first meal of the day are cooked up beginning at 6 AM.

Lunch specials change daily and include such local favorites as ham and cabbage, trout, shrimp, crab cakes, meat loaf, and turkey with dressing and yams. For dinner, try a seafood platter of flounder, scallops, oysters, dolphin or Spanish mackerel, each served with a choice of two sides: hush puppies, rolls, coleslaw, beets, peas, beans or other vegetables.

Kitty Hawk Pier Restaurant is a down-home place with lots of local patrons and flavor. You can find out what's biting here and even may see your dinner being reeled in off the nearby wooden planks. Most of the fish are caught right off the pier, within 200 feet of where you eat it. Better still, you can come as you are — even in your bathing suit.

Desserts include homemade cobblers (peach, apple, blueberry and cherry), straw-berry shortcake and a variety of pies. A children's menu is offered for the small fry. Everything is available to take out, but you'll enjoy eating in this oceanfront restaurant where salt spray stains the wide windows.

The restaurant serves three meals a day every day in summer. In the off-season only breakfast and lunch are available. Kitty Hawk Pier Restaurant is open April through November.

Rundown Cafe
$$ • N.C. Hwy. 12, MP 1, Kitty Hawk • (252) 255-0026

Opened in 1993, this Caribbean-style cafe has been a big hit with locals who live on the northern end of the beach and offers some spicy, unusual alternatives to traditional Outer Banks seafood. Named for a Jamaican stew, Rundown serves island entrees flavored with African and Indian accents. Try the conch chowder for an appetizer or one of several wild soups that change seasonally.

Specials shift nightly. Some of our favorites are blackened pork tenderloin, spinach-and-feta-stuffed chicken with roasted red pepper sauce and freshly grilled tuna topped with sesame vinaigrette. The steam bar here serves shellfish of all sorts, vegetables and steamed dinners. All the regular menu items also are terrific.

There's a full bar, and the bartenders can come up with some pretty potent concoctions. And there's Guinness Stout, Bass and Harp beers on tap. This is a casual, happening place often features live blues and jazz in the summer (see our Nightlife chapter). A rooftop deck is a great place to soak in the sunset, catch a few rays or just linger over a cool cocktail after a hot day in the sun. Lunch and dinner are available seven days a week. The Rundown is closed in December.

Ocean Boulevard
$$$ • N.C. Hwy. 12, MP 2, Kitty Hawk • (252) 261-2546

This warm, cozy, upscale eatery gives you a great feeling from the second you walk into the gold-walled dining room until you leave full and relaxed after consuming a fabulous meal. It opened in September 1995 and has quickly become one of the most popular places on the Outer Banks. Manteo residents drive 30 miles each way to treat themselves to a midweek dinner here. No wonder — it's owned by the same culinary masters who brought us the Blue Point in Duck (see previous entry). Ocean Boulevard has an intimate atmosphere, and the food is sophisticated.

This restaurant occupies the former 1949 Virginia Dare Hardware store, and you won't believe what the builders and decorators have done with the place. It's accented with warm woods, burgundy fabrics and forest-green chairs. Cobalt blue glasses and water pitchers grace every table top. There's even an open-air kitchen where you can watch the chefs work.

Selections are all prepared with locally grown herbs, spices, produce and just-caught seafood. Influences and ideas from around the world give the food here a flavor all its own, and the menu changes according to the season. For an appetizer, try seared rare tuna served with wasabi coleslaw and soy honey glaze. Four meal-size salads, one with seven types of lettuce, also are outstanding.

Entrees like cornmeal-crusted sea bass with roasted vegetables and black olive tapanade or macadamia-crusted mahi mahi served with rum-baked beans with passion fruit butter sauce are exquisite. And you can't go wrong by ordering any of the pastas, beef, shrimp with Portobello mushrooms or pork chops served with blue cornmeal onion rings.

Ocean Boulevard's wine list contains more than 100 selections, at least a dozen of which are served by the glass. Microbrewed beers and a full bar also are on hand. Six dessert offerings are to die for. We especially crave the white chocolate crème brûlée, The Blvd., and macadamia nut torte with caramel ice cream. A full line of after-dinner coffee drinks and herbal teas also is served.

This elegant eatery will please even the most discriminating diners. It's open year round for dinner only. During summers, doors are open seven days a week. Call for off-season hours. Reservations are highly recommended.

Art's Place
$, no credit cards • N.C. Hwy. 12, MP 2½, Kitty Hawk • (252) 261-3233

Serving good, basic meals for 19 years, this tiny eatery across from the ocean is a Kitty Hawk standby well known among locals. The food here isn't fancy, but it's cheap, filling and all-American. Sausage gravy is the most popular breakfast entree, although Art's also serves the usual eggs, pancakes and biscuits. The same entrees are available for lunch and dinner, with daily specials such as fried chicken, shrimp and clam strips and cheeseburgers — each served with french fries, coleslaw and a cucumber and onion salad. Jalapeno poppers are a hot bet for an appetizer, and calamari is also available most of the time. The eatery is open seven days a week year round. Reservations are accepted but seldom necessary.

Argyle's Cafe and Bake Shop
$ • U.S. Hwy. 158, MP 2½, Kitty Hawk • (252) 261-7325

Formerly on the Beach Road in Nags Head, this scrumptious bake shop now includes a sit-down restaurant and full delicatessen. In 1997 Argyle's added a dinner menu and scaled back on its breakfast offerings. Even though the new hours (10 AM to 9:30 PM) won't feed the early morning crowd anymore, Argyle's Bake Shop is still our favorite place for pastries and fresh bread. The cinnamon rolls are giant and sticky, smothered with just enough frosting to guarantee you'll lick your fingers. A new tropical juice and espresso bar was added recently, so you can now enjoy a gourmet beverage with your treat.

For lunch, Argyle's serves hamburgers, french fries, chicken tender strips, prime rib, seafood platters, Philly cheese steaks and a full line of huge deli sandwiches — all made on freshly baked bread with the finest Boar's Head meats and cheeses. The chicken salad

---

INSIDERS' TIP

Coastal Cactus in Kill Devil Hills offers a party menu to go — great for large groups and charter boat outings. The meals are packed in microwavable heat-in containers. Call (252) 441-6600 for details.

here is the best on the beach. You can also choose from loads of meal-size chef and garden salads and veggie burgers. The owners are glad to accommodate special dietary needs. The dinner menu is geared toward families looking for reasonably priced hearty meals that will please any palate. Meals are made fresh to order and include the gamut of wholesome American food: surf and turf, chicken Parmesan, ribs, filet mignon, shrimp scampi, fettuccine Alfredo and stuffed shells. All dinners include a house salad. Argyle's also has a full bar, and wine and beer are available.

All kinds of desserts are also among the offerings. Cannolis, cookies of all shapes and sizes, at least a half-dozen flavors of cheesecake, fresh fruit pies, turtle and Snicker's pie, mousse tortes and an array of other unreal sweets are available, like the meals, to eat in or take out. Argyle's cooks also cater parties and weddings and will make special cakes for any occasion. Argyle's is open for lunch and dinner every day all year and has a Sunday Brunch every week.

Keeper's Galley
$$ • U.S. Hwy. 158, MP 4, Kitty Hawk
• (252) 261-4000

Keeper's Galley now is run by Rufus Pritchard Jr., the same fellow who owns the Dunes Restaurant in Nags Head (see subsequent entry). But the menu is slightly different here, and Keeper's Galley serves breakfast, lunch and dinner seven days a week in-season.

Breakfast, which is available until noon, features waffles, eggs, pancakes, country ham, grits, toast, biscuits, vegetarian breakfast sandwiches and fish roe stirred into eggs. For lunch, try a Reuben, cold plate, shrimp or tuna sandwich, homemade seafood gumbo or a big bowl of clam chowder. Dinner entrees change daily but include such regular offerings as prime rib, crab cakes,

seafood fettuccine, chicken and a surf and turf platter. For dessert, the turtle cake is simply scrumptious. Keeper's Galley has a children's menu and a full bar. Reservations aren't accepted.

Black Pelican Oceanfront Cafe
$$ • N.C. Hwy. 12, MP 4½, Kitty Hawk
• (252) 261-3171

This casual restaurant is in an old Coast Guard station and includes an enclosed deck overlooking the Atlantic. It's roomy and wide, with three separate levels, and features a huge bar with 12 TVs (see our Nightlife chapter). Hardwood floors, tongue-and-groove appointments, light gray accents, burgundy carpeting and black bentwood chairs all add to the comfortable ambiance of this moderately priced eatery.

Here, gourmet pizzas are cooked before your eyes in a wood-hearth oven. Try the steamed shellfish fresh from the sea. An extensive selection of appetizers are made from scratch. Dinner offerings include pasta and seafood specials, grilled or blackened to suit your taste. A children's menu is also available. Black Pelican serves lunch and dinner year round, seven days a week in summer.

Frisco's Restaurant
$$ • U.S. Hwy. 158, MP 4½, Kitty Hawk
• (252) 261-7833

Chefs at this restaurant pride themselves on using only fresh local seafood, choice beef, poultry and pasta. Entrees include traditional Outer Banks fish, great crab cakes and shrimp jambalaya. Specials change daily. All the desserts, including chocolate chess pecan pie, are homemade. Frisco's dining room is light and open with greenery throughout. Well-tended terrariums and aquariums filled with fascinating fish line the walls and gargantuan bar (see our Nightlife chapter). Lunch and dinner is served seven

INSIDERS' TIP

Two of the best desserts on Roanoke Island: coconut cake at the Full Moon Cafe on the waterfront and the chocolate-chip cannolis at Garden Pizzeria on U.S. Highway 64.

days a week during the summer. Call for off-season hours because this restaurant is open year round. A children's menu is available, and early bird prices are offered from 4:30 to 6 PM. Parents: Frisco's is very kid-friendly. Children love the decor, and your waitperson will hand each of the little ones crayons and a placemat to color.

John's Drive-In

$, no credit cards • N.C. Hwy. 12, MP 4¾, Kitty Hawk • (252) 261-2916

Home of the planet's best milk shakes, John's has been an Outer Banks institution for years. Some folk even drive two hours from Norfolk just to sip one of the thick fruit and ice cream concoctions, some of which won't even flow through the straw. Our favorite is the chocolate-peanut butter-and-banana variety, but you'll have to sample a few first and create some of your own combinations before making that call for yourself.

You can't eat inside here, but plenty of picnic tables across from the ocean are scattered around the old concrete building. Everything is served in paper bags to go. While you're waiting for your food, check out the faded photographs of happy customers who line the salt-sprayed windows of this diner. You may even recognize a few local friends.

Besides the milk shakes and ice cream sundae treats, John's serves delicious dolphin, trout and tuna sandwiches or boats with the fish crispy-fried alongside crinkle fries. Dogs love this drive-in too. If your pooch waits patiently in the car, the worker behind the window probably will provide him or her with a free "puppy" cup of soft-serve vanilla ice cream. We can't think of a better doggie treat on a hot summer afternoon.

John's drive-in is open from May through October for lunch and early dinner. It's closed Wednesdays, unfortunately (we could eat there seven days a week).

Tradewinds

$ • U.S. Hwy. 158, MP 4½, Kitty Hawk • (252) 261-3052

If you're in the mood for Chinese food, Tradewinds serves tasty Mandarin-style dishes. The chef here is willing to cook each meal to your specification, whether you prefer lightly steamed vegetables without a sauce or a variation on the seafood, chicken and beef entrees, which are always available. Carry-out is popular here, as it is at many Chinese restaurants, but the generous portions of succulent spicy and mild meals are best enjoyed in this dimly lighted eatery. Tradewinds has a full bar and is open for lunch and dinner all year.

La Fogata Mexican Restaurant

U.S. Hwy. 158, MP 4½, Kitty Hawk • (252) 255-0934
U.S. Hwy. 158, MP 14½, Nags Head • (252) 441-4179

A traditional Mexican restaurant, La Fogata got its name from the Spanish word for "campfire." All the owners, waiters and cooks are Mexican natives, but almost all of them speak English. We think they serve the best ethnic food for the price on the beach. After being open for four years, people still wait in line to eat here on weekend nights.

Airy, bright and decorated with paper piñatas, the interior of this ultra-casual eatery usually hums with Latin tunes; a mariachi band plays here frequently. Tables and booths all are set with bowls of slightly spicy homemade salsa, and the waiters never stop filling the baskets of crispy tortillas they serve as soon as they distribute the menus. Beware: We often fill up on chips and this authentic salsa before the meals arrive. All entree portions are generous, so save some room for the main course. Other appetizers we enjoy include the hot queso (cheese) dip and stuffed jalapeno peppers.

Specialties here are fajitas, beef and chicken tacos, enchiladas and chiles rellenos. The cooks make the dishes hot or mild, depending on your desire. Selections come in every possible combination, vegetarian varieties and à la carte if you want to try one of everything. (Actually, that's impossible here. The menu has more than 36 dinner selections, many starting at $6.) A full bar offers a wide selection of Mexican, American and imported beers, and mixed-drink and Margarita prices are among the lowest on the beach. La Fogata is open for lunch and dinner year round, seven days a week.

Kill Devil Hills

Coastal Cactus
$ • Seagate North Shopping Center, U.S. Hwy. 158, MP 5, Kill Devil Hills • (252) 441-6600

Entering their fifth season, Jim and Deby Curcio have introduced the best the Southwest has to offer to the Outer Banks. Visitors from Arizona, Texas, New Mexico and California have raved about the authentic regional flavor of the menu offerings at this affordable, casual eatery. The Curcios have recently added a separate lunch and dinner menu which has more than 60 choices of entrees, combination plates and à la carte items. They prepare all their food from scratch daily using fresh vegetables and meats and hot-off-the-grill tortillas. Start your meal with nachos piled high on the plate and covered with cheese, jalapenos, onions, tomatoes and your choice of beef, chicken or beans. It's all smothered in the Coastal Cactus' own fresh homemade salsa, which is bottled for purchase if you want to take some home. All the herbs and spices used here are imported directly from the Southwest.

For an entree, select their signature dish: sizzlin' fajitas served still smoking in a cast-iron skillet. You can choose from shrimp, steak, tuna, chicken, lobster or vegetarian combinations to fill them. Other offerings include tacos, enchiladas, burritos, chiles rellenos, tamales and tequila-lime shrimp. Desserts all are tempting and retain the Tex-Mex theme. Fried ice cream, banana chimichangas, apple enchiladas à la mode and coconut caramel flan are just some of the sweets from which you can choose.

Drinks are among our favorite features at the Cactus. The golden Margaritas are marvelous and made from scratch. There are also several other fresh-fruit varieties to sample. Wine, beer and other mixed drinks also are available in this peach and teal colored restaurant accented with authentic Southwestern artifacts and art. A children's menu is available. Separate smoking and nonsmoking dining rooms are provided. A Southwestern general store on the premises features Navajo pottery, Hopi jewelry, hot sauces and other unusual gift items. The Coastal Cactus is open year round seven days a week for lunch and dinner.

JK's Ribs
$ • U.S. Hwy. 158, MP 5¼, Kill Devil Hills • (252) 441-9555

Long known for serving the best pork ribs on the beach, JK's originally opened in the early 1980s, but the restaurant burned down several years later. Now, JK and his gang are back in a tiny eatery at the Grass Course. Again, they're serving those baby back ribs that have made mouths water for years. There's no table service here; you have to call in carry-out orders or pick up your own plate from the counter. A few tables allow you to eat inside, and outdoor tables are available too. Besides ribs, which are smothered in his famous dry spice so you don't have to deal with sloppy sauce, JK's serves grilled and roasted chicken, hamburgers, cold salads, coleslaw, red beans, freshly baked corn bread and thick brownies. Beer and wine are available. You can eat lunch and dinner here year round, including late night suppers. Limited delivery also is available with a minimum $12 order. Reservations are not accepted.

Henry's Beef & Seafood Restaurant
$ • U.S. Hwy. 158, MP 5½, Kill Devil Hills • (252) 261-2025

Locals love this low-priced, homey restaurant that has been serving breakfast, lunch and dinner for 10 years. Omelettes, hotcakes and egg combinations are filling ways to start the day, and they're served until 1 PM for late-risers. Lunch entrees include hamburgers, a variety of sandwiches, seafood platters and several homemade soups. For dinner, there's prime rib, fried oysters, chicken dishes, pasta, shrimp, scallops, soft-shell crabs in-season, flounder, trout, clam strips and daily specials. The hot fudge cake, apple pie and cheesecake are rich and decadent dessert options.

There's nothing fancy about Henry's. Diners eat at low booths lining the walls or on paper placemats spread across bare tabletops. The food is hearty and filling. Beer, wine and mixed drinks are served here. Reservations are accepted for large parties. And all-you-can-eat dinners are offered daily. Henry's is open year round, seven days a week.

Photo: Courtesy of J. Aaron Trotman

The decor of Outer Banks homes often brings the outdoors in.

Chilli Peppers

$$ • U.S. Hwy. 158, MP 5½, Kill Devil
Hills • (252) 441-8081

World fusion with a Southwestern twist
comes alive in the cooking at in this fun, always
bustling restaurant. Owner Jim Douglas has
worked in Outer Banks eateries for years and
has brought some of the most creative cooking
around to Chilli Peppers. If being adventure-
some is your style, you'll be wowed by the chefs'
wild collaborations. If you prefer a milder meal,
they can do that too and still tickle some un-
tapped taste buds. The menu here changes
frequently, with daily lunch and dinner specials
sometimes stunning even the regulars. Some
of our favorite entrees are the scallops, steak,
shrimp, pork and quail combinations, each as
tastefully presented as they are tasty. Chefs
Damon Krasauskas and Kenny McClean, both
graduates of renowned culinary schools, always
come up with something exciting. The nachos
appetizer is a meal in itself.

A full bar separate from the cozy dining room
offers fresh-fruit Margaritas, a nice wine selec-
tion and more than a dozen varieties of bottled
beer. Nonalcoholic fruit smoothies also are a
great bet in the early afternoon. Steamed sea-
food and veggies are served until closing. There's
usually something going on here late night (see
our Nightlife chapter) too. Chilli Peppers is an
extremely progressive restaurant with a laid-back
feel. Cacti, wooden chairs and hand-painted ac-
cents all add to the casual atmosphere. Lunch
and dinner are served here seven days a week
year round. Weekend brunches, featuring a
make-your-own Bloody Mary bar, are worth get-
ting out of bed for. Also, you can take home a
bottle of Chilli's award-winning original hot sauce,
barbecue sauce or hot salt. The T-shirts, too,
make great memorabilia of a delicious meal.

Coffee Talk

$ • U.S. Hwy. 158, MP 5¾, Kill Devil Hills
• (252) 480-2420

Owned and operated by locals Jeannine
and Keith Duke, this comfortable coffeehouse
is one of the few on the beach where you can
find a good cup of coffee and a pastry in the
evening hours.

Biscotti, homemade cakes, muffins, gour-
met cookies and bagels with three kinds of
cream cheese can be purchased here, either
to go or to enjoy while sitting at one of the
tables. To drink, choose from espresso,
cappuccino, lattes, caffe mocha, hot choco-
late, iced cappuccino, Italian sodas, gourmet
coffees and chai tea — spiced tea mixed with
milk. Health food items, Internet and e-mail
access and a variety of newspapers are avail-
able.

Coffee Talk is open from early morning
daily year round. Closing hours vary depend-
ing on the season and demand, so call
ahead.

Awful Arthur's

$$ • N.C. Hwy. 12, MP 6, Kill Devil Hills
• (252) 441-5955

An always-popular spot across from Avalon
Pier, this raw bar and restaurant is usually
crowded throughout the year. Wooden tables
are laid out along the oblong room, and a bar
stretches the entire length of the downstairs
eatery. Upstairs, a separate lounge offers an
ocean view. A live lobster tank and huge saltwater reef tank also offer interesting sea creatures to watch as you dine.

Arthur's is a comfortably casual place
where you won't mind peeling seasoned
shrimp or picking the meat from succulent crab
legs with sticky fingers. Seafood is the speciality here: Everything from scallops and oysters to clams, mussels, homemade crab cakes
and daily entree specials. The bartenders are
some of the fastest shuckers in town. Bass
Ale and several other varieties of beer are on
tap, or you can order from a full line of liquor
and speciality drinks. For landlubbers, several
non-seafood sandwiches are served.

At night, Arthur's is usually packed (see our
Nightlife chapter). A late night menu is available. Mondays are Locals' Nights, featuring

Most eateries will gladly pack a bag lunch for you to enjoy during
your visits to the beach. Just call ahead, and it'll be waiting for
you.

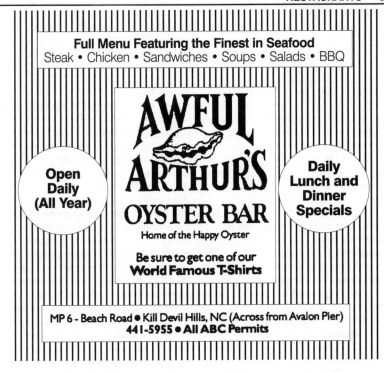

Full Menu Featuring the Finest in Seafood
Steak • Chicken • Sandwiches • Soups • Salads • BBQ

AWFUL ARTHUR'S OYSTER BAR

Home of the Happy Oyster

Be sure to get one of our
World Famous T-Shirts

Open Daily (All Year)

Daily Lunch and Dinner Specials

MP 6 - Beach Road ● Kill Devil Hills, NC (Across from Avalon Pier)
441-5955 ● All ABC Permits

drink and food specials all day. Arthur's T-shirts have been seen all over the world and are also local favorites. This eatery is open seven days a week year round for lunch and dinner.

Carolina Seafood
$$$ • N.C. Hwy. 12, MP 6¼, Kill Devil Hills • (252) 441-6851

For an elaborate, all-you-can-eat seafood buffet where "fried has died," try Carolina Seafood. Here, you can enjoy 25 items for less than $19.95 a person: salad, soups, hush puppies, garlic crabs, crab legs, scallops, stuffed shrimp and several types of fish served baked, broiled, blackened, steamed or sauteed. You even see the whole loin of fish here. Roast beef is cut to order, and a variety of desserts are included in the price. If you're not feeling hungry enough to tackle the buffet, Carolina Seafood serves crabs, scallops, shrimp and other seafood by the basket too. A children's menu also is available. This restaurant is open seven nights a week from May through Septem-

ber. It's open weekends only in the spring and fall.

Jolly Roger Restaurant
$$ • N.C. Hwy. 12, MP 6¾, Kill Devil Hills • (252) 441-6530

Serving some of locals' favorite breakfasts, this lively restaurant is open for three meals a day 365 days a year. Besides the traditional eggs, pancakes, sausage, bacon and toast, Jolly Roger has an in-house bakery that cooks up some of the biggest muffins and sticky buns you've ever seen. For lunch, choose from sandwiches, local seafood or daily $3.95 specials. During the week, there's an all-you-eat soup and sandwich bar for $4.95. Dinner entrees include homestyle Italian dishes, steaks, broiled and fried fish and a popular $8.95 prime rib special each Friday. All the desserts are homemade, and special orders are accepted for items to go. The food isn't fancy, but the portions are enormous. You'll have no excuse if you leave here hungry. Jolly Roger also offers steamed spiced shrimp in the separate bar area each afternoon and has live entertainment throughout the year (see our Nightlife chapter).

Great Dane Deli & Wrong Dog Cafe
$$ • Dare Centre, U.S. Hwy. 158, MP 7, Kill Devil Hills • (252) 441-2519

Formerly Petrozza's deli, this new eatery/delicatessen serves New York-style salads, sandwiches and bakery goods that will make Northeastern visitors feel at home and local Southerners appreciate what they've missed. With one of the largest deli sandwich selections on the beach, this cafe provides every kind of combination a hungry patron would want.

The menu carries the cafe's colorful canine name to its fun and creative heights. Every item is named for some kind of dog and is elaborated with a humorous play on words. It's a clever gimmick, because you can't resist reading through the whole menu. Once you do, you won't be able to decide which mouthwatering combo to order. How about the Bloodhound ("this sandwich can't miss, it'll track YOU down"), Black Forest ham and melted dill havarti cheese with mayo, Dijon mustard and onion on rye bread? Or the Greyhound ("big and fast and lean . . . bet on this one!"), lean pork sausage and seared bell peppers and onions with marinara sauce and melted mozzarella cheese on a half-loaf of Italian bread, served hot. There's even the Wright Dog (two beef franks on a poppy seed roll) and the Wrong Dog (a vegetarian sandwich with pesto sauce).

You can eat in or take-out at the Wrong Dog Cafe, but if you're looking for a nice break in the day, we suggest having a seat. The black-and-white checkerboard linoleum and unobtrusive, tasteful decor make this cafe a comfortable spot to relish a satisfying meal alone or with a friend. There's plenty worth taking home, also, including a range of gourmet pasta and vegetable salads, fantastic crusty breads and delectable desserts. A good selection of fine wine is also available to purchase. Dinner entrees, which include fresh bread, an appetizer sampler and a family-style salad, range from fettuccine Alfredo to chicken marsala to shrimp Florentine. Entrees can be ordered for take-out, also. Espresso, cappuccino, beer and wine are some of the drink options.

The Great Dane Deli & Wrong Dog Cafe is open Tuesday through Thursday from 11 AM to 7 PM. On Friday and Saturday the eatery is open until 8 PM. Hours are extended in-season.

Mako Mike's
$$ • U.S. Hwy. 158, MP 7, Kill Devil Hills • (252) 480-1919

Opened during the summer of 1995, this is the most outrageously decorated dining establishment on the Outer Banks. The fluorescent shark fins outside, decorated with swirls, stripes and polka dots, don't give even a glimpse into what you'll see once you step inside. Some patrons have described the experience as similar to being under water. We think it's almost like visiting an octopus' garden complete with three separate levels of dining, fish mobiles flying overhead, painted chairs, bright colors exploding everywhere and murals all along the deep blue walls.

The menu is big and varied. Entree salads — Greek, seafood, spinach, Caesar and fruit — are popular choices. Appetizers include hot crab dip and calamari. Dinner offerings are seasoned with Mediterranean, Cajun, Oriental and other exotic spices and include nine varieties of fresh pasta, chicken, several sorts of fish, beef, pork, vegetarian stir-fries, mixed grills, scallops, shrimp and dozens of other options. For dessert, try Key lime cheesecake, white chocolate mousse or chocolate passion cake.

This huge restaurant caters to couples, families and large groups. A small meeting room is available for business luncheons and private parties. A separate bar serves daily frozen drink specials in addition to dozens of bottles of beer and wine. A children's menu is provided. Dinner is available here daily most of the year. The restaurant closes Mondays and Tuesdays in the winter. Mako Mike's owner, Mike Kelly, also operates Kelly's Restaurant and Tavern and is part owner of Penguin Isle, both in Nags Head.

3rd Street Oceanfront Grille
$$$ • Sea Ranch Hotel, N.C. Hwy. 12, MP 7, Kill Devil Hills • (252) 441-7126

3rd Street Oceanfront Grille offers one of the few true oceanfront dining rooms on the

3RD. STREET OCEAN FRONT GRILLE

252-441-7126

Breathtaking Ocean View
Serving Southeastern Coastal Cuisine
Nightly Specials • Breakfast & Dinner • Sunday
Brunch • Reservations Accepted
Dancing Nightly

Quality Inn

the Sea Ranch

Located MP 7

Outer Banks. A wall of glass overlooks the Atlantic, allowing patrons at any table to get caught up in the rhythm of the waves. The menu features traditional Outer Banks seafood and steaks prepared with a Southern regional flair. Appetizers include fried green tomatoes with a remoulade sauce; grilled shrimp and grits with sauteed sweet peppers and red-eye gravy; and puff pastries filled with sauteed scallops, country ham, mushrooms and spinach in a Chardonnay shallot cream sauce.

A children's menu and nightly specials are available. Our favorite entrees include fresh egg fettuccine with scallops and shrimp tossed with bacon, sweet peas and a garlic cream sauce; grilled center-cut pork chop with an apple pecan compote; and sesame seed-crusted wahoo with a wilted spinach and soy ginger beurre blanc. The selections and service here are superb. A traditional breakfast also is served daily, and Sunday Brunch is served until noon every week. 3rd Street isn't open for lunch, and reservations are recom-

mended for dinner. The restaurant is open seven days a week year round.

Goombay's Grille & Raw Bar
$$ • N.C. Hwy. 12, MP 7½, Kill Devil Hills • (252) 441-6001

A fun place for food, drinks and just hanging out, Goombay's is owned by John Kirchmier, a 16-year veteran of Outer Banks restaurants and bars. "Good days and nights can always be found at Goombay's" is the fitting motto of this island-style eatery. Light and bright inside, with plenty of cool artwork, there's an outrageous fish tank and a wall-size tropical mural in the dining room. The ambiance is upbeat and casual, with wooden tables and chairs and a bare tile floor. The horseshoe-shaped bar, which is separate from the eating area, is a great place to try some of the delicious appetizers or drink specials that Goombay's serves. We especially recommend the spicy crab balls and sweet coconut shrimp. Some of the drink offerings, both alcoholic and children's cocktails, come with zany toys to take home.

For lunch or dinner, try a fresh pasta entree, locally caught seafood, a juicy burger topped as you wish, Southwestern sampling or one of the half-dozen daily specials that range from pork to barbecued shrimp and steak stir-fry. Everything here is reasonably priced and flavorful. A raw bar is open until 1 AM, serving steamed shrimp, oysters, vegetables and other favorites. Key lime pie is always a smart choice for dessert. Goombay's is open for lunch and dinner year round, seven days a week (see our Nightlife chapter).

Quagmires

$$ • N.C. Hwy. 12, MP 7½, Kill Devil Hills • (252) 441-9188

With two oceanfront decks, an upstairs snack bar and large downstairs dining room overlooking the Atlantic, Quagmires is entering its third summer season. It's owned and operated by John Kirchmier, who's already locally revered for his Goombay's Grille (see previous entry).

This casual restaurant caters to almost every dining whim. If you're sunning yourself on the beach midday and start to hear your stomach grumble, you can get lunch to go from the upstairs grill without even putting on shoes or throwing a shirt over your wet bathing suit. If you'd rather wait to dress for dinner, you'll feel well cared for — and fed — in the casual downstairs dining room. The giant U-shaped bar upstairs provides a great place to watch the waves and sip some of the best Margaritas and frozen drinks on the beach. There's a kid's menu and special treats just for the little ones. A volleyball court, horseshoe pit and even ring toss are set up in the sand behind this eatery in case the younger set gets bored while their folks dawdle over dinner. Don't be misled, though: Those games also are open to adults. Better still, in 1998 Quagmire's has added a new kids' playground.

The menu here features fresh local seafood, sandwiches, pasta, beef, chicken and some Mexican favorites. The desserts are fresh and fabulous. Live acoustic music is offered throughout the summer (see our Nightlife chapter). Quagmires is open seven days a week for lunch and dinner in-season.

Port O' Call Restaurant & Gaslight Saloon

$$$ • N.C. Hwy. 12, MP 8½, Kill Devil Hills • (252) 441-7484

This antique-adorned restaurant offers fresh seafood cuisine with entrees such as broiled shrimp stuffed with crabmeat and an array of seafood, veal, chicken, pasta and beef. Blackboard specials change nightly. Each dinner comes with fresh-baked bread, fruit and salads. The soups and chowders here are hot and succulent, and all the desserts are decadent. A children's menu also is offered.

Frank Gajar opened the restaurant 24 years ago, decorating it with a collection of Victorian furnishings. The dining room is warm and romantic, with flickering gas lights and brass accents. Port O' Call doesn't serve lunch, but there's a Sunday brunch buffet that lasts until 1:30 PM, and special early bird dinners are served from 5 to 6:30 PM. Live entertainment is offered in a large, separate saloon (see our Nightlife chapter). A full bar is available, and the gift shop/art gallery carries unusual, eclectic items. Port O' Call is open from mid-March through December.

The Thai Room

$$ • Oceanside Plaza, N.C. Hwy. 12, MP 8½, Kill Devil Hills • (252) 441-1180

Jimmy lets his patrons choose their own level of spice — from mild to blow-your-brains-out. When he asks, "Very hot?" — think twice. He means it. Besides the daily specials, the cooks have added a new buffet dinner so you can sample several of the wonderful offerings. More than a dozen American-style desserts are available. As for decor, it is unlike any other on North Carolina's barrier islands: authentically Thai with paper lanterns, Oriental portraits and red-tasseled lamps. Family members prepare

---

INSIDERS' TIP

Soft-shell crab sandwiches are an Outer Banks delight in the spring and early summer. No picking for meat necessary — eat 'em up, legs and all.

GOOMBAYS GRILLE & RAW BAR

MP 7 • Beach Rd. • KDH

Lunch & Dinner

Kids Menu

Local Seafood

Caribbean Specialties

Raw Bar

Call 441-6001 for info.

OPEN YEAR ROUND

Quagmires On The Beach

MP 7 1/2 • Oceanfront • KDH

Lunch & Dinner

Kids Menu

Local Seafood

Mexican Specialties

Oceanfront Decks

Call 441-9188 for info.

OPEN APRIL-OCTOBER

and serve each delectable meal — and they'll be happy to make suggestions if you're overwhelmed by all the options. The Thai Room is open for lunch and dinner March through December. All items also are available for carryout. The restaurant also has a full bar where you can indulge in exotic drinks and Thai beer while you wait for a table or take-out order.

Four Flags Restaurant
$$ • N.C. Hwy. 12, MP 8½, Kill Devil Hills • (252) 480-3733

In the former Mex-Econo building, which also once served as the Kill Devil Hills town hall, this family-owned eatery offers filling, reasonably priced meals for lunch and dinner. Lunch features fresh pasta, homemade soup and bread and a variety of salads and sandwiches. Dinner entrees include Angus beef steaks cooked to perfection and a large variety of local fresh seafood steamed, broiled or sauteed. Daily specials have included lobster, tuna and crab imperial. Try the new dish that's gotten rave reviews — Angry Pasta.

Brunch, available Saturday and Sunday, includes eggs Benedict, French toast, pancakes and frittatas. Children have their own menu here. Vegetarian offerings are always available. The decor is casual and comfortable. There's a full bar, complete with kiddie cocktails. Four Flags is open seven days a week year round.

Bob's Grill
$ • U.S. Hwy. 158, MP 9, Kill Devil Hills • (252) 441-0707

Bob's is open year round for breakfast, lunch and dinner. During the summer it also stays open from dinner straight through breakfast the next day from Wednesday through Saturday. Bob serves big, cheap breakfasts year round seven days a week until 3 PM daily — and that's hard to find around here. The blueberry pancakes are so big, they fill a whole plate. Eggs are made any way you want 'em, and the hash browns flavored with onions and peppers are some of the best around.

For lunch, try a hamburger, tuna steak or one of several traditional hot and cold sandwiches. Owner Bob McCoy cooks much of the food himself. A hot lunch special for $4.92, tax and drink included, is available every day. You can't leave town without trying Bob's No. 1 seller — Philly steak and cheese. Dinners feature the biggest cuts of prime rib on the Outer Banks, Cajun beer batter-dipped shrimp and fresh mahi mahi caught just offshore. The selection of salads is also good here. And you gotta save room for the hot fudge brownie dessert.

Bob's has a casual, diner-like atmosphere, with a regular-folk appeal that makes everyone comfortable. Even McCoy's well-known gruff motto, "Eat and get the hell out," has obviously not offended any locals, since the parking lot is packed with loyal customers more days than not. Service is fast and friendly, beer and wine are available, and everything can be ordered for carry-out. This grill closes from 3 to 5 PM daily, but it's open for three meals a day every day all year.

Chardo's
$$ • U.S. Hwy. 158, MP 9, Kill Devil Hills • (252) 441-0276

Owner Ron Chinappi is continuing the tradition of fine dining begun a decade ago by his father Rich Chinappi, a first-generation Italian American. Chardo's provides a cultural as well as culinary experience at this family-run establishment.

A quiet, fine restaurant specializing in seafood and meats with regional flavors of Italy, Chardo's serves an array of entrees and plenty of homemade pasta. Whether you're in the mood for spaghetti and meatballs or traditional Italian seafood, Chardo's will satisfy your palate. Veal chops are a speciality here, cut to order on the premises. There's a $9.95 steak and pasta special each Tuesday, Thursday and Sunday. Fresh sauteed or steamed vegetables and warm bread accompanies every entree.

Salads here are prepared with originality and flair. They include an interesting combination of garden vegetables and flavorful homemade dressings. The tableside Caesar salad especially is delicious. A full bar is set apart from the dining area. Chardo's wine list features top California and Italian varieties, and a coffee bar also is on hand for after-dinner speciality drinks. All the desserts are made daily; try a cannoli, tiramisu or napoleon for the perfect ending to a delightful dinner. Children can purchase half-portions of any entree for half-price. Several smaller rooms set off from the main dining area provide an intimate atmosphere for special occasions.

Chardo's sells specialty Italian meats, cheeses, breads and imported olive oil you can take home, and the restaurant caters. Chardo's is open all year for dinner. Call for winter hours.

Dare Devils Authentic Pizzeria
$ • N.C. Hwy. 12, MP 9, Kill Devil Hills • (252) 441-6330, (252) 441-2353

This pizza parlor has been in business for more than a decade and is known for its superb strombolis and hand-tossed pizzas.

Chicken wings, mozzarella sticks, nachos, Greek salads and pizza bread also are available here. Dare Devil's also has four types of beer on tap served in frosty glass mugs. The interior is low-key, with laminated tables and a long bar where you can eat. A big-screen TV in the corner features whatever hot sporting event happens to be going on. You can also order any item to take out. Dare Devil's is open seven days a week for lunch and dinner from March through November.

Dip-n-Deli
$, no credit cards • N.C. Hwy. 12, MP 9¼, Kill Devil Hills • (252) 441-4412

The perfect place for a healthy, quick, inexpensive lunch, this deli serves fresh tuna salad chock-full of chunky white fish, homemade chicken salad with just enough mayonnaise, veggie pitas with hummus and sprouts, chef's and Greek salads and a variety of cold plates. The Sou'wester, a thick sandwich of grilled wheat bread loaded with smoked turkey, Muenster cheese, mustard and hot peppers, is one of our favorites. And all their homemade soups could make a meal in themselves. The jalapeno poppers here are stuffed with three types of cheese.

The homemade cookies, Key lime pie and old-fashioned milk shakes are fantastic. For an unusual dessert treat, try the locally revered bumbleberry pie, bursting with rhubarb, apples, blackberries and raspberries. It's a taste sensation. Several flavors of hand-dipped Breyer's ice cream also are on hand. Dip-n-Deli serves beer, and everything in this casual eatery is available to eat in or take out. You can even get boxed lunches for fishing trips or beach picnics, and party platters are made to order. This enjoyable eatery is open Monday through Saturday for lunch year round.

Etheridge Seafood Restaurant
$$ • U.S. Hwy. 158, MP 9½, Kill Devil Hills • (252) 441-2645

The Etheridge family has long been synonymous with Outer Banks seafood, operating a commercial fishing fleet and wholesale fish company from the deep-draft docks in Wanchese. This 11-year-old restaurant serves almost all its fish right off the boats, so you know it's fresh. The casual, round dining room is nautically themed as well.

This is a real family-style restaurant where the waiters never stop pouring iced tea, and the food, though cooked to order, always seems to come fast. This is an ideal place to sample traditional Outer Banks-style seafood. For lunch, try a seafood pizza served with red or white garlic sauce. The Mill Landing egg rolls won the Wanchese Seafood cook-off several years ago and will win your approval too; they're stuffed with black olives, scallops, shrimp and fresh vegetables rolled into slightly crisp shells. Crab cakes here are divine, filled with fresh white meat and bursting with flavor. The sweet hush puppies are, in our opinion, some of the best on the beach.

For dinner, a five-course early bird special is served for $13.95 each day. Blackened Cajun crawfish with tomato basil sauce, broiled or fried platters with a sampling of several types of seafood and any of the traditional fish specials are sure to please. Landlubbers, too, will find something to their liking here with several beef and chicken entrees from which to choose. The soups make great starters. Each evening meal comes with a basket of crackers, a crock of cheddar cheese and the best seafood cheese spread you've ever tasted. There's even a children's menu, and a full bar is set off from the dining area. Etheridge's is open for lunch and dinner seven days a week from February through December.

Pigman's Bar-B-Que
$ • U.S. Hwy. 158, MP 9½, Kill Devil Hills • (252) 441-6803

Pigman's rib-man, Bill Shaver, is locally famous for his corny cable television commercials. He's also known for serving succulent North Carolina-style barbecue and walking his pet potbellied pigs around town. At this counter-service eatery, you can get beef, pork, chicken, and ribs barbecue. Try his new lowfat creations: catfish, turkey and tuna barbecue. Each dinner comes with homemade coleslaw, homemade hush puppies and baked beans and is served on disposable plates with plastic utensils. The sweet potato fries here are spectacular. Pigman's has a selection of gorgeous Southwestern jewelry and gifts for

sale. You can also purchase his hush puppy mix, all four Pigman barbecue sauces and Pigman meat rub at the restaurant. Pigman's is open for lunch and dinner seven days a week. It's closed January and February. Come on by and visit Pigman's critters behind the building. You might see one of his llamas, his miniature donkey or horse, or one of his smart, lovable potbellied pigs.

Peppercorns
$$ • Ramada Inn, N.C. Hwy. 12, MP 9, Kill Devil Hills • (252) 441-2151

With a wide, open dining room overlooking the Atlantic, Peppercorns and its team of chefs supervised by Ramada Inn Food and Beverage Director Robin Rector has been attracting the most discerning diners on the Outer Banks. Up-and-coming culinary master Randy Stitt is the sous chef. Mark Pennington offers multi-ethnic foods and aromatic Mediterranean dishes as the chef de cuisine. And executive chef Erik Speer brings a cosmopolitan flair to the entire menu with innovative appetizers, healthy grilled entrees and an array of finely crafted desserts.

Outer Banks favorites include locally caught shrimp and crab cakes. The soup du jour is always filling and delicious. Unusual dishes flavored with saffron, curry, Thai spices and chiles also will tempt those with extraordinary tastes. Entrees include prime rib crusted with spices, slow-roasted and served au jus; Atlantic salmon stuffed with crabmeat; or Italian risotto with shrimp, scallops and crabmeat. Each meal is served with several artfully prepared vegetables and a basket of interesting breads. Vegetarian entrees always are offered. There's a full bar and a children's menu. You'll especially want to save room for Erik's painted-plate desserts, some of which are so carefully manicured they appear as masterpieces after the artistically arranged meals. The seven-layer chocolate cake, New York-style cheesecake with a raspberry coulis or apple dumplings served with cinnamon caramel sauce will leave your palate begging for more. Peppercorns provides take-out food and room service for Ramada guests. This restaurant is open daily year round for breakfast, lunch and dinner. Custom catering also is available for events of any size.

Hurricane Alley
$$ • Sea Holly Square, N.C. Hwy. 12, MP 9½, Kill Devil Hills • (252) 441-1533, (252) 480-3667

After its premier summer in 1996, Hurricane Alley expanded into the former Impacciatore's Italian Cafe and took a lot of that bistro's great food along. Owners Charlie Cole and James Standen have created an exceptional combination of casual atmosphere and excellent food and drink.

With its good-natured, tongue-in-cheek nod to the Outer Banks annual storm scares, surfer scenes on the walls and homemade videos of the Outer Banks crowd in action shown on three large-screen TV screens, Hurricane Alley feels remarkably comfortable the minute you walk in. The long, curving wood bar is an inviting spot to eat your meal, or you can have a seat at several tables near the bar or in the large back room.

Food, including a variety of appetizers such as shrimp fritters, chicken wings, grilled scallops, clams, oysters and mini-crab cakes, is served all day until the wee hours. Most of the lunch menu, including sandwiches, 100 percent Angus beef burgers and fresh seafood is served until 11 PM. Don't miss the fabulous Caesar salad, served up plain or with a choice of chicken, shrimp or filet mignon. Dinner selections include beef, veal, poultry and gourmet pastas. Taking its cue from Impacciatore's, much of the menu reflects an Italian flair.

Desserts such as peanut butter pie and Kahlua chocolate cheesecake with Bailey's demi-glaze are all homemade, as are the bread and salad dressings. Hurricane Alley has a full bar, and it serves a variety of wines by the glass or bottle. Three beers, including one dark, are on tap, and there's a good selection of domestic, imported and microbrew beers. Hurricane Alley is open seven days a week for lunch and dinner. Live music is featured several times a month in the summer. See our Nightlife chapter for additional information.

The Fish Market
$ • U.S. Hwy. 158, MP 9½, Kill Devil Hills • (252) 441-7889

Serving traditional Outer Banks seafood in a down-home fish house atmosphere, this low-key restaurant has some of the friendliest employees in town. It's been open 19 years and has always been a favorite with locals and watermen. Lunch specials such as meat loaf, fish cakes and chicken and dumplings all taste just like Grandma used to make 'em. Dinner entrees from shrimp to tuna to mahi mahi come with hush puppies and two vegetables. Shrimp and crabs are steamed fresh daily. The clam chowder is among the best on the beach. Also, you won't want to skip dessert: chocolate turtle cake, Key lime pie and apple crunch are our favorites.

Besides the restaurant, which is lined with wooden chairs and tables, The Fish Market has a seafood market in its front foyer. One of the owners fishes commercially, so the seafood's usually fresh out of the ocean. A children's menu is offered. An L-shaped bar stretches around the wide room, and its offerings include all sorts of beer and mixed drinks. Live acoustic music is performed here on weekends year round (see our Nightlife chapter). This inexpensive restaurant is open for lunch and dinner seven days a week all year.

Flying Fish Cafe
$$ • U.S. Hwy. 158, MP 10, Kill Devil Hills • (252) 441-6894

This delightful restaurant is owned by George Price, who helped manage Penguin Isle for eight years before he decided to open his own restaurant. John Xenakis and Price purchased the former Osprey Island Grille, sandblasted off its pink and teal exterior and added their own special touches, and dishes, to create an island eatery serving an array of American and Mediterranean dishes. The interior is spruce green and adobe white with purple accents. Price's color photographs grace the walls. Brightly colored tablecloths adorn each table, illuminated by sconce wall lights crafted from wine boxes and by candles set in the center of each table or booth.

Chefs at Flying Fish roll their own pasta daily and offer an array of seafood, vegetarian and nontraditional toppings for the scrumptious noodles. Gourmet pot pies, salmon and roasted chicken are also always on the menu. Fresh fish is served four ways each night, and there's an Angus filet mignon and pork chops with caramelized onions for meat lovers. All entrees come with a starch of the day, veg-

etables and just-baked bread. Appetizers include Portobello mushrooms stuffed with shrimp, two types of soup, oysters Florentine and hot seafood dip. For dessert, try to resist the Grecian Urn, a waffle filled with ice cream and topped with glazed fresh fruit and whipped cream. Chocoholics will love the chocolate hurricane, a bed of chocolate with dark chocolate swirled through the top.

Lunch specials are served daily. And more than 40 types of wine are served by the bottle or glass. A children's menu also is available. Early bird dinner specials are discounted from 5 to 6 PM. The Flying Fish offers lunch and dinner every day year round. Reservations are recommended for dinner at this casual, innovative restaurant.

Millie's Diner
$$ • N.C. Hwy. 12, MP 10, Kill Devil Hills • (252) 480-3463

A fully restored 1940s dining car, Millie's made a hit from the moment it was delivered to the beach in summer 1996. Gleaming silver, Millie's initially attracted attention for its classy retro look. But it quickly got more notice for its gourmet menu. Food at Millie's is creative, distinctive and delicious. And considering the upbeat decor inside — art deco set off by burgundy and yellow walls and room fixings — this is a most extraordinary and satisfying place to dine.

Note the authentic 1950s jukeboxes (stocked with jazz, blues, funk and rock) in each of the dining room's eight booths. The dinner menu offers both light fare — which includes pan-seared scallops with Portobello mushrooms, plum tomatoes and carmelized shallots; or Millie's bruschetti with roma tomatoes, smoked mozzarella, sweet basil and olive oil — and full-blown entrees such as grilled Moroccan spiced New York strip with wild mushrooms and creamy potato gratin or Parmesan-crusted tuna with sage, basil and lemon butter. Other offerings, which change according to availability and season, include vegetable and polenta torte with eggplant, summer squash, tomatoes and roasted red pepper sauce and nightly fresh seafood specials.

The homemade desserts are no less imaginative. Selections have included such delights as steamed ginger pudding with butterscotch sauce. Lunch menu items include grilled Asian-spiced salmon with sesame noodles and spicy beef and mushroom burrito, in addition to out-of-the-ordinary sandwiches. Breakfast is added to the menu after Easter. And Millie's "World Famous" brunch, offered Saturday and Sunday in the off-season and every day in the summer, is all you could ever want in a brunch — fabulous omelettes, thick French toast with berries and cream, steak and eggs, mouthwatering salads, grilled quesadillas and wonderful specials.

Millie's prides itself in using the freshest food available, including organic produce, so the menu is flexible. An extensive wine list, imported, domestic and microbrewed beers and a full bar are available. Millie's also offers live music in the summer (see our Nightlife chapter). Millie's is open April through November. The diner serves daily in the summer, and six days a week in the off-season.

Colington Island

Colington Cafe
$$ • Colington Rd., 1 mile west of U.S. Hwy. 158, Kill Devil Hills
• (252) 480-1123

Step back in time at this cozy Victorian cafe, nestled among live oaks on Colington Road. This popular restaurant is only a mile off the Bypass. Once you've arrived, you'll feel worlds away from the bustling beach. It's tranquil and absolutely lovely in this restored old home set high on a hill. This is our favorite place to come for an intimate dinner, and the chefs prepare some of the most marvelous meals around for extremely reasonable prices. Three small dining rooms are adorned in tasteful decor. There's a separate bar upstairs where you can sip a glass of wine or imported beer while waiting for your table. Even the black painted plates are unusual and artistic.

Hot crab dip slathered on buttery crackers and bowls of homemade crab bisque are outstanding appetizers. Daily specials include wonderful pasta dishes, a mixed grill with hollandaise and the freshest filet mignon available. Seafood entrees change

depending on what's just been caught. Only fresh herbs and vegetables are used in cooking and as side dishes. Salads are served à la carte.

Owner Carlen Pearl's French heritage permeates her restaurant's delicious cream sauces, and she makes most of the irresistible desserts herself — from blackberry cobbler to chocolate tortes and crème brûlée. Colington Cafe is open for dinner only seven days a week, April through November. In the off-season, the cafe is open Christmas week and Thursday through Sunday from Valentine's Day through April 1.

Bridges Neighborhood Bar & Bistro
$$ • 1469 Colington Rd., Colington
• (252) 441-6398

Drive west three minutes from the bustling Bypass on winding two-lane Colington Road, and you'll be in the thick of Colington's charm. Bridges, a frame house tucked among tangled bushes and small gardens adjacent to a skinny canal, is just right for those who want to relax in an unpretentious, friendly atmosphere. Good food at affordable prices can be had at this homey bistro. Diners can relax with a drink before or after dinner on a screened-in porch that overlooks the canal. Inside, booths afford comfort while enjoying a meal in the light and airy dining room. Appetizers include seafood fritters with Cajun mayonnaise and mushroom ravioli with peanut ginger sauce. Lunch ranges from meat loaf with mashed potatoes, shrimp jambalaya or pasta of the day. Sandwiches like pork barbecue, sliced steak with grilled onion, fried oyster, fried fish and marinated grilled portobello mushroom are available day or night, and are served with a choice of fries, potato salad or baked beans. Seafood dinners, served with fries, coleslaw and hush puppies, are available after 5 PM. Seasonal entrees are other options: roasted pork loin chops with cornbread stuffing, apple gravy and vegetables; half-chicken, roasted with garlic and rosemary, potato and a vegetable; or linguine with shrimp, feta and Bridges' marinara. Homemade dessert, soup and salad are also on the menu, as well as a good selection of bottled wine, wine-by-the-glass and domestic, imported and microbrewed beers. Bridges is open from 11:30 AM to 10 PM every day year round.

Nags Head

The Sands
**$$ • U.S. Hwy. 158, MP 10, Nags Head
• (252) 441-1649**

This restaurant features country cooking for lunch and dinner year round, seven days a week. It's been serving ham and cabbage, stewed chicken, roast pork and seafood specials for nine years. Dinner entrees include Delmonico steak, prime rib, lobster tails, shrimp, tuna steaks, lemon pepper trout and daily specials. Each meal comes with unlimited trips to the salad bar, a baked potato, coleslaw, hush puppies and a basket of rolls. Desserts such as hot fudge cake, peanut butter pie, turtle cheesecake and three types of cobblers are made each day. A full bar and children's menu are offered. This food isn't unusual or artistic, but it's well-prepared and oh-so-filling. The Sands is very casual with wide wooden tables and booths. The thing we like best about this restaurant is that it serves thick, creamy she-crab soup every day — enough to make a meal in itself.

New York Pizza Pub
**$ • U.S. Hwy. 158 MP 10, Nags Head
• (252) 441-2660**

Spacious and welcoming, New York Pizza Pub offers — you guessed it — all the Italian food favorites you'd find in the North-

east. Its motto, "the ultimate family feast," is reflected in a menu that offers a wide range of selections: steaks, fresh seafood, pasta dishes, calzones, salads and soups. And of course, there's pizza — traditional hand-tossed, Chicago deep-dish, Sicilian or pan pizza is available in 19 gourmet styles. Try one laden with fresh broccoli, spinach, oven-roasted peppers, mushrooms, onions, garlic, ricotta, marinara and a pound of mozzarella cheese.

Sandwiches, heros, burgers and stuffed potatoes are also available. Specialty coffees and desserts can top it all off — if you have any room left. Or you can choose a domestic, imported or microbrewed beer or a glass or bottle of imported or domestic wine.

New York Pizza Pub is open year round for lunch and dinner.

Mrs. T's Deli
**$ • U.S. Hwy. 158, MP 10, Nags Head
• (252) 441-1220**

Owned and operated by a little local lady, her sweet daughter Shirley and two grandchildren when school lets out, this homey deli is a great bet for quick, satisfying lunches and some of the friendliest chatter in town. A big color TV plays year-old movies constantly, and the largest collection of antique cookie jars we've ever seen lines three walls. You serve yourself drinks here out of a wall of coolers stocked with everything from beer and Snapple to sodas and exotic fruit drinks. Menu items are scrawled in thick magic marker strokes on paper plates and cardboard squares hung behind the cash register.

Mrs. T's soups are laden with vegetables, pulled chicken and rich broth. Most of her three-dozen sandwiches are named after friends and family members who eat here. We like the Stacy sub with four types of melted cheese. And the three varieties of veggie burgers always get rave reviews. Club sandwiches are stacked so high they barely fit in your mouth. And all the meats and cheeses are fresh out of the deli counter, which also offers items by the half-pound or more to take home. The Outer Banks curly fries, lightly seasoned and made to order, are wonderful. Each entree comes with ripple chips and a pickle. Cakes, pastries and gourmet jelly beans are available for dessert, and lots of kosher food, including matzos, can be found all year. Mrs. T's serves lunch and dinner seven days a week from mid-March through early February. Everything here can be packaged to go.

Red Drum Taphouse
$$ • N.C. Hwy. 12, MP 10, Nags Head • (252) 480-1095

New in 1998, the Red Drum earned word-of-mouth praise from the moment it opened. The handsome red brick exterior presents an apt introduction to the very tasteful decor inside: glossy, deep rust-colored square tables, a gleaming redwood bar stretching across the back wall, big windows, a poster-size photo of an angler with his red drum catch, even a small fireplace that makes things cozy on cooler days.

Red Drum also serves up tasteful food. For lunch try chowder, wings or shrimp con queso for starters. Follow with more filling fare, including steamed snow crab legs, burgers, crab-cake sandwiches, chicken havarti, fish and chips or a blue-plate special that changes daily.

Dinner offerings include cowboy steak, a 16-ounce bone-in Angus rib steak, grilled and served with Red Drum onion rings; apple chops, a double pork porterhouse chop grilled with a hard cider glaze, served with sweet potato gratin and veggies; or bangers and mash,

grilled banger served over sour cream mashed potatoes with a Portobello mushroom gravy and veggies.

Grilled or fried fresh fish, pasta and vegetarian dishes are also available on this unique menu.

Sunday brunch is also served in-season after Easter. In addition to traditional items like omelettes and French toast, Red Drum also serves up mom-style chicken and dumplings, meat loaf, and poached egg over prime rib.

Red Drum serves lunch and dinner year round. Closing times — 10 PM weekdays and 10:30 PM weekends — are extended into the wee hours with entertainment. (See our Nightlife chapter.)

Kelly's Outer Banks Restaurant & Tavern
$$$ • U.S. Hwy. 158, MP 10½, Nags Head • (252) 441-4116

Kelly's is an Outer Banks tradition and one of the most popular restaurants year round. Owner Mike Kelly gives his personal attention to every detail, so the service and selections are always first-rate. This is a large, upscale eatery and a busy place. The decor reflects the area's rich maritime heritage and includes abundant examples of fish, birds and other wildlife. The tavern is hopping seven nights a week, even during winter (see our Nightlife chapter).

Dinner is the only meal served here, and it's offered in several rooms upstairs and downstairs. Kelly's menu offers fresh seafood dishes, chicken, beef and pastas. There's a raw bar for those who enjoy feasting on oysters and other steamed shellfish. An assortment of delicious homemade breads accompanies each meal. Kelly's sweet potato biscuits are succulent — we usually ask for a second basket. Desserts are flavorful and filling. A separate children's menu is available, complete with crayons and special placemats to color. Kelly's also caters private parties, weddings and any style event imaginable. The restaurant and lounge are open daily. Dinner is served between 5 PM and 10 PM.

Calico Jack's at The Carolinian
$$ • N.C. Hwy. 12, MP 10½, Nags Head • (252) 441-7171

Recently renamed, Calico Jack's is at the

same location in the Carolinian where Outer Banks guests have been served since 1946. Breakfast, lunch and dinner are offered daily during the season. Fresh seafood and nightly specials are available for supper. The restaurant has early bird discounts and a children's menu. The big dining room can easily accommodate large groups and conferences. The outdoor tiki bar has all sorts of beer, wine and tropical drinks. Free, live music is performed nightly on the deck in the summer. Dinner patrons also receive priority seating at the Carolinian's comedy club (see our Nightlife chapter).

Mulligan's Oceanfront Grille
$$ • N.C. Hwy. 12, MP 10½, Nags Head • (252) 480-2000

Serving seafood, steak and an array of pasta dishes, Mulligan's is a great place for lunch or dinner. Occupying the old 1949 Miller's Pharmacy building, the eatery is divided in half lengthwise by wooden and glass partitions. The south end is flanked by a long, low bar reminiscent of the TV show *Cheers*. Scores of old Outer Banks photographs, painted mirrors and other memorabilia decorate this comfortable full-service bar, where appetizers and light dinners are available.

The north half of Mulligan's is the restaurant, where excellent oysters, crab cakes and teriyaki chicken are available. Bread, a salad and potatoes or rice complete the main course, but be sure to save room for cheesecake and other delightful desserts. Live entertainment is featured here year round (see our Nightlife chapter). Mulligan's is open seven days a week all year.

George's Junction
$$ • N.C. Hwy. 12, MP 11, Nags Head • (252) 441-0606

Outside, George's Junction has a slightly exotic mystique, thanks to the unusual architecture of the former Restaurant By George. Inside, the expansive interior is a fitting setting for the largest all-you-can-eat seafood buffet on the Outer Banks. The dinner buffet offers 70 hot items and includes crab legs, hand-carved roast beef, ham, chicken, a variety of local seafood, a full salad bar, several varieties of bread and rolls baked daily and a delicious homemade dessert bar. A special price is set for children. The only restaurant big enough where customers can wait on line inside in the comfort of air-conditioning, George's is nicely decorated and includes a large lounge with a full bar. Patrons will feel comfortable in everything from jeans to evening gowns. George's serves dinner seven days a week in-season. The schedule varies in the off-season from March through November. Reservations are requested for parties of 10 or more.

CW's

$ • U.S. Hwy. 158, MP 11, Nags Head
• (252) 441-5917

For more than 23 years CW's has been serving food on the Outer Banks. Wayne Blackburn has owned this Colonial-style restaurant with the tall white columns since 1982. He offers traditionally prepared local seafood, steaks and baby-back ribs for dinner during summer. Breakfast, which is available year round, includes pancakes, eggs, bacon, oatmeal, hash browns, sausage and other early morning staples starting at $1.50 a meal. There's full bar service here and separate smoking and nonsmoking rooms. Original art, on loan from Seaside Art Gallery (see Arts), adorns the walls.

Tortuga's Lie Shellfish Bar and Grille

$ • N.C. Hwy. 12, MP 11, Nags Head
• (252) 441-RAWW

Our hands-down favorite haunt on the Outer Banks, this small, upbeat eatery is housed in a turquoise and white cottage across from the ocean near a great surf break. Tortuga's features an enclosed porch furnished with handmade wooden booths; an expanded bar seats more than two-dozen people. There's a sand volleyball court out back where pickup games always are being played — and watched from the outdoor picnic tables. This is one of the only places around where it's truly comfortable to eat alone. The bartenders and wait staff are some of the friendliest folk we know. The food is fabulous and creatively concocted. The atmosphere inside is fun and casual, with turtle-themed batiks hanging from the white walls and more than 100 license plates, some with pretty unusual personal messages, from across the country tacked to the low ceiling beams.

The menu here offers everything from 'gator bites — yes, the real thing — and delicious sandwiches to scrumptious seafood flavored with outrageous spices and a full raw bar that always has something steaming. The french fries are the best we've ever had. And the coco loco chicken entree (smothered with coconut, served with a side of lime curry dipping sauce for lunch and dinner) is something we crave at least once a week. Other dinner entrees include pork medallions, steak stir-fries, just-off-the-boat tuna steaks, succulent shrimp and pasta plates. Most meals come with finely flavored rice and beans, but the cooks will substitute fries if you ask. And the full lunch menu is offered until 10 PM. Sushi is served during the off-season on Wednesday nights, and the place usually is packed with locals. Desserts are creamy, delicious and change daily. Some of our favorites are turtle cheesecake and Tortuga's gargantuan chocolate chip cookies.

There's a full bar here with loads of speciality drinks. We also enjoy the Black and Tans, a combination of Bass Ale and Guinness, poured to almost overflowing in pint-sized glasses. If you're a beer lover and haven't discovered this duo yet, be sure to order one on your next trip to Tortuga's (see our Nightlife chapter). This hip, laid-back eatery is open seven days a week for lunch and dinner from late February through December. Call for winter hours.

Pier House Restaurant

$ • Nags Head Fishing Pier, N.C. Hwy.
12, MP 11½, Nags Head • (252) 441-5141

Offering an amazing ocean view on the beach, this family-style restaurant allows patrons to sit right above the ocean. You can feel the salt spray if you dine on the screened porch, and even inside the air-conditioned building, waves sometimes crash beneath the wooden floor's slats. This is a great, laid-back place to enjoy a big breakfast before a day of fishing or to take a break from angling on a hot afternoon. The staff is friendly, and all three meals of the day are traditionally prepared. Lunch includes sandwiches, soups and seafood specials. All-you-can-eat dinners also are popular picks. Each entree comes with coleslaw, hush puppies and french fries or baked potato. You can have your fish grilled, broiled

INSIDERS' TIP

Few Outer Banks restaurants have dress requirements. Most are happy if you wear a shirt, shorts or summer dress and don't track too much sand on the rug.

or fried, and if you clean the fish you catch, the folks here will cook it for you. Appetizers and desserts also are available. Free sightseeing passes come with supper so you can stroll along the long pier after your meal and watch the anglers and surfers. Pier House Restaurant is open seven days a week from March through November. Dinner is served during summer only.

The Wharf
$$ • N.C. Hwy. 12, MP 11½, Nags Head • (252) 441-7457

You can't miss this popular beach restaurant across from the Atlantic: It's the one with the long, long line of people out front. Folks arrive early for the ever-popular all-you-can-eat seafood buffet of Alaskan crab legs, fried shrimp, scallops, chowder, broiled catch of the day, clam strips, barbecue, prime rib, homemade yeast rolls, loads of vegetables and desserts — all for less than $15.95 a person. The atmosphere is very informal. A new $4.95 children's menu offers hamburgers, hot dogs, pizza, chicken tenders, a drink and all-you-can-eat dessert served on a souvenir Frisbee. Kids 3 and younger eat for free. The Wharf is open from Easter through October. Doors open at 4 PM during the summer. The Wharf is closed Sundays. Alcoholic beverages are not served here.

Las Trancas
$$ • N.C. Hwy. 12, MP 11¼, Nags Head • (252) 441-9330

Las Trancas offers both traditional Mexican fare and Tex-Mex style dinners. When it opened in 1995, the eatery was only the second of its kind on the Outer Banks. With native Mexican cooks, Las Trancas' food is as authentic south-of-the-border as you can get. The ambiance, with Mexican decor and music, is tasteful and not overdone. And Mexican food aficionados among us give this eatery two thumbs up.

All meals are served with rice and beans and fresh vegetables. There are plenty of choices that include fresh Outer Banks seafood cooked with a Mexican flair. Or try the fabulous chargrilled fajitas with chicken, steak or shrimp. Vegetarian selections in addition to a children's menu are available. You can top off your meal with a traditional Mexican dessert such as fried ice cream — if you have any room left.

Las Trancas also has on hand a good range of Mexican beer and specialty drinks, and there's a full bar on the premises. The restaurant is open daily May through September for dinner only.

Country Deli
$, no credit cards • Surfside Plaza, N.C. Hwy. 12, MP 13, Nags Head • (252) 441-5684

A laid-back eatery with items only available for take-out, Country Deli offers some of the biggest sandwiches on the beach. The Killer is always a hit, with ham, turkey, havarti and muenster cheese and hot peppers spread on a sub roll. Our favorite is the Goesway, where five kinds of cheese are melted on thick slices of toast and topped with crispy strips of bacon. There's a full deli counter here, so you can create your own sandwiches. Side salads of macaroni, pasta, potato and vegetables also are served. The owner offers several types of chips, but sour pickles come free with every option. Brownies and cheesecake are tempting dessert selections.

Don't leave without checking out the philosophical ponderings employees leave on the blackboard behind the cash register — they could change the way you think about the world while you're trying to decide what to order. Country Deli is open for lunch and dinner seven days a week during the summer and offers free delivery to Nags Head and Kill Devil Hills. This eatery is open for lunch only during the off-season (call for hours and days).

The Clove Italian Pizza Kitchen & Pub
$ • Surfside Plaza, U.S. Hwy. 158, MP 13, Nags Head • (252) 480-1988

One of the Outer Banks newest eateries, The Clove adds class and gourmet cooking to the traditional pizza parlor concept. Here, you don't just have beer with your pizza — you can choose from a whole list of microbrews. Pasta dishes, sandwiches and a complete Italian-food menu are available, along with gourmet and traditional pizzas. Check out the unique mural inside this interesting, well-crafted restaurant.

Seafare Restaurant
$$ • U.S. Hwy. 158, MP 13½, Nags Head
• (252) 441-5555

So how does one of the oldest and most successful of the array of seafood buffet places on the Outer Banks celebrate its 45th birthday? How about by cutting prices. The folks at Seafare have shaved about $4 off the buffet menu prices that were in effect during 1997.

For a restaurant that considers its tradition one of its strongest selling points, there are plenty of new things in store for 1998 at Seafare. The restaurant's backbone of a buffet returns with the crab legs and steamed shrimp, clams, mussels, crabs and scallops. The dinner menu has been expanded and — as might be expected with the arrival of new chef Lou Petrozza, formerly of the popular Italian deli of the same name in Kill Devil Hills — includes special new creations that feature fresh pasta and Italian recipes.

The rum dinner rolls and she-crab soup are still here, but they are joined with a "breads du jour" option, a yummy spinach salad with warm bacon dressing, and the new Nag's Head Clam Bake feature (with clams, mussels, shrimp, corn on the cob and all the other stuff you'd want to include at one of your own).

Seafare has a small bar with complete service. Dinner is served nightly from March through November. Reservations are not necessary, and the restaurant's outdoor playground helps keep the kids occupied while you wait for a table (remember, this place gets packed during summer). Ask about children's and senior discounts.

La Fogata Mexican Restaurant
$ • U.S Hwy. 158, MP 14½, Nags Head
• (252) 441-4179

At the front of the Outer Banks Mall, La Fogata (known by some locals as La Fa-Hardees, due to its location in a former fast-food place) joins its original Kitty Hawk sister with the same name in offering delicious Mexican food at affordable prices. These restaurants have a strong Outer Banks following, and the mall location has the same menu and similar decor as the first restaurant. See the listing in our Kitty Hawk section for more information.

Maione's
$$ • U.S. Hwy. 158, MP 14½, Nags Head
• (252) 480-3311

Owned by a New Jersey family who decided to relocate its popular Northern beach eatery to Nags Head, this restaurant opened in 1995 and serves a variety of homemade, traditional Italian and American offerings. Linguine with clam sauce, fresh-baked lasagna and fresh seafood specials are among the best selections. A huge array of pastas with flavorful sauces are always on the menu. Each entree comes with salad and bread, and you have a wide range of appetizers from which to choose. The tiramisu is sinfully delicious — and authentic — for dessert. A full bar and lounge area is separate from the dining room. Dinner is served throughout the summer seven days a week. Call for fall and winter schedules.

The Island's Eye
$$ • N.C. Hwy. 12, MP 16, Nags Head
• (252) 480-1993

This family-owned and operated restaurant opened in 1991 and offers a warm, soothing atmosphere and abundant greenery. The Island's Eye is open for dinner only, serving selections such as seafood broiled, pan fried, blackened or baked, and combination platters of beef, poultry and pasta. The barbecue shrimp is great for starters. A children's menu is available, and in the summer, dining specials are offered from 4:30 to 6 PM. The restaurant has a full bar. The Island's Eye is open from early spring through fall. Call for off-season hours.

Penguin Isle Soundside Grille
$$$ • U.S. Hwy. 158, MP 16, Nags Head
• (252) 441-2637

As night falls, waterfowl begin fluttering across the low-lying marshlands of Roanoke Sound, right outside the windows of this elegant soundside restaurant. Windsurfers in the distance cruise by beneath colorful sails, and brilliant sunsets abound. The sights outside the dining room are as lovely and tranquil as the ambiance inside. Penguin Isle is truly a peaceful place to enjoy a relaxing, intimate meal.

Here, the decor is tasteful and creative, with displays of local art, hand-carved decoys, lighted authentic ship models, enormous

mounted wine bottles and light wood accents around the airy dining room. White linen tablecloths cover every table, and the lights and slow jazz music are soft and low.

Not only a premier place to dine, Penguin Isle is also a wine destination. The staff is very knowledgeable, and the much-heralded Wine Spectator's Award of Excellence identified this restaurant's wine list as "one of the best in the world" for the past six years. Seasonal wine dinners also are offered in the off-season with advance registration.

A separate window-walled lounge with full bar, an abbreviated menu and small tables overlooks the sound. Patrons can also have a cocktail before dinner on the outdoor deck, and a lobby with comfortable couches affords an alternative place to await your table. Owners Doug Tutwiler and Mike Kelly combine their talents here to create a truly distinctive restaurant. Chef Lee Miller is one of only a handful of certified working chefs on the Outer Banks, and all the staff are friendly and professional.

Penguin Isle serves fresh local seafood, handmade pasta, certified Black Angus beef, chicken, duck, fresh-baked breads and many other appetizing offerings. Creative food pairings, also called fusion cookery, is the chef's specialty, but the seafood trio platter featuring fresh fish, shrimp and scallops is hard to beat. We also recommend grilled Gulf Stream tuna over homemade fettuccine. The seafood gumbo and bean cakes are also delicious for starters here. Penguin Isle's portions are generous, especially for such an upscale restaurant. All the desserts, of course, are delectable.

Only dinner is served here from March through January. Employees also will cater private parties, wedding receptions and almost any occasion on-site. A children's menu is available, and early dining specials are offered from 5 until 6 PM.

Soundside Pavilion
$$$ • U.S. Hwy. 158, MP 16½, Nags Head • (252) 441-0535

This wide, open eatery with a great view of the Roanoke Sound offers an all-you-dare-to-eat surf and turf buffet. In the same building as the family arcade, it's served nightly throughout the summer for $19.95 a person. Fresh fish, chicken, pasta, barbecue, oysters, clams, crab legs, vegetables, rolls, fresh-baked breads, fruit, a salad bar, homemade desserts and soft-serve ice cream all are included in the price. A $4.95 breakfast buffet offers eggs, pancakes, sausage, fruit, bacon, grits, French toast sticks, biscuits, sausage, ham, corned beef hash and other items. A bottomless cup of coffee or tea can be had for $1. A limited à la carte menu is also available. Cocktails, beer and wine are served nightly. Buses and large

groups are welcome. Breakfast and dinner are served every day in the summer. Winter hours vary, so call ahead.

Windmill Point

$$$ • U.S. Hwy. 158, MP 16½, Nags Head • (252) 441-1535

Magnificent views of the sound at sunset, marred only by the colorful sails of windsurfers, delight diners here. Famous for its memorabilia from the elegant ocean liner SS *United States*, this restaurant provides excellent cuisine to match the outdoor sights. There are two dining areas, tastefully furnished down to the tablecloths, linen napkins and comfortable chairs that hug rather than support you. Service is fast and unobtrusive. The upstairs lounge, which features the authentic kidney-shaped bar from the ship, complete with plaques from famous 1950s statesmen and actresses who sipped cocktails there, is a pleasant place to await your call to dinner.

Favorites from the menu include a seafood trio, poached or grilled with succulent sauces; and a seafood pasta entree of lightly seasoned scallops. The chefs also prepare roasted prime rib, sauteed duck, fettuccine primavera and capelli con scampi. Cooked with fresh herbs and creative sauces, the entrees get better each season. Windmill Point's menu features heart-healthy selections. A children's menu is also available. Dinner is served seven nights a week March through September.

Jennette's Pier Restaurant & Pub

$$ • N.C. Hwy. 12, MP 16½, Nags Head • (252) 480-6600

Entering its second season in 1998, Jennette's bills itself as "the restaurant with the million dollar view." No argument there — diners can look out one of the restaurant's many windows and see 5 miles north up the beach. Stormy weather dramatizes the view even more, with waves crashing up around the pier.

For breakfast, try eggs served with catfish, herring roe, steak or sausage, grilled ham or bacon. Eggs Benedict, omelettes and Belgian waffles are other offerings. Lunch items include sandwiches options like fried flounder, soft-shell crab, grilled Cajun chicken and Reubens. Hot plates and baskets — clam strips, oysters, shrimp or scallops, grilled pork chops — are also available, in addition to an interesting selection of appetizers. Dinners include prime rib, broiled and fried seafood platters, crab cakes, lobster tail, chicken, steak and pasta. A children's menu is available.

Specialty drinks and kiddie cocktails are offered from the pub. There is a also a "pub grub" menu with light fare including veggie burgers,

barbecue sandwiches, crab cakes, hot wings, chips and salsa, mozzarella sticks, she-crab soup and steamed shrimp. Jennette's serves three meals a day in-season. Hours are 6 AM to 9 PM. Pub grub is available from noon to 11:30 PM.

The Dunes
$ • U.S. Hwy. 158, MP 16½, Nags Head • (252) 441-1600

When a large crowd or big family is gathering for a meal, this 16-year-old restaurant can accommodate everyone in its three huge dining rooms. Breakfast at The Dunes is a locals' favorite — you can tell by the packed parking lot — where every early morning entree in every imaginable combination is offered. There's also a popular breakfast bar here during weekends in the off-season and daily in the summer. Lunches include great burgers and homemade crab cakes served with fries and coleslaw. The rib-eye steak sandwich is also a good choice.

Dinners feature local, well-prepared seafood at moderate prices and a huge salad bar. All-you-can-eat specials are selected often. There are also plenty of desserts to choose from, if you're not already too full. The Dunes serves beer and wine and has a children's menu for small fries. The service is fast and friendly. The restaurant is open from mid-February through Thanksgiving seven days a week in-season (call for winter hours). The Dunes is a nonsmoking establishment.

Owens' Restaurant
$$$ • N.C. Hwy. 12, MP 16½, Nags Head • (252) 441-7309

The oldest Outer Banks restaurant owned and operated continuously by the same family, Owens' is a local legend. In 1996 this upscale eatery celebrated its 50th anniversary, marking a half-century of good food and good service, which are well-appreciated by loyal patrons who return year after year.

Clara and Bob Owens first owned a small hot dog stand in Manteo. In 1946 they opened a 50-seat cafe in Nags Head on the deserted strip of sand that's now filled with hotels, rental cottages and thousands of vacationers who arrive each summer. The Owens raised their two children, Bobby and Clara Mae, in the restaurant serving breakfast, lunch and dinner during those early days. Today, Clara Mae and her husband, Lionel, run the family restaurant. R.V., Clara Mae's nephew, owns a restaurant by the same name on the Nags Head-Manteo Causeway. Clara Mae's daughter, Clara, runs a self-titled eatery on the Manteo waterfront. Together, this food-loving family serves some of the best traditional Outer Banks-style seafood on the beach.

Owens' Restaurant now seats more than 200 people and offers only evening meals. More than 90,000 dinners are served from this Beach Road eatery each season. The atmosphere is still homey, the food is still fresh and homemade, and the large lobby overflows with memorabilia of the barrier islands' and Owens family heritage. Even the building's architecture is reminiscent of the Outer Banks' past, patterned after an old Nags Head lifesaving station. The menu, however, combines modern tastes with traditional recipes. Owens' renowned Southern Thanksgiving buffet is worth experiencing just to sample the range of delights this restaurant is capable of creating.

Locally caught seafood, often fresh off the boat, is broiled, fried, sauteed or grilled each evening. Coconut shrimp, "Miss O" crab cakes and pasta are among the most popular entrees. There's a mixed grill for patrons who prefer prime rib with their fish. Live Maine lobsters, picked from the tank, are steamed just before they're placed on your plate. Homemade soups, including Hatteras-style clam chowder and lobster bisque, are delicious ways to start a meal. All of the homemade desserts are well-worth saving room for.

There's a full bar upstairs in the Station Keepers' Lounge where beer, wine, mixed drinks and special coffee concoctions are available. Light fare is also available upstairs. Owens' is open from mid-March through New Year's Eve. Dinner is served seven days a week.

Sam & Omie's
$$ • N.C. Hwy. 12, MP 16½, Nags Head • (252) 441-7366

Begun as a place for early morning anglers to indulge in a big breakfast before the Oregon Inlet charter fishing fleet took off, Sam & Omie's is one of the oldest family restaurants on the barrier islands. In fact, the famed Lost Colony production and Sam & Omie's both celebrated their 60th anniversary in 1997. Omie Tillett recently retired his boat The Sportsman, and he long ago sold this little wooden building at Whalebone Junction. The restaurant, however, retains its old beach charm and still serves hearty, homemade food cooked with traditional local recipes for breakfast, lunch and dinner.

This is a very casual place with wooden booths and tables and a full-service bar. Local fishermen congregate to contemplate the day's catch, and families flock to enjoy the low-priced, filling meals. Photographs of famous Gulf Stream catches line the walls, and the TV usually is tuned in to some exciting sporting event. For breakfast, omelettes are our favorite option. We like to make a meal of the rich she-crab soup and red chile poppers for lunch. Salads, sandwiches, hamburgers, fish fillets, turkey clubs and daily specials also are served. A steamer was added in 1998 for healthy steamed vegetables and fish. For dinner, try a soft-shell crab sandwich in-season or a prime rib entree on Thursdays. Sam & Omie's is open from early March through December, at least. Call for winter hours.

RV's
$$ • Nags Head/Manteo Cswy., Nags Head • (252) 441-4963

Celebrating its 16th year this summer, RV's is one of the most popular places on the beach for lunch and dinner. Just check the parking lot if you don't believe us. Owner R.V. Owens often stops by your table to greet you, offering his warm smile, a firm handshake and maybe an opinion or two as an appetizer to an abundant meal. You can eat at the full-service bar in this casual restaurant or sit at a table in one of the soundfront dining rooms. The seafood stew is extremely tasty and filled to overflowing with shrimp and scallops. Marinated tuna is a must for fish lovers. There's also a gazebo raw bar on an attached deck overlooking the water that takes on a life of its own in the evening. Prices here are really reasonable, and the atmosphere is lively and fun. RV's is open

from mid-February through Thanksgiving seven days a week.

Tale of the Whale
$$ • Nags Head/Manteo Cswy., Nags Head • (252) 441-7332

Family-operated and owned for 20 years, Tale of the Whale is situated right on the Roanoke Sound. You can enjoy the delightful views either looking through the expansive windows inside while savoring dinner, or out on the 75-foot deck and gazebo while sipping a refreshing cocktail. Newly decorated, this roomy establishment is bright and airy, with big wooden booths lining the walls. Tables fill out the center of the two dining rooms, and a 40-foot bar is on the north side where diners can watch sunsets and bird life dance on the water.

Tale of the Whale serves a variety of the freshest available food in generous portions. Seafood, lots of pasta, steaks and prime rib are staples of the menu. Specials, featuring everything from a mixed grill to broiled shellfish, are offered daily, and early-bird specials are available from 4 to 5 PM. Combination platters can be served fried or broiled. Desserts are homemade and baked on the premises. Tale of the Whale is open daily for dinner from April through October.

Basnight's Lone Cedar Cafe
$$ • Nags Head/Manteo Cswy., Nags Head • (252) 441-5405

One of the newer Outer Banks restaurants, Lone Cedar Cafe opened in the spring of 1996 to serve lunch and dinner. The Basnight family of Manteo operates this casual, upscale eatery where diners wearing everything from shorts to suits are welcome. In fact, it's not unusual to see the president pro tem of the state senate himself, Marc Basnight, talking with guests and removing dinner plates. Checkered green-and-white tablecloths cover every table. You'll notice the hunting motif with duck decoys and fishing memorabilia in honor of the former barrier island hunt club for which the eatery is named.

Appetizers are plentiful, ranging from on-

INSIDERS' TIP

Looking for a restaurant with a view that's right on the water? Try dining at Billy's Fish House Restaurant in Buxton. It's down-home and delicious.

ion straws to clam chowder, seafood bisque, clam and oyster fritters, hot crab balls and hot crab dip plus soups and other specials of the day. Lunch entrees start at $3.95 and include sandwiches and fresh local seafood. For dinner try black Angus beef, homemade pasta, sliced duck breast or fried or broiled seafood or order any of the evening specials. Each meal is accompanied by a salad, choice of potato, rolls and homemade corn bread. There's a full bar and an extensive wine list here. Desserts, home-baked daily, include pumpkin and pecan praline cheesecakes; pecan, peanut butter, lemon or Key lime pie; banana fritters and Lebanese chocolate cake.

This cafe offers a view of the water from every table and is open for lunch and dinner daily year round. Vegetarian and children's offerings are available. Reservations are not accepted.

The Oasis
$$ • Nags Head/Manteo Cswy., Nags Head • (252) 441-7721

This waterfront building was constructed as a restaurant in the 1940s, making it one of the oldest continuously operated eateries on the beach. Violet Kellam bought the building in 1950, and her grandchildren, Mike, Mark and Kellam France, took the place over several years ago. Framed black-and-white photographs of barefoot 1950s-era waitresses still flank the walls.

Open for breakfast, lunch and dinner April through Christmas, this restaurant offers a panoramic view of the sound. Breakfast includes traditional eggs, bacon and pancake options. Fresh seafood and hearty sandwiches are served for lunch. For dinner try a daily special or featured entree such as peppered salmon, blackened tuna or prime rib. The steam bar serves oysters, shrimp, clams, crab legs and live lobsters. The Oasis has a children's menu, and full bar service is available evenings. Diners coming by boat can tie up at the new 200-foot dock. Before or after a meal, patrons can stroll along the 100-foot pier or sit and admire the view from the 500-square-foot gazebo. Acoustic entertainment is offered in the summer. (See our Nightlife chapter.)

Roanoke Island

Manteo

Hurricane Mo's
$$ • Pirate's Cove Yacht Club, Manteo/ Nags Head Cswy., Manteo • (252) 473-2266

The former Pirate's Cove Restaurant & Raw Bar, this restaurant sits high atop Pirate's Cove Marina overlooking the Roanoke Sound. Owner Jeff Ashworth, who has been in the restaurant business for more than 20 years, wanted a toned-down, classic feel with an authentic Outer Banks focus. The restaurant serves traditional fresh seafood, steaks, prime rib and some Cajun selections. There are also vegetarian choices and a children's menu. Beer and wine are served, and the establishment has a brown bagging license for liquor, which will allow patrons to bring their own. Hurricane Mo's serves lunch and dinner in the summer. Call for off-season hours.

The Weeping Radish Brewery & Bavarian Restaurant
$$ • U.S. Hwy. 64, Manteo • (252) 473-1157

Next to the Christmas Shop on the main highway in Manteo, this large Bavarian restaurant includes an outdoor beer garden, separate pub, children's playground and two-story dining room. A European flavor prevails throughout. Traditional German meals include veal, sauerbraten and a variety of sausages. Homemade noodles, also called spaetzle, and cooked red cabbage are flavorful side dishes offering unusual tastes you won't find elsewhere on the Outer Banks. Continental cuisine also is available.

The restaurant's name comes from the radish served in Bavaria as an accompaniment to beer. Cut in a spiral, it's sprinkled with salt and packed back together. The salt draws out the moisture and gives the radish the appearance of weeping. Beer isn't served with radishes here (except by special request), but the brews are certainly the best part about this place. A microbrewery

opened at The Weeping Radish in 1986 offering pure, fresh handcrafted German beer without chemical additives or preservatives. You can watch this "nectar of the gods" being brewed on-site. Take home an extra pint to enjoy later. The Weeping Radish is open all year seven days a week for lunch and dinner.

Garden Deli & Pizzeria
$, no credit cards • U.S. Hwy. 64, Manteo
• (252) 473-6888

Shaded by pine trees, this tiny restaurant has a breezy outdoor deck perfect for summer dining. The cheerful, hometown crew at the eatery have watched their Garden grow into one of the most popular lunch spots for the working crowd in Manteo. Here, New York-style pizzas are cooked to order and packaged to go, if you wish. White pizza, one of our favorites, is topped with ricotta, mozzarella, Parmesan and Romano cheeses, broccoli and minced garlic. Traditional red sauce pizzas and specialty pizzas also are offered. The Philly cheese steaks, burgers, gyros and a wide assortment of deli sandwiches, homemade salads and antipasto salads are wonderful. Fresh tuna and chicken salad plates are just right for a light lunch or dinner.

For breakfast, bagels, muffins and sandwiches are available. Garden Pizzeria offers

free evening delivery to Roanoke Island and Pirate's Cove. The restaurant is open for breakfast, lunch and dinner Monday through Saturday year round. Garden also offers catering.

Big Al's Soda Fountain & Grill
$ • U.S. Hwy. 64, Manteo
• (252) 473-5570

You can't miss Big Al's, across from the Christmas Shop in downtown Manteo. The talk of the town since construction began the winter of 1996-97, locals anxiously awaited the early summer opening of this down-home eatery in the huge brand-new building. Owners Vanessa and Allan Foreman were originally planning to open a little ice cream parlor, but the concept expanded into a full-blown soda fountain and family restaurant. It's definitely a place to take the kids. With '50s decor and memorabilia, Big Al's is a great place to kick back and enjoy some good ol' American food and fountain treats. Plus, you can get fish so fresh, it's literally off-the-boat, says Vanessa. She should know because Allan catches most of it.

Children's meals are available for $2.95. Kids can also check out the game room, with a pinball machine, video games and a jukebox. There's even a dance floor. Big Al's serves lunch and dinner daily.

Darrell's Restaurant

$$ • U.S. Hwy. 64, Manteo
• (252) 473-5366

This down-home restaurant started as an ice cream stand more than 30 years ago and has been a favorite family-style eatery for the past two decades. It's common knowledge that Darrell's fried oysters are among the best in town. Menu items such as popcorn shrimp, crab cakes, grilled marinated tuna and fried scallops are teamed with french fries, coleslaw and hush puppies to provide more than enough to fuel you through the day. Soups such as Dare County-style clam chowder and oyster stew are hard to resist. Salads, sandwiches and steamed and raw seafood are additional options for the hungry diner. Meat-eaters will be satiated by offerings such as delmonico steak, barbecued minced pork and grilled marinated chicken. Daily seafood specials are served for dinner; a children's and light-eater's menu is available. The hot fudge cake is a must for dessert. Beer and wine are served. Darrell's is open for lunch and dinner year round but is closed Sundays.

Ron Saul's Bar-B-Q and Family Buffet

$, no credit cards • U.S. Hwy. 64, Manteo
• (252) 473-6464

The atmosphere is casual, and the food is spicy at this family-style restaurant known for its Carolina-style barbecue. The all-you-can-eat lunch and dinner buffets include fried chicken, coleslaw and other vegetables — besides the barbecue, of course. Rose Bay oysters are available all summer, and the fried and steamed shrimp are great. The ambiance is friendly — Ron enjoys his customers as much as they enjoy his ribs and sandwiches. Eat in or call for take-out. Ron Saul's also caters off-site pig pickin's and family barbecues. It's open Tuesday through Saturday for lunch and dinner in-season. Call for winter hours.

Clara's Seafood Grill and Steam Bar

$$$ • The Waterfront Shops, Manteo
• (252) 473-1727

Overlooking Shallowbag Bay and the state ship, *Elizabeth II*, this is one of our favorite Manteo eateries where diners can watch boats on the water and see birds diving for fish. A casual, relaxing restaurant with good service and equally admirable food, Clara's lunch menu has delicious sandwiches and salads, hot soups and an ever-changing specials board. We order the black beans and rice most frequently. All the dinners are excellent, especially the mixed grill of shrimp and shrimp kebabs, filet mignon and tuna. The she-crab soup, tuna kebabs and mixed grill are some other favorites at this classy establishment. Grilled fish specials are offered every day. Caesar salads are a cool alternative on warm summer evenings. And the steam bar showcases local seafood of all sorts.

Historic photos lining the walls will remind you of what Manteo's waterfront looked like in the early days. Since this restaurant is less than a 10-minute drive from The Lost Colony amphitheater, it's a good place to take in an early meal before the outdoor drama begins. Beer, wine and champagne are available, and brown bagging is allowed. A children's menu is provided. Lunch and dinner are served here March through December.

Full Moon Cafe

$$ • The Waterfront Shops, Manteo
• (252) 473-MOON

A cozy cafe overlooking Shallowbag Bay from its second-story vantage point, this eclectic eatery opened in late 1995 and consistently overflows with local and visiting patrons. Tablecloths line every table, and a plate glass window wall opens onto the water. The innovative cuisine here has a nouveau American flair. Most of the entrees and specials (which usually involve creative takes on pasta and seafood) are so unusual we haven't seen them anywhere else on the Outer Banks.

Hummus spread, baked brie and mushroom caps stuffed with shrimp are succulent appetizers. Lunch specials include gourmet sandwiches to satisfy everyone's tastes, vegetarian offerings, seafood, chicken and homemade soups, such as Hungarian mushroom, curried spinach and spicy tomato. Each en-

tree is served with corn chips and Full Moon's own salsa. A separate dinner menu offers enticing seafood dishes, stuffed chicken breasts, roasted eggplant with other vegetables smothered in marinara sauce and provolone cheese, and beef Charron covered in Portobello mushrooms and a Gorgonzola cheese sauce. All the desserts are delightful. Beer (including some microbrews) and a good selection of wines are available. You can eat inside the lovely little dining room, dine outdoors in the courtyard or take any meal to go. Reservations are accepted for parties of six or more.

Full Moon is open for lunch and dinner seven days a week in summer. Hours are more limited in the off-season, so call for specific schedules.

Poor Richard's Sandwich Shop
$, no credit cards • The Waterfront, Manteo • (252) 473-3333

One of Manteo's favorite downtown eateries, Poor Richard's changed ownership in 1998. But new owner Tod Clissold is not about to alter the easy charm and delicious food at this waterfront establishment. With half the work force in Manteo making a bull's-eye to Poor Richard's every day, this casual eatery is a local gathering spot that's reasonably priced with fast counter service and interesting offerings. Try the cucumber sandwich with cream cheese

— a cool meal that surprises your palate. Sandwiches are made-to-order, and specials are offered daily. Soups, meatless chili, hot dogs, salad plates, cookies and ice cream are also available. Breakfast includes scrambled egg and bacon sandwiches, bagels and cream cheese and fresh fruit. Steamed shrimp is available for lunch and dinner.

Whatever your mode of transportation — boat, bike, car or legs — Poor Richard's is a worthy fueling station. You can eat inside at a roomy booth or take your meal out on the back porch and enjoy the waterfront view — there always seems to be enough room for everybody. Poor Richard's is open daily in the summer for breakfast, lunch and dinner. Call for off-season hours.

1587
$$$ • Tranquil House Inn, Queen Elizabeth St., Manteo • (252) 473-1587

The owner of this critically acclaimed restaurant makes your mouth water just by reading his menu aloud. The offerings are unusual, extremely upscale cosmopolitan and some of the most ambitious of any Outer Banks establishment. Ambiance is elegant and romantic: the soft glow of intimate lighting, a gleaming copper-topped bar in a separate lounge area and polished wood and mirrors that reflect the lights sparkling off boats anchored in Shallowbag Bay. Executive Chef

Donny King creates a constantly changing menu that's always as fresh and fabulous as the food.

Homemade soups prepared each day include Mediterranean mussels and crayfish with spring vegetables and feta cheese in a light tomato broth. For appetizers, select sesame-encrusted colossal scallops with spicy vegetable slaw and soy-wasabi cream or grilled Portobello mushroom on a zucchini podium with balsamic-sauteed julienne vegetables. Salads, served à la carte, offer Boston Bibb, romaine and baby lettuce leaves with spring vegetables and herb-shallot vinaigrette.

Dinner entrees, each of which is an artistic masterpiece, range from crispy cornmeal rockfish with Louisiana-style crayfish butter sauce and chile-fried rice to an ocean panache of tiger prawns, mussels, scallops and fish tossed with vegetables and orzo pasta, finished with feta cheese. Another excellent choice is grilled filet mignon fanned with roasted garlic mashed potatoes and a wild mushroom and goat's cheese and Cabernet Ragout.

A children's menu offers simpler dishes for younger tastes. Vegetarian requests are welcome. The exquisite dessert creations are well worth saving room for, and are so beautiful that you may want to take a snapshot before digging in!

Named for the first year English colonists attempted to settle on Roanoke Island, 1587 serves a wide selection of wine and beer and permits brown bagging. This outstanding restaurant is open for dinner daily in the summer. Call for off-season hours. Reservations are requested.

The Green Dolphin
Restaurant and Pub
$ • Sir Walter Raleigh St., Manteo • (252) 473-5911

This downtown Manteo eatery has been a popular pub for more than 18 years. It's casual and comfortable inside, with wooden booths and tables fashioned from the hatch covers taken off old ships. This storied pub suffered serious smoke and water damage in a late summer fire in 1997, but the owners have the Dolphin back in the swim of things,

complete with a brand-new kitchen and remodeled bathrooms. Much of the same old nautical memorabilia lines the walls, and a long bar still stretches along the back of the restaurant.

Food here is simple, cheap and satisfying. Hamburgers, she-crab soup (some say it's the best on the Outer Banks), crab cakes, lasagna, manicotti, Italian sausage and french fries are just a few of the offerings served for lunch and dinner. Appetizers and desserts also are available, and the pub serves pizzas and small-fry portions for the kids. The Green Dolphin is open year round daily except Sundays. Live entertainment is usually offered Fridays (see Nightlife).

Anna Livia's Restaurant
$$ • The Elizabethan Inn, U.S. Hwy. 64, Manteo • (252) 473-3753

Opened in 1995, this restaurant has earned acclaim for its moderately priced, contemporary and traditional Italian cuisine and generous selection of seafood. Anna Livia's features a gourmet seasonal menu and nightly specials including chicken and ravioli with mushrooms in balsamic sauce; and veal caprese sauteed with tomatoes and mozzarella cheese with basil. Pasta and chicken also are served. The lunch menu offers daily specials, sandwiches and seasonal fresh salads. Desserts are homemade, and beer and wine are served. A variety of breakfast entrees and a weekend breakfast buffet also are available. Other features include a children's menu, seniors' discounts, and a completely smoke-free environment. A full carry-out menu is available. Banquet rooms are reserved for private parties. Anna Livia's is open daily year round; on Saturday, breakfast and dinner only are served. Call for winter hours.

Wanchese

Queen Anne's Revenge
$$ • Old Wharf Rd., Wanchese • (252) 473-5466

Named after one of Blackbeard's famous pirate ships that plied the waters off Carolina's coast during the early 1700s,

Queen Anne's Revenge is snuggled in a grove of trees in the scenic fishing village of Wanchese. It's one of our favorite Outer Banks restaurants, well off the beaten path at the end of a winding lane. Wayne and Nancy Gray have operated this outstanding restaurant since 1978. They use only quality ingredients, and their attention to detail really shows.

The restaurant has three dining rooms, one with a fireplace that provides a cozy ambiance during cold winter months. A large selection of appetizers is offered, including bouillabaisse (chock-full of fresh seafood) and black bean and she-crab soups. All the seafood here is excellent, from Blackbeard's Raving to the locally landed shellfish and fish served with the Wanchese platter. There's even Châteaubriand for two, carved at your table. Queen Anne's chefs make their own pasta; in fact, their fettuccine is a staple around Wanchese. All the desserts are homemade and served in generous portions. This lovely restaurant offers a children's menu and

a nice selection of beer and wine. The dining room serves dinner only seven days a week during the summer. Enjoy the Sunday lunch buffet from October through May. Queen Anne's is open all year, closing Tuesdays during the off-season.

Fisherman's Wharf
$$ • N.C. Hwy. 345, Wanchese
• (252) 473-5205

Overlooking the fishing port of Wanchese, the dining room of this family-owned restaurant offers the best views around of the Outer Banks' commercial fishing fleet. Windows form an entire wall of the dining room, so diners can see the seafood they might be served this evening being unloaded from the boats in the afternoon. The fish here is as fresh and local as it gets.

The Daniels family, of Wanchese fishing history fame, opens this restaurant for lunch and dinner from late March through November. Seafood plates complete with homemade hush puppies and good coleslaw are the best selections from a variety of items

on the menu. There's a grill, and landlubbers can order pasta and chicken entrees. Diners can enjoy oysters on the half shell as an appetizer. You'll want to save room for the homemade desserts. This is a casual eatery where families feel right at home. A children's menu is available. Fisherman's Wharf is closed Sundays.

Hatteras Island

Rodanthe, Waves and Salvo

Lisa's Pizza
$ • N.C. Hwy. 12, Rodanthe
• (252) 987-2525

Speciality pizzas, deli sandwiches, subs, calzones, chicken Parmesan and salads are among the most popular items at this 13-year-old restaurant. Lisa's also serves breadsticks, hot wings, garlic and cheese bread and New York-style cheesecake for dessert. Beer and wine are available. There's also a separate children's menu. Lisa's offers lunch and dinner seven days a week from early April through November. All items can be eaten inside this casual restaurant, carried out or delivered.

Down Under Restaurant & Lounge
$$ • Rodanthe Pier, off N.C. Hwy. 12, Rodanthe • (252) 987-2277

Ocean views are spectacular at this Australian-style restaurant, perched high over the pilings of Rodanthe's pier. You can sit at the bar in this warm and friendly eatery and watch the sun set over the sound, or you can enjoy your meal in the dining room and see the pelicans glide over Atlantic waves or the moon rise over the dark sea. Decorated with authentic Australian art and memorabilia, Down Under is a one-of-a-kind on the Outer Banks. Here, you'll find crabmeat and Western omelettes for breakfast. Lunch specialties include the Great Australian bite, similar to an Aussie burger, made with hamburger, a fried egg, grilled onions, cheese and bacon. Spicy fish burgers, vegemite sandwiches and marinated chicken sandwiches are good authentic options too. Kangaroo, a delicious meat that is very popular at Down Under, is imported from Australia for 'roo stew, 'roo burgers and kangaroo curry. And you've got to try stuffed jalapenos served with Down Under's famous sweet chile sauce.

Dinner selections include Down Under shrimp stuffed with jalapeno peppers and cream cheese wrapped in bacon. We also enjoy a side order of the foot-high onion rings and a Foster's lager or Cooper's Stout. Happy hour is from 3 to 6 PM daily. Steamed, spiced shrimp are 10¢ each. Parents will appreciate the children's menu,

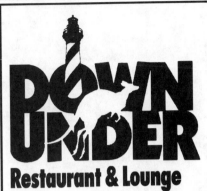
and kids will appreciate the extraordinary decor. Everyone will enjoy the view. Down Under is open seven days a week for breakfast, lunch and dinner from April through November. The restaurant is handicapped-accessible. Reservations are recommended.

Mid-Atlantic Market, Restaurant & Marina
$ • N.C. Hwy. 12, Salvo • (252) 987-1520

Serving some of the best hot lunches on Hatteras, this eatery is open year round seven days a week. Lunch specials, popular with local construction crews and watermen, include hot roast beef sandwiches with mashed potatoes and green beans, meat loaf made that morning, ham and cabbage, fried chicken, pork chops, hamburgers and barbecue. All the regular sandwiches, including fresh tuna and chunky chicken salad, are available. Popular side dishes are french fries and onion rings, and beer and wine can be bought to go. Mid-Atlantic also sells gasoline and has a boat ramp, travel trailer park and dock space for fishing boats.

Avon

The Barefoot Pub
$$ • N.C. Hwy. 12, Avon • (252) 995-6159

Local artwork lines the walls of this quaint and comfortable bistro with the beautiful curved oak bar and tasteful, casual decor. Starting his third season in Avon, owner/operator Kevin Carmichael wanted to design a gathering place that had character and informality with a touch of class. This rustic eatery and tavern is welcoming to both tourists and locals alike. The Barefoot Pub's food offerings are upscale, and mostly revolve around whatever fresh fish is in-season. A raw bar, sandwiches, crab cakes, fried shrimp and stone oven pizzas are also available. A wide variety of microbrewed beers and tap beer — Guinness, Bass, Foster, Pete's Wicked Ale — are yours for the asking. Tap beers are even rotated seasonally. Port wine is also sold by the glass. The pub is open April through December. Lunch and dinner is served daily in the summer.

Sea Robin Restaurant
$$ • off N.C. Hwy. 12, Avon • (252) 995-5931

This popular soundside restaurant offers wonderful, waterfront views. It's off the main highway and is a lot quieter than many Hatteras Island eateries. The Sea Robin serves eggs Benedict, steak and eggs, waffles and several other traditional breakfasts. For lunch, try oysters, clams, mussels, shrimp or crab legs from the steam bar. Appetizers include Buffalo wings, cheese sticks and jalapeno poppers. Dinner menus feature a full list of entrees, from the Sea Robin seafood platter and surf and turf to Cajun

You can sample fresh fish from these waters in many area restaurants.

fish and crabmeat saute. Wine and beer are served here, and a children's menu is available. This restaurant is open from March through November. In the summer it serves all three meals daily. Call for off-season hours.

Blue Parrot Cafe
$$ • The Castaways Hotel, N.C. Hwy. 12, Avon • (252) 995-6993

Serving breakfast and dinner daily from April through December, this casual cafe is adorned with an artistic surf theme and provides diners with a view of a marshy pond that usually accommodates several hungry ducks. Cooks offer eggs Benedict, blueberry pancakes, hash browns, toast, bacon and French toast for breakfast. Dinner entrees include steaks, seafood, chicken, pasta, vegetarian dishes and a special kids' menu. Fried flounder is available for $9.99 all night. The tempura shrimp and she-crab soup are great appetizers. And for dessert, we recommend French silk pie or chocolate pecan pie. California and Australian wines, as well as domestic, imported and microbrewed beers, are available. In 1988, patrons can order off a new and expanded menu that includes lobster tails, flounder Michael and 1-pound crab-leg dinners.

Reservations are recommended for parties of five or more. Every item can be packaged to carry out. Blue Parrot's staff also caters private parties or banquets.

Hodad's
$-$$ • N.C. Hwy. 12, Avon
• (252) 995-7866

This casual restaurant with surf boards and surfer pics decorating the walls is a perfect place to have a good filling meal without having to worry about changing from your beach garb.

Lunch offerings include sandwiches, burgers, quesadillas and mini-pizzas. For dinner, choose from pasta, beef or shrimp kebabs, steak, chicken, soups, salads or a daily fresh catch of the day. Beer and wine is also served.

Hodad's is open for lunch and dinner from St. Patrick's Day through Thanksgiving.

The Mad Crabber Restaurant & Shellfish Bar
$$ • N.C. Hwy. 12, Avon • (252) 995-5959

This lively place offers dinner nightly from April through November. It's not a fancy restaurant, but you'll find good, fresh seafood here and reasonable prices. It's a recipe for success that keeps people coming back — during summer the Mad Crabber usually is extremely busy. Steamed crabs and shrimp lead the way on the menu. Locally caught blue crabs, snow crabs, Dungeness crabs from the Pacific Northwest and Alaskan king crabs also are on hand. Of course, delicious crab cakes are the speciality.

If you're not feeling "crabby," try a pasta dish, the vegetarian platter or — for meat-lovers — a thick burger or juicy steak. And you must try the famous "mad platters," a pizza pie plate overflowing with crab legs, shrimp, oysters, crawdads, clams, scallops, mussels and, if requested, blue crab. All-you-can-eat specials are served on "Fat Tuesdays," along with $1 draft beers. Wine also is available. There's a special menu just for kids. A separate game room attached to the Mad Crabber has two pool tables for low-key fun.

Buxton

Cape Sandwich Company
$ • N.C. Hwy. 12, Buxton
• (252) 995-6140

A popular spot with both tourists and locals, Cape Sandwich Company serves breakfast, lunch and dinner during summer months to eat at an umbrella-shaded table outdoors, an eat-in bar or for take-out. Owners Bryan and Sylvia Mattingly are now into their fifth season and continue serving a consistently good array of salads and sandwiches, daily specials and enticing desserts. Imported beer and cappuccino are available, as are picnic items for the beach. Call for off-season hours.

Diamond Shoals Restaurant
$$ • N.C. Hwy. 12, Buxton
• (252) 995-5217

The parking lot at this eatery, which is within walking distance of several Buxton motels, always seems to be crowded around breakfast time. Here you'll find one of the best breakfasts on Hatteras Island, featuring all your early morning favorites. Diamond Shoals is closed for lunch; dinner offerings include plenty of seafood choices, featuring fried and broiled seafood and some good nightly specials. Steaks and other landlubber specials are also available.

In 1998 the owner added a remarkable new 200-gallon saltwater aquarium stocked with tropical and Gulf Stream sea life. Diners can get a close-up look at corals, anemones and a variety of fascinating marine creatures. Diamond Shoals is open March through December.

Tides Restaurant
$$ • N.C. Hwy. 12, Buxton
• (252) 995-5988

The driveway for this family-style restaurant is just south of the entrance to the Cape Hatteras Lighthouse, on the sound side. Traditional breakfasts are served here, with tasty homemade biscuits and blueberry and pecan pancakes. Dinner selections include a fresh catch of the day, steaks, chicken and ham. The stuffed potatoes are super. All the portions here are large, and the service is attentive. Beer and wine are available; brown bagging is allowed. This restaurant is open daily from Easter through Thanksgiving.

Labrador Oceanic Bistro
$$$ • N.C. Hwy. 12, Buxton
• (252) 995-3348

Under new ownership by Sylvia and Bryan Mattingly, owners of the popular Cape Sandwich Company (see previous entry), the Labrador Oceanic Bistro is open for lunch and dinner every day except Sunday, when brunch only is served. The decor is warm and inviting, with purple carpeting and lavender ceilings playing up the natural light provided through lots of windows. With a focus on New American cuisine, the restaurant offers the gamut of choices from sandwiches, soups and salads for lunch; to fresh fish, beef, pork, chicken, pasta and vegetarian for dinner. A wide variety of microbrews, beers on tap and wine are also available. And homemade desserts top it all off. A nonsmoking section is provided. Labrador Oceanic Bistro is open March through November from 11:30 AM to 10 PM.

Orange Blossom Cafe and Bakery

$$, no credit cards • N.C. Hwy. 12, Buxton • (252) 995-4109

Henry and Michel Schliff started Papagayo's Restaurant in Chapel Hill in 1978, and then relocated to Buxton where they opened the Orange Blossom. Now in its seventh year, this wonderful cafe serves great Mexican cuisine on Hatteras. The sandwiches made with thick, homemade Italian bread always are a good bet. This little spot also caters to vegetarians, serving a wide selection of meatless salads, sandwiches and entrees. The Orange Blossom starts the day offering an array of baked goods and keeps serving until mid-afternoon. The famous Apple Uglies, huge apple fritter-style pastries piled high with fruit, are our favorite early morning treats. This restaurant is open daily from 7 AM until 2 PM year round, except for December 15 through January 15, for take-out or eat-in.

Billy's Fish House Restaurant

$$ • N.C. Hwy. 12, Buxton • (252) 995-5151

Can you tell that this always-bustling eatery occupies a former fish house? If the simple wooden architecture and wharf-front location didn't give it away, you might notice something fishy when you glimpse down and see the slanted concrete floors sloped for easy washing so the fish scales could flow back into the sound. Billy's is now a down-home restaurant where everything is casual and easygoing. It also serves some of the best Outer Banks seafood prepared with traditional, local recipes. The tilefish is a popular choice, and we highly recommend the homemade crab cakes. All the seafood is fresh. Each entree comes with your choice of vegetables and hush puppies. Most of the foods are lightly fried with peanut oil (except the new pasta offerings, of course). And everything is served on disposable plates with plastic utensils. Billy's is open for lunch and dinner daily from early April through mid-November.

The Pilot House

$$$ • N.C. Hwy. 12, Buxton • (252) 995-5664

Set well off the road to capture spectacular, panoramic views of the sky, water and sinking sun, The Pilot House offers soundside dining amid a decor that's unobtrusively nautical. A separate upstairs lounge serves beer and wine. Capt. Bernice Ballance serves fresh local seafood such as oysters Rockefeller and clams casino for appetizers and homemade soups and bisque.

Dinner entrees include a catch of the day, a variety of shellfish and grilled steaks hand-cut to order. Salad and bread accompany each meal. Desserts are delicious, especially the hot fudge cake and French silk pie. Both children's and senior citizens' menus are available. The Pilot House serves only dinner seven days a week from mid-April through late fall.

Soundside Restaurant

$$ • N.C. Hwy. 12, Buxton • (252) 995-6778

With 30 to 50 items served for all three meals daily, this casual waterfront eatery has something for everyone. It's not a fancy place, but the food's good and filling.

Breakfasts include eggs, pancakes, sausage and, of course, bacon and coffee. Popcorn shrimp, oysters and clam strips are our picks for lunch, unless you prefer Hatteras-style chowder, gumbo or beef stew. For dinner, you can choose between prime rib cut to order, rib-eye steaks, fresh trout, crab legs or dozens of other entrees. Each comes with a trip to the salad bar, two vegetables and rolls. Desserts are a changing selection of cake and pie slices. Children can order off their own separate menu, and senior citizens receive a 10 percent discount.

Soundside is open year round for lunch and dinner. Breakfast is served in-season only.

Frisco

Quarterdeck Restaurant

$$ • N.C. Hwy. 12, Frisco • (252) 986-2425

Fresh, local seafood served broiled or fried, crab cakes packed with jumbo lump meat and Hatteras or New England clam

Bubba's Bar-B-Q

RIBS· CHICKEN· SLICED PORK ·TURKEY BEEF

All cooked on an open pit with hickory wood

Call The Hog Line - 995-5421 in Frisco
6 Miles South of Hatteras Light House

or 995-4385 in Avon
Located next to Food Lion
Try Bubba's Original Recipe Fried Chicken.

chowder are among the most popular offerings here. The Quarterdeck also has an 18-item salad bar and gives 10 percent off all dinners to folk who eat between 5 and 6 PM. For dessert, the coconut cream, lemon meringue and Key lime pies are delicious. Beer and wine are available as well as a children's menu.

This low-key spot occupies a 70-year-old building that housed Hatteras Island's original bar. For the past 20 years, the same family has owned and operated the Quarterdeck, which is open for lunch and dinner daily from mid-March through late November.

Gingerbread House Bakery
$, no credit cards • N.C. Hwy. 12, Frisco • (252) 995-5204

From this tiny cottage flanked by gingerbread-style fencing, breakfast and dinner are served seven days a week in-season. To start the day, sample egg biscuits, French toast, omelettes or waffles. If you'd rather indulge yourself in delicious baked goods, try a frosted donut, cookie or still-steaming bagel. By early evening, you can order a gourmet pizza made on the bakery's own homemade dough. Pan and hand-tossed thicknesses are offered in regular and whole wheat varieties. A whopping 30 toppings to choose from should satisfy virtually any craving. And a salad will round out your meal.

Ice cream, brownies and sweet breads all are great dessert options. You can eat inside this low-key little house or get your pizza and sweets to go. During the summer, the Gingerbread House also delivers from Buxton to Hatteras Village. And its bakers make super speciality cakes for any occasion. Call for off-season hours.

The South Shore Grill
$ • N.C. Hwy. 12, Frisco • (252) 995-5535

Formerly the Frisco Sandwich Shop, the new owners of this casual eatery promise the same quality and good food that hungry patrons depended on for more than 20 years at this favorite Hatteras Island establishment. Deli sandwiches, hamburgers, soups, salads, subs and the full range of popular appetizers and side dishes are offered. Vegetarian sandwiches are also on the menu. Diners order at the counter and eat at tables in the roomy dining room — no tipping! Comfortable and unassuming, South Shore Grill is a perfect place to stop on your way home from the beach. The restaurant is open daily from 11 AM to 11 PM year round.

Bubba's Bar-B-Q
$ • N.C. Hwy. 12, Frisco • (252) 995-5421

If you're in the mood for some genuine Carolina barbecue, you won't be able to miss Bubba's — just follow your nose to this famous roadside joint. The hickory fires start early here so the pork, chicken, beef, ribs and turkey can cook slowly over an open pit behind the counter. The late Larry "Bubba" Schauer and his wife, Julie, brought their secret recipe from West Virginia to Hatteras Island more than a decade ago — and the food has been drawing locals and tourists to their eatery ever since. Homemade coleslaw, baked beans, french fries and corn bread round out the meal and diners' bellies.

The homemade sweet potato and coconut custard pies, cobblers and other desserts are delectable. Mrs. Bubba's Double Devil Chocolate Cake is approaching celebrity status. Bubba's has a children's menu and a nice selection of beer and soft drinks. All items are available for eating in or taking out. Bubba's Sauce is now a hot commodity with barbecue fans and is sold at retail and specialty shops across the Outer Banks. Bubba's is open daily for lunch and dinner during the summer. Call for winter hours. You'll find a second Bubba's, (252) 995-4385, farther north on N.C. 12 in Avon, near the Food Lion.

Hatteras Village

Gary's Restaurant
$$ • N.C. Hwy. 12, Hatteras Village
• (252) 986-2349

In recent years, this restaurant has grown from a fast-food style eatery to a small cafe. You can relax over a cup of coffee and a great breakfast here or enjoy a nice lunch any day of the week year round. Breakfast treats include crabmeat omelettes, Belgian waffles, steak and eggs, homemade biscuits and fresh fruit cups. For lunch, choose from steamed shrimp, clams, deli or sub sandwiches and a variety of seafood entrees.

For dinner, choose prime rib, fresh local seafood or one of the nightly specials. Homemade cheesecakes and fudge cakes are divine desserts. Beer and wine are available, and carry-out is an option for any item. A separate smoking area is set aside inside. Gary's is open for breakfast, lunch and dinner daily except Tuesdays in-season. Call for off-season hours.

The Channel Bass
$$ • N.C. Hwy. 12, Hatteras Village
• (252) 986-2250

Owned by the Harrison family, well known for its fishing heritage, this canal-side restaurant has been a Hatteras Village institution for more than 30 years. You'll notice all of Mrs. Shelby Harrison's fishing trophies in the foyer. The Channel Bass has one of the largest menus on the beach, loaded with seafood platters, crab imperial crab cakes, veal and charbroiled steaks that the chefs slice in-house. An old family recipe is used for the hush puppies, and all the salad dressings are homemade. Make sure you try the homemade coconut, Key lime and chocolate cream pies. A private dining room is available, and large groups are welcome. The Channel Bass has early bird discounts and different dinner specials every night. A nice selection of beer and wine is served; brown bagging is allowed. A children's menu is available. Dinner is served seven days a week from mid-March through November.

Harbor Seafood Deli
$ • N.C. Hwy. 12, Hatteras Village
• (252) 986-2331

Harbor Seafood Deli serves breakfast and lunch, including daily seafood specials, homemade pasta, seafood salad and a wonderful shrimp pasta salad. Homemade desserts are delicious and can be enjoyed on the enclosed porch. This porch gets very busy in the late afternoons when charter boats return to the adjacent marina. Steamed shrimp and other munchies are available during the late afternoon hours if you want to watch all the activity, and hand-dipped Breyer's ice cream is a favorite dessert to sample while sitting in the hot sun.

One of the best aspects of this deli is that the owners will pre-pack breakfasts and lunches that you can pick up the next day to take on a charter fishing trip. Just call in the afternoon or early evening before you're scheduled to depart — and a hearty meal will be ready to go, probably even before you are. Harbor Seafood Deli opens at 6 AM daily. There's a $15 minimum purchase if you want to pay by credit card. Call for off-season hours.

Breakwater Island Restaurant
$$ • N.C. Hwy. 12, Hatteras Village • (252) 986-2733

If dining in a comfortable atmosphere with a stunning view of Pamlico Sound or relaxing with some live music on a deck at sunset sounds good, then this restaurant is the place for you. Here, a second-story dining room, deck and bar overlook a small harbor and stone breakwater, providing a unique feel to this locally loved outpost.

The dinner menu features fresh, progressive seafood dishes, prime rib, veal and pasta, all served in generous portions. Entrees are accompanied by a selection of vegetables, salad and fresh-baked breads. Live entertainment is performed atop the deck on summer Sunday evenings between 8 PM and midnight. Dinner is served seven days a week during the season. A good selection of beer and wine is available. Children's items are also offered. Check for winter hours.

Sonny's Restaurant
$$ • N.C. Hwy. 12, Hatteras Village • (252) 986-2922

This casual, family-run eatery serves breakfast and dinner seven days a week year round. Breakfast begins at 6 AM for fishermen and includes hash browns, grits, Western omelettes, ham and cheese omelettes

and hotcakes — just a few of Sonny's specialties. There's an $18.95 dinner buffet each evening, with an 18-item salad bar, breads, crabmeat bisque, soft-shell crabs in-season, sea scallops, popcorn and regular shrimp, prime rib, clams, oysters, macaroni and cheese, fettuccine Alfredo and desserts such as carrot and chocolate cake, rice pudding and a soft serve ice cream bar. Salad bar, soup and dessert are all included in the price.

Regular menu items range from steaks to seafood to pasta. Alcoholic beverages aren't served here, but you're welcome to bring your own. Sonny even will provide frosty beer mugs and wine glasses for you. Senior citizen and children's menus are offered. Reservations are accepted for large parties.

Ocracoke Island

The Fig Tree
$, no credit cards • N.C. Hwy. 12, Ocracoke Village • (252) 928-4554

The Fig Tree, a tiny delicatessen offering carry-out cuisine only, packs picnics for ferry boat rides and serves a variety of light lunches and baked goods. Veggie pockets here are stuffed to overflowing with lettuce, tomatoes, cucumbers, carrots, mushrooms, sprouts and feta cheese and topped with a choice of homemade dressing. Shrimp and tuna salad are made with just-off-the-boat seafood. You can also design your own sandwich from numerous selections of meats and cheeses to be served on bakery-fresh bread, a hearty bagel or inside a pita. Baked delights include jumbo cinnamon rolls, doughnuts, fruit and nut breads, breakfast biscuits and gourmet cookies. Heavier dessert items, also outstanding, range from chocolate swirl cheesecake atop brownie crumb crust to Ocracoke's own fig cake, each served whole or by the slice.

The Fig Tree also makes a traditional tomato sauce and cheese pizza, a white garden pizza and a Greek tomato pie, all with homemade crusts. The Fig Tree is open March through December.

Trolley Stop Restaurant
$ • N.C. Hwy. 12, Ocracoke Village • (252) 928-4041

Serving breakfast and lunch all year and adding dinners starting in mid-March, this affordable little eatery has counter-service only and basic, good food. Diners can eat inside on the long picnic tables after serving themselves drinks, or the staff will package any meal to go. Tables have also been added outside, so you can eat under the sun and ocean air. Breakfasts start at 99¢ for biscuit sandwiches. French toast, scrambled eggs, bacon, pancakes and grits are other offerings. For lunch, you can order all your favorite sandwiches including Italian subs, 6-ounce hamburgers, hot pastrami, barbecue and crab cakes. French fries, hush puppies and chips are served à la carte. Breakfast and lunch are served all day. The seasonal dinner menu is the same as the lunch fare. Large groups can call ahead to order boxed lunches, complete with sandwiches, chips and a cookie.

Cockle Creek Restaurant
$$ • N.C. Hwy. 12, Ocracoke Village • (252) 928-6891

This lovely seafood cafe is in the building that used to house Maria's Restaurant. It's owned by David Styron and his wife, Kari. The couple does much of the cooking themselves and produce some delightful, moderately priced dinners and offer a range of entrees. Linen tablecloths and oil lamps are attractive table appointments

in the three-level dining room, with soft jazz music piped in to create added ambiance. Dress is casual, but you could come for a special evening out and still feel intimate and elegant here.

Dinner entrees include grilled swordfish, local shrimp, scallops and crab, homemade lasagna and fresh-cut steaks. Locally caught deep-sea fish (grouper, tuna, and salmon) are also served here. The ravioli special, stuffed with flavorful cheeses, is superb. And each meal is accompanied by a baked potato or fries and salad or soup. A nice wine list and plenty of scrumptious desserts are added features, as are raw bar selections of all sorts of shellfish. Cockle Creek is open seven days a week for dinner only from late February through late November.

Pony Island Restaurant
$$ • N.C. Hwy. 12, Ocracoke Village • (252) 928-5701

A casual, homey place that lots of people come back to time and again, this restaurant features big breakfasts of biscuits, hotcakes, omelettes and the famous Pony Potatoes — hash browns covered with cheese, sour cream and salsa. Dinner entrees range from Chinese and Southwestern cuisine to a variety of interesting fresh seafood creations. The folks here even will cook your own catch of the day for you, as long as you've cleaned the fish first. Beer and wine are served, and homemade desserts add a great finishing touch to a tasty meal. The Pony Island Restaurant is adjacent to the Pony Island Motel. Breakfast here begins at 7 AM. The restaurant closes during lunchtime then reopens for dinner nightly from late March through November.

The Back Porch
$$$ • 1324 Country Rd., Ocracoke Village • (252) 928-6401

Whether you dine on the wide, breezy screened porch, eat in this quaint restaurant's small nooks or get seated in the open dining room of this well-respected restaurant, you'll find that dinners at the Back Porch are some of the most pleasant experiences on the Outer Banks. This older building was renovated and refurbished to blend with the many trees on the property. It's off the main road, surrounded by waist-high cacti, and is a quiet place to enjoy appealing entrees and comfortable conversation. Overall, it's one of our favorite restaurants

RESTAURANTS • 121

on the 120-mile stretch of barrier islands. It's well worth the two-hour trip from Nags Head, including the free ferry ride, just to eat here.

The menu is loaded with fresh herbs, vegetables and seafood, most of which is caught nearby. All sauces, dressings, breads and desserts are made right in the restaurant's huge kitchen. And each piece of meat is hand-cut. In addition to the quality ingredients, the chefs come up with some pretty outrageous taste combinations, and all of them seem to blend perfectly. The crab cakes with red pepper sauce are outstanding. And you won't want to miss the smoked bluefish or crab beignets appetizers. Non-seafood dishes are a tasty option as well. Our favorite is the Cuban black bean and Monterey Jack cheese casserole.

Reduced prices and smaller portions are available for children and senior citizens. And all the desserts are divine. Freshly ground coffee is served here, and the wine selections and imported beers are as ambitious as the menu. If you get hooked — like we are — you can try your hand at some of the restaurant's recipes at home after buying a *Back Porch Cookbook*. Be prepared, however. Some of these menu items are quite involved. After reading the recipes you'll be even more impressed with the upscale culinary concoctions served in this laid-back island eatery. Dinner is offered nightly here in-season.

Cap't. Ben's
$$ • N.C. Hwy. 12, Ocracoke Village
• (252) 928-4741

Serving Ocracoke locals and guests for 28 years, Cap't. Ben's is a casual restaurant that offers lunch and dinner every day from April through mid-November. Owner and chef Ben Mugford combines Southern tradition with gourmet foods to achieve a well-balanced menu. Ben is especially revered for his crabmeat, prime rib and seafood entrees. He also serves a mean Caesar salad and comes up with some good pasta and chicken creations as well. Sandwiches, crab cakes and shrimp salad are good bets for lunch, each served with chips or fries. Dinners come with soup and salad. And all the desserts are delicious and homemade. A large variety of domestic and imported beers is available, and the wine list complements the menu. The decor in this family eatery is nautical and friendly. The lounge is a comfortable place to relax if you have to wait for a table.

Howard's Pub & Raw Bar Restaurant
$ • N.C. Hwy. 12, Ocracoke Village
• (252) 928-4441

Always a fun, friendly place to go for a meal, this year Howard's Pub has just about doubled its floor space on the first level, giving diners, drinkers and dancers room to spread out and expand their possibilities. Even the beer list has grown — in 1997, the pub increased its number of different imported and domestic brews from 175 to 214, where it still hovers.

Howard's Pub is the only Ocracoke establishment that can boast it's open an average of 365 days a year, including Christmas. Owners Buffy and Ann Warner hail from West Virginia, where he was a senator and she worked for the governor as director of economic development. Their lifestyles have changed a bit since purchasing this pub. And you can tell they love it. This is a must-stop for everyone on Ocracoke, with great local flavor and guaranteed good times (see our Nightlife chapter). You can relax on the huge — also recently doubled in size — screened-in porch that stretches the length of this long restaurant — or sit inside at a wooden table.

The restaurant is the only raw bar on the island and is the home of the spicy oyster shooter. We love these raw oyster and Tabasco combinations, especially when washed down with an unusual imported beer. Howard's appetizers range from soups and salads to jalapeno poppers and hot wings. Lunch and dinner items include subs, burgers and fish sandwiches. Snow crab legs, fried shrimp and wine by the bottle were recently added to the menu. Buffy also added a Cabernet and a Chardonnay made by private label winery Jefferson Vineyard of Charlottesville, Virginia.

Within the not-so-distant future, a new upper deck will be added as part of the restaurant's three-part expansion. The top deck will afford a view of the ocean, sound, salt marshes and sand dunes. On a clear day, you'll even be able to see Portsmouth Island! There's a wide-screen TV, several

Photo: Courtesy of Elaine Fogarty

Enjoy ocean views while dining in a pier restaurant.

smaller ones, free popcorn and games such as chess, a Barrel of Monkeys and Trivial Pursuit to entertain. With the newly expanded dance floor, you'll have lots of room to dance to live music in the evenings. Food and drinks are served every day from lunchtime into the wee hours.

Cafe Atlantic
$$ • N.C. Hwy. 12, Ocracoke Village • (252) 928-4861

This traditional beach-style building was opened a few years ago by Bob and Ruth Toth. There's not much that's traditional about their innovative, fantastic food, however. Views from the dining room look out across marsh grass and dunes. The gallery-like effect of the restaurant is created with hand-colored photographs by local writer and artist Ann Ehringhaus.

There's a nonsmoking dining room upstairs and a smoking section downstairs. Lunch and dinner are served at this upscale yet casual eatery seven days a week in-season. And the Sunday brunches from 11 AM to 3 PM are the best we've found south of Duck. Brunch menus change weekly, but champagne and mimosas always are served. We're partial to the blueberry pecan pancakes, chicken and broccoli crepes and the huevos rancheros served over black beans in a crisp tortilla shell. Hash browns

come with almost every entree. And the flavorful food will fill you up at least until supper.

The Toths make all their soups, dressings, sauces and desserts from scratch. Lunches feature a variety of sandwiches and salads. Dinner entrees include caciucco, a combination of fresh fish, shrimp, scallops and mussels in marinara sauce served over linguine; and a wide range of beef, chicken, lasagna and other excellent seafood and pasta plates fill out the menu. Each meal is served with salad, rice or potato and steaming rolls just out of the oven. You've gotta leave room for dessert here, or take one of their outrageously ornate cakes, pies or cobblers home. A children's menu is available, and the restaurant has a nice selection of wine and beer. Cafe Atlantic is open from early March through October. Lunches may vary in the off-season, so call for hours. This cafe, though isolated on tiny Ocracoke, is certainly among the best dining experiences the Outer Banks has to offer.

Ocracoke Coffee
$ • Back Rd., Ocracoke Village • (252) 928-7473

The neatest place on the island to take care of those unavoidable caffeine and sugar needs, Ocracoke Coffee has enjoyed tremendous success since opening for the 1996 sea-

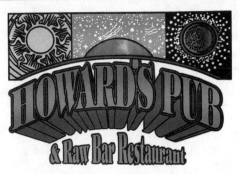

Live Entertainment and Big Green Tvs

**Fresh Local Shrimp,
Clams, Oysters
and Mussels**

**Burgers, Subs,
Salads, Pizza
and more!**

Over 200 Domestic and Imported Beers, Microbrews and Wines

Highway 12, Ocracoke Island • 928-4441 • AAA Approved • Serving 11:00am -2:00 am Daily

son. The aromatic eatery is filled with bagels, pastries, desserts, brewed coffee drinks, espresso, shakes, whole bean coffees and loose tea. The shop is nestled under tall pines on Back Road, within an easy walk of most anything in the village. We know you'll find your way here in the morning (everyone does), but why not shuffle in after dinner for something sweet as well? The shop's feel is way hip, but it's also cozy and inviting, and the folks frothing your concoctions are friendly as can be. For 1998 the shop is expanding the smoothie menu — look for more than 10 varieties for a cool respite from the summer heat.

Ocracoke Coffee is open daily from 7 AM to 10 PM. The shop closes December through March.

Island Inn Restaurant
$$ • Lighthouse Rd., Ocracoke Village • (252) 928-7821

This family-owned and operated restaurant at the Island Inn is one of the oldest establishments on Ocracoke. Its main dining room and airy porch are furnished in a traditional country style, with blue and white china to dine on and bright, nautical touches throughout. Breakfast and dinner are served here daily except in the dead of winter. Owners Bob and Cee Touhey make sure everyone, not just Inn guests, are welcome to eat here. Standard breakfast fare, such as pancakes, eggs and hash browns, is available. The cook also comes up with some unusual creations, such as oyster omelettes with spinach and bacon, and shrimp omelettes

---

INSIDERS' TIP

Call ahead and find out if the restaurant you are interested in has an early-bird special. Also, check the coupon section of the local Yellow Pages and look in the local newspaper for special deals at particular restaurants.

Seafood lovers will find many delectable dishes in Outer Banks restaurants.

Ocracoke's newest restaurant
welcomes you to enjoy a casual
meal overlooking scenic Silver Lake Harbor

Open 10am to 9:30pm

Brunch 10-12   Lunch/Dinner 10-9:30

P.O. Box 368
Ocracoke, NC 27960
Phone: (252) 928-3606

Proprietors
Darlene Styron
Chris Styron

drenched with melted Jack cheese, green chiles and salsa.

For dinner, locally landed seafood and shellfish entrees can be grilled, fried or broiled to your liking. Beef, pork, lamb, pasta and stir-fry dishes also are available, as are vegetarian offerings. All the breads and soups are made daily at this restaurant, and homemade pies are perfectly delicious. A selection of wines is served here, and a children's menu is available. Reservations are needed for large groups; the owners are happy to accommodate private party requests. Call for off-season hours.

Creekside Cafe
$ • N.C. Hwy. 12, Ocracoke Village
• (252) 928-3606

Overlooking Silver Lake Harbor from a second-story vantage point, the views from this 4-year-old restaurant are wonderful. A covered porch around two sides of the wooden building has ceiling fans and breezes to cool afternoon diners. Inside, the eatery is casual and friendly, serving brunch items daily and lunch and dinner from a single menu between April and early November. Soups, salads, seafood and pasta dishes are the afternoon and evening fare here. The blackened chicken sandwiches are so popular that the owners decided to package and sell the spices. French dips, fresh fish sandwiches, oyster baskets, crab cakes and Greek-style linguine with feta cheese and black olives all are great choices. For brunch, we recommend the Tex-Mex: scrambled eggs, onions, peppers, tomatoes and salsa served in a tortilla shell with a dollop of guacamole. Desserts include parfaits, cheesecakes, Key lime pie, tollhouse pie and pecan pie — all homemade. Beer and wine are available, and four champagne drinks offer unusual alcoholic creations.

If you're a night owl, or
at least like to stretch
your wings a bit on
vacation, there's always
fun and frolic to be
found here.

Nightlife

You've showered off the sand and sunscreen at the end of an active day at the beach — now you're ready to sample the Outer Banks after dark. Even Insiders here still think the best way to make the transition into the evening is to watch the best free entertainment we have: the sunset. For some mysterious, scientific reason, the sunsets on these barrier islands are consistent show stoppers. Intense colors bleed into the waters and stretch for miles into the horizon. Many evenings, we have to pull off the road on our way home from the job because the scene is so compellingly glorious. But the sun sinks fast, and the night is young. Fortunately, there's also lots to do under Outer Banks moonshine and starlight.

The Outer Banks after hours aren't like other resort areas. So many families come here — and so many early-rising anglers — that many people are bedded down for the evening by 9 PM. But in-season, when the beaches are loaded with vacationers, bars and dance floors across the barrier islands are hopping. And if you're a night owl, or at least like to stretch your wings a bit on vacation, there's always fun and frolic to be found in dozens of establishments from Corolla to Ocracoke.

Families also can enjoy a variety of early-evening entertainment options here. Miniature golf, go-cart tracks, movie theaters, bumper boats, even a small amusement park and a bowling alley are listed in our Recreation chapter. And don't forget *The Lost Colony* outdoor drama; that's detailed in our Attractions chapter.

But if what you want to do is unwind — or gear up, if that's more your style — there are plenty of places to shoot pool, catch sporting events on big-screen TVs, play interactive trivia, throw darts, listen to low-key acoustic music or boogie the night away to a rocking live band.

Local musicians play everything from blues to jazz to rock to hard-core alternative and country tunes. Outer Banks and out-of-town cover bands and those with original songs take the stage often during the summer season. Several nightclubs on the Outer Banks assess nominal cover charges at the door, usually ranging from $1 for dueling acoustic guitar duos to $10 or more for the national acts that grace these sands between mid-May and Labor Day. Many acoustic acts, however, can be heard for free.

If live music is what you're listening for, check *The Virginian Pilot's* weekly *Coast* magazine — available free at area grocery and convenience stores and motels — for up-to-date listings in its "Club Hoppin'" section and music scene info in the "After Dark" column by John Harper (see our Media chapter for more on the *Coast*). WVOD 99.1 FM and WOBR 95.3 FM give daily concert updates on evening radio broadcasts. (See our Annual Events and Arts and Culture chapters for more nighttime possibilities.)

Alcoholic beverages are available at most Outer Banks lounges until around 2 AM. Beer and wine are offered throughout the barrier islands. In Corolla and on Colington, Roanoke, Hatteras and Ocracoke islands, it is illegal to serve mixed drinks. However, with the exception of Colington Island, ABC stores sell liquor in each of those areas. And most nightclubs on those islands do allow people to brown-bag and bring in their own alcohol for the evening. Call ahead to make sure that's OK.

Several restaurants on the Outer Banks offer late-night menus or at least raw and steamer bar food until closing. Every nightclub operator will be glad to call a cab to take you home or to your hotel or rental cottage after an evening of imbibing. Beware: The legal drinking age in North Carolina is 21, and the blood-alcohol content necessary for a drunk-driving citation is only .08. So even if you've only had a couple of cocktails, play it safe and take a taxi. They are easy to hook up with, and it's a whole lot cheaper than court costs and license problems.

Although several area restaurants offer happy hour specials and most have bars within their establishments, we've only included those eateries that are open until at least midnight in this chapter. Check our Restaurants chapter for early-bird bar specials and sunset entertainment schedules. Several spots also feature outdoor acoustic music until dark — but this section is for those who like to come out with the stars.

www.insiders.com

See this and many other **Insiders' Guide®** destinations online — in their entirety.

Visit us today!

Corolla

Neptune's Grill & Arcade
Timbuck II Shopping Village, N.C. Hwy. 12 • (252) 453-8645

A laid-back burger joint offering dine in, take-out and delivery of good, cheap eats, this establishment has the only pool table north of Duck. Pinball, Foosball and a variety of video games are available here, and 24 different beers and a good selection of wine are sold until 2 AM. Dinners are served until 11:30 PM. In the summer, live acoustic and electric music created by various local talent and bands will be offered. Call ahead for schedules. Neptune's is open most of the year, seven days a week in season. Call for winter hours.

Planet Corolla
TimBuck II Shopping Village, N.C. Hwy. 12 • (252) 453-4644

Live acoustic music will be on-site at this easygoing bistro every Tuesday, and for four or five nights a week in summer. Dinner is served until 10 PM, and music will continue until midnight. A wide variety of wines and microbrews are available to quench the thirst. Call directly to find out more about the musical offerings.

Duck

Barrier Island Inn Restaurant and Tavern
Duck Rd. (N.C. Hwy. 12) • (252) 261-8700

A favorite nightspot in Duck village, the tavern is upstairs, separate from the restaurant. Folks enjoy fabulous sunsets overlooking Currituck Sound and indoor recreation including a pool table, dartboard and table-top shuffleboard. There's an outdoor deck where you can stargaze until closing time, and live acoustic music or bands can be heard most summer nights.

The tavern offers interactive TV trivia nightly year round, and QB1 interactive football is fun for armchair quarterbacks — especially with the free buffalo wings the tavern serves up during fall football season. Steamed shrimp, sandwiches and pizza are available late at the bar or around tables sized to accommodate any party. Barrier Island is open seven nights a week. Call for summer entertainment schedules.

Elizabeth's Cafe & Winery
Scarborough Faire, N.C. Hwy. 12 • (252) 261-6145

Join owner Leonard Logan for late-night "Jazz in the Grotto" at one of the most romantic, classy restaurants on the Outer Banks, hands down. National jazz acts entertain in the intimate atmosphere of the restaurant's wine cellar throughout the summer. Couples, singles and their friends can enjoy the tunes while feasting on Elizabeth's superb food from a limited late-night menu. Additional nights with live music may be offered in the peak season, so call for information.

This award-winning restaurant, with its lovely lace tablecloths and candlelit shadows dancing on the walls, is a delight. Elizabeth's is renowned for its extensive, superior selection of wines and has won *The Wine Spectator* magazine Best of the Award of Excellence for the past seven years. French beers are also served from the bottle. Reservations are necessary, as this is a small and very popular establishment. Elizabeth's is a nonsmoking eatery, but a special cigar and cigarette section is available on the outside porch.

Fishbones Raw Bar & Restaurant
Scarborough Lane Shops, Duck Rd.
(N.C. Hwy. 12) • (252) 261-6991

Opened in summer 1995, this raw bar and restaurant fast became one of Duck's most popular evening hangouts. It's open every day of the year and features a full bar with five beers on tap, 50 bottled beers from all over the world, various microbrews and a wine list. During summer, deck parties are held outdoors when the weather is good. It's a casual place to catch up on conversation with old acquaintances — or to make new ones.

Roadside Bar & Grill
Duck Rd. (N.C. Hwy. 12)
• (252) 261-5729

Low-key, casual and offering great food year round, Roadside is another of the newer Duck establishments that's been receiving rave reviews from locals and tourists alike. There's a full bar in this restored 1932 cottage, and an outdoor patio where live blues and jazz is performed Tuesday, Friday and Saturday evenings in-season. Appetizers and cocktails can be enjoyed under the stars, and you'll enjoy the hardwood floors and homey feeling inside as well. Roadside is open seven days a week.

Kitty Hawk

Rundown Cafe
N.C. Hwy. 12, MP 1 • (252) 255-0026

If you're looking for summertime blues and jazz — or just want to sip some frothy brews —

this Caribbean-style cafe is always an exciting spot to hang out on the north end of the beach. It's a great place to relax with friends, listen to some of the best music on the Outer Banks several nights a week or just sit a spell at the long bar. You'll be comfortable coming in here alone too. There's a rooftop deck that affords great views of the ocean and the opportunity to catch some cool breezes and conversation.

A variety of domestic and imported beers are on hand, and there is a full line of liquor (ask about the specialty rum and tequila drinks). Enjoy Guinness stout, Bass and Harp beers on tap. The steam and raw bar serves seafood and vegetables until closing. By the way, Rundown is a traditional Jamaican stew, and the decor reflects the cafe's unusual name. Call ahead for a rundown of the evening entertainment at Rundown, or just stop by and check out this happening haunt.

Frisco's
U.S. Hwy. 158, MP 4 • (252) 261-7833

A popular nightspot for locals year round, this restaurant features a large, three-sided bar and beautiful terrariums and aquariums throughout the dining area. It's open seven days a week, and karaoke gives everyone a chance to take the stage. Groups are welcome and encouraged here, and singles and couples will find a good time too. There are tables of all sizes in the lounge, and drink specials are served late into the night. There's even a wide-screen TV for sports fans. Call for entertainment schedules.

Black Pelican Oceanfront Cafe
N.C. Hwy. 12, MP 4 • (252) 261-3171

With 12 TVs and an enclosed porch overlooking the ocean, this Kitty Hawk hangout is a fun place to catch up on sporting events or just sit a spell at the bar. It's in a former Coast Guard station and still features hardwood floors, tongue-and-groove appointments and

---

INSIDERS' TIP

Don't forget that sharing a bottle of wine with a friend on a moonlit beach may be the best (and safest) entertainment you can get. Some towns don't allow glass containers on the beach, so check first. And make sure you don't leave any trash in your wake.

light gray accents reminiscent of days gone by. In the evenings its upbeat atmosphere is anything but antique. Live music is offered sporadically throughout the summer season, and interactive trivia is available for the contemporary crowd. Gourmet pizzas are a great treat for late-night munchies. The Black Pelican is open year round. Call for entertainment schedules.

Kill Devil Hills

Chilli Peppers
U.S. Hwy. 158, MP 5 • (252) 441-8081
World fusion food with a Southwestern twist is served at this small, innovative restaurant year round. The separate bar area out front always is teeming with partying people. Live entertainment and open-mike nights are featured year round. A full bar offers fresh fruit Margaritas, a nice wine selection and dozens of domestic and imported beers seven nights a week. Bartenders also serve nonalcoholic beers and fruit smoothies that complement any meal. There's an outdoor patio if you want to sip your drinks under the stars, and steamed seafood and vegetables are served until closing.

Awful Arthur's
N.C. Hwy. 12, MP 6 • (252) 441-5955
Loud, packed with people and about as popular as it gets on the Outer Banks, this rustic restaurant features a live lobster tank and long bar downstairs and a separate upstairs lounge that affords patrons an ocean view. Locals love to hang out here, especially on Mondays when there are food and drink specials all day. Live entertainment is offered in summer. A full bar offers up lots of cold beer on tap, and raw or steamed seafood is served late into the night. The TVs always seem to be tuned to the day's most popular sport-

ing events. The T-shirts here sell as well as the steamed shrimp. College students especially seem to enjoy Arthur's atmosphere, but people of all ages will find a good time here seven nights a week year round.

Jolly Roger Restaurant
N.C. Hwy. 12, MP 6¾ • (252) 441-6530
Adorned with hanging plants and colorful lights, the lounge at this restaurant is separate from the dining area. This is a casual place with a long, distinctive bar inlaid with seashells. There's almost always something going on here late into the night. Most summer evenings, there's live acoustic entertainment or a band. Outer Banks folk favorite Jamie Jamison plays a variety of country, rock and blues tunes every Thursday night and usually brings some musician friends with him. The Wilder Brothers perform often throughout the year, and the bar is open seven nights a week. There is also karaoke, and interactive TV, featuring games from sports to movie trivia, draws a regular audience. Prizes are even awarded to some of the big winners. Locals love this place, and you'll find people from their early 20s to late 60s hanging out here.

Sea Ranch Lounge
Quality Inn Sea Ranch, N.C. Hwy. 12, MP 7 • (252) 441-7126
A longtime tradition for Outer Banks' shaggers, this lounge in the Sea Ranch hotel features local musician Buzz Bessette Tuesday through Saturday year round. He plays a variety of dance music from the '50s to the '90s, and there's almost always someone cutting a rug on the dance floor. A full bar is open seven nights a week, and a large-screen TV is always on for added entertainment. Recorded beach music is played here on Sunday and Monday nights. Line-dance lessons and line dancing go on every Wednesday night. The

low-key atmosphere seems to attract a more mature crowd than other Outer Banks establishments.

Paradise Billiards
Dare Centre, U.S. Hwy. 158, MP 7 • (252) 441-9225

There are five pool tables at Paradise Billiards, and play is by the hour. The 50-inch TV includes a satellite system with a special sports package that provides plenty of national events that are tough to find anywhere else. Dartboards, pinball machines, Foosball and free interactive trivia are up and running until 2 AM. In addition to more than 40 beers and an extensive wine list, bartenders serve an expanded late-night menu featuring Cajun chicken wings, burgers and deli offerings until midnight.

You must be 21 or older to come to Paradise after 7 PM. If you're younger than 21 and want to shoot pool in the daytime, you have to bring an adult with you. Paradise Billiards is open daily year round.

Goombay's Grille & Raw Bar
N.C. Hwy. 12, MP 7 • (252) 441-6001

This popular nightspot teems with tourists and locals year round and is open seven nights a week. It's fun and colorful with a tropical island flair and flavor — and the bartenders all are local characters. Goombay's is Caribbean and casual, the kind of hangout where you're sure to feel right at home even if you've never visited the Outer Banks.

On Wednesdays live bands play here for an increasingly crowded "Locals Night" year round — visitors make it the-more-the-merrier in summer. A horseshoe-shaped bar is set to the side of the dining area, so you can lounge on a stool or high-backed chair in the bar area or have a seat at a nearby table after the dining room closes at 10 PM. Goombay's serves lots of imported and domestic beers, wine and mixed drinks until 2 AM. Be sure to try some of the special rum, vodka and tequila combos that come with toys to take home. Steamed shrimp and veggies are served until closing.

Quagmires
N.C. Hwy. 12, MP 8 • (252) 441-9188

"Quags," as many locals call it, is owned by the same groovy guy who runs Goombay's, so you know once you step inside or out onto one of the biggest open-air oceanfront decks on the beach, you're bound to have a great time. A horseshoe-shaped bar faces the Atlantic — everyone sitting on a stool is guaranteed a gorgeous view.

Frozen drinks are served outdoors or in, and the bartenders even pour pitchers of Margaritas so you don't have to keep getting up to fill your thin-stemmed, salt-encrusted glass. Beer, wine and mixed drinks are available, and there's a whole line of appetizers and munchies to sample through the night. Quagmire's is open seven days a week in summer, featuring live acoustic music many nights. On the sand below the bar, horseshoes, a ring toss and a beach volleyball court beckon people to come play if they need a break from partying in the lounge. Quagmire's is open daily April through October; call for the entertainment schedule.

Port O' Call Gaslight Saloon
N.C. Hwy. 12, MP 8½ • (252) 441-7484

One of the area's most unusual places to hang out — and one of the only local nightclubs that attracts national bands in summer — the Gaslight Saloon is decorated in an ornate Victorian style complete with overstuffed armchairs, antique wooden tables and a long mahogany bar. There's a nice dance floor here and an upstairs lounge (with separate bar) that overlooks the stage.

Port O' Call features live entertainment seven nights a week in-season and every weekend while the restaurant is open from mid-March through December. There's usually a cover charge here for the bigger-name bands. In recent years, Port O' Call has hosted such national acts as the ultra-hip trailer-park boogie of Southern Culture on the Skids, hirsute blues legend Leon Russell, eclectic rockers Fishbone, Southern rock cliche-mongers Molly Hatchet, and an array of first-rate reggae artists. Beer, wine and liquor are served until 2 AM.

Dare Devils Authentic Pizzeria
N.C. Hwy. 12, MP 8½ • (252) 441-6330

With a big-screen TV and four types of beer on tap, this wide, airy pizza joint is a cool place to kick back and enjoy an evening with friends. There are plenty of domestic and imported beers served in heavy glass mugs, along with a wine list and mixed drinks to sip at a table or while sitting at the bar. Each pizza is cooked to order, and there are a variety of appetizers, from plates piled high with nachos to hot wings sure to set your mouth on fire.

Shucker's Pub and Billiards
Oceanside Plaza, N.C. Hwy. 12, MP 8½ • (252) 480-1010

This pub and billiard room serves more than 75 types of beer and features the only 9-foot pool tables on the Outer Banks. A dozen billiard tables offer people the chance to play by the game or by the hour. Darts, Foosball and pinball are popular pastimes, and there are plenty of TVs for sports fans. Would-be pool sharks who get beached by too much cigarette smoke will be happy to know that Shucker's operates heavy-duty electronic "smoke-eaters" in every room. It's is open year round, seven nights a week until 2 AM. Wine is available, and Shucker's serves pizza and sandwiches until closing. You must be 21 or older to play in this pub after 9 PM.

Van's Pizza & Bar
U.S. Hwy. 158, MP 9 • (252) 441-5534

Van's features 50¢ draft beers and acoustic music every Thursday night for a $1 cover charge. On Friday and Saturday nights, live bands from the Outer Banks, Maryland, Virginia and other areas perform; the cover charge

Photo: Courtesy of the Dare County Tourist Bureau

Outer Banks nightlife includes outdoor adventures and club-hopping evenings.

is $3. The entire Van's menu — pizza, subs, pasta, fries, onion rings, stromboli, hot wings and more — is available until 3 AM when there's entertainment. Music is offered year round, and in the summer more nights with entertainment may be added. Van's opens at 11 AM daily.

The Pit
U.S. Hwy. 158, MP 9 • (252) 480-3128

One of the few clubs to offer entertainment for underage kids, in addition to national name acts for adults, The Pit has become wildly popular since it opened its expanded surf shop/cyberpub in 1997. Live music is offered five nights a week. Disco dance parties are held every Friday, and modern dance night is Sunday. The sound system for both live music and CDs really packs a sweet punch. Every Wednesday in summer, The Pit hosts all ages from 8 PM to 3 AM. All teens — or even younger kids if they're supervised — are welcome to dance to a com-

bination of rave and live music. No alcohol, of course, is served.

The rest of the week, patrons can sample the wide selection of microbrews and domestic and imported beers. A neat antique Foosball table, a pool table, darts and two computer terminals providing free Internet access all night are also available here. In 1998 The Pit added a full restaurant that serves such stomach fillers as burrito wraps, tacos and appetizers. Call for weekly entertainment schedules. See our Watersports chapter for more on the surf shop operation. The Pit is open year round.

Madeline's at the Holiday Inn
N.C. Hwy. 12, MP 9 • (252) 441-6333

A disc jockey spins Top 40 tunes here most summer nights, and there's a shag club on Mondays. The lounge serves beer, wine and mixed drinks year round and is a convenient place for guests of the hotel who don't want to worry about having to drive anywhere after enjoying an evening of fun.

Peppercorn's at the Ramada Inn
N.C. Hwy. 12, MP 9 • (252) 441-2151

Enjoy a breathtaking ocean view from the plate-glass window wall while visiting with friends and listening to acoustic soloists or duos in the Ramada Inn's intimate lounge area. Live music is performed daily throughout summer and often starts earlier here than elsewhere on the Outer Banks — sometimes they get started at 8 PM. This is an open, laid-back place with booths, tables and a full bar. The music is never too loud to talk over. But if you'd rather listen, some of the best guitar talent on the beach shows up here in season.

Hurricane Alley
Sea Holly Square, N.C. Hwy. 12, MP 9½ • (252) 480-3667, (252) 441-1533

Hurricane Alley immediately found its niche in summer 1997 as a hot spot on the barrier islands. Tucked away in the Sea Holly Square mall, it's a restaurant and nightspot combined, offering great food, Foosball, trivia games and three big-screen TVs. Instead of showing just the usual sports, homemade videos of regular people doing Outer Banks activities like surfing are displayed. But when something big is happening in the sports world, one of the sets will also feature those events.

Inspired by the ever-present threat of hurricane activity, owners Charlie Cole and James Standen felt Hurricane Alley should honor the resilient, rise-above-it spirit of the Outer Banks, hence the colorful name. Visitors and locals alike feel comfortable in the casual atmosphere here, where they can listen to music or enjoy food and drinks at the bar, seated at a table or outside on the deck.

A full-service pub with domestic and imported beers, three beers (one dark) on tap, a great wine selection and liquor service, Hurricane Alley features live blues, rock and alternative bands on Saturdays all winter and three to four times a week in summer. Acoustic music will also be offered. Call for an entertainment schedule. Appetizers, lasagna and Caesar salads are available until 2 AM.

The Fish Market
U.S. Hwy. 158, MP 9½ • (252) 441-7889

A local hangout popular with fishermen and Outer Banks natives, this low-key restaurant includes an L-shaped wooden bar and great barrier island flavor. The Fish Market serves all sorts of beers, and the bartenders shake and stir mixed drinks to suit any taste. On Sundays, step into a NASCAR speedway cheering section and prepare to get caught up in the fast-paced action broadcast from overhead TVs. The Fish Market features live acoustic music year round on Friday and Saturday nights and serves great locally caught seafood throughout the evening.

Millie's Diner
N.C. Hwy. 12, MP 10 • (252) 480-3463

Since it opened in 1996, this art-deco diner has become a favorite hangout for discerning Outer Bankers looking for some good food, music and talk in a classy, relaxed atmosphere. Serving up a great selection of wine and beer at the full bar, Millie's also boasts live jazz by local favorites performed periodically on Sunday nights. Don't be deceived by the narrow appearance outside this glittering silver diner — the inside is far roomier than you'd ever guess and is decorated in appealing art deco with yellow and burgundy appointments. You can sit at the counter-type bar and enjoy your brew, or stroll to the large back dining room to watch the entertainment.

Millie's will present live bands for entertainment occasionally on weekend nights throughout the summer. Even when there's no live music, check out the eclectic selection of rhythm and blues, funk and rock on the old-fashioned jukeboxes found at the bar and in the booths. Millie's serves American and European microbrews and two high-quality beers (the selections rotate) on tap. It's open seven days a week from Easter through Labor Day. Off-season hours will vary.

Colington Island

Blue Crab Tavern
Colington Rd., 1.5 miles west of U.S. Hwy. 158 • (252) 441-5919

A favorite afternoon and evening haunt for this island's fishing enthusiasts, Blue Crab includes an indoor bar, pool tables, video games and one of the best soundfront decks in the area. Anglers often pull their boats up to the rectangular deck and tie onto the wooden pilings to sip a few beers outdoors after work. Lots of local characters hang out here, and if you sit a spell, you're sure to hear what's biting where. Liquor is not available, but brews are cold and among the cheapest you'll find. There's a horseshoe pit out front if you feel like tossing a few around after you've tossed a few down.

Nags Head

Red Drum Taphouse
N.C. Hwy. 12, MP 10 • (252) 480-1095

One of the newest establishments on the beach, Red Drum pours 18 beers on tap — hence the name. These are no run of the mill brews — try Sierra Nevada, J.W. Dundee's Honey Brown, Woodpecker Cider, Black Radish or Pyramid Hefeweizen. All the domestics are available as well, and you can get wine by the glass or the bottle. Red Drum also serves liquor from its beautiful long redwood-colored bar.

Every Monday night in-season is open-mike night. On Thursdays local and out-of-town bands play a variety of music ranging from rock, blues and jazz to alternative. A minimum cover is charged. Beer specials are offered all night. A pool table, Foosball table and dartboard are in an adjacent bar area that's separate from the dining room. Why not try a little competition with the tunes?

The Comedy Club and Lounge at the Carolinian
N.C. Hwy. 12, MP 10 • (252) 441-7171

This is the oldest oceanfront summer comedy club in the country, featuring soon-to-be stars for more than 14 years now. Favorite TV comics Sinbad, Brett Butler and Drew Carey all tickled funny bones from this eclectically adorned stage. National comedians are booked every summer. Reservations are recommended; although the room is big, it often gets packed in season. There's a full bar here, and cocktail servers offer tableside service through-

out the show. One cover charge includes three comics who always put on hilarious acts — many that demand audience participation.

Doors open at 9 PM seven nights a week in season, and the laughter begins around 10 PM. During fall and spring, the comedy club is open only on weekends. Before the show, you can enjoy your favorite beverages from a bar on the outside, oceanfront deck. The Carolinian features free live music on the deck seven evenings a week in season, weather permitting. Priority seating in the comedy club is given to those who dine in the Carolinian's restaurant, Calico Jack's.

Mulligan's Oceanfront Grille
N.C. Hwy. 12, MP 10 • (252) 480-2000

Mulligan's is heralded as a popular evening hot spot and maintains its image as the Outer Banks own version of TV's *Cheers*. A wooden partition separates the long, three-sided wooden bar from the dining room, and loads of local memorabilia adorn the walls. Mulligan's serves microbrewed beers on tap or in iced-down bottles. Wine and liquor are available. Acoustic music is offered on weekends in the off-season, and Wednesday through Monday in summer. Light fare — appetizers and sandwiches — to munch on is served until 1 AM.

Kelly's Tavern
U.S. Hwy. 158, MP 10 • (252) 441-4116

Probably the most consistently crowded tavern on the Outer Banks, Kelly's offers live bands six nights a week in-season and an open-mike fest with a lip-synch contest and cash prizes on the only music off-night, Tuesday. Even during fall and winter, rockin' bands take the stage, and fun people always fill this place.

A full bar serves everything from suds to shots, and folks often line up around its three long sides two or three people deep. The big dance floor is usually shaking after 10 PM. If you're in the mood just to listen and watch, secluded booths surround the dance floor a few steps above the rest of the lounge, and tables are scattered throughout the tavern. A dartboard and fireplace adorn the back area, and beach memorabilia hangs in every corner. Featuring a tasty variety of foods served late into the night, a lounge menu offers appetizers and steamed shellfish. An old-fashioned popcorn popper even provides free munchies served in wicker baskets throughout the evening. Singles seem to really enjoy this tavern.

Tortuga's Lie Shellfish Bar and Grille
N.C. Hwy. 12, MP 11 • (252) 441-7299

Our favorite place to meet friends for a laid-back evening — or to hang out alone to chat with long-lost local pals — Tortuga's offers sporadic acoustic entertainment in summer and probably the most comfortable atmosphere you'll find on the Outer Banks most of the year. Owners Richard Welch, the eatery's longtime chef, and Bob Sanders often are on hand to greet guests themselves. They renovated their restaurant a couple of years ago — regulars are now used to the closed-in porch that includes custom-made wooden booths and ceiling fans. The bar also got bigger, winding around a corner to allow at least a half-dozen more stools to slide under the refurbished countertop.

Don't worry, however, if you loved Tortuga's just as it was, you'll still find the old license plates perched on the low, wooden ceiling beams, and the sand volleyball court remains ready for pickup games out back all summer. Bartenders serve Black and Tans in those same pint glasses — that's right, Tortuga's has Guinness and Bass Ale on tap. Longneck beers are served by the bottle or by the iced-down bucket. Shooters, mixed drinks and tropical frozen concoctions are sure to please any palate.

The steamer is open until closing, so you can satisfy late-night munchies with shellfish or fresh vegetables. Whether you're new in town or here to stay, Tortuga's is one place you won't want to miss. Most nights, it remains open until 2 AM. Tortuga's closes for a brief spell in December and early January.

Sticky Wicket Pub
U.S. Hwy. 158, MP 14 • (252) 441-6594

For weeks through the winter, we Outer Banks locals were intrigued by the marquee outside the shocking pink building on the By-pass that had housed the defunct Lance's Restaurant and Bar. "Something Wicket This Way Comes," it read. That portent proved true when the nice folks that run the Sticky Wicket Pub — one of our favorite spots in the southern part of Nags Head to hoist a pint — finally moved over from their former location in the Outer Banks Mall.

The Wicket crew gutted the old building, and the result is a much larger space than they had in the mall annex. They've also painted over the sore-thumb pink to try to blend in better with the surroundings — the Wicket's exterior is now a neutral, sand color with teal trim. With all the space, the Wicket features an expanded dinner menu (more seafood, steaks and pasta dishes) to go with their old pub favorites. A big S-shaped bar is more removed from the dining area in the new building, and there will be occasional acoustic entertainment. The pub features a full bar and more beer options than you can shake a sticky wicket at. Pool, a popular pastime at the old location, looks to be an in-season casualty for space reasons, but billiards will return in the slower months.

The Sticky Wicket Pub is open daily year round for lunch and dinner. Pub food is available until 1 AM in-season.

Maione's
U.S. Hwy. 158, MP 14 • (252) 480-3311

Across from the Outer Banks Mall, this authentic Italian restaurant has a separate lounge area featuring a full bar. Light, contemporary live music will be performed nightly in summer, and a late-night menu complements the entertainment.

Roanoke Island

The Oasis
Nags Head/Manteo Cswy.
• (252) 441-7721

With an airy, roomy setting right on Roanoke Sound, The Oasis lends itself perfectly to experiencing nightlife with authentic Outer Banks style. A 200-foot dock encourages revelers to come by land or by sea. Boaters can tie up to a 100-foot pier. You can get the best views of the renowned, eye-popping sound sunsets while sipping one of the daily drink specials out on the 500-square-foot gazebo by the dock, or you can sit at one of the tables facing the sound.

An impressive full-service bar also is an inviting spot to enjoy a cocktail. Spacious and decorated with just the right nautical and beach touches, this place makes you feel like kicking back and staying awhile. Twilight entertainment is offered all summer long, with live acoustic music on site three nights a week. The Oasis is open April through Christmas and serves lunch and dinner.

Route 64 Cafe
U.S. Hwy. 64, Manteo • (252) 473-6081

The after-work and NASCAR crowd on Roanoke Island has found itself on Route 64 with regularity since the cafe opened under new ownership on Independence Day 1997. On the barroom side of this little pub, just across from Manteo's Chesley Mall and R.D. Sawyer's Ford dealership, you'll find a friendly staff twisting tops and serving terrific food. The selection of more than two dozen beers includes all your favorite domestics, plus a few microbrews and imports.

Pool is a popular option at Route 64, and tournaments are held on periodic Sundays. You can count on the NASCAR race (or the other big sporting event of the day) being on the tube. This is one of the few spots in Manteo for late-night munchies: Sandwiches, salads and nightly specials (the food these folks serve belies the modest look of the place) can usually be whipped up until about midnight. Route 64 is open daily year round; call for off-season operating hours.

The Green Dolphin Restaurant and Pub
Sir Walter Raleigh St., Manteo • (252) 473-5911

Acoustic entertainers perform here on Fridays year round, featuring rock, folk, blues, beach and even light jazz tunes. There's a bar serving a variety of beer, and there's never a cover charge for live music. This pub is warm and comfortable, and it's made a great comeback after a summer 1997 fire caused considerable damage and closed its heavy wooden doors for several months.

There are wooden floors, booths and tables made from old ship hatch covers and Singer sewing machine stands. The staff is friendly, and locals like to hang out here. It's a fun place with a pool table and pock-marked dartboards set in a separate room. Check out the lovely old wooden cabinet with lockers — it's a holdover from the days when folks used to brown-bag their liquor into the establishment. The restaurant serves appetizers and sandwiches late into the night. Call for seasonal schedules of enter-tainment.

Hatteras Island

The Barefoot Pub
N.C. Hwy. 12, Avon • (252) 995-6159

Entering its third season on Hatteras Is-land, the Barefoot Pub has become a favor-ite gathering spot for locals and passers-through. Rustic but classy, this casual tav-ern and bistro is anchored by a curved oaken bar and adorned with local artwork on its dark painted walls. A wide variety of microbrews and dark beers are on tap. A potent port wine is also available by the glass. In summer the Barefoot Pub offers acoustic guitar entertainment every night. Call for schedules. The pub is open daily April through December.

Sandbar & Grille
N.C. Hwy. 12, Hatteras Village
• (252) 986-2044

Formerly the Lightship Tavern, the Sand-bar has been a hit since it opened on New Year's Eve in 1997. Even when there's no band playing at this rustic, casual establishment, you can hear a fabulous range of music on one of the 83 satellite radio channels. The station is chosen to fit the crowd — the staff says there are even a select few that do a great job clear-ing the house when closing time comes around.

Bands that play everything from blues and rock to jazz and alternative are featured every Friday starting at 10 PM. The cover charge is $4. On Wednesday nights a solo guitarist starts at 9 PM, and there is no cover. A pool table and Foosball are also on the premises. Call for en-tertainment schedules. Lunch and dinner are served all day every day. A late-night menu is available from 9 to 11 PM.

Ocracoke Island

Howard's Pub & Raw Bar Restaurant
N.C. Hwy. 12, Ocracoke Village
• (252) 928-4441

Our absolute favorite place to hear live bands — featuring the friendliest crowd of lo-cals and visitors around — Howard's Pub has an atmosphere and feeling all its own. Once you've visited, you'll plan to make at least a yearly excursion to this upbeat but laid-back place. We try to return at least once a month to get a fix of fun and to get away from it all. Howard's is open 365 days until 2 AM — the only place on the Outer Banks that can make that claim. It's also the only restaurant on Oc-racoke open year round.

The pub serves more types of beer than any place we know of — at least 214 different bottles line the top shelf above the bar, show-ing an unusual array of offerings from around the world that are always available at this oasis on the isolated island. There's an out-door deck here for catching sunsets or fall-ing stars. A huge, screened porch — com-plete with Adirondack rocking chairs for re-laxing in the evening breezes — wraps around one side of the spacious wooden building. The dance floor has more than doubled in size in recent years. A wide-screen TV offers sports fans constant entertainment, and six other TVs usually tune in to a variety of events. Howard's has a dartboard, backgammon, chess set, checkers, Trivial Pursuit, Barrel of Monkeys and card games available for free to playful patrons. Bartenders serve pizza, sandwiches and raw bar-style food until 2 AM and offer free chili Monday nights during football season.

Bands play at least three nights a week in season and can be heard here even on many winter weekends. Music ranges from rhythm and blues to bluegrass, jazz, rock and originals. Open-mike nights and karaoke are favorite events with locals and visitors alike. And the cover charge at Howard's is never more than a few dollars. Even when electric-ity fails the rest of the island, this pub is equipped with a generator so employees can keep on cooking — and keep the beer cold.

Jolly Roger Pub
N.C. Hwy. 12, Ocracoke Village
• (252) 928-3703

A waterfront eatery overlooking Silver Lake, this pub has a huge outdoor deck that's covered in case of thunderstorms. Local entertainers often perform live acoustic music here with no cover charge. Jolly Roger serves beer, wine and finger foods throughout summer.

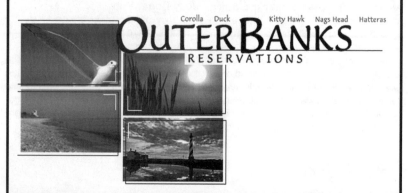
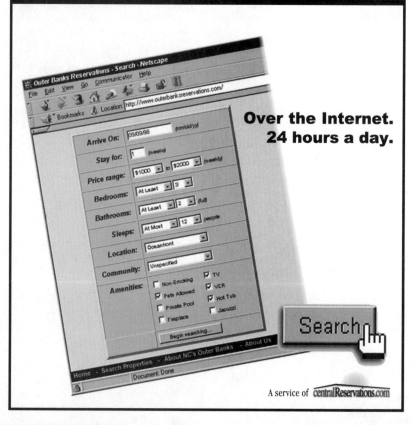

Weekly & Long-term Cottage Rentals

The vacationers who get the most out of their beach getaways are the ones who stay awhile — especially if they bring along their friends or family. If you really want to kick back and relax, renting a beach cottage for a week or more is the way to go. If you decide you never want to leave this vacation paradise, this chapter also includes long-term rental options to help you stake out a year-round place in the sand. A few rental companies even will lease properties by the month or season in case you just want to be here for the warm weather or during the quiet months when most other visitors have left the beach.

From the off-road wilderness of Currituck's National Wildlife Refuge in Carova, north of where N.C. 12's pavement ends, to the quaint hammocks of live oaks that line Ocracoke Island, rental cottages are scattered along almost every mile of the Outer Banks.

"Cottage" options range from small beach bungalows that sleep two to four people amid wooden crate-style furnishings to huge ocean-front mansions, sleeping 20, that come complete with columns, Jacuzzis, fireplaces, decks, porches and custom, upscale interior decorations. If you plan early enough and do your research, you can find short-term rentals to suit any taste, budget or number of guests in just about any locale you wish to be.

Weekly rentals are the most popular options, followed by seasonal and monthly leases. In the off-seasons, many cottage management companies also allow vacationers to rent homes for three- or four-day weekends, and they cut the rates at least in half. The peak season here is summer, from mid-June through August. Most companies rent cottages at least from Easter through Thanksgiving, with many offering year-round short and long-term leases.

In this chapter, we've tried to help you plan any vacation or long-term stay you might desire. Information is included on reservations, deposits, regulations, equipment rentals and, of course, cottage rental companies throughout the Outer Banks. If you plan on visiting in the summer, your best bet is to reserve that vacation getaway early, often by late March. It becomes more difficult to secure a weekly cottage rental after schools let out in June, but sometimes rental managers can squeeze you in if there's a cancellation.

Planning Your Cottage Vacation

Demand and prices for rentals vary according to the area of the beach you want to be on, proximity of the property to the ocean, amenities offered, the number of people the unit sleeps and the time of year during which you plan to stay. Traditionally, oceanfront properties are booked first. Cottages that are semi-oceanfront and in the central areas of the Outer Banks typically book up next. Soundfront and soundside properties tend to be reserved at a slower rate simply because they are farther from the ocean.

Descriptions of Locations

Rental properties right on the beach with no homes or lots between the cottages and the Atlantic are called "oceanfront" and are, by far, the most popular option for vacationers. Oceanside properties are those from which you can walk to the beach without having to cross a major street or road. In these houses, you can roll out of bed and be at the beach: The sand leading to that spectacular surf is right at your door. You can eat lunch at home without driving to another destination and fall asleep to the rhythm of the waves. You'll pay for those privileges, though, as these are the most expensive properties during in season. Off season rates can be very reasonable.

Semi-oceanfront cottages usually lie one lot behind an oceanfront lot or oceanfront house. Distance to the Atlantic varies, and some views are blocked by high sand dunes. There will be other rows of houses along roads or lanes between your cottage and the ocean. Often though, you can still watch the waves from these homes' upstairs windows and the higher decks.

Many cottages from Kitty Hawk through Nags Head are between the highways, west of the Beach Road but east of U.S. 158. You don't have to traverse the five-lane highway that way to get to the beach, but you can count on at least a five- to 15-minute hike to the sea. And you'll have to cross the two-lane Beach Road to get there. Traffic travels at a slow pace on this road: 35 mph. A word of caution: The pavement gets scorching hot in the summer sun, so don't venture out without wearing shoes when walking from a cottage between the highways to the ocean.

Soundfront or soundside locations gener-

ally mean that the homes face the waters of the sound on the western reaches of the Outer Banks. Families with young children, or those who don't mind a short drive to the ocean, often select these cottages because the sound is a shallow, warmer body of water to swim in than the Atlantic. These rental units are also considerably cheaper than those east of U.S. 158. You have to cross the five-lane highway to get to the Atlantic from these cottages, but you often can still reach the waves by walking or bik-ing less than a mile.

West-side rentals are those west of U.S. 158 but probably not too close to the sound. These are the least expensive cottages to rent, and most year-round rentals are found there.

Reading chapters on each area of the Outer Banks in this book should help you choose which places on the beach you'd prefer to visit. Whether your taste is for upscale elegant homes loaded with amenities in Corolla or quiet, cloistered neighborhoods in South Nags Head or off-the-beaten-path fishing villages in Frisco — each town and village has its own personality and price range. Once you know, generally, where you'd like to be and when you plan to arrive, call the rental companies in that area and request a brochure. Many rental companies cover wide expanses of the barrier islands and offer an array of options. Most have toll-free telephone numbers and will gladly send a free brochure to you. Read the cottage and location descriptions carefully so that you'll know exactly what you're renting, and make sure to confirm rates and extra expenses you might incur with your rental agent.

Reservations

When you make an advance reservation for a rental cottage, be sure you can provide a portion of the rent to secure your spot. Rental brochures are mailed between Thanksgiving and mid-January, in plenty of time for you to make informed choices about accommodations. Traditionally, most summer reservations are received by March or April; however, if

www.insiders.com

See this and many other Insiders' Guide® destinations online — in their entirety.

Visit us today!

you are unable to book as early as you would like or you decide at the last minute that you need an Outer Banks getaway, don't be discouraged. Rental managers say some cottages almost always can be found at the last minute.

Most cottages are equipped with full kitchens (including pots, pans and dishes), cable TVs, telephones and air conditioning. Many, however, require guests to provide their own towels and sheets or will provide these items for an extra fee. Of course, you'll almost always need to bring toiletries. Before booking your cottage, ask about what things you should pack to ensure that your rental unit is as comfortable as possible when you arrive. Rental managers also can answer questions about special needs, such as provisions to bring pets, or find nonsmoking or handicapped accessible houses.

If you vacation at the Outer Banks annually, most companies also offer the option of reserving time in the same property for the following year. It's not uncommon for visitors to rent the same cottage year after year. Some families even think of these weekly rentals as a second home at the beach.

Minimum Stays

During the off-season, some options exist for partial weeks and weekend rentals in cottages. During the summer, it's practically impossible to rent for less than a full week. Most weeks run either Saturday to Saturday or Sunday to Sunday. Long-term rentals are by the month, season or year. Hotels and motels are much more flexible for short-term stays but sometimes end up costing more if you want to spend a full week at the Outer Banks.

Remember, the off-season is a much cheaper time to rent cottages for the week

or long weekend on these barrier islands. Fewer people are around then. Most restaurants and shops stay open through Thanksgiving, and every year, more and more eateries and retail stores remain open almost all winter.

Cancellations

Rental brochures and lease agreements spell out each company's specific cancellation policy in detail. Most cancellations or transfers of any confirmed reservations are required in writing. You will probably lose all or part of your deposit and advance rent if the property you already have reserved is not re-rented. Make sure you read the small print and know what will happen if you decide you have to cancel.

Advance Rents

Money paid in advance is no longer considered a deposit. It's usually called advance payment or advance rent. Laws of the North Carolina Real Estate Commission involving renting or leasing property now govern most of these practices.

Details, explanations and rules are spelled out in rental brochures and again in your lease. Read the fine print and save yourself a potential headache. Personal checks are usually accepted for these advance rents, and some rental companies allow credit card transactions. In most cases, rent balances, taxes and other applicable fees and deposits are due 30 days prior to arrival. Final payments made upon check-in are usually required in the form of certified checks, travelers' checks or cash. Most rental companies do not accept personal checks at check-in.

Security Deposits

Besides advance rents, most rental companies also require people to pay a security deposit when they lease a cottage on the Outer Banks. The deposit can be as much as $500 for a week's stay; however; some properties do not require a deposit.

Security deposits generally are refundable if the cottage you've rented passes inspection. If anything is damaged or missing, expect a smaller refund or no refund at all. Rental company agents have the final word on this, so take as good care of your vacation property as you would of your own home. Cottages that accept pets, especially, almost always charge higher security deposits.

Hurricane Evacuation Refunds

Each rental contract has different specifications about whether you'll get your money back if the Outer Banks are evacuated for a hurricane. In many cases, partial or complete refunds are provided if a mandatory evacuation has been issued by the Dare County Emergency Management Control Group. Adjustments to your bill are made according to the number of days you were unable to occupy the property due to the mandatory evacuation.

Most rental managers say refunds are not provided for days you don't occupy the property once re-entry is permitted. Ocracoke property management companies also make special provisions for refunds in case the free state ferry boats can't run from Hatteras or Cedar Island to their island. Since it's almost impossible to visit Ocracoke without the ferries, unless you own a private plane, most rental companies will refund your rent and deposits if you can't get to Ocracoke because of interrupted ferry schedules. These policies also vary by business.

You might want to consider buying travel insurance, which will cover you if you're delayed because of traffic or airplane layovers, if you have to cancel due to illness or unexpected problems, or if there is natural disaster at your year-round residence that prevents you

from leaving home. It also will compensate you in the event of a hurricane evacuation on the Outer Banks. Many property agents now offer the insurance, usually at a charge of about four percent of your total bill.

Handling and Inspection Fees

Almost all rental companies charge a handling fee for processing information and an inspection fee to check out the cottages after you've gone. The total for both generally ranges from a few dollars to $50. This is a nonrefundable fee assessed on top of advance rents and security deposits.

Taxes

On the Outer Banks, all tourism fees are taxable. Rental charges and handling fees are taxed. If cleaning, pet or extermination fees are applicable, they are taxable too. Deposits are not taxable since they're generally returned. The North Carolina tax rate on lodging is 6 percent. The local/county lodging tax rate is 4 percent. Combined, the tax rate is 10 percent on rental charges and fees.

Pet Rules and Costs

Some rental cottages allow guests to bring along their pets. Most of the companies that manage these properties, however, require additional deposits and, often, additional fees. These extra costs help cover charges for spraying for fleas, ticks and other pests. Fees vary depending on the type of pet, type of house and management company. Pet fees generally are not refundable.

Check-In, Check-Out Times

Check-in times vary between companies. Most rental cottages allow you to get inside your temporary home between 3 and 6 PM. Guests check-in at the rental company before taking occupancy of the cottage. Be prompt, but don't be early. Cleanup crews need suffi-

Families can double-up in many of the vacation homes on the Outer Banks.

cient time to get your cottage in tip-top shape. Rental managers urge you not to try to occupy the cottage before it is ready. They understand your eagerness to settle into your cottage, but they simply are unable to let you do so.

Most checkouts occur between 9 and 11 AM. Again, it is important to check out on time to allow for necessary maintenance. Late fees may be imposed if you stay beyond checkout time .

Almost all Outer Banks cottages that rent by the week go from Saturday to Saturday. In recent years, however, many of the larger companies have been offering Sunday-to-Sunday or Friday-to-Friday rentals and checkout instead. If you have this option, you may want to consider these alternatives. Traffic to and from the beach will be lighter on those days.

Occupancy

The number of people each rental cottage can accommodate is listed in the rental brochure for each individual property. Often, this limit is determined by the number of beds available, including sleeper sofas. Septic and water capacity, however, also dictate how many people can stay in each unit, so be sure you don't exceed the maximum occupancy, or you may find yourself with more problems than you care to handle on vacation. Groups who try to get around rules governing occupancy could lose their money and risk eviction. Most agents would first give a warning, but why chance marring your vacation?

What's Furnished

Most rental cottages are fully furnished homes with appliances, TVs, toasters, microwaves, telephones and other necessities. Some also include extra amenities such as VCRs, stereos, board games, beach chairs, beach umbrellas, hammocks and outdoor

Glistening Sunrises . . .
Soothing Ocean Breezes . . .
Treasured Memories . . .
Discover the Magic
of our Beaches
with Extraordinary
Vacation Getaways.
BRITT REAL ESTATE
DUCK TO COROLLA
Call for a free rental brochure.
1-800-334-6315
1316 Duck Road Duck • Kitty Hawk
North Carolina 27949 • (252) 261-3566
www.brittrealestate.com • e-mail: BRITTDUCK@aol.com

grills. Kitchens generally are fully equipped with dishes, silverware and pots and pans.

Almost all rental companies, however, require guests to bring their own sheets and towels, paper products, detergents and personal toiletries. You can rent towels from many equipment rental companies (see the "Equipment Rentals" section of this chapter). You also can lease bicycles, in-line skates and other recreational equipment to take back to your cottage for the day or week.

If it's important to keep track of the time, bring a clock or radio. Otherwise, judge time by the sun and relax — after all, you're on vacation!

Mail and Phone Service

Some rental company agents will take phone or mail messages for you while you're vacationing on the Outer Banks, but it's better to take care of these requirements before you arrive. When you reserve a cottage, ask for the phone number at that location to leave with close friends, colleagues or relatives in case they need to contact you.

Some older cottages don't have telephones. Ask ahead if you really need one. All rental companies require their renters to foot the bill for long-distance charges.

Trash Pickup and Recycling

Town or county garbage collectors gather the trash from in front of most rental cottages at least twice a week during summer. Just put your bags in the bin or receptacle in front of the property, and make sure it sits beside the road before you leave. Recycling, however, is the renters' responsibility. You can carry bottles, cans, plastics, cardboard, newspapers and other items to a variety of Outer Banks recycling collection points located at town halls, fire stations and shopping centers. Rinse out all items and sort them according to material.

Many beach accesses also have recycling bins for you to deposit cans or bottles in as you leave the sandy seashore for the day. If there isn't one at the spot you choose to sun yourself, please pack up your trash and take it off the beach with you. For a complete list of recycling centers on the Outer Banks.

Equipment Rentals and Related Services

If you'd rather not take everything with you, equipment rental companies along the Outer Banks can provide almost everything you need except clothing. Strollers and wheelchairs with large wheels for easy movement in the sand, beach chairs, umbrellas, bikes, videos, VCRs, camcorders, cribs, high chairs, cots, fishing gear, linens, grills, camping equipment, watercraft . . . you name it, and you can probably rent it by the day, week or month.

Businesses that lease surfboards, Boogie Boards, Jet Skis, kayaks, boats, windsurfers, canoes and other watersports equipment are listed in our Watersports chapter. In this section, we've included companies that rent a wider range of items. Some rental companies even will deliver large equipment to your home, hotel or rental cottage. A few of these businesses are only open seasonally. If you need to rent items during the off-season, call ahead to check on availability and hours.

At Your Service
(252) 261-5286, (800) 259-0229

A vacation is supposed to be fun, right? So who wants to spend hours in a grocery store checkout line — or tied to other chores that eat up your precious beach time? At Your Service, a growing 10-year-old business on the Outer Banks, will take on those tiresome chores by acting as your personal concierge. They can help in acquiring babysitters (it's the oldest babysitting and eldercare service on the Outer Banks), stocking your vacation cottage with groceries and other necessities before you arrive, providing linens and cleaning service, ordering flowers and theater tickets and seeing to details to make a vacation run smoothly. Pamela Price, a former teacher and public relations professional, is the energetic owner

of At Your Service, and she has a well-trained and competent staff of around 60 employees. For more information, see our Education and Child Care chapter.

Ocean Atlantic Rentals
(800) 635-9559 information
Corolla Light, Corolla • (252) 453-2440
Duck Rd., Soundfront, Duck
• (252) 261-4346
N.C. Hwy. 12, MP 10, Nags Head
• (252) 441-7823
N.C. Hwy. 12, Avon • (252) 995-5868

If you've prepaid with advance reservations, Ocean Atlantic will deliver from any location. Beach umbrellas and chairs, bikes, cribs, TVs, VCRs, kayaks, linens, skates, grills, videos and watersports equipment are among the items this company leases.

Money's Worth Beach Home Equipment Rentals
(252) 453-4566, (252) 261-6999,
(800) 833-5233

With a minimum rental order of $20, all items are delivered to your vacation home on your check-in day and picked up after you check out.

This company is the only one that services the real estate companies directly. You do not have to be present for delivery or pickup service.

Lifesaver Rent-Alls
U.S. Hwy. 158, MP 1, Kitty Hawk
• (252) 261-1344
Lifesaver Shops, Kill Devil Hills
• (252) 441-6048, (800) 635-2764
information

Delivery is available. Beach equipment, bikes, baby supplies, linens, fishing supplies and beach wheelchairs are among the items this company leases.

Metro Rentals
U.S. Hwy. 158 and Colington Rd., Kill Devil Hills • (252) 480-3535

This company specializes in party supplies, party tents, construction equipment and beach-combing devices such as metal detectors.

Beach Outfitters
N.C. Hwy. 12, Ocracoke
• (252) 928-6261, (252) 928-7411

Beach Outfitters, at Ocracoke Island Realty, is open all year and accepts reservations.

INSIDERS' TIP

Leave all that bulky baby equipment at home. There are numerous rental outlets available, and some even deliver.

Free delivery and pickup are available on Ocracoke Island with full-week rental and prepayment. Items available to rent include beach chairs, towels, bikes and kitchen equipment.

Island Rentals
N.C. Hwy. 12, Ocracoke • (252) 928-5480

Affiliated with Sharon Miller Realty, Island Rentals leases beach equipment, croquet sets, Nintendo games, cottage supplies and many other items.

Cottage Rental Companies

In this section, we've listed rental companies, their physical locations, mailing addresses, telephone numbers, geographic areas in which they lease properties and the number of cottages these companies maintain. They're listed north-to-south, but many real estate companies overlap in their territory and cover a wide span of the Outer Banks, so read the range of each company in different areas. We've also provided information about what types of rentals are available, whether the companies rent by the year or by the week year round, whether they offer weekend rentals in the off-season, whether they have cottages that can accommodate pets and whether they rent handicapped-accessible units. For your own benefit, call each rental company you may be interested in leasing from as soon as possible to get someone to mail you a brochure with other specific information.

Corolla

Corolla B&B
Brindley & Brindley Realty and Development Building, Corolla
• (252) 453-3033, (800) 962-0201

Corolla B&B manages about 450 properties from Carova to Pine Island and Buck Island. Weekly rentals are available all year, and weekend rentals are offered during the off-season. Pets are accepted in some units.

Handicapped-accessible cottages also are available. Linens and toiletries are provided in all units.

Karichele Realty
TimBuck II Shopping Village,
N.C. Hwy. 12, •(252) 453-4400,
(800) 453-2377

Karichele Realty manages more than 100 properties from Carova to Duck that may be rented by the week. During the off-season, weekend packages are available. Pets are accepted in some units. Handicapped-accessible cottages also are available.

Duck

Britt Real Estate
N.C. Hwy. 12, Kitty Hawk
• (252) 261-3566, (800) 334-6315

Britt Real Estate manages 250 properties, including two handicapped-accessible homes, from Corolla to Southern Shores. Pets are ac-

cepted in some units. Weekend rentals are offered in the off-season.

Duck Real Estate
1232 Duck Rd., Duck • (252) 261-4614,
(800) 992-2976

Duck Real Estate manages 180 weekly rentals from Corolla to Southern Shores. Three-day golf packages also are available. Pets are accepted in some units. Some cottages are equipped for handicapped guests.

R & R Resort Rental Properties Inc.
N.C. Hwy. 12, Duck • (252) 261-1136,
(800) 433-8805 in Duck,
(800) 849-6189 in Corolla

R & R manages more than 350 weekly rental properties from Whalehead to Pine Island and Duck to Southern Shores. Many homes have private pools and hot tubs, and a number of them are suitable for hosting small weddings. Three-day rates are available. Some cottages allow dogs. A few units are handicapped accessible with elevators.

Real Escapes Properties
N.C. Hwy. 12, Duck, NC 27949
• (252) 261-3211, (800) 831-3211

Real Escapes manages more than 180 weekly rental cottages from Corolla to Southern Shores. The company prides itself on managing quality homes that are maintained by conscientious, caring owners. Call for copies of an illustrated brochure.

Twiddy & Company Realty
1181 Duck Rd., Duck • (252) 261-3521, (252) 453-3341, (800) 489-4339 in Duck, (800) 789-4339 in Corolla

Twiddy & Company manages more than 400 rental properties from Carova to Southern Shores. Pets are accepted in some units. Some units offer private pools and hot tubs.

Southern Shores

Southern Shores Realty
N.C. Hwy. 12, Kitty Hawk
• (252) 261-2111, (800) 334-1000

Southern Shores Realty manages 425 year-round and weekly rentals from Southern Shores to Duck. Weekend packages also are available year-round. Dogs are accepted in some units. Ramps and elevators are offered in some cottages.

Kitty Hawk

Atlantic Realty
U.S. Hwy. 158, MP 2½, Kitty Hawk
• (252) 261-2154, (800) 334-8401
100-M Sunset Blvd., Corolla
• (252) 453-4110, (800) 669-9245

This company manages more than 200 properties from Corolla to South Nags Head for year-round and seasonal rental. Pets are accepted in some units.

Kitty Dunes Realty
(252) 261-2171, (800) 334-DUNE

Kitty Dunes manages about 480 rental properties from Corolla to South Nags Head. Some can accommodate up to 22 people. Most properties rent by the week, but long-term rentals are offered in Colington Harbour (call the Kitty

Hawk office). Three-night weekend packages are often available, even during the summer. Pets are accepted in many units, and a few cottages are handicapped-friendly. Some properties include private pools and spas.

Joe Lamb Jr. & Associates
U.S. Hwy. 158, MP 2, Kitty Hawk
• (252) 261-4444, (800) 552-6257

This company manages more than 200 properties, including year-round rentals from Duck to South Nags Head. Three-night packages also are offered during the off-season. Pets are accepted in some cottages. Handicapped-accessible rentals also are available. Units in some developments include pool access. Many units also have private pools.

Resort Central Inc.
U.S. Hwy. 158, MP 2½, Kitty Hawk
• (252) 261-8861, (800) NAGS-HEAD

Resort Central manages 100 year-round and weekly rental properties from Corolla to Nags Head. Advanced reservations are available in the off-season for weekend packages. Some cottages allow pets, and some units are equipped with elevators.

Resort Realty
(252) 261-8383, (252) 261-8888, (800) 458-3830;

Resort Realty manages 430 weekly rental properties from Corolla to South Nags Head. Some three-night packages are available with a maximum of five days' notice. A few cottages allow pets.

Seaside Realty
U.S. Hwy. 158, MP 3, Kitty Hawk
• (252) 261-5500, (800) 395-2525

Seaside Realty manages 150 year-round and weekly properties from Corolla to South Nags Head. At least 300 additional timeshares also are offered in that area. Three-night packages are available during the off-season. Some of these units allow pets. Some accommodations have elevators.

Wright Property Management
U.S. Hwy. 158, MP 4¾, Kitty Hawk
• (252) 261-2186

Wright Property manages 150 year-round

Old Nags Head:
Authentic Outer Banks Architecture

For much of the 19th century, Nags Head was a getaway for the wealthy, a place to relax and recuperate; a safe haven from disease and so-called toxic vapors that doctors believed promoted illness. Summer after summer, growing families and networks of friends made this then-isolated beach one of the most popular of the East Coast's resort communities.

The Nags Head of yesteryear is still evident in a mile-long row of cottages that line the oceanfront east of Jockey's Ridge. Weathered and stately, about a dozen homes built between 1860 and 1940 best characterize the unique Nags Head-style architecture that has become one of the signatures of the Outer Banks. The Nags Head Beach Cottage Row Historic District is one of the few turn-of-the century resort areas remaining on the Eastern Seaboard that has maintained its original character, state historians say.

For the last two Septembers, Preservation North Carolina, a private nonprofit historic preservation group, has opened up many of the Nags Head cottages, with

— continued on next page

Photo: Courtesy of Drew Wilson

Have a seat, relax and enjoy the view.

the owners' cooperation, for public tours. Scores of people eagerly took the group up on the offer, strolling from house-to-house and meeting the owners, some of whom spent most every summer of their lives in the family's Nags Head oceanside retreat.

The beach cottages were designed to be functional and practical. Most notable for large porches lined with wind-proof built-in benches that wrap around three, even four, sides, the houses feature unpainted wooden siding, weathered by salt air to a deep brown, and angled porches and roofs. Shuttered windows offer ready shelter from sun and wind, but are easily propped open with an attached stick. Pilings boost the floors away from encroaching waves. And if the ocean came a little too close for comfort, the houses were made to be moved easily. Some already have been moved away from the surf four times.

Most of the homes are one- or two-storied and have three or four bedrooms. Stairwells to the upstairs are narrow and the steps are creaky and often uneven. In some places on the ground floor, you can see through cracks to the scrubby plants and sand beneath the house. All houses now have flush toilets, rather than relying on the former outhouses, but many still depend only on the original outdoor shower installed away from the living quarters. Former servants' quarters have been changed into spare bedrooms, offices or storage areas. Most cottages now have new kitchens in former breezeways, which separated the original kitchens from living space for safety reasons.

But what hasn't changed is the remarkable airiness and light that the rooms are effused in — and the way the steady slapping and sighing of ocean waves dominates the background sounds. The homes were all designed to foster air circulation; many cottage owners find no need for air conditioning. Sea breezes flip and billow tab curtains away from bedroom windows, affording occupants of one of these old beach cottages one of the best oceanfront vistas you can get on the Outer Banks.

Although there was already a thriving resort community near what is now Soundside Road in Nags Head, no one dared build near the Atlantic until 1866, when Dr. William Gaskins Pool decided to erect the first beachfront house on the Outer Banks. Pool, according to historical documents, paid $30 for 50 acres of land along the ocean. In the interest of securing companionship, he gave 130-foot-wide lots away to friends, who built their own homes. Eventually, others followed, and one of the oldest beachfront settlements in the state took hold. The thirteen original Nags Head cottages were built between the end of the Civil War and World War II's onset.

Some cottages that have been part of the Preservation North Carolina tours include:

The Windemere

Built by well-known builder S.J. Twine, who constructed many of the cottages along in the historic district, this one-story house was completed in the 1930s.

Fred Wood Cottage

This two-story house, also constructed by Twine, has two gable-end chimneys and a covered porch surrounding all four sides.

Whedbee Cottage

One of the few Civil War-era homes, this two-story frame home was finished in 1866.

Nixon Cottage

The third-oldest oceanfront cottage in the area, this home was originally a single-

— continued on next page

story structure. In the 1920s, a second floor was added and the lower floor was expanded.

Badham-Kittrell Cottage

Another house built by Twine, this 1928 home is one story with an L-shaped wing extending from the back of the house. The second level perches over the main living area.

Miss Mattie Midgett's Store

Moved from the soundside in 1933, this 1914 store supplied vacationers and locals with groceries, mail and the area's only telephone. It still houses the booty from years of beachcombing done by Miss Mattie's daughter, Nellie Myrtle.

Martha Wood Cottage

Possibly the oldest of the historic district's cottages, this two-story house was likely built in 1870 or earlier. It has two projecting dormers on the beach side and a small, L-shaped addition in the rear.

The Silver Cottage

Built in 1883, this home's original owner paid $6.06 in annual taxes. The cottage was moved back farther from the ocean after the 1997-98 nor'easters.

For more information about future tours, call Preservation North Carolina at (252) 832-1651 in Raleigh, or (252) 482-7455 in Edenton.

---

and weekly properties from Ocean Sands to South Nags Head. Weekend rentals also are offered. Some units accept pets.

Kill Devil Hills

Kitty Hawk Rentals/Beach Realty & Construction
U.S. Hwy. 158, MP 6, Kill Devil Hills
• (252) 441-7166, (800) 635-1559
N.C. Hwy. 12, Duck • (252) 261-6605
790-B Ocean Tr., Corolla
• (252) 453-4141

This company manages more than 600 properties, a few of which are handicapped-accessible, from Ocean Hill to South Nags Head. Some are available for year-round rental, but most rent by the week. Pets are accepted in some units. Outer Banks Golf Getaways, this company's lat-

est division, offers weekend golf/accommodation packages in area homes and hotels. Call (800) 916-6244 for more information.

Ocean Breeze Realty
100 E. Third St., Kill Devil Hills
• (252) 480-0093, (800) 633-4491

Ocean Breeze manages about 80 weekly and year-round cottages, condos, duplexes and townhouses from Ocean Sands to Manteo. There are swimming pools and tennis courts available for use at the condos, and some units will accept pets.

RE/MAX Ocean Realty
U.S. Hwy. 158, MP 6, Kill Devil Hills
• (252) 441-3127, (800) 548-2033,
(800) 334-6436

RE/MAX manages more than 300 units from Whalehead Junction through South Nags

Head. Year-round and weekly rentals are available. Three-night packages are offered during the off-season. Some allow pets, and some are handicapped-accessible. RE/MAX also offers rentals at the Barrier Island resorts in Duck and Kitty Hawk.

Sun Realty
U.S. Hwy. 158, MP 9, Kill Devil Hills
• (252) 441-7033, (800) 334-4745

Satellite offices are at Corolla, Duck, Kitty Hawk, Salvo and Avon. Sun Realty offers the largest inventory of rental properties on the Outer Banks, managing more than 1,100 properties from Corolla through Hatteras Island. Weekly, monthly and year-round rentals are available. A special program for handicapped guests, with a separate brochure, is offered. Pets are accepted in some units.

Nags Head

Bodie Island Rentals
N.C. Hwy. 12, MP 17, Nags Head
• (252) 441-2558, (800) 862-1785

This R.C.I. affiliate manages 23 timeshares and two wholly owned units in the Bodie Island Resort for weekly rental all year. Three-night rentals are offered during the off-season. An elevator is located in one building.

Cove Realty
Between N.C. Hwy. 12 and U.S. Hwy. 158, MP 13½, Nags Head
• (252) 441-6391, (800) 635-7007

Cove Realty manages 125 properties in Old Nags Head Cove and South Nags Head for year-round, weekly and student rental. Pets are accepted in some units. Weekend packages are available during the off-season. Guests have access, for a small fee, to a swimming pool and tennis courts in Old Nags Head Cove.

Nags Head Realty
U.S. Hwy. 158, MP 10, Nags Head
• (252) 441-4315, (800) 222-1531

Nags Head Realty manages more than 250 weekly rentals from the Crown Point development in the northern beaches to South Nags Head. Three-day rentals are offered during the off-season. Some units accept pets.

Outer Banks Ltd.
U.S. Hwy. 158, MP 10½, Nags Head
• (252) 441-5000, (800) 624-7651

Outer Banks Ltd. manages 250 weekly rental properties from Kitty Hawk to South Nags Head. Three-day packages are offered year-round as well. Some units have private pools or pool access. Several handicapped-accessible units are available.

Outer Banks Resort Rentals
U.S. Hwy. 158, MP 11, Nags Head
• (252) 441-2134

Marvin Beard represents the sales and rentals of timeshares only from Duck to South Nags as well as a few in Hatteras.

Sea Oats Realty
Pirate's Quay, U.S. Hwy. 158, MP 11, Nags Head • (252) 480-2325, (800) 933-2325

Sea Oats Realty manages weekly rentals from Duck to South Nags Head. Partial week rentals are available in the off-season. Some units include pool access. Pets are allowed in several units.

Stan White Realty & Construction, Inc.
U.S. Hwy. 158, MP 10½, Nags Head
• (252) 441-1515, (800) 338-3233
1232 Duck Rd., Duck
• (252) 261-4614, (800) 992-2976

Stan White manages 400 weekly and year-round rentals from Corolla to South Nags Head. Pets are allowed in some weekly rentals. Handicapped-accessible units are available. Corporate retreat and golf packages are offered.

Village Realty
U.S. Hwy. 158, MP 15, Nags Head
• (252) 480-2224, (800) 548-9688

Village Realty manages more than 260 rental properties in the development of the Village at Nags Head. A few year-round rentals are offered, but most lease by the week. Special weekend and golf packages are available. Some units include access to a beach club with an outdoor swimming pool, tennis courts, a game room and family activities. Golf and tennis lessons are available. A golf course, pri-

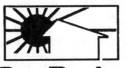

vate oceanfront access and two private sound-side piers also are on the premises. Some cottages allow pets. Some have elevators and can accommodate handicapped vacationers.

Roanoke Island

Pirate's Cove Realty
Manteo/Nags Head Cswy., Manteo
• **(252) 473-6800, (800) 537-7245**

Pirate's Cove Realty manages properties in the Pirate's Cove development for weekly rentals. Two-night weekends also are offered during the off-season. Some cottages accept pets. All units include access to an outdoor swimming pool, tennis courts, playground and free boat slips.

20/20 Realty
516 S. Main Hwy., Manteo
• **(252) 473-2020, (800) 520-2044**

This company manages primarily year-round rentals from Kitty Hawk to Manns Har-

bor. At least eight weekly rentals also are offered on Roanoke Island.

Hatteras Island

Dolphin Realty
N.C. Hwy. 12, Hatteras Village
• **(252) 986-2241, (800) 338-4775**

This company manages 70 properties, including homes and one-room efficiencies on Hatteras Island. Some are available for year-round rental. Pets are accepted in some units.

Colony Realty Corp.
N.C. Hwy. 12, Avon • (252) 995-5891, (800) 962-5256

Colony recently bought Water Side Realty and handles about 125 weekly units and approximately 40 long-term rentals in Avon, Buxton, Frisco and Hatteras. Most of the units, which are single-family cottages or condos, will accept pets. Three-day mini-

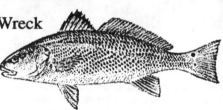 

A stroll on the beach is a mandatory part of your beach stay.

mum stays can be arranged in the off-season. Several handicapped-accessible units are available.

Hatteras Realty
N.C. Hwy. 12, Avon • (252) 995-5466, (800) HATTERAS

Hatteras Realty manages 270 properties on Hatteras Island for weekly rental only. Units may be rented by partial weeks during the off-season. Pets are accepted in some units. Handicapped-accessible cottages are available. More than half of this company's units are furnished with hot tubs. Every guest has free access to the pool and tennis courts at Club Hatteras.

Midgett Realty
N.C. Hwy. 12, Hatteras Village • (252) 986-2841, (800) 527-2903

Midgett Realty manages more than 350 properties from Rodanthe to Hatteras Village for weekly rentals. Three-night rentals are available during the off-season, and some units

accept pets. Several handicapped-accessible units are offered.

Outer Beaches Realty
N.C. Hwy. 12, Avon • (252) 995-4477 in Avon, (252) 987-2771 in Waves, (800) 627-3250

Outer Beaches Realty manages more than 400 rental cottages from Rodanthe to Hatteras Village. Weekly and three-day rentals are available. A few allow pets. Some handicapped-accessible properties also are offered.

Salvo Real Estate
N.C. Hwy. 12, Salvo • (252) 987-2343

Salvo Real Estate manages 35 weekly rentals in Rodanthe, Waves and Salvo. Three-night rentals are offered during the off-season. A few of these cottages allow pets.

Surf or Sound Realty
N.C. Hwy. 12, Avon • (252) 995-5801, (800) 237-1138

Surf or Sound Realty offers 190 cottages

on Hatteras Island. Pets are accepted in some units. Handicapped-accessible rentals also are available.

Ocracoke Island

Ocracoke Island Realty Inc.
N.C. Hwy. 12, Ocracoke Village
• (252) 928-6261, (252) 928-7411,
(800) 699-9082 reservations

Ocracoke Island Realty manages 112 weekly rental properties on Ocracoke. Three-night packages are available during the off-season. A few of these cottages allow pets.

Sharon Miller Realty
N.C. Hwy. 12, Ocracoke Village
• (252) 928-5711, (800) 955-0630

Sharon Miller Realty manages 130 Ocracoke Island properties, one of which is handicapped-accessible. Only weekly rentals are available during the peak season. In the off-season, three-day minimums are available. Pets are accepted in some units.

Year-round Rentals

Because the Outer Banks is primarily a vacation destination, not all rental companies will lease their properties to year-round residents. Some houses, apartments, duplexes and other units, however, are available for monthly, seasonal or year-round rentals.

The majority of long-term rentals are between the highways or west of U.S. 158 in Kitty Hawk, Kill Devil Hills and Nags Head, or on Colington, Roanoke and Hatteras islands. It's easiest to sign a year-round lease between October and March. If you're looking for a seasonal, summer rental, make arrangements through a real estate agent as early as possible, at least before Easter.

Check with rental agents to determine specific occupancy rules regarding rates, deposits, pets, furnishings, washing machines and dryers or other issues. Most companies require one month's rent plus a security deposit equalling one month's rent, and, often references from previous employers and landlords. Pet deposits can be hefty around here.

INSIDERS' TIP

Ask about Sunday-to-Sunday rental homes if you want to avoid sitting in long lines of traffic waiting to get on or off the beach in the summer. Some real estate companies listed in this chapter offer this option.

The following companies manage year-round rentals. After the name of the company and phone number, we give the areas in which they have year-round options. Most of these companies are listed in greater detail either above or in our Real Estate chapter. Also check local newspapers for classified listings of year-round rentals available.

Atlantic Realty, (252) 261-2154, Colington, Kill Devil Hills and Kitty Hawk

Colony Realty, (252) 995-5891 or (800) 962-5256, Avon, Frisco and Hatteras

Cove Realty, (252) 441-6391 or (800) 635-7007, Old Nags Head Cove and South Nags Head

Dolphin Realty, (252) 986-2241 or (800) 338-4775, Hatteras Island

Kitty Dunes Realty, (252) 261-2171, Colington Harbour, Kill Devil Hills and Kitty Hawk

Kitty Hawk Rentals/Beach Realty & Construction, (252) 441-7166, (800) 635-1559, Duck, west of U.S. 158, and between the highways in the central areas of the beach

Joe Lamb Jr. & Associates, (252) 261-4444, Kitty Hawk to Nags Head

Nags Head Realty, (252) 441-4315 or (800) 222-1531, Kitty Hawk to South Nags Head

Jim Perry & Company, (252) 441-3051 or (800) 222-6135, Duck to South Nags Head

RE/MAX Ocean Realty, (252) 441-3127 or (800) 548-2033, Kitty Hawk to Manteo

Resort Central, (252) 261-8861 or (800) 334-4749, Kitty Hawk to Manteo

Seaside Realty, (252) 261-5500, Kitty Hawk to Nags Head

Southern Shores Realty, (252) 261-2111 or (800) 334-1000, Duck to Kitty Hawk

Sun Realty, (252) 261-1152, (800) 334-4745, Corolla through Hatteras Island

20/20 Realty, (252) 473-2020, (800) 520-2044, Kitty Hawk through Roanoke Island

Stan White Realty & Construction, (252) 441-1516, (800) 338-3233, Kitty Hawk to Nags Head

Wright Properties, (252) 261-2186, Ocean Sands to South Nags Head.

Accommodations

When it comes to accommodations, just like every other thing on the Outer Banks, you can have it as restful or as rowdy as you choose. Visitors looking to stay a night, several days or a week can choose from a range of small family-owned seaside motels to multiple-story franchises of national lodging chains. The farther south you go, the fewer chain-owned accommodations you'll see; in fact, they almost disappear. In recent years, upscale elegant inns and a variety of bed and breakfast establishments have opened their doors — offering a little more luxury and personal attention than the traditional barrier island hotels. A new hotel in Corolla, only the second one on the northern barrier islands, is scheduled to be completed by midyear 1998.

A few of these motels and hotels require two-night minimums on the weekends, and many accommodations managers request at least three-day stays for Memorial Day weekend, July 4 weekend and Labor Day weekend, since those are, by far, the busiest times on these barrier islands. A lot of Outer Banks hotels also have suites, efficiency apartments and cottage units that rent by the day, week or longer. Of course, you can stay in any room in any of these accommodations for a week or longer if you wish.

Modest, beachy cottages that offer comfort and convenience line the Beach Road from Kitty Hawk through South Nags Head. Many families and groups of friends also choose to rent some of the thousands of cottages along the Outer Banks for a week's vacation or longer. Companies that lease these properties are included in our Weekly and Long-term Cottage Rentals chapter.

If you're planning a summer stay on the Outer Banks you should call early for reservations. Most accommodations are filled to capacity from mid-June through August. Usually, you can find walk-in rooms during the week; however, if you know the exact week or weekend that you're planning to visit, your best bet is to go ahead and book a room now.

Locations are indicated by milepost and town. Most of the hotels, motels and inns are scattered along the Beach Road. A few line U.S. Highway 158, which is also called the Bypass. Roanoke and Ocracoke islands also have several tucked beneath the trees off the beaten paths. If you're looking for more privacy, we suggest you check out the Bed and Breakfast listings.

Rates vary dramatically from one area of the Outer Banks to another, from oceanfront rooms to those across the highway, between in- and off-season times and especially depending on the amenities offered with each unit. In general, fall, winter and early spring prices are at least one-third lower than mid-summer rates — sometimes as little as $25 per night. The most expensive season, of course, is between mid-June and mid-August, when rates in general range from $50 a night for two people with two double beds to more than $150 per night in some of the fancier establishments.

Many hotels and motels honor AARP and

other discounts, and children stay free with paying adults in many of these accommodations.

Price Code

For your ease in checking out price ranges, we've created a dollar-sign key showing a range of the average cost for a double-occupancy one-night stay in a room with two double beds during peak summer season. Extra charges may apply for special weekends, additional people in the room, efficiency apartments or pets. These prices do not include local and state taxes. Unless otherwise indicated in the listing, all accommodations accept major credit cards.

$	**$60 and less**
$$	**$60 to $80**
$$$	**$80 to $125**
$$$$	**$125 and more**

Many accommodations owners have decided to keep their doors open all year to cater to fall fishing parties, spring visitors and people who like the Outer Banks best in winter when few others are around. If you prefer isolation at the beach and don't mind wind and temperatures in the 40s and 50s, November through February would be a good time to come. September and October, however, are our favorite months. The ocean is still warm enough to swim in, the daytime temperature seldom drops below the mid-60s, most restaurants, attractions and retail shops are still open, yet the prices are much cheaper and most of the bustling feeling is gone once school starts up again.

Deposits and Check-In Times

Most motels and hotels require deposits to hold advance summer registration. Policies vary between properties, but the average amount is 25 percent to 35 percent of the total reservation cost or one night's rate. Ask about specific provisions when reserving your room, and call to confirm your reservations before leaving for the Outer Banks.

Many proprietors require the balance of your bill to be paid on arrival. Be prepared with cash, traveler's checks or a credit card. Personal checks often are not accepted for this final payment. Again, ask when booking your room. Automated teller machines (ATMs) also are available at most local banks.

Before making reservations, be sure to check on the cancellation or refund policies. If you are concerned there might be a hurricane brewing during your visit, ask about refund policies in case of evacuation.

Check-in times also vary among accommodations. Most places won't allow you into their rooms before 2 PM but can hold them for you until 10 or 11 PM if necessary. If you know you'll get here earlier, ask about early check-in provisions or go ahead and just spend that first morning out on the beach. Public showers are provided at some beach accesses, so you can clean off before getting into your hotel room. Several motels, inns and bed and breakfast establishments also offer outdoor showers for their guests. Check-out times in general are between 10 AM and noon. Sometimes, later stays can be accommodated. Ask if you know you'll want to linger that last day.

Locations and Amenities

In this chapter, oceanfront means that the property has at least some rooms facing the ocean right on the beach. Most of these units have balconies and picture windows. Rooms on the ground level or behind sand dunes, however, may not have views of the Atlantic, even if they're just off the sandy shore. Ask about what's available, and clarify which type of location you'd prefer. Remember, you'll almost always pay more to watch the waves from your room.

Conveniences and luxuries included in rooms at motels, hotels, inns, efficiencies and bed and breakfasts usually vary, even in the same structure. Some include kitchenettes, king-size beds and Jacuzzis. Others may have double beds and an extra sleeper sofa for the kids. All have air-conditioning, and places that

remain open in the fall and winter also include heat.

Many motels and hotels, especially the older beachfront structures and newer high-rise units, also have meeting facilities, conference rooms and large common areas to accommodate family reunions, business workshops and tour groups. Although most newer accommodations are handicapped-accessible, many of the older motels and hotels are partially accessible, or not at all. It is always a good idea when making your reservation to check that your particular needs can be met. Also, if you are a pet owner and want the pooch to vacation with you, your pickings are going to be much slimmer. Most motels and inns do not allow pets, so assume that pets are not permitted unless otherwise noted.

Amenities run the gamut from the most basic (bed and shower only) to places that provide microwaves, refrigerators, televisions with free movie channels or videocassette recorders, telephones, fluffy bathrobes, fancy soaps, free coffee, cocktails and afternoon tea, gourmet breakfasts, bicycles and golf clubs. A few hotels offer "big-city" advantages such as room service, assistance with luggage and wake-up calls — but most don't, so read the descriptions carefully if you require such services, and call ahead with other specific questions.

All Outer Banks accommodations provide free parking for at least one vehicle per unit. Keep valuables with you rather than leaving them locked in the car. Some hotels offer safes in the main office for their guests to stow valued items.

Many motel, hotel and inn managers will provide recreation packages with your room, especially during the off-season. For the most part, golf courses, tennis facilities and health clubs are open year round. Call about these special combinations, or ask the proprietor about special discounts that might be available to guests. Walk-in or weeklong memberships are offered at most private facilities. Some accommodations also include volleyball courts, horseshoe pits, picnic tables, gas grills and small putting greens on-site for their guests.

Area Profiles

Accommodations in the northern beaches are much more upscale than on the rest of the Outer Banks, although you'll find a few luxury inns and bed and breakfast inns in Kill Devil Hills, Nags Head, Roanoke Island and on Ocracoke too. Corolla only has one place that allows people to stay for a night at a time; Duck boasts two such establishments. All three are elegant and guaranteed to make guests feel comfortable and well cared for; however, most travelers who stay in these villages rent individual cottages by the week.

Nearly all accommodations in the northern beaches area are along the main artery, N.C. Highway 12, which is known as Ocean Trail in Corolla and Duck Road in Duck.

Kitty Hawk was one of the first Outer Banks beach towns to develop a tourist trade, and some of the hotels and motels there are reminiscent of the early cottage courts. These primarily family-run businesses are small, clean and often cheaper than nationally known hotels. There's also a Holiday Inn Express on U.S. Highway 158 and a bed and breakfast inn on a golf course west of the highway.

Kill Devil Hills is the most central — and most populated — place on the barrier islands. Many of its accommodations are in walking distance of restaurants, shopping and recreational attractions. Quaint motels with fewer than two dozen rooms are common here, while big chain establishments with conference centers and bellhops are just across the street. Public beach and sound accesses abound in this town.

The Outer Banks' first resort destination was Nags Head, so here you'll find everything from a 1930s-era inn to the tallest hotel on the Outer Banks. Some accommodations retain the old-timey feel of cedar-shake-shingled cottages, while others have gone for the ultra-

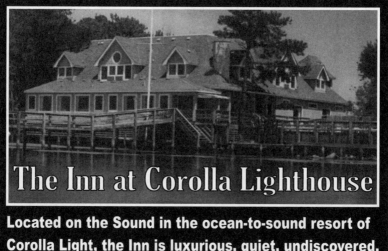
modern, multiple-floor look complete with elevators and room service from the in-house restaurant. Like Kill Devil Hills, but a lot more spread out and slightly less populated, Nags Head abounds with restaurants, retail shops and recreation.

Roanoke Island's accommodations range from modest cottage courts to fine, fabulous inns. Few are more than a bike ride away from the historic waterfront, and many are perfect for a romantic weekend getaway or cloistered honeymoon stay. Rental cottages aren't prevalent here because the large majority of the population, even in the summer, is made up of permanent residents; however, if you want to get away from the bustle of the beach and still be close to the sound, wetlands and wonderful historic attractions this island has to offer, you won't have difficulty finding a room to suit your tastes here.

Motels and hotels on Hatteras Island are, in general, more laid-back than on other parts of the barrier islands. There are now two national chains on the island (one in Buxton and one in Hatteras), but family-owned and operated places still dominate the accommodations here. Many of these units are no-frills without phones in the rooms or fancy furnishings, but if you're looking for an affordable place to stay along quieter stretches of beach, don't overlook Hatteras Island's short-term room, inn and efficiency options.

Ocracoke Island's lodgings are, in general, the most personal on the Outer Banks. Here, you'll find old inns, newer motels, upscale bed and breakfast inns, efficiency apart-

INSIDERS' TIP

Plan ahead to avoid getting caught in traffic on "turnover" day when visitors make a mass exodus off the islands. If you leave long before or after check-out times, traffic will be much lighter.

Photo: Courtesy of J. Aaron Trotman

Nothing beats a day at the beach.

ments and even a few folks who will rent you a room in their house, sometimes right next to their own. This laid-back little island is separated from the rest of the world by free ferryboat rides (see our Getting Here, Getting Around chapter). It's a great place to escape from it all. There are also plenty of accommodations, quaint boutiques and great restaurants to please almost anyone here.

Corolla

The Inn at Corolla Lighthouse
**$$$$ • 1066 Ocean Tr., Corolla
• (252) 453-3340, (888) 546-6705**
The Inn at Corolla Lighthouse is a luxurious place where guests can plan their days around an incredible array of recreational activities available nearly at their doorstep — or they may wish simply to relax in full view of the sparkling waters of Currituck Sound and bask in the serenity of this beautifully appointed facility.

The year-round inn opened during the 1995 season in the ocean-to-sound resort community of Corolla Light. The upscale development is laced with wooded walking and biking trails and offers every leisure amenity a vacationer could dream of: an indoor sports center with an Olympic-size pool, hot tub, saunas, clay

tennis courts, racquetball courts and fitness equipment; an oceanfront complex that boasts two outdoor pools, a video game room, restaurant and exclusive access to the beach; play areas for basketball, shuffleboard, tennis, horseshoes and more; and terrific shops and restaurants nearby (see our Shopping and Restaurants chapters). Guests of the inn have unlimited access to all of the resort's facilities. There is a nominal fee for use of the indoor tennis courts, but all other courts are free.

Guests may also use the inn's own soundfront swimming pool, hot tub and private 400-foot pier on Currituck Sound. The inn furnishes bicycles to guests so they can take leisurely tours of the resort's landscaped grounds.

Sailing excursions, guided kayak trips, windsurfing, parasailing and personal watercraft (Jet Skis, Waverunners and others) are available at a watersports rental site on the resort. A championship golf course is also nearby. Ask about new tour packages that arrange for you to stay at multiple Outer Banks inns. Each participating property cooperates to create a mutually beneficial arrangement where you can enjoy your favorite activities at different Outer Banks locales without having to make separate reservations. The tours will focus on lighthouses, birdwatching or bicycling. Other available tours include horseback riding on the beach and an off-road adventure that encompasses a historic tour of Corolla.

The inn's 41 guest rooms include kitchenettes, cable TVs, radios, VCRs and private baths. Many also have fireplaces and whirlpool tubs. The rooms are designed for single or double occupancy, and many are equipped with sleeper sofas too. Guests can enjoy a free continental breakfast daily.

The Inn at Corolla Lighthouse has a two-night minimum stay on weekends and charges $15 per night for each additional person. Special rate packages are offered throughout the year. Be sure to call their toll-free number for more information.

Duck

Sanderling Inn Resort
$$$$ • 1461 Duck Rd., Duck
• (252) 261-4111, (800) 701-4111

The Sanderling Inn Resort is situated on 12 acres of oceanside wilderness about 5 miles north of Duck Village. Here, heavy strands of beach grass, sea oats, pines, fragrant olives and live oaks provide a natural setting for an elegant, enjoyable vacation. The Sanderling was built in the style of the old Nags Head beach homes with wood siding, cedar-shake accents, dormer windows and porches on each side. Rocking chairs line the wide porches, providing a relaxing way to pass sultry afternoons while overlooking the ocean or sound.

All 87 rooms at the Sanderling are comfortable, lush and oh-so-accommodating. The inn provides all its guests with lounging robes, luxury soaps, toiletries and a welcome gift featuring North Carolina products. A continental breakfast and afternoon tea also come with each room.

The main lobby and gallery of the Sanderling offer a warm welcome to weary travelers. Decorated in an English country theme, they're adorned with contemporary finishes and accented by polished wood floors and wainscotting. The inn's main building has 29 rooms, all with kitchenettes. Audubon prints and artwork line the walls. Another 32 rooms in Sanderling Inn North are filled with wicker furniture and equipped with a refrigerator and wet bar. The 26 rooms in the newest South Wing each have a king-size bed, wet bar, refrigerator and a microwave. Six of the units in the South Wing are deluxe suites that feature two televisions with VCRs (one in the bedroom and one in the living area), a double sleeper sofa and a stereo with compact disc player (1½ baths). Some suites also have Jacuzzis. All Sanderling rooms have telephones and televisions with remote control and cable.

Accommodations here are designed for the comfort and privacy of two guests per room, but sleeper sofas and cribs are available for an additional charge.

A separate building at the Sanderling houses excellent conference and meeting facilities including the Presidential Suite, complete with Jacuzzi bath, steam shower and two decks — one overlooks the ocean and the other overlooks the sound. For an additional charge, the inn's housekeeping staff provides laundry service with a 48-hour turnaround. Room service is provided by the on-site, upscale Sanderling Inn Restaurant (see our Restaurants chapter).

This is a complete resort with private beaches, a health club with expansive exercise rooms, an indoor pool, a separate whirlpool room, locker rooms, saunas, an outdoor pool, tennis courts and a natural walking or jogging trail. The Audubon Wildlife Sanctuary and Pine Island Tennis and Racquet Club are nearby. A seasonal outdoor pavilion and three three-bedroom houses were also recently added to Sanderling's already extraordinary offerings.

Full package deals are available for New Year's Eve, Valentine's Day, honeymoons and winter escapes. Packages generally include one or more meals at the Sanderling Inn Restaurant, full use of the health club and indoor pool, welcoming gifts and other extras. Some seasonal discounts are available. Weekend guests must stay both Friday and Saturday nights during the summer, and a three-day minimum stay is required for in-season holidays. Wheelchair access is provided for all buildings on the property, and handicapped-accessible rooms are available. The Sanderling Inn is open year round.

Photo: Courtesy of J. Aaron Trotman

The Currituck Lighthouse is a great place to view the beautiful scenery of the Outer Banks.

Advice 5¢

$$$$ • 111 Scarborough Ln., Duck
• (252) 255-1050, (800) 238-4235

Starting its fourth season in 1998 as the only bed and breakfast north of Kitty Hawk, Advice 5¢ offers four guest rooms and one suite and exudes an air of casual simplicity. Here, Nancy Caviness and Donna Black provide all their guests with private baths, rocking chairs and decks. The suite also includes cable TV, a stereo and Jacuzzi bath. Hardwood floors and juniper appointments, comfy Lexington cottage furniture, ceiling fans, quilts, colorful bath towels, linens and greenery galore lend this idyllic beach getaway a crisp, unaffected atmosphere. Just three-tenths of a mile from the ocean, this sunny, spacious bed and breakfast has beautiful views of both sea and sound.

A common area with a fireplace for those chilly off-season evenings is a popular gathering spot for guests. A continental breakfast buffet of fresh fruit salad and just-baked breads and muffins is served daily in the common room. Afternoon tea tempts guests with more homemade delights as well as hot and cold beverages. At day's end, or when the weather doesn't cooperate, you can try your hand at a puzzle or round up some folks for an intense game of Scrabble. If quieter pursuits are what you crave, the den on the guest floor level is the perfect place to delve into one of a variety of good books available here.

Two outdoor showers allow beachgoers to wash off after a long day in the sun. A locking storage shed also provides protected shelter out of the elements for storing bicycles, Boogie Boards, golf clubs and other gear. An in-ground pool across the street and tennis courts are available for guests.

All rooms at this establishment are nonsmoking. It is not accessible to the handicapped, and young children cannot be accommodated here. Advice 5¢ is open year round.

Kitty Hawk

3 Seasons Bed & Breakfast

$$$$ • off U.S. Hwy. 158, MP 2, Kitty Hawk • (252) 261-4791, (800) 847-3373

This bed and breakfast inn is tucked away from the ocean and highways at Sea-

...find a place to call home

Advice 5¢

a bed & breakfast

"life's too short to wear tight shoes"

Scarborough Lane in Duck

for reservations, (800) 238-4235
www.theouterbanks.com/advice5

scape Golf Course on the west side of the Bypass. Golf enthusiasts find this location ideal: The putting green is in front of the property, and the 9th hole is behind it. You barely have to get out of bed before bellowing, "Fore!"

Just two-and-a-half blocks from the ocean, 3 Seasons sits on a high sandhill, so guests can enjoy views of the Atlantic. Even if you've never swung a 9-iron, you'll enjoy unwinding and relaxing at this charming establishment. Susie and Tommy Gardner have been operating the bed and breakfast since 1992. It's a five-bedroom house, and four of the rooms are available for double occupancy. Each guest room has a private bath and TV. The decor feels like home — comfortable and "beachy." Guests can gather around a fireplace in the common area or take in the ocean breezes off the canopied deck. The Jacuzzi on the deck also creates a big splash. A tennis court and a swimming pool are available for guests to enjoy.

Complimentary cocktails are served afternoons on the enclosed patio. Guests can also enjoy a full breakfast cooked to order daily between 8 and 10 AM. Bicycles are available for a ride to the beach or along trails nearby. The entire establishment is nonsmoking, although smoking on the outdoor deck is fine. Note that 3 Seasons is not equipped to accommodate children younger than 18 or the handicapped. Two-night stays are required on summer weekends, and a three-day minimum is requested for holiday weekends. This quaint inn is open March through November.

Outer Banks International Hostel
$ • 1004 W. Kitty Hawk Rd., Kitty Hawk • (252) 261-2294

The only hostel on these barrier islands, the Outer Banks International Hostel opened its doors in April 1996 and has made it possible for travelers on a budget to enjoy their stay in comfortable, clean accommodations that won't break the bank. The former elementary school building is nestled on 10 acres in Kitty Hawk Village not far from where the Wright Brothers visited. As part of Hostelling International American Youth Hostels, this facility is a year-round, very inexpensive no-frills operation — and there are no curfews or chores in the deal. You're just expected to clean up after yourself. All ages are welcome, and a friendly staff is on hand to help you plan your stay on the Outer Banks.

Amenities include shared kitchen facilities, a common lounge area with cable TV and books, a barbecue and campfire area and a large front porch with Adirondack chairs. Guests can choose from sleeping in separate male and female dormitories with four beds per room or couple/private and family/group rooms. Private rooms with private baths are available. Sheets and towels, bikes, canoes and kayaks can be rented here. Boogie Boards, surfboards, fishing gear and beach chairs are also available to rent. Guests are welcome to enjoy basketball hoops, croquet and boccie ball in the spacious yard. Volleyball, badminton, tennis and shuffleboard are other fun options.

As veteran international travelers already know, hostels are reputed to be safe, friendly places where it's easy to meet other adventurers like yourself. The Outer Banks International Hostel is as affordable as you get on the barrier islands, and you can have a pleasant, memorable stay to boot. Rooms cost $15 a night for Hostelling International members. Call for other rates. Reservations are required for groups. There is an additional charge for a private room with a private bath. Children younger than 12 are charged half-price.

Sea Kove Motel
$$$, no credit cards • N.C. Hwy. 12, MP 3, Kitty Hawk • (252) 261-4722

This family-owned and -operated establishment rents 10 one-bedroom efficiency units, 10 two-bedroom units and one cottage by the week only from April through November. It's across from the ocean and includes full-size kitchens and televisions in each apartment. A playground and outdoor pool also are available.

Beach Haven Motel
$$$ • N.C Hwy 12, MP 4, Kitty Hawk • (252) 261-4785

This small motel sits across the road from its own private beach and includes two buildings with a total of six semi-efficiency units. Owner Joe Verscharen makes sure his motel provides guests all they need for a peaceful and relaxing stay. A practical, homey atmosphere prevails at this motel, where each room has a refrigerator, microwave, hair dryer, cable TV, telephone and porch chairs. Coffee is provided in each room at this uniquely groomed establishment, which Verscharen boasts has earned a Grade A cleanliness rating year after year from the Dare County Health Department.

Beach Haven is in uncrowded surroundings with natural beach landscaping that will remind visitors of a lovely oasis. Guests can loll on the elevated deck and enjoy the scenery. A grass-carpeted picnic area with tables and a gas grill are on the premises. You can practice your classic stroke on a putting green situated on the cashmere lawn, where you might also show off your talents in a game of croquet.

Economy rooms sleep two people, and deluxe rooms can accommodate up to four guests. Cribs are provided for infants. The decor throughout reflects a contemporary beach look with rattan and wicker furniture. Joe lives at the motel and promises to make your stay as pleasant as possible. Beach Haven is open late March through mid-November.

Holiday Inn Express
$$$ • U.S. Hwy. 158, MP 4¼, Kitty Hawk • (252) 261-4888, (800) 836-2753

Situated on the east side of U.S. 158, Holiday Inn Express has an outdoor swimming pool and is a short walk to life-guarded

Silver Lake Inn & Motel

New Victorian Suites with Hot Tubs

Nestled in a grove of oaks overlooking Silver Lake.
Enjoy the spectacular view from our Lounge.

The Silver Lake Inn & Motel is a family operation.
"We do truly care!"

For reservation call:
(252) 928-5721

P.O. Box 303
Ocracoke, NC 27960

Kitty Hawk Beach, where guests can use the motel's private access and oceanfront deck. All the motel's 98 rooms are spacious and have cable TV, telephones and refrigerators. Some also have couches, and half have microwaves. Most offer two double beds and some rooms have queen beds. All are attractively furnished in soft beach decor.

The inn provides a complimentary continental breakfast bar for guests each morning in the lobby. Nonsmoking and handicapped-accessible rooms are available at this Holiday Inn Express. Children 17 and younger stay free if accompanied by an adult. Meeting rooms accommodate up to 10 people, and year-round group rates are available. This motel is in walking distance to shopping and several restaurants. It's open all year.

Buccaneer Motel and Beach Suites
$$ • N.C. Hwy. 12, MP 5½, Kitty Hawk • (252) 261-2030, (800) 442-4412

Repeat business is the name of the game at the Buccaneer, where folks who stayed here as teenagers are now bringing their grandkids for visits. New owners Sandy and Dave Briggman have fostered the authentic Outer Banks charm that's made the Buccaneer a place vacationers come back to year after year. Travelers have their choice of one- and two-bedroom units, and efficiency apartments with one to four bedrooms are avail-

INSIDERS' TIP

When hurricanes threaten the Outer Banks, Ocracoke Island is evacuated up to 36 hours earlier than the rest of the barrier beaches. There are no bridges to this island, and visitors' safety on the ferries is the prime concern of emergency managers.

able for those wishing to stay longer. Each unit has a refrigerator, cable TV and a microwave.

While the Buccaneer is across the highway from the beach, there are no other buildings between it and the ocean, and guests only have to cross a small sand dune to reach the surf. A dune-top deck and private beach access make enjoying the Atlantic from this accommodation almost as easy as if the motel were on the ocean. Other amenities provided include a large, outdoor swimming pool with adjoining deck; a children's playground; basketball and volleyball courts; a horseshoe pit; charcoal grills and a fish-cleaning station. Ten percent discounts are offered on all weekly stays, and AARP and other discounts are honored during the off-season. The motel is not handicapped-accessible. The Buccaneer is open year round.

Kill Devil Hills

Tan-a-Rama Motel Apartments
$$$ • N.C. Hwy. 12, MP 6, Kill Devil Hills • (252) 441-7315

Two regular motel rooms and 33 one- and two-bedroom efficiency units are offered at this oceanside motel. Most of the rooms are oceanfront, and all have been newly renovated. Four upstairs oceanfront suites each include a separate bedroom with two double beds, a sitting room with a double bed and a full kitchen. Oceanfront and courtside efficiencies have two double beds plus a sitting room and kitchen. Phones and cable TVs are provided in all units.

Guests of the Tan-a-Rama will enjoy its outdoor pool, and the kids will love the new playground. The Avalon Fishing Pier is on the north side of this motel, so there are plenty of recreation possibilities nearby. Kids 6 and younger stay free here. This motel is open year round.

Days Inn Mariner Motel
$$$ • N.C. Hwy. 12, MP 7, Kill Devil Hills • (252) 441-2021, (800) 325-2525

A total of 70 units — 58 of which are on the ocean — comprise the accommodations here: 33 offer two double beds in a single room and 37 are one- and two-bedroom apartments with complete kitchens. Each room and apartment includes a telephone, refrigerator and cable TV. All the rooms were also refurbished recently with a fresh, contemporary beach look.

There's easy access to the Atlantic, and the units are spacious enough to offer flexible living arrangements for families or groups. This motel's recreation area has facilities for volleyball, and an outdoor swimming pool and showers are just off the ocean. Nonsmoking and handicapped-accessible rooms are available. All Days Inn programs are honored, and AARP discounts are available. The Mariner is

open mid-February through November, with rates discounted by 50 percent in the off-season.

Quality Inn Sea Ranch Hotel
$$$$ • N.C. Hwy. 12, MP 7, Kill Devil Hills • (252) 441-7126, (800) 334-4737

The Sea Ranch was one of the Outer Banks' first resort properties to include recreational amenities, a restaurant, lounge and retail shops. This hotel is family-owned and operated, with a five-story oceanfront tower and a two-story building that contains 50 motel-style rooms and 28 luxury apartments with full kitchens. Each unit has a cable TV and HBO, a refrigerator, microwave and telephone. The apartments have glass-enclosed oceanfront balconies, two bedrooms and two baths. They typically rent weekly, but some also can be rented nightly depending on occupancy. About 25 of the hotel rooms have oceanfront views. Nonsmoking rooms are available, and the hotel is handicapped-accessible.

Amenities at the Sea Ranch include room service (a rare find on the Outer Banks) from the hotel's upscale restaurant, Third Street Oceanfront Grille (see our Restaurants chapter). The lounge has a dance floor and nightly entertainment (see our Nightlife chapter). If you're in the mood for exercise, the Sea Ranch has a heated indoor pool that's open year round on the premises, and across the road is a recently expanded Nautilus fitness center frequented by both locals and visitors. A women's boutique and hair salon also are on-site (see our Shopping chapter). The Sea Ranch is open all year.

The Chart House Motel
$$$ • N.C. Hwy. 12, MP 7, Kill Devil Hills • (252) 441-7418

With an eye-catching blue mural depicting dolphins dancing through the waves painted on the front of this building, you can't miss the Chart House Motel. David and Kristin Clark, the hosts of this 18-unit motel live in the large oceanfront brick Colonial beside it, close enough to offer their personal touch. Built in

1966, the Chart House is a popular spot with six efficiency apartments and 12 motel rooms. Each unit has two double beds, a color TV, a telephone, refrigerator, microwave and coffee maker. The one-room efficiencies also have fully equipped kitchens, and five of these units connect with regular motel rooms to accommodate larger groups and families. Nonsmoking rooms are available. This motel is not equipped for the handicapped.

The Chart House sits perpendicular to the ocean, so direct ocean views are not available. A small pool and patio are away from the road. The Outer Banks Nautilus & Athletic Club (see our Recreation chapter) is across the street, and two local favorite restaurants are also in walking distance: the Jolly Roger and Goombays (see our Restaurants chapter). The motel is open mid-March through November.

Nettlewood Motel
$-$$ • N.C. Hwy. 12, MP 7, Kill Devil Hills • (252) 441-5039

Locally owned and operated for 23 years, the Nettlewood is a favorite of the older set who like to come to the beach in small groups and who appreciate a small, clean motel. The Nettlewood has 22 rooms with one or two double beds and 16 efficiency units with two double beds and complete kitchens. All rooms have refrigerators, telephones and color TVs

with remote controls and cable. Rooms rent by the day during the week, but three-night minimum stays are required during summer weekends.

Across the street, four 1,500-square-foot apartments each offer three bedrooms and two baths and can accommodate up to eight people. These larger units rent weekly. There's also a large in-ground swimming pool on-site for guests. The Nettlewood is open year round.

Nags Head Beach Hotel
$$$$ • N.C. Hwy. 12, MP 8, Kill Devil Hills • (252) 441-0411, (800) 338-7761

This 97-room, four-story hotel has exterior and interior corridors and was recently renovated inside and out. It's across the street from the ocean, so some guest rooms here have views of the Atlantic, while others afford glimpses of the Wright Brothers National Memorial. Twelve of the first-floor guest rooms open directly onto the outdoor courtyard and pool.

Each room has a microwave, refrigerator, color TV with remote control, cable and free HBO, a telephone and private balcony or patio, with nonsmoking and handicapped-accessible rooms available. A complimentary continental breakfast featuring cereals, pastries, juices, coffee, tea and fresh fruits is served daily in the lobby from 6 until 10 AM. Discounts are available to AARP members. Children 18 and younger stay free in their parents' room, and pets are welcome for a $5 per day additional charge. During summer holidays, three-night minimum stays are required. The Nags Head Beach Hotel is open all year.

Comfort Inn North
$$$$ • N.C. Hwy. 12, MP 8, Kill Devil Hills • (252) 480-2600, (800) 854-5286

Only nine years old and one of the newer oceanfront motels on the Outer Banks, this three-story property includes 121 rooms that open along exterior corridors. They're filled with natural light and decorated tastefully. The building is T-shaped, so not all rooms have views of the Atlantic; however, oceanfront units also offer private balconies.

Some rooms at this Comfort Inn have refrigerators and microwaves, while most have full baths, cable TV and HBO, telephones and coffee makers. Nonsmoking and handicapped-accessible rooms are available. Guests here can enjoy the hotel's oceanfront pool. Other amenities include a game room and coin-operated laundry facilities on-site. A complimentary breakfast is provided. Children 18 and younger stay free with an adult. A three-night minimum stay is required on summer holiday weekends. Managers honor AARP discounts. The Comfort Inn is open all year.

Cherokee Inn Bed and Breakfast
$$$ • N.C. Hwy. 12, MP 8, Kill Devil Hills • (252) 441-6127, (800) 554-2764

This historic bed and breakfast inn owned by Kaye and Bob Combs was originally operated as a hunting and fishing lodge. The house still has the cozy feel exuded by the original tongue-and-groove cypress. Just 500 feet from the beach, the Cherokee has been operated as an inn for the past 21 years and has been a bed and breakfast for the last 11 years. If you stay here, you'll learn about your lodging's history from its second-generation proprietors

Cherokee Inn

Bed and Breakfast
Only 500 Feet From Beach!
500 N. Virginia Dare Trail, M.P. 8
Kill Devil Hills, N.C. 27948
(800) 554-2764
http://www.chaela.com/cherokeeinn

who are surrounded by four generations of family just a short distance away.

Six guest rooms are available on the second floor of this three-story building. Wicker furniture and floral accents in each room help create a bright, homey atmosphere. All units include private baths, remote color TVs and ceiling fans, and there is central air conditioning. Five of the rooms offer queen-size beds, and one room has a queen and a twin bed. Although telephones aren't in each room, there is a phone in the first-floor common area that's reserved for inn guests. A wraparound porch with picnic table, swings and lounge chairs allows guests to catch cool ocean breezes during the heat of summer.

A continental breakfast is included in room rates. Bicycles, beach chairs and an outdoor shower are available for all guests. No smoking is allowed in this inn. In July and August, two-night minimum stays are required on weekends. The Cherokee Inn Bed and Breakfast is open April through October.

The Tanglewood
$$$$ • N.C. Hwy. 12, MP 8¼, Kill Devil Hills • (252) 441-7208

This family-oriented motel has an outdoor

swimming pool, a boardwalk to the ocean with a deck for sunbathing and an enclosed outdoor bathhouse with hot and cold water for a relaxing shower after a day at the beach. Other amenities include a fish-cleaning station, picnic tables and grills. The Tanglewood is open March through November. Weekly rentals are preferred during the summer; daily rentals are also available.

Cavalier Motel

$$$ • N.C. Hwy. 12, MP 8½, Kill Devil Hills • (252) 441-5584

A variety of rooms is available at this court-yard motel on the oceanfront. Three one-story wings enclose the two swimming pools, a volleyball court, children's play area and shuffleboard courts. The Cavalier has 40 rooms with double and single beds and six one-room efficiency units with two double beds and kitchenettes right on the beach. Some rooms have full baths, while others just have shower stalls. All are equipped with telephones, refrigerators, microwaves, cable TV and free HBO.

Besides these units, the motel offers 13 cottages that rent by the week. Pets are allowed in the cottages only. There is some handicapped access here, and ramps are on the premises.

Parking is available outside each room, and the covered porch with outdoor furniture is just right for relaxing with a free cup of coffee while watching the sunrise. An observation deck sits atop the oceanfront section. This is a well-maintained, family-oriented property and is reasonably priced for daily or weekend rentals. Children 5 and younger stay for free in their parents' rooms. The Cavalier Motel is open year round.

Days Inn Oceanfront Wilbur & Orville Wright

$$$ • N.C. Hwy. 12, MP 8½, Kill Devil Hills • (252) 441-7211, (800) 329-7466

An oceanfront property on a wide stretch of beach, this facility opened as an Outer Banks motel in 1948. It was built to resemble an old mountain lodge and offers an inviting lobby decorated in the nostalgia of Old Nags Head where guests can read the newspaper and sip a cup of free coffee. The room is further enhanced by Oriental rugs on polished hardwood floors and a fireplace large enough to take away the chill on cold beach evenings during the off-season.

Guests here enjoy balconies with old-fashioned furniture and nice views. All 52 rooms have been renovated and furnished with 1990s decor. There are singles, doubles, kings, king suites and efficiency units that sleep six and include a living room, adjoining bedroom and complete kitchen. All rooms have telephones, cable TV and refrigerators. Oceanfront rooms also have microwaves. Nonsmoking and handicapped-accessible rooms are available. The hotel has interior and exterior corridors, and suites have entrances to both.

A complimentary continental breakfast is available throughout the year. Hot apple cider and popcorn are served around the fireplace during the winter, and lemonade and cookies are served in the summer. Leisure amenities include a large outdoor pool, sun deck, volleyball court, barbecue pit for cookouts and a boardwalk to the beach.

Children 12 and younger stay for free here. AARP discounts also are honored. There's a three-night minimum stay for summer holiday weekends, and Saturday check-ins aren't allowed unless you plan to stay for a week. Daily and weeklong rentals are available throughout the year.

Best Western Ocean Reef Suites

$$$$ • N.C. Hwy. 12, MP 8½, Kill Devil Hills • (252) 441-1611, (800) 528-1234

All 70 one-bedroom suites in this newer oceanfront hotel are decorated and arranged like luxury apartments with a contemporary beach decor. The views are great, and you'll find everything you need for a truly luxurious beach vacation. Each room has a telephone, cable TV, free coffee and a fully equipped galley-style kitchen. The bath area has a double vanity.

Nonsmoking and handicapped-accessible rooms are available. Upper-floor rooms have private balconies overlooking the ocean. Some first-floor units open onto the oceanfront pool and courtyard, while others offer a private patio. The Ocean Reef is one of the few facilities on the beach to have a penthouse suite; this one boasts a private Jacuzzi and rooftop deck.

A heated, seasonal outdoor pool and a whirlpool are available to guests in the courtyard, and the exercise room features the latest equip-

ment and a sauna. Other amenities include a laundry facility on the premises and year-round bar and food service available at Crocker's. Children 17 and younger stay free with adults here. A two-day minimum stay is required on summer weekends. Ocean Reef is open all year.

Colony IV Motel
$$$ • N.C. Hwy. 12, MP 8½, Kill Devil Hills • (252) 441-5581, (800) 848-3728

This modern family-owned and -operated oceanfront motel is well-maintained and offers lots of amenities. Managers Cindy and Tom Kingsbury provide ample hospitality for moderate prices as well as an outdoor heated pool with a Jacuzzi and patio, a nine-hole miniature golf course, two picnic areas with grills, a children's playground, a dune-top gazebo, a video game room, horseshoe pits, a private beach with lifeguard and other outdoor activities. A complimentary continental breakfast is served every morning. Laundry facilities are available on the premises.

The motel has 87 units, 14 of which are efficiencies. Most offer two double beds, although rooms with king-size beds are also available. Telephones, refrigerators, microwaves, TV with remote control and cable and clock radios are provided in each unit. Some rooms have direct access to the beach, while others have a small balcony overlooking the ocean. The efficiencies have an eating area

and, when combined with adjoining rooms, create a good arrangement for family vacationers. Nonsmoking units are available.

Children 12 and younger stay free here. Discounts of 10 percent are provided for AARP and active military members. The motel is also handicapped-accessible. A three-night minimum stay is required on summer weekends. The Colony IV Motel is open February through November.

Budget Host Inn
$$$ • U.S. Hwy. 158, MP 9, Kill Devil Hills • (252) 441-2503, (800) BUD-HOST

This motel is on the Bypass, about two blocks from the ocean. All 40 rooms are tastefully furnished and well-maintained, with either king-size beds or extra-length double beds. Each unit has a telephone, cable TV and tub/shower combination. Refrigerators and microwaves are available upon request. The lobby also has a guest refrigerator, microwave and a coin-operated laundry room.

The entire second floor of the inn has been made into a nonsmoking, no pets floor. Handicapped-accessible rooms are also available here. The motel offers two family rooms that sleep six to eight people comfortably. The property maintains an indoor heated pool for year-round use, and a small picnic area is just south of the motel. Free coffee and tea are available in the lobby each day. Pets are accepted. Cribs are provided free of charge, and children 16 and younger stay free with an adult. The Budget Host Inn is open year round.

First Flight Inn
$$ • N.C. Hwy. 12, MP 9, Kill Devil Hills • (252) 441-5007

Of the 55 units at this oceanfront inn, 15 are efficiency apartments. Most have two double beds per room, and five have one double bed. Each room has cable TV and a refrigerator. Microwaves are available in 32 rooms. Although telephones aren't in each guest room, there are two pay phones on the premises. This is a family-oriented inn with an outdoor swimming pool and deck, fish-cleaning station and outdoor showers. You can also count on free coffee brewing in the office from 8 AM to 10 AM each morning. Children 12 and younger stay free. On summer holiday weekends, there's a three-day minimum stay. First Flight Inn is open from April through October.

See Sea Motel
$$ • N.C. Hwy. 12, MP 9, Kill Devil Hills • (252) 441-7321

A small, family-run motel across the street from the ocean, See Sea offers 20 rental units, including 11 motel rooms, five efficiencies, three two-bedroom apartments and one three-bedroom cottage. The motel rooms and efficiencies rent by the day (the apartments and cottage require a one-week minimum stay in season). All units have a refrigerator, telephone and cable television. There's also a pay phone on the premises. A coin-operated laundry is on-site and free coffee is provided.

Amenities here include an outdoor swimming pool, fish-cleaning facility, fish freezers, a picnic area and gas grill. Nonsmoking rooms are offered, and children 14 and younger stay free. See Sea Motel is open from March through December.

The Anchorage
$$ • N.C. Hwy. 12, MP 9, Kill Devil Hills • (252) 441-7226

All 17 units at this oceanfront motel include full kitchens and cable TV. There are nine efficiencies that rent by the day or week all four

seasons. Eight cottages rent only by the week during the summer. Pets are accepted here. The Anchorage is open year round.

Holiday Inn
$$$$ • N.C. Hwy. 12, MP 9½, Kill Devil Hills • (252) 441-6333, (800) 843-1249

This oceanfront hotel has 105 rooms, many with spectacular ocean views. Banquet and conference facilities here can accommodate 10 to 300 people. An on-site restaurant and lounge provide room service (see our Restaurants chapter), and guests can use the on-site video arcade game room and coin-operated laundry. An outdoor pool and Jacuzzi are other features.

All rooms include telephones, cable TV with remote, microwaves and refrigerators. This Holiday Inn has two nonsmoking floors and handicapped-accessible rooms. Children 18 and younger stay free here, and AARP members receive a 10 percent discount. Weekends require three-night minimum stays during summer. The Holiday Inn is open all year.

Ramada Inn at Nags Head Beach
$$$$ • N.C. Hwy 12, MP 9½, Kill Devil Hills • (252) 441-2151, (800) 635-1824

This five-story, 172-room oceanfront hotel was built in 1985. It's popular with tour groups and hosts many meetings throughout the year. All rooms have balconies or patios, cable TV with pay-per-view movies, small refrigerators and microwaves. Bellhop and room service are available here. Nonsmoking, handicapped-accessible and pet rooms are offered. Meeting facilities are on the fourth floor overlooking the ocean. Several suites are available to fit a variety of conference and workshop needs.

For guests, an indoor swimming pool and Jacuzzi are just off the second floor atop the dunes and surrounded by a large sun deck. A flight of steps takes you onto the beach where volleyball is a popular pastime. Food and beverage services are available at the oceanfront Gazebo Deck bar adjacent to the pool.

Peppercorns, the hotel's fine oceanview restaurant, serves breakfast and dinner year round and offers lunch on the deck during the summer (see our Restaurants chapter). The Ramada Inn is open all year.

Tanya's Ocean House Motel
$$$ • N.C. Hwy. 12, MP 9½, Kill Devil Hills • (252) 441-2900

This seaside motel is an Outer Banks legend offering unique, individually designed accommodations the owners call Carolina Collection Rooms. Legend has it that original owner, Tanya Young, and a designer friend decided to do a theme room at the motel. Their ideas got a little out of hand, and they ended up selecting separate themes for each room. There's the Carolina Party Room, Jonathan Seagull's Nest and dozens more. No two rooms at this motel are alike.

Tanya's has 47 rooms, including a few normal rooms that have been converted back from the original designs over the years. All units have refrigerators and cable TV with HBO. Oceanfront rooms also offer microwaves. Telephones are not provided.

Guests here can enjoy a 40-foot outdoor pool surrounded by umbrella-shaded picnic tables. Free coffee is provided throughout the day. During summer, there's a two-night minimum stay on weekends. The seventh night is free if you stay a week. Children younger than 18 stay free at this motel, and AARP discounts are honored. Tanya's is open April through mid-October.

Miller's Outer Banks Motor Lodge
$$$ • N.C. Hwy. 12, MP 9½, Kill Devil Hills • (252) 441-7404

An oceanfront motel with 30 efficiency units and eight regular rooms, Miller's Outer Banks Motor Lodge only rents its oceanfront units by the week during the peak season. Other units, however, can be occupied by the day. Each room has cable TV, a refrigerator and microwave. Handicapped-accessible units are available. Also on-site are a washer and dryer, a playground, an outdoor swimming pool, and a restaurant. Children 9 and younger stay free here. Miller's is open from February through November.

Quality Inn John Yancey
$$$$ • N.C. Hwy. 12, MP 10, Kill Devil Hills • (252) 441-7141, (800) 367-5941

This family hotel is on a wide beach that's lifeguarded during the summer. Shuffleboard courts, an outdoor heated pool and a playground are on the premises.

The hotel has 107 rooms, most of them doubles, housed in three buildings. The oceanfront units each have balconies or patios so you can watch and hear the waves from your room. Cable TV with optional in-room movies, small refrigerators and telephones are in each room. Ten units also offer microwaves, five have fully equipped kitchens and three include hot tubs. Coffee makers and coffee are provided in all rooms. About half of the rooms are nonsmoking, and there are handicapped-accessible units.

Another feature here is a coin-operated laundry. VCRs, movies and free coffee are available in the lobby. This Quality Inn has 24-hour front desk and maintenance service, a rare find on the Outer Banks. Children 12 and younger stay free, and you can rent rollaway beds to accommodate additional kids. A two-night minimum stay is required on summer weekends. AARP and other discounts are honored. The Quality Inn John Yancey is open all year.

The Ebb Tide
$$ • N.C. Hwy. 12, MP 10½, Kill Devil Hills • (252) 441-4913

The ocean is just across the road from this family-run motel, which has 34 rooms with refrigerators, microwaves and cable TV. Three seaside apartments across the street are right on the beach. Handicapped-accessible rooms are available. Guests have full use of the outdoor pool, picnic table and restaurant on the premises. Children younger than 12 stay free. The Ebb Tide is open from mid-March until early October.

Nags Head

Ocean Veranda Motel
$$$-$$$$ • N.C. Hwy. 12, MP 10½, Nags Head • (252) 441-5858, (800) 58BEACH

A well-maintained oceanfront property, Ocean Veranda offers 16 standard rooms, 14 efficiencies and one honeymoon suite with a king-size, canopy waterbed. Standard rooms are large and have two double beds, refrigerators and cable TV. Nonsmoking rooms are available. Efficiencies have complete kitchens with microwaves and coffee makers and can adjoin other rooms to accommodate larger families of up to five people. Rollaways and cribs are available for a small charge. Some rooms on the second level offer partial ocean views.

Complimentary morning coffee is offered in the office. Other amenities include an outdoor pool and two gazebos, horseshoe pits, a children's playground, picnic area and barbecue grill. Children younger than 6 stay free. A small charge for extra persons in the rooms is applicable. Ocean Veranda is open January through November.

Beacon Motor Lodge
$$$ • N.C. Hwy. 12 MP 10¾, Nags Head
• (252) 441-5501, (800) 441-4804

Visitors will find lots of options for seasonal and off-season stays at this family-oriented, comfortable oceanfront lodge. The James family has owned the 47-room Beacon Motor Lodge since 1970, offering one-, two- and three-room combinations that include motel-type rooms and efficiencies, plus two cottages. Nonsmoking rooms are available. The attractive rooms, finished in mauve, turquoise and peach, are all equipped with small refrigerators, phones and cable TV with remote control. Most units also have microwaves.

Guests can gather on the oceanfront patio, a grand place for enjoying the beach scene from a comfy lounge chair. Oceanfront rooms open onto a large, walled terrace affording wonderful views of the ocean from early morning until moonrise. Amenities include two children's pools, a large fenced-in, elevated outdoor pool with tables and umbrellas, a playground, patios with grills, an electronic game room and laundry facilities. Some provisions have been made for handicapped guests, including a ramp for beach access.

Inquire about discounts and weekly rentals (credit cards are not accepted for some discounts). The Beacon Motor Lodge is open late March through late October.

Colonial Inn
$$ • N.C. Hwy. 12, MP 11½, Nags Head
• (252) 441-7308, (800) 345-9405

The Colonial Inn sports oceanfront rooms, efficiencies with full kitchens and nine apartments with separate bedrooms, kitchens and full baths. All 38 rooms have televisions. While the inn is an oceanfront establishment, it also offers an outdoor pool. Colonial Inn is open from April through November.

Old London Inn
$$ • N.C. Hwy. 12, MP 12, Nags Head
• (252) 441-7115

The Old London Inn is split in two sections with some efficiencies on the west side and the rest on the east side of the Beach Road. Many units are oceanside. These are larger than the westside group and feature two double beds and a rollaway, plus a full kitchen; they accommodate up to five people. Smaller rooms are available with a double and a single bed to sleep up to three people. All remaining rooms offer two double beds. All rooms have cable TV and full-size refrigerators. The westside efficiencies are not heated. Children younger than 12 stay free. Prices reflect single or double occupancy; for each added person you pay $6. The Inn is open from the last week of March until mid-October.

Sea Spray
$$ • N.C. Hwy. 12, MP 12, Nags Head
• (252) 441-7270

This down-to-earth beachfront establishment has a little bit of everything including eight rooms, 16 efficiencies and four cottages. All rooms feature two double beds, and some efficiencies have queen-size beds. All units have TVs. Handicapped-accessible rooms are available. The cottages with two and three bedrooms are across the street from the main establishment. Sea Spray is open March 1 through November.

Nags Head Inn
$$$$ • N.C. Hwy. 12, MP 14, Nags Head
• (252) 441-0454, (800) 327-8881

This sparkling white stucco building with blue accents and plush bermudagrass lawns is a tasteful contrast to the older Nags Head-style cottages nearby. Designed for family enjoyment, the oceanfront inn features a sunny lobby where greenery thrives. Also at ground level are offices and covered parking for guests.

Guest rooms begin on the second floor of this five-story building, and all oceanside rooms afford panoramic ocean views from private balconies. Rooms on the street side do not offer balconies, but the view of the

Know the difference between a business trip and a vacation? We do.

Our independently owned and operated ocean front luxury hotel is a cut above the familiar chain establishments. We're here primarily for your vacation enjoyment. All rooms have a refrigerator, free HBO, spacious floor plan, and the most luxurious furnishings on the beach. Honeymoon suite, private balcony, king rooms and non-smoking rooms available. Indoor/outdoor heated pool and spa.

We offer 450 feet of beautiful dunes, plus limited covered parking. Visit Nags Head's newest and nicest ocean front hotel.

The Nags Head Inn

1-800-327-8881
nhi@interpath.com

Roanoke Sound from the fifth floor rooms is notable. All rooms have small refrigerators, cable TV with HBO, phones and full baths. Nonsmoking rooms are available, and there are handicapped-accessible rooms on each floor. The Nags Head Inn also features one suite with an adjoining sitting room, wet bar and Jacuzzi — a perfect honeymoon setting.

A small conference room with adjoining kitchen/sitting area can accommodate about 30 people comfortably. The heated, all-weather swimming pool is on the second floor with a deck overlooking the ocean. During the summer months, the glass doors are removed, providing a completely wide open lounging and sitting area for your enjoyment. Of course, it's nice and toasty in the pool area in the winter months, so don't forget to pack bathing suits; the kids will love you for it.

Tour groups are welcome. The inn is open all year.

Silver Sands Motel
$$ • N.C. Hwy. 12, MP 14, Nags Head • (252) 441-7354

Silver Sands, which sits across the road from a beach access, has 26 rooms that offer simple, basic decor (rustic pine walls and crate furniture) along with such amenities as refrigerators and cable TV with HBO. Guests are offered either two double beds or one queen-size bed. One handicapped-accessible room is available.

A separate two-story building offers rooms on the upper level with balconies for ocean views. The main building offers 16 units near the outdoor swimming pool. Complimentary coffee is provided for guests. For the location,

---

INSIDERS' TIP

Some restaurants (and not just pizza places) will deliver to Outer Banks motel rooms.

you can't beat the price. It's open Easter through November.

Oceanside Court
$$ • N.C. Hwy. 12, MP 15½, Nags Head • (252) 441-6167

There's nothing like an oceanside stay on the Outer Banks. That's what you'll get here, and you can choose from a room, efficiency or cottage. This small establishment offers six efficiencies with cable TV and full kitchens; two rooms with microwaves, refrigerators and cable TV; and seven cottages. Phones are not available in any of the units. The court is open from March 1 to November 30.

Surf Side Motel
$$$$ • N.C. Hwy. 12, MP 16, Nags Head • (252) 441-2105, (800) 552-7873

This attractive five-story motel is situated on the oceanfront, and rooms face north, south and east for ocean views. Some rooms have views of the Roanoke Sound as well. All rooms have private balconies and are decorated attractively in muted beach tones. Nonsmoking rooms are available. Refrigerators, cable TV and phones are standard room features. Some microwaves are available, and the honeymoon suites feature king-size beds and private Jacuzzis. An elevator provides easy access, and handicapped-accessible rooms are available. An adjacent three-story building offers rooms and efficiencies with either ocean or sound views.

Complimentary coffee and sweets are provided for early morning convenience, and the staff hosts an afternoon wine and cheese social hour for guests. You can choose between an indoor pool and Jacuzzi that are open all year and an outdoor pool for swimming in warm weather. The Surf Side is open all year.

If you're interested in deep-sea fishing, Surf Side charters a boat for expeditions from Oregon Inlet. Call Oregon Inlet Fishing Center, (252) 441-6301, for reservation information.

Sandspur Motel and Cottage Court
$$ • N.C. Hwy. 12, MP 15¾, Nags Head • 441-6993, (800) 522-8486

At the Sandspur you can choose from a room, efficiency or cottage stay. All rooms feature two double beds, cable TV, ceiling fans, refrigerators and microwaves. The efficiencies also have stoves. The rooms have no phones, but a pay phone is on the premises. The motel also has a coin-operated washer and dryer. The Sandspur closes in December and reopens March 1.

First Colony Inn
$$$$ • U.S. Hwy. 158, MP 16, Nags Head • (252) 441-2343, (800) 368-9390

Back in 1932, this gracious old structure was known as Leroy's Seaside Inn. Today, the landmark hotel has been moved and refurbished, but it's still a favorite for those who like the ambiance of a quiet inn. The old Nags Head-style architecture, resplendent under an overhanging roof and wide porches, has been preserved and now is listed in the National Register of Historic Places. This is as close as you'll come to what it must have been like 66 years ago when the little hotel first opened. The First Colony received a historic preservation award from the Historic Preservation Foundation of North Carolina.

The Lawrence family, with deep roots in the area, rescued the hotel from demolition in 1988. The building was sawed into three sections for the move from its oceanfront location to the present site 4 miles south between the highways. It took three years of rehabilitation to return the inn to its original appearance. The interior was completely renovated and now contains 26 rooms, all with traditional furnishings and modern comforts.

In the sunny breakfast room, you can enjoy a complimentary deluxe continental breakfast and afternoon tea. Upstairs, an elegant but cozy library with books, games and an old pump organ is a favorite place to read the paper or meet other guests. A great selection of jazz and classical music wafts throughout the reception area.

Each room is individually appointed in English antique furniture. Special touches, such as tiled baths, heated towel bars, English toiletries, telephones, TVs, individual climate control and refrigerators, are standard. Some rooms offer wet bars, kitchenettes, Jacuzzis, VCRs and private balconies; some also include an additional trundle bed or day bed for an extra person. The first floor is wheelchair-accessible, and one room is designed for handi-

First Colony Inn®

The Outer Banks' Only Historic
Bed and Breakfast Inn

6720 South Virginia Dare Trail • Nags Head, NC • **(800) 368-9390**

capped guests. Smoking is not permitted in the inn.

Guests are invited to relax at the 55-foot swimming pool and sun deck behind the inn or to follow the private boardwalk across the street to the oceanfront gazebo.

This magnificent year-round inn provides easy access to the ocean and is close to many shops and restaurants in Nags Head. The inn has a policy of one night free for stays of five weeknights or longer but must include consecutive Sunday, Monday, Tuesday, Wednesday and Thursday stays.

Islander Motel
$$$$ • N.C. Hwy. 12, MP 16, Nags Head • (252) 441-6229

The Islander is a small, popular oceanfront property, due in part to its attractive landscape and well-maintained rooms. Most rooms have an ocean view, and all rooms have either a balcony or patio.

Some of the first-floor units do not offer ocean views because they are tucked behind the dunes. The motel has 24 rooms

and two efficiency apartments. The rooms are large, frequently refurbished and feature either mostly double or queen-size beds. One king is available. All have sitting areas, coffee makers and refrigerators. Some first-floor units offer kitchenettes.

Guests will enjoy the pool and private dune walk to the ocean. This property is convenient to all Nags Head restaurants, shops, recreational outlets and attractions. You'll find the comforts of this attractive motel more than adequate. The Islander is open April through October. They can be reached on the Internet.

Blue Heron Motel
$$$ • N.C. Hwy. 12, MP 16, Nags Head • (252) 441-7447

The Blue Heron Motel is considered one of the Outer Banks' best-kept secrets among the small motels in the area. The family-owned facility provides a year-round indoor swimming pool, a spa and outdoor pools. The Gladden family lives on the premises and pays careful attention to the management of the property. It's in the midst of fine Nags Head restaurants

INSIDERS' TIP

Bring along a camera when heading for the kayak or canoe. The Outer Banks is threaded with canals that take you to where the wildlife is. A long lens will help get you close in and still not disturb the bears, deer, birds, alligators, fish and turtles.

and offers plenty of beach for those who come here to relax.

Nineteen rooms offer double or king-size beds, and 11 efficiencies sleep up to four people and provide full kitchens. All units have refrigerators, microwaves, coffeepots, cable TV, phones and shower/tub combinations. Handicapped-accessible rooms are available. Second- and third-floor rooms offer private balconies. The Blue Heron Motel is open all year and offers weekly rates.

Vivianna

$$-$$$ • N.C. Hwy. 12, MP 16, Nags Head • (252) 441-7409

You can't beat the views at the oceanfront Vivianna, and with the number of folks who return here year after year, something must be going right. The Midgett-Senf family has owned the motel since 1960. Expect to find 15 rooms here that are mostly apartments with kitchens and grand ocean views. Handicapped accessible rooms are available. All rooms have double beds, cable TV and microwaves. The motel is open March 1 through December 1.

Owens' Motel

$$ • N.C. Hwy. 12, MP 16, Nags Head • (252) 441-6361

The Owens family has owned and operated this attractive motel, one of the first on the beach, for more than 42 years. Adjacent to the family's famous restaurant (see our Restaurants chapter), this property across the highway from the ocean is well-maintained. You'll love the family atmosphere!

The Owens' three-story oceanfront addition includes efficiencies with large, private balconies. Each room has two double beds, a tile bath and shower and a kitchen. Cable TV also is standard in the guest rooms.

The motel swimming pool on the west side of the property offers guests an alternative to the ocean. Easy access to Jennette's Fishing Pier and a comfortable oceanfront pavilion with rocking chairs also will entice you. Owens' Motel is open April through October.

Sea Foam Motel

$$$ • N.C. Hwy. 12, MP 16½, Nags Head • (252) 441-7320

Twenty-nine rooms, 18 efficiencies and

three cottages make up this attractive oceanfront motel. Efficiencies accommodate two to four people, and cottages sleep up to six comfortably. The efficiencies and cottages rent weekly; inquire about rates. Rooms are tastefully decorated in mauve and green and some have washed-oak furniture. All rooms have cable TV with HBO, refrigerators, microwaves and phones. Some have king-size beds, and each has a balcony or porch with comfortable furniture. Some units in the one- and two-story buildings have ocean and poolside views.

Children are welcome, and they will enjoy the playground. Other features include a large outdoor pool, children's pool, sun deck, shuffleboard area and a gazebo on the beach for guests' pleasure. Sea Foam Motel is within walking distance of restaurants and Jennette's Fishing Pier. Free coffee is provided until 11 AM, and a special family plan allows children younger than 12 to stay free with parents. Sea Foam Motel is open March through mid-December.

Quality Inn Sea Oatel

$$$$ • N.C. Hwy. 12, MP 16½, Nags Head • (252) 441-7191, (800) 440-4386

This year-round Quality Inn has an excellent oceanfront location near restaurants, recreation, shops and Nags Head attractions. Each of the 111 rooms is tastefully furnished; nonsmoking rooms are available.

This inn is one of the nicest places to stay on this end of Nags Head. Pets are allowed free-of-charge in the off-season from Labor Day to Memorial Day. The front desk is open 24 hours a day, and all rooms conform to Quality Inn's high standards. Each room has a coffee maker, microwave and refrigerator, telephone and cable TV with HBO. You'll also find a coin-operated laundry, snacks and ice. A sheltered gazebo is on the beach. Inquire about Lost Colony and other package options. The inn is open all year.

Dolphin Motel

$$ • N.C. Hwy. 12, MP 16½, Nags Head • (252) 441-7488

The Dolphin Motel features 46 rooms and 12 efficiencies. Some rooms have queen-size beds, but most have double beds. Two nice features are the breezeway to the beach and an outdoor pool. All rooms and efficiencies have cable TV. Nonsmoking rooms are available. The Dolphin Motel opens the last Friday in March and closes the last Saturday in October.

Whalebone Motel
$$$$ • N.C. Hwy. 12, MP 17, Nags Head • (252) 441-7423

The Whalebone Motel is open all year and has standard motel rooms and efficiencies divided among three buildings. One efficiency has one king, one double and two single beds. Three have king-size beds, and others feature one double and two single beds. Some units have two double beds. All accommodations feature stoves, refrigerators and cable TV with HBO. Pets are welcome at $4.50 a night.

Comfort Inn South
$$$$ • N.C. Hwy. 12, MP 17, Nags Head • (252) 441-6315, (800) 334-3302

The Comfort Inn South, a seven-story oceanfront hotel situated in a quiet residential neighborhood, is one of the few accommodations in this area and the tallest building on the Outer Banks. The light peach-and-teal exterior gives this hotel a clean, contemporary beach look. The 105-room hotel has deluxe oceanfront rooms with magnificent views from private balconies; oceanside and streetside rooms are available too. All rooms have remote cable TV, phones, refrigerators and microwaves. Nonsmoking rooms are offered too. A honeymoon suite with Jacuzzi is popular, as are rooms with king-size beds. One handicapped-accessible room is available. Corporate meeting rooms can accommodate groups of up to 350 people.

The oceanfront pool and deck are favorite gathering places. Other amenities include a children's pool, game room and playground. These features make this hotel appealing to families and business groups alike. A deluxe complimentary continental breakfast is offered in the lobby. Jennette's Fishing Pier is only a block away. The Comfort Inn South is open all year.

Fin 'N Feather Motel
$$-$$$ • Nags Head-Manteo Cswy., Nags Head • (252) 441-5353

A small motel along the water's edge, the Fin 'N Feather is popular with anglers and hunters. If you're planning to come in the fall or spring, call well in advance for reservations. This motel's proximity to Pirate's Cove Yacht Club is convenient for anyone headed out for a day on the open seas. There's a boat ramp here too.

Housekeeping units are available year round, featuring double-bed efficiencies. Each

efficiency has a stove and refrigerator and is equipped with cooking utensils. The renters take care of all their needs here. The rooms are clean and comfortable with blue and white decor. Large windows open onto the water from either side and offer stunning views of the sound.

Roanoke Island

Manteo

Island Motel
$$ • U.S. Hwy. 64, Manteo
• (252) 473-2434

The Island Motel is the former Bide-a-wee Motel and has been completely remodeled. In the heart of Manteo, convenience is a hallmark at this neat little motel. Most of the 14 rooms have their own microwave or full kitchen. The main building has a great room where you can meet and greet other guests. Each room has cable TV, air conditioning and two double beds. Fold-away

beds are available for children. Daily, weekly and monthly rates are offered. Amenities include courtesy bikes, fishing poles, other sports equipment and surfing lessons. Nonsmoking and smoking rooms are available, but smoking is not allowed in the main house. This motel is open all year.

The Elizabethan Inn
$$$ • U.S. Hwy. 64, Manteo
• (252) 473-2101, (800) 346-2466

The Elizabethan Inn is a year-round resort facility with spacious shaded grounds, country manor charm and Tudor architecture that reflects the area's heritage. Only 7 miles from the beach, the hotel consists of three buildings providing more than 80 rooms, efficiencies and apartments, plus conference facilities, a health club, gift shop and a restaurant. Nonsmoking and handicapped-accessible rooms are available. All rooms have cable TV with HBO, refrigerators and direct-dial phones. Rooms are available with a king-size bed or two queen-size or double beds, and two rooms

n a world of mediocrity
there are still those
who strive for excellence.

PO Box 970,
305 Fernando St.,
Manteo,
NC 27954

(252) 473-5511
toll free
(877) 473-5511

THE
ROANOKE
ISLAND INN

have whirlpool baths. All rooms are comfortable and well-suited for a quiet, Roanoke Island vacation.

Anna Livia's Restaurant, on the premises, features excellent contemporary and traditional Italian cuisine and a bounty of seafood dishes (see our Restaurants chapter). The lobby is filled with interesting antiques, and a friendly staff welcomes you. A small shop offers a selection of fine gifts, local books, souvenirs and personal items.

The inn's Nautics Hall Fitness Center, the largest and most complete health club in the area, is available for guests (see our Recreation chapter). Guests may also use the outdoor pool and a heated, competition-size indoor pool. There's another nice touch: Guests have free use of bicycles to tour the nearby village or travel the paved bike path.

Inquire about special rate packages. Some pets are welcome at $10 per night, so call for more information. The inn is open all year.

Roanoke Island Inn
$$$$ • 305 Fernando St., Manteo
• (252) 473-5511

With the sparkling Roanoke Sound and quaint Manteo waterfront just a stroll away, you'll find yourself easing into the relaxed village pace the moment you step up to this attractive inn. The distinctive white clapboard inn with dark green shutters offers the atmosphere of a gracious, restored residence with the comforts of a small, well-designed bed and breakfast. The furnishings are handsome, reflecting the meticulous care of the owner, designer-architect John Wilson IV. The ambiance is laid-back and friendly.

An eight-room addition designed for the guests' privacy gives each room a private entrance, private bath, TV and phone. Guests can choose to stay in the quaint bungalow behind the inn complete with an antique tub and furnishings, wet bar and refrigerator. You'll enjoy browsing through a collection of Outer Banks-related books and artwork in the lobby, and a light breakfast is offered in the butler's pantry.

The grounds are private and landscaped with gardenia, fig bushes and other native plants. A picturesque pond complete with koi and sweet-smelling lotus plants is a great place to relax. Dip nets are provided so guests can experience netting crabs along the bay's edge. Bicycles are furnished for touring the town and nearby historic attractions, including the Elizabeth II and the Outer Banks History Center.

The inn opens in the spring, usually around Easter, and closes sometime in the fall.

The White Doe Inn
$$$$ • Sir Walter Raleigh St., Manteo
• (252) 473-9851, (800) 473-6091

The White Doe Inn retains the charm of its Queen Anne-style heritage and offers

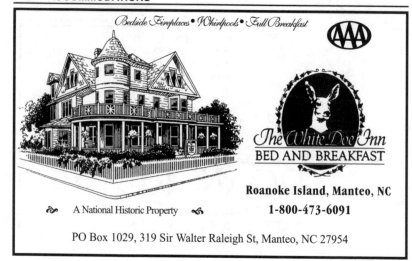

guests an elegant escape in its rooms and hideaways. The inn offers seven guest rooms and one suite, each with its own personality. Each room has a private bath and fireplace. Honeymoon suites are available. The large, wraparound porches are the perfect place to relax and be pampered. Guests have full use of the study-library, formal parlor-living room, foyer and dining room of this stately old home. Afternoon tea and coffee are served. Bob and Bebe Woody work hard to fulfill their guests' every need. The inn serves a full Southern-style breakfast every morning, a good time for guests to gather to read the newspapers, enjoy the fine food and prepare for a day of exploring historic Manteo and Roanoke Island. This is a nonsmoking establishment, but smoking is allowed on the porch.

The White Doe is in a quiet neighborhood in downtown Manteo and is a perfect point of departure to explore the town on foot. Everything is within easy reach. The inn is truly beautiful, and guests won't be disappointed. Special events for up to 30 people can be accommodated. It's a perfect place for weddings, anniversaries, reunions or retreats. The inn is open all year, and off-season rates are available.

Scarborough House
$$ • Fernando and Uppowac Sts., Manteo • (252) 473-3849

The Scarborough House, owned by Phil and Sally Scarborough, opened in 1995. Relax in one of four tasteful guest rooms, each with its own refrigerator, microwave and private bath. Nonsmoking rooms are available. Queen- or king-size beds are available. New for 1998 is a loft room with a king-size bed with canopy and a whirlpool. This inn is appointed with period antiques and other fine furnishings. A continental breakfast is served daily. Bicycles are available for guests' enjoyment and provide the best way, in our opinion, to discover downtown Manteo. Everything about this accommodation reflects the owners' care and personal touch. The Scarborough House is open year round.

Duke of Dare Motor Lodge
$ • U.S. Hwy. 64, Manteo
• (252) 473-2175

On the main street and only a few blocks from the Manteo waterfront, this family motel provides the basics in accommodations: clean rooms with full baths, cable TV and phones. All rooms have queen-size beds. Handicapped-accessible rooms are available. The lodge also has an outdoor pool.

The Creef family has owned and managed the motel for more than a quarter-century. The Duke of Dare is an inexpensive, family-oriented motel that's close to shopping, restaurants and attractions. It is open all year.

"A Quiet Island, Friendly Hosts, and a Warm Outer Banks Welcome!"

SCARBOROUGH INN ON ROANOKE ISLAND

P.O. BOX 366 MANTEO, NC 27954 (252) 473-3979

Scarborough Inn

$$ • U.S. Hwy. 64, Manteo
• (252) 473-3979

Across from The Christmas Shop, this small inn is a delightful and friendly place to stay. The two-story structure was modeled after a turn-of-the-century inn. Each of the guest rooms is filled with authentic Victorian and pre-Victorian antiques and other interesting furnishings, mostly family heirlooms.

Each room and piece of furniture has a story, and the Scarboroughs create a casual, comfortable atmosphere as they relate the history behind some of the pieces. The inn's six rooms are set away from the street. Each has two double beds, cable TV, phone, microwave, private bath, small refrigerator and coffee maker. Tasty muffins for the morning are delivered the night before, an especially nice treat for early risers.

Rooms in the two-story inn have exterior entrances and open onto a covered porch. The four rooms in the annex offer two suites with two separate rooms as well as two smaller rooms; all are tastefully furnished, and one is handicapped-accessible. The Barn has two king rooms that are light and airy. All six rooms are equipped with wet bars and small storage spaces for kitchen utensils and miscellaneous items. House-trained pets are allowed in some rooms at no extra charge, but they cannot be left alone in the rooms.

Complimentary bicycles are available, and there's a glider swing in the backyard. Travelers will appreciate the owners' care and attention. We're sure your stay here will be most pleasant. It's open year-round.

Tranquil House Inn

$$$$ • 405 Queen Elizabeth Ave., on the
waterfront, Manteo • (252) 473-1404,
(800) 458-7069

You will be charmed by this lovely 25-room country inn on Shallowbag Bay that's modeled after an old hotel that stood on this site from just after the Civil War until the 1950s. Although the inn looks authentically aged, it is only 11 years old, so all sorts of modern conveniences are included: TVs with HBO, telephones and private baths. Two of the 25 rooms, which are on the second floor, are one-bedroom suites that feature a queen-size bed and a separate sitting room with sofa and two TVs. All are individually and delightfully decorated.

Large rooms on the third floor have high ceilings. Nonsmoking rooms are available, and the inn has one handicapped-equipped room. A ramp to the first floor makes rooms on that level accessible to all. You're sure to enjoy the hospitality and fine surroundings.

The spacious second-floor deck faces east toward the bay. The Elizabeth II sailing ship is docked across the water. Shops along the wa-

Ocracoke Students Urged To Preserve Unique Dialect

by *Lane DeGregory*
(As appeared in *The Virginian-Pilot* & *The Ledger-Star*)

Most students learn the right way to speak in school. But eighth-graders on this tiny Outer Banks island learn that the way they speak is right — although unusual and sometimes ungrammatical.

When they call their teacher "a real buck," he thanks them for the term of friendship. When students talk about "goin' a-fishin'," he merely asks what they caught. And if the class says a certain lesson was "goodsome," their instructor accepts the compliment — without correcting the language.

"Kids get enough of what's wrong in the classroom," North Carolina State University Professor Walt Wolfram explained. "Just because a certain way of speaking isn't socially acceptable, that doesn't make it linguistically right or wrong.

"I'm interested in children learning respect for their language," said Wolfram. "If they understand and appreciate their own dialect, they'll be better able to preserve it."

Wolfram, an English professor who specializes in regional dialects, spent 1993 conducting a $2,000 study of Ocracoke's unique language.

If young people don't learn to appreciate the individuality of their speech, he said, outside influences such as visitors, television and mass media will homogenize their brogue.

"They're finally getting to absorb from an English standpoint what they hear all day long," said Gail Hamilton, the school's eighth-grade history teacher. "I don't think they

— continued on next page

all realized what they had in their dialect. But now they can — and they're beginning to make sense of it."

Ocracoke is a 15-mile-long barrier island that is inaccessible except by ferry boat. Although it hosts thousands of tourists each summer, the historic village does not have a full-size grocery store, movie theater or even a laundromat. But the 700 permanent islanders have a distinctive dialect all their own.

According to a 40-page paperback curriculum that Wolfram and N.C. State graduate student Natalie Schilling-Estes wrote specifically for Ocracoke School, the island's rare tongue dates from 1715 and contains features of Appalachian English, New England pronunciation, Elizabethan English, Irish and a variety of mainland Southern dialects.

The 'Bankers' brogue, however, has evolved distinctively on isolated Ocracoke. Many of the island's watermen traveled along the Atlantic seaboard for business, working in fisheries and shipyards, delivering goods. They returned with aspects of other accents, which mingled with traditional speech and tourists' tongues.

Village teenagers say they're "skuddin' a ride" instead of catching one. Cashiers "tag your sack" when they charge purchases to a credit account. And a favorite Ocracoke saying about the tide asks, "Ween's eet hoih toide on the souind soide?"

Wolfram said such idioms and seeming errors are not wrong at all. He calls linguistic changes in vocabulary, sentence structure and pronunciation "dialect grammar differences" — and teaches the students to recognize and appreciate them.

Additions from the class included the following:

Breakwatered: built a bulkhead to save shorelines from erosion

Heist the window: open the window

Feeling tolerable: feeling all right

"I learned that I talk weirder than most people. But I'm just using the words they use around the island," student Ben Strange said. "It never really occurred to me before. I just said them because they sounded right. If everybody talked the same everywhere, it sure would be boring."

Wolfram has studied African-American English, Puerto-Rican dialects and Native

— continued on next page

American versions of traditional language. But Ocracokers have the best chance of preserving their distinct dialect, he said, because they are so proud of it. Natives who realize what is special about their speech are less likely to allow it to erode.

"Last summer, some tourist girls called me and my friends hillbillies for the way we talk," Ocracoke native Charlene Garrish said. "That got me upset then.

"Now, I'd just look at them and say, 'Our way of talking is part of our history. It's the way we've done things for years.

"And we're proud of the unique way we say things down here."

Dictionary of Ocracoke Dialect

Call the mail over: Distribute the mail; "Is the mail called over yet?"

Chunk: To throw; "Chunk the rock in the water."

Haint: A ghost; "Some people think they've seen haints."

Poke sack: A bag; "Did you put the duck in the poke sack?"

Russian rat: A large rodent technically known as a nutria; "Look at that Russian rat!"

Wampus cat: A fictitious cat, used to refer to a rascally person; "He's a classic example of an off-island wampus cat."

Winard: Moving into the wind; "We have a better catch going winard."

Dingbatter: An outsider who moved to the island; "He's no better than a dingbatter."

Quamish: Feeling bad, having an upset stomach; "I'm feeling quamish today."

Mommuck: To hassle, irritate, annoy; "I've been mommucked."

terfront are just a few steps away, and the marina behind the inn is convenient for those arriving by boat.

The inn's exquisite restaurant, 1587, specializes in gourmet cuisine and offers an extensive selection of wines (see our Restaurants chapter). Guests have free use of bicycles. Tranquil House Inn is open all year.

Dare Haven Motel
$ • U.S. Hwy. 64, Manteo
• (252) 473-2322

The Dare Haven, a family-run motel suited to the cost-conscious vacationer, is toward the north end of Roanoke Island and is a favorite place for families and fishing enthusiasts — there's enough room here to park your own boat and trailer. Visitors planning to attend The Lost Colony or visit any of the other Roanoke Island attractions and historic sites of Fort Raleigh will find this location convenient. The motel also is close to the beaches and many other Outer Banks attractions.

The 26 motel-style rooms are basic, clean and comfortable and have cable TV and telephones. Most rooms are decorated in traditional Outer Banks-style, with paneled walls and wraparound porches. All rooms are on ground level.

Craft lovers will want to visit the on-site Crafts Galore shop, which offers supplies for plastic and canvas needlework, stenciling, dolls and other handicrafts as well as works by local artists and crafters.

Call for special rates for groups and extended stays. The motel is open all year.

Wanchese

C.W. Pugh's Bed and Breakfast
$$ • Old Wharf Rd., Wanchese
• (252) 473-5466

A truly charming bed and breakfast, C.W. Pugh's occupies a renovated house that is more than 100 years old. Situated next door to Queen Anne's Revenge (see the Restaurants chapter), the inn has three guest rooms. Baths are on the first and second floors, and a parlor and seating area is the setting for a complimentary full breakfast. Antique furniture and some reproductions add to the appeal of this bed and breakfast.

The spacious lawn is appealing for those who like some elbow room, and the winding lanes of Wanchese are perfect for bicycle rides. This bed and breakfast is situated near the end of the road where, at one time, Mr. Pugh was a lighthouse keeper at Marshes Light, a house built on pilings in the water. Pugh's duty was to help keep the channel waters open and safe for passing ships in an area where shifting sands fouled the entrance to the harbor. These days, there is an electric light out on the sound instead. Nancy Gray, whose husband, Wayne Gray, is the owner of Queen Anne's Revenge, has managed this bed and breakfast for 11 years.

This country setting, not far from historic Manteo and the beach, is a good choice for anyone looking for quiet relaxation. Children are welcome. It's open from Easter through Thanksgiving.

Island House of Wanchese Bed and Breakfast
$$$ • 104 Old Wharf Rd. Wanchese • (252) 473-5619

This old home, built in 1902, celebrates its fourth year as a bed and breakfast in 1998. Furnished in period antiques with Oriental rugs and cabana fans, the small but cozy estab-

lishment offers many comforts including private baths, cable TV and radios in every room, beach towels and chairs, complimentary bikes and a hot tub for guests. All rooms have one double bed.

Of course, a bed and breakfast would not be complete without a hearty morning meal. Island House offers a breakfast buffet often including casseroles, grits, fresh fruit, sweets and juice. This is a nonsmoking establishment, but smoking is allowed on the porch. Children 12 and over are welcome. Island House is open April through November. Summer rates apply from May 15 to September 15.

Hatteras Island

Rodanthe

Hatteras Island Resort
$$ • N.C. Hwy. 12, Rodanthe
• (252) 987-2345, (800) 331-6541

Plenty of leisure activities await guests at this large oceanfront resort next to the Hatteras Island Fishing Pier. The two-story building includes 22 motel-type rooms, each with two double beds, a dressing room and shower and 10 efficiencies featuring queen beds and full kitchenettes. Each of the 12 oceanfront rooms and efficiencies offers an ocean view.

A second building behind the dune offers 10 additional motel-type rooms.

The 25-acre oceanside property also has 35 two-, three- and four-bedroom cottages arranged in clusters. Cottages rent weekly; inquire about rates. All units are comfortably furnished and have cable TV. In-room phones are not available, but pay phones are on the premises. Pets are allowed in the cottages only. Inquire about the fee.

Families will enjoy the outdoor oceanfront swimming pool, kiddie pool, large patio area, volleyball and basketball. The Hatteras Island Fishing Pier is right out front on the Atlantic and draws a lot of people to the resort. The motel is open April through November.

Sea Sound Motel
$-$$ • Sea Sound Rd., Rodanthe
• (252) 987-2224

Sea Sound is between N.C. 12 and the ocean and offers efficiencies and regular motel-style rooms. The efficiencies have fully equipped kitchens including microwaves. Motel rooms feature either one double and one twin bed or two queen beds. All accommodations have heat and air conditioning, color TV and phones, and most rooms have coffee makers. There's an outdoor pool on the premises with a deck and hot tub. Sea Sound also features an outdoor grill, picnic area with table and small basketball court.

Avon

Avon Motel
$$-$$$ • N.C. Hwy. 12, Avon
• (252) 995-5774, (800) 243-5774

This terrific 45-unit establishment has been in business for more than 40 years and offers a perfect starting point to enjoy everything Hatteras Island has to offer. The Avon has standard, oceanside motel rooms and a handful of efficiency apartments. Motel rooms come with either two double beds, one queen-size or one king-size bed, and they all have microwaves, compact fridges and coffee makers. The efficiencies have either two or three rooms with a variety of bed setups along with fully equipped kitchens. All rooms and efficiencies have air conditioning, cable with free HBO and in-room phones (local calls are free). For the anglers in the group, there is a lighted fish-cleaning station at the motel, and there is a guest laundry.

The motel is in the neighborhood of tackle shops, a fishing pier, four-wheel-drive beach accesses, windsurfing and beach shops, res-taurants and gift stores. The Cape Hatteras Lighthouse is 6 miles away, and (listen up, windsurfers) the famous "Canadian Hole" is within 4 miles.

Castaways
$$$$ • 40393 N.C. Hwy. 12, Avon
• (252) 995-4444, (800) 845-6070

The hallmark of this year-round oceanfront establishment is the spaciousness of its 68 rooms, spread over five floors and offering oceanfront or dune views. Rooms feature king- and queen-size beds. Most rooms have wet bars, refrigerators and private balconies. Only first-floor rooms do not offer ocean views because they are tucked behind the dunes. Non-smoking connecting rooms, rollaways and cribs are available. Meeting and conference facilities accommodate up to 200 people.

Amenities here include a heated, competi-tion-size indoor swimming pool and hot tub. The wide, unspoiled beaches at Castaways are beautiful and perfect for swimming, sun-bathing and enjoying the beach. A boarded

walkway leads you across the dunes and onto the beach.

The on-site Blue Parrot Cafe (see our Restaurants chapter) is attractively decorated in a tropical island motif. The ambiance, delicious fresh seafood and leisurely pace put guests into a real vacation mood.

Castaways is closed in December. Inquire about special rate packages.

Buxton

Cape Hatteras Motel
$$$$ • N.C. Hwy. 12, Buxton
• (252) 995-5611, (800) 995-0711

When you arrive in Buxton, you'll see the Cape Hatteras Motel situated on both sides of the road. Owners Carol and Dave Dawson maintain this motel, parts of which have been here for more than 32 years. The 28 efficiency units are popular with anglers, surfers and folks who just plain enjoy Hatteras Island's beaches. Windsurfers especially like this facility because it is near the Canadian Hole, one of the best windsurfing spots on the East Coast (see our Attractions chapter).

Efficiencies sleep up to six comfortably, offer double beds as well as queens and kings and have full kitchens. The newer, more modern townhouses and efficiencies are on the ocean. The motel has an outdoor swimming pool and spa. The motel's position at the north end of Buxton is convenient not only to pristine uncrowded beaches but also is near restaurants and services, making this a very popular place in the busy summer season. There are no nonsmoking rooms, but the motel does offer a ZonTech clean air machine.

Efficiencies rent weekly, but nightly rentals also may be available, depending on supply. Book reservations early. Cape Hatteras Motel is open year round.

Outer Banks Motel
$$ • N.C. Hwy. 12, Buxton
• (252) 995-5601, (800) 995-1233

Situated next to the Cape Hatteras Motel, this establishment offers 11 motel-style rooms,

six efficiency units and 17 two- and three-bed-room cottages. Units accommodate from one to nine people comfortably, and about 80 percent of the units provide an ocean view. Nonsmoking rooms are available. Rooms and efficiencies offer enclosed porches with sliding windows and screens, perfect for a relaxing evening listening to the ocean. The pine-paneled rooms have tiled baths, microwaves, toasters and small refrigerators. Efficiencies have fully equipped kitchens. All units have cable TV and telephones.

The owners also have 14 additional cot-tages in Buxton Village, a mile from the ocean, near Connor's Market. Because these units are not oceanfront, rental rates are quite a bit lower. If you rent one of these cottages, you are welcome to use the motel pool and beach facilities. The cottages are clean, simply furnished and provide the basics for family vacationers, including cable television.

The motel has a coin-operated laundry, fish-cleaning station and a guest freezer to store your big catch. If you enjoy crabbing, or if you just want to paddle around on the Pamlico

Sound, the motel has several row boats that guests may use free of charge. There's even a library in the office in case you want to grab a good book on your way to the beach. This motel is open year round.

Lighthouse View Motel
$$$ • N.C. Hwy. 12, Buxton
• (252) 995-5680, (800) 225-7651

Lighthouse View is easy to find on the big curve in Buxton, where the Hooper family has been serving vacationers for more than 38 years. The 73 units include a choice of motel rooms, efficiencies, duplexes, villa units and cottages. Most units are oceanfront, and all are oceanside. (The rate guideline above pertains to motel rooms.) The well-maintained complex has an outdoor pool and hot tub, and surfers, windsurfers and anglers enjoy the proximity to ocean and sound.

Rooms have cable TV, phones, full baths and daily maid service. Efficiencies accommodate two to six people and are equipped with complete kitchens. The oceanfront villas offer balconies on both the oceanside and soundside, so you can enjoy sunrises and sunsets. The six duplexes offer two decks and sleep up to six people each. Efficiencies and villas usually rent on a weekly basis and there is a three-night minimum stay, but they can be rented nightly when available. Note that there is no daily maid service for the villas, efficiencies and duplexes, but

linens can be exchanged. Cottages are rented by the week only. Efficiencies, duplexes, villas and cottages are fully furnished. Handicapped-accessible one-room efficiencies are available.

Falcon Motel
$$ • N.C. Hwy. 12, Buxton
• (252) 995-5968, (800) 635-6911

The Falcon offers some of the best prices for accommodations on the Outer Banks. The traditional Outer Banks-style rooms here appeal to family-oriented guests who appreciate moderate prices, accommodations with character and the peaceful environment of Hatteras Island. The Falcon, owned by Doug and Anne Meekins, is known for its attention to detail, which is apparent in the clean, well-maintained rooms and grounds.

This motel includes 35 units with 30 rooms and five fully equipped apartments, all at ground level. All rooms have double beds. Nonsmoking rooms are available. The spacious rooms have a light, airy feel and include cable TV with HBO. Many rooms have refrigerators and microwaves. Some have wooden deck chairs on a wide, covered porch. Park right outside your door.

Guests have use of the swimming pool and boat ramp as well, and you'll find a shaded picnic area with barbecue grills amid mature oak trees, away from the road. The landscaping includes martin and bluebird houses and planted shrubs and flowers that attract the local bird population. Don't miss seeing the osprey platform on the soundside area beyond the trees. As you can tell, Anne Meekins is a devout bird lover and enjoys sharing her interests with guests.

The Falcon Motel is in the heart of Buxton, within easy walking distance of several shops and restaurants, including Diamond Shoals Restaurant (see our Restaurants chapter) across the street. The beach is a short walk away.

The rate guideline above pertains to the rooms only; apartments rent mostly on a weekly basis. The motel is open from March through mid-December.

Comfort Inn of Hatteras
**$$$$ • N.C. Hwy. 12, Buxton
• (252) 995-6100, (800) 432-1441**

The Comfort Inn is in the heart of Buxton, close to the beach and shops. The 60 units with exterior access are standard motel-style rooms with kings or double beds. Rooms are decorated in attractive, soft beach colors; all have cable TV with HBO, refrigerators and direct-dial phones and microwaves. Nonsmoking and handicapped-accessible rooms are available.

Free ice and complimentary guest laundry is available. A complimentary continental breakfast is served in the lobby. Guests have use of the outdoor swimming pool, gazebo

and the three-story watch tower, the latter two providing panoramic views of the ocean, the sound and nearby Cape Hatteras Lighthouse (see our Attractions chapter). AARP and Triple A discounts are honored.

Comfort Inn of Hatteras Island has ample parking for boats and campers and is open year round.

Tower Circle
$, no credit cards • Old Lighthouse Rd., Buxton • (252) 995-5353

This small motel, just off N.C. 12, is the closest lodging to the Cape Hatteras Lighthouse

Atlantic View Motel

Hatteras Village, North Carolina
1-800-986-2330

(see our Attractions chapter) and is one of the friendliest spots on the Outer Banks. The Gray family, which has owned Tower Circle for 26 years, treats their guests like old friends, and many of them are. Guests sit on the porch, swap stories and enjoy the atmosphere.

The 19 units, including eight duplexes, five suites and two efficiency apartments, all open onto the porch, have cable TV and sleep from two to six people comfortably in either queen- or double-size beds. All suites and apartments have complete kitchens. Some have two bedrooms, while others are two-room efficiency apartments. None of the units have phones, but microwaves are available. All linens are furnished for the apartments, and fresh linens can be delivered. Handicapped-accessible rooms are available.

It's just a short walk to restaurants and stores or the beach. Tower Circle is open April through November.

Surf Motel
$ • Old Lighthouse Rd., Buxton
• (252) 995-5785

The ocean is only a one-block walk from this motel managed by Bea and Jack Goldman, which is one reason it's so popular with surfers, windsurfers, anglers and family vacationers. Four motel-style rooms, eight efficiencies and one apartment are available here. The rooms offer double or single beds; the efficiencies sleep two or four comfortably and have full kitchens; the apartments, featuring two separate bedrooms and 1.5 baths, are popular with families of up to five people. The decor features carpeting and traditional Outer Banks-style wood paneling.

INSIDERS' TIP

Bring extra beach towels so you don't have to borrow bath ones from your hotel.

Amenities include an outdoor, enclosed hot and cold shower, barbecue grills, fish-cleaning stations and a freezer for your daily catch. Daily maid service is provided.

The Surf Motel is open March through mid-December.

Cape Hatteras Bed and Breakfast
$$-$$$ • Old Lighthouse Rd., Buxton • (252) 995-6004, (800) 252 3316

This bed and breakfast inn is popular with windsurfers (the owners are both windsurfing enthusiasts), surfers and couples who just want to get away. The two-story inn offers several styles of accommodations from which to choose. All six units are nonsmoking and are on the first floor, and each has its own entrance opening onto a covered porch that runs the length of the building. Two of the rooms offer two double beds, and the rest have queen-size beds. The inn has two efficiency units: The two-room unit features a bedroom with a queen-size bed, a living room with a sleeper sofa

and a full kitchen; the one-room unit has a queen-size bed and kitchenette. All units have cable TV and private baths. Refrigerators, microwaves and phones are not provided in the rooms.

Amenities include a common dining and living area upstairs where a complimentary full gourmet breakfast is served, color cable TV, VCR, stereo, a small library, and outdoor showers. Beach gear, coolers, bicycles, fishing rods and beach toys are available along with lockable storage for surf and sailboards. Daily maid service is provided. Weekly rentals are available, with special accommodations available for honeymooners. It's open year round, but we recommend that you call after November to be sure.

Cape Pines Motel
$ • N.C. Hwy. 12, Buxton
• (252) 995-5666, (800) 864-2707

Cape Pines Motel, in the center of Buxton just a mile south of the Cape Hatteras Lighthouse, is a nicely maintained one-story facility with private exterior entry to each room. Steve and Hazel Totton have owned this property since 1988.

Each of the 26 rooms offer cable TV and a full bath. Furnishings have a contemporary beach look. Some rooms have queen-size beds, and nonsmoking rooms are available. Guests will also find three apartments, each offering separate bedrooms, a living room and a full kitchen. In the summer season, the apartments rent on a weekly basis only. Mini-efficiencies also are available with microwaves, coffee makers and refrigerators.

Stretch out and relax around the pool and the lawn. The flowers and landscaping are some of our favorites on this end of the island - a splash of color along the main road through Buxton all summer. You'll also find picnic tables and charcoal grills. Fish-cleaning tables and a pay phone are on the premises. Cape Pines is close enough to walk or bike to shopping, attractions and the beach. The motel is open year round.

Pamlico Inn
$$$ • 1 mi. south of Cape Hatteras School on the sound, Buxton
• (252) 995-6980

The Pamlico Inn features three suites overlooking the sound. A large wraparound deck, hot tub and hammock on the sound are pleasant places to enjoy the outdoors. Owners Scott and Brenda Johnson have a sailboat and canoes accessible for free to their guests and offer complimentary boat rides on the sound.

All rooms have spectacular soundfront views, queen-size beds, private baths and TVs. The inn offers special packages, including ones for anniversaries and honeymoons. It's open year round.

Hatteras Village

Durant Station Motel
$$$ • N.C. Hwy. 12, Hatteras Village
• (252) 986-2244

Durant Station Motel caters to families, anglers and outdoor enthusiasts. Amenities in-

clude an outdoor pool and fish-cleaning stations for the day's catch. Limited handicapped access is available.

This property offers one motel room and 29 apartments, each individually owned and furnished. The one-, two-and three-bedroom apartments rent weekly or nightly depending on availability. The apartments have a minimum two-night stay in season. The motel room rents nightly, weekly or monthly. Each of the apartments is comfortably furnished. All rooms have cable TV, and two rooms have phones. Linen service is provided. Daily maid service is not available.

Durant Station is open April through November.

Sea Gull Motel
$$ • N.C. Hwy. 12, Hatteras Village • (252) 986-2550

Most nights at this motel, you can raise the window, catch the ocean breezes and listen to the breaking waves about 125 yards away. The Sea Gull is a well-maintained motel at the northern end of scenic Hatteras Village, and patrons will enjoy the quaint, quiet charm and friendly ambiance of this popular, established accommodation. Guests enjoy walking on the beach and along nearby Pamlico Sound or relaxing in the shade on a lazy afternoon. Sea Gull Motel has spacious grounds and a walkway to the beach.

Other amenities include an outdoor pool, a wading pool for the kids, picnic tables, grills and fish-cleaning tables. A few shops are within walking distance, and Gary's Restaurant, just across the street, serves three meals daily (see our Restaurants chapter).

Guests will find a variety of accommodations, including 35 motel-style rooms. Nine rooms offer ocean views. Rooms offer a combination of double beds or queen-size beds, and some rooms have refrigerators and microwaves. Six apartments and four efficiencies offer fully equipped kitchens. Handicapped-accessible rooms are available. The large, comfortable rooms rent nightly, while the apartments and efficiencies require a three-day minimum stay. All rooms have cable TV and phones.

The motel is open March through November.

General Mitchell Motel
$$ • N.C. Hwy. 12, Hatteras Village • (252) 986-2444, (800) 832-0139

This oceanfront motel is named for Billy Mitchell, the aviation pioneer of the U.S. Army Air Service, who proved the value and power of airplanes against naval vessels by sinking two retired battleships off the coast of Cape Hatteras from his plane. The newly remodeled facility, on the left as you enter Hatteras Village from the north, is popular with anglers,

divers, vacationers and travelers alike. Two buildings house 33 motel-style rooms and 15 efficiencies with full kitchens. Some have ocean views. The rooms vary in size and offer double beds, king-size beds or two doubles and one single bed. Efficiencies have a two-day minimum stay.

Amenities include an outdoor pool and Jacuzzi, a lighted fish-cleaning pavilion, picnic area, freezer for storing the day's surf catch and a wooden walkway to the beach. Last but not least, they serve a traditional continental breakfast. The motel is open year round.

Atlantic View Motel
$$ • off N.C. Hwy. 12, Hatteras Village • (252) 986-2323, (800) 986-2330

The office of Atlantic View is close to the main road, but the motel itself is situated down a quiet paved lane. The beach is just a few minutes' walk away. The motel offers 20 motel rooms and eight efficiencies. The rooms are larger than standard, and all are fully carpeted and have two double beds and cable TV. Efficiencies have fully equipped kitchens. Handicapped-accessible rooms are available. Phones are near the main unit. High dunes prevent ocean views.

This is a particularly nice place for families. Guests and their children will enjoy the play area, in-ground swimming pool, smaller kiddie pool, volleyball nets, basketball hoop and complimentary bikes. Shankie and Donna Peele, owners of the Atlantic View, cater to small families, but some rooms connect to accommodate larger groups. For travelers on a tight budget, this motel is a good choice. The Atlantic View is open year round.

Seaside Inn at Hatteras
$$$-$$$$ • N.C. Hwy. 12, Hatteras Village • (252) 986-2700

This inn is actually the site of the first motel built on the Outer Banks in 1928. It's been lovingly refurbished, and owners Sharon and Jeff Kennedy offer guests something special here. On N.C. 12 in Hatteras Village, the Seaside features 10 guest rooms (five have separate sitting areas) with fully modernized bathroom facilities, and some with Jacuzzi's. All rooms feature either king- or queen-size beds with fine linens. Each room has a distinct personality, size and floor plan. The inn offers a full breakfast served in a quaint dining room that includes freshly squeezed juices, hot coffee and tea and a menu that changes daily. Selections may include hot biscuits, ham and eggs or homemade granola, fresh fruit, French toast or a Hatteras-style seafood breakfast. There are always choices to accommodate different tastes.

One room is available for visitors with pets for a $10 fee. The inn requires a 50 percent

deposit a week before your stay. It is not handicapped-accessible, but the innkeepers are willing to work to accommodate challenged visitors. This is a nonsmoking establishment. Seaside Inn can handle small gatherings, weddings and parties, and it's open year round.

Hatteras Harbor Motel
$$ • N.C. Hwy. 12, Hatteras Village • (252) 986-2565

This soundfront motel in the heart of Hatteras Village is convenient to restaurants, shops and services and is adjacent to the Hatteras charter boat fleet. Visitors can park their cars and walk or bike to most places in this sleepy community. We like this motel because of its location and cheerful staff.

Hatteras Harbor Motel has 15 rooms (each with two double beds and a full bath), four two-bedroom efficiency apartments and two studio efficiencies. All rooms have cable TV, microwaves, refrigerators and telephones. Nonsmoking rooms are available. Daily maid service and fresh linens are provided. Guests will enjoy the in-ground pool (complete with a kiddie wading pool) and the long, shaded porches that are perfect for watching the daily village activities.

Some rooms allow pets. Inquire about the fee. The motel, a longtime favorite of anglers and budget-minded travelers, is open year round. Inquire about off-season rates.

Hatteras Marlin Motel
$ • N.C. Hwy. 12, Hatteras Village • (252) 986-2141

Hatteras Marlin Motel, owned and operated by the Midgett family, is in sight of the harbor fishing fleet, restaurants and shops. The 40 units are divided between three buildings and consist of standard motel rooms with king- or double-size beds and one-bedroom efficiencies. A newer building near the back of the property away from the road offers a pair of two-bedroom suites with combined living, kitchen and dining areas. From this building, built along a canal, you can often see ducks waddling around in the grassy areas of the yard.

The two older buildings near the road share parking with Midgett's Gas Station and convenience store. All rooms are well-maintained and have cable TV and telephones. Accommodations sleep one to six people comfortably and rent weekly or nightly depending upon availability. The motel has an in-ground swimming pool and sun deck. Hatteras Marlin Motel is open all year.

Holiday Inn Express
$$$$ • N.C. Hwy. 12 at Marina Way, Hatteras Village • (252) 986-1110

The Holiday Inn Express is at the tip of Hatteras Island and is open 24 hours a day. It offers standard rooms with two double

On beautiful Ocracoke Island

OCRACOKE HARBOR INN

Enjoy the view from your own private deck overlooking Silver Lake Harbor. With 16 rooms and 6 suites, we feature continental breakfast, in-room refrigerators, boat docking, suites w/jacuzzis and a waterfront hot tub.

Phone: (252) 928-5731 or (888) 456-1998
P.O. Box 940, Silver Lake Road Ocracoke, NC 27960

beds or king-size beds and suites with two double beds or a king-size bed plus a separate living area with a fold-out double bed sofa. All rooms feature microwaves, refrigerators and cable TV with HBO. Nonsmoking rooms are available. Handicapped accessible rooms and suites are available. A laundry facility is available to guests. Suites have additional amenities, such as coffee makers, irons and boards, kitchen counter space with sink and round kitchen tables with four chairs. The second-floor rooms have private balconies. Rooms with ocean and sound views are available, and first-floor rooms feature private patios. They also have an outdoor pool. The inn is open year round.

Ocracoke Island

Berkley Center Country Inn
$$$, no credit cards • N.C. Hwy. 12
• (252) 928-5911

Two buildings situated on 3 acres house this nine-room bed and breakfast on Ocracoke Harbor. The Manor House, built in 1860, was remodeled in 1950. The Ranch House dates from the mid-1950s, and the architecture and cedar exterior create an impression of age and quality. Both buildings are furnished in reproduction antiques, and all interior walls, floors and ceilings of the

Manor House are made of hand-carved wood panels of redwood, pine, cypress and cedar.

Berkley Center is adjacent to the Park Service offices and ferry dock but away from the congestion that one might anticipate from seasonal visitors. Lots of trees provide comfortable privacy. A complimentary continental breakfast consisting of fresh breads, fruits, preserves and coffee is available in the breakfast room of the Manor House. There is also a guest lounge here and it offers the only television at the inn. Staying here is a real opportunity to get away from the hustle and bustle of everyday life. Guests also have the choice of relaxing on one of the porches overlooking the lovely lawn and enjoying the company of other guests.

All rooms are spacious and have been furnished in classic fashion. Double sinks in the baths and large closets are among the nice features here. The inn has nine rooms, with private baths in seven of them (two rooms share a large bath, which would be ideal for a family). Phones are not provided in the rooms. Berkley Center is open April through October.

Thurston House Inn
$$, no credit cards • N.C Hwy. 12
• (252) 928-6037, 928-7961

The Thurston House Inn is a relatively new accommodation on Ocracoke Island, but the structure itself was built in the 1920s. The former home of Capt. Tony Thurston Gaskill, it is now on the Register of Historic Places in North Carolina. Renovated in 1996 by the captain's granddaughter Marlene Mathews and her husband, Randal, the inn offers five rooms, each with a private bath. A phone is available on the premises, but the rooms offer true solitude minus phones and TVs. All are air conditioned, and three downstairs rooms have private decks and entrances. The rooms feature either king-,queen-, or two twin-size beds.

Guests will enjoy relaxing on the covered porch, where they can soak in a wisteria- and ivy-covered yard. The parlor is another option for get-togethers with other guests. A full breakfast is part of the package. Children older than 12 are welcome. This is a nonsmoking establishment. The inn is within walking distance of Silver Lake, Ocracoke Lighthouse and various stores, restaurants and historic sites. Local airport pickup is available. Reservations are recommended. A three-day notice is necessary for cancellation. The inn is open year round.

Joyce's Motel
$$$$ • Silver Lake • (252) 928-6461

Joyce's Motel offers water views of Silver Lake from a large deck. Four of the smaller efficiencies are larger than standard motel rooms. Each is set up with a queen bed and queen sofabed. The two larger efficiencies have two queen beds and a queen sofabed plus a full-size refrigerator, range, microwave, coffee maker, toaster and kitchen utensils. Daily housekeeping is offered; linens are furnished. Swimming privileges are available about 100 yards from the motel at a nearby pool. Room amenities include phones, cable TV with HBO, heat and air conditioning. Nonsmoking rooms are available. Boaters will love the location — you can pull your boat up at the establishment's 10-slip boat dock. Joyce's is open March through Thanksgiving.

The Anchorage Inn and Marina
$$$-$$$$ • N.C. Hwy. 12
• (252) 928-1101

The Anchorage Inn, which resembles a small resort, overlooks Silver Lake and the village. Besides accommodations, the inn has a marina and fishing center, recreational amenities, an outdoor cafe and gift shops nearby. The attractive five-story red brick building with white trim has elevator access to each floor.

Accommodations here offer some of the best bird's-eye views available of the harbor and Ocracoke Village, especially from upper-floor rooms. Most of the rooms have some view of Silver Lake Harbor. Each of the motel-style rooms has a king- or queen-size bed or two double beds, full bath, direct-dial phone, and cable TV with The Movie Channel. The fourth-floor units are nonsmoking rooms, and handicapped-accessible rooms are available. Pets are allowed in some rooms for a $10 fee.

The Anchorage Inn offers its guests a complimentary continental breakfast, a private pool with a sun deck situated on the harbor and an on-premises boat dock and ramp. The gazebo at Silver Lake is a perfect place to watch an early evening sunset. Guests can walk to restaurants, shops and the historical sites on Ocracoke Island. Bike rentals are available. Fishing charters, which depart from the dock across the street, can be booked with the inn's receptionist or from your room. The motel is open year round.

Pony Island Motel
$$ • N.C. Hwy. 12 • (252) 928-4411

At the edge of Ocracoke Village, a short distance from Silver Lake Harbor, Pony Island Motel offers 50 units. The grounds are spacious and inviting. For nearly 25 years, owners David and Jen Esham have hosted families and couples in search of peace and solitude on Ocracoke Island.

Most of the units have either single or double occupancy, but the motel offers some rooms that accommodate up to five people. Each room has color cable TV with Showtime, and the efficiencies provide fully equipped kitchens. Rooms are refurbished regularly, but maintain a traditional decor with paneled walls. Nonsmoking rooms and one handicapped-accessible room are available.

The motel has been recently remodeled and now has bedroom suites featuring from one to four additional rooms per suite. The rooms are spacious and have wet bars and refrigerators.

The motel is in walking distance of the Ocracoke Lighthouse and other island attractions. Bike rentals are available. The large pool, deck, picnic tables and lawn offer plenty of room for family activities. The Pony Island Restaurant, a locals' favorite, is right next door (see our Restaurants chapter). The motel is open year round.

Edwards of Ocracoke
$-$$ • Pony Island Rd. • (252) 928-4801

This refurbished motel, away from the center of Ocracoke and off the main route near The Back Porch Restaurant, consists of eight motel rooms, three efficiencies, six apartments and two cottages. Most all of the units have screened porches, and some open onto a veranda. Phones are available in most units, and there is cable TV. The cottages rent weekly, and the efficiencies require a three-day minimum stay. Some have refrigerators. The rate guideline above pertains to nightly rentals of the motel rooms only.

The motel offers inexpensive accommodations in a family setting with a carefully landscaped green lawn, flower beds and pine trees. Pets are allowed in some of the cottages for an extra charge. The motel is open Easter through New Year's.

Bluff Shoal Motel
$$ • N.C. Hwy. 12 • (252) 928-4301

Bluff Shoal Motel, a small seven-unit facility on the village's main street, has carpeted and paneled rooms that open onto a long porch. Each room has a private bath, small refrigerator, telephone and cable TV with Showtime. Nonsmoking rooms are available. A two-bedroom efficiency apartment also is available. Bluff Shoal Motel is across the street from The Pelican Restaurant and is in walking distance of the post office, community store and village shops. Owners Jennifer and Wayne Garrish keep the motel open all year.

Pirate's Quay
$$$$ • Silver Lake • (252) 928-3002, (800) 995-0630

This extraordinary hotel directly across from the Coast Guard Station in Ocracoke Village opened in 1987 and provides some of the most luxurious accommodations available on a nightly basis anywhere on the Outer Banks. The hotel is made up of six

Beach House

P.O. Box 578
Ocracoke, NC 27960
(252) 928-1411
Hostess: Martha

individually owned condo suites, each with living room, dining room, full kitchen, two bedrooms and one-and-a-half baths. Non-smoking rooms are available. Units on the top floor have cathedral ceilings. Two decks off each suite, a waterfront gazebo and docking facilities make the most of the harborfront location.

Each condo suite accommodates five adults and children and has a Jacuzzi and cable TV with Showtime. All suites are beautifully furnished and have kitchens stocked with all the dishes, cookware and gadgets you need. From Pirate's Quay (pronounced "key"), guests can walk or bike to quaint nearby shops, restaurants and other attractions. The hotel is open year round.

The Island Inn
$$$ • N.C. Hwy. 12 • (252) 928-4351

The Island Inn, owned by Cee and Bob Touhey, provides a variety of accommodations suitable for single adults, couples and families with children. Originally built as an Odd Fellows Lodge in 1901, the main building has served as a school, a private residence and naval officers quarters. It was restored by former owners and has been recognized in *Country Inns of the Old South*, *Southern Living*, *Cuisine* and *The Saturday Evening Post*.

The owners had their first date on Ocracoke Island and vacationed here for many years; they have returned to live and work. The main building is a nonsmoking establishment. Many of the 35 rooms have been refurbished, reflecting the inherently romantic style of this country inn. The main building houses individual rooms and suites, all uniquely furnished with antiques and quilts, as if they were separate guest rooms in a private home, providing a restful ambiance. The adults-only rooms and suites accommodate a wide range of needs. If you're looking for a contemporary feel, ask for the Crow's Nest, which offers spectacular views of the postcard-pretty village.

Across the street, a much newer 19-unit, two-story structure includes two honeymoon rooms with king-size beds. Families with children will find these casual accommodations a welcome retreat. The inn also rents a number of cottages, some of which accommodate pets with no fee attached, and has a heated swimming pool that is kept open as long as weather permits. Cable TV with free Showtime is available in every room. The inn has an on-site restaurant (see our Restaurants chapter), a large lobby for lounging and a covered porch with rocking chairs. The inn closes for a few weeks in January but otherwise is open year round.

Oscar's House
$$ • One block from Silver Lake Harbor • (252) 928-1311

Oscar's House was built in 1940 by the keeper of the Ocracoke Lighthouse and was first occupied by the World War II commander of the Ocracoke Naval Base. Stories abound about Oscar, who lived and worked on the island for many years as a fisherman and hunting guide. This four-room bed and breakfast guesthouse is managed by Ann Ehringhaus, a massage therapist, local fine art photographer and the author of Ocracoke Portrait.

The house retains the original beaded-board walls, and all rooms are delightfully furnished. One upstairs bedroom has a loft that creates a comfortable setting. You won't find private baths, but sharing is easily managed. The large kitchen with a big table is available to guests; however, the stove is off limits. Ann serves a complimentary full breakfast to all guests and will gladly adhere to special preferences for vegetarian or macrobiotic meals. Smoking is allowed on the back deck only. Ann also offers therapeutic massage.

Oscar's House also offers an outdoor shower (there's one inside too), a dressing room and a deck area complete with barbecue grills. Meals can be eaten inside or outdoors. Oscar's House is within walking distance of all village shops and restaurants, and bicycles are free for guests. Ann will also gladly transport guests to and from the Ocracoke Airport, which is open to single- and twin-engine planes. This bed and breakfast is open from April to October.

Boyette House
$$-$$$$ • N.C. Hwy. 12 • (252) 928-4261

Jon Wynn presides over this very pleasant motel that opened more than 18 years ago. The Boyette House has more than doubled in size since 1994, and Boyette House II is now open. The newer addition offers wide porches and wicker furniture, which create a comfortable atmosphere. Ceiling fans stir the air on warm summer evenings. Each of the rooms in the newer section is well-appointed with a queen-size bed, breakfast bar, microwave, refrigerator and coffee maker. Most rooms also have wet bars and steam baths; all rooms have phones and remote cable TV. The two luxury suites on the third floor each have a private porch, picture windows on three sides, a Jacuzzi and steam bath.

Boyette House I is a 12-unit, two-story wooden structure offering comfortable hotel-style rooms. Each room has a private bath, remote TV and a refrigerator. Ten of the rooms have two double beds, and the other two offer one double bed. The five units on the first floor have ramp access, and wheelchairs will fit through the doors into the rooms and bathrooms, but you can't turn around once in the bathroom. They do, however, have one fully handicapped accessible room. Rocking chairs line the wide upper and lower decks fronting all rooms, which are nice places to read and relax. The lobby is a comfortable reading area as well, and visitors can borrow from the house selection of books. Guests will enjoy the complimentary coffee bar in the mornings.

Whether you're staying at Boyette House I or II, the sun deck in the back is perfect for sunbathing. You'll also find a hot tub here and hammocks under the trees out front.

You can arrange to be picked up at the boat docks or the airport free of charge. Boyette House is in walking distance of Silver Lake and the restaurants in Ocracoke. The motel is open most of the year, but its best to call ahead during the winter months just to make sure.

Sand Dollar Motel
$$ • Sand Dollar Ln. • (252) 928-5571

This quaint establishment is in the heart of Ocracoke Village behind The Back Porch Restaurant (there are no street signs). Fresh flowers welcome guests to the lobby. You're likely to be greeted by Roger Garrish, the property's personable owner, who is a great source for info on the island. The Sand Dollar has 11 rooms and a two-bedroom cottage. Two of the rooms are efficiencies, featuring small microwaves and coffee makers; all rooms have refrigerators and cable TV. Bedding options include queen- and double-size beds. One special room is connected to the pool and has a private deck and a king-size bed. Non-

smoking rooms are available. Guests can enjoy a continental breakfast and a dip in the pool. Repeat visits are common at this neat little place, so book your stay early. The inn is open from April 1 to mid-November.

Silver Lake Motel
$$-$$$ • N.C. Hwy. 12 • (252) 928-5721

Silver Lake Motel sits among a grove of trees along the main street of Ocracoke Village. The Wrobleski family built the two-story, 20-room motel in 1983 and has added another building since then. Featuring long porches and rooms paneled in California redwood, this motel is well-known for its rustic appeal and comfort; most of the furniture in the older rooms was built by the owners. Wooden shutters, pine floors and wallpapered baths create a cozy atmosphere.

The 12 suites in the newer building feature private porches with hammocks and wicker furniture, affording views of the lake. Rooms adjacent to these suites can be opened to provide for larger families. Suites, which offer living rooms and full kitchens, have wood floors, wallpapered baths and Victorian-style furnishings and wall coverings. End units have their own 7-foot-wide Jacuzzis overlooking Silver Lake - a relaxing environment indeed. Rooms offer king, queen or double beds. All the rooms have cable TV with Showtime. A common area in the older section of the motel serves as a dining room and lounge.

The Silver Lake Motel offers families comfortable and attractive rooms. A deep-water dock is provided for those arriving by boat. Handicapped-accessible rooms are available. It is open year round.

Ocracoke Harbor Inn
$$$ • across from the Coast Guard Station on Silver Lake Harbor
• (888) 456-1998

This is a brand new 16-room, six suite inn that overlooks Silver Lake Harbor. You can dock your boat right out front. Accommodations, decorated in an island motif, include private decks, hot tubs, microwaves, refrigerators, TVs, phones, coffee pots and hair dryers. There are king- and queen-size beds, and most suites have two-person Jacuzzis. Boat and beach equipment rentals are available. A continental breakfast is served. Nonsmoking rooms and two handicapped-accessible rooms are available. The inn is open year round.

The Castle
$$$$ • on Silver Lake • (252) 928-3505, (800) 471-8848

The Castle is a brand-new bed and breakfast in a renovated historic Ocracoke structure that was originally built during the 1950s, '60s and '70s. It features nine rooms, two with queen beds and Jacuzzis, one with a queen bed and double sofabed, one with a queen and two twin beds, three with a double and a twin, and two with queen beds. The suite features a queen bed and a walk-in shower. Three rooms have TVs. The upstairs sitting room has a communal TV. Two downstairs rooms are handicapped-accessible. All rooms have private baths, and two have lakefront views. A two-night stay is required on weekends. The Castle serves breakfast: quiche, muffins, pastries, coffee, tea and juice. It's open year round except for the Thanks-

giving and Christmas holidays. Smoking is allowed only on the porches and decks. Children older than 14 are welcome.

Harborside Motel
$$ • across from Silver Lake Harbor
• (252) 928-3111

This charming motel offers 18 rooms and four efficiencies, all well-kept and comfortable. All rooms have cable TV, phones and refrigerators. Most rooms offer two double beds, one has three and two have one double bed. Guests can use the waterfront sun deck, docks and boat ramp across the street. Nonsmoking rooms are available.

Harborside has its own gift shop offering a wide selection of clothing, books, gourmet foods and small gifts. Other shops and restaurants of Ocracoke Village are in walking distance. The Swan Quarter and Cedar Island ferry docks are nearby. This property has been owned by the same family since 1965, and its hospitality and service are well-established. All rooms are refurbished on a regular basis.

A complimentary breakfast of homemade muffins, coffee, juice and tea is provided. The motel is open Easter through mid-November.

Blackbeard's Lodge
$$ • Back Rd. • (252) 928-3421, (800) 892-5314

Bob Martin and his family have owned and operated Blackbeard's Lodge for 16 years. This three-story motel is right across the street from The Back Porch Restaurant.

This family-oriented property offers a wide variety of accommodations to suit almost anyone's needs. All 36 units, which accommodate from two to 10 people, have private baths, cable TV with Showtime, linen service and daily maid service. Eight of the units are efficiency apartments, some with adjoining rooms. All of the apartments offer fully equipped kitchens but no microwaves. Among the amenities at this 36-room motel, which includes suites, are refrigerators, whirlpool baths, king-size beds and wet bars. A 7-foot deep above-ground heated pool and bicycle rentals are also available.

Some units require a minimum stay of three nights. Ask about group rates and special rates for school trips. Blackbeard's Lodge is open April through October.

Beach House Bed and Breakfast
$$ • N.C. Hwy. 12 • (252) 928-1411

Located in a renovated 80-year-old home, this bed and breakfast is furnished with antiques and collectibles and offers three guest rooms. Two rooms have two queen beds, and the third room offers a double bed. All have private baths. Guests are served breakfast catered by the Fig Tree Bakery & Deli (the menu wasn't set by presstime).

The establishment features a lounge where guests can relax and a porch with a swing and rocking chairs. Beach House is a nonsmoking accommodation. Look for it on the sound side of Cafe Atlantic as you enter town. The airport is but a half-mile away. Shuttle/van service is free and includes ferry pickup. They are open year round.

Crews Inn Bed and Breakfast
$, no credit cards • Back Rd.
• (252) 928-7011

The Crews Inn is a great place to really get

away from it all. No phones or TVs will disturb your privacy here. Three rooms have private baths, and two share a bath. All rooms have double beds. The wraparound porch is an especially nice spot for guests to gather because the bed and breakfast is surrounded by large live oaks and is far enough away from traffic to make chatting easy. This is a nonsmoking establishment, but smoking is allowed on the porch. The inn serves mostly a continental but occasionally a full breakfast. Crews Inn is open year round.

Pelican Lodge
$$-$$$ • across from fire station
• (252) 928-1661

Built as a lodge, the Pelican features a full sit-down breakfast. The four rooms, one with two double beds and the others with one double bed, are spacious, carpeted and have private baths. Nonsmoking rooms are available. Amenities include cable TV, a small pool and free use of bicycles. The lodge is open year round.

Our rugged, low-slung coastline offers some of the prettiest places you could ever want to camp.

Camping

If you favor roughing it, even if it's in a luxurious camper, then surely you must experience camping on the edge of the North American continent. Our rugged, low-slung coastline offers some of the prettiest places you could want to camp at. Waves, wind and wildlife provide night symphonies and create long lost lullabies that just can't be heard inside hotel rooms. Between mid-March and late October, the weather along the barrier islands often is ideal for outdoor accommodations — and the soft sand of most area campsites makes a much more comfortable bed than the hard dirt floor of other campgrounds.

Even local Insiders like to get away for a weekend, leave their nearby homes, pitch a small tent and enjoy the Outer Banks as nature intended. Each year, more than 100,000 people camp in the National Park Service campgrounds. Thousands of others spend memorable vacations outdoors at privately owned facilities.

In its early days as a summer tourist destination, the Outer Banks overflowed with campgrounds. Anglers, boaters and hunters seemed to prefer sleeping outdoors. There also was not an abundance of motels and rental cottages.

Recent development, however, has encroached on some of the formerly wide open spaces. Several of the area's original campgrounds have long since closed, but at least 20 campgrounds, some with hundreds of sites, still are available on Colington, Roanoke, Bodie, Hatteras and Ocracoke islands. Many of these facilities are right off the ocean, behind high dune walls, open to the sun and wind. Others are secluded along the sound or in wooded hammocks.

Several Outer Banks campgrounds are seasonal, open only during warm weather and offering only cold showers. Others are year-round, residential parks that include electric and water hookups, sewage disposal, cable TV, laundry facilities, swimming pools, game rooms, full bathhouses — even on-site general stores. A few campgrounds also rent fully furnished recreational vehicles that sleep up to six people in addition to renting lots for travelers to park their own RVs. Tents, of course, are accepted at almost every camping facility.

All Outer Banks campgrounds have drive-up sites and roads suitable for any vehicles. Wilderness camping is not allowed anywhere, including open, undeveloped areas such as Kitty Hawk Woods, Nags Head Woods and Buxton Woods. Camping also is prohibited on the beach.

If you're looking for the ultimate backwoods escape, wilderness camping is permitted on Portsmouth Island — about a 20-minute boat ride south of Ocracoke. This uninhabited, isolated island has no permanent residents and is inaccessible except by boat. It's the perfect place to get away from it all and experience the barrier islands the way they once were. See our Daytrippin' chapter for more information on Portsmouth Island.

Campgrounds along the Outer Banks are either privately owned or managed by the National Park Service. Unless otherwise noted, private campgrounds accept major credit cards. Many take advance reservations — and we recommend making reservations if you plan to stay in July or August.

Summer is certainly the warmest time to sleep outside, but we enjoy camping in spring or fall when the barrier islands seem a different place and the air is crisp and cooler. If you're going to camp in-season, however, bring lots of bug repellent. Many campgrounds are in wooded areas or along the sound where mosquitoes sometimes outnumber people by the millions. Also bring long-sleeved, loose-fitting shirts and long pants to wear after the sun sets.

Be alert to sudden storms, and get a weather report before setting up camp for the night. Hurricane season runs from June through November. See also our Beach Information and Safety chapter.

All National Park Service campgrounds on the Outer Banks operate under a common policy and charge the same fees, except for the Ocracoke campground, which is on the National Park Reservation Service between Memorial Day and Labor Day (see this chapter's Ocracoke Island section for details). Other Park Service campgrounds accept only cash on arrival and don't take reservations. Sites are assigned on a first-come, first-served basis. Call the Park Service, (252) 473-2111, for additional information about any of their Outer Banks campgrounds.

www.insiders.com

See this and many other **Insiders' Guide®** destinations online — in their entirety.

Visit us today!

The National Park Service provides lifeguards at Coquina Beach, the Cape Hatteras Lighthouse, south of the Frisco Pier at Sandy Bay, and on Ocracoke Island. Swimming, shelling, surfing, fishing and sunbathing are allowed virtually everywhere on the Outer Banks. So pack your duffle bags and coolers, pull out those hiking boots and tent stakes, and get ready to really enjoy all the outdoors has to offer.

North of Oregon Inlet

Colington Park Campground
Colington Rd., Little Colington Island
• **(252) 441-6128**

Less than 3 miles west of the Bypass, past the first Colington Road bridge by Billy's Seafood, Colington Park Campground is situated on the quiet, calm waters of the sound — a stone's throw away from the best crabbing bridge on the Outer Banks (see kidstuff). Fishing and boating opportunities also abound in the areas around this campground.

Heavily wooded, tucked beneath tall pine trees, this campground originally was a tent-only area but has since been redesigned to accommodate recreational vehicles too. It's open year round, and reservations are accepted. Tent campers, however, are limited to two-week stays at a time.

All 55 sites at this facility have water, power and picnic tables. Grills are not provided, and open fires are prohibited, so bring your own grill or camp stove if you plan to cook. Hot showers, toilets, laundry facilities and a swing set on the property offer amenities to campers. There's also an on-site general store.

Air conditioning is available to recreational vehicles for $2 a night. Camping rates start at $14 per night for tents with two people and $16 a night for RVs with two people. The campground accepts personal checks. Pets are allowed on leashes.

Joe & Kay's Campground
Colington Rd., Little Colington Island
• **(252) 441-5468**

About a mile west on Colington Road, before you get to the first bridge, Joe & Kay's Campground has 70 full hookup sites that are rented on a yearly basis. An additional 15 tent sites also are available from April through November. Rates are $12 a night for two people, with a $2 per night charge for each additional person. Reservations aren't accepted, so sites are secured on a first-come, first-served basis. Credit cards and personal checks are not accepted.

Oregon Inlet Campground (NPS)
N.C. Hwy. 12, Bodie Island
• **(252) 473-2111**

The northernmost National Park Service campground on the Outer Banks, this facility offers 120 sites along the windswept dunes just north of Oregon Inlet. If you're arriving from the north, look for the campground entrance on the east side of N.C. 12 just before you cross the Bonner Bridge. It's on the ocean almost directly across from the Oregon Inlet Fishing Center.

Water, cold showers, modern toilets, picnic tables and charcoal grills are available here. There aren't any utility connections, but dumping stations are nearby.

Most of these sites are in sunny, open areas on the sand. Park rangers suggest that campers bring awnings, umbrellas or other types of shade. You also may need mosquito netting and long tent stakes here.

Oregon Inlet Campground is open from April through September. Campers are limited to a two-week stay. Reservations are not accepted, and sites are assigned on a first-come, first-served basis. Fees begin at $12 per night. Golden Age Passport holders receive a 50 percent discount. Note that only cash is taken — this campground does not accept credit cards or personal checks.

Roanoke Island

Cypress Cove Campground
U.S. Hwy. 64, Manteo • (252) 473-5231

Cypress Cove is a wooded, year-round, family vacation campground across from the Christmas Shop on Roanoke Island in Manteo. A total of 60 sites are available, including 27 tent sites with shade and 33 sites with hookups for RVs. Reservations are accepted, and pets are allowed on leashes.

Amenities at Cypress Cove include a playground, basketball court, batting cage, horseshoe pits, a nature trail with an osprey lookout and a fishing pond stocked with bass, bream and catfish where no fishing license is required. Boat and camper storage is available on-site. Hot showers, restrooms, picnic tables, grills and drinking water also are on the premises. There's an on-site dump station here. And laundry facilities are within walking distance at a nearby shopping center.

Rates are seasonal, with fees going up in the summer and on holiday weekends. Tent sites begin at $17 a night and RV sites start at $20 a night. Additional charges apply for additional people and sewer hookups.

Besides providing camping accommodations, Cypress Cove also rents 15 fully furnished trailers and air-conditioned "Kamper Kabins" that sleep one to six people. Rates run from $35 to $75 per night, depending on which cabin is used and how many people sleep there. Some units have up to three bedrooms and efficiency-style kitchens. Weekly rentals also are available.

Hatteras Island

Cape Hatteras KOA
N.C. Hwy. 12, Rodanthe
• (252) 987-2307, (800) 562-5268

A large campground about 14 miles south of the Bonner Bridge across Oregon Inlet, Cape Hatteras KOA has about 300 sites, including one-to-two-room "Kamping Kabins." Friendly, attentive staff greet campers as they arrive at this well-equipped campground. The campground is open March 15 through November and accepts reservations.

Besides hot showers, drinking water and bathhouses, Cape Hatteras KOA offers campers a dump station, laundry facilities, two pools, a hot tub, a playground, a game room, a restaurant and a well-stocked general store. Campers here can even take in a round or two of miniature golf, or a whirl on the campground's "Fun Bike" — a low-slung three-wheeler to ride inside the park. The ocean is just beyond the dunes for fishing and swimming, and a 200-foot soundside pier is the perfect place to fish, crab, or just sit and watch spectacular sunsets. There's even a recreation program at this campground, offering varied activities in the summer.

Rates are seasonal. Summer charges for tent sites with two campers are $29.95 per night, while sites with water and electric hookups cost $33.95 per night for two people. Full hookups are $35.95 nightly.

These cabins aren't fully furnished, but they do have beds. Rates are $49.95 per night for one-room units and $59.95 nightly for two-room cabins.

Lisa's Pizza Shoreline Campground
N.C. Hwy. 12, Rodanthe • (252) 987-2525

This soundside campground is open from Easter through Thanksgiving for recreational vehicles and tents. Windsurfers especially en-

---

INSIDERS' TIP

Use sturdy tent stakes designed to hold in sand — or you'll surely have open-air, starlit sleeping quarters.

Beach walkers investigate a large buoy that washed up during a storm.

joy this campground because they can sail right up to some sites.

Six sites have electrical and water hookups and cost $14.50 per night. Tent sites also include water and cost $11.50 nightly. Hot showers and picnic tables are on-site, but grills aren't provided, so bring your own camp stove if you plan to cook — or grab a pizza from Lisa's! Pets are allowed. Reservations are accepted — but not required. Personal checks are accepted, but not credit cards.

North Beach Campground
N.C. Hwy. 12, Rodanthe • (252) 987-2378

In the village of Rodanthe, North Beach Campground sits alongside the ocean south of the Chicamacomico Lifesaving Station. Here, 110 sites, all with water and electric hookups, offer campers both tent and RV accommodations and a wide range of amenities. Hot showers, bathhouses, picnic tables, a laundry facility, an outdoor swimming pool and a pump-out station are available on-site. There aren't any grills here, and open fires aren't allowed, so bring your own grill or camp stove if you want to cook.

North Beach Campground also has a grocery store that sells LP gasoline, kerosene, regular gas and virtually any convenience store item you might need. Pets are allowed on leashes. Reservations are accepted.

The campground is open from March through November. Rates begin at $14.50 a night for tents. Full hookups start at $19.50 a night.

Camp Hatteras
N.C. Hwy. 12, Waves • (252) 987-2777

A 50-acre, world-class campground, Camp Hatteras is a complete facility that's open year round and offers every amenity campers could desire. The site includes 1,000 feet of both ocean and sound frontage. Nightly, monthly and yearly reservations are accepted.

Most of Camp Hatteras' 320 sites have full hookups, concrete pads and paved roads. There's also a natural area near the Atlantic available for about 50 tents. Campers will find laundry facilities, hot showers, full bathhouses, picnic tables and grills on the premises.

For recreation, this campground provides

INSIDERS' TIP

Check out our Daytrippin' chapter for more camping choices within several hours of the Outer Banks.

Photo: Courtesy of Jeanne Reilly

two swimming pools, a clubhouse, a pavilion, a marina, fishing, two tennis courts, a 9-hole miniature golf course, volleyball, basketball and shuffleboard on-site. The grounds are extraordinarily well-kept and more organized than most comparable facilities. Sports and camping areas are separate, so sleeping outdoors is still a quiet experience here — even if you're napping midday.

Rates vary throughout the year, with full hookups running from $24.95 per night to $38.95 per night. Tent sites cost between $20.95 and $27.95 nightly. Personal checks are accepted. Pets are allowed on leashes.

Ocean Waves Campground
N.C. 12, Waves • (252) 987-2556

Open mid-March through mid-November, Ocean Waves Campground is a seaside resort with sites for RVs as well as tents. There are 68 spaces with full hookups. Twenty-five of those sites are concrete paved.

Three bathhouses, hot showers and laundry facilities are available. Campers also will enjoy the game room, picnic tables and an outdoor pool. New paved roads are an added convenience.

Rates for a family of four with two children younger than 12 are $18 to $20 per night for a full hookup and $13 to $15 per night for a tent site. Cable TV hookups and 50-amp service also are offered for $2 per night.

Kinnakeet Campground
Off of N.C. Hwy. 12, Avon
• (252) 995-5211

Just a quarter-mile from the Avon fishing pier, this soundside campground is geared toward families. Kinnakeet Campground is open year round and offers RV as well as tent sites. Reservations are recommended, and a dump site is available.

This Avon outpost has 53 full hookup sites and 15 tent sites. Each site has a picnic table, access to hot showers, toilets, drinking water and electricity. Avon Shopping Center is adjacent, offering tackle, groceries, a gas station and propane refills. No grills are available, and open fires are prohibited. So bring your own grill or camp stove if you plan to cook. A laundry facility is on-site.

Rates for two people begin at $12 a night year round for full hookups and $10 a night for tents. The cost for each additional person is $5 per night. Pets are allowed on leashes.

Sands of Time
Harbour and North End Rds., Avon
• (252) 995-5596

This year-round Avon campground has 51 full hookup sites and 10 tent sites, some with full shade. Water is available at every site. Hot showers, flush toilets, laundry facilities, a dump site and a pay telephone also are offered to all campers.

Besides swimming, fishing and sunbathing at the nearby beach and sound, visitors at Sands of Time will enjoy volleyball, horseshoes and picnic tables. Cable TV connections also are available for $2 extra per night. Grills aren't provided, and open fires are not allowed, so bring your camp stove if you want to cook.

Residents are permitted to live in this campground year round, and pets are allowed on leashes. Reservations are accepted and recommended for summer stays. Rates for tent sites are $16 a night in-season and $14.50 a night off-season. Rates for full hookups are $20.00 a night in-season and $18.00 a night off-season. Credit cards are not accepted.

Cape Woods Campground
Buxton Back Rd., Buxton
• (252) 995-5850

This off-the-beaten-path campground sits on the south side of Buxton in stands of poplar, pine and live oak trees. It includes 120 sites, 25 for tents, 29 with electric and water hookups, and 66 sites with full hookups. Cape Woods is open from March through November and accepts reservations.

Campers at this full-service facility will find two hot showers, fire pits, grills, picnic tables and two bathhouses, one of which is handicapped-accessible. You'll also find a laundry room, outdoor swimming pool, playground, volleyball court, and horseshoe pits. A general store on-site sells ice and LP gas. Freshwater fishing is allowed in the canals that run around this campground, where bass frequently are found. Pets are allowed on leashes.

In-season rates for a family of four begin

Camping near the ocean affords views like nowhere else.

at $18 a night for tents, $20 a night for water and electric and $23 a night for full hookups. Cable TV also is available for $2 extra per night on full hookup sites. Monthly and seasonal rates are available for all sites, and the campground accepts personal checks. Good Sam discounts are honored. Campers paying in advance get the seventh night for free.

Cape Point Campground (NPS)
Off N.C. Hwy. 12, Buxton
• (252) 473-2111

The largest National Park Service campground on the Outer Banks, Cape Point is about 2 miles south of the Cape Hatteras Lighthouse, across the dunes from the Atlantic. This campground has 202 sites — none with utility connections. It's open from Memorial Day Weekend through Labor Day Weekend but does not accept reservations.

Flush toilets, cold showers, drinking water, charcoal grills and picnic tables are provided here. Each site has paved access. A handicapped-accessible area is available, and a dumping station is nearby.

The campground is a short walk away from the ocean where world-class fishing and surfing abound. Most of these sites sit in the open, exposed to the sun and wind. Bring some shade, long tent stakes, lots of bug spray and batteries. Cost is $12 a night, and pets are allowed on leashes. Credit cards are not accepted.

Frisco Cove Marina and Campground
N.C. Hwy. 12, Frisco • (252) 995-4242

Part of a full-service marina on the Pamlico Sound, Scotch Bonnet offers mostly tent sites but has a good selection of permanent sites with utilities. Tent sites cost $13 a night, and full hookup is $20 nightly. The campground is open March 1 through Christmas.

Frisco Woods Campground
Frisco Woods, off N.C. Hwy. 12, Frisco
• **(252) 995-5208, (800) 948-3942**

This 30-acre campground in Frisco Woods is one of the best privately owned facilities on the Outer Banks. Developed by Ward and Betty Barnett, the soundside property boasts abundant forest and marshland beauty and at least 300 sites in a wooded wonderland.

Electricity and water are available at 150 campsites. Full hookups are offered at 35 other sites, and there are 90 tent sites in this shady spot.

Amenities include an in-ground swimming pool, picnic tables, hot showers, a small country store, propane gas and public phones. A recreation room with games and a TV lounge are also on-site. Windsurfers prefer this campground because you can sail right to the sites on the sound. Crabbing, fishing and hiking through the woods also are enjoyable activities for campers staying at Frisco Woods.

In-season rates for two people begin at $18 a night for tent sites, $21 a night for electric and water and $24 a night for full hookups. Each additional adult costs $4 per night. Cable TV is available for an extra $2 per night. Air conditioners and heaters are available for $3 a day.

A one-bedroom log cabin that sleeps four can be rented for $39.95 per night. The two-bedroom log cabin that sleeps six rents for $49.95 per night.

Frisco Woods is open March through November, and reservations are accepted. Pets are allowed on leashes.

Frisco Campground (NPS)
N.C. Hwy. 12, Frisco • (252) 473-2111

Our favorite spot for tent camping on the Outer Banks, Frisco Campground is operated by the National Park Service and sits about 4 miles southwest of Buxton. Just off the beach, next to Ramp 49, this is the area's most isolated campground. Its undulating roads twist over dunes and around small hills, providing privacy at almost every site. Some tent areas

are so secluded in stands of scrubby trees that you can't even see them from the place you park your car. This campground is a welcome find for folks who like to camp away from civilization.

Frisco Campground has 127 no-frills sites, each with a charcoal grill and picnic table. Flush toilets, cold water showers in bathhouses and drinking water are available. There aren't any hookups here, but RVs are welcome. A wooden boardwalk crosses from the campground to the ocean.

Reservations aren't accepted, and only cash is taken (no credit cards). Cost is $12 per night. Pets are allowed on leashes. Frisco Campground is open from Memorial Day weekend through Labor Day weekend. Golden Age discounts are honored.

Hatteras Sands Camping Resort
Eagle Pass Rd., Hatteras Village
• **(252) 986-2422, (800) 323-8899**

A well-maintained campground near the Hatteras Village ferry docks, Hatteras Sands is about a 10-minute walk from the ocean and is open March through November. Reservations are accepted up to a year in advance. Pets are allowed on leashes.

This campground has 104 sites with water and electricity, 43 sites with full hookups that includes cable TV and 25 tent sites. Pull-through sites for people who don't want to unhook their campers from their cars also are available. Each site has drinking water and a picnic table. Grills aren't provided, and open fires are prohibited, so bring your own grill or camp stove if you plan to cook.

Hot showers, five-star bathhouses and laundry facilities are on-site here. There's also an Olympic-size swimming pool, a game room and a mini-mart that stocks all sorts of camping supplies. A canal winds through this campground, offering fishing and crabbing opportunities. Campers also can walk to village shops and restaurants from this Hatteras resort.

Rates for tent sites run from $20.95

INSIDERS' TIP

Campers need to check weather forecasts frequently. Storms can pounce quickly, and it's best to be prepared.

nightly in the off-season to $26.95 nightly in the summer. Sites with hookups range from $24.95 through $33.95 per night. Hatteras Sands also rents six RVs, called "Camping Condos" that include beds and water. Electricity is available outside these units. Cost is $51.95 per night. There's also a "chalet," a small single-wide mobile that includes two bedrooms, a full kitchen and bathroom and a fold-out couch that sleeps one adult or two small children. The chalet rents for $395 a week, or $60 a night in the off-season and $700 per week, or $100 a night in the summer. The minimum stay at the chalet is three nights, with a $100 security deposit required. Some special rates and a 10 percent discount are available to Good Sam Park members.

Village Marina Motel & Campground
N.C. Hwy. 12, Hatteras Village
• (252) 986-2522

Open year round, this soundside campground includes six tent sites as well as 30 hookups with electricity, water and cable TV for recreational vehicles. A bathhouse with hot showers, a boat ramp, a small store, boat slips, picnic tables and grills are on site. Even tent sites, which cost $17.99 per day for two adults, include electrical outlets. Recreational vehicle sites cost $19.99 per day for two adults. Additional adults cost $2 per person per site. Children younger than 12 stay free. One small pet per site is permitted, as long as it's leashed. Personal checks are accepted, but not credit cards.

Ocracoke Island

Teeter's Campground
Cemetery Rd., Ocracoke Village
• (252) 928-3135, (800) 705-5341

Near the heart of Ocracoke Village, tucked in a shady grove of trees, Teeter's Campground offers nine full-hookup sites, 16 sites with electricity and water and 10 tent sites. Rates for two people begin at $15 a night for tents, $18 a night for electric and water and $20 a night for full hookups. Almost an anomaly on the Outer Banks, green grass lines this semi-wooded campground, creating a soft bed beneath thin tent floors.

Hot showers are available here. Six new charcoal grills were installed at tent sites just in time for the 1998 season, and a picnic table sits at every site. There aren't any laundry facilities on Ocracoke, so don't plan to machine-wash any clothes while camping here.

Teeter's Campground is open March 1 through November. Reservations are recommended on holiday weekends. Credit cards are not accepted.

Beachcomber
N.C. Hwy. 12, Ocracoke Village
• (252) 928-4031

Less than a mile from Silver Lake and the nearest beach access, Beachcomber campground has 29 sites with electricity and water and six tent sites. Rates for two people begin at $15 a night for tents and $18 a night for electric and water hookups. There's a $2 charge for each additional person.

Hot showers and fully-equipped bathrooms are available here. Picnic tables and grills also are on the premises. Remember: There aren't any laundry facilities on all of Ocracoke Island.

Pets are allowed at Beachcomber as long as they're leashed. The campground is open from late March through late November, depending on the weather. Reservations are recommended if you plan to camp here during the summer.

Ocracoke Campground (NPS)
N.C. Hwy. 12, Ocracoke Island
• (800) 365-CAMP

An oceanfront campground 3 miles east of Ocracoke Village and just behind the dunes, this National Park Service campground maintains 136 campsites. No utility hookups or laundry facilities are available here, but there are cold showers, a dumping station, drinking water, charcoal grills and flush toilets. As in all Park Service campgrounds, there's a 14-day limit on stays at Ocracoke Campground. The facility is open from Easter Weekend (April 5, 1996) through September.

Since most of these sites sit directly in the

sun, we suggest bringing awnings or some sort of shade to sit under. Long tent stakes also are helpful to hold down tents against the often fierce winds that whip through this campground. The constant breeze, however, is a welcome relief from summer heat. Bug spray is a must in the summer.

Ocracoke is the only National Park Service campground on the Outer Banks that operates on the National Park Reservation Service. Call the toll-free number to book a site in late spring or during summer. Major credit cards are accepted.

Since the phone number is almost always busy, we recommend reserving your campsite in writing. Reservations are not accepted during the off-season, so sites are assigned on a first-come, first-served basis, with cash only (no credit cards). All sites at Ocracoke Campground cost $13 per night in the summer, and $12 nightly during the off-season.

Old-fashioned stores
offer polished shells and
candy by the pound.
Sophisticated shops
sell estate jewels
and lavish linens.
New Age boutiques
beckon buyers with
glittering crystals and
mystical music.

Shopping

Barrier island shops extend from Corolla to Ocracoke, like a strand of pearls lazily draped in a velvet-lined case. Reclining on a sandy bed that's caressed from the east and west by salty kisses, each establishment offers surprises that remind one of an anniversary gift list: something paper, something gold, something wood, something copper. Cuddled within all the twists and turns, shoppers discover buys that range from the necessary to the novel. Old-fashioned stores offer polished shells, picturesque postcards and candy by the pound. Sophisticated shops sell estate jewels, cantaloupe soap slices and lavish linens. New Age boutiques beckon buyers with glittering crystals, bejeweled belly chains and mystical music.

Outer Banks stores are eclectic by necessity. We really have only one season to capture our slice of the pie, which must be stretched to last all year. As a result, many stores offer groceries, clothing and gifts under one roof. You can browse sandy island markets where crowded shelves yield everything from Red Delicious apples or generic toothpaste to imported pâté and fine French wine.

Buyers for our shops travel around the country and the world to bring back unique items: Louisiana hot sauce, Mexican candelabras, Celtic music, Polish glass ornaments and African batiks. You'll also find handcrafted works by local artisans and artists (see our Arts & Culture chapter). Pottery, basketry, painting, sculpture, carved ships and waterfowl, stained glass and handpainted furniture are available to enhance your surroundings.

The adventurous will want to check out our surf and sport shops for watersports paraphernalia and windsurfing equipment, Rollerblades, team sporting goods and tennis and golf needs. Our surf shops have racks of stylish clothing as well as surfing supplies (see our Watersports chapter). Tackle shops (listed in our Fishing chapter) fulfill the angler's dream.

Food stores run the gamut from those where you'll have difficulty finding whole-wheat products to a few that reserve shelf space for health food and imports. We have an abundance of seafood stores that carry fresh fish such as tuna, dolphin, wahoo, king mackerel, bluefish, snapper, croaker and flounder, along with crabs, shrimp, mussels, clams and oysters in season. The seafood at Seamark Foods — one is next to Wal-Mart in Kitty Hawk, another at the Outer Banks Mall in Nags Head — is reasonably priced, fresh and diverse enough to compete with more traditional seafood stores. The Food Lion grocery chain has five stores spaced along the Outer Banks, so there's no need to carry perishables from home if you're coming for an extended stay.

Whatever you may have forgotten to bring along — film, sunscreen or beach towels — you can find at large department stores, including Wal-Mart and Kmart. And what vacation would be complete without books? Many of the Outer Banks stores specialize in works by North Carolina authors. Manteo Booksellers is a cozy shop that will order whatever they don't have — check out their surprising Latin American section (see our Annual Events chapter introduction for book-signing information).

Many shops have seasonal hours, and some close down from December to March. During the height of the summer season, the majority are open seven days a week (some with extended evening hours). A good many shops in Southern Shores, Kitty Hawk, Kill Devil Hills and Nags Head are open year round, though not every day. Corolla and Hatteras shopping tends to be more seasonal, but don't discount those shops in both spots that keep their doors open through the fall and winter. During winter bluefin tuna season, some Hatteras shop doors will open to take advantage of the visitors.

Here are some of our favorite shopping

spots on the Outer Banks, organized by community beginning at the northern reaches of Corolla and Duck and running south through Ocracoke Island. Please bear in mind that since we have a limited tourist shopping season, our shops generally can't offer discount prices. Still, we don't jack up prices as some resort areas do. We are grateful for our visitors. When you purchase goods on the Outer Banks, you are helping us extend services to help handle the massive influx of visitors that flock to our shores in the summer, allowing us to live here year round. As part of our gratitude, we offer terrific service, quality goods, variety and a hometown greeting that's second to none. And just to show how much we do appreciate you, we'll share an Insiders' secret: There are unbeatable sales on the Outer Banks during our shoulder seasons. Spread the word!

Corolla

Corolla, about 10 miles north of Duck, offers convenient and novel shopping along N.C. Highway 12. We begin at the northernmost point.

Monteray Shores Shopping Plaza
N.C. Hwy. 12

The plaza is anchored by Food Lion and speckled with several spots to buy ice cream or other goodies to nibble between stops on your northern beach shopping excursion. The plaza has public restrooms and plenty of parking.

Gray's Department Store is here and has become an Outer Banks clothing tradition for men and women. Celebrating its 50th year in 1998, it offers name-brand swimwear and sportswear, a wide variety of top-quality T-shirts and sweatshirts and everyday shoes. Gray's has four other locations: at Scarborough Faire in Duck, in Kitty Hawk at U.S. Highway 158, MP 4, at TimBuck II Shopping Center in Corolla and in Nags Head at the Croatan Center on U.S. 158, MP 14.5. The Duck, Kitty Hawk and Nags Head locations are open year round. Both Corolla locations are open Easter through Thanksgiving.

Ocean Annie's sells handcrafted functional and decorative pottery, jewelry, wind chimes and fine gifts and gourmet coffee. You can shop at four other locations: Outer Banks Mall, U.S. 158, Nags Head; Scarborough Faire, N.C. 12, Duck; N.C. 12, Hatteras Landing, Hatteras Village; and Island Shops, N.C. 12, Avon. The Nags Head shop is open year round. The other locations operate on a seasonal basis opening mid-to late March and closing after Christmas.

Outer Banks Outdoors is an outfitter for hiking and climbing clothing and offers a variety of T-shirts, ladieswear and children's clothing, plus jewelry and souvenirs. This sporting goods business is operated by Kitty Hawk Kites and features an outdoor climbing wall in the courtyard. Kayak tours and hang gliding lessons are available. Other locations are in Nags Head at the Kitty Hawk Connection, across from Jockey's Ridge, U.S 158, MP 12; in Avon on N.C. 12; Hatteras Landing, Hatteras Village; and in Manteo on Queen Elizabeth Street on The Waterfront. The Nags Head shop is open all year. The Corolla and Avon shops are open Easter through December (see our Recreation chapter for more information).

Birthday Suits is a beachwear boutique that features casual sportswear and accessories for the entire family. The store is packed with an extensive line of swimwear for men, women and children. Look for swimwear in bra sizes, long torso, maternity, mastectomy and competition suits, and check out the selection of sunglasses, shoes, accessories and swim goggles. Owners Greg and Jill Bennett keep up with the times, and their shops (also at the Beach Barn, U.S. 158, MP 10, Kill Devil Hills; Scarborough Lane, N.C. 12, Duck; and Hatteras Landing on N.C. 12 in Hatteras Village) reflect their desire to provide the latest fashions for all body types. The Kill Devil Hills store is open year round. The Corolla, Duck and Hatteras shops are open from March through New Year's.

Bacchus Wine & Cheese carries one of the most extensive selections of domestic and imported wines on the Outer Banks as well as wine accessories and delicious deli sand-

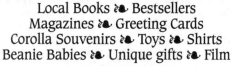

wiches. This shop also will put together special party platters and gift baskets.

TimBuck II Shopping Village
785 Sunset Blvd., N.C. Hwy. 12
• **(252) 453-4343**

TimBuck II features a variety of shops and several restaurants. Ground-level parking, covered decks, public restrooms and a recreation area with playground equipment, hammocks and swings are features. The village is open from Memorial Day to Labor Day from 10 AM to 9 PM. But individual shop schedule may vary as some attempt to keep their doors open year round. Keep in mind that operating hours during shoulder seasons will also differ from store to store.

Joan's is returning for its sixth season at TimBuck II. Owner Joan Estes offers complete interior design and furnishing services. Her boutique has home furnishings and accents including upholstery, dressers, nightstands, silk flower arrangements, lamps, pictures and wall hangings. We've found exquisite glass decanters, mango soap, lotus flower candles and hydrangea flower arrangements that took our breath away. Joan tries to keep her shop open all year. An Insider had a heyday purchasing a dozen or so bars of her intoxicating soaps for Christmas gifts.

Tar Heel Trading Company carries American handcrafted decorator items, accessories and serving pieces, puzzle boxes, pottery, wind chimes and designer jewelry. This popular business has several locations. At the Corolla shop look for cottage decor, including art for the walls and exquisite blown glassware. The Tar Heel location in Duck features handcarved decoys and kitchen and bath accessories. At Sea Holly Square, where they've almost doubled the size of the shop, you'll find handmade women's clothing — more like wearable art — including silk reversible jackets and stoles. Look for handprinted linens and an expansion of their designer jewelry lines. All branches, including the Duck shop on N.C. 12 and the Kill Devil Hills shop at MP 9½ are open March through December.

Looking for Beanie Babies? Corolla Book, Card & Gift Gallery has those popular little critters as well as beautiful gifts and items for the entire family — posters, candles, Corolla souvenirs, greeting cards, florals, Jelly Bellies, jewelry and local T-shirts and hats. A large children's department sells hats, shirts, toys, books and games. And the store offers a wide selection of local books and bestsellers in hardcover and paperback. It's open from Easter through Thanksgiving.

Carolina Moon is one of our favorite places on the Outer Banks to shop for jewelry, cards and New Age notions. For more information, see the listing on the main, Kill Devil Hills location under the Beach Barn Shops listing. Michael's Gems and Glass is a fun shop for kids of all ages. Their two locations offer rocks and minerals, fossils, marbles and other toys plus sterling silver jewelry. The Tanger Outlet Stores (formerly Soundings Outlet Mall) location on U.S. 158 in Nags Head is open year round. The Corolla store is open Easter through Thanksgiving.

Cotton Gin includes quality clothing and gifts including Department 56 collectibles, Tom Clark gnomes, decoys and carvings. The store's primary location is a sprawling barn-red building on U.S. 158 on the Currituck mainland. The Corolla shop features gifts, unique bedding and bath and kitchen supplies. It's open Easter through Thanksgiving.

Island Gear sells T-shirts, souvenirs, lots of glassware, swimsuits, sportswear and sweats. Look for their other shops in Scarborough Lane in Duck and at Nags Head's Tanger Outlet Mall, U.S. 158, MP 16. The Nags Head shop is open year round. The Corolla and Duck shops are open March through Christmas. Simply Southwest offers a wide variety of goods with the Southwest flair. Look for boots, hot sauces, home accessories, silver and Native American jewelry and ladies apparel. It's open March through November.

Gourmet Kitchen Emporium and Confectionery features a full line of specialty foods including pasta, jams, jellies and hot spicy stuff. Also offered are unique culinary gadgets, kitchen accessories and appliances, gift baskets, linens and cookbooks. It's open March through December.

Corolla Light Village Shops
N.C. Hwy. 12

Corolla Light offers just a couple of shops

arranged in a quaint seaside setting, but there's lots of variety found within. You can shop for anything from clothing and cappuccino to gourmet food, handcrafted gifts and baked goods here. In the same vicinity as these shops you'll find a post office, ABC package store and Winks, a convenience mart with gas pumps. The pumps are important to note because there are so few of them in the northern beach areas.

Mustang Sally's offers ladies' and men's contemporary sportswear, handpainted and embroidered one-of-a-kind articles of clothing, accessories and jewelry such as necklaces made of glass, iron or wooden beads, rings and hand-cut stones. You'll also find an assortment of handcrafted gifts like handpainted boxes, pottery and ironworks. Gift certificates are available. Look for other Mustang Sally's locations in Village Square Shops in Duck and at TimBuck II in Corolla. All three shops are open Easter through Thanksgiving.

If you're looking for all things surfing, dude, Gary can, like, hook you up at the Corolla Surf Shop. This is the only surf shop on the northern Outer Banks, and this store and the new shop at TimBuck II carry a great selection of surfboards, plus clothing, shades and shoes. Rentals and lessons are available. Ocean Threads specializes in swimwear for the entire family and features maternity, mastectomy and long-torso suits. This shop is packed with lots of sportswear for men and women including a good selection of name brands such as Billabong, Airwalk, Rusty, Arnette, Oakley, Emeric, Janco, Roxy, Quicksilver, Rusty Girl and more. The shop carries hats, stickers and incense and is an authorized Beanie Babies dealership. Check out the Monteray Shores Plaza location too. The Corolla Light location features the Gourmet Garage, with gourmet foods, gifts and gift baskets. Ocean Threads also is located at the Outer Banks Mall, U.S. 158, Nags Head.

Duck

You can shop 'til you drop in Duck village. This waterside community has maintained its quaint personality while adding numerous shops along the water's edges and among the shade trees across the narrow, winding Duck Road (N.C. Highway 12).

The complexes here range from just a couple of shops to the denser setups such as Scarborough Faire, where individual stores stretch back into a woody setting. In the more elaborate locations, you can satisfy your shopping needs on foot, though most other nearby shops are within walking distance too. Below is a listing of shops and centers found south to north — the direction folks travel while headed to Duck from the lower Banks.

Duck Soundside Shoppes
N.C. Hwy. 12

The accent is on clothing and gifts at this soundside location. But there's also a tackle shop (see our Fishing chapter) nestled among the shops geared to women. For a touch of magic, visit Papa's Garden, which features a full line of women's clothing and a vast array of unusual jewelry and gemstones; aromatherapy products including candles, oils and books; and an extensive line of handcrafted gifts and decorative accessories for your home and garden. It's open year round. The Dolphin Song specializes in brass and bisque sculptures and collectibles with ocean and marine themes, plus unique gift items and accessories to promote awareness of wildlife and the environment. Look for both Papa's Garden and the Dolphin Song shops in Kill Devil Hills at U.S. 158 at MP 6 and in Hatteras Landing. All locations are open year round.

For fine women's apparel, unique jewelry and accessories, stop in at La Rive Boutique. The focus is on handpainted clothing featuring motifs such as fish, flowers, fruit, cats and dogs. These are rendered in bold colors to give a contemporary feel. Many of the clothing lines come from California, so the fabric used is wearable year round. Speaking of a great feel, check out their cotton cashmere clothing — it's the ultimate. The shop is open year round.

Everything you need to add country charm to your home can be found at The Farmer's Daughter, including home accessories, crafts, decoys, collectibles (such as Department 56, Boyd's Bearstones and Byer's choice babies) and a variety of gift items such as lighthouses, statues, T-shirts and Christmas decorations. Look for the Nags

Head location at U.S. 158, MP 16. Both shops are open year round.

The Duck Duck Shop
1181 Duck Rd. (N.C. Hwy. 12)
• (252) 261-8555

The Duck Duck Shop, located between Scarborough Faire and Twiddy Real Estate, operates as a gift shop and post office. It features selected local North Carolina decoys, greeting cards, postcards, books and prints and is open year round.

Scarborough Faire and Scarborough Lane
N.C. Hwy. 12

These adjoining complexes feature a series of boutiques and businesses in a garden setting. The facade of the latter is reminiscent of the architecture of old-time lifesaving stations. The buildings are set into a grove of trees, and the shops are connected by a walkway through the woods, creating one of the shadiest spots in Duck in midsummer. You'll find an ice cream shop here if you really need to cool down and a fudge shop for your sweet tooth.

We'll start with a selection of the Scarborough Faire shops. At Rainbow Harvest you'll find all made-in-the-U.S.A. items. The shop's jewelry line features gold and silver creations by Ed Levin. You can purchase candles and Christmas ornaments, posters and knickknacks with lighthouse and Corolla horse motifs. Rainbow Harvest is an animal lover's paradise chock-full of animal figurines and gift items with animal motifs. You'll find United Design Collectibles, which include lions and tigers and teddy bears, plus penguins, frogs and lots more. Handcarved wooden marine mammals and animal mobiles abound. Also look for the TimBuck II location. The Duck shop is open year round; the Corolla shop is open May through Thanksgiving.

Elegance-of-the-Sea features custom-designed wreaths and arrangements. In addition, the shop carries baskets, silk flowers, candles, oil lamps, collector's dolls and carvings. New for 1998 is a selection of fresh flowers. It's open Easter through New Year's. Sara DeSpain is celebrating her 25th year and offers a wide range of gold, gems and diamond jewelry of her own creation. She features the original designs of 30 artisans in a special gallery section here. DeSpain accepts limited commissions and is open Easter through Christmas.

Toy-rific is a great children's store for rain or shine activities. Look for top-of-the-line playthings for infants, toddlers and older kids including stuffed animals, puzzles, beach toys, trains and kites. It's open March through Christmas. Kid's Kloset is one of the few children's clothing boutiques on the Outer Banks. You'll find summerwear and swimsuits with name brands such as Citris and La Blanca sized for newborns to preteens. The shop is open March through November.

Island Bookstore sells established works of fiction, discount hardcover bestsellers, a wide variety of nonfiction, children's books and specialty selections. The collection of works by Southern authors is extensive, and you also can find audio books and jazz and blues on compact disc. Special orders are welcome. The shop is open year round. The Solitary Swan features cherry, pine and walnut furniture and accessories such as porcelains, glassware and pewter, plus traditional crafts and outdoor garden pieces, decoys and folk art. The shop is open year round.

Now we'll move on to Scarborough Lane. Stop at the Island Trader for sterling silver jewelry and a variety of gifts and home and garden accessories. It features loads of baskets and candles, kitchen linens and plenty of North Carolina food products with a hot flair — hot sauces, chutney and barbecue sauces. The shop is open March through November. Exotic Cargo features woodcarvings and pottery from Indonesia and Thailand plus silver jewelry, handbags, book bags and hats. There are two other locations — at Timbuk II in Corolla and at the Croatan Center, U.S. 158, MP 14½ in Nags Head. The Nags Head shop is open all year. The northern locations are open March through Thanksgiving.

There are two Salt Marsh shops on the Outer Banks specializing in unique children's toys from the educational to the just-plain-fun. They also carry a line of conservation-oriented items. Look for glow-in-the-dark playthings, stickers, puzzles, stuffed animals, baby gifts, collectibles, building toys and much more. The Nags Head shop at

the Kitty Hawk Connection, U.S. 158, MP 13½, features irresistible gifts, T-shirts, clothing, jewelry, books and fun and educational toys.

Osprey Landing
N.C. Hwy. 12

Osprey Landing is a smaller shopping area overlooking the sound. If you get hungry, The Afterdeck Bar and Grille, a delightful cafe, is here (see our Restaurants chapter). Books & Things offers all kinds of hardbacks and paperbacks, children's and local books plus a variety of cookbooks, collectibles, chimes, framed prints and maps. It's open Easter through Thanksgiving. The Board Room is a stimulating shop featuring challenging intellectual games plus high-quality jigsaw puzzles and lots of mind-boggling magic tricks. The shop is open March through December.

Loblolly Pines Shopping Center
N.C. Hwy. 12

Loblolly Pines is a complex of shops and eateries where you can purchase anything from a postage stamp to precious gems. You can whet your appetite with an ice cream cone or sweet treat as well. Look for a rental shop, bicycle business, shoe store and another fine T-shirt shop in this center.

Yesterday's Jewels carries an interesting collection of old and new jewelry, including gold and sterling silver. It's open Easter

through December. The Phoenix offers high-quality fashions, jewelry and accessories. The hand-sewn hats are beautiful, and you will find other unique items here that you won't find anywhere else on the Outer Banks. The selection includes handmade shell lamps made by Richard Hoosin, using methods created by Louis Tiffany. The shells used in the shades come from all over the world.

Duck Trading Company
1194 Duck Rd. (N.C. Hwy. 12)
• (252) 261-0491

This is a variety shop you won't want to miss. If you like North Carolina-made products, you'll love the selection of crafts and collectibles, Tar Heel specialty foods, cookbooks, peanuts and other goodies. The staff will put everything together in a charming gift basket. It's open year round.

Duck Village Square
N.C. Hwy. 12

Practical as well as tasty needs can be met at this soundside location. You'll find Kellogg's True Value, where you can shop for all your hardware and building supply needs. Kellogg's also has a garden center and a selection of outdoor furniture. For your convenience, they have two other locations: one in Kill Devil Hills on N.C. 12 at MP 9½, a second in Manteo on U.S. 64/264. All stores are open year round. Choose from an extensive variety of affordable wines and beers from all over the world and a wide variety of sandwiches and wood-fired pizza at The Village Wine Shop and Deli, which is open all year.

Duck Common
N.C. Hwy. 12

This beautifully landscaped setting offers something for men, women, children and even pets. Confetti Clothing Company offers casual sportswear for the whole family. It stocks clothing made by small design firms — you won't find that mass-manufactured look here — but there's more to Confetti than designer threads. The shop carries novelty items and home accessories and has an interesting pet department complete with gourmet dog bones, catnip and an array of leash apparel with funny inscriptions. Check out the home furnishings including authentic, old Mexican furniture — one-of-a-kind items you won't want to miss. Also look for home accessories, silver and ceramic gifts. This eclectic shop is open year round.

Cravings, open year round, is an appropriately named gourmet shop (see our Restaurants chapter). Just one sip of Northwest Market Spice Tea, and you'll be hooked. Run by the folks who operate Confetti, the shop features gourmet coffee and tea, cappuccino, blended ice drinks and iced teas. You can buy your favorite beverage already made or take home your own special package. You'll find fresh coffee beans and fresh bagels and baked goods.

Wee Winks Square
N.C. Hwy. 12

Wee Winks is a practical stop for a wide variety of needs. This is the home of Wee Winks Market, the perfect quick stop for those last-minute food and gas purchases or for picking up a newspaper. If you're interested in fresh produce, Green Acres Produce, only open during the summer season, has fresh-from-the-farm vegetables and fruits. You'll also find an ABC package store at this location.

We dare you to make it through the Lucky Duck without buying at least one remembrance of your visit. Every nook and cranny is filled with unique home accessories, local arts and crafts, pictures, shells, woven throws, bath items, books and even fudge. This store, open from March through December, is a must-see in Duck.

Stop by Beach Essentials, open March through October, for virtually everything for a beach outing, including boogie boards, lotions, rafts and lots more. Children are fascinated by the shop's hermit crabs. Artisan's Boutique offers an eclectic combination of ladies' apparel, T-shirts, women's hats, shoes, jewelry and some gift items, all of which bring to mind the artist's touch. It's open March through December. At Lady Victorian you'll find contemporary styles for today's woman. Outfits and suits are the emphasis here, and you'll find lots of cotton, silk and linen plus quality dresses, evening wear, intimate apparel, travel accessories and personal items such as bath products, soaps and powders. Lady Victorian is open year round.

Tommy's Gourmet
N.C. Hwy. 12 • (252) 261-8990

Tommy's is a place to pick up delicious, fresh-baked goods such as pastries, turnovers, breads, bagels and doughnuts. You'll find a complete deli featuring roasted ham and chicken, ready-to-eat spiced shrimp, sandwiches, fresh salads, fresh-baked pies and daily luncheon specials. Tommy's is famous for its Angus beef steaks that are aged for 21 days. All steaks are cut to order. Tommy's maintains an extensive wine selection and carries lots of imported beers in addition to a full range of groceries. It's open March through New Year's.

Duck Waterfront Shops
N.C. Hwy. 12

These cool shops — both in location and what they have to offer — provide all kinds of great shopping opportunities. Sunset Ice Cream is just the spot to sip or slurp your refreshments. The entertainment here is provided by dozens of mallards and other web-footed friends paddling around in the Currituck Sound shallows just below the railings. It's open Easter through Thanksgiving. At Duck's General Store you'll find a wide variety of unique gifts. Some of the most popular items include finely crafted sterling silver jewelry, a wide selection of T-shirts, sweatshirts and hats, postcards and humorous greeting cards, books on North Carolina and the Outer Banks, ship models, picture frames, gourmet sauces, candy, weather instruments and other unusual gifts including B.D. Whort, the redneck frog fountain. It's open year round.

Islands, under new ownership in 1998, offers casually comfortable, lightweight women's clothing, a designer clothing section for children and a line of men's apparel made from vintage Hawaiian fabric. Islands has a large aromatherapy section with lotions, soaps and candles. You'll also find lots of artistic gifts and jewelry including sterling silver baby gifts and music, picture frames and stuffed animals. It's open year round.

Barr-EE Station and Catalogue Outlet features unbelievably low prices on name-brand men's and women's clothing, shoes and accessories priced up to 50 percent off the regular retail price. And Barr-EE Station Swimwear Outlet, just two doors down, sells discounted name-brand swimwear at up to 50 percent off.

For one-of-a-kind clothing for women and children, visit Donna Designs, a unique shop featuring handpainted artwork — crabs, fish, turtles, flowers and frogs, to name a few subjects — on cotton T-shirts including crop-top tees for adults and children, sweatshirts, sundresses and French terry. New for 1998 is a line of gifts and home decor items called "Out Of The Blue" featuring lampshades and lamps, glassware, toy chests and children's tables and chairs all handpainted in Donna's inimitable style. Her work is tasteful, colorful and rendered in a meticulous fashion. Insiders know they always will find top quality, artistic goods here. The other retail locations are at Kitty Hawk Connection in Nags Head (across from Jockey's Ridge State Park) and at Monteray Plaza in Corolla. The Duck shop is open March though New Year's. All the other shops are open Easter through New Year's.

The Kid's Store has toys for kids of all ages. The selection includes stuff for the beach, craft kits, wildlife and museum replicas, and infants' and children's T-shirts in sizes ranging to pre-

teens. Visit their other location in Surfside Plaza in Nags Head. Both shops are open March through Thanksgiving.

Southern Shores

The Marketplace
U.S. Hwy. 158, MP 1

The Marketplace in Southern Shores, which is the large shopping center on your left at MP 1 as you drive onto the Outer Banks off the Wright Memorial Bridge, is anchored by a Food Lion grocery store and CVS pharmacy. Food Lion, a large North Carolina-based chain, has five stores on the Outer Banks, and CVS (formerly Revco) has several additional locations as well. Listed are a few of the specialty shops that fill out the Marketplace selection.

Total Communications is an Outer Banks source for pagers, cellular phones and two-way radios for individuals and businesses. Weekly

rentals are available along with Internet access. Paige's carries a full line of women's casual and elegant wear in sizes 2 to 26. Look for accessories such as scarves and belts, fashion jewelry and even peach syrup and body chocolate. Paige's is open year round. Southern Bean, a fantastic little coffeeshop with fresh bagel sandwiches, tempting desserts and all those frothy, high-octane concoctions that'll make you say "au lait!" is tucked into The Marketplace as well (see Restaurants for more information).

Kitty Hawk

Shopping in Kitty Hawk is geared toward year-round residents. In Kitty Hawk, you'll find nationally recognized store chains plus local mom-and-pop shops. You may be wondering how the previously mentioned Marketplace shopping complex can be in Southern Shores, while The Shoreside Centre, just across U.S. 158, is in Kitty Hawk. To avoid

confusion, bear in mind that everything on the south side (the Coastal Chevrolet and Wal-Mart side) of U.S. 158 is considered to be in Kitty Hawk.

Central Garden & Nursery
U.S. Hwy. 158, MP ¼ • (252) 261-7195

This is a family owned and operated business that's been serving the Albemarle area for 32 years. The garden center sells indoor plants, shrubs and trees plus perennials and annuals. A landscape architect is available to assist with landscape planning. The nursery is behind Coastal Chevrolet at the eastern foot of the Wright Memorial Bridge. It's open year round.

Islander Flags
U.S. Hwy. 158, MP 1
• (252) 261-6266

All designs at Islander Flags are appliqued, including custom artwork and U.S., state and foreign emblems. You can buy decorative banners, windsocks, flagpoles and accessories. The Kitty Hawk shop is open year round and is next to Coastal Auto Mart.

The Shoreside Centre
U.S. Hwy. 158, MP 1

This center features national chains including Wal-Mart, Radio Shack, Subway, The Dollar Tree, Cato's and McDonald's. The shops are open year round. Seamark Foods is an upscale grocery store with a terrific bakery, deli and salad bar. Seamark has an extensive selection of cheeses and wines as well as other gourmet foods not always available in other supermarkets on the Outer Banks. Seamark carries a large selection of fresh fish, shellfish (including live lobsters) and everything else you need to fix a seafood feast. There's another location in Nags Head at the Outer Banks Mall, U.S. 158, MP 15, 441-4121. Both stores are open year round.

Carawan Seafood
U.S. Hwy. 158, MP 1 • (252) 261-2120

Situated on the lot in front of The Shoreside Centre, Carawan's is locally owned and sells fresh local fish and shellfish in season. The store also carries a modest but excellent selection of wines and beers, gourmet food items, lures and tackle. It's open year round.

Three Winks Shops
U.S. Hwy. 158, MP 1

This modest group of businesses is in the same vicinity as The Shoreside Centre. Included are an ABC package store, an express Chinese take-out food shop and a discount golf shop (see our Golf chapter for more information).

Ambrose Furniture
U.S. Hwy. 158, MP 2 • (252) 261-4836

South of the Aycock Brown Welcome Center is Ambrose Furniture, a family owned and operated furniture showroom that has been in business in the area for more than 50 years. The store has a free design service and a qualified staff to assist you with your selection of furniture, blinds and housewares. Check out the Corolla location at Monteray Shores Plaza. Both locations are open year round.

Winks Grocery
N.C. Hwy. 12, MP 2 • (252) 261-2555

Winks is what shopping is supposed to be like at a beach store — a sometimes-sandy floor, beach music filling the air and a laid-back atmosphere. Winks has a deli, lots of edibles and plenty of beach supplies, beer, wine and deli sandwiches plus sweatshirts and T-shirts. The shop is open year round.

Whalebone Surf Shop
U.S. Hwy. 158, MP 2½ • (252) 261-8737

This shop is jammed with all the hot looks in beach fashions, swimwear, surfwear and travel gear. This is a true local surf shop, and owner Jim Vaughn is popular with the area's top surfers. Whalebone also has a Nags Head location on U.S. 158 at MP 10. The Nags

Head shop is open year round. The Kitty Hawk location is open March through Thanksgiving.

Wave Riding Vehicles
U.S. Hwy. 158, MP 2½ • (252) 261-7952

Wave Riding Vehicles is the largest surf shop on the Outer Banks. WRV has beach fashions, swimsuits and gobs of T-shirts in all the way-cool brands (see our Watersports chapter for surfing equipment information). They also offer snowboarding equipment and apparel. It's open year round.

Seabreeze Florist
U.S. Hwy. 158, MP 3 • (252) 261-4274

Seabreeze specializes in fresh flowers and arrangements by designers on staff. Dried arrangements incorporate shells and flowers to create tasteful beach mementos. Nautical baskets are very popular, and Seabreeze delivers balloons, plants and flowers for all occasions. Weddings are a specialty. Seabreeze offers worldwide FTD and Telaflora services. It's open year round.

East Coast Softspa and Jacuzzi
Quail Run Business Center, 500 Sand Dune Dr., Ste. 8 • (252) 261-8588

Visit East Coast Softspa and Jacuzzi for a downright relaxing and hydrotherapeutic way to spend the day. The company sells, ser-

vices and rents Softubs and portable spas, which set up easily indoors or out. New in 1998 are Jacuzzi brand acrylic spas. Located behind Pizzazz Pizza, East Coast is open year round.

Ace Hardware
U.S. Hwy. 158, MP 3½ • (252) 261-4211

Ace sells everything the do-it-yourselfer needs for home- or cottage-improvement projects. Other Ace Hardware stores are in Corolla on N.C. 12; in Nags Head on U.S. 158, MP 11½; in Manteo on U.S. 64/264; and in Avon on N.C. 12. All locations are open year round.

Bert's Surf Shop
U.S. Hwy. 158, MP 4 • (252) 261-7584

Bert's carries a full line of swimsuits, T-shirts and other beachwear along with the obligatory surfing gear and souvenirs (see our Watersports chapter for more information). Bert's has a second location at U.S. 158, MP 10½, Nags Head. Both shops are open year round.

COECO Your Office by the Sea
U.S. Hwy. 158, MP 4 • (252) 261-2400

COECO is a complete office supply store featuring computer supplies, stationery and other accessories. You can rent typewriters, and a fax service is available. It's open year round.

Kitty Hawk Plaza
U.S. Hwy. 158, MP 4

Kitty Hawk Plaza offers quality shopping experiences with the emphasis on home improvement. Decor by the Shore designs complete home furnishing packages assembled by a team of design specialists; it's open year round. Daniels' Homeport specializes in housewares and accessories such as candle holders, wine racks, lamps, window treatments and wicker and outdoor furniture.

Crafter's Gallery
U.S. Hwy. 158, MP 4½ • (252) 261-3036

Across from Daniel's is Crafter's Gallery, a spacious year-round marketplace featuring only handmade, one-of-a-kind crafts, pottery and jewelry, much of it created by local artists. The shop has a large inventory of country crafts including cloth baskets, handpainted gourds and furniture and more. It's open year round.

Kill Devil Hills

Shopping is something to look forward to along U.S. 158 and the Beach Road in Kill Devil Hills — there's a little bit of everything along this stretch. (Kill Devil Hills is also a good place to head to if you're hungry for fast food: U.S. 158, here known as "French Fry Alley," has a Taco Bell, Burger King, Wendy's, McDonald's and Pizza Hut.)

Second Hand Rose Thrift Shop
U.S. Hwy. 158, MP 5½ • (252) 441-0352

This shop is brimming with consignment items (mostly old) and some antiques, but there are some new items, jewelry, decorative accessories and clothing for the entire family. You'll find household items, knickknacks, books, records, tapes, jewelry and more here. It's open year round.

Seagate North Shopping Center
U.S. Hwy. 158, MP 6

At the north end of Kill Devil Hills, Seagate North offers a variety of shopping experiences. T.J's Hobbies and Computer Rx carries hobby and craft materials, model cars, airplanes and boats, rockets and kites plus radio control supplies for models and railroading equipment. The shop, open year round, has metal detectors too. It also offers computer sales, service and consultations.

Mom's Sweet Shop and Beach Emporium will remind you of an old-fashioned ice-cream parlor where you can choose from 24 flavors of ice cream and yogurt. They even make their own fudge. Browse around the emporium for souvenirs; it's open all year. Movies, Movies rents videos and provides all the services you would expect; it's open year round.

Outer Banks Flag Shoppe offers more than 330 in-stock designs of decorative house flags, sports flags (including those popular NASCAR designs), state and county flags and boat flags. There is also custom flag-making service. Shop here for a variety of kites and hundreds of windsocks. A color catalog is available for mail orders. The shop is open year round.

Hatteras Swimwear specializes in custom-made swimsuits for our custom-made bodies. At I Love Country, gifts, crafts and woodworking are the focus plus teddy bears galore and the popular Beanie Babies. The shop takes special orders and is open March through December. Lenscape Photos, open year round, is a full-service photography shop that carries film and offers a variety of portrait options and a state-of-the art machine for previewing your negatives.

Norm Martinus at Nostalgia Gallery specializes in antiques, vintage paper, antique advertisements, custom matting and framing. If you're looking for picture framing perfection, this is the place to go, and it's open year round. Martinus is the co-author of *Warman's Paper*, an encyclopedia of antiques and collectibles. He's a real Insider on the subject and a local favorite. Stop and chat with him — he holds a warehouse of knowledge and is very personable. The store is open year round.

Cooke's Corner
U.S. Hwy. 158, MP 6 • (252) 480-0519

Cooke's Corner features a surf shop, a children's clothing store, a women's apparel shop, a health food store and a NASCAR sports paraphernalia shop. Anchoring Cooke's Corner is Speedway Sport Shop, owned by Mr. Cooke himself, offering NASCAR hats, shirts, cars, mugs and sunglasses year round. My Kid features children's clothing from newborn to 16. The shop offers organic cotton fabrics, swimsuits and swim diapers, hats and baby gifts. They provide free gift wrapping and are open year round.

Daily Menu features organic foods including refrigerated, frozen, bulk and fresh organic produce as well as herbs and spices, cleansing and beauty-care products and free facials. It's open year round. Casual Creations & Craftworks features women's clothing, some with painted fabric, along with crafts such as bird and fish carvings. It's open year round.

Awful Arthur's Beach Shop
N.C. Hwy. 12, MP 6 • (252) 449 2220

This shop is a haven for Awful Arthurs paraphernalia inspired by the popular oyster bar next door. You'll find T-shirts, sweatshirts, golf shirts, hats, beach towels and glassware bearing the eatery's infamous logo. Shop here for beach needs including beer and groceries, beach chairs and umbrellas, fireworks, seashells, tackle, coolers and hermit crabs. It's open mid-March through Thanksgiving.

The Dare Centre
U.S. Hwy. 158, MP 7

On the west side of U.S. 158, The Dare Center is anchored by Belk's Department Store and Food Lion. Look for a variety of eateries here, including a new Chinese take-out or eat-in restaurant, China King, with very reasonable prices. You'll also find Hosanna, featuring Christian books, cards, T-shirts and mu-

sic. Outer Banks Sports Locker specializes in sporting goods, sportswear and fitness equipment by companies such as Nike, Starter, New-Era, Russell, Champion, Diamond, Wilson, Spalding and DeLong, to name a few. Martial arts and weightlifting needs are available here, and they handle uniform printing requests and have a full line of trophies and awards.

Good Vibes Video is a rental shop that offers box-office hits and esoteric art films. The Dare Center location is open all year; Good Vibes' Corolla shop at TimBuck II shopping center is open Easter through Thanksgiving. Hairoics is a full-service salon where the staff has a great sense of humor but takes your coiffure seriously. Hairoics is open year round. Atlantic Dance is a dance studio as well as a great little boutique for children and adults featuring shoes, leotards, tights, bags and skirts.

North Carolina Books
U.S. Hwy. 158, MP 7½ • (252) 441-2141

In the Times Printing building, North Carolina Books is chock-full of secondhand paperback books and a selection of reduced-price hardcover books. You can bring in your old paperbacks and use them as credit toward the purchase of other secondhand books from the store. The store also has new books and tapes and is open year round.

Stop 'n' Shop
N.C. Hwy. 12, MP 8½ • (252) 441-6105

Insiders consider this little treasure trove a hidden gem that's well worth discovering. More than your average gas and goodies store, the Stop 'n' Shop offers an upscale convenience alternative. A 4,000-square-foot expansion, completed in April, means almost double the space of the original store and much more of all the good things on hand. The deli (which starts serving fresh bagels, hot coffee and breakfast sandwiches at 6:30 AM year round) uses top-quality Boar's Head meats, and the store boasts a wide variety of gourmet food products and one of the best selections of wine and microbrewed beers on the beach. There are large selections of beach necessities and fishing stuff, and Stop 'n' Shop sells and rents beach equipment such as boogie boards, sand chairs, umbrellas and rods and tackle. There's even an impressive variety of daily newspapers. During the summer season, the store is open until 1 AM.

The Trading Post
N.C. Hwy. 12, MP 8½ • (252) 441-8205

Here's a good general store to buy things for the beach. It carries T-shirts, souvenirs, swimwear and convenience grocery items and is also a branch post office. It's open year round.

SunDaze
U.S. Hwy. 158, MP 8½ • (252) 441-7272

Located just south of the Kill Devil Hills Post Office, SunDaze features islandwear, fine sterling silver jewelry and a good selection of accessories such as sunglasses, hats, belts and bags. If you're into all things reggae, this is the Outer Banks' best outlet for rasta-tinged CDs and accessories. Check out the shop's incense, aromatic oils and candles. It's closed in January and two weeks in February.

The Bird Store
U.S. Hwy. 158, MP 9 • (252) 480-2951

The Bird Store carries a complete line of antique and new decoys featuring local carvers. Antique fishing gear, fish prints and original art are also on display. It's open Easter through Christmas.

Jim's Camera House
U.S. Hwy. 158, MP 9 • (252) 441-6528

Jim's is a full-service photography store that offers film developing (including one-, two-, four- and 24-hour service) and is stocked with camera and black-and-white darkroom supplies. The shop sells beautiful frames and albums and offers professional photography service and studio facilities. Custom framing and matting are available. Jim's is open year round.

Charlotte's Web Pets and Supplies
U.S. Hwy. 158, MP 9 • (252) 480-1799

Charlotte's is a well-stocked pet shop featuring fish, commercial and residential fish tank maintenance, birds, reptiles, small animals, pet food and supplies. It's open year round.

Lifesaver Shops
N.C. Hwy. 12, MP 9

Lifesaver Shops features several practical stops. Lifesaver Rentals fills rental needs and offers thrifty bargains — these folks rent it all! Look for beach umbrellas, chairs, TVs, VCRs, baby equipment, cottage supplies, portable radios, microwaves, charcoal grills and even blenders. They offer linen service complete with sheets, pillowcases and bath towels. Look for surfboards, ocean kayaks, boogie boards, snorkel and fishing equipment and bikes galore. It's open March through November. Nana's Thrift Store, open year round, is a consignment shop featuring men's, women's and children's clothing, housewares, antiques, jewelry and bedding.

Nags Head Hammocks
U.S. Hwy. 158, MP 9½ • (252) 441-6115, (800) 344-6433

You can't miss the setting, with its palm trees and lush landscaping. At the shop you'll find the famous, durable, high-quality handmade hammocks; single- and double-rope rockers, footstools and bar stools; single and double porch swings; "slingshot" swings; captain's chairs; and double recliners. You can also purchase items via mail-order year round. Nags Head Hammocks has other showrooms at Timbuk II in Corolla, Duck village on N.C. 12, on N.C. 12 in Avon, and in Point Harbor (Currituck County) on U.S. 158.

Seashore Shops
N.C. Hwy. 12, MP 9½

There's a cluster of interesting places here including a small year-round eatery (the Dip-n-Deli) for ice cream, subs, sandwiches and soups plus gift and art shops. Sea Isle Gifts and Lamp Shop, open from March through December, carries ceramic, wood, metal, shell-filled and other lamps and a variety of shades, repair kits, shells, souvenirs, gifts, home accessories and jewelry. A picture frame shop and gallery, Frames at Large provides custom framing services, and its gallery displays prints, watercolors, etchings and posters of seascapes. It's open year round.

The Bike Barn
Wrightsville Ave., MP 9½
• (252) 441-3786

The Bike Barn, located behind Taco Bell between the Beach Road and the Bypass, sells a wide variety of bikes and services all types. Skilled mechanics are on staff. It sells a full line of parts and accessories too. Serious bikers will appreciate name brands such as Caloi, Jamis, Diamondback Giant, Trek and more. The shop rents 18-speeds and 21-speed hybrids, gear bikes and beach cruisers. The shop is open year round. The Corolla location, at Monteray Shores Plaza, is open March through Thanksgiving.

Roanoke Press and Croatoan Bookery
U.S. Hwy. 158, MP 9½ • (252) 480-1890

This shop is owned by the same folks who publish *The Coastland Times* newspaper and operate Burnside Books in Manteo. Here you'll discover secondhand and new books; both bookstores carry an extensive line of books about North Carolina and the Outer Banks. It's open year round.

Sea Holly Square
N.C. Hwy. 12, MP 9½

This is a complex (recently painted yellow) with shops, boutiques and a restaurant/bar, Hurricane Alley (see our Restaurants chap-

ter), connected by boardwalks around a central deck. The popular Tar Heel Trading Company has a shop here (see our Corolla shopping section). Blue and Grey specializes in Civil War memorabilia such as books, posters, prints and flags. The store is open late March through December. Skaters and bikers will want to check out KDH Cycle and Skate for bicycle and Rollerblade sales, rentals (including mopeds) and repairs. The shop is open year round.

Island Dyes
N.C. Hwy. 12, MP 9½ • (252) 480-0076

Island Dyes offers T-shirts and a full line of women's clothing, reggae and Grateful Dead T-shirts and tobacco accessories.

Beach Barn Shops
U.S. Hwy. 158, MP 10

On the west side of the bypass, the Beach Barn Shops is a great place to stop to purchase gifts. It houses Birthday Suits, a popular swimsuit and sportswear shop (see our Corolla shopping section), and Carolina Moon, a great place for finding unusual gifts, scents, pottery, stationery and greeting cards. The shop has an outstanding line of jewelry of all kinds — you'll find pieces you've never seen before. Be sure to see the delightful Christmas ornaments, many with a whimsical touch. The shop has a New Age ambiance and a fine collection of esoteric gifts. You also can shop at their Corolla location in TimBuck II from Easter through Christmas. The Kill Devil Hills store is open year round.

Nags Head

Nags Head is a shoppers' mecca with its boutiques along the Beach Road, U.S. 158 and the Nags Head/Manteo Causeway, and larger shopping destinations such as the Outer Banks Mall and the Tanger Outlet Stores on U.S. 158.

Ben Franklin
U.S. Hwy. 158, MP 10 • (252) 441-7571

Across the street from the Food Lion Plaza, Ben Franklin carries clothing for all ages and everything you need for the beach. There are some great buys on ladies' dresses here. It is open Easter through Christmas.

Food Lion Plaza
U.S. Hwy. 158, MP 10

Besides Food Lion and CVS pharmacy, this plaza has food shops like Mrs. T's Deli (see our Restaurants chapter) and TCBY yogurt shop. Whalebone Surf Shop is nearby, and Nags Head News is a well-stocked bookstore and newsstand featuring the largest selection of magazines on the Outer Banks. It also sells a variety of national newspapers and is open year round.

Nature's Exotics
N.C. Hwy. 12, MP 10½ • (252) 480-1999

This pet shop features an incredible bunch of creatures ranging from hand-fed, domestically raised parrots, cockatiels and macaws to prairie dogs, hedgehogs, bunnies, ferrets, reptiles and freshwater and saltwater fish. If Nature's Exotics, which is open year round, doesn't have what you're looking for, the staff will help you find it. Also in stock is a full line of pet paraphernalia.

The Christmas Mouse
U.S. Hwy. 158, MP 10½ • (252) 441-8111

This holiday-oriented shop is brimming with Christmas collectibles, Cairn Gnomes, papier-mâché Santas, Snow Babies, porcelain dolls, unique ornaments and nautical-

and Midwestern-themed trees. It is open year round.

Central Square
U.S. Hwy. 158, MP 11

Across the highway from Secret Spot, you'll find the weathered cottage-style complex of shops and offices called Central Square. This is the location of several service-oriented businesses including the weekly newspaper, *The Outer Banks Sentinel* and the Dare County Arts Council (see our Arts and Culture chapter). There's a new flea market-type shop that sells lots of inexpensive gifts and snacks. Walk through the covered and connecting boardwalks to experience the entire venue. Edith Gallery is the new shop on the block here. Edith Deltgen is an artist who showcases some of her unusual sculptures here. She offers antiques, collectibles and even delicious German chocolate, and her store is open year round.

The Merry-Go-Round Thrift Store
N.C. Hwy. 12, MP 11½ • (252) 441-3241

This delightful thrift shop features knick-knacks, jewelry, books, household items, baby paraphernalia and lots of clothing. There are some reasonable antique finds here, and the store is open all year.

Pirate's Quay
U.S. Hwy. 158, MP 11½

You'll find an eclectic grouping of clever boutiques, stores, offices and eateries here. Look for tobacco, jewelry, crafts and clothing in these shops.

If anyone has ever admonished you to "get a hobby," drop by the new year-round shop, OuterRageous Hobbies, and check out the shop's specialties: wooden ships and NASCAR models. For jewelry that captures the feel of the sea, visit Devi's. Goldsmith Tom Hampton and his wife, Anne, a designer, offer nautical and seashore jewelry priced for the locals, including their line of original shell jewelry. Look for traditional gems here along with a diamond line. The Hamptons also do repairs. The shop is open year round six days a week.

Island Magic sells contemporary fashions and wooden crafts from Bali. The colorful wood masks, carvings, handpainted fish and jew-

Photo: Courtesy of Bruce Roberts

This store was built to look like a lighthouse.

elry are especially appealing. Cloud Nine is an adventure in clothing, accessories and other discoveries from around the world. Owner Ginny Flowers has beads and lots of them. Other finds include recycled glass, Grateful Dead merchandise, T-shirts made by locals and visitors, beautiful batiks and treasures from Africa and Nepal. Cloud Nine also carries gold and silver jewelry. Bring in your sea glass and have a custom necklace made. It's open Easter through Thanksgiving.

The Quacker Connection, open March through December, features decoys, country crafts, antiques and a large selection of country collectibles. Doug, the resident carver, is often carving or painting a decoy, so take a moment to see this classic craft being performed. Need a one-stop shop for all your vacation gear? Check out Wings, where you'll find souvenirs, beach clothing, boogie boards, bathing suits, beach chairs, umbrellas and fudge. There's another location in Kitty Hawk, U.S. 158, MP 3½. Both shops are open year round.

Twila Zone
N.C. Hwy. 12, MP 12 • (252) 480-0399

Owner Jo Ruth Patterson stocks Twila Zone with vintage clothing from the 1920s to the 1970s. She offers hats, accessories, costume jewelry, old toys and fine-quality vintage furnishings. Look for vintage Levi's and textiles plus collectibles, old books, records and various accessories.

Something Fishy
N.C. Hwy. 12, MP 12 • (252) 441-9666

Here's a fun shop swimming in the artistic fish-print clothing of Sherrie Lemnios, who has been creating fish prints for 12 years. Clothing, jewelry, toys and crafts all have a fish theme. The shop features items from the Outer Banks and all over. It's open Easter through December.

Gulf Stream Gifts
N.C. Hwy. 12, MP 12 • (252) 441-0433

Gulf Stream features contemporary nautical gifts, jewelry and lighthouse and dolphin memorabilia. The store is open from Easter until Thanksgiving.

Austin Fish Company
U.S. Hwy. 158, MP 13½ • (252) 441-7412

Austin's is a Nags Head fixture near Jockey's Ridge. It's a full-service seafood store that also serves as a gas station with some of the lowest prices on the beach. It's open March through November.

Kitty Hawk Connection
U.S. Hwy. 158, MP 13½ • (252) 441-4124

Kitty Hawk Connection is home to Kitty Hawk Kites and Kitty Hawk Sports, which are situated at opposite ends of the complex. Kitty Hawk Kites is one of the most colorful stops on the Outer Banks and sells just about any kite, windsock or banner imaginable. It can supply everything you need for a great vacation on the Outer Banks, including quality men's and women's sportswear and outerwear, sandals, T-shirts and sweatshirts. This shop also offers toys, and in-line skates are for sale or rent here. (See our Watersports chapter for exciting sporting opportunities offered by these folks.) Other locations are in Monteray Shores Plaza, N.C. 12, Corolla; TimBuck II, N.C. 12, Corolla; Wee Winks Square, N.C. 12, Duck; and Island Shops, N.C. 12, Avon. Look for a new shop in Ocracoke Village. The Nags Head location is open year round. All other locations are open March through December.

Kitty Hawk Sports carries popular name-brand clothing, boogie boards, accessories and sunglasses plus windsurfing and kayaking gear. It offers all sorts of sporting opportunities (see our Watersports chapter). Check out the other locations at Wee Winks Square, N.C. 12, Duck, and Timbuk II, N.C. 12, Corolla. The Nags Head shop is open all year. The northern beach shops are open March through December.

Also in the complex is Salt Marsh (other locations are in Corolla and Duck), a conservation-conscious shop filled with irresistible gifts, T-shirts, clothing, jewelry, books and fun and educational toys. A portion of the profits from the store are donated to wildlife and environmental associations. There is a location of Donna Designs here, along with How Sweet It Is — the place to stop for homemade ice cream, tasty deli sandwiches and delicious ice cream cakes. To satisfy a yearning for all types of fudge, stop by The Fudgery.

Surfside Plaza
U.S. Hwy. 158, MP 14

This is a great mix of shops you won't want to miss. You'll find everything from comic books to contemporary clothing and crafts. There are several food shops here (including a Subway) in case you get hungry.

Surfside Casuals has more swimsuits than just about any other store on the beach. This shop also carries an extensive line of casual wear for men and women. Look for other locations in Rodanthe on N.C. 12; Avon on N.C. 12; Duck at Duck Soundside Shops on N.C. 12; and Corolla at TimBuck II on N.C. 12. All shops are open Easter through Thanksgiving.

Sea Holly Hooked Rugs has a beautiful display of finished pieces including small rugs, chair pads, coasters and seat cushions in traditional rug hooking rather than latch hooking. It also sells rug-hooking kits that are designed and put together by owner Jean Edmonds. All-wool fabrics are used throughout. The craft is true American folk art, and summer workshops are offered on Wednesday from 1 to 4 PM beginning in June.

Beach Peddler, open Easter through October, sells everything you'll need at the beach and also has jewelry, shells, postcards, souvenirs, gifts, hats, hermit crabs and T-shirts. Darnell's offers hermit crabs, shells, fudge and nautical gifts.

Joy By the Seaside is a cross-stitch shop with a wide variety of fabrics for everyone from the novice to the experienced stitcher. Accessories include Mill Hill beads, specialty threads, DMC and Anchor floss. Special orders and mail ordering is offered. Adults and kids alike will love Outer Banks Cards and Comics, a collector's paradise that features sport and nonsport cards and a massive collection of comic books, both foreign and domestic. It also sells action figures, T-shirts and holds Magic card tournaments during winter. It's open year round. Art lovers will enjoy We're Art year round for posters, prints, local artwork and custom framing or ready-made frames.

Croatan Center
U.S. Hwy. 158, MP 14½

This is a fun group of shops featuring gifts from around the world, fine jewelry, CDs and shoes. Lion's Paw, open year round, features a variety of women's resort wear clothing and accessories. Halloran & Co., in the same shop as Lion's Paw, offers sterling silver jewelry, 14-karat gold and gemstones and sterling silver watches. Soundfeet Shoes, open year round, will fulfill your sole's desire in footwear. It offers a wide variety of men's, women's and children's casual and fancy shoes and sandals including popular sports shoes by Reebok and Nike.

Sea Trader's Exchange, open year round, features nautical gifts, home accessories and Yankee Candles. You'll also find fudge, candy, toys and shells. If you're looking for new and used CDs, look no further than Outer Banks Music, which offers a wide variety of music for all tastes. It also sells music videos, T-shirts, posters and accessories. If they don't have something in stock, ask Steve or Lisa to special order it for you; they can usually turn such requests around in a couple of days at no extra charge. It's open all year.

Capt. Marty's Tackle Shop
U.S. Hwy. 158, MP 15 • (252) 441-3132

This full-service fishing and hunting mecca carries an incredible array of sporting goods such as rods, reels and bows, and also offers virtual-reality archery, bait and more. This shop boasts of being the largest of its kind on the East Coast, and the staff, including Marty himself, are all pros in the field. It's open year round. (See our Recreation chapter for more information.)

Outer Banks Mall
U.S. Hwy. 158, MP 15

The Outer Banks Mall is open year round. Seamark Foods (see The Shoreside Centre listing in our Kitty Hawk section) anchors the center of the complex, which is home to a mix of shopping, service, entertainment and dining businesses, including a two-screen RC Theatres location (see our Recreation chapter), North China Restaurant (see our Restaurants chapter), a dry cleaner, coin-op laundry, a thrift shop, a Sears catalog store and a Heilig-Meyers furniture store. Vintage Wave offers '70s clothing, recycled Levi's and silver jewelry. It is open year round.

Also found outside the main, enclosed mall are two of our favorites places: Video Andy has a good selection of videos including British, Chinese, Latin American and French films and lots of children's flicks. Video Andy rents videos and players year round. And locals can't wait until New York Bagel opens for the season. These goodies are ALWAYS fresh. Their Everything Bagel, topped

with your choice of cream cheese or egg salad, is killer.

The interior of the mall is fascinating. It features a replica of the Wright Flyer — the flying machine crafted by the Wright Brothers — as well as colorful papier-mâché critters that hang from the ceiling. Insiders go to the mall for these sites alone! There are snack and sandwich choices in the mall. Also, look for an eyewear shop, Hallmark shop and a jewelry shop.

The Mule Shed features ladies apparel and lovely purses, gifts and wedding, household and outdoor garden items such as statuary and a sweet little brass bunny doorbell. Lady Dare is a charming boutique for women with full figures. It features clothing and accessories for the office and the beach, including the Outer Banks' largest selection of full-figure swimwear and sportswear. It's open year round. Sea Witch Gifts features sea motif gifts and pottery, shell vases and fascinating birdhouses. Check out T-Tops Racing for Winston Cup souvenirs. And just across the hall at T-Tops Shirt Expo, you can choose from T-shirts, shorts, hats, mugs and souvenirs. It's open year round. Stop at Uncle Milty's for cool drinks and lots of ice cream choices.

Island Tobacco stocks imported cigars, tobacco and cigarettes, smoking accessories such as imported pipes and pipe lighters, along with darts and dart boards, pool cues, accessories and the accompanying paraphernalia. Check out the Corolla location at TimBuck II; it's open Easter through Thanksgiving. Habitat Earth carries groovy knit dresses, wild pants, couch throws with dancing bears, jewelry, CDs and more; it's open year round. Waves Music has a wide variety of CDs and cassettes, music accessories and music videos. The emphasis here is on alternative, pop and rock music. It's also open year round.

Samson and Delilah offers lingerie and apparel for both men and women plus a host of accessories such as hosiery, jewelry, hats, belts, ties and purses. Shop here for bed, bath and massage products. Free gift wrapping is offered, and the business also sends birthday and all-occasion reminder cards. They keep a customer and bridal registry. It's open year round. Jam's World is packed with islandwear and kid's clothing, and Harrell's Carpet and Home Accents is a fun stop for rugs, baskets, prints, interesting key hangers and other decorator items.

Collector's Galley has a fascinating mix of collectibles and antiques including kid's Tonka trucks, dolls and flags. Lil Grass Shack offers bathing suits for women in sizes 3 to 28 as well as children's swimwear. Look here for girls', women's and men's sportswear. It's open year round. You'll also find Ocean Threads, which specializes in swimwear (see our entry on Corolla Light Village Shops). Ocean Annie's has a shop here that offers wonderful gift items including lots of pottery. Check out their iris and sunflower pottery; it's lovely.

Forbes
U.S. Hwy. 158, MP 15½ • (252) 441-7293

You can't come to the beach without picking up a box of saltwater taffy. Forbes, an Outer Banks tradition, moves into a new building in Nags Head for the 1998 season. The Forbes folks hope to be in their new digs by Memorial Day. Stop in for a box or three of the company's famous homemade gooey goodies. The shop, which is open year round, also features a gift and souvenir selection.

The Chalet Gift Shop
N.C. Hwy. 12, MP 15½ • (252) 441-6402

Celebrating its 23rd year at the same Beach Road location, The Chalet is one of the nicest stores on the beach. The gifts, collectibles and souvenirs here are exquisite. Collectors will love the selection of David Winter Cottages, Harbour Lights, Lilliput Lane, Collectible Dolls, Legends, Michael Garman, Rick Cain, Iris Arc Crystal and Madam Alexander dolls. The collection of 14-karat gold and sterling silver jewelry is gorgeous. The shop also carries fine home accessories and just about anything you'd need for the beach. Mail orders are welcome; it's open March through December.

Souvenir City
N.C. Hwy. 12, MP 16 • (252) 441-7452

This Beach Road shop is a family owned business run by Pat and Kathy Preston. One of the most impressive collections of beach memorabilia around is joined by tons of T-shirts, jewelry, miniature lighthouses and hermit crabs. Going to the beach? Pick up your boogie boards, suntan lotion, hats and rafts here. Prices are reasonable too. It's open March through Thanksgiving.

Captain's Corner
U.S. Hwy. 158, MP 16½ at Whalebone Junction • (252) 441-6786

For 18 years, Captain's Corner has offered a variety of local and North Carolina-made nautical gifts and crafts including lighthouses, light-house lamps and tide clocks, plus jewelry and beach glass. They also offer silk ties and scarves. It's open all year.

The Dare Shops
N.C. Hwy. 12, MP 16½ • (252) 441-1112

These folks have been in business since 1959. They offer fine jewelry such as necklaces, bracelets and rings featuring beautiful gold, silver, diamonds and other gemstones. Look for shell accessories and gifts here as well. It's open Easter though Christmas.

Tanger Outlet Mall
U.S. Hwy. 158, MP 16½ • (252) 441-7395

Tanger is a discount outlet shopping center brimming with great buys in all sorts of merchandise, from clothes to dishes. These are nationally known names, so we don't give extensive store descriptions. We've listed some of our favorites below to get you started. Once you park, you'll wander for hours here. Bring plenty of cash! And when you get hungry, take a break at Stone Oven Pizza (see our Restaurants chapter).

All shops in the Tanger complex are open year round. Look at Westport Ltd. and Westport Woman for clothing and lots of accessories. You can pick out a complete outfit with all the trimmings, including jewelry and stockings. They have great sales here! Pfaltzgraff has dishes, glasses and knick-knacks. London Fog is very popular with locals and visitors alike who stop here for their yearly coat purchases. Check out the great buys on a vast selection of outerwear including casual jackets and rainwear. At Rack Room Shoes you can outfit the entire family with quality discounted tennis shoes and casual and dressy year-round footwear.

You'll adore Corning/Revere Ware Store, a great kitchen supply shop. Of course you'll find traditional Corningware with pretty designs, but the shop's also chock-full of gadgets that make your kitchen experiences easier. Stock up on quality shirts, pants and sweats for men, women and children at Bugle Boy — you'll find plenty of jeans here. We've found fashionable short leather boots at Nine West that really last, plus lots of dressy and casual shoe selections for women only. The Dress Barn has great sweaters (dressy, sporty and casual dressy) for women and some super tops for all occasions. Wallet Works has a tremendous selection of classy wallets and purses and some exquisite, well-made luggage.

Publishers Warehouse has a large collection of books, including large, coffee-table art books. Claire's Accessories overflows with hair accessories, jewelry, fashionable clear plastic purses for kids, sunglasses, those little fuzzy cloth key chain books and hats. Kids love this shop. The prices are extraordinary. For a few dollars, the little ones feel like they've had a big shopping spree.

Cahoon's
N.C. Hwy. 12, MP 16½ • (252) 441-5358

Cahoon's is a large, family owned grocery and variety store that's been around for more than three decades. It's a nice change of pace from city-size supermarkets. Dorothy and Ray Cahoon bought the store shortly before the Ash Wednesday Storm of 1962 and, despite what must have been a rather wild start, continue to stock everything you'll need for your visit to the beach, including good meats that butcher Robert Heroux cuts to perfection. The store is near Jennette's Pier and is open March through Thanksgiving.

Whalebone Seafood
U.S. Hwy. 158, MP 16½ • (252) 441-8808

Whalebone is run by the Daniels family, known locally for their commercial fishing roots. It's a full-service seafood market selling whatever's in season. It's open Easter through October.

Caribbean Corners
Nags Head/Manteo Cswy.

This collection of shops is a gaily painted cluster of buildings on the sound with plenty of parking in front. Music wafts across the breezy decks, where you can relax at the picnic tables between visits to the charming boutiques and businesses. My Sister's Closet is a women's fashion paradise featuring unique junior and contemporary misses styles; it's open year-round. At this shop the motto is: "It's not an age, it's an attitude." His Shells by Brenda features handmade nautical seashell

mirrors, ornaments, lamps, jewelry, candles, a large assortment of shell gifts and baskets plus picture frames. It's open year round.

Nature's Treasures features handcarved gourds (including those fashioned into birdhouses and feeders), rattles, drums, bowls and planters. It offers gifts such as pottery, custom lamps, decoys and a line of buckskin and rawhide pioneer-type bags. Look for celestial items such as handpainted Mexican clay sun and moon wall pieces. It's open March through December.

Hungry? What's Your Scoop will appeal to the tummy with ice cream and sandwiches. Outer Banks Posters & Prints is slammed full of nature-oriented prints and educational posters of dinosaurs, solar eclipses and atoms. These folks are the producers of the popular Apollo IX poster of the Outer Banks, which you can purchase here. The shop is open year round.

Pil Pel lives up to its motto, "A Bathing Suit for All," with an assortment of swimsuits to suit nearly every preference for men, women and children. You can mix and match tops and bottoms for just the right fit. Bra sizes go up to DD. Look for a variety of T-shirts and souvenirs and a coffee bar featuring cappuccino and pastries. It's open mid-April through Thanksgiving.

Blackbeard's Treasure Chest
Nags Head/Manteo Cswy.
• (252) 441-5772

Blackbeard's is a variety gift shop featuring T-shirts, beach accessories and apparel, seashells, jewelry and local crafts. They also have a Christmas room, where you can buy a miniature tree and ornaments. It's open March through October.

Shipwreck
Nags Head/Manteo Cswy.
• (252) 441-5739

Shipwreck is another gift store with a nautical twist. Look here for local crafts, driftwood, nets, shells and other sea treasures piled everywhere. It's open March through Thanksgiving.

Roanoke Island

Shopping on Roanoke Island runs the gamut from small shopping centers and businesses along U.S. Highway 64/264 to a col-

Shoppers have a chance to add to their fine art glass collection during their Outer Banks excursions.

lection of stores near Shallowbag Bay called The Waterfront Shops.

Downtown Manteo and Surrounding Area

Pirate's Cove Ship's Store
Pirate's Cove Yacht Club, Nags Head/ Manteo Cswy. • (252) 473-3906

This marina store has a nice selection of active sportswear, including Kahalas, a Hawaiian line of beautifully hand-screened and batiked clothing. The shop also carries gifts, picture frames, wind-up crabs, marina supplies and groceries as well as a line of 14-karat gold jewelry with a fishy flair. It's open year round.

Caimen Gardens
U.S. Hwy. 64/264 • (252) 473-6343

This shop sells a little bit of everything for your home and gardening needs. Look for lots of annuals, perennials, fruit trees, salt-tolerant plants and a full line of vegetation that will thrive on the Outer Banks. They sell house plants, blooming plants, seasonal plants, mulch, potting soils and fertilizers. Shop in the year-round Christmas room or the home accents room.

You'll also find planters, statuary, fountains, water garden supplies such as pond liners, pumps and lily pads, and a selection of other aquatic plants and local art. It's open year round.

Island Produce
U.S. Hwy. 64/264 • (252) 473-1303

Island Produce offers fresh seasonal vegetables and fruits. It also has flowering plants for the garden and home, including beautiful lilies, pumpkins and Christmas trees in season. They are open April until Christmas.

Jeanine's Cat House
U.S. Hwy. 64/264 • (252) 473-1499

Cat lovers will revel in this shop that abounds in delightful gifts and necessities ranging from "purr-ty" cat earrings to beds and carrying cases for the furry felines. Cat motif sculptures, wall art, clothing, collectibles, cards and stationery fill this pussycat palace. Jeanine's is next to the Christmas Shop and is open daily year round.

The Christmas Shop & The Island Gallery
U.S. Hwy. 64/264 • (252) 473-2838

We cover this fabulous shop in our Attractions and Arts and Culture chapters, but a few items that will be showcased in 1998 bear not-

SHOP DOWN

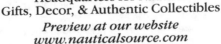

ing. Expect to find Christopher Radko glass ornaments and Polonaise glass ornaments from Poland, designed by American artist Patricia Breen and only available in 43 places in the country (they're usually displayed in museums). Other collectibles include Byer's Choice Christmas figurines dressed in the period of Dickens, a brand-new angel display and plenty of carolers. New for 1998 is an expansion that features a new wing that resembles a country store; it's just off the art gallery. You'll find lots more candles, collectible glass, candy and art as a result of the additional 4,000 square feet. This stop is at the top of our list! Parking is plentiful in lots on both sides of the road. It's open year round.

Chesley Mall
U.S. Hwy. 64/264

Food-A-Rama and CVS pharmacy hold down the fort here as well as a Hallmark shop, video store, film shop and hometown pharmacy. Chesley Mall is a year-round shopping venue. Island Pharmacy is an old-fashioned store where you can buy prescription and over-the-counter medicines, sundries, film and gifts and take advantage of the UPS and Airborne Express services in the back of the store. There are plenty of gift items, including glass and china knickknacks and some cute stuffed animals.

Qwik Shot is a professional portrait studio that also serves your film and developing needs. They can provide a fast turnaround on your vacation film; one-hour processing for 3½-by-5 and 8-by-10 prints is available. J. Aaron Trotman Photographs at Quik Shot provides photography services for family reunions, weddings, portraits and commercial needs. They have a lovely selection of frames and prints — a new addition is the hand-thrown pottery by Laura Trotman. The glazes are exquisite.

The Video Store has an array of first-rate drama, comedy, adventure and martial arts, horror and children's movies. They even have some $1 videos. It also rents VCRs, Super Nintendo, Nintendo and Sega Genesis games. Susan's Hallmark carries a wide variety of party supplies, religious products, candy (try the

spicy jelly beans), cards, stationery and photo albums.

Sybil's of Manteo
U.S. Hwy. 64/264 • (252) 473-6696

Sybil's is a ladies' and children's clothing boutique that features sportswear and evening wear. These folks specialize in one-of-a-kind clothing at affordable prices. Take advantage of the full-service beauty parlor that's here. Sybil's is open year round.

Burnside Books
U.S. Hwy. 64/264 • (252) 473-3311

Burnside carries office and art supplies and a good selection of historical and children's books. Upstairs you'll find used hardback and paperback books and a North Carolina book section. It's open all year.

Hotline Thrift Shop
U.S. Hwy. 64/264 • (252) 473-3127

West of the Dare County Public Library, Hotline Thrift is a fund-raising shop for Outer Banks Hotline, a crisis intervention service that also operates a shelter for battered women and their children. Hotline is quite possibly the most popular secondhand store on the Outer Banks. The inventory includes furniture, toys, books, knickknacks and clothing for men, women and children. It's open year round.

Wanchese Pottery
107 Fernando St. • (252) 473-2099

This artistic shop is a small business near The Waterfront on Fernando Street, where customers can watch local potters Bonnie and Bob Morrill at work (see our Arts and Culture chapter). The shop is known locally for its beautiful, useful art, and it also features handmade baskets and fresh cooking herbs. It's open year round, but call for winter hours.

Manteo Furniture
Sir Walter Raleigh St. • (252) 473-2131

Manteo Furniture stocks a large selection of home and cottage furnishings ranging from traditional to contemporary. The store, which has

INSIDERS' TIP

Keep an eye out for great swimsuit bargains during the winter.

been in operation for nearly 54 years, offers down-home friendly service. Allow yourself plenty of time to browse through the many rooms of furnishings in this 48,000-square-foot showroom/warehouse. The company sells a full line of General Electric appliances and offers financing and free delivery. It's open year round.

Manteo Booksellers
105 Sir Walter Raleigh St.
• (252) 473-1221

Housed in charming quarters dotted with wing chairs, cozy corners and quaint antiques, Manteo Booksellers is a must-browse for every reader. Three rooms are packed with books ranging from literary classics to delightful children's stories. The Outer Banks and Latin American sections (they also have books in Spanish) are excellent, as are the historical, self-help, Civil War and North Carolina fiction areas. The cookbook selection is extensive.

The bookstore has a busy calendar filled with book signings and free readings by authors, poets and storytellers. This shop alone is definitely worth the trip to Manteo! Be sure to give the store cat, Stunt, a pat on the head (if he'll have it, that is). Manteo Booksellers is open year round.

My Secret Garden
Sir Walter Raleigh St. • (252) 473-6880

Next door to Manteo Booksellers, My Secret Garden features Tiffany-style lamps, custom wreaths and swags, unique garden accessories and statuary, handmade birdhouses and Mary Engelbreit cards and collectibles. They offer handpainted furniture including mirrors, lamps, dressers and servers plus indoor fountains, Muffy Vanderbears and Beanie Babies, the Lady Primrose bath line and pottery. This is a charming shop with lots of gift ideas. It's open year round.

Candle Factory
Sir Walter Raleigh St. • (252) 473-4950

This lovely shop is filled with beauty and fragrance. Handmade candles abound in a variety of shapes and sizes as well their signature seashells recreated in candle form. All giftware is American-made and includes Burt's Bees personal-care products such as soaps, creams and bath salts. Ironwork, blown-glass plantation rope baskets, fine pewter and brass, aromatherapy products and the popular Winelight kits are also available. It is open year round.

The Waterfront Shops
Queen Elizabeth Ave.

Lining the Manteo Waterfront is an attractive four-story complex with businesses, restaurants, residential space and covered parking. Two delightful restaurants, Full Moon Cafe and Clara's Seafood Grill and Steam Bar, are good choices for shopping intermissions (see our Restaurants chapter).

Charlotte's is a quality women's boutique that features traditional and contemporary fine and casual clothing, accessories and gifts. You must see the beautiful sweater collection, including ones by designers Lisa Nichols and Michael Simon. They carry Sak and Kaminski bags. The helpful staff is attentive and professional, and the store is open year round.

Waterfront Salon and Boutique is a full-service beauty salon for men, women and children, situated on the waterfront side of this shopping arcade. Pamper your nails, face and hair here. The boutique features some gold, sterling and fashion jewelry. They carry colorful casual to dressy clothing. It's open year round.

Island Nautical is an Outer Banks headquarters for nautical gifts and decor. Owners Jack and Marilyn Hughes have devoted this shop exclusively to marine-related merchandise, including authentic maritime artifacts such as spinnakers, life rings, portholes and authentic and reproduction lanterns; quality weather instruments; marine-style clocks; and an array of tide clocks, ship model kits, a ship-in-a-bottle collection and much more. Authentic Greek fishermen's hats are available here, and it's the only place in the area to find out-of-print maritime books as well as current selections. It's open all year. Island Trading Company is the Hughes' other venture, featuring fine pewter, crystal and English china gifts and accessories from such names as Woods of Windsor, Pimpernel, Vera Bradley Designs and Glassmasters, plus original artwork and limited-edition prints. It's open year round.

Ken Kelley and Eileen Alexanian are the owners of Diamonds and Dunes, a full-service jewelry shop. The "designing couple" produce fine handcrafted work, drawing on more than two decades of experience in the jewelry business.

Outer Banks boutiques are filled with take-home treasures.

Services include everything from setting stones and sizing rings to creating one-of-a-kind keepsakes. They showcase their very own lighthouse bracelet that features the five Outer Banks lighthouses. They'll also be offering Belgian diamonds and gold, silver or gem-studded ear pins to give you the three-earring look without all the holes. Ken and Eileen are members of the American Gem Society. The store is open year round.

The Toy Boat Toy Store is an exciting stop for high-quality toys, both fun and educational. It's a fun shop for any age. The shop has won a merchandising achievement award from *Playthings Magazine* for store design. These toy experts are doubling the size of their shop for the 1998 season. They will offer more toys — all with the same slant toward educational, developmental and creative items. Among the newer toy lines offered at the Toy Boat are products by BRIO, Small Miracles Dressups and a Lamaze Infant Development System line of infant toys. It's open year round.

The Cloth Barn
Etheridge Rd. • (252) 473-2795

Returning to U.S. 64, head north toward Manns Harbor and turn left onto Etheridge Road. Drive a short distance, and you'll be at a store packed nearly floor to ceiling with fabrics, notions and patterns. The selection of woven tapestry cloth is unbelievably beautiful. You'll want to wear it, cover your walls in it and just roll around in this eye-catching fabric. The Cloth Barn closes mid-December through mid-January.

Dare County Mainland

Nature's Harmony
Shipyard Rd., Manns Harbor • (252) 473-3556

This is a full-scale nursery with three greenhouses, specializing in herbs, perennials and wildflowers. The store offers a plant maintenance service for your office or home. Nature's Harmony sells pottery and garden-related accessories plus fertilizers and mulches. Landscaping services are available. It's a lovely, peaceful spot that's open from February through Christmas.

Wanchese

After you cross Roanoke Sound westbound on the Nags Head-Manteo Causeway and pass Pirate's Cove, make a left at the next intersection onto N.C. Highway 345, which will take you to Wanchese. Turning to the right

Hatteras Island • Hatteras Island • Hatteras Island • Hatteras Island

onto Old Wharf Road (less than a mile from the intersection with U.S. 64/264), you'll find Nick-E Stained Glass, a studio and gallery, which is a veritable stained-glass wonderland featuring the original creations of Ellinor and Robert Nick (see our Arts and Culture chapter).

Carriage House Nursery
275 C.B. Daniels Sr. Rd., Wanchese
• (252) 473-4759

The Carriage House Nursery offers a selection of perennials, bedding plants, hanging baskets, vegetable plants, herbs and topiaries. During the summer, the nursery sells vegetables grown on the premises with an emphasis on unique peppers. New for 1998 is a gift section.

Hatteras Island

Even though you may not find the large number of shops you'd find in Nags Head, Kill Devil Hills or Duck, the ones in the Hatteras area are unique in character and carry fine quality items. We love the selection of handmade goods that share space with the typical souvenir and gift items found all along the Outer Banks.

Every year it seems there are more shops on Hatteras Island. Some shops here are adopting year-round schedules, but most of them still close for at least a month or two during the winter.

Rodanthe

Rodanthe has several general stores where you can find groceries, camping and fishing supplies, bait and seafood — the vacation necessities. Read on for some additional arty shopping experiences.

The Waterfowl Shop
N.C. Hwy. 12 • (252) 987-2626

The Waterfowl Shop is a sports photography gallery featuring the work of Richard Darcey, an award-winning former photographer for *The Washington Post*. The shop also offers gifts, such as new and used working decoys, tide clocks and wind speed indicators. It's open March through January.

Olde Christmas at Rodanthe Gift Shop
N.C. Hwy. 12 • (252) 987-2116

Stop here to browse one of the most complete cross-stitch departments on the Outer Banks. The shop has unusual gift items including statuary, lighthouse afghans and a selection of nautical Christmas ornaments. In 1998 they are offering an expanded needlework department. It's open April though December.

Pamlico Station
N.C. Hwy. 12

This two-story shopping center sits on the east side of N.C. 12 in Rodanthe and houses a nice selection of shops and services as well as the post office for Rodanthe, Waves and Salvo. The Village Video rents TVs, VCRs, Nintendo systems, camcorders and movies. Also available are blank VHS tapes, head cleaners, rewinders, 8-mm film and VHS-C audio tapes. At Lee's Collectibles you'll find North Carolina lighthouse T-shirts and figurines, beach supplies, unusual gifts, mugs, cards, antique bottles, shells, coral, toys and hermit crabs. We could spend hours browsing here. For an artistic venue, visit the Upstairs Art Gallery (see our Arts and Culture chapter), open April through October. The Fudgery will satisfy your sweet tooth.

Bill Sawyer's Place
N.C. Hwy. 12 • (252) 987-2214

Just a short distance south of Pamlico Station is Bill Sawyer's Place, which carries an assortment of gifts, a huge collection of shells, bait and tackle and cold beer. Sawyer also rents boogie boards. It's open April through October.

The Island Convenience Store
N.C. Hwy. 12 • (252) 987-2239

This is a one-stop shopping place for groceries, bait and tackle, gasoline and deli stuff including breakfast foods, sandwiches, pizza and fried chicken. You can take your food with you or eat at the tables. The store also carries souvenirs, gifts and beach supplies and offers 24-hour AAA wrecker service and auto repair. It's open year round.

Waves

Waves is home to just a few businesses including Hatteras Island Surf Shop (see our Watersports chapter) and Michael Halminski's Photography Gallery (see our Arts and Culture chapter).

Salvo

Salvo is a sleepy little village, but it has a few shopping stops that we've highlighted.

Fishin' Hole
N.C. Hwy. 12 • (252) 987-2351

In 1998 the Fishin' Hole marks its 22nd year as a general tackle shop. But the shop, open April through mid-December, also sells plenty of beach supplies and groceries.

Mid-Atlantic Market
N.C. Hwy. 12 • (252) 987-1520

Stop here for groceries, cold beer, hot meals, sandwiches, subs, daily specials and a boat ramp. It's open year round.

Avon

The Fisherman's Daughter
N.C. Hwy. 12 • (252) 995-6148

The Fisherman's Daughter features pottery from all over the United States. Local art and photography are available in the upstairs room. Gift items include brass nautical items and furnishings, Christmas ornaments, a large line from Department 56 Christmas, T-shirts with Outer Banks themes, cotton afghans with various designs including lighthouses, lots of gold and silver jewelry and Beanie Babies and Yankee Candles. It's open Easter through mid-December.

Avon Shopping Center
N.C. Hwy. 12 • (252) 995-5362

Avon Shopping Center, which is actually a general store, is a local favorite for fresh-cut meats, but they also have most everything else you'd expect from an all-purpose shop. Souvenirs, beachwear, groceries, all kinds of fishing supplies, beach chairs, quick-serve foods, gas and free air are all available. It's open year round.

Hatteras Wind & Surf
N.C. Hwy. 12 • (252) 995- 6275

Hatteras Wind & Surf has a full line of skateboard gear, Tim Nolte surfboards, windsurfing equipment sales and rentals and summer apparel with an emphasis on shorts. They also operate as a consignment shop for windsurfing goods. (See our Watersports chapter for more information on windsurfing lessons and kayak tours.)

Summerwind Shops
N.C. Hwy. 12

Island Spice and Wine is a little bit of wine heaven. Specializing in California, Italian and French wines, it has some tasty accompaniments, including gourmet foods and cheeses. How about a gourmet gift basket? You can sneak in some neat kitchen gadgets or cute cookie cutters. They offer wine accessories such as wine racks, serving ware, barbecue tools, Gourmet Kitchen cooking supplies and cookbooks. How about specialty beers and an extensive section of Oriental food products? New for 1998 is an expanded gift section that includes lots of North Carolina food products such as delicious sauces and preserves and a genuine organic North Carolina cooking wine flavored with basil, tarragon and rosemary. Check out the line of collectibles, huge mug selection, angel items and whimsical salt and pepper shakers. It is open year round. Brenda's Boutique offers a nice selection of casual clothing, including women's sportswear, swimwear, T-shirts and sweats. The shop also has a line of sterling silver jewelry. It's open Easter through mid- December.

Country Elegance
Harbor Rd. • (252) 995-6269

As you head south, if you turn right on Harbor Road at the only stoplight south of Whalebone Junction, you'll come across this store. Owned and operated by Lois and Dallas Miller, it features wearable art, country collars, bonnets, handpainted shirts, antique quilted heirlooms, whimsical art, designer dolls and Southwestern decorator items. There are also wood items, cake candles and lots and lots of lace.

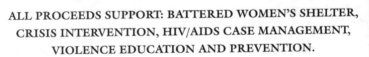

The Hatteras Island Plaza
N.C. Hwy. 12

This Avon plaza is anchored by Food Lion. Another Ace Hardware is here as well. Beach Bites is a well-rounded bakery/deli featuring fresh tuna salad, sliced meats and cheeses and pizza kits. It's the home of the Outer Banks Elephant Ear (tasty sticky buns), Key lime pies, jumbo cookies, gourmet muffins and home-made breads. It's open March through December.

Home Port Gifts is one of the loveliest upscale gift shops on the Outer Banks. Here original artwork, fine crafts and exquisite jewelry in fine silver and 14-karat gold (much of it with a nautical theme) will tempt you. You'll also find quality accessories for the home and nautical antiques. We especially like the custom Tiffany-style stained-glass pieces, nautical sculptures, handcarved decoys, terra cotta sculptures and sea candles by Sally Knuckles. The work of about 120 local artists is on display at Home Port, which enters its 10th year in 1998. The folks here say you can spend anywhere from a nickel to about $2,500 — there's something here for everyone.

Buxton

A 5-mile drive south of Avon brings you to the village of Buxton, where you'll discover things are more spread out and range from a general store and bait and tackle shop to specialty boutiques. Buxton's supermarket, Conner's Cape Hatteras Market, offers groceries and basic supplies year round. Beach Pharmacy II can help with prescription needs and sundries; they also offer UPS shipping and Western Union services.

Daydreams
N.C. Hwy. 12 • (252) 995-5548

Daydreams has earned a reputation for having stylish clothing and a selection of top name brands such as Patagonia and Birkenstock. The shop, open March through Christmas, carries clothing for men, women and children, plus accessories and jewelry.

Hatteras Outdoors
N.C. Hwy. 12 • (252) 995-5548

Hatteras Outdoors adjoins Daydreams and has all the coolest clothing for surfing enthusi-asts. You can find Cape Hatteras T-shirts, sweats and just about everything you need for the beach, including umbrella rentals and children's games and toys. The shop rents and sells boogie boards, rents surfboards and provides surfing accessories (see our Watersports chapter).

Dillon's Corner
N.C. Hwy. 12 • (252) 995-5083

Here's a terrific bait and tackle shop that carries all kinds of fishing rods, including custom-built ones. You'll find a charming little shop that features gifts, Yankee Candles, jewelry, pottery, T-shirts and a bevy of Beanie Babies. It's open year round.

Bilbo's Plaza
N.C. Hwy. 12

Bilbo's is the right stop for flowers, cards and beach equipment. Moonshine Florist and Hallmark Shop can help you celebrate special occasions while you're away from home with its selection of stuffed animals, balloons, candy and flowers (delivery service available). It's open year round. Hatteras Wear is a seasonal shop filled with dresses, adult and kid T-shirts, swimwear, beach stuff, jewelry, sunglasses and suntan products. It's open Easter through Thanksgiving. At Buxton Under the Sun you'll find all kinds of beach equipment, clam rakes, boogie boards and surfboards, and a car rental and taxi service. It's open year round.

Natural Art Surf Shop
N.C. Hwy. 12 • (252) 995-5682

Natural Art is owned by Scott and Carol Busbey, two serious surfers who love the sport and the lifestyle. During the 22 years the shop has been in business, it has gained the reputation for being "the surfer's surf shop," meaning they specialize in surfing rather than all water board sports. Surfers from everywhere and all walks of life have been coming here for years. Scott, who has his own line of boards called In The Eye, manufactures custom boards and does repairs. Carol makes clothing (her hand-sewn women's and men's tops and children's shirts and dresses are unique and colorful) and tries to find time to surf. The shop rents surfboards, boogie boards, swim fins, wetsuits and surf

videos and sells all the necessary surfing gear and great T-shirts. It's open March through December. (See our Watersports chapter for more information.)

Osprey Shopping Center
N.C. Hwy. 12

Osprey is behind Natural Art Surf Shop and the Great Salt Marsh Restaurant and has an ABC package store. Ocean Notions Gift Shop has a nice selection of gifts including candles, bath products and nautical gifts as well as women's and men's clothing and a small selection of children's apparel. Look no further for beach supplies and a selection of gold and silver jewelry. It's open March through mid-December. Turn toward the ocean on Light Plant Road to find The Old Gray House gift shop. Baskets, woodwork, stitchery, miniatures, dolls, shells, potpourri and more fill the shelves in this old house, maintained as it must have looked at the turn of the century.

Buxton Village Books
N.C. Hwy. 12 • (252) 995-4240

Comfortably nestled in what was once the summer kitchen of an island house, Buxton Village Books is open for its 15th year. This charming space is packed with lots of good reads, including all the current bestsellers, hard-to-find Southern fiction and saltwater fly-fishing titles. In a room overlooking Pamlico Sound, you can browse over a delightful selection of notecards and stationery. The shop has a public fax machine; ask about the shop's mail-order catalog. It's open year round. Check out their other locations in Hatteras Village at Hatteras Landing and at Hatteras Island Plaza in Avon.

Buttons N Bows
N.C. Hwy. 12 • (252) 995-4285

Are you looking for original Outer Bank's cross-stitch patterns? You'll find those and lots more here. Owner Laurie Farrow's cute shop offers a large assortment of Outer Banks-oriented cross-stitch patterns. Farrow's own exclusive designs for beach scenes, local maps and birds are included. This shop also carries notions, candles, jewelry, and gift items , and other patterns and offers cross-stitch classes. It's open March through November.

INSIDERS' TIP

Try the mouthwatering homemade deli salads at Conner's Market in Buxton.

Frisco

Scotch Bonnet Gifts
N.C. Hwy. 12

Frisco is home to Scotch Bonnet Gifts, a shop with great fudge, custom and silk-screened T-shirts, hermit crabs and other gifts. They also sell and rent boats and Jet Skis. The shop is at the Frisco Cove Marina and Campground (see our Camping chapter).

Pirate's Chest of Frisco
N.C. Hwy. 12 • (252) 995-5118

Pirate's Chest opened in 1953, making it the oldest gift shop on Hatteras Island. If you've been searching for a coconut pirate head, you'll find one here. The shop also has exotic shells and coral, jewelry, handmade Christmas shell ornaments, T-shirts, scrimshaw, children's books and learning tools, cookbooks and light-house collectibles — a mountain of things for the whole family to enjoy, including hermit crabs. It closes for a few weeks after Christmas; otherwise it's open year round.

All Decked Out
N.C. Hwy. 12 • (252) 995-4319, (800) 321-2392

This is a furniture factory owned by Dale Cashman. He and his crew handcraft outdoor furniture such as picnic tables, Adirondack chairs, benches, wooden recliners and hammocks, and they will ship anywhere in the United States. Stop by and have a seat. It's open year round.

The Frisco Market
N.C. Hwy. 12

The Frisco Market is directly across from the entrance road to Ramp 49 and Billy Mitchell Air Field. The market stocks all sorts of groceries, beer, wine, reading material, gas and beach supplies. Frisco Rod and Gun specializes in fishing and hunting equipment. You'll find everything you need for a hunting or fishing trip on the Outer Banks, including offshore and inshore fishing equipment, fly-fishing equipment, guns, ice, bait, tackle and one of the best selections of knives we've seen anywhere. They also carry camping supplies, name-brand outdoor apparel, Sperry Topsiders and T-shirts and offer free air. They are open year round.

Sandy Bay Gallery
N.C. Hwy. 12, Hatteras Village • (252) 986-1338

This gallery puts an emphasis on showcasing Outer Banks artists. Sandy Bay is filled with original watercolor and acrylic paintings and local photography. Potters, jewelers, glass artisans and paper, wood, stained glass and fiber artists all have wares on display. Glass boxes with silver trim by Mary Anne feature a geometric collage of colored and clear glass — they are exquisite. The gallery is open March through Christmas Eve.

Hatteras Village

Hatteras Village offers a mixture of services including drugs and groceries and a few gift stops mixed in. And don't overlook the ferry terminal's Ship's Store, located in the lobby — it offers a selection of T-shirts, coffee mugs, coloring books and souvenirs.

Burrus' Red & White Supermarket
N.C. Hwy. 12 • (252) 986-2333

Burrus' carries freshly cut meats and has a full-service deli and salad bar, Eight O'Clock coffee, fresh produce, frozen foods, dairy products and health and beauty aids. It's open year-round.

Nedo Tru Value Shopping Center
N.C. Hwy. 12 • (252) 986-2545

This is really just one store, but it carries lots of things you'll need for fun and sun on the beach and beyond, including small appliances, bed and bath supplies, books, toys, sporting goods, fishing equipment, clothing, shoes and boots for the whole family and more. The store also has Makita tools and an automotive section. It's open year round.

Hatteras Harbor Marina Store Gift Shop
Hatteras Marina, N.C. Hwy. 12 • (252) 986-2166

The marina gift store has jewelry, name-brand sportswear, fishing supplies, unique gifts, deck shoes and other items. It's open year round.

Lee Robinson General Store
N.C. Hwy. 12 • (252) 986-2381

The original Lee's opened in 1948 but was replaced by a replica several years ago. We're glad it kept the old look, including the wide front porch and the wooden floors. Owners Belinda and Virgil Willis carry everything you need for a vacation at the beach, plus something you wouldn't necessarily expect to find at a beach general store: a great selection of fine wines. The store also carries groceries (including gourmet items), chocolates, fudge, books and magazines, T-shirts, sweatshirts, jewelry and gifts, plus sundries such as film, lotions, boogie boards and hats. You can rent bicycles here too. We like to buy a Coke (in a glass bottle!)and something to snack on for the ferry ride to Ocracoke. It's open year round.

Ocracoke Island

Shopping in Ocracoke is casual, interesting and easily managed on foot. Small shops

are scattered throughout the village and along the main street, on sandy lanes and in private homes. You'll also discover that some dockside stores have the feel of a general store and carry everything you need. Ocracoke Village shops offer a variety of local crafts, artwork, quality accessories for the home, antiques, beachwear, books, music and magazines as well as the ubiquitous T-shirts and even a few souvenir mugs. An ABC package store is adjacent to the Ocracoke Variety Store.

Ocracoke Variety Store
N.C. Hwy. 12 • (252) 928-4911

Ocracoke Variety is on N.C. 12 before you enter the village from the north. Shop for groceries and fresh meat, beer, wine, T-shirts, beachwear and accessories, ice, gifts, books, magazines, camping and fishing supplies, household items, health and beauty aids. True Value Hardware is conveniently located next door. There's a bulletin board posted at the front entrance featuring menus of the local restaurants and community information. They're open all year.

Pirate's Chest Gifts and T-shirts
N.C. Hwy. 12 • (252) 928-4992

Pirate's Chest is a must-stop just to peruse the variety of merchandise sold here: T-shirts, souvenirs, jewelry, local shells, books, scrimshaw, coral, lighthouse prints, 14-karat

gold jewelry, Joan Perry sculptures and more. It's open March through November.

Island Ragpicker
N.C. Hwy. 12 • (252) 928-7571

Island Ragpicker will catch your eye with an attractive mixture of bells, baskets and handwoven rugs displayed on the porch and everywhere inside. Owners Mickey Baker and Carmie Prete offer fine quality crafts (some by local craftspeople), handmade brooms, cards, decoys, pottery, dishes, jewelry and casual cotton apparel. Look for local and nature books, short story collections and self-help books along with an amazing assortment of easy-listening music. The Ragpicker has great cards too. It's one of the few Ocracoke shops open all year.

Cork's Closet Thrift Store
N.C. Hwy. 12 • (252) 928-7331

Cork's is a great example for other thrift stores. The fun is in discovering unique island objects among the large inventory of new and used clothing, housewares, collectibles, books, antiques, toys and local crafts. Cork's Closet is between Styron's General Store (see subsequent listing) and Harbor Road.

Sally Newell Interiors
N.C. Hwy. 12 • (252) 928-6141

Sally Newell, a member of the American Society of Interior Designers, designs commercial and residential interiors. Her service includes furnishings and accessories, carpeting and window treatments. It's open year round.

The Community Store
Ocracoke Waterfront • (252) 928-3321

On the waterfront, The Community Store is a place to shop for essential items. You can also rent videos here. We like to grab an ice cream from the cooler. It's open year round.

The Gathering Place
N.C. Hwy. 12 • (252) 928-7180

Across the parking lot on the harbor, The Gathering Place (located in a century-old building) boasts a front porch complete with an old swing. It's a great place to rest and view the boats on the harbor. Inside, the shop has a collection of local crafts, pottery from North Carolina, Margaret Furlong collectibles, Hanover lighthouse clocks, tide clocks and lighthouse lamps. For 1998 they've added a boutique featuring the April Cornell collection — an Outer Banks exclusive — as well as a variety of sundresses, hats and sandals. Upstairs you'll find small antiques and art including English stained glass and the artwork of Frans Van Baars, Jim Wordsworth and others. Shipping is available year round. The shop is closed in January.

Joyce's of Ocracoke Gifts & Clothing
Ocracoke Waterfront • (252) 928-6461

On the waterfront, Joyce's occupies the first floor space of Joyce's of Ocracoke Motel and Dockage. Owner Joyce L. Barnette offers well-made, comfortable men's and women's apparel, including a very nice collection of classic, sophisticated clothing for women in sportswear and dressier island styles. Joyce also offers an intimate apparel section. The shop carries lovely accessories for the home, such as collectors items with frogs, cows, rabbits, fish, shells and teddy bears. Other great finds here are handcrafted fashion jewelry in all price ranges, mobiles, gifts, cards, stationery, wrapping paper and T-shirts with unique designs. It's open March through Thanksgiving.

Harborside Gifts
N.C. Hwy. 12 • (252) 928-3111

Harborside is one of the many pleasant surprises for visitors to Ocracoke. Quality sportswear for the family, a gourmet food section, gift basket service (some readymades are available), teas, cooking items, pottery, books and magazines share the shop with an interesting collection of T-shirts and — look up! — a model train that chugs along overhead throughout most of the store. You'll also find domestic and imported wine and beer. It's open Easter through Thanksgiving.

Philip Howard's Village Craftsmen
Howard St. • (252) 928-5541,
(800) 648-9743

Village Craftsmen has become an Ocracoke landmark. It's been in business 29 years, but it isn't as easy to find as, say, the local lighthouse. The shop is on the narrow, sandy lane known as Howard Street, a nice walk from the main street. The shop has an abundance of North Carolina crafts, including pottery, rugs, books, soaps, candles and jams. You can buy stoneware and tie-dyed T-shirts here too.

Philip Howard, the owner, is an artist and sells his pen-and-ink and watercolor prints in the shop. A fine selection of cassettes and CDs features Celtic, blues, jazz and bluegrass music. Musical instruments, such as catpaws and strumsticks, help set a creative mood at this out-of-the-way place. The instruments are lightweight and simple to play. You can pick up a mail-order catalog at the shop or have one mailed to you year round. The shop closes for the month of January.

Over the Moon
British Cemetery Rd. • (252) 928-3555

Over the Moon is a wonderful shop filled with handmade contemporary crafts. More than 150 artists provide work such as jewelry, porcelain and Brian Andreas' Storypeople — books, prints and sculptures with insights painted on the work. These folks also offer pins and magnet cards, Metamorphicards and hammock chairs. Pace yourself; this is a place to linger. It is open Easter through Thanksgiving.

Ocracoke Island Hammocks
British Cemetery Rd. • (252) 928-4387

These folks assemble their own 100 percent handwoven hammocks on the premises, and you are welcome to come and watch the process. The shop offers island mementos, lighthouse afghans, jewelry and unique candles. You'll find a wide variety of bath and body and aromatherapy products and gourmet foods. It's open Easter through Christmas.

Teach's Hole
Back Rd. • (252) 928-1718

Come listen to the tales of the notorious Edward Teach — better known as Blackbeard the Pirate — at Teach's Hole. The "piratical piratephernalia," as George and Mickey Roberson call their collection, includes a gift shop and exhibit. More than 1,000 pirate items, including a life-size re-creation of Blackbeard in full battle dress and artifacts from the 17th and 18th centuries, form the exhibit. There is a fee to view it; for more information, see our Kidstuff chapter. Items in the gift shop include pirate toys, music boxes, movies and more than 100 pirate book titles, plus maps, flags, hats, T-shirts, costumes, ship models and treasure coins. It's open Easter though Thanksgiving.

Albert Styron's General Store
N.C. Hwy. 12 • (252) 928-6819

On the street as you approach the Ocracoke Lighthouse, Styron's dates back to 1920. Despite renovations, the store retains the appearance of an old general store. Make your purchases from a wide selection of cheeses, coffee beans, bulk spices and natural foods as well as beer, wine, T-shirts and lighthouse and general merchandise. It's open March through January.

Ocracoke Adventures
Corner of N.C. Hwy. 12 and Silver Lake Rd. • (252) 928-7873

Ocracoke Adventures is appropriately named because the merchandise runs the gamut, including Christmas gifts, bird feeders, prints, shells, film and sundries. You can also sign up for eco and kayak tours, educational programs and children's activities. Your kids will thank you for the memories! (See our Kidstuff chapter for more details.)

Deepwater Pottery & Books
To Be Red
School Rd., Ocracoke • (252) 928-7004

This is an eclectic shop filled with artistic and functional gifts and books as well as an on-site pottery studio that generates stoneware and raku pieces. Choose from a varied selection of plates, bowls, pitchers and decorative pottery. Browse through the paperback section featuring fiction, nonfiction and children's books. Other items include handmade candles and glass, journals and stationery. They have a special bath section filled with soaps and other great-smelling bath luxuries. The shop is open March 1 through Christmas.

Ride The Wind Surf Shop
N.C. Hwy. 12 and Silver Lake • 928-6311

Open April through Christmas, Ride the Wind offers complete surfing equipment and gear, ladies' and men's clothing, shoes, sandals, handbags, suntan lotions, watches and jewelry. Obviously it's more than just a surf shop! See our Watersports chapter for surf and boogie board rental and kayak tour information.

Island Tee's and Gifts
Harbor Loop Rd. • (252) 928-6781

Located in a home built in 1910, this shop offers stacks of T-shirts in every size and color.

Look for children's wear, beach shoes, bathing suits, shorts and sweatshirts. Gift items include shell-decorated picture frames, wind chimes, books, jewelry, beach toys and a roomful of Christmas ornaments and decorations crafted by locals.

Ocracoke Coffee
Back Rd. • (252) 928-7473

Wow! This is a mouth-watering, aromatic shop filled with bagels, pastries, brewed coffee drinks, espresso, smoothies, shakes, whole bean coffee and loose tea. How about a sesame bagel topped with Italian herb cream cheese washed down with a frozen root beer float? Get the picture? Ocracoke Coffee is open daily from 7 AM until 9:30 PM.

Heart's Desire
Back Rd. • (252) 928-4104

This shop features fine crafts by artisans from across the country. You'll find pottery, silver jewelry, blown and cast glass and papier-mâché, folk art, stained-glass windows and copper work, plus beach glass jewelry and beach glass mirrors. Also showcased here are small antiques and collectibles including medicine cabinets, chairs, small benches, shelves and children's paraphernalia such as cribs and wagons. The shop is open April through December.

Whatever your interests, you'll find outlets for them here. There's never enough time to see everything the Outer Banks has to offer.

Attractions

Even after you've made the rounds at our most famous attractions — the beloved candy-striped Cape Hatteras Lighthouse, the world-renowned Wright Brothers National Memorial and the long-running *The Lost Colony* outdoor drama — so much more remains to be seen and done here that even natives always find new adventures every year. Attractions are available to fit every mood, age and price range.

We're not just the home of two of the most significant events in the nation's history — the first English-speaking colony and the first powered flight — we're also gifted with an extraordinary coastline. Between lighthouses, lifesaving stations, wild horses and shipwrecks, visitors can get lost in our long, lively barrier island history. In between, you can kick back, take off or glide away. There's no better place to do virtually nothing but relax or to do every conceivable activity — barring mountain climbing and downhill skiing.

There are wide-open wildlife refuges across the islands and fluorescent-lighted fish tanks at the state aquarium. You can dive into history by boarding a 16th-century representative sailing ship or scuba dive beneath the Atlantic to explore a Civil War shipwreck. Whatever your interests, you'll find outlets for them here. There's never enough time to see everything the Outer Banks has to offer.

In this chapter, we have highlighted our favorite attractions. There are many others you'll discover on your own, and locals will gladly share their own secret spots. Many of these places have free admission or request nominal donations. We begin with the northernmost communities and work southward. Each area has its own section, so pick your pleasure.

Also, be sure to read our chapters on Recreation, Shopping, Arts and Culture, Watersports, Fishing and Nightlife for more exciting, educational and unusual things to do on the Outer Banks.

Corolla

Pine Island Audubon Sanctuary
N.C. Hwy. 12, Sanderling

Ducks, geese, rabbits, deer, fox and dozens of other animals make this 5,400-acre wildlife refuge on the northern Outer Banks (between Duck and Corolla) their home. Hundreds of other species fly through the skies during annual migrations. Set between remote villages of sprawling vacation rental cottages, Pine Island Audubon Sanctuary is a secluded outdoor enthusiast's paradise and a major resting area for birds along the great Atlantic flyway.

Live oaks, bayberry, inkberry, pine, yaupon, holly and several species of sea grass also grow naturally in this wild, remote wetland habitat. The Pine Island Clubhouse and grounds are privately owned, but if you're a member of the Audubon Society, tours are available.

Hikers, bikers and strollers can park at Sanderling Inn to access a 2.5-mile clay trail through a portion of the sanctuary. The path is maintained and is open year-round to the public.

Kill Devil Hills Lifesaving Station
Off N.C. Hwy. 12, Corolla

Built in 1878, the Kill Devil Hills Lifesaving Station is now the setting for Outer Banks Style, (252) 453-4388, a specialty shop in Corolla. The interior doesn't look anything like the old outpost, but the exterior appearance, a peaked roof and crossed timber frame, remains relatively unchanged.

The U.S. Lifesaving Service was established in the late 19th century, and stations were built every 7 miles along the Outer Banks. Crews lived in the wooden structures throughout winter months, patrolling the beaches for shipwrecks and survivors. This station, which was moved almost 30 miles north of its original location, is especially significant because it was frequented by the Wright brothers during their several sojourns to the barrier islands. The Kill Devil Hills Lifesaving Station crew assisted Orville and Wilbur with their early experiments in flight, and some crew members witnessed the world's first powered airplane soar over the sand dunes.

This lifesaving station was brought from Kill Devil Hills to Corolla in 1986, and then restored and renovated. History buffs are welcome to visit Outer Banks Style and the lobby of Twiddy & Company Realtors (behind the station) for free, where a collection of memorabilia used by the lifesaving service and the Wrights is on display.

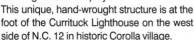

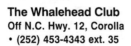

See this and many other **Insiders' Guide®** destinations online — in their entirety.

This unique, hand-wrought structure is at the foot of the Currituck Lighthouse on the west side of N.C. 12 in historic Corolla village.

The Whalehead Club
Off N.C. Hwy. 12, Corolla
• **(252) 453-4343 ext. 35**

Overlooking the windswept wetlands of Currituck Sound, this grand dame of days gone by was once the Outer Banks' biggest, most modern structure. It was built in 1925 as a hunt club for a wealthy industrialist's French wife who had been denied admission to the nearby all-male hunt clubs that dotted the barrier island marshes. The Whalehead Club remains one of the area's most charming attractions and affords a romantic trip back in time to an era of lavish accommodations, elaborate ornamentation and Gatsby-like galas that guests once enjoyed in this great house.

Currently, county officials and a dedicated group of volunteers are trying to raise funds to bring the Whalehead Club back to its former glory. The copper-roofed retreat needs restoring. The ballroom's cork floor is crumbling. The once-grand exterior is battered. Proceeds from tour fees are earmarked for restoration efforts, and officials and volunteers are also hoping to include a wildlife museum on the first floor. Recently, the 1902 Louis XIV low-signature Steinway piano that sat in the mansion for more than a half-century was sent out for repairs. For the time being, the newly revitalized instrument can

be seen at the Currituck County satellite office in Corolla.

Today, visitors can still see the structure's solid mahogany doors and interior walls. The Tiffany globes from the former chandeliers, custom designed in a waterlily motif, can be seen alongside the dining room fireplace's slate hearth. The 16-room basement, which once housed an extensive wine cellar and root cellars for potatoes and onions, is no longer used for its original purpose. The bathrooms, one of the first on the Outer Banks to contain hot and cold indoor plumbing — with both salted and unsalted running water available to fill claw-foot tubs — still look inviting to vacationing house guests.

Outside, the area's first in-ground swimming pool, which once flanked the premises, has long since been demolished. The footbridge and boathouse, however, remain. You can walk the grounds of this historic hunt club for free. Tours of the mansion are offered from 10 AM to 4 PM daily from June through September. Since the Whalehead Club is staffed on a volunteer basis, hours may change according to availability of staff. There is an entry fee. Call for prices and updates.

Currituck Beach Lighthouse
Off N.C. Hwy. 12, Corolla
• **(252) 453-4939**

The Outer Banks' northernmost lighthouse, this red-brick beacon was built in 1875 just north of the Whalehead Club in Corolla. The 214 steps to the top bring you eye to eye with the 50,000-candlepower lamp that still flashes every 20 seconds. This 158-foot-tall lighthouse is open from Palm Sunday weekend through Thanksgiving from 10 AM to 5 PM seven days a week, weather permitting. Visitors are not permitted to climb the tower during high wind conditions or lightning storms. In summer's extended daylight, the lighthouse is open until 6 PM. There is a $4 entry fee per person. The Corolla Wild Horse Fund maintains its headquarters at the base of the tower, and a museum and giftshop are also on the premises.

The Lighthouse Keepers' House, a Victo-

rian dwelling, was constructed from pre-cut, labeled materials shipped by the U.S. Lighthouse Board on a barge and then was assembled on-site. In 1876, when the Keepers' House was completed, two keepers and their families shared the duplex in the isolated seaside setting. The house was abandoned when the lighthouse became automated and keepers were no longer needed to continually clean the lenses, trim the wicks, fuel the lamp and wind the clockwork mechanism that rotated the bright beacon.

Today, the Keepers' House is listed on the National Register of Historic Places. Outer Banks Conservationists Inc. assumed responsibility for its restoration in 1980. Exterior reconstruction already is complete, and the interior is nearly restored.

The Keepers' House is open only 12 days per year, and occasionally by special arrangement. Since the interior of the quarters is very small, public tours of the facility are not possible on a regular basis. Call for more information if you are interested in viewing the house.

Corolla Chapel
Old Corolla Village Rd., Corolla
• (252) 453-4224

Tucked two-and-a-half blocks behind the Currituck Beach Lighthouse, the Corolla Chapel is a charming little gem worth seeing. The best way, no doubt, would be to attend one of the weekly interdenominational services that are given at the chapel year-round. The church is locked most other times, although it's delightful enough to be appreciated plenty just from the outside.

Originally built in 1885, a vestibule, bathroom and storage area were added in 1992. Now gleaming white and by all appearances in perfect condition, the little chapel has had its share of hardship. Battered about by hurricanes in 1894 and 1933, some say it was moved 4 feet south by both storms. After the sound lapped at its floors one too many times, the whole structure was propped higher onto five cinder block stacks in 1992.

In its younger years, the church was used primarily by Missionary Baptists, although

The Wild Horses of Corolla

Corolla's wild horses are part of the mystique of the Outer Banks: a symbol of the roots, endurance, and resilience of an isolated land and its tough inhabitants. They also may become the symbol of the toll taken by breathtaking growth in Corolla.

Close-up

Visitors to the northernmost stretches of barrier beach no longer see pastoral views of horses grazing on golf courses or newly-planted lawns. They no longer see the majestic beasts loping on oceanside sands. They won't even see closeups of the few that were corralled until recently at the Currituck lighthouse.

There are no horses left in Corolla, and there are renewed fears concerning the fate of the ones fenced in the nearby Currituck National Wildlife Refuge.

Believed by many to be descendants of Spanish mustangs, the wild horses have the compact, stocky confirmation and, according to one scientist, the genetic markers of the Barb horses that were brought to the Outer Banks as early as 1523 by Spanish explorers. One native Outer Banker who has studied the "Banker ponies" said they may be the oldest breed of horse in North America.

— continued on next page

Photo: Courtesy of Drew Wilson

Wild horses no longer roam free in Corolla.

Before development in Corolla took off like a shot in the mid-1980s, wild horses ranged unmolested among the sea grasses and dunes of the northern barrier islands. A late discovery for developers, the area didn't have electricity until 1968, telephone service until 1974, or a public paved road until 1984. Tourists driving on the new road were charmed that undomesticated horses milled freely in plain view. Less than ten years later, horses were lounging in shade under rental cottage decks, nosing through garbage cans and strolling nonchalantly through the grocery store's automatic door. Tourists took to feeding and petting them — or attempting to. Close calls with horse bites and kicks became part of the local lore.

Tragically, many horses were struck by vehicles on N.C. Highway 12. A group of local citizens established the Corolla Wild Horse Fund in 1989 to protect the animals after three pregnant mares were killed. The group rallied public support, managing to have the county pass an ordinance to help protect the horses from harm. Signs were posted along the road: Wild Horse Crossing; You Are Entering A Wild Horse Sanctuary; Do Not Feed Horses. Bumper stickers proclaiming "I brake for wild horses" began materializing on cars. Horse souvenirs from the lighthouse giftshop became one of the most popular Corolla memorabilia. The wild horses, in fact, quickly established themselves as the area's most popular attraction.

Still, horse fund volunteers and staffers were unable to protect their charges — at least 17 steeds had died after colliding with cars and trucks. Finally, after a poll revealed that most people wanted to preserve the horses in their own environment instead of relocating them, the fund erected a mile-and-a-half long fence, stretching from sound-to-sea near where the pavement ends in Corolla. The idea was not to enclose the wild animals, but to allow them to roam freely — but safely — in the more than 1,600 acres of public and private land north of the fence. On March 24, 1995, the wildings were herded behind the fence. But the Corolla wild horse story was not yet over.

Like clever children, within no time a group of 10 horses waded 1,500 feet on a shallow sandbar out into the Currituck Sound to get around the fence. Led by a dominant mare called Butterscotch, the herd was apparently determined to get back to the sweet cultivated grasses they'd become spoiled on in Corolla. Equally stubborn horse fund members herded the recalcitrant ponies back behind the fence at least four more times. Exhausted, frustrated and discouraged, members of the fund finally concluded that the horses would outlast them. Reluctantly, the group found homes for them on a farm on mainland North Carolina.

For a while, it seemed all was well. After the forced relocation, area horse lovers took comfort in knowing that at least the 40 or so remaining members of the herd remained safe and wild behind the fence. Visitors yearning for a peek at the beautiful creatures could still see some up close in a 2-acre paddock at the Currituck Beach Lighthouse. Two mares with permanent injuries inflicted by vehicles were boarded on the grounds, along with their two foals. Amused tourists might be treated to a visit by a lovesick blood bay stallion named Okisko, who would come and go around the fence at whim to commune with his sweetheart. Bold and persistent, Okisko would enter the enclosure through the gate, cutting in line in front of tourists. He would then put on an entertaining display: kick up his heels, whinny impressively and prance and paw playfully until a horse fund member would cajole him away. Convinced the charming beast was unstoppable anyway, he was soon allowed to move in — although he continued to leap the fence when he craved his freedom.

With the group no longer in crisis mode, the horse fund became inactive. An employed staff member and founding member, Rowena Dorman willingly resigned in 1996. Another founder and the group's main engine, Debbie Westner, resigned the next year, shortly after finding good homes for the mares and their foals.

— continued on next page

In the fall of 1997, Virginia residents in Sandbridge, about 25 miles up the beach from Corolla, reported seeing some wild horses wandering in populated Sandbridge and the nearby Back Bay National Wildlife Refuge. With the permission of Virginia Beach officials, five horses were carted away to an unknown fate. By December, another horse strolled into view, but this one was captured by Sandbridge-area horse lovers, treated by an equine veterinarian, and transported back to Corolla.

North Carolina and Currituck County officials, meanwhile, said they had no way to help the horses if they strayed into Virginia. The Corolla Horse Fund lacked both the means and the resources to do anything to protect the horses anymore, organizers said. No state or federal law was in place to preserve them; however, Sandbridge residents who agreed with North Carolina's official declaration that the wild horses are an important cultural resource organized an effort to help protect them — eventually, perhaps by constructing a fence on the northern end of the preserve. They also promised to bring any more strays back to North Carolina while they're working on a solution.

The next few years will determine the final fate of the Corolla wild horses. In the Outer Banks' balance between growth and preservation, the horses may be the most immediate test run. As horse fund organizer Dorman conceded in an interview shown in the 1996 UNC public television production *Wild in Corolla*, narrated by North Carolina native Charles Kuralt, the tension may be weighted to the disadvantage of the horses.

"They've survived 400 years," Dorman said. "But they can't survive this development."

originally the house of worship was supposed to be interdenominational. Catholic masses were first said at the church in 1917 and continued to be offered on a sporadic basis throughout World War I and World War II for Coast Guard personnel stationed nearby. In 1938, the Baptists dropped Corolla from their circuit, and church trustees maintained control of the facility, inviting visiting ministers from numerous denominations to conduct services.

Corolla native and church trustee John Austin outlived all the trustees, and when he died in 1984, sole ownership of the chapel was passed on to his son, Norris Austin, who granted a 99-year lease to the present building. Austin says the church of his youth, where he fondly remembers all the townfolk gathered to give thanks the day WWII ended, is not much different than the pretty little chapel he still attends today. Except now there's a heat-pump in place of the former potbellied stove, he says.

Pastor John Strauss has been the sole minister of the Corolla Chapel parish since 1987, when he held his first service on Easter Sunday. Today about 35 residents are members of the congregation, and 16 are associate members. In the summer months though, up to 140 folk attend services, spilling out the doors of the 120-seat church. To meet the demand, the pastor now holds two services every Sunday from May through the end of September. Strauss says the annual Easter sunrise service regularly attracts hundreds of worshipers. In 1997, in fact, a record-breaking 650 worshipers attended the sunrise service, which is held outside by the pool and dunes at nearby Corolla Light. Three additional Easter services are also conducted later in the morning at the church. Interdenominational services are held every Sunday year-round. Catholic Mass is conducted every Wednesday evening. Services are held more frequently in the summer. Call for scheduling information.

Duck

U.S. Army Corps of Engineers Field Research Facility

N.C. Hwy. 12, Duck • (252) 261-3511

Set on a former Navy weapons test site, the Waterways Experiment Station of the U.S. Army Corps of Engineers has helped scientists study ocean processes for 20 years. This 173-acre federally owned scientific mecca has

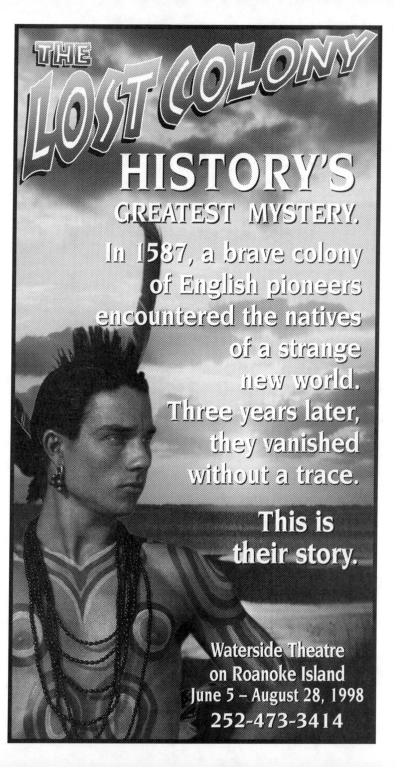

gained a reputation as one of premier coastal field research facilities in the world. Just north of Duck village, the site includes state-of-the-art equipment to monitor sand movement, wave forces and water currents, temperatures and sedimentation. Its 12 full-time employees regularly host dozens of scientists from around the globe to conduct experiments on sand movement, beach erosion and coastal dynamics. Last summer, during the world's largest near-shore research experiment, billed Sandy Duck '97, 250 coastal engineers gathered at the research facility in the most ambitious effort ever undertaken to study the near-shore zone of breaking waves to determine the causes of beach erosion.

The grounds, research station and 1,840-foot-long pier at the Duck experiment station are open weekdays from mid-June through mid-August. Federal researchers conduct free 1½-hour walking tours of the facility at 10 AM. The tours are outside and can be strenuous, so be prepared. Access to beach areas will depend on ongoing research experiments.

Besides the pier itself, the U.S. Army Corps of Engineers' experiment station owns a 125-foot observation tower and a 35-foot-tall Coastal Research Amphibious Buggy, the CRAB, which carries people and equipment from the shore into the sea. The Corps works in cooperation with the U.S Army and Navy and the National Oceanic and Atmospheric Administration, using the latest technically advanced equipment to improve the design of coastal navigation projects. Research conducted at the station could eventually alter the way engineers design bridges; help people pick sites for beach nourishment projects; improve projections about where the shoreline might erode; determine how and why sandbars move; and predict what effect rock jetties might have on Oregon Inlet.

Kitty Hawk

Kitty Hawk Public Beach & Bathhouse
N.C. Hwy. 12, MP 4, Kitty Hawk

Across the road from the ocean, a bathhouse and small, free parking area offer visitors a place to go on the beach as soon as

they arrive on the Outer Banks at Kitty Hawk. If you get here too early for check-in, you can change into bathing suits here and enjoy a few hours at the ocean until it's time to head to your hotel or beach cottage. Public showers also are available to rinse off after one last stop in the sand on the way home.

Kitty Hawk Village
Along Kitty Hawk Rd., west of U.S. Hwy. 158, Kitty Hawk

If you want to check out one of the islands' oldest neighborhoods and see where the Wright brothers stayed when they first visited the Outer Banks by ferry, head west on Kitty Hawk Road, turning just north of the 7-Eleven in Kitty Hawk. This winding, two-lane street dead-ends after about 3 miles at Kitty Hawk Bay. Drivers pass through at least two centuries in the process.

The old post office for this isolated village still stands on the north side of the road and has been restored to become the town's new police station. Several two-story farmhouses still stand along the shady streets and shallow canals. Boats on blocks and fishing nets tied to trees are strewn along back yards. On warm weekend afternoons, families still ride horses down the live oak-lined lanes, waving to neighbors sitting on their covered porches. You can forget you're at the beach in this quaint, quiet community on the western shores of the Outer Banks.

Kill Devil Hills

Wright Brothers National Memorial
U.S. Hwy. 158, MP 8, Kill Devil Hills
• (252) 441-7430

Set atop a steep, grassy sand hill in the center of Kill Devil Hills, the trapezoidal granite monument to Orville and Wilbur Wright is within easy walking distance of the site of the world's first powered airplane flight. Below where this lighthouse-style tower now stands, on the blustery afternoon of December 17, 1903, the two bicycle-building brothers from Dayton, Ohio, changed history by soaring over a distance of more than 852 feet and staying airborne for 59 seconds in their homemade flying machine. The monument was

Photo: Courtesy of Bob Reardon

It's not unusual to see dolphins frolicking in these Atlantic waters.

erected in Orville and Wilbur Wright's honor in 1932.

In the low, domed building on the right side of the main drive off U.S. 158, the National Park Service operates a visitors center, gift shop and museum. Here, people can view interpretive exhibits of man's first flight and see displays on later aviation advancements. Explanations of the Wright brothers' struggles to fly include parts of their planes, engines and notes. Reproductions of their gliders are displayed in the flight room, and rangers offer free guided historical tours year round.

Outside the exhibit center, four markers set along a sandy runway commemorate the takeoff and landing sites of each of Orville and Wilbur's December 17 flights. Reconstructed wooden sheds replicating those used at the Wrights' 1903 camp and hangar also are on the grounds and open to visitors. These sheds are furnished with tools, equipment and even cans of milk like the brothers used.

A short hike takes you from the visitors center to the monument hill, but if you'd rather drive or ride, parking is available closer to the base of the hill. Paved walkways make access easier, but cacti and sand spurs abound in the area. Also, be wary that the walk up the monument hill is longer and more strenuous than it looks, so it's best to go at a leisurely pace. On a hot summer day, consider visiting the site in the morning or late afternoon, when the sun is not as strong. This seemingly simple structure is most powerful when you can really contemplate the immensity of the brothers' accomplishment.

Besides tours, the Exhibit Center at the Wright Brothers National Memorial offers a variety of summer programs. Grounds and buildings are open to vehicles from 9 AM until 5 PM Labor Day through Memorial Day. Hours are from 9 AM to 6 PM in the summer. Thirty minute flight-room talks are given by rangers every hour on the hour year-round.

Cost for entry at the guard gate is $2 per person or $4 per car.

Kitty Hawk Aero Tours
Behind the Wright Memorial, off Colington Rd., Kill Devil Hills
• (252) 441-4460

For a bird's-eye view of the Outer Banks and a unique perspective on how fragile the barrier islands really are, take a 30-minute air tour over the land and ocean in a small plane.

A short runway and parking lot sit behind the Wright Brothers' monument. In front of a tiny ticket booth, blue and yellow airplanes beckon adventurers to fly the same skies that hosted the world's first flight. Pilots will gear tours to passengers' wishes but usually find a few dolphins splashing near the shores or dip over the rare maritime forests on the islands' western reaches. Views are breathtaking, and the experience is one that's not to be missed. Bring your camera for this high-flying cruise.

Rates are $23 per person for parties of three to six; $28 per person for parties of two; and $27 per person for parties of four on larger planes.

Biplane flights in an open-air cockpit authentic 1941 Waco also are available from the same site starting at $48 per person. These 15-minute trips take you back in time, complete with goggled leather helmets. Pilots fly south to Jockey's Ridge State Park and back to the Wright Brothers' monument.

Air tours are offered year round, weather permitting. Advance reservations are accepted.

Nags Head Woods Ecological Preserve
Ocean Acres Dr., Kill Devil Hills
• (252) 441-4381, (252) 441-2525

If you've had a little too much sun, or if you'd just like to spend time in a secluded forest on a part of the Outer Banks few people get to see, allocate an afternoon for the Nags Head Woods Ecological Preserve, west of U.S. Highway 158.

The Nature Conservancy, a privately funded organization dedicated to preserving pristine ecosystems, oversees this maritime forest. Although Nags Head Woods is privately owned — it is not a park — it is an example of a successful private-public partnership. A large portion of the land was donated to the non-profit group by the Town of Nags Head. Trails are open to visitors on weekdays from 10 AM until 3 PM, while members of the Nature Conservancy are welcome anytime.

More than 4 miles of trails and tiny footbridges wind through forest, dune, swamp and pond habitats. There's an old graveyard near the site of an early 20th-century farming community that once included a school, church and dozens of homes. The maritime forest itself is well-hidden on the west side of the Outer Banks, and many rare plant and animal species abound within this virtually untouched ecosystem. See our Natural Wonders chapter for more information.

There is a small visitors center, gift shop and gazebo near the entrance. The staff offers a variety of free field trips, including guided bird walks and kayaking excursions during warm months. No camping, horseback riding, loitering, bicycling, firearms, alcoholic beverages, picnicking or pets are allowed in the preserve.

Write to the Nature Conservancy at 701 W. Ocean Acres Drive, Kill Devil Hills, NC 27948. All donations are welcome, and memberships start at $25. Monies support the preserve's environmental education and research programs.

Nags Head

Jockey's Ridge State Park
U.S. Hwy. 158, MP 12, Nags Head
• (252) 441-7132

The East Coast's tallest sand dune and one of the Outer Banks most phenomenal natural attractions, Jockey's Ridge has been a favorite stop for tourists for more than 150 years. In the early 1970s, bulldozers began trying to flatten the top of the dune to make way for a housing subdivision. A Nags Head woman, Carolista Golden, single-handedly stopped the destruction and formed a committee that saved Jockey's Ridge.

State officials made the sand hill a protected park in 1975, but the dunes are unruly subjects. The sand mountains have migrated southwest in fits and starts over the decades. In the past 25 years, the steepest side of the

Coming Soon to a Beach Near You

Can't believe how much there is to do on these bountiful barrier islands? Just wait — there will be more to come soon.

Major additions and renovations are planned at one already popular Outer Banks attraction, previews of the Wright Brothers' centennial celebration are steaming forward as 2003 looms nearer, and a huge museum dedicated to the history and mystique of area shipwrecks is in the works. Plus, there's a hoped-for beachcomber's museum in the talking stages, based on the massive collection of one Nags Head woman who walked Outer Banks beaches twice daily for most of her 74 years.

The North Carolina Aquarium at Roanoke Island is one of the three state aquariums slated for enlargements and improvements. Although groundbreaking was scheduled initially at the Outer Banks site for the fall of 1996, a state budget shortfall held up the $30 million project. Each facility was expecting $10 million to enhance their exhibits and double in size, and Roanoke Island was first in line. Relieved aquarium officials finally announced in 1997 that the funds were put in the budget.

New displays planned at the aquarium include a half-round tunnel that will provide

— continued on next page

Photo: Courtesy of Elaine Fogarty

Roanoke Island Festival Park is perched alongside Shallowbag Bay.

visitors with a view into the habitat and behavior of native marine life; a 185,000-gallon open ocean tank stocked with sharks, rays, sea turtles, groupers and other native species; and river otters, reptiles, aquatic snakes and wading birds exhibited in their natural habitat.

The focus of new aquarium will be on "Waters of the Outer Banks," which will draw visitors into a tour of native aquatic life in its natural environment, starting at the Alligator River and continuing through the freshwater and saltwater marshes to the offshore waters. Within the ocean tank, viewers will see a replica of the USS *Monitor* shipwreck that will be home to a wide variety of reef fishes. A skylit atrium with 50-foot trees will house the new freshwater habitat.

Planning and design work has been completed and renovation of the North Carolina Aquarium was under way in 1998. The project should be completed in 1999. The facility will remain open throughout most of the expansion, but some areas may be closed temporarily while work is ongoing.

The 100th anniversary of Orville and Wilbur Wright's first successful motor-powered flight on Dec. 17, 1903 near Kill Devil Hills will likely be the biggest event that the Outer Banks has ever seen. At least that's what the First Flight Society intends it to be. It might be years down the road, but the nonprofit group is already stirring the coals so the occasion will be regarded as a must-show full-scale national celebration. Preparation at the site is nearly complete. The monument at the Wright Brothers National Memorial has already been restored; its beacon has been repaired and brightened; its pylon has been rededicated. On July 27, 1998 the first annual air race, where 30 experimental aircraft will fly over the airstrip near the monument, will be held. On National Aviation Day, August 19, speakers will come to the monument to honor Orville Wright's birthday. Next, the 95th anniversary of the brothers' flight will honor Dr. John Paul Stapp, a practitioner of aviation medicine, and Col. Joe Kittinger, the first man to solo a balloon across the Atlantic, for their contributions to aviation.

Much more is in store as the anniversary gets closer every year. Stamps and coins honoring the brothers already have been issued or commissioned. Officials hope a proposed $17 million visitors' center at the Wright Brothers National Memorial will be funded and completed by 2002. A federal panel is also expected to be created to handle the full-scale plans for the centennial. First Flight Society members say the celebration will last for a least a week and attract national and international officials, leaders and celebrities. So mark your calender, and plan ahead for the Outer Banks' biggest day.

The Graveyard of The Atlantic Museum will trace the 400-year maritime history of North Carolina's Outer Banks. The 18,768-square-foot facility will be beside the Hatteras Village ferry docks, and will include artifacts, interactive displays, multimedia films and presentations, classroom and exhibit space and information about the 1,000 or more ships that went down off the shores of the barrier islands between Carova and Cape Lookout.

The voyages of Sir Walter Raleigh and the "lost colony" pioneers, pirate and privateer raids, German submarine attacks, and numerous groundings, ghost ships, and storm fatalities will be explored at the $5 million museum.

Some of the artifacts that are planned to be displayed will include a shipwreck commissioner's log book from the Civil War, which describes bombardment by blockade runners and hundreds of photographs and relics. Other items the curators hope to secure for exhibits are a hand-hewn juniper oar that members of the U.S. Lifesaving Service used to row their surfboat through the breakers during a daring turn-of-the century rescue, a cannon ball fired from a Confederate gunboat off the Outer Banks, a seaman's journal he kept during 51 years of voyages, and a marine toilet off the steamer *Proteus*, which sank near Hatteras during World War I. Museum officials

— continued on next page

have also asked for permission to display some of the newly discovered artifacts from what is believed to be Blackbeard's pirate boat.

The public, nonprofit museum has been working on securing funds and artifacts since 1988. As of spring of 1998, the facility needed to raise more than $3 million. A model of the museum has been completed and can be seen at the East Carolina Bank in Hatteras Village. The Graveyard of the Atlantic Museum, which will include a gift shop and cost about $5 per person for admittance, was targeted to be open by the start of the 1998 tourist season. The opening date has been pushed ahead as the museum board searches for funding sources, however. For more information call (252) 986-2995.

The Nellie Myrtle Beachcomber's Museum: It could happen. Here's an example where there's more than enough fascinating items to display, but no place to show 'em off. Nellie Myrtle Pridgen, born in Nags Head in 1918, strolled the ocean shores of the Outer Banks and the sands of Jockey's Ridge twice daily for more than 60 years before she died in 1992. She collected a massive amount of ocean rejects and beach glass in the process — a collection valuable for the story it tells about the barrier islands, the ocean and Nellie Myrtle — and about the these lands before tourism changed its face.

Friends and family have decided to meet and formulate a plan of action for setting up a museum. In the meantime, the items are stored safely away, many just the way Nellie left them. Jars of bird feathers and beach glass, pieces of fulgurite, hundreds of bricks, some vases, lengths of rope, toys, buttons, false teeth, pottery, driftwood, buoys — all found during her daily walks — are still stacked where Nellie put them. Most important, she left behind a library of hundreds of articles about the Outer Banks.

We hope we'll have a chance to see Nellie's collection in the near future. Stay tuned.

---

hill has shifted more than 1,500 feet to the southwest. Jockey's Ridge is also getting shorter. At the turn of the century, the highest mound was estimated at 140 feet tall. In 1971, it was about 110 feet tall. Development has blocked replenishment of the sand, and nearby grasses have caught the blowing sand before it reaches the ridge.

Today, the 1.5-mile-long, 420-acre-plus dune — which varies from 90 feet to 110 feet in height — is open to the public year round until sunset. It's a popular spot for hang gliders, summer hikers, small children who like to roll down the steep slopes and teenagers who delight in flinging and flipping themselves dramatically down the sandy hills. In 1997, more than 940,000 people visit Jockey's Ridge, making it one of North Carolina's most popular parks.

Getting to Jockey's Ridge has been easier since state Department of Transportation workers installed a crosswalk across U.S. 158 a few summers ago. If you park at Kitty Hawk Connection, where the colorful flags are flying on the east side of the highway, you can walk across the road and enter the state park on foot. If you'd rather drive in, park headquarters is near the northern end of a parking lot off the west side of U.S. 158. You'll notice an entrance sign at MP 12, Carolista Drive in Nags Head.

A new visitor's center, a museum and a giftshop were recently completed near park headquarters. Centered around the theme of wind and how it affects Jockey's Ridge, the

---

INSIDERS' TIP

The Lost Colony Children's Theater tours the Outer Banks mid-July though mid-August. Call the Waterside Theater, (800) 488-5012, for dates and location. If you're around before Halloween, check out The Haunted History Tour of Waterside Theater between Oct. 24 and Oct. 31. Call the theater for information — it's a scream!

The top of a castle is all that remains of this miniature golf attraction that was slowly swallowed up by the Jockey's Ridge sand dune.

free museum features photo displays of the history and recreation at the dune and a diorama of the animals that inhabit the area. Information panels of plants and animals and an auditorium where slide shows and videos are shown is also at the facility. Maps available from the park ranger indicate walking areas. Two trails — the new Soundside Nature Trail, a very easy 45-minute walk, and Tracks in the Sand, a moderate 1.5-mile trek — are on-site for hikers looking for a change of scenery. Jockey's Ridge State Park offers natural history programs throughout the summer, including stargazing and wildlife discovery evening hikes and early-morning bird-watching and natural history discovery adventures. Programs for kids are also offered, but rangers warn that they fill up early and many require advance registration. Sheltered picnic areas also are available for leisurely lunches. Call for program schedules.

It's a long, hot hike to the top of the ridge, but it's well worth the work. Bring shoes or boots. Don't try it barefoot; you'll burn your feet. Also, some lower areas around the dune are covered with broken glass. From the top of Jockey's Ridge, you can see both ocean and sound. Cottages along the beach look like tiny huts from a miniature train set. Kite-flying and hang-gliding enthusiasts catch the breezes that flow constantly around the steep summit, shifting the sand in all directions. The desert-like appearance of the sand dunes reveals strange but artistic patterns of winds and of footprints made by people climbing the hills.

If your mobility is impaired, there's a 360-foot boardwalk that affords wheelchairs and baby strollers a slightly sloping incline onto a wooden platform overlooking the center of the dune. For the visually handicapped, audio guides are available at the park office. Park rangers can also provide a ride to the top of the dune if you call in advance.

Newman's Shell Shop
N.C. Hwy. 12, MP 13½, Nags Head
• (252) 441-5791

This bright pink establishment on the ocean side of the Beach Road is an Outer Banks shell shop, tourist attraction and local museum. Newman's was the first store on the beach, opening in 1939. It's remained a family-owned business throughout the years and stocks shells from all over the world. Owner Susie Stoutenberg displays a labeled collection of shells from as far away as India and Peru. A large variety of gifts, local and imported crafts and accessories also are arranged in attractive displays.

Wind chimes, shell sculptures and jewelry made from ocean artifacts abound at this charming seaside shop. There's even a display of antique guns, pistols and swords that have been in the family for many years. After being in business for more than a half-century, Newman's has supplied thousands of Outer Banks visitors with reminders of their summer sojourns to the beautiful barrier island beaches.

Besides shells and crafts, many of which are made on the premises, Newman's is known for its hermit crabs. On the last Saturday in July, the shop hosts a Hermit Crab Race that has become increasingly popular with the younger set (see our Annual Events chapter). So select your crustacean critter early and start training for the big event.

Newman's Shell Shop is open seven days a week in season. See our Shopping chapter for related information.

Old Nags Head
N.C. Hwy. 12, MP 12-13 and Soundside Rd., Nags Head

Most of the villages on the Outer Banks began as small soundside communities. Just south of Jockey's Ridge, there's a narrow road leading toward the sound appropriately dubbed Soundside Road. Here, some of the original, old-style Outer Banks homes still teeter toward the water on stilts. Some of the houses were repaired with timbers that washed ashore from shipwrecks. Others have succumbed to the rising tides or the shifting sands of Jockey's Ridge.

On the ocean end of the street, along the Beach Road in both directions, some of the original seaside cottages still cling to the shore. Called the "unpainted aristocracy" by one Outer Banks author, these sprawling wooden houses reflect their age in the weathered, dark brown cedar-shake siding and shutters. Many grandchildren and great grandchildren of the original landowners who built these first beach homes still inhabit the historic structures each summer.

Gallery Row
Between U.S. Hwy. 158 and N.C. Hwy. 12, MP 10½, Nags Head

A green sign off the east side of U.S. 158 indicates the entrance to an artisans' alley known as Gallery Row in northern Nags Head. Here, Glenn Eure's Ghost Fleet Gallery, featuring Glenn's eccentric oil paintings on strangely shaped tree limb-mounted canvases, sits across the street from Jewelry by Gail's handmade gem creations. Morales Art Gallery offers an array of works by area and out-of-town artists in its sprawling showrooms. Lighthouse Gallery and Gifts has hundreds of bright beacons in every style and size, and Ipso Facto Gallery shows unusual artifacts from all over the globe.

Most of these shops are open year round and are free for people who just want to browse. To learn more, see the Galleries section in our Arts and Culture chapter.

Roanoke Island

The Elizabethan Gardens
Off U.S. Hwy. 64, Roanoke Island
• (252) 473-3234

Created by the Garden Club of North Carolina Inc. in 1960 to commemorate the efforts of Raleigh's colonists at establishing an English settlement, these magnificent botanical gardens offer an exquisite, aromatic environment year round. They include 10½ acres of the state's most colorful, dazzling flora. The flower-filled walkways are the perfect contrast to the windblown, barren Outer Banks beaches.

Six full-time gardeners tend more than 1,000 varieties of immaculately manicured trees, shrubs and flowers in the Elizabethan Gardens, which you'll find north of Manteo. Translucent

---

INSIDERS' TIP

To see Jockey's Ridge from the back, drive down Soundside Road to the end and make the first right. There's a parking lot where you can leave your car, so take a stroll and get a different perspective on this phenomenon.

emerald grass fringes marble fountains, and beauty blooms from every crevice.

Visitors enter at the Great Gate into formal gardens along curving walkways carefully crafted from brick and sand. The bricks were handmade at the Silas Lucas Kiln, in operation during the late 1800s in Wilson, North Carolina. The tree-lined landscape is divided into a dozen gardens.

Although this botanical refuge is breathtakingly beautiful all year, offering different colors and fragrances depending on the season, it is, perhaps, the most striking in spring. Azaleas, dogwood, pansies, wisteria and tulips bloom around every bend. Rhododendron, roses, lacecap and other hydrangea appear in May. Summer brings fragrant gardenias, colorful annuals and perennials, magnolia, crape myrtle, Oriental lilies and herbs. Chrysanthemums and the changing colors of leaves signal the beginning of autumn and camellias bloom from late fall through winter.

In the center of the paths, six marble steps down from the rest of the greenery, the crowned jewel of the Elizabethan Gardens awaits discovery. A sunken garden, complete with Roman statuary, tiered fountains and low shrubs pruned into geometric flower frames springs from the sandy soil. The famous Virginia Dare statue nearby is based on an Indian legend that says Virginia, the first English child born in America, grew up among Native Americans (see our Roanoke Island chapter).

The Elizabethan Gardens are open daily from 9 AM to 5 PM except Saturday and Sunday in December, January and February. Shoulder season hours are adjusted according to available daylight. The gardens are closed Christmas and New Year's Day. From June 1 through September 1, the gardens will stay open until 7 PM. Admission is $3 for adults, $1 for youths ages 12 through 17 and free for children younger than 12.

There is no fee in the winter. Season passes are offered for $7.

Wheelchairs are provided. Most paths are handicapped-accessible. Some plants are for sale in the garden gift shop. The gardens also are a favorite wedding locale, and a meeting room is available for a fee to community groups up to 100 people.

Fort Raleigh National Historic Site
Off U.S. Hwy. 64, Roanoke Island
• (252) 473-5772

Don't visit Fort Raleigh and expect to see a fort. What exists on the site is a small earthworks fortification. It's no daunting barricade, but is a lovely spot drenched in American history. On the north end of Roanoke Island, near the Roanoke Sound's shores, Fort Raleigh marks the beginning of English settlement in North America.

Designated as a National Historic Site in 1941, this more than 500-acre expanse of woods and beach includes the "outerwork" — an area built intentionally away from living space — where 1585 colonist Joachim Gans smote copper, along with the National Park Service's Cape Hatteras National Seashore visitors center and headquarters, and a nature trail. An outdoor exhibit about the Freedman's colony, a community the government established for escaped slaves between 1862 and 1867, is also on-site. Fort Raleigh incorporates Weirs Point and Fort Huger, significant historic markers to radio and war, respectively.

At the Roanoke Island base of the bridge to Manns Harbor, Weirs Point is an attractive public beach on the Croatan Sound. Free parking is available at the turnoff on Roanoke Island just before the end of the bridge. The brackish water is warm and shallow and perfect for kids. The beach is also wide enough to allow for a good game of Frisbee or a pleasant family picnic. About 300 yards north of Weirs Point, in 6 feet of water, lay the remains of Fort Huger. This was the largest Confeder-

INSIDERS' TIP

The Wright brothers did not achieve their feat of flight off Kill Devil Hill, as many mistakenly believe. Their machines went aloft on the level sands below the hill, between what is now the monument and the visitors center at the Wright Brothers Memorial.

ate fort on the island when Union troops advanced across the Outer Banks during the Civil War battles of 1862. The island has migrated quite a bit in the last 130 years. The fort used to sit securely on the north end on solid land.

In 1901, from a hut on Weirs Point beach, one of the unsung geniuses of the electrical age began investigating what was then called "wireless telegraphy." Reginald Fessenden held hundreds of patents on radiotelephony and electronics but died without credit for many of them. In a letter dated "April 3, 1902, Manteo," Fessenden tells his patent attorney that "I can now telephone as far as I can telegraph. . . . I have sent varying musical notes from Hatteras and received them here with but 3 watts of energy." The world's first musical radio broadcasts were completed on this soundside sand of the Outer Banks.

Picnic benches, a Dare County information kiosk and restrooms are provided at Weirs Point. Watch for stumps and broken stakes in the water. The tide also creeps up quickly, so beware of needing to move beach blankets away from its encroaching flow.

The Fort Raleigh visitors center offers interpretive exhibits in its small museum. A 17-minute video provides an introduction to this historic site. Here, the 400-year-old Elizabethan Room from Heronden Hall in Kent, England, is on display. William Randolph Hearst had the room transported to the United States after he had it removed from an authentic 16th-century house. The furnishings, carved mantelpiece, paneling, stone fireplace and blown glass in the leaded windows offer a glimpse of America's origins across the ocean.

Self-guided tours and tours led by Park Service personnel are available at this archaeologically significant site. Programs vary depending on the time of day and year. The Thomas Hariot Nature Trail is a short, self-guided trail with pine-needle paths that lead to the sandy shores of Roanoke Sound. Some believe that Sir Richard Grenville first stepped ashore here on Roanoke Island in the late 16th century.

Interpretive programs on African-American history, European colonial history, Native American history and Civil War history are offered in the summer. Fort Raleigh National Historic Site is open year round from 9 AM until 5 PM seven days a week. Hours are extended in the summer. Fort Raleigh is closed Christmas Day.

The Lost Colony
Off U.S. Hwy. 64, Waterside Theatre, Roanoke Island • (252) 473-3414, (800) 488-5012

The nation's longest running outdoor drama, this historical account of the first English settlement in North America is a must-see for Outer Banks visitors. Pulitzer Prize-winning author Paul Green brought the history of English colonization to life through an impressive combination of Elizabethan music, Native American dances, colorful costumes and vivid drama on a soundside stage in 1937. His play continues to enchant audiences today at Waterside Theatre, near Fort Raleigh, on Roanoke Island.

After record-breaking attendance in 1997, the 60th anniversary of *The Lost Colony* production, the 1998 season also promises to be exciting. Not only will the audience have use of bigger bathrooms and concession areas, but they will, for the first time, sit in brand-new stadium seats, rather than the rough-hewn benches in place for decades. In essence, it will be almost a totally new amphitheater. The pre-show production both leading to and inside the theater that was revamped considerably last year by Tony-award-winning Broadway designer William Ivey Long will again be part of the show. Spectacular new scenery and costume designs will be featured changes in the 61st season.

The Lost Colony is a theatrical account of Sir Walter Raleigh's early explorers who first settled on the shores near the present day theater in 1585. (Andy Griffith got his start playing Sir Walter Raleigh for several seasons). Children and adults are equally captivated by the performers, staging and music; many locals see the show every year and always find it spellbinding. If you have youngsters, come early and have them sit in the very front row by the stage. They'll never stop talking about it! It can get chilly on evenings when the wind blows off the sound, so we recommend sweaters, even in July and August. Mosquitoes at this outdoor drama also can be vicious, especially after a rain, so bring plenty of bug repellent. The theater is wheelchair-accessible and the staff is glad to accommodate special customers.

Once you arrive, settle back and enjoy a thoroughly professional, well-rehearsed, technically outstanding show. The leads are played by professional actors. Most of the backstage personnel are pros too — and it shows. Supporting actors are often locals, with some island residents passing from part to part as they grow up. On August 18, a local infant is chosen to reenact Virginia Dare's birthday.

All shows start at 8:30 PM and are performed nightly except Saturday. The season opens June 5 and runs through August 28. Tickets are $14 for adults, $7 for children 12 and younger and $13 for senior citizens. Adult-accompanied children 12 and younger are admitted at half price for Sunday and Monday night performances. Those 65 and older are admitted for $12 on Fridays. North Carolina residents will be admitted for half-price on Fridays and Sundays in June. Groups of 20 or more can call for a discount.

This is probably the most popular summertime event on the Outer Banks, and we recommend you make reservations, though you can try your luck at the door if you wish. You can make paid mail reservations by writing The Lost Colony, 1409 Highway 64/264, Manteo, North Carolina 27954; or you can reserve tickets by phone. Tickets can also be purchased at 70 outlets across the Outer Banks. Call for locations. Unpaid reservations will be held at the box office for pickup until 7:30 PM. If a production is rained out, ticket holders can come back any other night any other week, month or year.

North Carolina Aquarium
Airport Rd., Roanoke Island
• (252) 473-3493

Down a winding road northwest of Manteo near the Dare County airport, the North Carolina Aquarium at Roanoke Island offers an air-conditioned, indoor excursion that's open all year.

Accessibly set up and labeled to provide a detailed glimpse of sea life along North Carolina's barrier islands, this educational attraction includes an 8,400-gallon, wall-size, well-lighted shark tank; a video of on-site osprey nesting near the parking lot; state laboratories and a marine reference library; and a touch-me tank where visitors can pet horseshoe crabs and watch saltwater fish scurrying through shallow ponds.

Fluorescent lights glow like jewels along long, darkened corridors where sea turtles float on iridescent driftwood, long-nose gar bump against the glass walls of their world, and octopi and burrfish dive through their tanks, swirling sand. Sea life starts out with freshwater species at the aquarium, shading through brackish to saltwater. A wetlands exhibit features freshwater turtles and amphibians, including some small alligators. Be aware that because the aquarium is in the process of expansion, some exhibits may not always be available to view. Call ahead for updates.

Visitors can view films on marine and biological topics. Staff members conduct summer daytime field trips and talks for all age groups. Check at the front desk for a monthly calendar of events, or consult *The Coast* free weekly newspaper. The aquarium caters to groups of any kind and can supply meeting facilities in its conference room, seminar room or 240-seat auditorium. There's also a great gift shop with marine-related collectibles, books and T-shirts.

To reach the aquarium, drive north from Manteo on U.S. 64 W. Turn left on Airport Road, following signs to the airport. After the big 90-degree turn in the road, the aquarium will be on the right. It's open year-round from 9 AM to 5 PM every day except Thanksgiving, Christmas and New Year's Day. Admission is $3 for adults, $2 for senior citizens and active military, $1 for children ages 6 to 17 and free for children younger than 6. Aquarium Society members are admitted free.

Mother Vineyard
Off Mother Vineyard Rd., Roanoke Island

The oldest-known grapevine in the United States grows on Roanoke Island. When the first settlers arrived here, the Outer Banks were covered with wild grapes. Arthur Barlowe wrote to Sir Walter Raleigh in 1584:

". . . Being where we first landed very sandy and low toward the water side, but so full of grapes as the very beating and surge of the sea overflowed them, of which we found such plenty, as well there as in all places else, both on the sand and on the green soil, on the hills as in the plains, as well on every little shrub, as also climbing toward the tops of high cedars, that I think in all the world the like abundance is not to be found."

The Mother Vine is one of those ancient grapevines, so old that it may have been planted even before Europeans arrived in the New World. Certainly it was already old in the 1750s, as records attest, and scuppernong grape vines do not grow swiftly. Another story is that this vine was transplanted to Roanoke Island by some of the Fort Raleigh settlers. Whichever story is true, the Mother Vine is more than 400 years old, and it's still producing fine fat, tasty grapes. In fact, for many years, a small winery owned by the Etheridge family cultivated the vine on Baum's Point, making the original Mother Vineyard wine until the late 1950s.

Mother Vineyard Scuppernong, the Original American Wine, is still produced by a company in Petersburg, Virginia. It is a pink wine, quite sweet, similar to a white port or Mogen David. You can find it at many Outer Banks groceries.

The Mother Vine is on private property and a bit out of the way. To find it, drive north from Manteo on U.S. 64. About .75 miles past the city limits, turn right on Mother Vineyard Road. Go less than a half-mile, where the road makes a sharp turn to the right at the sound. About 300 feet past the turn, on the left, the patient old vine crouches beneath a canopy of leaves, twisted and gnarled, ancient and enduring. Please stay on the road if you're sneaking a peek.

The Christmas Shop and The Island Gallery
U.S. Hwy. 64, Manteo • (252) 473-2838, (800) 470-2838

The original Outer Banks ornament shop and a perfect excuse for celebrating Santa year round, the Christmas Shop and Island Gallery offer an exquisite world of fantasy and festive delights. Edward Greene opened this unique store on June 1, 1967. It remains the only one of its kind, although others have tried to emulate its wide array of holiday statues, decorations and unusual collectibles.

This shaded shopping complex includes seven rambling, multilevel buildings. Each room is furnished with well-restored antique furniture (that's not for sale). The trip will fill visitors with wonder.

The Christmas Shop stocks about 60,000 items from 500 companies and cottage industries. Creations from more than 100 artists and craftspeople from across the country are included in the inventory, says Greene, a former New York City actor who decorated Christmas trees for area department stores. Whole walls are filled with toys, pottery and handcrafts. Others overflow with baskets, carvings, miniatures, handmade jewelry, ornaments, seashells, candles and Christmas cards. The shop's 125 switches control innumerable atmospheric lights that give everything a magical glow. There's even a year-round Halloween room, an old-fashioned candy store, a card and stationery shop, a basket shop, sun-catchers and fun things for kids. And this fascinating store recently got even bigger: In 1998, Greene added 4,000 square feet to the building.

The Christmas Shop is open Memorial Day through mid-September, Monday through Saturday from 9:30 AM to 9 PM and Sunday from 9:30 AM to 6 PM. From mid-September through Christmas, hours are Monday through Saturday from 9:30 AM to 6 PM and Sunday from 9:30 AM to 5:30 PM. The shop is open from 9:30 AM to 5:30 PM daily January 1 through March 1. It's closed Christmas Day.

Weeping Radish Brewery
U.S. Hwy. 64, Manteo • (252) 473-1157

Historians say the first beer made in America was brewed on Roanoke Island. In 1585, they write, English colonists made a batch to befriend the Native Americans — or maybe to calm their own nerves. Roanoke Island today boasts its own brewery at a Bavarian-style eatery called The Weeping Radish, 1 mile south of downtown Manteo.

On the shaded grounds just south of downtown Manteo, a full-time brewmaster makes both light and dark lager beers, which can be sipped on-site at the restaurant or taken to go in 1-liter refillable bottles and six-packs of their Fest brew. Weeping Radish beer in 22-ounce bottles is sold at area retailers. Notice the artistic labels that depict local landmarks.

Free, daily tours of the brewery are offered throughout the year. You can also sample the frothy mugs afterward in the pub or outdoor patio tables.

An annual OktoberFest is held the weekend after Labor Day. Events and activities include oompah bands and German folk dancers (see our Annual Events chapter). Locals find this a favorite evening spot in the off-season. Visitors will feel at home too. There's even a colorful playground for the kids.

Historically Speaking Customized Evening Entertainment
(252) 473-5783

Nicholas Hodsdon and Douglas L. Barger, both seasoned actors and performers, offer made-to-order programs for tour groups, conferences or conventions. They'll either come to the group or have the group meet them at the fellowship hall of St. Andrew's Episcopal Church in Nags Head. Each program can be adopted to meet any situation, and both are delightful alternatives to pub-hopping. The entertainment is available year-round on a as-requested basis.

Call for additional information. The two presentations offered by Historically Speaking are: "Sea Song Sing-Along," featuring Outer Banks Folk Music and Sea Songs, with entertaining commentary on 400 years of coastal Carolina history, and "The Troubadour," a staged and costumed "living history" visit with a gentleman of Queen Elizabeth's court. Meet a 400-year-old standup comic who leads songs and weaves in the history of Roanoke Island's colonization between playing on seven Renaissance instruments. Historically Speaking also offers step-on guides and receptive services for motor coach groups. See our Getting Here, Getting Around chapter for more information.

Mill Landing
N.C. Hwy. 345, Wanchese

Near the end of a winding 5-mile road, past a long expanse of wide, waving marshlands overflowing with waterfowl, Wanchese is well off the beaten path of most visitors (see the section on Roanoke Island in our Area Overviews chapter) and remains one of the most unspoiled areas on the barrier islands. At the very end of N.C. 345, one of the most picturesque and unchanged areas of the Outer Banks is often overlooked: Mill Landing, which embodies the heritage of the Outer Banks. Here, active fishing trawlers anchor at the fish scale-strewn docks, their mesh still dripping seaweed from the wide roller wheels. Watermen in yellow chest waders and white rubber boots (known locally as Wanchese wingtips) sling shark, tuna and dolphin onto cutting room carts. Pieces of the island's past float silently in the harbor, mingling with remade boats that are still afloat and sunken ships that have long since disappeared.

The fish houses at Mill Landing include Wanchese Fish Company, Etheridge's, Jaws Seafood, Quality Seafood, Moon Tillett's and others. These houses ship seafood to restaurants in Hampton Roads, Baltimore, New York, Boston and Tokyo. Scallops, shrimp and crabs are available here in season.

Wanchese Seafood Industrial Park
615 Harbor Rd., Wanchese
• (252) 473-5867

A 69-acre industrial park on a deep harbor at Wanchese, this state-supported facility was built in 1980 with $8.1 million in state and federal funds. It was designed to attract large-scale seafood processing companies to set up shop on the secluded Roanoke Island waterfront. After federal promises about stabilizing Oregon Inlet failed to materialize, few deep-draw fishing trawlers could afford to keep risking the trip through the East Coast's most dangerous inlet.

Oregon Inlet continued to shoal terribly through the 1980s, and the seafood park remained largely vacant until 1994, when some smaller area businesses and fish processing plants began establishing themselves there. Unpredictable weather patterns still affect the channel's navigability.

Today the 29-lot industrial area is about 60 percent full. There's a Marine Maintenance Center, Coastal Engine and Propeller, Harbor Welding, Wanchese Trawl and Supply, the state's oyster planting program offices, Bay Country Industrial Supply (they make fish boxes), Carolina Welders, Wanchese Boat Builders, O'Neal's Sea Harvest and the Weeping Radish bottling warehouse.

The seafood park is an educational attraction for anyone interested in how fish are commercially caught, cut, packed, processed and

Photo: Courtesy of Bob Reardon

The Wright Brothers National Memorial sits on the highest hill in Kill Devil Hills. The view is worth the hike.

distributed. Visitors are welcome to watch boat builders work or watermen unload their catches at the wide docks. Park Director Rodney Perry also will arrange free tours of the facility for families or groups with advance notice.

The state seafood park hosts the annual Wanchese Seafood Festival the last Saturday in June each summer when businesses open their doors — and kitchens — to the community. (See our Annual Events chapter for details.)

Pirate's Cove Yacht Club
Manteo-Nags Head Cswy., Manteo
• (252) 473-3906, (800) 367-4728

This busy 152-slip marina is surrounded by upscale permanent and rental waterfront homes and has a ship's store that can supply almost every maritime need. Reservations are accepted for dock space. A growing number of charter fishing boats run Gulf Stream trips from Pirate's Cove most of the year (see our Fishing chapter).

Besides fishing supplies, the Ship's Store at Pirate's Cove sells sportswear, T-shirts, souvenir hats and drink huggers, groceries and ice.

The community at Pirate's Cove includes more than 600 acres, much of which is marshland. Plans call for 627 residential homes, townhouses and condominiums to eventually be developed on the site. All residences have deepwater dockage and access to a clubhouse, pool and tennis courts (see our Real Estate chapter). A boardwalk winds throughout the waterfront at Pirate's Cove where you can watch the charter boats returning from sea in the late afternoon.

Downtown Manteo
Off U.S. Hwy. 64, Queen Elizabeth,
Budleigh and Sir Walter Raleigh Sts.,
Manteo

Named for a Roanoke Island Native American who accompanied English explorers back to Great Britain in the 16th century, Manteo is one of the oldest Outer Banks communities and has long been a commercial and governmental hub for the area.

When Dare County formed in 1870, and Manteo became the county seat, there were only a few houses lining the sandy lanes along Shallowbag Bay. Today hundreds of permanent residents make this Roanoke Island town their home, and many more county residents commute here from other towns to work. Insiders' Guides® corporate headquarters have moved to bigger quarters on Budleigh Street, where many of the county and town offices also are scattered in older office buildings up and down the street. The Dare County Courthouse, one of the oldest in use in the state, bookends Budleigh and Sir Walter Raleigh streets, and faces the Waterfront Shops, an upscale shopping plaza. New restaurants and bed and breakfast inns beckon tourists from other areas, and thousands of visitors arrive each summer to explore this historic waterfront village. (See the Roanoke Island section of our Area Overviews chapter.)

On the wooden wharves of Manteo's Waterfront, 53 modern dockside slips with 110- and 220-volt electrical hookups offer boaters overnight or long-term anchorage. A comfort station with restrooms, showers, washers and dryers also serves vessel crews and captains. There's plenty of shopping and dining within walking distance in Manteo — or better yet — break out the bikes. This is the perfect town to enjoy on your two-wheeler.

Across the street from the Waterfront, in the center of the downtown area, small- to medium-size shops, eateries and businesses offer everything from handmade pottery to candles, all in a four-square-block area. There's plenty of free parking across from Manteo Booksellers on Sir Walter Raleigh Street. Watch time limits on curbside spots: You will be ticketed if you overstay your limit.

Around the southeast point of the Water-

front, the town's American Bicentennial Park is tucked in between the courthouse and a four-story brick building that houses shops and condominiums. There's an emotionally moving inscription under the cross. Picnic benches afford a comfortable place to rest and enjoy the view across the bay, where the state's 16th-century representative sailing ship *Elizabeth II* rocks gently on small sound waves.

If, as most visitors do, you reach the Banks via U.S. 158, you can get to Manteo by continuing south until you reach Whalebone Junction. Bear right onto U.S. 64 at the traffic light near RV's restaurant. Continue across the causeway and high-rise bridge past Pirate's Cove, then bear right at the Y-intersection, staying on U.S. 64. Turn right at either of the town's first two stoplights to go downtown.

The Waterfront
Manteo docks, Manteo • (252) 473-2188

Overlooking smooth wooden docks along Shallowbag Bay, the Waterfront is a 34-unit condominium and marketplace at the head of downtown Manteo. This four-story complex is styled in Old World architecture, open around a breezy courtyard, built above a ground-level parking garage. Three-hour free public parking is available in this shaded facility.

The Waterfront's second level contains 20,000 square feet of retail space, including a jewelry shop, toy store, nautical gift store, European-style cafe, hair salon and seafood restaurant. The third and fourth levels are entirely residential. Some condominium owners keep their boats at the backdoor docks on the Manteo harbor.

Roanoke Island Festival Park and the Elizabeth II
One Festival Park, Manteo
• (252) 475-1500, (252) 475-1506
24-hour events line

An expansion of the Elizabeth II Historic Site, Roanoke Island Festival Park is the newest — and most ambitious — attraction on the Outer Banks. Funded by a $10 million state appropriation, the new history, education and cultural arts project will include an 8,500-square-foot hall of interactive exhibits; a film theater featuring *The Legend of Two-Path*, a 45-minute film depicting the first landing of English settlers from the Native American perspective; an outdoor performance pavilion with lawn seating for 3,500 people; an art gallery and public meeting space; a museum shop; and the *Elizabeth II* sailing vessel.

Visitors can explore the evolution of Roanoke Island and the Outer Banks from the late 16th century though the early 1900s through living history interpretation, exhibits, film, and visual and performing arts programs.

The *Elizabeth II*, designed as the centerpiece for the 400th anniversary of the first English settlement in America, is a representative sailing ship similar to the one that carried Sir Walter Raleigh's colonists across the Atlantic in 1585. Interpreters clad in Elizabethan costumes conduct tours of the colorful, 69-foot ship.

Although it was built in 1983, the *Elizabeth II*'s story really began four centuries earlier, when Thomas Cavendish mortgaged his estates to build the *Elizabeth II* for England's second expedition to Roanoke Island. With six other vessels, the original *Elizabeth* made the first colonization voyage to the New World 1585 and landed on the Outer Banks.

There wasn't enough information available about the original vessels to reconstruct one, so shipbuilders used the designs of vessels from 1585 to build the state boat. Constructed entirely in a wooden structure on the Manteo waterfront, the completed ship, *Elizabeth II*, slid down hand-greased rails into Shallowbag Bay in front of a crowd of enthusiastic dignitaries and locals in 1983.

Stretching 69 feet long, 17 feet wide and drawing 8 feet of water, the *Elizabeth II* cost $750,000 to build and was funded entirely through private donations. Its decks are hand-hewn from juniper timbers. Its frames, keel, planking and decks are fastened with 7,000 locust wood pegs.

Every baulk, spar, block and lift of the state ship are as close to authentic as possible, with only three exceptions: a wider upper-deck hatch for easier visitor access; a vertical hatch in the afterdeck to make steering easier for the helmsman; and a controversial pair of diesel engines that were installed in the *Elizabeth II* in 1993. The 115-horsepower motors help the grand sailing ship move under its own power, instead of relying on expensive tug boats that had to tow it before. Now, the vessel can cruise up to 8 knots per hour with no wind and travel for up to 40 hours without refilling its two 150-gallon gas tanks. The state ship stays on the Outer Banks most of the year, but during the off-seasons, it sometimes travels to other North Carolina ports, acting as an emissary for its Roanoke Island home and serving as the state's only moving historic site. Roanoke Island Festival Park is open year round. Hours vary according to season. Admission is $8 for adults, $4 for students and free for children under 5. Group rates are available.

Outer Banks History Center
Roanoke Island Festival Park, One Festival Park, Manteo • (252) 473-2655

Near the waterfront and next to the site of the Festival Park's new amphitheater and interactive museum, the Outer Banks History Center is the most remarkable repository of North Carolina state and regional history collected in any place.

More than 25,000 books, 4,500 official documents of the U.S. Coast Guard and the U.S. Life Saving Service, 30,000 photographs, 1,000 periodicals, 700 maps and hundreds of audio and video recordings are housed in this regional library. Special collections include the David Stick Papers, 324 paintings in the Frank Stick collection, the Cape Hatteras National Seashore Library, the Cape Lookout National Seashore Oral History collection and the Aycock Brown Tourist Bureau collection of 17,000 photographs. There are maps of the area more than 400 years old here.

Opened in 1988 near the *Elizabeth II* visitors center building, the Outer Banks History Center includes a comfortable reading room with long tables for research. A new gallery with rotating exhibits opened in 1998. North Carolina natives will enjoy exploring their own history here. Visitors will find the Outer Banks legacy equally enchanting.

Most of the collections included in this library belonged to Outer Banks historian David Stick, who still lives in Kitty Hawk. The author of many books on the Outer Banks, Stick gathered much of the information during his years of research and writing. Stick's father, Frank Stick, helped found the Cape Hatteras National Seashore as part of the National Park Service.

Staffers at the history center are knowledgeable and happy to help anyone access the facility's vast resources. Journalists, history buffs, students, archaeologists, writers and even interested tourists will find the stop well worth their time. The reading room is open year round from 9 AM until 5 PM Monday through Friday and 10 AM until 3 PM Saturday. Gallery hours are 10 AM to 4 PM Monday through Friday and 10 AM to 3 PM on Saturday, year round. The Outer Banks History Center is a public facility and is open free of charge.

OBX Air Tours
Dare County Regional Airport,
408 Airport Rd., Roanoke Island
• (252) 473-3222, (888) 289-8202

OBX offers a variety of tours of the beautiful barrier island attractions. From the northernmost points of the Outer Banks in Corolla down to Hatteras Village and Ocracoke and all points in between, OBX can give you a perspective on the barrier islands that you'll never forget. Tours start at $25 per person. Passengers can also customize their own tour. Biplane rides are available. Located across from the North Carolina Aquarium, vacationers are welcome to stop by in person to make a reservation during the busy summer season, or call for further information.

Ye Olde Pioneer Theatre
113 Budleigh St., Manteo
• (252) 473-2216

With an old-timey candy counter and fresh buttered-popcorn smells filling the front lobby, this historic moviehouse is our favorite place to see films on the Outer Banks. The original Manteo movie theater, built in 1918, burned. The one still showing first-run films today opened in 1934.

It's the oldest theater operated continuously by one family in the United States. George Washington Creef was the founder.

Today, his grandson, H.A. Creef, sells tickets from the street-front window. The carbonarc projector that had been used since 1947 was replaced in 1997. A rare find for old movie buffs, the occasional breakdowns that used to happen during screenings added to the theatre's charm. But even with the new machinery, the Pioneer has the best old-time feel, history and prices you can find anywhere: $3 for all tickets.

One movie is shown at 8 PM each night, as long as there are at least three people in the theater. Listings change weekly, on Fridays. Check the billboard in downtown Manteo, or call the theater for current listings.

Bodie Island

Bodie Island Lighthouse and Keepers' Quarters
West of N.C. Hwy. 12, Bodie Island
• (252) 441-5711

This black-and-white beacon with horizontal bands is one of four lighthouses still standing along the Outer Banks. It sits more than a half-mile from the sea, in a field of green grass. The site, 6 miles south of Whalebone Junction, is a perfect place to picnic.

In 1870, the federal government bought 15 acres of land for $150 on which to build the lighthouse and keepers quarters. When the project was finished two years later, Bodie Island Lighthouse was very close to the inlet and stood 150 feet tall and was the only lighthouse between Cape Henry, Virginia, and Cape Hatteras. The inlet is now migrating away from the beacon, which is the third to stand near Oregon Inlet since the inlet opened during an 1846 hurricane. The first light developed cracks and had to be removed. Confederate soldiers destroyed the second tower to frustrate Union shipping efforts.

Wanchese resident Vernon Gaskill served as the last civilian lightkeeper of Bodie Island Lighthouse. As late as 1940, he said, the tower was the only structure between Oregon Inlet and Jockey's Ridge. Gaskill helped his father strain kerosene before pouring it into the light. The kerosene prevented particles from clogging the vaporizer that kept the beacon burning.

Today, the lighthouse grounds and keeper's quarters offer a welcome respite during the drive to Hatteras Island. Wide expanses of marshland behind the tower offer enjoyable walks through cattails, yaupon and wax myrtle. A boardwalk will keep your feet dry.

The National Park Service added new exhibits to the Bodie Island keepers quarters in 1995. The visitors center there is open daily from mid-March through December. Hours are 9 AM to 6 PM, except after Labor Day when the facility closes at 5 PM. The lighthouse itself is not open, but you can look up the tall tower from below when volunteers are present to open the structure. Even a quick drive around the grounds to see the exterior is worth it.

Coquina Beach
N.C. Hwy. 12, Bodie Island

Once one of the widest beaches on the Outer Banks, Coquina Beach, 6 miles south of Whalebone Junction, was heavily damaged during 1993 and 1994 storms. The National Park Service expanded and repaved parking areas, and in 1996 it opened a spanking new bathhouse, restrooms and outdoor shower facilities.

This remote area, miles away from any business or rental cottage, is still a superb spot to fish, surf, swim or sunbathe. The sand is almost white and the beach and offshore areas are relatively flat.

Drawing its name from the tiny butterfly-shaped coquina clams that burrow into the beach, at times almost every inch of this portion of the federally protected Cape Hatteras National Seashore harbors hundreds of recently washed up shells and several species of rare shorebirds. Coquinas are edible and can be collected and cleaned from their shells to make a fishy-tasting chowder. Local brick makers also have used them as temper in buildings.

The Laura A. Barnes
Coquina Beach, N.C. Hwy. 12,
Bodie Island

One of the last coastal schooners built in America, the *Laura A. Barnes* was completed in Camden, Maine, in 1918. This 120-foot ship was under sail on the Atlantic during a trip from New York to South Carolina when a nor'easter drove it onto the Outer Banks in 1921. The *Laura A. Barnes* ran aground just north of where it now rests at Coquina Beach. The entire crew survived. In 1973, the National Park Service moved the shipwreck to its present location, where visitors can view the remains of the ship behind a roped-off area that includes placards with information about the *Laura A. Barnes* and the history of lifesaving .

Oregon Inlet Fishing Center
N.C. 12, Bodie Island • (252) 441-6301,
(800) 272-5199

Sportfishing enthusiasts, or anyone remotely interested in offshore angling, must stop by this bustling charter boat harbor on the north shore of Oregon Inlet. Set beside the U.S. Coast Guard station on land controlled by the National Park Service, Oregon Inlet Fishing Center is a federal concessionaire, so all vessels charge the same rate. A day on the Atlantic with one of these captains may give rise to a marlin, sailfish, wahoo, tuna or dolphin on the end of the line. See our Fishing chapter for details.

Oregon Inlet Coast Guard Station
N.C. Hwy. 12, Bodie Island

In the last century, the federal government operated two lifesaving stations at Oregon Inlet. The Bodie Island station was on the north side of the inlet. The Oregon Inlet station was on the south. Both of these original facilities are now closed. The Oregon Inlet station sits perilously close to the migrating inlet, the victim of hurricanes and decades of neglect. The

Bodie Island station has been replaced by the current Coast Guard facility behind the Oregon Inlet Fishing Center.

Opened in 1991 with wide boat docks and an ample parking area, the Oregon Inlet Coast Guard station includes a 10,000-square-foot building, a state-of-the-art communications center, maintenance shops, an administrative center and accommodations for the staff. Coast Guard crews have rescued dozens of watermen off the Outer Banks. They also aid sea turtles and stranded seals by helping the animals get back safely to warmer parts of the ocean.

Oregon Inlet and the Bonner Bridge
N.C. Hwy. 12, Oregon Inlet

Sea captains call this the most dangerous inlet on the East Coast — and with good reason. Since 1960, at least 26 lives and an equal number of boats have been lost at Oregon Inlet. The inlet continues to shoal alarmingly as officials wrestle with ways to keep the passageway open.

The only outlet to the sea in the 140 miles between Cape Henry, in Virginia Beach, and Hatteras Inlet, Oregon Inlet lies between Bodie Island and Pea Island National Wildlife Refuge. It is the primary passage for commercial and recreational fishing boats based along the northern Outer Banks; however, in recent years, the channel has shoaled so much that many deep-draw vessels have not been able to get to sea.

Federal officials have refused to authorize or fund construction of jetties, rock walls that some scientists say would stabilize the ever-shallowing inlet. Environmentalists and other scientists oppose the proposed $100 million project, saying it would cause increased erosion on beaches to the south. The debate continues and the sand keeps building up in the area's only outlet to the Atlantic.

Oregon Inlet was created during a hurricane in September 1846, the same storm that opened Hatteras Inlet between Hatteras Village and Ocracoke Island. It was named for the side-wheeler Oregon, the first ship to pass through the inlet.

In 1964, the Herbert C. Bonner Bridge was built across the inlet. This two-lane span finally connected Hatteras Island and the Cape Hatteras National Seashore with the northern Outer Banks beaches. Before the bridge was built, travelers relied on ferry boats to carry them across Oregon Inlet.

Hurricane-force winds blew a dredge barge into the bridge in 1990, knocking out a center section of the span. No one was hurt, but the more than 5,000 permanent residents of Hatteras Island were cut off from the rest of the world for four months before workers could completely repair the bridge. The bridge is slated for complete reconstruction in the near future, although state officials say the span is still perfectly safe.

Four-wheel-drive vehicles can exit N.C. 12 on the northeast side of the inlet and drive along the beach, even beneath the Bonner bridge, around the inlet. Fishing is permitted along the catwalks of the bridge and on the beach. Free parking and bathrooms are available at the Oregon Inlet Fishing Center. There are also parking and portable toilets on the southern end of the bridge. This trip is especially beautiful at sunset.

Hatteras Island

Pea Island National Wildlife Refuge
Pea Island, N.C. Hwy. 12,
• (252) 987-2394

Pea Island National Wildlife Refuge begins at the southern base of the Herbert C. Bonner Bridge and is the first place you'll come to if you enter Hatteras Island from the north. The beach along this undeveloped stretch of sand is popular with anglers, surfers, sunbathers and shell seekers. On the right side of the road, heading south, salt marshes surround Pamlico Sound, and birds seem to flutter from every grove of cattails.

Founded on April 12, 1938, Pea Island refuge was federally funded as a winter preserve for snow geese. President Roosevelt put his Civilian Conservation Corps to work stabilizing the slightly sloping dunes, building them up with bulldozers, erecting long expanses of sand fencing and securing the sand with sea oats and grasses. Workers built dikes near the sound to form ponds and freshwater marshes. They planted fields to provide food for the waterfowl.

With 5,915 acres that attract nearly 400 observed species of birds, Pea Island is an outdoor aviary well worth venturing off the road, and into the wilderness, to visit. Few tourists visited this refuge when Hatteras Island was cut off from the rest of the Outer Banks, and people arrived at the southern beaches by ferry. After the Oregon Inlet bridge opened in 1964, motorists began driving through this once isolated outpost.

Today, Pea Island is one of the barrier islands' most popular havens for bird watchers, naturalists and sea-turtle savers. Endangered species from the loggerhead sea turtle to the tiny piping plover shorebirds inhabit this enchanted area. Pea Island's name comes from the "dune peas" that grow all along the now grassy sand dunes. The tiny plant with pink and lavender flowers is a favorite food of migrating geese.

If you enter the refuge from the north on N.C. 12, note the new roadbed that was completed in December 1995. This 3-mile stretch of highway had to be moved more than 300 feet west of its former site to get it farther away from the waves. During 1994, state officials had to shut down the two-lane road at least three times because the ocean had washed across it, spilling up to 2 feet of sand in some spots.

To keep the road clear and provide a more permanent pathway through the Outer Banks, transportation engineers decided to re-route the most threatened portion of the pavement closer to the sound. The project cost taxpayers about $3 million. Since 1990, state transportation officials have spent more than $31 million trying to keep N.C. 12 open. They invested another $18 million in routine maintenance on the road. Special efforts have included a $1.8 million beach nourishment project to pump sand back on the beach and $920,000 worth of sandbags stacked along the shore. Against the objections of Dare County officials, the sandbags were removed during the summer of 1996 because state officials deemed them a temporary measure that would be harmful to the shoreline if they remained in place any longer.

Four miles south of the Bonner Bridge's southern base, at the entrance to the new portion of N.C. 12, the Pea Island Visitor Center offers free parking and easy access to the beach. If you walk directly across the highway to the top of the dunes, you'll see the remains of the more than century-old federal transport

Oriental. Her steel boiler is the black mass, all that remains since the ship sank in May 1862.

On the sound side of the highway, in the marshes, ponds and endless wetlands, whistling swans, snow geese, Canada geese and 25 species of ducks make winter sojourns through the refuge. Savannah sparrows, migrant warblers, gulls, terns, herons and egrets also alight in this area from fall through early spring. In summer, American avocets, willets, black-necked stilts and several species of ducks nest here.

Bug repellent is a must on Pea Island from March through October. Besides insects, ticks may also cause problems. Check your clothing before getting back in the car, and shower as soon as possible if you hike through any underbrush.

North Pond Trail
N.C. Hwy 12, Pea Island

A bird watcher's favorite, this handicapped-accessible nature trail begins at the visitors center parking area and is about a mile long, a 30-minute brisk walk to the sound and back. The trail runs along the top of a dike between two man-made ponds that were began in the late 19th century and completed by the Civilian Conservation Corps. The walkway includes three viewing platforms, marshland overlooks and mounted binoculars.

Wax myrtles and live oaks stabilize the dike and provide shelter for scores of songbirds. Warblers, yellowthroats, cardinals and seaside sparrows stop here during their spring and fall migrations. If you whistle the correct calls into the brush and wait quietly, they'll answer in a symphony.

The U.S. Fish & Wildlife Service manages Pea Island refuge's ecosystem carefully. Workers plant fields with fescue and rye grass to keep the waterfowl coming back. Besides migrating birds, which don't occupy the island during summer, pheasants, muskrats and nutria live along these ponds year round. This short journey through a virtually unspoiled area will enhance any stay on the Outer Banks. If you crave quiet, fresh air, isolation and, above all, an opportunity to commune with wildlife, you'll want to walk the North Pond Trail. The trail is open to foot traffic only. This area is about 4 miles south of Oregon Inlet.

Pea Island Visitor Center
N.C. Hwy. 12, Pea Island
• **(252) 987-2394**

A recently paved parking area, free public restrooms and the Pea Island Refuge Headquarters are 4 miles south of the Oregon Inlet bridge on the sound side of N.C. 12. Refuge volunteers staff this small welcome station year-round and are available to answer questions. Visitors can see exhibits on wildlife, waterfowl and bird life. There is also a small gift shop. In the summer, the facility is open seven days a week from 9 AM to 4 PM. In the off-season, the center is open Thursday through Sunday from 9 AM to 4 PM. It's closed Christmas Day. Free nature trail maps are available, and in summer months, special nature programs are offered.

Hunting, camping and driving are not allowed in the refuge. Open fires also are prohibited. Dogs must be kept on leashes on the east side of the highway. Firearms are not allowed in the refuge; shotguns and rifles must be stowed out of sight even if you're just driving straight through Hatteras Island. Fishing, crabbing, boating and other activities are allowed in the ocean and sound but are prohibited in refuge ponds.

About 3 miles south down N.C. 12, there is kiosk just beyond the Refuge Headquarters that marks the site of the remains of the nation's only African-American lifesaving station. Pea Island was established with the rest of the U.S. Lifesaving outposts in 1879 and was originally manned by mostly white crews. Black men were confined to tasks like caring for the horses that dragged surfboats through the sand.

The year after the station was set up, however, federal officials fired Pea Island's white crew members for mishandling the Henderson shipwreck disaster. Black personnel from other stations were placed under the charge of Richard Etheridge, who was of Native American and African-American descent. The new crew carried out their duties honorably.

Pea Island's surfmen rescued countless crews and passengers of ships that washed ashore in storms or sank in the seething seas. Etheridge became known as one of the best prepared, most professional and daring leaders in the service. One of the crew's most famous rescues was in 1896 when the captain

of the *E.S. Newman* sounded an SOS off Hatteras Island's treacherous shores, an area also known as The Graveyard of the Atlantic.

In 1992 the U.S. Coast Guard Service, a latter-day version of the Lifesaving Service, dedicated a cutter to the Pea Island crew. About a dozen of the African-American surfmen's descendants witnessed the moving ceremony. A plaque on board the big ship commemorates the lifesaving crew's heroism.

Hatteras Shipwrecks
N.C. Hwy. 12, Hatteras Island

Big winter blows and even smaller summer storms often unveil incredible sunken treasures on the Hatteras Island beaches. Pirate gold is hard to come by, but shipwreck remnants, old bottles and beach glass abound. Each shift in wind seems to change the scenery for souvenir seekers who care to comb these quiet shores. You don't need a shovel or even a metal detector to unearth broken teacups, hand-blown whiskey bottles or the rotting remains of a cork.

Chicamacomico Life Saving Station
N.C. Hwy. 12, Rodanthe • (252) 987-1552

With volunteer labor and long years of dedication, this once decrepit lifesaving station is now beautifully restored and open for tours. Its weathered, silvery-shingled buildings sparkle on the sandy lawn, which is surrounded by a perfect picket fence. Even the outbuildings have been brought back to their former uses.

Chicamacomico was one of the Outer Banks' original seven lifesaving stations, opening in 1874 at its current site. The present boathouse building was the original station but was retained as a storage shed when the bigger facility was built. Under three keepers with the last name of Midgett, Chicamacomico crews guarded the sea along Hatteras Island's northern coast for 70 years. Between 1876 and the time the station closed in 1954, seven Midgetts were awarded the Gold Life Saving Award; three won the silver; and six others worked or lived at Chicamacomico. Perhaps the station's most famous rescue was when surfmen pulled crew members from the British tanker *Mirlo* off their burning ship and into safety.

Today the nonprofit Chicamacomico Historical Association oversees and operates the lifesaving station. Volunteers set up a museum of area lifesaving awards and artifacts in the main building and have recovered some of the lifesaving equipment for the boathouse. Volunteers take school groups on tours of the station, showing them how the breeches buoy helped rescue shipwreck victims and explaining the precise maneuvers surfmen had to follow on shore.

Costumed re-enactments of beach apparatus drills are held every Thursday in summer from 2 through 5 PM. The building is open from 11 AM to 5 PM Tuesday, Thursday and Saturday in-season. Hours may be extended if volunteers are available. The interior restoration was completed in 1998, and new photo, video and lifesaving service artifacts are on display. To help support the lifesaving station and the Chicamacomico Historical Association, send donations to the association at P.O. Box 140, Rodanthe, NC 27968.

Salvo Post Office
N.C. Hwy. 12, Salvo

If you're heading south on N.C. 12 through Hatteras Island, slow down as you leave Salvo, and try to spot a tiny whitewashed building with blue and red trim on the right side of the road. That's the old Salvo Post Office, which was the country's smallest post office until an arsonist burned about half of it down in 1992. It sat atop low rails in the postmaster's front yard. Villagers moved it to in front of a new postmaster's house each time one came aboard.

The wooden structure had beautiful gilt post boxes surrounding the small glass service window, but it didn't have a bathroom, air conditioning or a handicapped-accessible ramp. Although community volunteers rallied and rebuilt their little post office quickly, the federal government refused to reopen the outpost, which was originally erected in 1901. Today, Salvo residents drive to Rodanthe to pick up their mail.

Canadian Hole
N.C. Hwy. 12, Avon

If a breeze is blowing, pull off the west side of the road between Avon and Buxton (1.5 miles south of Avon), into the big parking lot on the sound. Known as Canadian Hole, this is one of America's hottest windsurfing spots — and a magnet for visitors from the great white North. Whether you ride a sailboard or not, this sight is not to be missed. On windy afternoons, more than 100 windsurfers spread out along the shallow sound, their brightly colored butterfly sails gently skimming into the sunset. There's a nice bathing beach here, so bring chairs and coolers, and plan to watch the silent wave riders, some of whom are famous in windsurfing circles. The state recently expanded the parking area here. See our Watersports chapter for more details.

The Monitor
Off Cape Hatteras, in the Atlantic Ocean

Launched January 30, 1862, the *Monitor* is one of the nation's most famous battleships. It's watery grave is the first National Underwater Marine Sanctuary. Divers sanctioned by the National Oceanic and Atmospheric Administration have spent years trying to retrieve the four-pronged propeller from the ironclad boat, which rests upside down in 230 feet of water about 17 miles off Cape Hatteras.

The *Monitor* was owned by Union forces and was their counterpart to the Confederate ship *Virginia* during the Civil War. The *Virginia* was the world's first ironclad warship, built from the hull of the Union frigate *Merrimac*, which Southern forces captured and refitted. On March 8, 1862, the tent-shaped steamer *Virginia* cruised out of Norfolk to challenge a blockade of six wooden ships. By day's end, the *Virginia* had sunk two of those Union ships and damaged another.

Built by Swedish-American engineer John Ericsson and appropriately dubbed the "cheesebox on a raft" for its unusual design, the *Monitor* was a low-slung ironclad that included a revolving turret to carry its main battery. This strange-looking ship arrived in Norfolk on March 9 and soon battled the *Virginia* to a draw. Retreating Confederates eventually destroyed the *Virginia*. The *Monitor* was ordered to proceed farther south.

The New Year's Eve storm of 1862 caught the Union ironclad off Cape Hatteras, far out in the Atlantic. The *Monitor* sank and 16 sailors were lost. Its whereabouts were unknown until university researchers discovered the *Monitor* in 1973.

Although they haven't been able to retrieve the heavy propeller, federally permitted scuba divers have brought a few small artifacts off the Monitor's waterlogged decks. They've recovered bottles, silverware and china pieces. In 1983, they even brought up the ship's distinctive four-blade anchor, which is on display at the Mariner's Museum in Newport News, Virginia. More artifacts may be retrieved in a late spring 1998 dive.

Cape Hatteras National Seashore
Hatteras Island Visitors Center, off N.C. Hwy. 12, Buxton • (252) 995-4474

About 300 yards south of Old Lighthouse Road, a large wooden sign welcomes visitors to the Cape Hatteras National Seashore and Hatteras Island Visitors Center. Turn left if you're heading south, toward the split-rail fence, and follow the winding road past turtle ponds and marshes. (See our Natural Wonders chapter.)

If you turn left at the fork in this road, you'll head toward the Cape Hatteras Lighthouse and the National Park Service Visitors Center. Turn right, and you'll wind up at the Cape Point campground. Surf fishing, sunbathing, swimming, surfing and four-wheel driving are allowed along most areas of the beach here year round.

The visitors center is near the lighthouse, past a newly expanded parking area. It's in the former house of the assistant lighthouse keepers, which was built in 1854. This two-story, wooden frame home was renovated in 1986 and is adjacent to the smaller keepers' quarters. It houses an extensive museum of lifesaving artifacts and lighthouse memorabilia. Free exhibits include information on shipping, wars and Outer Banks heroes.

A small bookstore in the visitors center sells literature on lifesaving stations, lighthouses and Hatteras Island history. Clean restrooms also are available here. Volunteers offer a range of summer interpretive programs on the visitor center's wide, covered front porch. Activities change seasonally, with fall and spring programs also conducted. Call ahead for a schedule, or pick one up at the information desk inside.

The visitors center is open from 9 AM to 5 PM daily from September through mid-June and from 9 AM to 6 PM from mid-June through Labor Day. It's closed Christmas Day.

Cape Hatteras Lighthouse
Off N.C. Hwy. 12, Buxton
• (252) 995-4474

The nation's tallest brick lighthouse, this black and white striped beacon is open for free tours throughout the summer and is well worth the climb for hearty hikers. It contains 268 spiraling stairs — 257 which are open to the public — and an 800,000-candlepower electric light that rotates every 7.5 seconds. Its bright beacon can be seen about 20 miles out to sea.

The original Cape Hatteras Lighthouse was built in 1803 to guard the "Graveyard of the Atlantic." The tower sat by its present location near Cape Point. Just off this eastern edge of the Outer Banks, the warm Gulf Stream meets the cold Labrador Current, creating dangerous undercurrents around the ever-shifting offshore shoals.

Standing 90 feet tall and sitting about 300 yards south of its current site, the first lighthouse at Cape Hatteras was fueled with whale oil, which didn't burn bright enough to illuminate the dark shoals surrounding it. Erosion weakened the structure over the years, and in 1861, retreating Confederate soldiers took the light's lens with them, leaving Hatteras Island in the dark.

INSIDERS' TIP

Ospreys can be seen nesting atop poles, dead tree limbs and even sailboat masts in the spring and early summer. The huge birds-of-prey are loyal parents, and it's quite entertaining to watch them carrying scraps to fortify their nests and hunting for fish for their young. If you find a good spot, you may even be able to see the offspring squawking for food while their mom and dad go shopping.

The lighthouse that's still standing was erected in 1870 on a floating foundation and cost $150,000 to build. More than 1.25 million Philadelphia baked bricks are included in the 180-foot tall tower. A special Fresnel lens that refracts the light increases its visibility.

Although the lighthouse is still holding its ground, the beach around its octagonal base is eroding rapidly. Workers stacked sandbags around the structure and have added three rock groins in the ocean nearby to stop sand movement. The National Park Service plans to move the lighthouse 2,900 feet inland if the federal government funds the estimated $9.8 million project.

Staffed entirely by volunteers, the Cape Hatteras Lighthouse is open all the way to the outdoor tower at the top. The breathtaking view is like looking off the roof of a 20-story building, and the free adventure is well worth the effort. The climb is strenuous, so don't attempt to carry children in your arms or in kid carriers. Climbing is permitted starting at 9:30 AM from Easter weekend through Columbus Day. In the summer, the tower is open until 4 PM. In the shoulder seasons, the lighthouse closes at 2 PM. Hours are subject to change, so call first. Climbing is always subject to weather conditions.

The Altoona Wreck
Cape Point, Buxton

Four-wheel-drive motorists should enter the beach at the end of Cape Point Way on Ramp 44. Here, the Outer Banks jut out into the Atlantic in a wide elbow-shape curve near the Cape Hatteras Lighthouse. The beaches in this area offer some of the barrier islands' best surf fishing. Two rules of the beach: Do not try to drive on the beach in anything but a four-wheel drive (not to be confused with front-wheel drive) and be sure to let the proper amount of air out of the tires on your sports utility vehicles when traversing sand (see our Beach Information and Safety chapter).

If you can't drive on the beach, park on solid ground near the road and walk over the ramp to a foot trail. The path begins at the base of the dune and veers off at a 45-degree angle. At the edge of a seawater pond, about a 10-minute walk from the parking area, you'll glimpse the remains of the ancient shipwreck *Altoona*.

Built in Maine in 1869, the *Altoona* was a two-masted, 100-foot-long cargo schooner based in Boston. It left Haiti in 1878 with a load of dyewood bound for New York. On October 22, a storm drove it ashore near Cape Point. Lifesavers rescued its seven crew members and salvaged some of the cargo, but the ship was buried beneath the sand until a storm uncovered it in 1962. The sea has broken the big boat apart since then, but you can still see part of the bow and hull bobbing in the waves.

Diamond Shoals Light
In the Atlantic Ocean, off Cape Point, Buxton

You can't really visit this attraction, except in private boats, but you can see this unusual light tower from the eastern shore of Cape Point and from the top of the Cape Hatteras Lighthouse. Its bright beacon blinks every two seconds from a steel structure set 12 miles out in the sea.

Diamond Shoals once held a lighthouse, but waves beat the offshore rocks that held the lighthouse so badly that federal officials gave up the project. Three lightships have been stationed on the shoals since 1824. The first sunk in an 1827 gale. The second held its ground from 1897 until German submarines sank it in 1918. The third beamed until 1967 when it was replaced by the current light tower.

Diamond Shoals, the rocks around the tower, are the southern end of the treacherous near-shore sandbars off Hatteras Island.

Buxton Woods Nature Trail
Cape Point, Buxton

Leading from the Cape Point Campground road about .75 miles through the woods, the Buxton nature trail takes walkers through thick vine jungles, across tall sand dunes and into freshwater marshes (see our Natural Wonders chapter). Small plaques along the fairly level walkway explain the area's fragile ecosystems. People who hike this trail will learn about the Outer Banks' water table, the role of beach grass and sea oats in stabilizing sand dunes, and the effects salt, storms and visitors have on the ever-changing environment.

Cottonmouths seem to like this trail too, so beware of these unmistakably fat, rough-scaled snakes that can be dull brown, yellow, gray or almost black. If you see one, let it get away — don't chase it. If it stands its ground, retreat.

This hike is not recommended for handicapped visitors or young children, but picnic tables and charcoal grills just south of the nature trail provide a welcome respite for everyone. The walk is well worth it for hearty nature lovers who don't mind mingling with the outdoor elements.

Frisco Native American Museum
N.C. Hwy. 12, Frisco • (252) 995-4440

This fascinating museum on the soundside of N.C. 12 in Frisco is stocked with unusual collections of Native American artifacts gathered over the last 65 years, plus numerous other fascinating collections. Opened 11 years ago by Carl and Joyce Bornfriend, the museum boasts of one of the most significant collections of artifacts from the Chiricahua Apache people and has displays of the work of other Native American tribes from across the country, ranging from the days of early man to modern time. Hopi drums, pottery, kachinas, baskets, weapons and jewelry abound in homemade display cases. Many visitors are astonished at the variety, amount and eclectic appeal of the displays in the museum. A souvenir gift shop offers Native American art, crafts, jewelry, educational materials, toys and books. Native craft items made by about 40 artisans from across the country are also available for sale.

The book section and natural history center have recently been expanded. With advance notice, the Bornfriends will give guided tours of their museum and lectures for school and youth groups. Call for prices. The museum property also includes outdoor nature trails through 3 acres of woods, with a screened-in pavilion, a large pond and three bridges on the land. Hours are 11 AM to 5 PM Tuesdays through Sundays, year round. Admission is $2 per person or $5 per family. Seniors are charged $1.50.

Hatteras-Ocracoke Ferry
N.C. Hwy. 12, Hatteras Village
N.C. Hwy. 12, Ocracoke Island
• (252) 986-2353, (800) BY FERRY

The only link between Hatteras and Ocracoke islands, this free state-run ferry carries passengers and vehicles across Hatteras Inlet daily, year round, with trips at least every hour from 5 AM to midnight. A fleet of 10 ferry boats, some 150 feet long, carry up to 30 cars and trucks each on the 40-minute ride. (See our Getting Here; Getting Around chapter.)

You can get out of your vehicle and walk around the open decks, or stay inside the car if it's cold. A passenger lounge a short flight of steps above the deck offers cushioned seats, wide windows and free 15-minute video depictions of the villages you're about to visit. On the lower deck, telescopes give people a chance to see sea gulls and passing shorelines up close for a quarter. Free, always clean restrooms also are on the deck; however, there's no food or drink to be found on this 5-mile crossing, so pack your own picnic. Beware if you decide to break bread with the dozens of birds that fly overhead. After they eat, they, too, look for free bathrooms. And they'll follow — overhead — all the way to Ocracoke.

A souvenir shop is located at the Hatteras ferry docks selling everything from coloring books and Frisbees to sweatshirts and coffee mugs. Drink and snack machines also are on-site.

A daytrip to Ocracoke is a must for every Outer Banks visitor, whether you're staying in Corolla or Kill Devil Hills. (See our Ocracoke chapter for details.) The free ferry is the only way to get there besides by private boat or airplane. On summer days, more than 1,000 passengers ride the flat boats.

If you arrive at Ocracoke Island on the ferry, there's a 12-mile drive through open marshlands and pine forests before you get to the village. N.C. 12 picks up at the ferry docks and continues, two lanes, to the end of the island. On the left, some wide open beaches await avid four-wheelers and anyone who likes to have a piece of the seaside to themselves.

A National Park Service oceanfront campground is on your left just before you get to the village. Ocracoke itself is a quaint fishing village that has recently grown into a popular tourist destination. About 800 people live on Ocracoke Island year round. Boutiques, seafood restaurants, craft shops and other retailers line the quiet, twisting lanes, but most are open only during the summer season. We recommend you park your car somewhere near the waterfront and rent a bicycle to tour this picturesque, isolated island.

Ocracoke Island

Ocracoke Pony Pens
N.C. Hwy. 12, Ocracoke Island

According to local legends, ships carrying the first English colonists to America made their initial landing at Ocracoke Inlet in 1585. The flagship *Tiger* grounded on a shallow shoal. Sir Richard Grenville ordered the vessel, including a load of horses purchased in the West Indies, unloaded so the ship would float again. Some of the sturdy beasts, it is said, swam ashore to run wild on Ocracoke.

Other theories say the ponies were refugees from Spanish shipwrecks. A few practical people insist they were merely brought to Ocracoke by early inhabitants and allowed to roam freely because — on an island miles from anything else in the Atlantic — there is really no reason to fence in a herd of horses. In any case, Ocracoke's "wild" horses have survived on this Outer Banks island for at least two centuries. In the late 1900s, old-timers said, hundreds ran around eating marsh grass and splashing in the shallow salt marshes.

As populations grew, however, some of the animals were auctioned off. Boy Scout troops used to round up the wild horses annually. When the National Park Service began overseeing the federal seashore, they began managing the wild herd. Today, about two dozen ponies live in a large penned area off N.C. 12, about 6 miles southwest of the Hatteras-Ocracoke ferry dock. There's a small parking area off the road and a raised, wooden observation platform overlooking the mile-long fenced pasture. Sometimes the horses come right up near the road, posing for pictures. Other times, especially in bad weather, they huddle in shelters closer to the sound and can't be seen.

Don't climb into the horse pen or attempt to feed or pet the ponies. These are wild animals that can kick and bite. See our Ocracoke chapter for additional information.

Hammock Hills Nature Trail
N.C. Hwy. 12, Ocracoke Island

A .75-mile nature trail north of Ocracoke Village, Hammock Hills covers a cross-section of the island. The 30-minute walk begins near the sand dunes, traverses a maritime forest and winds through a salt marsh. Hikers can learn how plants adapt to Ocracoke's unusual elements and the harsh barrier island weather.

Bring your camera on this scenic stroll. We highly recommend bug repellent in spring and summer months. Watch out for snakes in the underbrush.

Teach's Hole
Back Rd., Ocracoke Island
• (252) 928-1718

Blackbeard is the focus at this shop, which has special exhibits for kids. For a complete description, see our Kidstuff chapter.

Ocracoke Island Visitors Center
N.C. Hwy. 12, Ocracoke Village
• (252) 928-4531

This seasonal visitors center at the southern end of N.C. 12 is a clearinghouse of information about Ocracoke Island. It's run by the National Park Service across from Silver Lake. If you're arriving on the island from the Hatteras ferry, stay on the main road, turn right at the lake and continue around it, counterclockwise, until you see the low brown building on your right. Free parking is available at the visitors center.

Inside, there's an information desk, helpful staff, a small book shop and exhibits about Ocracoke. You can arrange to use the Park Service's docks here, and pick up maps of the winding back roads that make great bicycle paths.

INSIDERS' TIP

If you climb the Cape Hatteras Lighthouse, look across the Atlantic toward the south from the tower to see flashes from Diamond Shoals Light Tower set on rocks in the ocean.

The visitors center is open March through December from 9 AM to 5 PM. Hours are extended in the summer. Rangers offer a variety of free summer programs through the center, including beach and sound hikes, pirate plays, bird-watching, night hikes and history lectures. Check at the front desk for changing weekly schedules. Restrooms are open to the public in season.

Ocracoke Island Museum and Preservation Society
Silver Lake, Ocracoke Village
• (252) 928-7375

By the Cedar Island ferry docks built by David Williams, the first chief of the Ocracoke Coast Guard Station, this two-story, white-frame house was moved to its present location on National Park Service land in 1989. It's east of the Park Service parking lot, on the same side of Silver Lake as the Coast Guard Station. It was recently restored and is now managed by the Ocracoke Preservation Society as a museum and visitors center. A visit to this museum provides a wonderful peek into Ocracoke as it once was, with old furnishings donated by local families and original photographs of natives filling every room. The kitchen even has its table set in authentic old silverware and dishes. Upstairs, the museum has a small research library that the public can use with museum personnel's permission. This free museum is open daily from 9 AM to 6 PM from April 1 through November.

Ocracoke Village Walking Tour
West end of N.C. Hwy. 12, around Ocracoke Village

The easiest ways to explore Ocracoke are by bicycle and on foot. The narrow, winding back lanes weren't meant for cars. And you miss little landmarks and interesting areas of the island if you try to drive through too quickly. People on Ocracoke are generally very friendly, and you'll get a chance to chat with more locals if you slow down your touring pace through this picturesque fishing village.

To take a walking tour of Ocracoke, park in the lot opposite the visitors center. Turn left out of the lot and walk down N.C. 12 around the shores of Silver Lake, past the sleepy village waterfront. You'll pass many small shops, boutiques and some large new hotels: the Anchorage, Harborside and Princess Motel. Keep walking until you see a small brick post office on your right.

Opposite the post office, a sandy, narrow street angles to the left. This is Old Howard Street. It winds through one of the oldest and least changed parts of the village. Note the humble old homes, the attached cisterns for collecting rain water and the detached kitchens behind these historic structures.

Continue walking past Village Craftsman. After about 400 yards, Howard Street empties onto School Street. Turn left, and you'll see the Methodist church and K-12 public school that serves all the children on Ocracoke. With graduating classes of less than a dozen students, this is the state's smallest public school.

The church is usually open for visitors, but use discretion if services are in progress. And please wipe your feet as you go in. On entering, note the cross displayed behind the altar. It was carved from the wooden spar of an American freighter, the *Caribsea*, sunk offshore by German U-boats in the early months of 1942. By strange coincidence, the Caribsea's engineer was Ocracoke native James Baugham Gaskill, who was killed when the boat sank. Local residents say that several days later a display case holding Gaskill's mate license, among other things, washed ashore not far from his family home.

Ocracoke has had a Methodist Church since 1828. The current one was built in 1943 from lumber and pews salvaged from older buildings. A historical-sketch pamphlet is available in the vestibule for visitors.

On leaving the church, walk around the north corner of the school, past the playground, onto a narrow boardwalk. This wooden path leads to a paved road beyond it. Turn left. This was the first paved road on the island and was constructed by Seabees during World War II.

After walking less than a mile down this road, turn right at the first stop sign. A few minutes' walk along this narrow, tree-shaded street will bring you to the British Cemetery where victims of World War II are buried far away from their English soil. (See the subsequent listing in this section.) It's on your right, set back a bit from the road and shaded by live oak and yaupon. The big British flag makes it easy to spot.

To return to the visitors center, walk west until you reach Silver Lake, then turn right. You'll pass craft shops, a hammock shop and several boutiques along the way. (See our Shopping chapter for details.) If the weather's nice, we suggest a stop for an outdoor drink at the waterfront Jolly Roger, the Creekside Cafe upstairs above the bicycle stand, or Howard's Pub on the highway before heading back to the ferry docks. See the Ocracoke Island section of our Area Overviews chapter for additional information.

Ocracoke Inlet Lighthouse
Southwest corner of Ocracoke Village

The southernmost of the Outer Banks' four lighthouses, this whitewashed tower also is the oldest and shortest. It stands 75 feet tall, a good walk away from any water and has an iron-railed tower set askew on the top. The lighthouse isn't open for tours or climbing, but volunteers occasionally staff its broad base, offering historical talks and answering visitors' questions. Inquire about possible staffing times at the visitors center or National Park Service offices.

Ocracoke's lighthouse is still operating, emitting one long flash every few seconds from a half-hour before sunset to a half-hour after sunrise. It was built in 1823 to replace Shell Castle Rock lighthouse, which was set offshore closer to the dangerous shoals in Ocracoke Inlet. Shell Castle light was abandoned in 1798 when the inlet shifted south.

The beam from Ocracoke's beacon rotates 360 degrees and can be seen 14 miles out to sea. The tower itself is brick, covered by hand-spread, textured white mortar. The walls are 5 feet thick at the base.

On the right side of the wooden board-walk leading to the lighthouse, a two-story, white cottage once served as quarters for the tower's keeper. The National Park Service renovated this structure in the 1980s. It now serves as the home of Ocracoke's ranger and the structure's maintenance supervisor.

To reach the light, turn left off N.C. 12 at the Island Inn and go about 800 yards down the two-lane street. You can park near a white picketed turnoff on the right. Visitors must walk the last few yards down the boardwalk to the lighthouse.

Styron's General Store
Ocracoke Village, Ocracoke Village
• (252) 928-6819

One of the oldest establishments on Ocracoke Island, Styron's General Store opened in its present location in 1920. Former owner Al Styron tore down his family's store on Hog Island, near Cedar Island, and loaded the cypress walls into his boat. He carted Styron's Store to Ocracoke and rebuilt the business there. Today, Styron's great-granddaughter, Candy Gaskill, runs the family business.

Ocracoke doesn't have a full-size grocery store, but Styron's stocks a variety of items ranging from ordinary to fascinating. Wooden milk crates and apple boxes hold gourmet wines imported from Australia and France. Metal fish baskets are filled with fresh onions and red potatoes. Shelves along the sides are stacked with Chinese roast duck mix and Thai sesame oil. The simpler things like whole wheat flour are still sold here, but there's also an amazing mix of virtually everything anyone would need.

The store's been expanded over the years, but the front room retains some of its past, proudly displayed amidst the new-fangled fodder: Burgundy leather-bound ledgers contain records of every transaction made in the store since 1925. The antique, gilt cash register that Al Styron installed is now on display in the store. The former feed scale holds storeroom keys. The original safe and a multi-drawer roll-top desk all are displayed and used, as they have been for nearly a half-century.

Besides food and general merchandise, Styron's offers two wooden tables and a dozen ladder-backed chairs for customers to sit a spell or sip one of Candy's locally famous fresh milk shakes. Styron's store sits on the corner of Point Road, about two blocks before the lighthouse. It's open from 8 AM to 5 PM Monday through Saturday, and from 10 AM to 5 PM on Sunday. Styron's is closed January through March. The store stays open later during summer months.

Photo: Courtesy of J. Aaron Trotman

There is more to the Outer Banks than just sand and waves.
Grab a canoe and explore the flora, fauna, and wildlife.

British Cemetery
British Cemetery Rd., Ocracoke Village

Beneath a stead of trees, on the edge of a community cemetery, four granite gravestones commemorate the crew of the British vessel HMS *Bedfordshire*. This 170-foot trawler was one of a fleet of 24 antisubmarine ships that Prime Minister Winston Churchill loaned the United States in April 1942 to stave off German U-boats. On May 11 of that year, a German submarine torpedoed and sank the British ship about 40 miles south of Ocracoke.

All four officers and 33 enlisted men aboard the *Bedfordshire* drowned. U.S. Coast Guard officers stationed on Ocracoke found four of the bodies washed ashore three days later. They were able to identify two of the sailors. Townspeople gave Britain a 12-by-14-foot plot of land and buried the seamen in a site adjacent to the island's cemetery.

Since then, Coast Guard officers have maintained the grassy area within a white picket fence. They fly a British flag above the graves, and each year, on the anniversary of the sailors' deaths, the local military establishment sponsors a ceremony to honor the men who died so far from their own shores.

Portsmouth Island
South of Ocracoke Island, by private boat access

The only ghost town on the Eastern Seaboard, Portsmouth Village is about a 20-minute boat ride south of Ocracoke Island and was once the biggest town on the Outer Banks. Today, the 23-mile-long, 1.5-mile-wide island is owned and managed by The National Park Service as part of Cape Lookout National Seashore. Wilderness camping, hiking, fishing and other activities are available on the wide beach. Free, self-guided walking tours of the village are an outstanding way to see how islanders lived in the 19th century.

Capt. Rudy Austin runs daily round-trip boat shuttles throughout the summer from Silver Lake on Ocracoke Island across the Pamlico Sound to Portsmouth Island. His boat leaves at 9:30 AM from the docks and picks up passengers on Portsmouth at 2 PM. Cost is $15 per person for groups of six or more people. For groups of less than six, the charge is $20 per person. Kids up to age 12 are half-price. The scheduled trip to Portsmouth Island is available from June through September, and is available at flexible times in the off-season. Other trips in the surrounding area can also be arranged. Call at least one day ahead for reservations, (252) 928-4361 or (252) 928-5431.

Generally you'll experience smaller waves and shallower water in the sound than in the ocean. Why not consider taking the kids there to play?

Kidstuff

From the toddler sifting sand to the teen battling Terminator II, kids of all ages find plenty of fun-filled opportunities on the Outer Banks. You can ride killer waves, gently examine a horseshoe crab, cast a line in our "fishy" waters, soak in the legend of the villainous Blackbeard or quietly commune with nature while kayaking through coastal canals.

In this chapter, we take you on a journey that promises to be a mind and body experience. Don't limit your browsing to this chapter, though. You'll find kids activities such as water slides, minigolf and horseback riding in our Recreation, Attractions and Watersports chapters. Boogie and sand boarding are local favorites that you won't want to miss (check out our Watersports chapter for board rental information).

Many of our activities occur under sunny skies, so bear in mind these safety tips: Please don't forget the sunscreen, and heed our red-flag warning system for ocean swimming. Parents: Don't leave a child of any age unattended, even for a few seconds while near the water — sound or ocean. The surf can be powerful, currents are insidious, and the water's sandy bottom can form deep holes or drop-offs. Don't let the appearance of surfers in the water lull you into a false sense of security. Lay your beach blanket down in a lifeguard-patrolled area. You may want to choose one close to a beach access bathroom for convenience sake (there's at least one public bathroom per township at the larger beach accesses). See our Beach Information and Safety chapter for locations of stands and mandatory ocean safety rules.

Another tip you may want to consider: Head soundside for a break from the ocean waves. As we've mentioned, you have to remain vigilant around any body of water, but generally you'll experience smaller waves and shallower water in the sound. This Insider's 7-year-old daughter definitely prefers the calmness of the sound to the sea (see our Jockey's Ridge write-up in this chapter for a good sound entrance).

If you're heading seaside, call your local radio station for tide times (see our Media chapter). Tidal pools are formed by the receding high tide. Kids will have fun examining these habitats. You can pick up a variety of marine-oriented story books at the library or local bookstores to identify what they discover. In fact, local author Suzanne Tate, from Nags Head, has published a series of children's books that personify sea creatures, such as Crabby, Nabby and Mary Manatee, to make them more accessible to children.

For more brainstorming activities, check out all the National Park sites: Fort Raleigh and the *Elizabeth II* on Roanoke Island, and The Wright Brothers National Memorial in Kill Devil Hills. The North Carolina Aquarium on Roanoke Island has a touch tank with live marine specimens that's perfect for kids. See our Attractions chapter for details.

For some "free" wheeling fun, don't overlook our bike paths (see our Getting Here, Getting Around chapter). It doesn't cost a penny to in-line skate, walk or bike on these. (Check with each township; some paths forbid in-line skating). If you didn't come with helmets, bikes or blades, see our Recreation chapter for rental information.

Under Sunny Skies

The Great Colington Crab Experience
Colington Rd., Big Colington Island

This Kidstuff adventure will have you wrestling with a crab — at least one dangling safely from the end of your fishing line.

Outer Banks waters teem with blue crabs that make tasty dinners when steamed and picked. Melt some butter, set out the finger bowls with a splash of lemon, and dine Outer Banks style.

There are soundside piers in Kitty Hawk on Kitty Hawk Bay (off West Tateway and Windgrass Circle) and in Kill Devil Hills on Orville Beach between Durham and Avalon streets. Plenty of folk also stop at the Oregon Inlet Fishing Center and drop a line from the rocky water's edge on both sides of the marina docks. But we'll steer you to crab heaven on Big Colington Island. Head to the area below the second bridge on Colington Road, near the firehouse. There's a parking lot for about a half-dozen cars.

The best time to crab is early morning or late evening when it's not so hot. You can buy a crab trap and bait, but frugal Insiders put a chicken neck on the end of a string to entice the crab, then use a long-handled net to bring it in. Just wiggle the net over a large bucket, and the crab will release its grip without you having to handle it. Nets can be found in any shop that sells generic beach supplies. You can go to the fish-cleaning stations at the marinas and ask for fish scraps to keep costs down to a minimum — crabs hang on real well to a fish head and tail. Throw back the small crabs (less than 5 inches at greatest shell width) — they'll be just right when you return next season. Besides, it's easier to pick the giant ones (more than 6 inches), and you get more meat.

The Children's Theater
on location outdoors · (252) 473-2127

Take a break from the sand and water with a trip to the theater. Actors from *The Lost Colony* perform classics weekly from July to early August at various Outer Banks locations. Past performances included *James and the Giant Peach* and *The Princess and the Pea*. Expect excellent acting from these thespians who hail from across America. Shows generally are performed

Wednesdays (at the Manteo waterfront) and Fridays at 11 AM. Tickets for kids generally run $3; adults, $2. Call The Lost Colony office for exact dates, locations and show titles.

Fishing Fun Headboat-Style
Pirate's Cove Yacht Club, Nags Head/ Manteo Cswy., Manteo · (252) 473-5577

It's high time you introduced your kids to fishing, whether you fish or not. We know the perfect way to do just that, and you don't even have to touch a fish or bait a hook if you're the squeamish type.

The 65-foot *Crystal Dawn* headboat (meaning it charges by head or per person) makes half-day excursions into the sound and inlet to bottom-fish for flounder, trout, sea mullet, pigfish, spot and croaker. Experienced mates will service your rods and reels, which are supplied, if you want them to. Just follow the mate's easy instructions, and drop your line overboard. When you feel it hit the bottom (the line will slacken), lock the reel in place and wait for a nibble. You won't be casting or trolling on this trip. (If you're looking for more advanced fishing experiences farther offshore, check out our Fishing chapter.)

There's a place on the boat to get out of the sun if you just want to cruise and not fish. Make sure you supervise your tykes carefully. The deck can get slippery, so running is strictly forbidden. Life vests are available for anyone wishing to don one. No fishing license is necessary. Fishing trips are limited to 50 people.

Snacks and sodas are sold on board, but feel free to bring a small cooler of drinks and food with you. Wear deck or tennis shoes, and carry sunscreen and a jacket. The sound waters are generally much calmer than offshore waters, so your chances of getting seasick are less in the sound. See our Fishing chapter for tips on avoiding an "upheaval" at sea.

In-season hours June 1 through August 31 are from 7 AM until noon and 12:30 PM

INSIDERS' TIP

Nags Head Woods summer children's nature camps feature programs on estuarine studies, canoeing and identification of small mammals, insects, reptiles and marine life.

Photo: Courtesy of J. Aaron Trotman

The surfing bug takes hold!

until 5 PM. Adults and kids 11 and older pay $25, children 10 and younger pay $20; prices include bait and tackle. During May, September and October, the boat departs daily at 8 AM and returns at 1 PM.

Several other headboats operate in the area: the *Miss Oregon Inlet* at Oregon Inlet Fishing Center; the *Miss Hatteras*, which runs out of Oden's Dock in Hatteras Village; and *Capt. Jack*, on the Manteo Waterfront. These boats offer similar packages and are described in our Fishing chapter. See our Recreation chapter for sunset- and moonlight-cruise information.

Dune Magic at Jockey's Ridge
U.S. Hwy. 158, MP 12, Nags Head
• (252) 441-7132

Ride the wind! Jockey's Ridge State Park in Nags Head is the ideal place to experience all kinds of wind-related fun. Try your hand at hang gliding (see our Attractions chapter), kite flying and sand boarding (pick up the required

permit for free at the park's offices; this activity is only allowed October 1 through May 31).

Climbing the dunes is great exercise, and the view from the top is worth the trek. Take in views of older soundside cottages to the west as well as ocean and sound views to the east and west, respectively.

Rolling down the dunes is for the brave-at-heart only. Your speed picks up rapidly, and it's hard to monitor where you're going. But it is the ultimate adventure of the sandy kind! Watch out, though: You may get an earful of sand! Running down the dunes is probably easier. A soundside beach with a parking lot is nearby at the park's southwest corner; a dip in the predominately shallow water here is perfect after a roll down the hill.

State park rangers offer more than 20 programs for children each summer including Beginner Astronomy, Seine the Sound and Tracks in the Sand. There are picnic tables here, and in case you can't climb the dunes,

Revitalize with a dip in the salty sea.

Photo: Courtesy of J. Aaron Trotman

you can still get a good look from the boardwalk. If you make arrangements in advance (call the listed number), a ranger will drive physically challenged visitors up the dune in a four-wheel vehicle. (See our Attractions chapter for more details about the dunes, including more handicapped-accessibility information.)

The park headquarters are north of the dune and west of U.S. 158 on Carolista Drive.

Kitty Hawk Sports
N.C. Hwy. 12, Corolla • (252) 453-4999
U.S. Hwy. 158, MP 13½, Nags Head
• (252) 441-6800, (800) 948-0759

Kids ages 6 to 13 are invited to attend a four-hour camp held several times a week during June, July and August. For $35, they'll learn kayaking basics from experienced instructors. The program features kayaking, beach exploration, fish and bird identification and salt marsh studies. All children must be swimmers and comfortable in the water. Kids become familiar with nets, body boards, kayaks, binoculars and masks and snorkels. Parents are invited to attend. The camp is offered

at Kitty Hawk Sport's Corolla (on N.C. Highway 12) and Nags Head locations. The clinic includes trips to Roanoke Sound and the ocean.

Free watersports clinics are held weekly, mid-June through August. Youngsters ages 8 through 16 learn the basics of surfing, skim boarding and body boarding. They are introduced to ocean- and beach-safety rules and the proper way to handle equipment. Once again, kids must know how to swim. Registration is required for the two-hour clinic, so call the listed number. The clinic is held oceanfront at the Ramada Inn in Kill Devil Hills.

Kitty Hawk Kites
U.S. Hwy. 158, MP 13½, Nags Head
• (800) 334-4777

Kitty Hawk Kites offers a Family Fun Camp each summer from June through August at their Nags Head location across from Jockey's Ridge. Kids get familiar with hang-gliding basics while their parents are taking hang-gliding lessons. The program includes rides in a hang-gliding simulator, rock-wall climbing, juggling and yo-

yo demonstrations, make-a-kite lessons and lunch (peanut butter and jelly sandwiches, chips, cookies and soda). A family of three pays $175, and that includes the parents' lessons. Each additional family member pays $35; nonmembers pay $45. The camp is held Thursdays and lasts three hours. Kids ages 5 through 12 may participate. Call the listed number for times.

If hang gliding is not your bag, Kitty Hawk Kites also offers a kayaking biology tour for ages 7 and older. Use a dip net, and identify Pamlico Sound marine life such as periwinkles, crabs and baby shrimp. All equipment is supplied, including the touring-style kayaks and paddling instruction. All participants use personal flotation devices, and kayaking sites include the Audubon Pine Island Sanctuary and Pamlico Sound. Parents are encouraged to participate. The tour is offered June, July and August for $30 a person.

For some free fun at Kitty Hawk Kites in Nags Head, come Wednesdays from 1 to 4 PM for Kid's Day. From mid-June through August, kids can face-paint, make kites, meet Wilbear Wright (KHK's "beary" mascot), witness juggling and yo-yo demonstrations, or take a ride in the hang-gliding simulator. The activities change weekly. The only charge is $3.50 for the kite-making kit.

Ocracoke Adventures
N.C. Hwy. 12 at Silver Lake Rd., Ocracoke • (252) 928-7873

Ocracoke Adventures offers daily programs for kids, including kayak eco-tours in Pamlico Sound and a host of activities for kids who can swim, including boogie-boarding or surfing lessons. Kayakers explore the fragile environment and identify plants and animals. Kids also can design a fish print T-shirt (paint, shirt and fish are supplied). The charge for the programs was not available at press time. Reservations are recommended during the summer months. Call the listed number for more information.

Rain or Shine

Nags Head Bowling
U.S. Hwy. 158, MP 10, Nags Head • (252) 441-7077

Yes, Nags Head Bowling offers fun for kids, but we also noticed that parents can bowl peacefully here too while little ones are totally enthralled. This facility sports kiddie bumpers that run the length of the lane, so even barely-walking tykes can knock down pins every time. We watched one toddler bowl for an hour straight while the adults carried on a serious game unhindered at the lane beside him. There are lightweight 6-pound balls available for the toddlers. Just turn them toward the pins, and away they go.

Games cost $2.85 each; shoes rent for $2. Nags Head Bowling is open from noon until midnight daily. If you are sensitive to smoke, try bowling early in the afternoon. See our Recreation chapter for evening specials.

There is a great selection of video games in the entrance including Tekken 2, Ultimate Mortal Kombat, Ms. Pac-Man, Stargate pinball and air hockey. Games run from 25¢ to 75¢. You must be 21 to play pool in the on-site bar unless you are accompanied by an adult. Yes, there is a snack bar!

Double L Bird Ranch and Petting Zoo
Back Rd., Buxton • (252) 995-5494

Here's a golden opportunity to experience the exotic on Hatteras Island. At the Double L you'll see anything from a small zebra finch to a blue-and-gold macaw. You can interact with these feathered friends in the aviary by hand-feeding them, or even offering them a little affection by scratching their heads. The larger birds put on a show at 10 and 11:30 AM and 1 PM. The ranch is open year round Tuesday through Saturday from 10 AM until 2 PM. Adults pay $5, and kids, $3 (this admission includes the bird show). Groups larger than 20 persons are eligible for reduced rates.

While you're on Hatteras Island, check out the Frisco Native American Museum and the Cape Hatteras Lighthouse, two stops sure to interest kids. (See our Attractions chapter for more information on these sites.)

Soundside Pavilion
U.S. Hwy. 158, MP 16½, Nags Head • (252) 441-2575

The Soundside Pavilion is a haven for gamers of all ages and skill levels. There are more than 100 up-to-date games packed in five rooms. Prices are reasonable, and there's a centrally located snack bar with light snacks, including soda, chips, candy and imported and domestic beers for adults. Games range from 25¢ to several dollars each. Several bill-changer machines are available. Kids and adults can play traditional games like pool, air hockey, Skee-Ball, basketball, pinball and Foosball. Video game fans can take on Tekken 2, Ultimate Mortal Kombat, Area 51 or Soul Edge. Become the master of Terminator 2 Judgement Day, challenge Virtua Cop 2 and try your luck at one of several Bally slot machines. For 50¢ you can pick a CD tune from the Wurlitzer and boogie down while you steer, shoot, putt, drive and aim your way into arcade oblivion.

The restrooms are large and clean. Security cameras scan the complex. There are even old-fashioned kiddie rides and an authentic stuffed African lion in the front hallway. For indoor fun, Soundside Pavilion is a hit with a bullet! In season, the Pavilion is open seven days a week. Operating hours cut back in January.

Teach's Hole
Back Rd., Ocracoke • (252) 928-1718

This Ocracoke stop is sure to fascinate the younger crowd. All you have to do is mention pirates, and they'll be begging you to take them to Teach's Hole. The pirate shop features a historical exhibit about Blackbeard, with several dioramas set up at eye level just for kids. Other displays include pirate weapons, old bottles and Blackbeard in full battle dress. Kids also can play a letter search game (for 50¢) throughout the exhibit and do a rubbing of Blackbeard's face on a woodcut by artist Elizabeth Seitz. A souvenir coin is included in the game.

A stop in the shop is a must because it's filled with more than 1,000 pirate items (see our Shopping chapter for more information). The exhibit costs $1.50 for adults and kids taller than 40 inches. Kids shorter than 40 inches are admitted free. Teach's is open Easter through Thanksgiving.

Photo: Courtesy of Jill Cutchin

Miles of shoreline offer endless opportunities for kid-type fun.

Photo: Courtesy of Jill Cutchin

Kids can wile away hours playing in the sand.

Village Playhouse
Between U.S. Hwy. 158 and N.C. Hwy. 12, MP 14, Nags Head • (252) 441-3277

Yo, paintball enthusiasts! This indoor amusement park is your kind of place. Adolescents and adventurous adults can shoot each other with pellets of paint in a long room filled with bunkers, foxholes and great hiding places. Headgear, camouflage clothing, a gun and 100 rounds of paint are provided for $15 a person. Meanwhile, the younger set can crawl or bounce through an inflated three-section moonwalk for 30 minutes at $3 each. Just so toddlers aren't jostled too much, they have a mini-habitat all to themselves to climb around in that's filled with colored plastic balls. There's also a video arcade, Skee-Ball, basketball and other games where winners can cash in paper tickets for prizes at a toy counter. Also enjoy air hockey, pool and Foosball at this indoor game palace. This place is perfect for rainy afternoons, cold winter weekends and kids' birthday parties.

A food court serves all sorts of appetizers and quick entrees including pizza and ice cream. An antiques shop beneath the same roof gives parents a place to shop and escape from the gleeful squeals. Village Playhouse is open Friday through Sunday year round. During the summer, it's open daily from 11 AM until 11 PM.

The Outer Banks is alive
with more than 300
practicing visual,
performing and
literary artists
residing within
its boundaries.

Arts and Culture

The Outer Banks is alive with more than 300 practicing visual, performing and literary artists residing within its boundaries. Living against such a stimulating backdrop as the Atlantic Ocean, their work is shaped and honed by the natural elements and deeply influenced by the islands' physical isolation. Artists soak in the rolling seas, summer sunshine and wind-swept marshes. Then these impressions are used to enliven canvas, stone, clay, metal, wood and cloth.

You can get a feel for this fascinating visual arts arena, which runs the gamut from conceptual art to classical painting, by attending several annual events. One of the longest running of these is the Dare County Arts Council's Frank Stick Art Show, which was started back in 1978. The show is held at the Ghost Fleet Gallery in Nags Head every February and features more than 150 artworks. (Frank Stick, 1884-1966, was a legendary illustrator and wildlife artist who moved to the Outer Banks in the 1940s.) The reception that marks its opening always is packed, and hundreds of local artists exhibit recent work during the event that lasts a little more than three weeks (see our Annual Events chapter for more information).

For some family fun of the artistic kind, set aside the first weekend in October for the arts council's annual Artrageous Art Extravaganza, which features hands-on creative booths with cookie decorating, hat creations, weaving, face painting and much more. Fashion shows, food, live music, art collaborations and local art and craft booths highlight the two-day event. During an elegant Sunday auction, fine art by adults and children is put on the block (see our Close-up in this chapter). Dedicated volunteers who coordinate the weekend event seem to outdo themselves year after year. It's never the same old thing!

Another must-see is the New World Festival of the Arts each August on downtown Manteo's waterfront, an ideal site for showcasing the talents of approximately 80 local and national artists and artisans. Look for painting, photography, jewelry, pottery and an assortment of handcrafted items. The two-day event was first held in 1982. If you would like to show your work or need more information about the festival, see our Annual Events chapter. The literature for this show usually comes out in January.

Private visual art studios scattered from Corolla to Ocracoke are another option for the art-seeker. Many of these local artists offer lessons mostly in watercolor and other painting techniques. We do have a large concentration of landscape painters here, but our 35 or more commercial art/craft galleries are packed with expressions as individualistic as grains of sand. Galleries offer art ranging from the hand-hewn decoy to the delicately painted Russian black lacquer box.

Not all art events have regular public venues, but they also feed the collective creative scene and therefore are noteworthy. One such example is the formation of Zen Iron. Three artists/crafters have joined forces to create welded iron sculptures — some as tall as 8 feet — that have a geometric thrust. This trio of Outer Banks residents, Jude LeBlanc, Robbie Snyder and Mark Thompson, works with scrap metal and then airbrushes the works. The final product is an impressive work of art that marries the fundamental to the metaphysical. The works are currently on display outdoors at the Roanoke Island Festival Park. They also can be seen in Kitty Hawk in front of Gulfstream Publishing on U.S. Highway 158, MP 1.

As Outer Banks artists like Zen Iron continue to emerge, civic, government and private business groups begin to notice that the Outer Banks is slowing turning into a bonafide art community. The Town of Nags Head took the lead in 1997 by setting aside funds to purchase art for its brand new municipal complex. A committee was appointed and already new works, including handcarved wood swans, vibrant oil paintings of old Nags Head cottages and mystical photographs of spiraling lighthouse stairs and misty coastal scenes, adorn the walls of the building. The town is working to establish a large body of work that it would like to turn into a public art tour.

The performing arts also flourish on the Outer Banks. Local theater groups present historic plays, comedies and dramas both seasonally and year round. Music streams from our nightclubs, and standup comics performing summer stints tickle our funny bones (see our Nightlife chapter). And symphonies, vocal groups and individual classical, folk and pop artists enliven our local auditoriums year round. What we can't generate ourselves in the way of cultural experiences, we import with the help of volunteer-based nonprofit organizations.

Thanks to the efforts of the Dare County Arts Council, Outer Banks Forum, The Theater of Dare, the Roanoke Island Historical Association (producers of *The Lost Colony*) and the Roanoke Island Festival Park, residents and vacationers on the Outer Banks enjoy exposure to local, regional and national cultural opportunities.

We begin our pilgrimage with a description of the area's major arts organizations and follow with a north-to-south excursion through the Outer Banks' eclectic galleries and other creative venues. We promise the journey will be as ever-changing and fresh as our climate.

Organizations

Dare County Arts Council
Central Square, U.S. Hwy. 158, MP 11, Nags Head • (252) 441-5617

Celebrating its 23rd year in 1998, the Dare County Arts Council supplies the Outer Banks with a wide variety of creative opportunities with the help of countless volunteers, generous patrons and members and some state

and county support. Past programs the council has sponsored include The National Tap Ensemble, The North Carolina Dance Theatre and the Neva Russian Folk Dancers. Each program usually includes a series of school performances and a public performance. This nonprofit group operates under the direction of Sandra Maddox and has a permanent office at the previously listed address. Office hours are 10 AM to 5 PM Monday through Friday year round. Visitors can stop by the DCAC office (it doubles as a gallery) to view a series of annual shows, including a spring art exhibition and a photography show, or to gather information on arts events here and nationwide. DCAC also offers slide lectures and life-drawing opportunities.

Stay in touch with these folks, especially in the fall of 1998, when they launch the North Carolina Shakespeare Festival September 10 through 12. It's still in the planning stages, but Insiders gleaned enough information to tantalize you. The three-day event will be highlighted by a performance of Shakespeare's *Merry Wives of Windsor*, performed by the North Carolina Shakespeare Festival from High Point, North Carolina. The group will perform in the local schools and do two public performances. The long weekend promises to be alive with music, culture and Elizabethan festivities, all part of Dare County's rich heritage.

The council is affiliated with the North Carolina Arts Council as the local distributing agency of the state's Grassroots funds. The DCAC also subsidizes other area arts organizations such as International Icarus, a nonprofit art exhibition honoring man's first powered flight, held each December at three Nags Head galleries (see our Annual events chapter), Theater of Dare, The Writer's Group and the Outer Banks Forum.

The arts council publishes a quarterly newsletter for members and is compiling a directory of artists. Memberships generally range from $10 for students and $20 for practicing artists to $50 for families and $100 for businesses.

Elizabeth R & Company
(252) 473-1061

Elizabeth R & Company is a producing organization that sponsors scholarly research projects centered on North Carolina history and professional films and audios that interpret history. The organization holds theatrical performances at the Pioneer Theatre in downtown Manteo each summer. *Elizabeth R*, starring English actress Barbara Hird, is a one-woman show featuring the life of Queen Elizabeth I that plays in Manteo during the summer season and tours internationally throughout the rest of the year. *Elizabeth R* was part of the 1995 Edinburgh Festival in Scotland and has been performed in London and across the mid-Atlantic United States. Along with *Elizabeth R*, summer audiences will be treated to a comedy with music, *Bloody Mary and the Virgin Queen* and *Jack Tales*, a series of musicals for children. Ticket prices vary. Call the previously listed number for more information. Dinner packages are available.

Outer Banks Forum
(252) 261-1998

The Outer Banks Forum is the area's performing arts organization. Since 1983 the Forum has produced an annual calendar of events from October through April. It has sponsored performances by such notable groups as the National Opera Company, Atlanta Brassworks and the Virginia Beach Chorale. Each season represents a variety of musical and dramatic styles ranging from orchestral to bluegrass and opera to folk tales. Performances are held in January, March, April, October and December (see our Annual Events chapter). Call for an updated listing. The programs are held at Kitty Hawk Elementary School. A season's subscription costs $30.

Roanoke Island Festival Park
Elizabeth II State Historic Site, Manteo
• (252) 475-1500

This brand-new state park, on the former Ice Plant Island at the *Elizabeth II* site across from the Manteo waterfront, is scheduled to be complete for summer 1998. The site includes an 8,500-square-foot hall of interac-

tive exhibits; a film theater featuring *The Legend of Two-Path*, a 45-minute film depicting the first English landing on Roanoke Island from the Native American point of view; an outdoor performance pavilion with lawn seating for 3,500 people that showcases visiting symphonies and theater groups; and an art gallery, which already is in full swing. The North Carolina School of the Arts will conduct a summer institute for about 50 students on the site and will offer a variety of cultural programs in music, dance and drama. Already the gallery has hosted several art shows, including the 1997 North Carolina Arts Council fellowship winners exhibition. National, regional and local artists also will be showcased here. Admission to the gallery is free. See our Attractions chapter for more information on what the Festival Park offers.

Roanoke Island Historical Association
1409 U.S. Hwy. 64/264, Manteo
• (252) 473-2127

The dramatic arts have a unique outlet on the Outer Banks in *The Lost Colony* outdoor drama, staged throughout the summer in a waterside theater on Roanoke Island (see our Attractions chapter). Perpetuated by the Roanoke Island Historical Association, *The Lost Colony* — celebrating its 61st season in 1998 — entices 120 actresses and actors, who hail from across the nation, to answer the casting call for the symphonic drama that chronicles the fate of the first English settlement to America.

Unfolding in 1998 are new set designs, created by production designer and renowned Broadway costume designer William Ivey Long. Long was inspired to create a new opening scene that would reflect the work of 16th-century artist John White whose renderings of Algonkian Indian life are some of the only visual links we have with those lost days. Also look for some new set surprises in Act II, the "Queen's Chamber."

Many of the *Lost Colony* thespians also try out for the Lost Colony's Children's Theater that wows junior audiences during the summer months with classics such as *The Princess and the Pea* (see our Kidstuff chapter).

This Event Isn't Just Good; It's Artrageous!

Every October, hundreds of Insiders gather in Kill Devil Hills at the Dare County Family Recreational Park on Mustian Street to celebrate the arts. The Dare County Arts Council, a local nonprofit organization, sponsors the two-day Artrageous Art Extravaganza the first weekend in October. It includes an all-day cultural arts festival on Saturday and finishes off the weekend with an evening art auction on Sunday. The festival, celebrating its 9th year in 1998, is designed to stimulate creativity and generate an artsy kind of fun.

Multiple booths are set up where children can enjoy face painting, hair wrapping or hat making, learn to fashion a musical instrument, paint a flower pot or work on a collaborative piece with their peers. The youth groups have turned out some unique creations including a mammoth paper-mâchè rock or a large mural with an outer-space theme. There's no admission fee on Saturday but a $1 contribution per booth is suggested.

You'll enjoy diverse entertainment. Each year's line-up is different, but past festivals

— continued on next page

Photo: Courtesy of DCAC

"I can outpaint you with my eyes closed!"

have included local musical groups, a balloon-tying clown, vintage-wear fashion shows and even educational workshops such as recycling with an art twist. Area artists and artisans set up booths to sell their creations. You can purchase a handpainted wine glass, a dog-hair hat, a watercolor painting or beach-glass jewelry. The surprises are endless but none can compare with the intent looks on the children's faces as they move from booth to booth creating their own works of art. Adults have a chance to kick back on Sunday evening and enjoy cocktails and hors d'oeuvres while bidding on local art and exciting golf, dinner and getaway packages. Things get hot and heavy when people from all walks of life start bidding, and everyone enjoys the friendly competition. There are lots of laughs as everyone struggles to keep hold of his or her favorite painting, photograph, drawing, handwoven hat or one-of-a kind necklace. The adult auction also includes children's art that was created during Saturday's festival, and sometimes these pieces summon the highest prices. Money sure can't buy you love, but there are plenty of parents in the audience who grab up these works and prove that love surely can earn some cash for a worthy cause!

Proceeds from both days directly benefit the local arts council, which disperses profits to needy artistic causes in the community. A scholarship fund was set up last year so local kids could pursue extracurricular art experiences like music camp or art classes, and for years, money has also been put into a fund for a future Outer Banks youth center.

Artrageous is open to the public. You don't have to be a local to enjoy the entire weekend or take a piece of local art home with you. That special painting of a Nags Head landscape or ocean cottage may be just the thing to keep you from pining away for the Outer Banks until you return once again to our sandy haven. The location has changed over the years for the days event but it looks like the current one will be more permanent. The adult auction is usually held at the Village at Nags Head Beach Club at milepost 15 on the Beach Road. Call the Dare County Arts Council at 441-5617 for an update on times, location and ticket information for the Sunday auction. This is one of our biggest off-season events. Join us Insiders on the first weekend in October. We promise it will be Artrageous!

Others take on roles as time-warped sailors for hilarious and educational interpretive tours of the *Elizabeth II*. So it's important to note that while the main play has a historic thrust, its players are aspiring performing artists that bring talent in a wider venue to the Outer Banks. A full day of special events, including free children's theater selections, interpretive park tours and special performances, takes place on Virginia Dare's birthday, August 18. Call the Lindsey Warren Visitor Center at Fort Raleigh, (252) 473-5772, for a schedule.

If you are interested in joining the Roanoke Island Historical Association, write to them at: 1409 Highway 64/264, Manteo, NC 27954 or call the previously listed number. Contribution details vary. You may become a member and/or contribute to the annual fund or their endowment fund.

The Theater of Dare
(252) 441-6726

The Theater of Dare was established in 1992 with a grant from the Outer Banks Forum. Its members bring quality live theater to the Outer Banks by taking part in all phases of production, from directing and set design to performing. The Theater of Dare produces three main stage productions a year from fall to spring. TOD embodies the true spirit of community theater by welcoming the amateur and professional thespian alike. The organization thus far has produced hits such as *Arsenic and Old Lace*, *Steel Magnolias* and *The Odd Couple*.

The Theater of Dare lacks a permanent rehearsal space, but most of its performances are held at Manteo Middle School. Season tickets cost $22 for nonmembers

This aerial view shows Waterside Theatre, the venue for *The Lost Colony*.

and $20 for members. Different levels of membership are available. The minimum category calls for a $10 donation or active participation in two productions within one year. For more information about membership, volunteering, auditions or production dates, call Julia Sheer at the previously listed number.

Galleries

Corolla

Dolphin Watch Gallery
TimBuck II Shopping Village, Ocean Tr., Corolla • (252) 453-2592

Dolphin Watch Gallery features the works of owner/artist Mary Kaye Umberger. This artist creates hand-colored etchings on handmade paper drawn from scenes indigenous to the Corolla area including wildlife, ducks and other waterfowl, seascapes and lighthouses. Other art pieces here include pottery, stoneware, carvings of marine life and wax sculptures (candles shaped by hand, with flower petals molded by the artist's fingertips). The gallery is open year round; call for off-season hours.

Glitz Gallery
TimBuck II Shopping Village, Ocean Tr., Corolla • (252) 453-6788

This shop features an eclectic mix of art and crafts. Shop here for antique glass jewelry fashioned by artists from around the world. Handpainted clothing and furniture are popular finds along with carved figurines and the folk art-style paintings of Nags Head artist Susan Vaughan (see her listing under our Studios section in this chapter). Glitz is open year round; call for off-season operating hours.

Outer Banks Style
1122 Ocean Tr., Corolla • (252) 453-4388, (800) 261-0176

Outer Banks Style offers viewers a taste of local art, crafts, furniture and home accessories in its Corolla shop. Owner Gary Springer has stocked the gallery with works by popular Outer Banks painter James Melvin and photographer Ray Matthews. Check out Troy Spencer's reproduction signs. Recently acquired is Story People by Brian Andreas, artist and storyteller. This line of fanciful art includes prints, sculptures, books and furniture decorated with short prose. The shop is open year round seven days a week. Hours vary, so call ahead.

Take Home Something Special
To Remember the Outer Banks

Come See Gallery Row

Morales Art Gallery
(Originals & Prints)

Glenn Eure's Ghost Fleet Gallery

The Lighthouse Gallery & Gift Shop
(The Lighthouse Store)

Jewelry By Gail

Ipso Facto Gallery

Sally Huss Gallery

Gallery Row

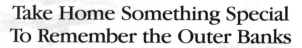

The Center for Fine Arts, Jewelry, & Crafts
Mile Post 10.5
behind the Christmas Mouse in Nags Head
Between the Highways

Duck

Greenleaf Art Gallery
1169 Duck Rd. (N.C. Hwy. 12), Duck
• (252) 261-2009
U.S. Hwy. 158, MP 16, Nags Head
• (252) 480-3555

Greenleaf galleries offer their guests a chance to experience exquisite fine crafts and paintings from nationally and regionally known American artists at their two gallery locations in Duck and Nags Head. The emphasis is on mid-Atlantic painters at the Nags Head location.

Approximately 300 artists and artisans are represented by Greenleaf galleries, offering a good geographic variation. Featured are one-of-a-kind, handcrafted jewelry, ceramics, wood, glass and furnishings, plus sculpture, acrylic and watercolor paintings, etchings, lithographs and mixed-media pieces. Expect to find both the delightful and serious at Greenleaf, anything from a huge, whimsical praying mantis to the works of some of the nation's finest glass artisans.

The Duck gallery closes December 23 and reopens in mid-March. It's open daily the rest of the year, with extended hours in the summer. The Nags Head location has the same schedule but is closed on Sunday year round. Call for an exhibition calendar.

Fine Art Furnishings
Barrier Island Shoppes, N.C. Hwy. 12, Duck • (252) 261- 2669

Renee Hilmire features complete place settings of handpainted glassware and accessories with bright colors and lots of floral designs. Insiders love her daisy and iris themes, and her more abstract selections are lots of fun. Hilmire hand-paints floor mats as well as offers her original paintings at her shop, which is tucked away on the second floor of this shopping complex. The shop's open year round. Call for hours.

Kitty Hawk

Crafter's Gallery
U.S. Hwy. 158, MP 4, Kitty Hawk
• (252) 261-3036

You are entering a handmade one-of-a-kind craft haven here. Crafter's features mostly country crafts coupled with some contemporary styles. The gallery offers cloth and wicker basketry, handmade dolls, cards and handpainted wooden knickknacks. The scene changes as the artists who show here change, but usually the thrust is on handmade crafts. (See our Shopping chapter for details.) The gallery is open all year.

Shattered Dreams Stained Glass
N.C. Hwy. 12, MP 4, Kitty Hawk
• (252) 255-0364

The original creations in stained glass here have an emphasis on nature. Jae Everett creates brilliant work that employs both subtle and bright colors. Tropical birds, tree frogs and lush flora come to life in her glasswork. She specializes in custom-made panels and custom-designed lamps. Her window pieces vary in size from a Christmas ornament to a full-length door or window panel. Special design contracts are welcome. The gallery is open year round, but hours fluctuate. Call for a schedule.

Kill Devil Hills

The Wooden Feather
Seagate North Shopping Center, U.S. Hwy. 158, MP 5½, Kill Devil Hills
• (252) 480-3066

The Wooden Feather presents award-winning, handcarved decoys and shorebirds as well as driftwood sculptures. The gallery features an outstanding collection of antique decoys. Hours are Monday through Saturday during the summer season, and it is closed

---

INSIDERS' TIP

Pocosin Art Center in Columbia, about 40 miles west of Manteo, is a great stop for artists and art enthusiasts. The center features classes, such as pottery and painting, and hosts exciting events such as the annual Snow Goose Contra Dance. The center operates as a museum. Art is also for sale here.

during January. Call for an off-season schedule.

Nostalgia Gallery
Seagate North Shopping Center, U.S. Hwy. 158, MP 5½, Kill Devil Hills
• (252) 441-1881

Norm Martinus specializes in paper memorabilia that deserves mention in any art chapter. He has to know his stuff as the coauthor of *Warmon's Paper*, an encyclopedia of antiques and collectibles. You'll find oodles of advertising art at Nostalgia as well as the original art of Matinus' daughter, Lee. Revel in old prints of Maxfield Parrish and Norman Rockwell. Martinus offers full-service custom framing and matting. Insiders know that he's one of the Outer Banks' finest framers. See our Shopping chapter for more tips of what Nostalgia has in store for you. The shop is open year round.

First Flight Shrine
Wright Brothers National Memorial Visitors Center, U.S. Hwy. 158, MP 8, Kill Devil Hills • (252) 441-7430

While the First Flight Shrine is not a commercial art gallery, it has a body of portraiture that deserves recognition in any Arts and Culture chapter. For more than 30 years, the First Flight Society has inducted one or more individuals into the Shrine who have accomplished an outstanding "first" that has enhanced the development of aviation. Hanging in the same room as a replica of Wilbur and Orville Wright's first flyer are more than 55 faces of great aviators such as Amelia Earhart, Adm. Richard E. Byrd, Neil Armstrong and Col. Edwin Aldrin. The portraits are produced annually and exhibited through a partnership with the National Park Service at the Wright Brothers National Memorial Visitor Center (see our Attractions chapter for operating hours of the Memorial).

Nags Head

Lighthouse Gallery and Gifts
Gallery Row, 301 E. Driftwood St., Nags Head • (252) 441-4232, (800) 579-2827

Owners Cheryl and Bruce Roberts have put together a shop dedicated to the "Keepers of the Light." They've built their gallery as a replica of an original Victorian-style lighthouse that represents the U.S. Lighthouse Service at its prime at the turn of the 20th century.

Open every day in summer, and every day but Sunday from Labor Day to Easter, this shop features lighthouse art and artifacts including hundreds of lighthouse models, collectibles, brass nautical memorabilia such as compasses, sextants and octants (both authentic and reproduction), books, jewelry, prints, paintings from all over the United States and local artwork. You must see the special collection of lighthouse books with photography by Bruce, who offers unique and breathtaking views of these beloved sentinels. Cheryl's book, *Lighthouse Children*, is definitely worth a read. The first publishing has sold out, and the subject of lighthouse families will be featured this fall in a series on PBS.

Add your name to the Outer Banks Lighthouse Society newsletter mailing list at the gallery, or call for information about joining the Society that boasts 600 members.

Sally Huss Gallery
Gallery Row, 300 E. Driftwood St., Nags Head • (252) 441-8098

Sally Huss Gallery features the upbeat original art and prints of the California artist of the same name. Huss creates impressionistic paintings done in bold colors and featuring childlike scenes. Her designs, which are coupled with cheerful sayings, are transferred onto mugs, gift wrap, T-shirts, cards and key chains. Adults and kids alike will get a kick out of her lighthearted creations that are dotted with toucans, mermaids, elephants, hearts and sailboats. The gallery is open all year.

Ipso Facto Gallery
206 Gallery Row, Nags Head
• (252) 480-2793

The merchandise at Ipso Facto — antiques, curios and objects of art from all over the world — is eclectic, and it's reasonably priced too. Look for furniture, ethnic trinkets, such as Mexican holiday candleholders, and original paintings. Ipso is really more of an antiques shop than a gift shop. It's a great place to browse, ooh and aah and, of course,

TUE - FRI
0 am - 6pm
SAT
0 am - 3 pm

Photo: Courtesy of Mary Ellen Riddle

Outer Banks galleries are chock-full of a variety of fine arts and crafts.

find a treasure to take home. Ipso Facto Gallery is open year round; it's closed Sunday.

Morales Art Gallery
107 E. Gallery Row, Nags Head
• (252) 441-6484
Scarborough Faire, N.C. Hwy. 12, Duck
• (252) 261-7190, (800) 635-6035

Mitchell and Christine Lively at the Morales Art Galleries have made financial success a personal reality for many struggling artists by showcasing their work and producing fine-art prints that are shown at their large gallery in Nags Head and at their second gallery in Duck. Morales Art Gallery is the oldest art venue on Gallery Row; the late Jesse Morales first opened the doors in 1971. Today, the Morales galleries and their Fine Art Print Shop (at the Nags Head location) carry fine original local, regional and nationally known art. Showcased here are the works of Larry Johnson, Pat Williams, Dennis Lighthart, Pat Troiani, Tony Feathers, William "Red" Taylor and E.M.

"Liz" Corsa. Expect to find limited-edition prints by the Greenwich Workshop, Mill Pond Press, Hadley House, Somerset Publishing and Wild Wings. If you want to view a major collection of original seascapes, this is the place to come.

Morales began offering a new service in 1998: Large format printing from 50 inches to 150 feet. The commercial uses are unlimited. Mitchell says there are only three of these printing machines in North Carolina. Uses include floor graphics, court room displays, backlit signage and fine-art reproductions. The quality is excellent.

If you're searching for specific art or artists, the gallery's laser disc computer system stores more than 40,000 images that you can pore over to find the perfect piece. Featured in the print shop here are breathtaking fine-art prints by premier nature painters.

Mitchell, who owns the business with his wife, Christine, has been framing and publishing art for more than two decades. The couple's dedication to the arts has been felt

INSIDERS' TIP

Stumpy Point, just 30 minutes from Roanoke Island, may someday be the new home for a dinner theater. Area theater enthusiasts are looking to turn an old schoolhouse into a theater and art center. Call (252) 473-5423 for information.

community-wide, especially in their generosity to the Dare County schools. A member of the Professional Picture Framers Association, Morales Galleries offers a wide variety of choices in custom framing. Mitchell is also an inventor; stop by and ask him about the mat cutter he designed. Call for weekly show and exhibit information at the Scarborough Faire location in Duck.

The Nags Head Gallery is open year round; call for the Duck schedule.

Glenn Eure's Ghost Fleet Gallery of Fine Art
Gallery Row, 210 E. Driftwood St., Nags Head • (252) 441-6584

Glenn and Pat Eure, owners of the Ghost Fleet Gallery, run an original art establishment that primarily features his work. A printmaker, Eure creates in a variety of forms including etching, woodcutting, collagraphy, serigraphy and relief carving and painting in addition to drawing, oil, acrylic and watercolor painting and woodcarving. He's recently completed a series of collagraphs (thin collages run through a printing press) honoring Wilbur and Orville Wright's first flight. The fine-art prints, each hand-pulled by the artist, contain flight imagery ranging from da Vinci's time to the present. Glenn also specializes in large canvases that bulge out from their frames — irregular shapes that are painted in a nonobjective style. He produces lighthearted watercolors that feature boat scenes. Most have two small skiffs laying in wait in a sandy cove and romantically tied together by one anchor. He personalizes these with names and special dates. Many have the Cape Hatteras, Ocracoke or Currituck lighthouses in the background.

The Eures rotate other artists' work in the West Wing Gallery and the Second Dimension gallery located a flight up. In the off-season Eure hosts several community shows: The International Icarus Show in December commemorates the Wright Brothers' first flight; the second is the Frank Stick Memorial Art Show each February sponsored by the Dare County Arts Council and a county public school art show. The two former shows draw more than 100 artists into the exhibition arena, and opening nights attract more than 800 art lovers to the gallery. Running in the West Wing during the Frank Stick exhibition is The Heart Show, an invitational that features art that speaks to matters of the heart. Approximately 35 paintings, sculpture, drawings and conceptual artworks cover the walls and floor of the intimate space. Poetry readings also are held year round at the gallery (see our Annual Events chapter).

The Ghost Fleet Gallery is open year round. Hours are cut back some in January and February.

Jewelry by Gail
Gallery Row, 207 Driftwood St., Nags Head • (252) 441-5387

Gail Kowalski is a designer-goldsmith who has won national recognition for her creations in precious metals and stones. Most of the jewelry designed and made here falls into the "wearable art" category. Check out Selections by Gail, a department of very high quality but moderately priced handmade jewelry from all over the world. Kowalski personally selects each piece exhibited here. "Charming Lights" sterling and gold lighthouse jewelry collection is a recent addition to the gallery. Images of the four local lighthouses are fashioned into earrings, pendants and charms. The gallery is open Monday through Saturday and is closed in January.

Seaside Art Gallery
N.C. Hwy. 12, MP 11, Nags Head • (252) 441-5418

Original etchings and lithographs by Picasso, Whistler, Rembrandt and Renoir are among the thousands of original works of art on display at the Nags Head location of Seaside Art Gallery. Sculptures, paintings, drawings, Indian pottery, fine porcelains, Mexican silver jewelry including the work of William Spratling, seascapes and animation art from Disney and Warner Brothers are spread throughout numerous rooms in this expansive gallery. Seaside is a Gold Circle dealer for Disney Classic Figurines. The prints by David Hunter are meticulously rendered and range from biblical portraiture to peaceful coastal scenes.

The gallery hosts several competitions annually including an international miniature art show (see the May listings in our Annual Events

chapter). Printmaking workshops also are held here each year by David Hunter. The gallery is open seven days a week year round.

Anna Gartrell's Art & Photography By the Sea
N.C. Hwy. 12, MP 10, Nags Head
• (252) 480-0578

Gartrell's artistry is evident in her expressive watercolors and photography. Her work seems to brighten every darkened recess in your being. Original is the key word here. A deeply spiritual woman, Gartrell said she revels in "God's explosive beauty frozen forever for you." Examine her series of jeweled and crystal wave photos, depictions of wild storms, sunrises and sunsets, ducks, dunes, wild stallions and lighthouses, crystal flounders and amazing sea angels. Take a bit of Outer Banks brightness home with you. A photo of a skyscape that Gartrell shot recently has been accepted into the National Aeronautics & Space Museum art collection for special art shows.

The gallery is open daily, but hours are flexible. The owner posts a note on the door daily with the day's operating hours.

Yellowhouse Gallery and Annex
N.C. Hwy. 12, MP 11, Nags Head
• (252) 441-6928

Yellowhouse Gallery and Annex houses one of North Carolina's largest collections of antique prints and maps. Thousands of original old etchings, lithographs and engravings are organized for browsing in several rooms of one of Nags Head's older beach cottages. Established in 1969 the gallery features Civil War prints and maps; prints of botanicals, fish, shells and birds; and old views, antique maps and charts of the Outer Banks. Yellowhouse Gallery also offers a huge selection of decorative and fine-art prints and posters as well as souvenir pictures and maps of the Outer Banks. If the picture you want is not in stock, Uncle Jack, the genial proprietor, will order it for you.

Yellowhouse Annex next door offers fast, expert custom framing, matting, mounting and shrink-wrapping. Archival framing is also available. The Yellowhouse Annex is open daily except Sunday all year. Winter gallery hours vary, but you can call the annex for more information.

Roanoke Island

The Silver Bonsai Gallery
905 Hwy. 64/264, Manteo
• (252) 475-1413

The Silver Bonsai Gallery features the fine metalsmithing work of Kathyrine Holton and Ben Stewart. These artists create original one-of-a-kind jewelry (pins, necklaces, earrings, rings), fine-art metal sculptures, lighthearted wind chimes, sculptural family trees and even ornate headwear. The sterling silver dragonfly earrings, studded with gems are to die for. While the majority of the wares are metal by nature, the shop also features handmade candles and quilts. Overall, the thrust is functional art. The metalwork in particular is meticulously handcrafted and a great new addition to the Outer Banks art scene. The shop is open year round.

Island Art Gallery
The Christmas Shop, U.S. Hwy. 64, Manteo • (252) 473-2838

The work of more than 100 artists is displayed in this adjunct to the popular Christmas Shop. The gallery, which has been operating for 32 years, is open daily year round. It consists of several large rooms of paintings, sculptures and works in other media ranging from decoys and lighthouse art to photographs and paintings of Outer Banks landscapes. Look for works by Patricia Breen and Christopher Radko as well as the well-known P. Buckley Moss. Check out the jewelry nook that's filled with locally handcrafted work and a touch of the international too, including fascinating Russian brooches.

The shop is expanding and will have a brand-new 4,000-square-foot addition opening that fronts U.S. 64. The idea is to create an old-fashioned general store featuring collectibles and an expanded candy, candle and stationery department. The addition will have Christmas dinner all set in a model dining room — complete with full-size fireplace, dining table and a crystal chandelier that's displayed in conjunction with the glass ornament shop that's also part of the new space. Another windfall of the expansion — more art gallery space. Ask shop personnel for information on the New World Festival of the Arts held each August under the guidance of Christmas Shop owner Edward Greene.

Wanchese Pottery
107 Fernando St., Manteo
• (252) 473-2099

Customers can watch local potters Bonnie and Bob Morrill at work in their studio in downtown Manteo. This shop is known locally for its beautiful, useful art graced with delicate, lead-free glazes. This Insider bought a handsome mug here that holds a generous amount of coffee, sits easily without wobbling and has an exquisite glaze that turns a morning routine into an artistic awakening. Choose dinnerware, oil lamps, hummingbird feeders, mugs, bowls and pitchers among other items. The shop also features some handmade baskets and fresh cooking herbs.

Wanchese Pottery is open year round. Winter hours are 1 to 5 PM Thursday, Friday and Saturday.

Manteo Gallery
The Waterfront Shops, Manteo
• (252) 473-3365

Manteo Gallery offers one of the best selections of nautical art in the area and features Outer Banks scenes and garden scenes, florals, wildlife, aviator and Americana prints, including works by Charles Wysocki, Linda Nelson Stocks and Elizabeth Mumford. The gallery offers limited-edition and open-edition prints, antique prints and maps, photography and original art. It also features the inspirational paintings and drawings of Duck artist Ellie Grumiaux, whose pen and ink Outer Banks scenes are published regularly in *The Virginian-Pilot's* weekly tabloid, *The Coast*. Grumiaux offers local scenes done in watercolor including landscapes with an emphasis on some of coastal North Carolina's old cottages, stores and countryside structures.

The Manteo Gallery is on the Manteo Waterfront and is open year round. It's closed Sunday during the off-season.

The Frame Shop
200 Sir Walter Raleigh St., Manteo
• (252) 473-1929

This gallery and frame shop recently has moved from a side alley to a prime Manteo location complete with showcase windows. Kim Keene is the driving force behind the wonderfully interesting space. It's a full-service frame shop offering reasonable prices and top-quality craftsmanship.

One- and two-person art shows are held here monthly except in January and February (but the gallery is still open during these months). You'll find prints and original sculpture, paintings and drawings including the work of Frank Sparrow, who creates curious shadow boxes,

Heed the piper's call to visit the Elizabethan Gardens.

and Linda Ritchie Crassons, whose colored pencil drawings are excellent. It's hard to describe her work because it's so personal, but it does exude a reverence for nature and the inner life of humankind. Genna Miles, a local fiber artist showcases her handspun, hand-dyed, crocheted and embellished hats that push the boundaries of craft to the fine-art edge. These are one-of-a-kind creations that exude elegance and individuality. It's not unusual to see locals sporting Mile's "crowning" achievements at gala affairs, at the pizza parlor or at an art show. It's important to note that The Frame Shop is one of the only galleries on the Outer Banks where you'll find black-and-white photography.

The shop is open year round, Monday through Friday from 10 AM to 5 PM and Saturday from 10 AM to 3 PM.

Hubby Bliven, Wildlife Art
Ananias Dare St., Roanoke Island
• (252) 473-2632

Bliven runs a full-service frame shop and wildlife art gallery that features his own work. He also operates a Civil War museum on the premises (see our Area Overviews and Attractions chapters). Bliven's shop is the place to go if you are looking for lighthouse photos that include all eight North Carolina sentinels framed together or as individual prints. This group includes the

Prices's Creek lighthouse in Southport, a rare find. Bliven was very fortunate to be given access to photograph this structure that's on private property. His shop is open year round.

Nick-E Stained Glass
813 Old Wharf Rd., Wanchese
• (252) 473-5036

The studio and gallery are a stained-glass wonderland featuring the original creations of Ellinor and Robert Nick. Shop for colorful panels, windows, lamps, personalized ceramic light-switch plates and sun catchers here. Special orders are welcome. Nick-E is open year round.

Hatteras Island

Upstairs Art Gallery
Pamlico Station, Rodanthe
• (252) 987-1088

The Upstairs Art Gallery features works by James Melvin, Chris Haltigan and other Carolina artists. You can purchase limited-edition prints, Green Heron stained glass, Black Hills gold jewelry, painted furniture, pottery and original watercolors. The gallery is above Lee's Collectibles. It's open April through October, six days a week and is closed on Sundays.

Gaskins Gallery
N.C. Hwy. 12, Avon • (252) 995-6617

The focus at Gaskins Gallery is on original local art and custom framing. Artists and owners Denise and Elizabeth Gaskins exclusively feature original family art, including their own watercolors and those of their 83-year-old grandmother, who began painting several years ago. The paintings generally are coastal scenes or florals. You'll also find handpainted glassware, decorated with brilliant flowers, and even some abstract designs. The gallery, which also has decorator prints and posters, is open year round.

Browning Artworks
N.C. Hwy. 12, Frisco • (252) 995-5538

This fine-art and craft gallery, which opened in 1984, has a reputation for showcasing top-notch North Carolina crafters, including many local artists. The collection includes the creations of 200 artisans who make stained and blown-glass, handweavings, porcelains, pottery, copper work, forged wrought-iron work and stoneware. Wood turners, many of whom use North Carolina woods, have a variety of crafts showcased here. Browning's jewelry selections are breathtaking, incorporating a variety of colorful semiprecious stones to form necklaces, rings, pins, bracelets and earrings. Several dozen jewelry designers are featured, including the breathtaking and colorful creations of Outer Banker Austin Cake.

The gallery also exhibits paintings and prints, such as the exclusive collection of Linda Browning's watercolor skyscapes and Dixie Browning's watercolor scenes as well as the color photography of Ray Matthews and Michael Halminski. Both photographers have a passion for the coastal scene. Antique tribal weavings by Majid are a beautiful attraction. Art and craft demonstrations are held on their deck by the artists whose work is featured. Call for a schedule. Proprietors Linda and Lou Browning also maintain a bridal and gift registry for residents and visitors and will ship your selections.

Browning Artworks is open year round.

Sandy Bay Gallery
N.C. Hwy. 12, Hatteras Village
• (252) 986-1338

This casual yet upscale gallery features original fine art and crafts with an emphasis on Outer Banks artists. Located in a 1940s-era Hatteras Island house, Sandy Bay is filled with original watercolor and acrylic paintings and photography by local artists. You'll also find regional and national fine-art crafts by potters, jewelers, glass artisans and paper, wood, stained glass and fiber artists. The handcarved decorative waterfowl, including egrets, blue herons, sandpipers and dowitchers, have grace and personality. The wood's grain is masterfully employed in the carving process to lend movement to curving necks, wings and feathers. Glass boxes with silver trim by Mary Anne feature a geometric collage of colored and clear glass reminiscent of Mondrian's paintings. You also can choose from a nice selection of prints. It's open March through Christmas Eve.

Ocracoke Island

Sunflower Center
Back Rd., Ocracoke Village
• (252) 928-6211

If you take the road that runs in front of the Back Porch Restaurant and drive around the loop, you'll find this shop. Sunflower Center combines contemporary and traditional East Coast arts and crafts, but most of the artists featured here are from Ocracoke. Only original art is exhibited. Other items here include fused glass, stained glass, art glass, pottery and handcrafted jewelry.

Owner Carol O'Brien offers weekly summer workshops in oil and acrylic painting, plus pastels and drawing. Watercolor classes are offered all summer for $25 an hour. A school of arts and crafts is provided Easter through October for adults. O'Brien features one type of media biweekly such as oil paintings, acrylic works, pen-and-ink or mixed media, in an upstairs gallery. A recent addition to the gallery is a section that includes aromatherapy products, Long Life herbal teas, Nature's Way herbs and other health products. The gallery is open daily Easter through Thanksgiving.

Deepwater Pottery
School Rd., Ocracoke Village
• (252) 928-7004

Artistic and functional stoneware and raku pottery are made here. You can choose from functional dining and kitchenware and decorative raku pottery with copper glazes. The shop carries an assortment of gifts. See our Shopping chapter for more details. It's open from March 1 through Christmas.

Village Craftsmen
Howard St., Ocracoke Village
• (252) 928-5541

The artwork in this well-known shop and gallery includes North Carolina pottery, handmade wooden boxes, jewelry and other original items. The focus is on excellent craftsmanship and variety. Owner Philip Howard also sells his pen-and-ink and watercolor prints here. See our Shopping chapter for more about this local landmark, open year round except the month of January.

Island Artworks
British Cemetery Rd., Ocracoke Village
• (252) 928-3892

Owner-artist Kathleen O'Neal has lived on Ocracoke for more than 20 years. "Art jewelry" aptly describes most of the finds here. O'Neal does all the copper enameling and silver and goldsmithing work herself. The artwork is done by local and North Carolina artists mostly, such as large, contemporary-style watercolors of island scenes by Debbie Wells and glass mosaic tile work by Libby Hicks. Local photography, sculptural assemblages created by O'Neal, glass art, basketry and mixed-media art are just some of the exciting discoveries at Island Artworks. It's a real fine-art experience. You won't find any mass-produced items here. The shop is open from mid-March until Christmas.

Over The Moon
British Cemetery Rd., Ocracoke Village
• (252) 928-3555

Over The Moon features handmade contemporary crafts from 150 artists across the nation. Shop here for jewelry, porcelain and Brian Andreas' Story People — books, prints and sculptures adorned with insightful sayings. See our Shopping chapter for other items found here. The shop is open from Easter through Thanksgiving.

The Old Ocracoke Gathering Place
N.C. Hwy. 12, Ocracoke Village
• (252) 928-7180

This turn-of-the-century building is chock-full of interesting finds, including a collection of local crafts and pottery from across North Carolina. Look here for artwork by Frans Van Baars, Jim Wordsworth and other creative folk. See our Shopping chapter for more on this artsy hotspot. It's open year round except for January.

Heart's Desire
Back Rd., Ocracoke Village
• (252) 928-4104

This shop features a variety of fine crafts including pottery, glass works, jewelry, folk art, copper works and beach glass creations. Heart's Desire is open April through December.

Studios

These are private studios that can be approached by appointment only.

Kitty Hawk

Dunehouse Pottery
(252) 261-9062

Dunehouse Pottery features the collaborative work of Shawn Morton and his mom, Lyditch. Shawn creates hand-thrown stoneware pottery that Lyditch glazes with exotic and North Carolina fish. Dunehouse is a working studio, and the Mortons welcome your calls. Shawn and Lyditch co-create bowls and stoneware platters, handpainted tile trays done in contemporary and classic designs. Lyditch's nosegay patterns and fish are delicate images that are painted with a skilled hand. Shawn's hand-thrown work is simple yet graceful. He uses lead-free glazes for his functional pots. The studio is open year round; call for an appointment.

Pat Troiani
(252) 261-4659

Pat Troiani is one of the Outer Banks top watercolorists. She teaches her craft at her Kitty Hawk studio and primarily works in a realistic style. She's produced some gorgeous renditions of the Whalehead Hunt Club in the winter, beautiful florals and various coastal scenes. Her work is sold at Morales art galleries and the Island Art Gallery at the Christmas Shop in Manteo. She offers classes twice weekly. Class size is limited to seven students. Troiani emphasizes color, composition and drawing instruction. Call for an appointment.

Kill Devil Hills

Marsh Ridge Studio
115 Ridge Rd. • (252) 441-6581

Award-winning watercolorist Chris Haltigan offers lessons and original art for sale in her private studio. She describes her work as impressionism and contemporary realism featuring scenes from the Outer Banks and general locale. The word "radiant" well describes her work, which is characterized by iridescent sound waters and atmospheric early morning boat scenes. The passage of light gets special attention in her pieces. Haltigan's work appears on the 1998-99 edition of *The Beach Book*, the local phone book.

Call for an appointment to see Haltigan's work. The studio is open year round.

E.M. Corsa
(252) 480-0303

Think Beatrix Potter. Now throw in some sophistication and humor, and you have an idea of the depth and delight of E.M. "Liz" Corsa's work. Her original watercolors appeal to the young and old alike featuring humanized wild and domestic animals. Insiders chuckle over her most recent painting of crows — portrayed as music students who are caught passing "notes" (musical notes that is) by their maestro. Corsa's inspiration comes from nature and family and is coupled with her unique sense of humor. She's a published writer of humorous magazine essays who combines images and titles in a thought provoking and fresh manner. Corsa takes commissions and will unveil a line of greeting cards, clothing and limited-edition prints in the summer of 1998. Her work is on display at Morales galleries in Duck and Nags Head. Call the previously listed number for more information.

Carol Trotman
(252) 441-3590

Painter Carol Trotman specializes in floral watercolors. Her work is so spectacular she was invited to show her watercolors at the American Horticultural Society in the spring of 1996 as a one-woman exhibition. Trotman's complicated garden scenes as well as poetic profiles of single blossoms are exceptional. Her work has been reproduced on cards, and you can purchase these or original work by calling the artist for an appointment or by visiting Greenleaf Gallery in Duck and Sandy Bay Gallery in Hatteras Village.

Monahan Studio
(252) 441-8735

Pat Monahan is a local artist who offers classes that introduce students to the work of modern artists from Cezanne to Jasper Johns. Her own works ranges from crazy found object sculptures to lively watercolors. Monahan teaches painting and introduces watercolors first, but she encourages her students to explore their own paths. She holds daytime classes only and also offers life-drawing workshops. Call for an appointment.

Susan Vaughan
(252) 480-3301

This is a working studio where Vaughan paints in a folk art-style. She produces town portraits in acrylics that are very popular on the Outer Banks. Prints are available including her representations of Manteo, Kill Devil Hills, Duck, Elizabeth City and Corolla. Vaughan also paints local scenes, and she welcomes commissions. Her work is on display at the Island Gallery at the Christmas Shop in Manteo, The Frame Shop in Manteo and Glitz Gallery in Corolla. Call the previously listed number for commission information.

Kathryn Rose Boutchyard
(252) 441-3448

This is a working studio where Boutchyard fashions one-of-a-kind beach glass and shell jewelry using sterling silver, 14-karat gold and gold-filled metals. Boutchyard collects her "gems" from Outer Banks beaches, then polishes and tumbles them and combines them with metal to create necklaces, rings, pins and bracelets that can be seen gracing many local folk. Her name has become synonymous with quality and grace. Call for an appointment.

Steve Lautermilch
Colington Harbour • (252) 480-0060

Steve Lautermilch is a professional photographer and poet who offers weekly private and group classes in writing, dream work and meditation. His photography is displayed at Glenn Eure's Ghost Fleet Gallery in Nags Head and Greenleaf Galleries in Duck and Nags Head. Lautermilch works mostly in color, and his subject matter encompasses both nature and people. His pictures have an ethereal feel, speaking to the inner nature of the life force. He is a meticulous camera man and believes that understanding your dreams and relaxing with meditation can enhance creativity. After viewing his work you may think he's on to something. Call for an appointment.

A Halley's Comet Production
(252) 473-1713

Clockman Craig Robb creates one-of-a-kind designs that can personalize a variety of clock styles. Photos, logos, original artwork, handprints and more can be incorporated in his work. Some of Robb's clocks have shown up in fine-art shows, so he's an artist as well as a craftsman. He also creates photo calendars that make wonderful year round gifts.

Nags Head

Ray Matthews Photographer
(252) 441-7941

Ray Matthews has been living on the Outer Banks for more than 25 years during which time he has developed a love for nature that is presented masterfully in his prints. While the Outer Banks is a real haven for the photographic arts, the height of excellence is represented in Matthews' work. He is a consummate custom-slide printer as well as a commercial photographer. His work is shown at Browning Artworks in Buxton, The Christmas Shop in Manteo, Greenleaf galleries in Duck and Nags Head and Outer Banks Style in Corolla. Call for an appointment. He is available year round.

Roanoke Island

The Hat Lady
(252) 473-1850

This is the working studio of Genna Miles who creates fine-art wearable hats in one-of-a-kind-only designs. Miles employs spinning and crochet techniques with natural, hand-dyed fibers and trinkets to set off these artistic creations that will warm your head and your heart. Her baby bonnets crafted in 100 percent cotton are precious. Miles takes commissions, or her work can be seen at The Frame Shop in Manteo and in many of the annual Outer Banks art exhibitions where, at times, she breaks away from headwear and creates fiber and mixed-media sculptures that reflect her love for nostalgic items and thrift-store treasures.

John Silver
(252) 473-6240

John Silver is full-time artist who's made a big splash with his brilliant watercolors of old beach cottages and beach scenes. His use of cobalt blue is breathtaking! You can feel the heat rise off his beach scenes that are drenched in nostalgia. He has an annual show at a private cottage every November, but you can call his studio to see his work year round.

Petie Brigham
(252) 475-1515

Petie Brigham is a newcomer to the Outer Banks, but already she has made her mark on the art scene. Brigham specializes in landscape painting with the focus on sound and seashore scenes. She works in alkyds, a form of oil paint that's characterized by brilliant colors. If you had to explain

The Lost Colony outdoor drama re-enacts Roanoke Island's 16th-century history nightly during the summer.

Brigham's work in a word, you would do well to choose "atmospheric." She takes commissions and works in a variety of sizes from the miniature to the mammoth. Call for an appointment.

Hatteras Island

Michael Halminski Studio and Gallery
Midgett Way, Waves • (252) 987-2401

Outer Banks seascapes and landscapes dominate the photography collection displayed at this studio. The bird photos are inspiring, especially his egret pictures. Call for an appointment. Halminski also has a fine collection of cards that features his work.

Russell Yerkes
Sandy Bay Gallery, N.C. Hwy. 12, Hatteras Village • (252) 986-1283

Yerkes is an award-winning watercolorist who likes to create a sense of mystery in his lush paintings. He focuses on fish and creates fluid patterns and personalities in his creatures that usually have a deeper meaning than just an aquatic scene. Yerkes operates this gallery year round. He does commissions and his work can be seen here and at the two Greenleaf Gallery locations, in Nags Head and Duck.

Juried Art Exhibitions

The Outer Banks offers several juried art exhibitions each year. While the traditional definition of juried implies that work is selected for showing by judges, most shows here have an open-entry policy, and the work is judged for excellence and originality. Most shows have an entry fee that averages $10 to $15. Here we've listed the major shows in the area; for detailed information, call the galleries mentioned or the Dare County Arts Council, (252) 441-5617. New shows are always cropping up, so keep in touch with the arts council. See our Annual Events chapter for more art activities.

Nags Head

Dance Studios

Frank Stick Memorial Art Show
Glenn Eure's Ghost Fleet Gallery, Gallery Row, 210 E. Driftwood St., Nags Head • (252) 441-5617

This February show is open to Dare County residents and Dare County Arts Council members. One piece of work can be entered. Size restrictions apply. All genres of art are welcome; some restrictions apply.

International Miniature Art Show
Seaside Art Gallery, N.C. Hwy. 12, MP 11, Nags Head • (252) 441-5418

Any artist may enter this May show held at Seaside Art Gallery. Work entered cannot exceed 40 inches. The show features mini-paintings, drawings, sculpture, wood-turned bowls, collages and more.

International Icarus Art Show
Various locations, Nags Head • (252) 441-6584

Open to any artist this show is held in December at Glenn Eure's Ghost Fleet Gallery, the Seaside Art Gallery and the DCAC Gallery. The show's theme always revolves around flight as the show was created to be an annual nod to man's first powered flight.

Atlantic Dance Studio
Dare Centre, U.S. Hwy. 158, MP 7, Kill Devil Hills • (252) 441-9009

This studio run by Victoria Toms is a super addition to the Outer Banks creative scene. Toms brings with her an outstanding history of professional dance experience. She studied under the Martha Graham School of Contemporary Dance and the Joffrey Ballet. Atlantic Dance Studio offers lessons for adults and children in tap, ballet, jazz, gymnastics and modeling. During the summer of 1998, the studio will offer a summer camp featuring those genres. Locals and visitors are welcome — both beginners and professionals.

A boutique carries garments, shoes, bags and dance paraphernalia — all the items dancers need to keep them on their toes.

Island Dance Studio
3017 Virginia Dare Tr., Nags Head • (252) 441-6789

Sophia Sharp has been teaching dance on the Outer Banks for 18 years. She offers classes in ballet, jazz, tap, and preschool movement. Sharp's studio closes during the summer, so she caters mostly to local folks. She teaches children and adults.

From art extravaganzas and chili cookoffs to poetry readings and zippy kite competitions, we manage to put together dozens of special events at creative venues.

Annual Events

When it comes to annual events on the Outer Banks, the environment and history are on our side. We have our time-honored cornerstones that draw national audiences: the festivities scheduled each December that surround the anniversary of man's first powered flight and the annual celebrations that revolve around Virginia Dare's birthday. Our environment is the calling card for national surfing championships, hang-gliding events and world-class fishing tournaments. May 1998 marked the arrival of Olympic hopefuls for the American Canoe Association's Marathon Team Trials.

As for venues, we manage to make do without an abundance of large event sites. Often our public buildings do double-duty. We use school auditoriums and gyms. Our patience for more high-quality annual events is rewarded as our calendar of happenings grows longer and richer every year.

Our vigilance and special location helped us again secure the Babe Ruth World Series in August. Also in 1998 we introduce the Roanoke Island Festival Park (RIFP), a breathtaking new state facility complete with a visual arts gallery, 230-seat film theater, an outdoor pavilion with lawn seating for 3,500 people and an 8,500-square-foot exhibit hall. Already, local audiences have experienced exciting events there including the North Carolina Arts Council Artist's Fellowship Show and a local presentation of *The Fantastics,* performed by Dare County's Little Big Theater Company. This summer, the North Carolina School of the Arts in Winston-Salem will be in summer residence at the Festival Park, offering public drama, dance and musical performances. Four big annual concerts (targeted for Memorial Day, Fourth of July, Labor Day and mid-autumn) will be held at the pavilion. Country chart-toppers Diamond Rio got the fun started on Memorial Day weekend 1998.

Our restaurants offer the annual Taste of the Beach, featuring talented chefs with awe-inspiring credentials. Our St. Patrick's Day Parade that promenades down the Beach Road in Nags Head each March is said to be the largest in the state. Retail stores, art galleries, the Outer Banks Chamber of Commerce and state sites also sponsor happenings such as dramatic vignettes, printmaking workshops, nature films, luncheons, lectures and book signings.

Manteo Booksellers in downtown Manteo holds a signing every week from mid-June through Labor Day. These generally begin at 1 or 2 PM and last two hours. Authors of local and national repute have participated, including National Book Award winner Bob Shacochis and Pen Hemingway Award winner Mark Richard. Book subjects include both serious and humorous nonfiction and fiction works. Occasionally they schedule an evening reading by an author; call (252) 473-1221 for more information on these free happenings.

Check out our Arts and Culture chapter for other options. The Outer Banks Forum, (252) 261-1998, offers a variety of musical performances, drama and comedy plays in February, March, May, October and December. Look to the Theatre of Dare, (252) 441-6726, for comedy and drama performances in late February/early March, May and November. The Dare County Arts Council (DCAC), (252) 441-5617, is planning a Shakespearean festival in fall 1998.

It's the Time of the Season

As you might expect in an area so subject to seasonality, the number of festivals and events varies in a way that's in large part tied to the calendar.

The winter months are the leanest when it comes to annual public events. Your best bet for scheduled activities is to call the DCAC at the number listed previously, or the Roanoke Island Festival Park's 24-hour events line — (252) 475-1506 or (252) 475-1500. In January 1998, the DCAC held a free fine-arts slide series in conjunction with the North Carolina Museum of Art's community outreach program. The group also offered a workshop bimonthly — "Drawing, Painting, Coffee & Conversation" — that provided an opportunity for professional and nonprofessional artists to meet and work together.

The RIFP, across Shallowbag Bay from the Manteo Waterfront, had a fabulous showing of floral oil paintings by a Lexington, North Carolina, artist, coupled with a tea and sherry reception featuring live piano music and mouth-watering delicacies. Monthly gallery receptions and shows are free to the public. The park is open Monday through Friday from 9 AM to 5 PM.

January also is a great time to visit our wildlife refuges and do some birdwatching. Waterfowl flock to our wetlands in droves, and the variety you'll find here is breathtaking. Naturally such excursions are free — a pair of binoculars is all you need. The Cape Hatteras Bird Club, (252) 995-4777, offers a guided bird walk, and the Pea Island National Wildlife Refuge, (252) 473-1131, has observation platforms throughout the refuge. Look for migrant warblers, heron, egrets and Savannah sparrows and at least two dozen species of ducks. Thousands of snow geese, Canada geese and tundra swan winter here as well. See our Natural Wonders chapter for more information.

Jockey's Ridge State Park in Nags Head, (252) 441-7132, offers various programs in winter including bird walks on Saturday mornings, and the North Carolina Aquarium on Roanoke Island, (252) 473-3494, hosts programs and films. If you enjoy cards, seniors can play open and duplicate bridge at the Thomas A. Baum Senior Center in Kill Devil Hills, (252) 441-1181 (see our Real Estate and Retirement chapters), evenings and afternoons during the week.

Traditionally, February is a big cultural arts

month. The calendar was full in 1998 with exhibitions, musicals, theater productions and even opera. March is a mixed bag when it comes to events — both indoors and out. Check our listing for Kitty Hawk Kayaks, (252) 441-6800, (800) 948-0759, in our Watersports chapter. They always have a few interesting trips planned. Call the DCAC for its monthly schedule as well.

Easter events such as egg hunts and so forth will fluctuate, depending on when Easter occurs. Many stores and businesses offer egg hunts, and these are usually advertised on the radio, in the local papers or on marquees. April is a pivotal month for Outer Bankers. Easter marks the beginning of our tourist season, so visitors can expect more events and more people. The bluefin tuna seasons ends, and the tasty dolphin (also known as mahi mahi, and not to be confused with the dolphins of *Flipper* fame) begin to show. Fishing tournament season officially starts. The Outer Banks Senior Games, hosted by the Baum Senior Center and detailed in this chapter, are held in April.

May is a holiday month, so plenty of activities will be planned by local businesses and nonprofit groups. Kitty Hawk Kayaks offers at least a half-dozen paddling excursions and the ACA Marathon Team Trials for their Surf Kayak Rodeo competitions held in September.

June is filled with exciting activities. EcoCamps are offered by the Nags Head Woods Preserve, (252) 441-2525, for children of all ages, but registration must be received before June. The National Park Service, (252) 473-2111, offers free educational activities and programs from mid-June through Labor Day. The film theater at Roanoke Island Festival Park will be in full swing early in June when it hosts Molasses Creek, an Ocracoke band. Country star Ricky Van Shelton is scheduled to perform in the RIFP pavilion as part of Manteo's biggest annual celebration, Dare Day.

The July 4 night skies dazzle, as various townships put on fireworks shows that cityfolk say are some of the best they've seen. Some Nags Head residents claim they can see three displays in one night from homes with high elevations. Boats gather in the sounds and sea for the occasion; lights sparkling in the darkness from vessels large and small add to the evening affairs. There are fireworks displays from Corolla to Ocracoke.

When autumn rolls around, kayaking, kiting and king mackerel tournaments highlight the calendar. If Halloween is your bag, you'll love to stop by the Christmas Shop in Manteo where they have a room or two devoted to this spooky holiday. Also, check out our listing for the annual Haunted History tours of Waterside Theater for a fun and educational scarefest.

Holiday festivities fill up December's Outer Banks calender. The annual Hotline Festival of Trees is a don't-miss event. Why not take the year off from trimming a tree and purchase a one-of-a-kind, fully decorated tree at this special charity event?

We've indicated admission or entry fees whenever possible for the events we've highlighted. For fishing tournament fees call the marina noted. These fees vary greatly depending on the category you enter.

From art extravaganzas and chili cookoffs to poetry readings and zippy kite competitions, we manage to put together special events at creative venues in all corners of our crazy little world. So without further ado, we lift the curtain on our annual offerings.

January

The Dare County Schools Annual Art Show
Glenn Eure's Ghost Fleet Gallery, 210 E. Driftwood St., Gallery Row, Nags Head • (252) 441-6585

For one week in mid-January, the Dare County Schools put together an art show that showcases works by kids from seven public schools, grades K-12. If you like children's art, this is the show for you. It's not surprising that the work is exceptional, what with the large population of adult artists living on the Outer Banks. Artist or not, parents here are very supportive, and many kids have taken years of private art lessons.

The works range from delightful watercolors to wild chairs crafted after the student's favorite artist. The Georgia O'Keefe and Picasso chairs were awesome at the most recent exhibition. This show is primarily for viewing — it's difficult to wrestle work away from parents. Don't expect to make any purchases, although some high school students may be more inclined to sell for some pocket money. The show's reception is on a Sunday, generally at 2 PM. Call for more information. Admission is free, and you can't beat the brownies and other goodies they serve.

February

The Frank Stick Memorial Art Show
Glenn Eure's Ghost Fleet Gallery, 210 E. Driftwood St., Gallery Row, Nags Head • (252) 441-5617

This art show celebrated its 20th year in 1998. It's held in early February and features the work of more than 160 artists (see our Arts and Culture chapter). If you want to submit work, you must be a Dare County resident or a member of the Dare County Arts Council, which sponsors the show. Stop in for the reception, which is always held at 2 PM on the first Sunday of the month, or leisurely view the show throughout the month of February. The reception is free. The 1998 entry fees for artists were $15 for nonmembers and $10 for members submitting one work. The works are judged for merit and excellence, with $150 and $50 prizes given to the winners. Visitors also vote for the "Peoples Choice Award." Judges from outside the local area are chosen.

Expect a varied palette here. Art ranges from traditional floral watercolors to thought-provoking conceptual pieces. Area artisans show off pottery, stained glass and meticulously handcarved and painted waterfowl. Artists working in three-dimensional formats showcase wire, bronze, wood and iron sculpture. Jewelers present sterling silver metalworks. Shadow boxes filled with found objects intrigue us, and party dresses and hats become wall art or part of three-dimensional paintings. Photography entries have ranged from the breathtaking aerial overview that shows the fragility of our barrier

This Bud's for the creator of these amazing sand sculptures.

islands to a crazy nude coupled with collage items. The printmaker has a heyday with etchings, woodcuts, collagraphs and seriographs from the totally abstract to the representational.

This is the best venue to see what area artists have been producing of late. Many artists go out on a limb introducing new styles (at least new for them!). It's a fun show, and the reception becomes an annual get-together for locals and visitors alike.

"A Literary Evening"
Glenn Eure's Ghost Fleet Gallery, 210 E. Driftwood St., Gallery Row, Nags Head • (252) 441-6584

This free event is held in mid-February as part of the month-long Frank Stick Memorial Art Show. Members of the Dare County Writers Group and other guests read original recent works. Poetry as well as humorous essays have a forum here. We even have witnessed barking dogs as part of one off-the-wall performance (but that's not the norm). The group, sponsored by the Dare County Arts Council, meets monthly on Thursdays at the Kill Devil Hills branch of the Dare County Library. It's open to all writers, and meetings are informal. Admission to "A Literary Evening" is free.

Outer Banks Forum
Kitty Hawk Elementary School, U.S. Hwy. 158, MP 1, Kitty Hawk • (252) 261-1998

The Outer Banks Forum introduced the National Opera Company's performance of Rossini's *The Barber of Seville* in late February 1998. The playbill doesn't always herald opera; the palette is varied (see our Arts and Culture chapter for more information on what the OBF offers audiences). Performances usually are scheduled at 7:30 PM. Admission is $10 at the door or by subscription.

March

Dare County Arts Council Photography Show
DCAC Gallery, Central Square, U.S. Hwy. 158, MP 11, Nags Head • (252) 441-5617

The Dare County Arts Council holds a photography show that hangs for three weeks and includes an evening reception. It's open to professional and amateur photographers. Call for information or write P.O. Box 2815, Kill Devil Hills, NC 27948. There is no admission fee to the show or reception, but artists pay a registration fee — $15 for members of the Dare County Arts Council, $25 for nonmembers. Generally, artists show three works. Expect the images to run the gamut from the beginner showcasing a Polaroid snapshot of kids to the mature artist submitting high-quality advertising art, coastal scenes, infrared photography or fine art black and white photos. The exhibition will be in its fourth season in 1999.

St. Patrick's Day Parade
N.C. Hwy. 12, Nags Head • (252) 441-4116

The St. Patrick's Day Parade — sponsored in 1998 by Kelly's Restaurant, East Carolina Radio and Falcon Cable — is held the Sunday before St. Patrick's Day every year. The parade begins at the Nags Head Fishing Pier at MP 12 on the Beach Road and proceeds north to about MP 10. Reputed to be the largest parade of its kind in North Carolina, the event is always fun for the whole family. Float participants throw candy, so wear something with pockets! Kelly's serves free hot dogs and sodas after the parade, and there's an evening of live entertainment at Kelly's under a tent. All events are free.

Pirate's Cove Inshore/Offshore Fishing School
Pirate's Cove Yacht Club, Manteo/Nags Head Cswy., Manteo • (252) 473-1451, (800) 762-0245

In its sixth year in 1999, this one-day, mid-March program features North Carolina fishing experts conducting hands-on round-table sessions at Pirate's Cove Yacht Club. The three-session program will be held at the club's

restaurant, clubhouse and fitness center. Pick up an entry form at Capt. Marty's Fishing and Hunting Tackle Shop on U.S. 158 in Nags Head (see our Shopping chapter) or at Pirate's Cove Yacht Club. The day is rounded out with a pig-pickin' and beer social at Capt. Marty's. The fee is $100 per person. Anglers of all skill levels are welcome. Offshore fishing and bait-rigging is demonstrated.

April

Kitty Hawk Kites Annual Easter Egg Hunt
U.S. Hwy. 158, MP 12, Nags Head • (252) 441-4124, (800) 334-4777

This event is held at Kitty Hawk Kites in Nags Head, with the specific date dependant on when Easter falls. Kids will enjoy the chalk coloring contests, a variety of games and, of course, an Easter egg hunt on the premises. Small fries will get a kick out of meeting KHK's fuzzy brown mascot Wil-Bear Wright. All activities are free.

Kelly's Midnight Easter Egg Hunt
Kelly's Outer Banks Restaurant, U.S. Hwy. 158, MP 10½, Nags Head • (252) 441-4116

Adults enjoy searching for treats by flashlight. It's lots of fun, and it's free. Anyone 21 or older may participate in this late-night egg hunt on the restaurant premises. The event's exact date depends on when Easter falls. Participants find eggs that may be empty or contain prizes such as gift certificates, free drink coupons or free T-shirt coupons. Stop in the tavern prior to the event for a drink or some great light fare at reasonable prices. The Mediterranean pizza is killer!

Taste of the Beach
Location varies • (252) 441-4116

Local restaurants and beverage distributors provide the public with a taste of their best Outer Banks treats in mid-April. Enjoy seafood and pasta specialties, fine wines and beers and a whole lot more, all at one central location. Past venues for the event have included the Outer Banks Mall and the large, empty store space at the Dare Centre. The admission fee is usually $10. We advise you to get there early. It's a very popular event with locals; in fact, it's as much a social get-together as it is a sampling of the culinary delights the beach offers in some of the finest restaurants around. When asked about the best places to eat on the Outer Banks, we usually just hand over our guidebook — it's hard to make a choice. This festive event does a good job of luring you to specific eateries.

The Outer Banks Senior Games
Thomas A. Baum Senior Center, 300 Mustian St., Kill Devil Hills
• (252) 441-1181

The Outer Banks Senior Games celebrated its 10th year in 1998. Dare County seniors 55 and older are eligible to compete in this competition that features shuffleboard, billiards, spin casting, golf, bowling, horseshoes, table tennis and much more. All ages are welcome to watch and cheer for the competitors in this mid-April event.

A modified version of the games is offered for challenged seniors. Volunteers work with each individual needing assistance. Games for this group can include door basketball and rubber horseshoes. The local group of seniors sends hundreds of competitors to state competitions every year. Some even have gone on to the national contest. The festivities include dinner at a local restaurant. The registration fee is $6 to participate in four events including the arts competition (see next listing) and includes lunch on opening day and on track and field day.

The Outer Banks Silver Arts Competition
Thomas A. Baum Senior Center, 300 Mustian St., Kill Devil Hills
• (252) 441-1181

This is the art component of the Outer Banks Senior Games featuring an exhibition of talent and craftsmanship in the visual, literary, heritage and performing arts. The events last for several days culminating in a free evening performance at the Kitty Hawk Elementary School. The $6 games registration fee covers entry into the arts competition.

Wines of the World Weekend
Pirate's Cove Yacht Club, Manteo/Nags Head Cswy., Manteo • (252) 473-1451, (800) 762-0245

Partake in an afternoon winetasting for $25 and enjoy discussions with wine experts under a tent at Pirate's Cove Yacht Club. Dinner follows at Penguin Isle in Nags Head and features a multi-course menu accompanied by wines that complement the fare. Dinner is $55 per person. This is a fun opportunity to gain knowledge while imbibing the curriculum! Call the above number to make a reservation and get directions to the site. The Pirate's Cove complex is massive, but the guard at the gate gives good directions. The 1998 event was held late in April, but the weekend has been scheduled in February in years past. Call early in the year to be sure.

Outer Banks Chamber of Commerce Small Business Expo
The Marketplace, U.S. Hwy. 158, MP 1, Southern Shores • (252) 441-8144

The local chamber sponsors a free expo that showcases the products and services of local businesses. Booths are set up in the former Food Lion building to explain retail products, and demonstrations are given. You'll find a big variety, from furniture retailers to water service and insurance companies. The expo occurs in late April and is an all-day affair. Call for details and to procure an information packet if you're interested in participating.

INSIDERS' TIP

If you want to enter the local Frank Stick Art Show but are not a Dare County resident, just join the Dare County Arts Council, and you'll qualify. You'll have a chance to win a cash prize, show your work and help support the arts with your entry fee.

Windfest 99
Frisco Woods Campground, N.C. Hwy. 12, Frisco • (252) 995-5208, (800) 948-3942

Wind lovers will enjoy this event, which also benefits charity. All donations go to the Cape Hatteras Meals on Wheels program. Bed down at the campground for a fee (see our Camping chapter) and enjoy the rest of the event for a donation. Windsurfing reps will offer free demos; join in the regatta and end each evening of the three-day festival with a cookout. The folks at Frisco Woods promise lots of wind and good company. Bring your own wind rider or use one of theirs. The donation covers your meals.

May

Hatteras Village Offshore Open Billfish Tournament
Hatteras Harbor Marina, N.C. Hwy. 12, Hatteras Village • (252) 986-2166

Anglers contend for prizes as they fish to catch and release the biggest billfish. A meat fish category is included for the largest tuna, dolphin and wahoo caught daily. The three-day fishing tournament is held in early May and sponsored by the Hatteras Village Civic Association. This is a Governor's Cup-sanctioned event, so anglers competing in the Governor's Cup challenge can include this tournament in their fishing schedule. All competitors must enter Level 1 for $500; two additional levels — Level 2 at $700 and Level 3 at $300 — are not mandatory. Fishing begins at 8 AM, and lines come out of the water promptly at 3 PM. Festivities with food and drink are usually held each evening. The event closes with an awards banquet. The tournament is open to the public.

Mollie Fearing Memorial Art Show
Central Square, U.S. Hwy. 158, MP 11, Nags Head • (252) 441-5617

This exhibition replaces the annual spring art show sponsored by the Dare County Arts Council. Mollie Fearing, one of the founders of the local cultural arts group, The Sea And Sounds Arts Council, which was the precursor of the current DCAC, died in 1997. To honor this former mayor of Manteo's efforts to promote the arts, the council voted to name their spring fling after Fearing. The show is open to all artists, and $2,000 in cash awards are given. It runs mid-May through late June and is open for public viewing (see our Arts and Culture chapter for gallery hours). Entry fees for 1997 were $15 for members and $25 for nonmembers. Call for membership, reception and entry information.

Hang Gliding Spectacular
Jockey's Ridge State Park, U.S. Hwy. 158, MP 12, Nags Head • (252) 441-4124, (800) 334-4777
Currituck County Airport, U.S. Hwy. 158, Barco • (800) 334-4777

Spectators and participants cover the dunes at the park every year to attend the longest-running hang-gliding competition in the country (1998 marks the 26th consecutive year). Pilots from all over the world compete in a variety of flying maneuvers including an aerotow competition. Beginning hang-gliding lessons are given. The event is sponsored by Kitty Hawk Kites, and a complimentary street dance and an awards ceremony add icing to the cake! Annual inductions to the Rogallo Hall Of Fame (Francis Rogallo is the father of the Flexible Wing Flyer — the prototype for the modern hang glider) will close the ceremony. Hang glider pilots who have achieved their Hang One are welcome to compete. The public is invited to view the event for free. Participants pay $35.

British Cemetery Ceremony
British Cemetery Rd., Ocracoke Island • (252) 928-3711

May 11 marks the commemoration of the 1942 sinking of the British trawler HMS *Bedfordshire*. A British official is sent to Ocracoke each year to attend this U.S. Coast Guard service. Four bodies of British naval seamen are buried in the British Cemetery. Their ship was stationed off Ocracoke to protect our shores during the beginning of World War II. The armed trawler was torpedoed and sunk by a German submarine on

The largest St. Patrick's Day parade in eastern North Carolina is held in Nags Head.

May 11. All perished, and the four bodies were the only ones recovered; they were buried by island residents. A plaque at the cemetery memorializes the men: "If I should die think only this of me that there's some forever corner of a foreign field that is forever England." This event is free. (See our Attractions chapter for more historic information.)

Nags Head Woods 5K Run
Nags Head Woods Preserve, Ocean Acres Dr., Kill Devil Hills
• (252) 441-2525

Folks from all walks of life run side by side through Nags Head Woods in this annual event that's held on a Saturday in early May. The run is limited to the first 400 runners to register. To participate, write Nags Head Woods 5K Run, 701 W. Ocean Acres Drive, Kill Devil Hills, NC 27948. Entry fee is $15 for adults, $10 for children 12 and younger and $7.50 for the post-run party that features music, food and drinks. Proceeds benefit Nags Head Woods.

Ocracoke Arts and Crafts Festival
Howard St., Ocracoke • (252) 928-6711

More than a dozen booths are set up to display wares including pottery, woodwork-ing, paintings, photography and glassware on Howard Street. Folks generally park at the Ocracoke School or nearby Ocracoke United Methodist Church. There's no admission fee. The festival date varies year to year but usually occurs in mid- to late May.

International Miniature Art Show
Seaside Art Gallery, N.C. Hwy. 12, MP 11, Nags Head • (252) 441-5418, (800) 828-2444

Artists from all over the world compete for cash prizes in this exhibition of miniature art. Past shows (the event was in its sixth year in 1998) have seen more than 450 works from 38 states and 12 countries. The work includes paintings, sculpture and drawings of all styles. The art is available for viewing for about two weeks. The reception occurs in late May. Call the above number for a prospectus for this annual event.

Memorial Day Weekend Arts & Crafts Fair
Ramada Inn, N.C. Hwy. 12, MP 9½, Kill Devil Hills • (252) 261-3196

Sponsored by the Outer Banks Women's Club, the fair showcases a wide variety of wares such as carved wooden birds, dolls and traditional, functional crafts. Admission is $1.

Pirate's Cove Memorial Weekend Tournament

Pirate's Cove Yacht Club, Nags Head/ Manteo Cswy., Manteo • (252) 473-3700, (800) 537-7245

This tournament is for pure fun only. No money prizes are awarded, but contenders can go home with a trophy. There is a $150 team entry fee. Anglers head offshore to fish for billfish, tuna, dolphin and wahoo. All billfish are released, and there is a prize for the largest release and the combined weight of the three largest meat fish caught per team. Call for entry dates and more information.

June

Dare Day Festival

Downtown Manteo • (252) 473-1101 ext. 319

Always held the first Saturday of June, Dare Day features arts and crafts, food (including yummy soft-shell crabs!), national and local musical entertainment and an evening street dance. The free event is sponsored by the Town of Manteo and Dare County. Ricky Van Shelton is the 1998 headliner. The free concert, which had generally been held on Queen Elizabeth Street in downtown Manteo, will be held in 1998 at the pavilion at Roanoke Island Festival Park, located at the Elizabeth II State Historic Site, across Shallowbag Bay from the Manteo Waterfront.

Rogallo Kite Festival

Jockey's Ridge State Park, U.S. Hwy. 158, MP 12, Nags Head • (800) 334-4777

This two-day, free, family fun fly in early June celebrates the beauty of kite flying and honors the father of hang gliding, NASA scientist Francis Rogallo. It is open to kite enthusiasts of all ages and features stunt kites, home-builts, kids' kite making and flying

competitions, and an auction where you can bid on display and demo stunt kites. Rogallo, the inventor of the flexible wing, generally makes an appearance. The event, sponsored by Kitty Hawk Kites, celebrates its 17th year in 1998.

The Art of Larry Johnson

Morales Art Gallery, Scarborough Faire, N.C. Hwy. 12, Duck • (252) 261-7190

North Carolina watercolorist Larry Johnson exhibits his work for a week during early June. Johnson will be on hand part of the week to demonstrate how he creates his beautiful beach scenes. Call for exact times and dates.

Roanoke Island Festival Park Gallery Art Show

Roanoke Island Festival Park, Elizabeth II State Historic Site, across from Manteo Waterfront • (252) 475-1500

At this show, Michael John Davis will display shadow box art that is meticulously handcrafted and accented with a philosophical twist. Three-dimensional images appear in the handpainted boxes coupled with a thought-provoking saying. Davis has won many Excellence Awards for the work he's exhibited in the local Frank Stick Memorial Art Show (see our February listings). The show runs all month and features a reception in early June. This is a free event.

Outer Banks Outdoors Kayak Jamboree

Waterworks Tower, Manteo/Nags Head Cswy., Nags Head • (252) 441-4124, (800) 334-4777

Try out new kayaks and explore Outer Banks salt marshes and channels from 9 AM until sunset in late June. Guides are available, and there are kayaks for rent if you don't bring your own. The event also features paddling exhibitions, demonstrations of new equipment, hourly tours and games. The event is in its fifth year in 1998. Call for a calender of special paddling and water events scheduled all week long.

The Art of Linda Nye
Morales Art Gallery, Scarborough Faire, N.C. Hwy. 12, Duck • (252) 261-7190

This Ohio watercolorist will exhibit her work for a week mid- to late-June at this northern beach gallery. She'll also demonstrate how she creates her landscapes and florals free of charge. Call for times and dates.

Hatteras Marlin Club Billfish Tournament
Hatteras Marlin Club, off N.C. Hwy. 12, Hatteras Village • (252) 986-2454

Celebrating its 39th year in 1998, the Hatteras Marlin Club Billfish Tournament offers a week of competition fishing and entertainment to participants and their guests. Teams head for offshore waters looking to catch the biggest billfish or meat fish including blue marlin, tuna, dolphin and wahoo. Evenings are filled with socials that include entertainment, cocktails, appetizers and dinner. The tournament is for members and anglers invited by the tournament committee. Write for membership and tournament information to Box 218, Hatteras, NC 27943. Registration costs $1,500.

Wil-Bear's Festival of Fun
Kitty Hawk Connection, U.S. Hwy. 158, MP 12, Nags Head • (252) 441-4124, (800) 334-4777

Children of all ages are thrilled by kite flying, yo-yo stunts, face painting and free balloons. The star of the day is Wil-Bear Wright, the colorful Kitty Hawk Kites mascot. This free event is held in mid-June.

The Art of Scott Gibbs
Morales Art Gallery, Scarborough Faire, N.C. Hwy. 12, Duck • (252) 261-7190

Scott Gibbs wows visitors with his fantastic Ostrich and Rhea handpainted eggs. The Ohio artist's work will be on display for a week in late June and early July. He'll demonstrate his craft during part of the week. There is no charge to watch, view the work or ask questions. Call for dates and times.

Wanchese Seafood Festival
Harbor Rd., Wanchese • (252) 441-8144

This event features the Blessing of the Fleet (the Outer Banks and, more specifically, Wanchese are home to a sizeable recreational and commercial fishing fleet), arts and crafts vendors, educational displays, crab races, children's games and lots and lots of seafood. The festival celebrates its 16th year in 1998. It's held the last Saturday in June, and admission is free and open to the public. As with most fairs, you'll pay for any trinkets you purchase, and there is a cost of about $10 for a heaping plate of seafood.

Windrider National Championship & Sailing Jamboree
Location to be announced • (800) 334-4777

This two-day event, sponsored by Kitty Hawk Kites and Outer Banks Outdoors, features windsurfing and sailing demos and lessons, plus races and a barbecue. Novice sailors can contend. Experience the thrill of multi-hull sailing in a tri-hull Windrider sailboat. Free demonstration sails begin at 9 AM and continue through sunset. The late June event is free to watch. Pre-register for boat rental. The registration fee is $40.

The Art of Liz Corsa
Morales Art Gallery, Scarborough Faire, N.C. Hwy. 12, Duck • (252) 261-7190

Liz Corsa's delightful watercolors are a must-see and will be on display for a week during late June. Several days will be set aside for Corsa to demonstrate her watercolor style to interested viewers. Corsa is rapidly becoming known for her whimsical and intelligent animal art that could be described as modern-day Beatrix Potter wrapped in plenty of humor. Call for times and dates.

Duck Village Art Show
Various locations, Duck • (252) 441-5617

This outdoor show was a smash hit in 1997 (its first year), so the Dare County Arts Council decided to keep it going. Artists and crafters set up booths and tents and sell wares to visitors walking through the quaint village. You can tour the whole show on foot. Refreshment booths offer cool drinks. Expect work to include paintings, drawings, pottery, glassware and more. This is a late June event.

July

Youth Fishing Tournament
Piers from Kitty Hawk to Nags Head • (252) 441-5464

This tournament is a low-key pier- and surf-fishing competition for kids ages 4 to 16. The cost is 50¢ per person, and you register at all oceanfront fishing piers from Kitty Hawk to Nags Head. It's sponsored by the Nags Head Surf Fishing Club, North Carolina Beach Buggy Association and the North Carolina Sea Hags. The event is held in early July. It lasts from 8 AM until 1 PM, ending with an awards ceremony at the Outer Banks Mall in Nags Head.

Sand Sculpture Contest
On the beach north of Ocracoke Village • (252) 995-4474

This artistic endeavor kicks off Fourth of July festivities on the island. Kids and adults are welcome to participate in the early morning event. You can work alone or in groups. Past events have seen sand transformed into turtles, jumping dolphin, pirates and ships. There's no entry fee for the contest. Call for times and location.

Independence Day Parade and Fireworks Display
Ocracoke Village • (252) 928-6711

This festive parade featuring about a half-dozen floats makes its way through the streets starting around 3 PM on July 4. Local shopkeepers and residents get creative making floats for what's dubbed the village's biggest annual event. The parade moves down N.C. 12 from Captain Ben's Restaurant through Ocracoke Village. The evening ends with a gala fireworks display at Lifeguard Beach. Ocracokers say it's the best Fourth of July celebration on the Outer Banks.

Teach's Lair Marina 4th of July Party
N.C. Hwy. 12, Hatteras Village • (252) 986-2460

This evening gala features live music, and

fireworks are set off on the beach across from the marina. There is no charge to come. We suggest grabbing a seat on the beach for the best view.

Manteo Independence Day Celebration
Manteo Waterfront • (252) 473-1101

Activities run from 1 to 9 PM and include a Wacky Tacky Hat Contest, children's games, food and other concessions, musical entertainment and a street dance from 6 to 9 PM, when a fireworks display begins. The event is free.

Fireworks in Hatteras Village
Ferry docks

The fireworks sponsored by the Hatteras Village Civic Association and the Volunteer Fire Department start at 8:30 PM at the Hatteras Docks at the end of the fishing village. There is no admission fee.

Fireworks Festival and Fair
Whalehead Club, N.C. Hwy. 12, Corolla

The historic hunt club is the backdrop for the fireworks and fair that begin at 4 and run to 11 PM. The Currituck County Board of Commissioners and the Corolla Business Association host this event. Expect fun, food, live musical entertainment and, of course, pyrotechnics galore. Admission is free.

Seamark Foods Children's Tournament
Pirate's Cove Yacht Club, Manteo/Nags Head Cswy., Manteo • (252) 473-1451, (800) 537-7245

Special Olympics athletes are invited to attend this annual mid-July fishing tournament that allows kids to fish from area headboats. All tackle and bait is supplied. Call for more information, or write Barry Martin at P.O. Box 1997, Manteo, NC 27954 for entry fee information.

Annual Wright Kite Festival
Wright Brothers National Memorial, MP 8, Kill Devil Hills • (252) 441-4124, (800) 334-4777

This mid-July family event involves kite flying for all ages and also includes free kite-making workshops, stunt kite demos and children's games. The event, sponsored by

Photo: Courtesy of Bob Reardon

These Boy Scouts are prepared to march in a local parade.

Kitty Hawk Kites and the National Park Service, celebrates its 20th year in 1998. You can watch for free. Adults are invited to participate in kite contests. Call for fees.

The Art of Dave Cordas
Morales Art Gallery, Scarborough Faire, N.C. Hwy. 12, Duck • (252) 261-7190

Ohio artist David Cordas will exhibit his work mid-July as part of a weeklong exhibit and demonstration series held at Morales each summer. His work typifies classic watercolor; he uses a loose, flowing technique to create landscapes and beach scenes. There's no charge to watch Cordas demonstrate his art or to view the work. Call for dates and times.

Hermit Crab Race
Newman's Shell Shop, N.C. Hwy. 12, Nags Head • (252) 441-5791

Kids of all ages love this fun — and funny — event featuring hermit crabs. Seventy-five to 100 contestants vie for prizes on the last Saturday in July. Kids bring their own pet crabs or purchase one at the shell shop. There is no entry fee.

The Art of Dennis Lighthart
Morales Art Gallery, Scarborough Faire, N.C. Hwy. 12, Duck • (252) 261-7190

Lighthart will exhibit his watercolors and demonstrate how he create luminous coastal and rural landscapes. Call for times and dates.

Printmaking Workshop
Seaside Art Gallery, N.C. Hwy. 12, MP 11, Nags Head • (252) 441-8563, (800) 828-2444

Two artists, David Hunter and Glenn Eure, team up to present the art of etching and the collagraph. Watch the artists demonstrate their craft, ask questions and view work in early July. No charge.

North Carolina School of the Arts International Orchestra
Roanoke Island Festival Park, Elizabeth II State Historic Site, across from Manteo Waterfront • (252) 475-1500

Late July and early August, this top-notch group will perform in the Festival Park's pavilion as a final tribute to the summer-long institute held by the arts school at the Roanoke Island state site. Ticket information, times and the agenda were not available at presstime. Call for more information.

First Flight to World Flight
Dare County Regional Airport, Airport Rd., Manteo • (252) 473-2600

This cross-country race is sponsored by

the Experimental Aircraft Association. All aircraft are home-builts and will be flown by the pilots who constructed them. On the first of the event's two local days, aircraft will be on display at the Dare County Regional Airport; the launch is scheduled for the following day, with a destination of Oshkosh, Wisconsin. This is a late July event.

August

Annual Wacky Watermelon Weekend
Kitty Hawk Connection and Kitty Hawk Sports, U.S. Hwy. 158, MP 12, Nags Head • (252) 441-6800

This is the 14th year for this watermelon-centered event, which begins with a parade led by the state's Watermelon Queen and includes an Olympic watermelon toss, big league watermelon bowling, carving, long-distance seed spitting and watermelon consumption. The most energized event of the day is the Kamikaze Watermelon Drop — kids join in the on-premises tower and drop watermelons. Register at Kitty Hawk Sports' Nags Head store. The event is free.

Nags Head Woods Benefit Auction
The Sanderling Inn, N.C. Hwy. 12, Duck • (252) 441-2525

This annual benefit helps support the Nags Head Woods Ecological Preserve. The event is held the first weekend in August, and 1998 marks its eighth year. The benefit features food, cocktails, jazz and a huge silent and main auction featuring original art, jewelry and fantastic vacation packages. Auction sponsor tickets cost $100; admission is $50.

Annual Herbert Hoover Birthday Celebration
Manteo Booksellers, Sir Walter Raleigh St., Manteo • (252) 473-1221

Browse through this superb bookstore, munch on three cakes (each one inscribed with either "Happy," "Birthday" or "Herbie"), sip some famous "Herbert Sherbert" punch and chat with Hoover fans at this tongue-in-cheek free event. The reason for the fun? It's all done purely for the sake of having a celebration. The

day includes an author signing. Look for a special display of Hoover memorabilia. Come eat, drink and think Herbert Hoover!

Annual Senior Adults Craft Fair
Thomas A. Baum Center, 300 Mustian St., Kill Devil Hills • (252) 441-9388

Local senior citizens provide the crafts for this 25-year-old community project sponsored by the Outer Banks Women's Club. Admission is $1.

Alice Kelly Memorial Ladies Only Billfish Tournament
Pirate's Cove Yacht Club, Manteo/Nags Head Cswy., Manteo • (252) 473-6800, (800) 367-4728

The tournament, sponsored by Pirate's Cove, is in its ninth year and honors the memory of local fishing enthusiast Alice Kelly, who died in her 30s from Hodgkin's disease. Kelly was a high-spirited woman whose love for fishing inspired many local women to try (and fall in love with) the sport. Women form teams and arrange for charter boats to carry them out to sea. The tournament occurs in early August in 1998. Call for entry fee information.

United States Boomerang Association Outer Banks Competition
Kitty Hawk Connection, U.S. Hwy. 158, MP 12, Nags Head • (252) 441-4124, (800) 334-4777

This tournament presents the opportunity to learn how to throw a boomerang, thanks to instruction from some of the top boomers in the nation. The event features competition and lessons along with free stunt-kite demos and kite-making workshops. The two-day event is open to novice throwers. Workshops are held the second day. Registration fee is $30. Competition fees for individual events range from $5 to $10. The public is invited to watch free of charge.

Pirate's Cove Billfish Tournament
Pirate's Cove Yacht Club, Manteo/Nags Head Cwsy., Manteo • (252) 473-6800, (800) 367-4728

Pirate's Cove Yacht Club hosts a billfish release tournament that celebrates its 15th year in 1998. Contenders fish for several days trying to catch and release the largest billfish. A meat fish (tuna, dolphin and wahoo) category, in which a prize is awarded for the largest catch, adds to the fun. The tournament is an official part of the N.C. Governor's Cup Billfish Series and occurs mid-month. Call for entry fee information.

Babe Ruth World Series
Manteo High School, Coy Tillett Field, Wingina St., Manteo • (252) 473-1101

Ten baseball teams from across the nation meet in Manteo mid-August for a week of World Series championship games. Youths ages 16 to 18 contend for the top spot while the stands are filled with cheering well-wishers and professional talent scouts. Get in on the inside track by witnessing future collegiate, minor and major league players in action. Family passes and individual tickets will be available at area banks and at the Dare County Recreational Park in Kill Devil Hills beside the library off Mustian Street. An individual pass costs $35; a family pass costs $50.

New World Festival of the Arts
Manteo Waterfront • (252) 473-2838

Coordinated by The Christmas Shop, this mid-August event makes downtown Manteo come to life every year. The outdoor two-day show, which is in its 16th season, features 80 artists showcasing fine art and crafts including pottery, jewelry, paintings and more. Outdoor booths and tents line the waterfront. There is no admission fee. Call for booth registration fees.

National Aviation Day
Wright Brothers National Memorial, U.S. Hwy. 158, MP 8, Kill Devil Hills • (252) 441-7430

Explore planes galore at this free mid-month event. Aviation enthusiasts will enjoy viewing about 25 different types of single-engine aircraft ranging from the antique to modern-day models. The schedule is not firmed up until a few days before the event so that weather conditions can be taken into consideration. Past events have included a flyover with Air Force and Navy planes, jets from Langley Field and the Blue Angels. The day's festivities include free admission to the memorial.

Virginia Dare Day Celebration
Fort Raleigh National Historic Site Visitors Center, U.S. Hwy. 64/264, Roanoke Island • (252) 473-5772

This event, held August 18, commemorates the birth of Virginia Dare, the first English child born in the New World. The celebration features a daylong series of special happenings. Past events have featured members of the cast of *The Lost Colony* singing and dancing, and demonstrations of arms from that period in history. Call the National Park Service for details. This event is free.

Virginia Dare Night Performance of The Lost Colony
Waterside Theatre, U.S. Hwy. 64/264, Roanoke Island • (252) 473-3414, (800) 488-5012

Also on August 18, *The Lost Colony* celebrates Virginia Dare's 1587 birth by casting local infants in the role of the baby Virginia Dare. Tickets cost $14 for adults and $7 for children 11 and younger. (For more on the famous outdoor drama, see our Arts and Culture chapter.)

Labor Day Arts & Craft Show
Ramada Inn, U.S. Hwy. 158, Kill Devil Hills • (252) 261-3196

This Labor Day weekend event features traditional functional and country crafts and is sponsored by the Outer Banks Women's Club. Admission is $1.

September

"The Allison" Crippled Children's White Marlin Release Tournament
Pirate's Cove Yacht Club, Manteo/Nags Head Cwsy., Manteo • (252) 473-6800, (800) 537-7245

A charitable tournament that raises funds for handicapped kids, The Allison is in its sixth year. Travel offshore to the infamous Outer Banks fishing grounds and search for billfish and other pelagic species. All billfish caught are released. Bait and tackle are provided. The event takes place the first weekend in September. There are four categories; entry in category 1 ($700) is mandatory. Costs for the other categories are $500 for category 2 (which simply gives anglers a chance to up the ante), $500 for category 3 (which is the pool for the daily prize) and $400 for category 4 (the prize for the largest meat fish). Call for more information.

Weeping Radish Restaurant and Brewery Oktoberfest
U.S. Hwy. 64/264, Manteo
• (252) 473-1157

The Weeping Radish hosts its 13th Oktoberfest in 1998 during the second week in September. Expect a family-oriented outdoor celebration featuring Bavarian-style food, an oompah band, children's games, specially brewed German beer and a chance to win a trip to Germany. There is no admission fee.

Outer Banks Triathlon
Roanoke Island • (252) 480-0500

In its 14th year in 1998, the triathlon is held in early September. Entrants swim 0.6 miles, bike 15 miles and run 3.1 miles. The swimming segment is held at the ol' swimming hole at the north end of Roanoke Island; the running and biking thirds are done at the Dare County Regional Airport. Individuals can participate in all three events, or a team of three can split up the events. The entry fees for individual entrants are around $45 for Triathlon USA members and $50 for nonmembers. Team entries are $95 for Triathlon USA members and $105 for nonmembers. The event is limited to 300 participants.

Labor Day Arts and Crafts Show
Hatteras Civic Center, N.C. Hwy. 12, Hatteras Village • (252) 995-5179

This traditional arts and crafts fair is sponsored by the Hatteras Island Arts and Crafts Guild and features pottery, dolls, clockmaking, shellwork and countless other goodies. There is no admission fee.

Outer Banks Surf Kayak Festival
Ramada Inn, N.C. Hwy. 12, Kill Devil Hills • (252) 441-6800

Sponsored by Kitty Hawk Sports, this event (in its third year in 1998) is fun to watch or participate in. Expect surf kayak events for paddlers with intermediate and advanced skills. There are men's, women's, high-perfor-

mance and sit-on-top categories as well as a junior division. Included are cash prizes, demonstrations, used kayaks for sale, mini clinics, food and reduced rates if you stay at the Ramada Inn. Call for entry fee information.

NOWR Annual Outer Banks Surf Kayak Rodeo
Rodanthe Pier, N.C. Hwy 12, Rodanthe
• (252) 441-6800, (800) 948-0759

This mid- to late September event, held by the National Organization of Whitewater Rodeos, is in its third year in 1998. It features rodeo and traditional kayak surfing for the experienced and the novice kayaker. There are men's, women's and junior divisions. The two-day festivities include a silent auction, boat raffle, boat demos, food and music. Profits help promote recreational boating and to protect our rivers. Call Kitty Hawk Kayaks at the listed number for fees and dates.

Hatteras Village Civic Association Surf Fishing Tournament
Hatteras Village Civic Center, N.C. Hwy. 12, Hatteras Village • (252) 986-2579

The event celebrates its 16th year in 1998. Surf-fishing fans meet the third week in September for this tournament during which anglers fish for a wide variety of eligible species including drum, bluefish, trout and more. Call for registration fees and information.

First Citizens Bank Big Sweep
Dare County beaches • (800) 27-SWEEP

This is a local waterway cleanup that's hooked into a statewide and national event. Trash picking runs from 9 AM to 1 PM on the third Saturday in September. Folks have flocked to the waterways for 12 years (as of 1998) to do their civic duty. Obviously, it's free. Call the above number for more information.

Ocean Fest
Rodanthe Pier, N.C. Hwy. 12, Rodanthe
• (252) 441-6800, (800) 948-0759

Participate in surf kayak and rodeo clinics and watch boat demos at this late September event. The five-day program features paddle races, surf ski sprints, an outrigger race, contests, raffles, music, food and parties. Call Kitty Hawk Kayaks for prices and dates.

ACA Surf Kayaking National Championships
Rodanthe Pier, N.C. Hwy. 12, Rodanthe • (252) 441-6800, (800) 948-0759

Events at this American Canoe Association happening include traditional surf kayaking. Competition categories include the International & High Performance K-1 Men, Women's and Juniors (both expert and novice), Wave Ski and open categories. The three-day event features a silent auction, boat raffle, free kayak demos and nightly parties. Call for fees and times.

North Beach Sun Trash Festival/ Operation Beach Sweep
N.C. Hwy. 12, Duck • (252) 449-2222

This *North Beach Sun*-sponsored festival is the end-of-the-day treat for beach cleaners. Beach Sweep participants receive a ticket to the event, which features live music and a North Carolina barbecue dinner. Drop a bag of trash off at designated sites, and you'll get into the festival free. Call for trash drop-off site information.

Eastern Surfing Championships
Buxton oceanfront • (252) 995-5785, (800) 937-4733

Competition is open to Eastern Surfing Championship Association members only, but it's a fun and free spectator event. Watch as surfers grab their boards and head to the ocean to pit their skills against the waves and their fellow competitors. For more information, write to Box 400, Buxton, NC 27920.

October

OBX Paddle Race
Roanoke Sound • (252) 441-6800, (800) 948-0759

This two-day event is sponsored by Kitty Hawk Kayaks and features a race to benefit clean water. The 12-mile professional race and the 5-mile recreational races are held in Roanoke Sound. The mid-to late October benefit includes a raffle, silent auction, demos and clinics. Cash awards are given

to the top six finishers in each class competing in the pro race. Some cash (but mostly prizes) is awarded in the recreational race. Entry fees for the pro race range from $30 to $40. Recreation race fees range between $15 and $25. The lower fees apply in each category for early entries received by mail by October 7. Call the above number for more information.

Outer Banks Homebuilders Association's Parade of Homes & Home Show
Homes from Corolla to South Nags Head and Manteo • (252) 255-1733

The OBHA opens new and remodeled homes to the public for this early October event. There's a $7 fee to tour about 20 participating homes. The four-day event also features a Home Show (the location wasn't set at presstime) that presents exhibits about products, builders, lending agencies and services available to the consumer. Expect about 75 exhibits of home improvement items from hot tubs to tiles. Door prizes are distributed. Proceeds go to Habitat for Humanity and a scholarship fund.

Outer Banks Chamber of Commerce Health & Fitness Expo
Site to be announced • (252) 441-8144

A variety of free health screenings and information are offered, including blood pressure, blood sugar and cholesterol tests. The expo is held in mid-October from 9 AM until 3 PM. Call closer to the event's date for more information on what's offered and for a site update.

Artrageous Art Extravaganza Weekend
Dare County Arts Council, Central Square, U.S. Hwy. 158, MP 11, Nags Head • (252) 441-5617

Artrageous, started in 1990, is a community art festival and auction sponsored by the Dare County Arts Council (see our Close-up in the Arts and Culture chapter) the first weekend in October. Children and adults are invited to spend Saturday painting, weaving and creating various arts and crafts. All art supplies are provided. Listen to local musicians young and old, eat tasty food and witness art in the making by professionals. Artists sell their wares, lining the DCAC parking lot. Collaborative paintings by children are auctioned on Saturday; a more formal adult auction, complete with hors d'oeuvres and cocktails, takes place on Sunday (admission to Sunday's auction is usually $10). There is no admission fee to Saturday's events. Average price for booth activities is $1.

Outer Banks Stunt
Kite Competition
First Flight Middle School, Run Hill Rd., Kill Devil Hills • (252) 441-4124, (800) 334-4777

Entrants compete on the Eastern League Circuit of the American Kiting Association. The program features novice, intermediate and expert challenges, workshops and demos. Kids enjoy making kites. Ballet competitions, music and team train competitions highlight the event. The public can watch for free. The registration fee is $40. Individual competition fees range from $10 and $20. Proceeds benefit First Flight schools. The fun is free to watch. Contact Kitty Hawk Kites for more information on this 11th annual competition.

Outer Banks King
Mackerel Festival
Pirate's Cove Yacht Club, Manteo/Nags Head Cswy., Manteo • (252) 473-6800, (800) 537-7245

Anglers are invited to enter this annual mid-October fishing tournament sponsored by Pirate's Cove Yacht Club. Contenders try to catch the largest king mackerel. Entry fees generally range from $200 to $300 per boat.

Red Drum Tournament
Frank and Fran's Fisherman's Friend, N.C. Hwy. 12, Avon • (252) 995-4171

Two hundred anglers fish the surf and try to catch the largest red drum during this late

October event, sponsored by this popular Avon tackle shop. Fees range from $25 to $75 per person. Limited space is available for this four-day tournament.

Kelly's-Penguin Isle Charity
Golf Tournament
Village of Nags Head, U.S. Hwy. 158, MP 15, Nags Head • (252) 441-4116

Six-person teams play 18 holes for charity during late October. Proceeds benefit the Outer Banks Community Foundation. Fees per team generally run around $400.

Teach's Lair Shootout King
Mackerel Tournament
Teach's Lair Marina, N.C. Hwy. 12, Hatteras Village • (252) 986-2460

In this tournament, anglers try their luck in capturing the largest king mackerel. It's held in Hatteras Village at the end of October. Entry fees range from $200 to $300. The tournament is open to the public.

Octoberfest at Frisco
Woods Campground
Frisco Woods Campground, N.C. Hwy. 12, Frisco • (252) 995-5208

Here's a great way to enjoy autumn on the Outer Banks and help out the community's Meals On Wheels program. Octoberfest events include a pig-pickin' with all the trimmings, live music, crafts, a bake sale and a rummage sale. This free, late October event is sponsored by Ocean Edge Golf Course, Frisco Woods Campground and Bubba's Bar-B-Que. Donations to the charitable cause are welcome.

Haunted History Tour at
Waterside Theatre
Waterside Theatre, U.S. Hwy. 64/264, near Fort Raleigh • (252) 473-2127

Sponsored by the Dare County Jaycees and The Lost Colony, the Haunted History

Tour is more than your average Halloween spook house. The 45-minute tours led by lantern-toting guides are jam-packed with mysterious historic characters such as Virginia Dare and Blackbeard, plus a bevy of scary ghosts and goblins. The look is so authentic and the tales so eerie, even the grownups get a little nervous every now and then. Legends and true stories come to life as they are recounted by talented storytellers in period garb. Tickets generally run about $10 for adults and $5 for children. The tours are usually given for several days preceding Halloween. They start at 7:30 PM nightly and run at 15-minute intervals until 10:30 PM or so. Bundle up: Sometimes the wait can get lengthy, but we think it's absolutely worth it.

Halloween Trick or Treat
Tanger Factory Outlets, U.S. Hwy. 158, Nags Head • (252) 441-7395

This event, held from 5:30 to 7:30 PM, brings out all the little ghosts and ghouls on October 31 when the stores give out free candy.

November

Mt. Olivet United Methodist Church Bazaar & Auction
300 Ananias Dare St., Manteo
• (252) 473-2089

For this event, the church is filled with all sorts of goodies including books, kitchenware, antiques and baked treats. Get there early — this is a very popular event. Browse table after table covered with exciting finds — something old, something new. The day features a late afternoon/early evening auction. There's no charge.

Surf and Sand Triathlon
Kitty Hawk Sports, U.S. Hwy. 158, MP 12, Nags Head • (252) 441-4124, (800) 948-0759

Paddle a boat up the coast, run down the beach, then paddle a surfboard out and back (hands only). The water's still warm, so it's a great way to kick off the winter Outer Banks style. Activities include a paddle sports fash-ion show and a party. Call for reservation information.

The Art of Berge Missakain
Seaside Art Gallery, N.C. Hwy. 12, MP 11, Nags Head • (252) 441-5418, (800) 828-2444

This show features the work of Armenian artist Berge Missakain. All month his vibrant paintings will be on display and highlighted by an evening reception at the end of the month.

The Invitation Inter-Club Surf Fishing Tournament and Open Invitation Tournament
Cape Hatteras Anglers Club, N.C. Hwy. 12, Buxton • (252) 995-4253

Anglers head to the Hatteras beachfront to cast a line for a wide variety of species in hopes of returning with the largest catch. The event is sponsored by the Cape Hatteras Anglers Club.

Turkey Shoot & Pig Picking
The Promenade, U.S. Hwy. 158, MP 1, Kitty Hawk • (252) 261-2666

Celebrating its 18th year in 1998, this Kitty Hawk Fire Department-sponsored event is held in mid-November. It's a major fund-raiser for the firefighters. Ticket prices for 1997 were $8 for adults and $4 for kids. The fee includes the turkey shoot, annual auction and dinner and pig picking. The full agenda was not ready at presstime, but fire department personnel plan to include some fun new events for kids this year. Call closer to the event date for more information.

Christmas Arts and Crafts Show
Cape Hatteras School, N.C. Hwy. 12, Buxton • (252) 995-5179

This late-November show is sponsored by the Hatteras Island Arts and Crafts Guild. Crafts include pottery, dolls, shellwork and woodworking. Admission is free.

Christmas Arts & Crafts Show
Ramada Inn, N.C. Hwy. 12, Kill Devil Hills • (252) 261-3196

The two-day show, held in late November,

is sponsored by the Outer Banks Women's Club. Expect to find a wide variety of crafts, including woodworking, pottery, dolls and more. Admission is $1.

Hangin' With Santa
Kitty Hawk Kites Connection, U.S. Hwy. 158 MP 12, Nags Head • (252) 441-4124, (800) 334-4777

Late November, kids can have their photo taken with Santa in a demonstration hang glider. There's no charge, and photos are available while supplies last. Feel free to take your snapshots if supplies run out. Call for times.

December

Outer Banks Forum Concert — Sheer Pandemonium
Kitty Hawk Elementary School, U.S. Hwy. 158, MP 1, Kitty Hawk • (252) 261-1998

Holiday music as well as traditional music of Scotland, Ireland and the British Isles performed on a variety of interesting instruments such as wine glasses, hammer dulcimers and the Greek bouzouki highlight the event. Expect some Irish dancing at this early to mid-December event. Tickets cost $10. (See our Arts and Culture chapter for more on the Outer Banks Forum.)

Kites with Lights
Jockey's Ridge State Park, U.S. Hwy. 158, MP 12, Nags Head • (252) 441-4124, (800) 334-4777

This magical, multicolored light show illuminates winter skies when stunt kites adorned with Christmas lights are sent sky high and dance to traditional Christmas carols. Sponsored by Kitty Hawk Kites, the early December event is free to the public and begins at sunset.

Outer Banks Hotline's Festival of Trees
Ramada Inn, N.C. Hwy. 12, Kill Devil Hills • (252) 473-2774

This popular auction and fund-raiser, in its 10th year in 1998, takes place in early December. Businesses and individuals donate fully decorated Christmas trees and other holiday items to be auctioned and delivered to buyers. Proceeds benefit Hotline's crisis intervention program and needy families in the area. Admission is free. Past trees have been decorated with collectible Beanie Babies, handwoven tapestry wear and accessories and CDs. The festive evening includes a social at 6 PM; the auction begins at 8 PM.

Christmas Parade and Christmas on The Waterfront
Downtown Manteo • (252) 473-2774

This morning hometown parade makes its way through downtown Manteo. The festivities include food, Christmas crafts, entertainment and an appearance by Santa at The Waterfront. The events are sponsored by the town of Manteo and are free.

Elizabeth II Christmas Open House
Roanoke Island Festival Park, Elizabeth II State Historic Site, across from Manteo Waterfront • (252) 473-1144

This holiday gala features Elizabethan-themed refreshments, music and free tours of the *Elizabeth II*. The exact date for the event is usually set by November.

Man Will Never Fly Memorial Society International Annual Seminar and Awards Program
Comfort Inn South, N.C. Hwy. 12, MP 17, Nags Head • (800) 334-4777

This tongue-in-cheek organization tries to prove every year that man never really flew and abides by the motto, "Birds Fly, Men Drink." The banquet is held annually in conjunction with the anniversary of the first flight and is open to the public. The food is prepared buffet-style and features meat as well as seafood. Call for ticket and reservation information.

Wright Brothers Anniversary of First Flight
Wright Brothers Memorial, U.S. Hwy. 158, MP 8, Kill Devil Hills • (252) 441-7430, (800) 334-4777

Every December 17, bands play, planes

The Manteo Waterfront hosts festivities year round that
bring demonstrating artists to the soundfront.

fly over and the monumental feats of Orville and Wilbur are recalled. Speakers generally include military personnel, local dignitaries and individuals who have dedicated their lives to the advancement of flight technology. There is no charge.

International Icarus 98
Glenn Eure's Ghost Fleet Gallery, 210 E. Driftwood St., Gallery Row, Nags Head • (252) 441-6584
Seaside Art Gallery, N.C. Hwy. 12, MP 11, Nags Head • (252) 441-5418
Dare County Arts Council Gallery, U.S. Hwy. 158, MP 11, Nags Head • (252) 441-5617

This international art show is a theme show that celebrates the mystery and beauty of flight. Each year a flight-related theme is chosen, and artists submit original art in all genres to compete for a multitude of top-dollar prizes.

The art is displayed through the month of December at three Nags Head galleries. A children's component is included. Call the listed numbers to get on the mailing list. The art is part of the countdown to the year 2003, when the world celebrates the 100th anniversary of Wilbur and Orville Wright's first flight achievement in Kill Devil Hills. Children enter for free. Adult entries run between $10 and $15. A commission is taken for sold work by International Icarus — a nonprofit group.

Christmas Parade in Hatteras Village
Hatteras Village Community Center, N.C. Hwy. 12, Hatteras Village • (252) 986-2370

The event features floats, a bike-decorating contest, prizes for the best-decorated home and business, refreshments and caroling at the community center. There is no charge.

Families return year
after year, generation
after generation, to
dash among the waves,
explore tidal zones for
sealife and canvass
the shores for
colorful shells.

Natural Wonders

Move over Dorothy and tap those ruby slippers no more. For Insiders know "there's no place like the Outer Banks!" This barrier island system is one of the most physically remarkable habitats in the United States. Unique natural phenomenon coexist here to back that claim. The Atlantic Ocean laps at our eastern border, and a series of sounds moisten our western edges. Our middle is riddled with connecting waterways and vital wetlands. The Gulf Stream and the Continental Shelf's edge influence us from a mere 37 miles away. Cradled within our boundaries are several unusual maritime forests, and Cape Hatteras marks the dividing line for northern and southern animal and plant species presenting variety that drives nature lovers wild.

Because of our geographic location and environmental offerings, animal lovers from the world over come to the Outer Banks to sight rare pelagic birds, breaching humpbacks and nesting waterfowl. Even manatees and harbor seals have visited our waters. Anglers can ply the waters for anything from the humble flounder to the majestic blue marlin. Botanists study our ancient live oaks. Writers hole up in wooden beach cottages and ponder how poetically the wind howls. In fact a new book on the science, beauty and mystery of the wind is due out in July 1998, written by local author Jan DeBlieu and published by Houghton Mifflin. Families return year after year, generation after generation, to dash among the waves, explore tidal zones for sealife and canvass the shores for colorful shells.

While the old timers will rightfully argue that things have changed dramatically here during the last 25 years, there's always been a constant: Nature rules with an ironclad hand. Our dependency is clear: She feeds us, creates and crumbles livelihoods, offers unlimited free entertainment, is the muse to the artist and sends us scurrying for shelter when she's in bad temper.

In this chapter we'll introduce you to the land and its wonders, our bountiful waters and our crazy Outer Banks weather. While we've divided our Natural Wonders chapter into these three sections, we suggest you remember that in reality, nature composes an Outer Banks symphony that cannot be divided without sacrificing the whole. You, our guest, can feel free to enjoy any part, big or small.

Our roles as environmental stewards are an essential part of Outer Banks' life. This stewardship is manifested in efforts to protect our waters, marine life and beaches by stopping huge conglomerates from drilling for natural gas off the coast. You can join our efforts (the Outer Banks is your vacationland, after all) by learning more about LegaSea, an environmental group that was instrumental in stopping Mobil Oil from drilling for natural gas off the coast years back. They have another fight on their hands with Chevron now wishing to do the same. LegaSea and many Outer Banks residents wish to preserve this wonderland to share with their descendants and the many visitors who come to this non-polluted haven. Visit the group's website at www.LegaSea.org.

Insiders also have self-imposed, state and national restrictions on game fish. We support tag and release programs and escort infant loggerhead sea turtles off the sand and into the water. Young and old alike participate annually in a nationwide coastal cleanup. All we ask of our visitors is that you treat the area's fragile ecosystem with care. This vacation paradise is home not only for us, but also for our less vocal friends who thrive on the air, sea and land.

The Land

It doesn't take long to realize that the Outer Banks' barrier island system — a small stretch of sand — contains vast variety in topography. Geologists refer to the Outer Banks and similar land forms as "barrier islands" because they block the high-energy ocean waves and storm surges, protecting the coastal mainland. Winds, weather and waves create the personality of the slender strips of sand. Inlets from the sounds to the sea are ever shifting, opening new channels to the ocean one century, and closing off primary passageways the next.

Sand forms a partnership with the sea to create a wonderland that sweeps from Carova down through the Cape Hatteras National Seashore to Ocracoke Island. At Jockey's Ridge State Park in Nags Head, huge migrating dunes heralded as the largest sand hills on the East Coast create one of the most popular attractions on the Outer Banks (see our Attractions chapter).

It is an amazing sight to see the sand moving ribbonlike as the wind whips across the dunes. Human forms, insignificant against the towering backdrop, dot the landscape, climbing the dunes, like ants, to fly kites, hang glide or simply view the sound and ocean from atop an 85-foot-high ridgetop. At sunset, the visual drama intensifies. The forms coming and going become stark silhouettes. Come nightfall, the dunes are silent, but wildlife is there, apparent by animal tracks. Foxes roam the area as do deer and opossum, and vegetation thrives in the sand. Wild grapes and bayberry, along with black cherry and Virginia Creeper are found along the park trail.

Sand is a challenge and a blessing. It thwarts seaside gardeners who replace their sandy land with mainland dirt to grow vegetables. Outer Bankers have a long-standing love/hate relationship with the gritty stuff: We play in it, pour it out of our shoes daily and constantly suck it into vacuums, but we know that this moveable earth has played a vital role in the formation of our natural habitat.

The next time you stroll along the shore, notice the vegetation such as sea oats and spartina climbing the sloping dunes. Wind-blown sand collects behind these pioneer plants, which often grow in otherwise barren soil. With the right combination of currents and breezes, a dune can grow large enough to protect areas that lie behind them, forming tall barriers against the salty sea spray, hence allowing the birth of maritime forests. Our habitat has generated several such phenomena that interest the naturalist and layperson alike. Nags Head Woods and Buxton Woods are good examples of gifts of the dune.

Nags Head Woods

Lo and behold! There's a maritime forest flourishing on the Outer Banks that seems to defy the rules of nature. Normally, vegetation that is constantly battered by salt and wind is stunted and minimal. In the Nags Head Woods preserve, 1,400 acres of maritime forest contain a diversity of flora and fauna that's nearly unheard of in a harsh barrier island climate. This forest has been able to thrive due to a ridge of ancient sand dunes, some 90 feet high, that has shielded the land from the effects of the sea. The woods also owe their diversity to the supply of fresh water beneath the forest. The high dunes absorb and slowly release rainwater into the underlying aquifer, swamps and freshwater ponds. Wild horses once roaming the entire Outer Banks exposed this cool, fresh water by digging with their hoofs. The area has three dozen year-round ponds and some seasonal ones that appear in the winter and dry up in the summer.

Botanists have identified more than 300 species in the forest, which is a mixture of maritime deciduous forests and maritime swamp forests. This combination is rare, existing in fewer than five places in the world. Because of its rarity, Nags Head Woods is classified as a globally endangered forest system. Many hardwoods in the forest are said to be as much as 300 to 400 years old. The oldest tree in Nags Head Woods is thought to be a 500-year-old live oak, but tests indicate that woody plant species were growing in the area more than 1,000 years ago.

Plant lovers will appreciate the woods year round. The forest is lush with ferns, pines, cedars, mosses, grasses, cattails, bamboo, seaside morning glory, spotted wintergreen, wild olive, sassafras, black willow, mistflower, sweet gum, swamp rose, blazing star and hundreds more species. Several species rare to North Carolina occur in the forest: the wooly beach heather, water violet, Southern twayblade and mosquito fern.

The most diverse population of reptiles and amphibians on the Outer Banks have found a permanent home in Nags Head Woods. These include five species of salamanders, 14 species of frogs and toads, more than 20 species of snakes and multiple species of lizards and turtles. This unusual forest is a nesting spot for more than 50 species of birds and is home to a wide variety of mammals including raccoons, river otters, gray fox, white-tailed deer and opossum.

Insiders like to enter the forest in the fall. Cooler weather and fewer mosquitoes make the trek more appealing, and you have plenty of visiting birds and waterfowl to look for. Several species of heron and egrets, including the great blue heron, little blue heron and snowy egret, are common to the woods. Mallards nest in the woods, as do the red-shouldered hawk and the mourning dove. Several species of songbirds may serenade you as you walk through the forest. In the fall you may hear the music of the Eastern kingbird, barn swallow, house wren, ruby-crowned kinglet or the magnolia warbler.

Hikers can traipse three trails. The Center Trail is a half-mile long and features a scenic pond overlook. The 2-mile-long Sweetgum Swamp Trail takes about an hour to hike. The Blueberry Ridge Trail is 3.5 miles long, and the hike is well worth it for the beautiful views of the woods and water.

Dogs, four-wheel-drive vehicles and bikes are tolerated on the road that runs through Nags Head Woods, but they are not allowed in other parts of the preserve. Year-round preserve hours are 10 AM to 3 PM, but the days of the week it's open varies with the season. It is closed on Sundays and open Saturdays during the summer only. These visitation limitations help preserve the natural habitat. Call their information line at (252) 441-4381 for hour information and special programs. There's no fee to enter, but a $2 donation is requested.

The Nags Head Woods Preserve, (252) 441-2525, is overseen by The Nature Conservancy, an international nonprofit conservation organization. If you wish to contribute to The Nature Conservancy, send your donation to 701 W. Ocean Acres Drive, Kill Devil Hills, NC 27948.

Buxton Woods

Buxton Woods on Hatteras Island is the largest maritime forest in North Carolina. The 3,000-acre forest sits on the sole source of drinking water for the inhabitants of the area from Avon to Hatteras Village. Measuring 3 miles wide and 50 feet high at the tallest ridge, this land mass has the capacity to act as a storage area for freshwater. Only 900 of the 3,000 acres are owned by the National Park Service. The state of North Carolina bought an additional 800 acres to protect as the North Carolina Coastal Reserve. The county also designates Buxton Woods as a special environmental district.

Buxton Woods is a much simpler ecosystem than Nags Head Woods because it sticks out 30 miles farther into the ocean and doesn't have the protection that the Nags Head forest has; however, compared to the surrounding land at the Cape Hatteras National Seashore, Buxton Woods holds incredible diversity.

The woods lie at the meeting place for several Northern and Southern species and have a viable population of dwarf palmetto and laurel cherry. There's a mix of wetlands and forests that are a combination of both Northern

Battling Against Time and Tide

A showdown with time and tide has arrived at a pivotal phase for two vital Outer Banks attractions: the Cape Hatteras Lighthouse and the Oregon Inlet water-way. Millions of dollars that federal, state and county governments have desperately sunk into sandbags,  jetties and dredging have held off Mother Nature so far, but coastal engineers have a frustratingly willful foe. Like fickle, unruly offspring, nature's sand and water are not so easily harnessed, and the clock is ticking louder by the minute.

There's a lot at stake. The battle to save the lighthouse and to stave off the sand in the inlet is probably the most dramatic struggle that Outer Banks residents and officials have had on their plates in the last 10 years. Interminable and behind the scenes, many visitors — even locals — are not privy to the crisis at hand. Yet it may be the best illustration of the inherent difficulty of controlling the forces of nature.

An attentive traveler may wonder why Bonner Bridge, which connects Nags Head to Hatteras Island over the inlet, spans over stretches of as much sand and marsh as water. If they're especially alert, they'll notice Oregon Inlet at low tide looks easier to navigate by four-wheeler than by boat. They're right. To the growing

— continued on next page

Photo: Courtesy of Drew Wilson

The proposed move of the Cape Hatteras Lighthouse has sparked considerable debate.

dismay of officials, watermen and year-round residents, the inlet is indeed shrinking.

Slashed out between South Nags Head and the northern tip of Hatteras Island by a hurricane in 1846, Oregon Inlet clearly wants to do what inlets have always done on the Outer Banks — close. Inlets allow for a vital exchange of water, nutrients and aquatic life between sound and sea, and historically they come and go as they please. Some last as little as several days, and others last several hundred years. Coastal scientists said they have doubts that the inlet would entirely close; more likely if left alone, the channel would become impassable as the inlet continues its slow southerly slide.

Every year, the U.S. Army Corps of Engineers dredges the Oregon Inlet channel, but it's getting more difficult to maintain. Many people think the only way to keep the waterway open is to construct two jetties to block sand from clogging the channel. But the project would cost about $100 million, the federal government is so far unwilling to fund it and conservationists say the rock walls could cause erosion and deplete sealife. It's not just the cost: Many believe it's a losing battle anyway, and that it's smarter to just let nature take its course. But both sides agree that dredging, if it's done right, can at least keep the channel navigable for a while.

Despite strong opposition to rock walls, even the staunchest environmentalist is pained to contemplate the impact the closing could have on the economy, safety and lifestyles of the residents that depend on the inlet. Watermen and boaters would lose the only passage to the Atlantic between Hatteras Inlet and Virginia. The entire fishing industry and related offshoots that depend on the inlet providing access to the Atlantic would relocate or go under. Tourism would lose an important focus. The Bonner Bridge, Hatteras Island's only connection to the mainland and the northern Outer Banks, could be endangered, or pointless.

Meanwhile, down the road a bit, Cape Hatteras Lighthouse is teetering on the edge of a watery grave. No less majestic than when it was built 128 years ago, the nation's tallest brick beacon has lost most of the beach that buffered it from stormy seas and wind-driven waves. Situated on a picturesque corner of sand that juts into the most dangerous waters of the Atlantic, the handsome spiral-striped tower in 1870 was a quarter-mile from the sea. But with erosion around its octagonal base stripping the beach at a rate of 12.8 feet per year, less than 120 feet of sand remain in front of the landmark.

Like Oregon Inlet, government officials have frantically tried to prevent what would be inevitable if they did nothing. The National Park Service has spent at least $3 million studying options to save the 208-foot black-and-white structure. Sandbags have been piled at its base. Rock jetties that deflect waves have been reinforced. In 1997 the Park Service finally decided that the only option that will guarantee Cape Hatteras Lighthouse will exist for future generations is to move it. A team of professors that year had backed a 1988 National Academy of Science study that recommended relocating the lighthouse a half-mile from the ocean. The federal government later allocated $2 million of the $12 million cost of the project, which was intended to be used for the project's required environmental studies. But a citizens' group that wants to shore up the lighthouse at its present location renewed its lobbying efforts to find funds for a small jetty. Although federal officials promised the additional funds would be forthcoming to safely relocate the Cape Hatteras Lighthouse 2,900 feet southwest of the current site in Buxton in spring of 1999, opponents of the move have cast doubt that the proposal is the best solution. They believe that the landmark would lose its historic significance if it was taken from its present post.

Again, like its troublesome neighbor to the north, Oregon Inlet, some people think the lighthouse is best left to the elements. Although scientists said the 3,000 tons of

— continued on next page

masonry is plenty sturdy enough to withstand being lifted on hydraulic jacks, set on rails and slid inland, many fear the move likely could result in a pile of black-and-white rubble.

Engineers say there is an 80 percent chance that the Outer Banks' favorite landmark would topple in a category 4 hurricane or in three northeasters that hit one after another. Park Service officials warn that time is running out if we want to ensure that our grandchildren can also experience the thrill of climbing the tower's 268 stairs to gaze out over the beautiful waters and sands of the Outer Banks. Opponents of the move agree, but urge quick action to shore up the beach in front of the light. Meanwhile, the famous beacon remains stalwart at its tenuous anchor on the eroded beach. For now.

deciduous maritime forests and Southern evergreen maritime forests. Nowhere else on Hatteras Island will you find the diversity in mammal population as in Buxton Woods. The woods are home to white-tailed deer, gray squirrels, eastern cottontail rabbits, raccoons and opossum. A bird's-eye view shows an overall ridge and lowlands throughout the area. In the woods is Jennette's Sedge, one of the largest, most highly developed and diverse freshwater marsh systems found on a barrier island in North Carolina (see our Attractions chapter for more information on Buxton Woods).

Alligator River National Wildlife Refuge

On the mainland to the west of Roanoke Island is the Alligator River National Wildlife Refuge. The refuge encompasses 150,000 acres of wetlands and wooded fields and is home to black bears, white-tailed deer, gray fox, bobcats, raccoons, mink, beaver, squirrels, possum, river otter, nutria, alligators and the protected red wolves.

In 1987, federal wildlife officials released four pairs of red wolves onto the refuge that covers parts of mainland Dare, Hyde and Tyrrell counties. Another 12 animals were confined to chain-link pens in a secluded thicket where volunteers and five full-time biologists fed them and administered to their health and reproductive needs.

More than 50 red wolves have been set free in this area so far, and at least 25 pups have been born in the wilds of northeastern North Carolina. In 1990 a female wolf born on the refuge gave birth to her own litter of pups

— proving that the creatures could adapt to their surroundings and reproduce beyond a single generation. These shy, skittish animals have only one natural predator — humans. Local officials say they have no records of red wolves becoming aggressive with people.

See our Attractions chapter for more information on visiting the refuge. For guided programs information call: (252) 473-1131.

Audubon Wildlife Sanctuary at Pine Island

Audubon is a northern Outer Banks, 5,000-acre wildlife sanctuary at Pine Island, and is a protected habitat for deer, birds, rabbits and a huge variety of plant life. There is an unmarked 2-mile trail you can walk, but the sanctuary is not really a park for people. While you are allowed to wander down the path, there is no planned parking. The land is primarily soundside marshland with lots of pine trees and waterfowl. The sanctuary runs 3 miles long north to south and is approximately 200 yards wide from east to west.

Cape Hatteras National Seashore

The Outer Banks should get a medal for firsts. Not only do we claim First Flight and the first English pioneers to colnize in the new world, but Cape Hatteras was the first seashore in the United States to become a national seashore (1953). The park covers 85 percent of Hatteras Island, which stretches south of the Bonner Bridge for 33 miles to Hatteras Inlet.

The beaches are clean and uncrowded. Subtle beauty abounds in the park. The swaying sea grasses, shifting sands and tenacious vegetation appear monochromatic at first glance. A closer study reveals pleasant surprises. Delicate white-petaled flowers with scarlet centers and lush purple flowers grow entwined in the roadside brambles. In the marshes, sea lavender, morning glories and marsh aster add color. In the early morning or late afternoon, you can usually see dozens of brown marsh rabbits nibbling grasses along the roadside. All along the seashore, ghost crabs burrow in the sand and can be seen scurrying about by day and night — a pure delight for children. One of the more spectacular sights is the occasional glow of phosphorous visible in the waves breaking on shore on a dark night. Sometimes even the crabs glow eerily.

The park offers visitors a respite from the frenzy of living in a resort community. It's a peaceful ride down N.C. 12 and always a welcome one except when the ocean washes away the dune and claims the road. There are several attractions in the park borders that appeal to the nature lover, including the Pea Island National Wildlife Refuge featuring more than 5,000 acres of wildlife refuge. The refuge is both a year-round and seasonal home for nearly 400 species, including the snow goose, Canada goose and whistling swan. During the fall you can watch large flocks of snow geese ascend from their watery resting places. Their flight is breathtaking. This section of the park may be one of the most poetic spots on the Outer Banks. The waterfowl are just far enough away to appear untouched by the human element. You can get up-close views of them through binoculars and a camera's lens. Photographers also enjoy this stretch for the interesting tree lines and sunsets on the salt marsh. Plan to stop and bird-watch at the platform available just off the road.

The North Pond Trail, on Pea Island, is another bird watcher's option. The Ocracoke pony pens and Hammock Hills Nature Trail across from the Ocracoke Campground are several more hotspots in the Cape Hatteras National Seashore. See our Hatteras Island section in the Attractions chapter for more information on these sites, and see our Beach Information and Safety chapter for off-road driving and lifeguard information within park boundaries.

In Buxton, at the tip of Cape Hatteras, is an area of beach only approachable by four-wheel drive vehicles. Locals call this "The Point," and it serves as a well-used haven for surf-casters. The sea is powerful at this spot, marked by strong currents, deep holes and shoals and opposing waves crashing into each other. Wildlife writers and anglers alike call it heaven. The bottom topography created by strong shoaling and The Point's proximity to the Gulf Stream and its spinoff eddies justify calling this wet and sandy spot a real Outer Banks natural wonder (see our Fishing chapter).

Whale watching is an exciting option for park visitors, though sightings are not restricted to the park boundaries. There are more species of whales passing by the coast of North Carolina than anywhere in Eastern North America. Mostly groups of small- to medium-toothed whales make passage both far offshore and in sight of the beach. Deeper offshore is the migration path for killer and blue whales.

The three largest species are the sperm whale, humpback and fin whale. The sperm whales make their way past our coast in the springtime. In the winter you can see both humpback and fin whales.

The humpbacks are particularly visible from the shore. They can be seen breaching and lunge feeding. In the latter action, the whale blows a bubble net to corral fish, then leaps through it open-mouthed to gulp in everything.

Pilot whales can be seen offshore year round. Even the most endangered species, the Northern right whale, was identified while scratching its head on an Outer Banks sandbar. We've also had rare washups of the dense beaked whale. Offshore sightings have been made of the Cuvier's beaked whale, and the first live sighting of the True's beaked whale was made 33 nautical miles southeast of Hatteras Inlet. Exactly one year later from this sighting, in May 1994, a type of bottle-nosed whale about 25 to 30 feet long was seen. Biologists suspect this particular mammal may be a new species.

Whether you're sitting on the beach with binoculars or viewing the creatures from an

A drive near any Outer Banks body of water is likely to provide glimpses of shoreline birds. Like this egret.

offshore charter boat, whale watching is an awe-inspiring pastime.

Whales are a hard act to follow, but let's face it — it's a rare visitor who comes to the park who doesn't delight in filling all available pockets and pails with shells. Hatteras Island dog-legs to the west, making it one of the farthest points out on the Eastern Seaboard. Its steep beaches cause high-energy wave action, so unbroken shells rarely make it to the shore. But the sea tosses up lovely blue mussels, quahog, jackknife clams, slipper shells, baby's ears, jingle shells and oysters. A good time to search for shells is at changing tides, after high tide or following a storm. If you're seeking whole shells, continue south to Ocracoke Island, where the beaches have gentle slopes.

The Water

Estuary, Sound and Salt Marsh

Fly over the Outer Banks in a small plane, and it will become clear that this string of islands is more an offspring of the sea than the land. With more than 2.2 million acres of sounds and bays between its barrier islands and mainland, North Carolina ranks behind only Alaska and Louisiana in the amount of estuarine acreage. With 2 million acres covered by the vast Currituck-Albemarle-Pamlico sound system, the Outer Banks region ranks second in size only to the Chesapeake Bay in terms of water surface area. Each day, more than 15 billion gallons of water pass into the barrier islands' estuaries. The bulk of it flows into the Pamlico Sound, and then into the Atlantic through four major Outer Banks inlets. The Albemarle Sound, the mouth of which sits west of Kitty Hawk, is fed by seven major rivers and is the largest freshwater sound on the East Coast. The Currituck Sound, also freshwater, lies northeast of the Albemarle. Due south of these bodies of water are two brackish sounds, the Roanoke and the Croatan. Farther south is the saltwater Pamlico Sound. Nestled in the crook of this sound, where Cape Hatteras indents toward the sea, is the famous Canadian Hole, one of the nation's top windsurfing spots (see our Watersports chapter).

The Outer Banks landscape is also defined by its salt marshes. The marshes shelter the barrier islands from the sounds, and cordgrass and other vegetation break much of the wave action and act as safe havens for marine life.

The wetlands are nursery grounds for many of the fish we enjoy dining on. Ninety percent of all commercial seafood species must spend at least part of their life cycle in the salt marsh. They spawn offshore and then release their eggs into the inlets, where currents carry them into the marsh. Oysters, crabs, shrimp and flounder flourish in the calmer waters of the marsh, which offer places to hide and lots of food. The salt marsh is also attractive to waterfowl and other bird species, which find food here.

The Sea

Perhaps the sea in its entirety is too huge for the human mind to comprehend, but it is only through trying to understand her that you come to appreciate the Outer Banks fully. The ocean dominates the islands, influencing their weather, land, flora, fauna and the lifestyle of the people. Scientists work daily at the U.S. Army Corp of Engineers Field Research Facility in Duck studying currents to understand erosion. Outer Banks' history is steeped in harrowing accounts of lifesaving efforts — the sea is not always a kind mistress — and the economy is heavily based in sea-oriented tourism, the commercial seafood industry and recreational fishing. Newcomers who arrive here to work in these livelihoods and those who come merely to visit the sandy, windswept edge of a continent are affected by the Atlantic Ocean.

The position of Cape Hatteras, jutting into the Atlantic, puts us in near the Continental Shelf's edge, which is approximately 37 miles southeast of Oregon Inlet and near the junction of three ocean currents, the Deep Western Boundary Current, Gulf Stream and Shelf Current. These physical combinations create a nutrient-rich habitat for sea life, resulting in a world-renowned offshore fishing hotspot and a wonderland for pelagic birds. Our proximity to the toasty Gulf Stream current is one of our most prestigious calling cards.

Gulf Stream

A forceful flow of water in the Atlantic Ocean passes off the Outer Banks' shores every day. The Gulf Stream is a swift ribbon of blue sea that has been flowing by since time immemorial. Powered by forces arising from the earth's rotation and the influence of the winds, the energy and warmth it emits has had a profound effect on mankind. While the stream's course is influenced somewhat by gales, barometric pressure and seasonal changes, the general flow remains fairly constant, creating a dichotomy: While the stream is ever-present, its contents are ever-changing. Millions upon millions of tons of water per second are carried along this ancient path. Swept along are fish, microscopic plants and animals and gulfweed that originates in the Sargasso Sea.

Gulfweed lines the edge of the Stream creating a habitat for baitfish. You can easily pull up a handful of vegetation and find it teeming with life. The weed offers protection to infant fish, turtles, crabs, sea horses and the most peculiar sargassumfish. Endangered loggerhead sea turtles less than 2 weeks old, their egg beaks still intact, have been spotted in the weed.

Flying fish are always fun to watch, although what we see as antics is actually the fish's sprint for life as it glides about 200 to 300 yards to escape a predator. The offshore life cycle is fascinating, and nowhere is it more evident than at the Gulf Stream.

Pelagic Bird-watching

You don't have to be a bird lover to realize you have entered a unique bird-watching area as you tool down N.C. 12 through the National Seashore. Off in the distance, in the wetlands, a variety of species feed and sun. What is not so obvious is the gold mine of pelagic species offshore, where bird-watchers can witness both common and rare birds that never come to our shores.

Local fishing headboats have been taking bird-watchers to the deep water for years. In fact, the sightings are so fruitful, a good part of Capt. Allan Foreman's charter boat business involves these trips. Foreman's *Country Girl*, (252) 473-5577, which fishes out of Pirate's Cove Yacht Club on Roanoke Island, is a 57-foot headboat built to carry large parties offshore. Down in Hatteras, Capt. Spurgeon Stowe runs bird-watching excursions aboard the 72-foot *Miss Hatteras*, (252) 986-2365, from Oden's Dock (see our Fishing chapter for more information). Bird enthusiasts spend the day searching for more than two dozen species that live on the water.

The petrel and shearwater families are the largest groups of birds available to bird-watchers here. Traveling from the Caribbean and the coast of Africa, these species leave their winter climate to spend summer off the Outer Banks.

Among the petrels, the black-capped petrel is probably one of the most common to North Carolina waters. Twenty-five years ago this species was believed to be on the verge of extinction. No one knew where the birds were. Scientists now say that the world's population hangs out in the Gulf Stream off the Outer Banks area. For comparison's sake, Florida bird-watchers may see one or two black-capped petrels per trip, whereas trips departing from the Outer Banks can yield as many as 100 sightings on a good day.

What's exciting about these trips is that you have the chance to view species that only come to land to breed, but when we speak of land, we refer to oceanic islands, not any place you can easily bump into these creatures. These birds are highly adapted for life on the sea. They could be mistaken for gulls or ducks, but as a group they are quite unique. Their tubular nostrils allow them to drink salt water and then expel the salt.

A much rarer bird sighted off North Carolina is the white-faced storm petrel. In a good year, one or two sightings are recorded. This bird shows up in the late summer or early fall and is very difficult to spot anywhere else in the world.

While bird-watching off the Outer Banks, Mike Tove, a biologist from Cary, North Carolina, discovered two species of petrel that were rarely seen near North America. One of them, called the herald petrel, up until 10 years ago was known from only a handful of recordings going back to the 1920s.

"In 1991 boats started venturing offshore farther than usual," Tove said. "We started finding them. It's now a bird we see a half-dozen times a year. People come great distances looking for them."

Tove officially presented to discovery another rare species in May 1991. "I had a bird that was identified as a Cape Verde petrel," he said. Prior to Tove's sighting, resurrected field notes revealed only three other recorded sightings of the bird.

This species was entirely unknown in the United States and is extraordinarily rare anywhere in the world. "And we're seeing them with almost predictable regularity in late spring in very deep offshore waters past the edge of the Continental Shelf," he said. Tove's sightings form the baseline data for research. All the birds have been well-documented with photographs.

You don't have to have a doctorate, as Tove does, to enjoy bird-watching. If you want to get a glimpse of these offshore species here are a few tips:

• Bring fairly low-power, waterproof binoculars (Zeiss or Leitz 7X or 8X are excellent).

• Don't bother to bring your spotting scope; if you're a photographer, bring a telephoto lens to help document rarities.

• Constantly scan the horizon and wave tops for birdlife, and call out your sighting with the boat as reference; for example, 6 o'clock is directly off the stern.

• Don't wait to try and identify the bird before calling it out; many eyes on the bird will aid in that. Identification is often very difficult, and to do it accurately you must have a great deal of field experience and ability to interpret flight and molt patterns, often during heavy seas.

• Expect long periods where no birds are seen, but be prepared for the appearance of a good number and variety. Always take good notes on any unusual species before consulting your field guide. Describe and sketch exactly what you saw without allowing outside influences to color your recollection.

• Offshore bird-watching can be an exciting new adventure. If you haven't spent any time on the water, don't allow your fears to get the best of you. Captains won't take you out if the weather is too risky, and you can follow our tips on preventing sea sickness (see our Fishing chapter). Happy bird-watching!

Weather

By the end of this guidebook, you may well be tired of the word "variety." It aptly describes not only the above-mentioned natural wonders but our weather as well. We find the weather to be more changeable on the Outer Banks than our inland counterparts. Business owners who specialize in outdoor attractions are plagued by phone calls when the skies turn dark:

"Is the cruise going to be canceled? Can you fish in the rain?"

We tell our visitors that because the weather is so mercurial, wait 10 minutes and those dark clouds very possibly may be gone. There's variation from town to town. It may be pouring in Corolla, but it's sunny skies in Manteo. Torrential rains could send beachgoers scattering at noon, but 20 minutes later the heavens are beaming. Get the picture?

It seems to rain less in the winter, while late summer evenings hold their share of window-rattling thundershowers. The good part is that the skies are usually clear during the day. The bad part is that unless you are a heavy sleeper, you may awaken from the booms on and off between midnight and 3 AM. In summer 1996, the weather was unusually cool. Temperatures soared a few times into the high 90s, but overall, we had a remarkably cool summer season. In 1997 we had mostly temperate summer days and a very dry spell. Warm temperatures lasted into December with just a few frozen mornings tossed in. Some nature watchers noticed few pecans and roadside bunnies and wondered if the lack of rainfall played a part; however, there was less mold and mildew. We sure did sleep better all summer though, and then reveled in fall's fantastic weather.

The Atlantic Ocean, which is slow to warm and cool and heats to a maximum of about 80 degrees in the summer, affects the air temperatures. Our nearness to the sea keeps summer air temperatures about 10 degrees cooler than our mainland counterparts. In the winter, disregarding the wind chill factor, our air temperatures do just the opposite. Air flowing over the Gulf Stream toward us warms the winter air.

Nor'easters, occurring most often in the fall and winter, plague homeowners and fishermen alike. The high winds keep boats at the docks, sometimes knocking out three to seven work days. These same winds wreak havoc on precariously perched oceanfront property. If the high winds coincide with the high tide and, heaven forbid, the full moon, powerful storm waves cover the land and cause beach erosion, structural damage and both ocean and soundside flooding.

March has seen a few nasty storms too, including the infamous Ash Wednesday Storm that struck on March 7, 1962, and the more recent March Storm in 1993 when winds were clocked at 92 mph. The sound waters rose 8 to 10 feet causing great damage. Year-round residents see all this nasty weather as a trade-off for living in such a paradise. While we tend to highlight the more extreme weather patterns here, there are far more absolutely gorgeous days occurring year round.

The wind blows most of the time at an average of 8 to 10 mph. Occasional gale force winds range from 30 to 35 mph. And then there are hurricanes.

Hurricanes

For the first time since this Insider has lived on the Outer Banks (12 years), there was no real hurricane scare all season. June through November marks our hurricane season, and usually we have to evacuate or at least board up once every year. All the southeastern shore of the United States is prone to hurricanes, but because of low elevation, lack of shelter and, especially, because they're way out in the Atlantic Ocean, the barrier islands of North Carolina are especially vulnerable to storms. Forecasters and almanac writers say a hurricane strikes the Outer Banks about once every nine years. A major one tears through the area every 42 years on average.

When Dare County officials order evacuations of the islands, everyone — from vacationers who already have paid for their week's stay to permanent residents who don't want to leave their homes behind — is ordered to leave the Outer Banks. Newspaper, radio and television reports will notify the public about mandatory evacuations and when bridges into the area may reopen for people to return. Make plans early to take pets and elderly people off the islands — and scope out a shelter or safe place to stay on the mainland. Watch the Weather Channel (channel 25 in the local cable listings) for early warnings or signs of a storm, and then obey your common sense: Stay off the beach and out of the water, especially during electrical storms.

For more information about emergency storm procedures, call (252) 473-3355 (Dare County), (252) 232-2115 (Currituck County) or (252) 928-1071 (Ocracoke).

Tornadoes spawned by hurricanes are among the worst weather-related killers. When a hurricane approaches, listen for tornado watches and warnings. (A tornado watch means tornadoes are expected to develop. A tornado warning means a tornado has actually been sighted.) When your area receives a tornado warning, seek inside shelter immediately, preferably below ground level. If a tornado catches you outside, move away from its path at a right angle. If you don't have time to escape, lie flat in the nearest depression, ditch or ravine.

Hurricane watches mean a hurricane could threaten the area within 24 hours. Evacuation is not necessary at that point. If a hurricane warning is issued, visitors should leave the Banks and head inland using U.S. 64/264 or U.S. 158, following the recently installed green and white "Hurricane Evacuation Route" signs. Always heed instructions of local authorities.

The Dare County Civil Preparedness Agency officials issued the following guidelines.

Hurricane Safety Rules

By late May of each year, recheck your supply of boards, tools, batteries, nonperishable foods and the other equipment you will need if a hurricane strikes.

Keep a battery-powered radio close by to listen to the latest weather reports and official notices. When you hear the first tropical cyclone advisory, listen for future messages. This will prepare you for a hurricane emergency well before watches and warnings are issued.

If your area comes under a hurricane watch, continue normal activities, but stay tuned to the Weather Channel or to local radio stations (see "Media" in the Services and Information Directory). Stay alert, and ignore rumors.

If your area receives a hurricane warning, keep calm until the emergency has ended. Leave low-lying areas that may be swept by high tides or storm waves. If time allows, se-

cure mobile homes with heavy cables anchored in concrete footings, and then leave for more substantial shelter. If possible, move automobiles to high grounds as both sound and sea can flood even central spots on the Outer Banks.

Moor boats securely before the storm, or haul them out of the water to a safer area. Once boats are secure, leave and don't return to them until the wind and waves have subsided.

Board up windows or protect them with storm shutters or tape. Danger to small windows is mainly from wind-driven debris. Larger windows may be broken by wind pressure. Secure outdoor objects that might be blown away, uprooted or propelled into the house. Garbage cans, garden tools, toys, signs, porch furniture and other harmless items become missiles of destruction in hurricane winds. Anchor outdoor items or store them inside before the storm strikes.

Store drinking water in clean bathtubs, jugs, bottles and cooking utensils. Water supplies can be contaminated by hurricane floods.

Check battery-powered equipment. A radio may be your only link with the world outside. Emergency cooking facilities, lights and flashlights also are essential if utilities are interrupted.

Keep automobiles fueled. Service stations may be inoperable for several days after the storm strikes.

Remain indoors during the storm. Keep pets and children inside, and don't attempt to travel by foot or vehicle. Monitor weather conditions on the radio or television. Once the hurricane has truly passed (don't be fooled by the relative calm that may return as the hurricane's eye passes):

Seek necessary medical care at the nearest Red Cross disaster station or health center.

Stay out of disaster areas. Unless you are qualified to help, your presence might hamper first-aid and rescue work.

Unless you're injured or are transporting

INSIDERS' TIP

The National Park Service maintains a .75-mile trail through Buxton Woods; access is near the Cape Hatteras Lighthouse. It is important to stay on the trail because cottonmouth snakes live in the woods year round.

someone who is injured, do not travel until advised by the proper authorities.

If you must drive, be careful along debris-filled streets and highways. Roads may be undermined and could collapse under the weight of a car.

Avoid loose or dangling wires and report them immediately to North Carolina Power or the nearest law enforcement officer.

Report broken sewer or water mains to the county or town water department.

Prevent fires. Lowered water pressure may make fire-fighting difficult.

Check refrigerated food for spoilage if power has been off during the storm.

Stay away from river banks and streams.

Check roofs, windows and outdoor storage areas for wind or water damage.

As Insiders, we know that even an award-winning swim team competitor has no business in the water when the red flags are up.

Beach Information and Safety

Folks come from the world over to dip in our salty waters, bask in our sunlight and wiggle their toes in our sand. The seaside in the summer can be as calming as an environmentally-controlled bath, but only if you obey a few, very important rules. What we want to stress is that every body of water and every shoreline is unique. Each comes with a set of uncompromising rules.

Following are some tips we've gathered to help make your stay a comfortable and safe one.

The Ocean

The sea is the eternal soother but it also can be a harsh mistress. If red flags are flying, don't go in the water at all. This warning applies to swimmers of all skill levels. As Insiders, we know that even an award-winning swim team competitor has no business in the water when the flags are up. Even wading during a red flag warning is very risky. Broken bones have occurred simply from being knocked down in the surf. Rough water also produces floating debris that can come from nowhere. Even if you see surfers in the water, stay out! The ocean's character is complex. Here are a few water safety points to bear in mind.

Water Sense

• Never swim alone.
• Never swim at night.
• Observe the surf before going in the water, looking for potentially dangerous currents.
• Nonswimmers should stay out of the water and wear life jackets if they're going to be near the water.
• Swim in areas with on-duty lifeguards, or use extreme care.
• Keep nonswimming children well above the marks of the highest waves.
• Keep an eye on children at all times, and teach them never to turn their backs on the waves while they play at water's edge.
• Don't swim near anglers or deployed fishing lines.
• Stay 300 feet away from fishing piers.
• Watch out for surfers and give them plenty of room.

INSIDERS' TIP

It may seem harmless enough to dig a deep hole by the sea, but you must always use caution. It's impossible to know the substructure of the beachfront or dune or sand pile where you might be frolicking. Sand can collapse, and it can take an unsuspecting, well-meaning digger with it. In summer 1997 there was a tragic incident of fatal sand suffocation after a man had dug a deep hole and placed a lounge chair in it. Obviously these events are very rare, but keep in mind the possibilities when playing in the sand.

Losing Control in the Waves

If a wave crashes down on you while you are surfing or swimming, and you find yourself being tumbled in bubbles and sand like a sheet in a washing machine, don't try to struggle to the surface against it. Curl into a ball, or just go limp and float. The wave will take you to the beach, or you can just swim to the surface when it passes.

Backwash Current

A backwash current on a steeply sloping beach can pull you toward deeper water, but its power is swiftly checked by incoming waves. To escape this current, swim straight toward shore if you're a strong swimmer. If you're not, don't panic; wait and float until the current stops, then swim in.

Littoral Current

The littoral current is a "river of water" moving up or down the shoreline parallel to the beach. It is created by the angled approach of the waves. In stormy conditions, this current can be very powerful due to high wave energy.

Rip Currents

Rip currents often occur where there's a break in a submerged sandbar (see the diagrams in this chapter). Water trapped between the sandbar and the beach rushes out through the breach, sometimes sweeping swimmers out with it. You can see a rip; it's choppy, turbulent, often discolored water that looks deeper than the water around it. If you are caught in a rip, don't try to swim against the current. Instead, swim across the current parallel to the shore and slowly work your way back to the beach at an angle. Try to remain calm. Panic will only sap the energy you need to swim out of the rip.

Undertow

When a wave comes up on the beach and breaks, the water must run back down to the sea. This is undertow. It sucks at your ankles from small waves, but in heavy surf undertow it can knock you off your feet and carry you offshore. If you're carried out, don't resist. Let the undertow take you out until it subsides. It will only be a few yards. The next wave will help push you shoreward again.

Jellyfish

Watch for jellyfish floating on the surface or in the water. While some can give little more than an annoying stinging sensation, others can produce severe discomfort. The Portuguese man-of-war is sometimes blown onto Outer Banks beaches and can be recognized by its distinctive balloon-like air bladder, often exhibiting a bluish tint. Man-of-war stings can be serious. Anyone who is stung by the tentacles and develops breathing difficulties or generalized body swelling should be transported to the nearest emergency facility for treatment. In extreme cases, death can result from anaphylactic shock associated with man-of-war toxin exposure.

Treatment for jellyfish stings includes vinegar or meat tenderizer applied to the affected area. Don't rub the wound site, since rubbing can force toxins deeper into the skin. Pain relievers can also allay some discomfort. Infections can occur, so it's also a good idea to see a doctor.

Services

Emergency Assistance

Many areas of the Outer Banks don't have lifeguards or flag systems warning you to stay out of the water. Keep in mind that help can be a long way off, and an emergency is not the time to learn about ocean safety. As you've learned after reading about the ocean currents listed above, water conditions here call for unusual vigilance. We are vigilant about hanging

Rip Currents

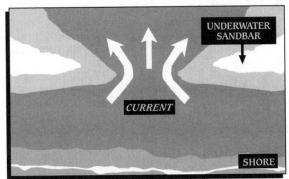

Rip currents form when water breaks through a nearshore sandbar (see figure above) or is diverted by a groin or jetty (see figure below) and rushes out to sea in a narrow path.

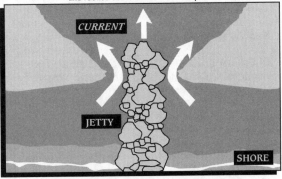

Rip currents can extend 1,000 feet offshore and travel up to 3 miles an hour.

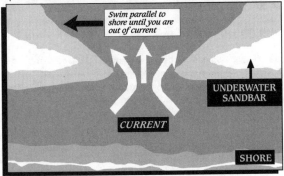

If caught in a rip current, don't panic. Do not swim against the current. Swim parallel to shore until you are out of the current, or float calmly until it dissipates.

red warning flags, but sometimes they are removed by souvenir-seeking scavengers. It's always best to listen to local radio stations or call municipal headquarters for daily water conditions anytime you plan to enter the ocean, despite the season. Accidents can and do occur. If you have an emergency and need the rescue squad, dial 911 for help. Please remember that this number is for emergencies only.

Lifeguards

Lifeguards are provided by Lifeguard Beach Service Inc., Nags Head Ocean Rescue and the National Park Service at fixed sites along the Outer Banks. Lifeguard Beach Service guards are on the beach from Memorial Day weekend through Labor Day weekend. Their hours at the designated sites are 9:30 AM to 5:30 PM daily, but hours and locations (see below) are subject to change without notice. Always use caution before entering and/ or swimming in the ocean, and be alert for red warning flags and red-and-white warning posters.

Ocean Rescue Services, (252) 441-5909, are provided by the town of Nags Head to that town's beaches. This service is also provided to Kitty Hawk and Southern Shores through a contracted arrangement. Guarded beaches are available daily beginning Memorial Day weekend through Labor Day, 10 AM until 6 PM.

Within the Cape Hatteras National Seashore, lifeguards will be on duty daily beginning Memorial Day weekend at Coquina, Frisco and Ocracoke beaches and starting June 21 at the Cape Hatteras Lighthouse. Lifeguard service ends after Labor Day.

In 1998 ocean lifeguard stands will be located at the following Dare County beaches:
• In Duck: Ocean Pines, North Snow Geese Drive, Barrier Island and Plover Drive
• In Southern Shores: Hillcrest and Chicahawk

• In Kitty Hawk: Kitty Hawk Public Beach and Bird Street
• In Kill Devil Hills: Helga Street, Haymen Street, Fifth Street, Third Street/Sea Ranch, Second Street, First Street, Asheville Drive, Woodmere Avenue, Raleigh Street, Sutton Avenue/Comfort Inn, Ocean Bay Boulevard, Oregon Street, Cavalier Motel, Clark Street, Outer Banks Beach Club, Martin Street, Atlantic Street, Holiday Inn/Ramada Inn and John Yancey Motel
• In Nags Head: Bonnett Street, Epstein Street and Hargrove Street, Enterprise Street, Juncos Street (LBS supplies lifeguards at the Nags Head Inn area)
• On Hatteras Island: Coquina Beach
• On Roanoke Island: Old Swimming Hole (10 AM to 6 PM), on the sound at the Airport.

Alcohol

The effects of alcohol can be amplified by the heat and sun of a summer afternoon, so be aware. It's illegal to operate boats or motor vehicles if you've had too much to drink, and enforcement officers keep an eye out for violators, so practice moderation. Alcohol and swimming can be a potentially deadly combination. Even small amounts of alcohol can give you a false sense of security.

Safety in the Sun

It's amazing how many red-bodied folk we see lying on the beach, limping into restaurants or, worse yet, waiting in medical centers while visiting the Outer Banks. Yes, we know. The sun feels so good. Combined with the sea air, it seems to have a rejuvenating effect. Actually any form of tan or burn is now considered damaged skin. While we can't stop visitors and Insiders alike from toasting themselves, these tips will help keep you comfortable.

Start out with short periods of sun exposure when you first arrive. It seems like most folk initially overdo it and have to be careful for the rest of their stay. The summer sun is pretty intense, and you'd be surprised how much of a burn your skin can get in 20 or 30 minutes on a afternoon in July. We always take our umbrella to the beach to keep our exposure within reasonable levels. You might want to do the same.

Use ample sunscreen (SPF 15 or higher) whenever you're in the sun for any length of time. We always put an extra coat on our noses, cheeks, lips and any other high-exposure spots. We also apply sunscreen at least 20 minutes before we go out, since it takes a while for it to become fully effective.

Avoid the hottest parts of the day, from 10 AM until 2 PM, when the sun's rays are the strongest. It's a great time to take a break from the beach and explore some of the other fun things listed in this guide.

Don't be afraid to cover up on the beach. Just remember: Healthy, protected skin is a sign of good sense.

Pets

Dogs must be on a leash unless they are in the water. Park rangers do patrol the beaches regularly, and they will approach you if your dog is running free. Voice command control is not enough. Save yourself some money and leash up; fines range around $50. For that price, you could purchase a nice meal or a fancy souvenir!

Litter

If you're getting ready to throw down a soda bottle or candy wrapper, it might help if you remember that while you may be staying at the ocean, which essentially belongs to everyone on the planet, you are also littering in a year-round community. Inevitably what is tossed in one backyard winds up gracing the lawn of another due to the wind factor. With that in mind, you'll want to secure all trash and trash bags carefully so the wind can't make mischief. Feel free to pick up any stray trash. It's not uncommon to see locals doing just this. Don't be shy — after all, we've already established that the ocean is yours too!

If you can't find a trash can that isn't already overflowing, please find another appropriate spot to dispose of potential litter. A good idea too is to look into our recycling efforts when you first get to the Outer Banks.

Beach Driving

Off-road access is possible on the Outer Banks but only in designated spots and at certain times of the year. It is mandatory that you use a four-wheel-drive vehicle Checking with each township for specific rules is necessary, and some places even require a permit.

Generally you can ride on the beach in Kill Devil Hills and Nags Head from October 1 through April 30. You must have a permit to do so in Nags Head. Southern Shores and Kitty Hawk prohibit driving on the beach at all times. As far north as Corolla and Carova in Currituck County, there are designated spots where you can drive on the beach. Hatteras Island operates under the guidance of the National Park Service, (252) 473-2111, so any questions you have concerning off-road driving can be referred to them.

Driving is not allowed on the beach at Pea Island National Wildlife Refuge (the area from Rodanthe Pier north to Oregon Inlet), but as you move south, you will see access areas marked by a picture of a Jeep where you can travel on the beach. Obviously those Jeeps with an X marked through them are spots where beach driving is prohibited. It's a good idea to stop at one of the National Park visitors centers or campgrounds and chat with a ranger before you take to the beach by wheels. They can supply up-to-date information on unusual conditions like eroded beach areas that could prove hazardous to you and your vehicle. See our Recreation chapter for information on all-terrain vehicles.

Year-Round Beach Driving Areas-NPS

Here is a list of areas that are open year round in the National Park for beach driving:

Photo: Courtesy of Elaine Fogarty

Don't forget to check out the Bodie Island Lighthouse during your sight-seeing adventures.

• From Ramp 23 to Ramp 34, the area that stretches from the south end of Salvo to the north side of Avon.

• The beach around Cape Point, which continues all the way to Frisco Campground. You can also enter the beach at Cape Point Campground and head north to the Point or south to Frisco.

• Hatteras Ferry dock to Hatteras Inlet.

• The north end of Hatteras Inlet, depending on how much beach front is available.

• The South end of Ocracoke Island toward the village to the beach behind the airport.

Seasonal Beach Driving Areas-NPS

These National Park areas are open to vehicular traffic on a seasonal basis:

• Ramp 20 to Ramp 23, from Rodanthe to Salvo, closes the end of May until the second week in September

• Ramp 34 to Ramp 38, the area in front of the village of Avon closes at the end of May until the second week in September.

Driving Rules & Safety Tips

The maximum speed for beach driving is 25 mph, but even that can be too fast on a crowded day. The speed limit is strictly enforced by park rangers. In some spots, like Coquina Beach where the sand is soft, you may have to drive even slower than 25 mph.

Beach drivers follow the same rules that apply when driving on asphalt: Keep to the right, pass on the left, etc. All vehicles must be street legal with valid plates, insurance and inspection stickers and driven by a licensed individual. Seat belts must be worn by anyone in the front seat. Standing is not allowed in any vehicle. If you are riding in the back of a pickup truck, you must sit on the bed, not on the side rail or wheel well.

INSIDERS' TIP

Lifeguard Beach Service Inc., a member of the United States Lifesaving Association, has been providing beach service and ocean rescue to Dare County since 1958.

Jeep passengers must be seated and may not stand and hold on to the roll bar. No open containers of alcohol are allowed in the vehicle.

Pedestrians have the right-of-way at all times on the beach regardless of where they are in relation to your vehicle. Look out for children, pets, sunbathers and anglers. Many folks fall asleep on the beach and are groggy as a result. Expect the unexpected. The wind can hamper hearing, so use caution when approaching pedestrians. If the wind is blowing away from them and toward you, they may not hear your approach.

When leaving the sand, please keep your eye on pedestrian traffic on the Beach Road also. The edge of the Beach Road sometimes grabs the car a bit and can pull you to one side or another abruptly. Just make sure you give a wide berth to anyone walking near you. And a note to pedestrians themselves:

Wear light clothing at night if you intend on walking near car traffic. While most folk respect driving safety rules, some come to the beach to really let their hair down. Pedestrians need to be as conscientious as drivers on both sand and road.

Vehicle Preparation

Many, many drivers get stuck because they don't let air out of their tires before driving on the beaches. The National Park Service says its rangers generally drive with 20 pounds of pressure in their tires. This applies to vehicles of any size, from large trucks to smaller models. Lowering the pressure also helps prevent the engine from overheating when traveling through soft sand. Make sure to use a tire gauge when inflating and deflating; in fact, the process can seem a bit time-consuming when you're raring to get out on the beach, so you may want to buy two gauges and put one of your passengers to work! Rangers advise reinflating tires when returning to the paved roads. Please don't block the beach ramps to lock hubs or deflate tires. We suggest pulling well off to the side of the ramp or using the parking areas found at most vehicle accesses.

Driving On Sand

Once on the beach, try to drive on the firm, wet section of the beach below the high tide line and follow in someone else's tracks if you can. Areas that don't have any tracks might have been avoided for good reason. Watch out for areas of the beach with shell-laden, reddish sand and depressions where there is just a bit of standing water. These areas can be very soft.

Restricted Areas

You are not allowed to drive on, over or in between the dunes for any reason at anytime. The dunes and their fragile vegetation create our protective barrier and are vital to the environment. Even if you see tire tracks at the toe of the dune, do not follow them. You will be penalized if caught. Pleading ignorance won't work. Please obey all the area designations that you'll find on the beaches. Often, portions of the beach are roped off to allow shorebirds and turtles to nest. These areas change throughout the seasons, so areas that were open in April could be closed in August. Through traffic can be curtailed by these closings, especially at high tide. Stay alert for the changes, and respect the limitations. There are substantial fines for violators.

Courtesy

When driving down by the water line, always drive (or walk) behind surf anglers. You don't want to snap their nearly invisible monofilament fishing line or upset their fishing activity.

Be Prepared

Rangers are not allowed to tow stuck vehicles, so use caution. Here's a list of essential gear you'll want to have on hand in case you do get stuck: shovel, tire pressure gauge, tow rope, fire extinguisher, flashlights (two or more), bumper jack (with some boards to place beneath it), blankets, drinking water and snacks. A car phone is also handy.

We have dozens of activities to challenge the mild-mannered and chill the daredevils.

Recreation

The Outer Banks is a resort area offering many amusements that families can enjoy together, such as biking, mini-golfing and dolphin tours. There are also plenty of activities to challenge the mild-mannered and chill the daredevils, with hang gliding, Jet Skiing and parasailing. Some activities are unique to these windswept barrier beaches; others are just ways to spend time relaxing or having fun under the sun on these beautiful islands.

You can spend an afternoon walking the wide beaches searching for shells and pieces of bright cobalt beach glass that have been polished smooth by the sand and seasons of waves. Buy the kids a kite and help them send it soaring atop the wafting winds. Bird-watching opportunities abound in the wildlife refuges north of Duck and south of Pea Island. Nags Head Woods offers both a shady respite during the heat of summer and a great place to take secluded hikes through one of the most marvelous preserved maritime forests on the Atlantic seaboard. Horseshoes and pickup volleyball games are scattered along many public beach accesses for those who prefer working up a sweat and finding a little friendly competition. Bike paths line roads along the sounds and the sea, through towns and even along the Wright Brothers National Monument. If you just need to get to sea for a while and enjoy the Outer Banks from a different vantage point, riding the state ferry to Ocracoke Island is one of our favorite year-round pastimes. Best of all, each of those activities is free!

If you don't mind lightening your wallet to try something different, we've devoted entire chapters in this book to watersports, with everything from surfing and windsurfing to sailing and scuba diving; fishing, from Gulf Stream charter trips for giant bluefin tuna to inshore headboat expeditions or pier fishing; and golf, where new courses are cropping up each season to test your skills in sea breezes.

This chapter includes overviews on all the other recreational opportunities and adventures we could think of: tennis, biking and in-line skating, athletic clubs, horseback riding and go-carts — all guaranteed to get your blood flowing. Write-ups on hang gliding, parasailing and airplane tours promise to send even the most landlocked spirits soaring. If you want to get in or on the water, try slipping down a twisting waterslide, seeking a school of dolphin on a boat trip or enjoying a pirate tour while cruising around the Pamlico Sound.

When you're in the mood for more solid ground, check out one of our many miniature golf courses, from par 3 natural grass greens to crazy courses complete with moving obstacles and horrific clowns. You can tour northern beaches on rented all-terrain vehicles where N.C. Highway 12's pavement ends; or, if you've had a little too much fun in the sun, there are sections on indoor activities such as bowling alleys, movie theaters and noisy, state-of-the-art video arcades. Don't forget to check out our Kidstuff chapter for additional activities geared toward the children.

If bingo is your bag, several fire stations and civic clubs along the barrier islands host regularly scheduled sessions in the early evenings throughout the summer. Colington Island's Volunteer Fire Department off Colington Road, 441-6234, and Nags Head's Fire Department on U.S. Highway 158 just south of the Outer Banks Mall, 441-5909, are home to two of the area's more popular part-time bingo parlors.

For home entertainment, video rental stores also are scattered from Corolla to Ocracoke. Most stores don't require memberships, and they almost all rent videocassette recorders you can take back to your hotel room or vacation cottage for a night or a week.

Each season it seems, some new pastime springs from these sandy shores. The area's first paintball war zone opened in 1995. Two new minigolf courses opened their greens for the 1996 season, and a new go-cart track opened in 1997. Even Insiders who have lived here for years have not yet experienced all the recreational opportunities the Outer Banks has to offer. We sure have fun trying though.

Airplane Tours

The best way to get a feel for how fragile these barrier islands are is to take a plane ride above the Outer Banks. Small planes offer tours daily most of the year from Corolla through Ocracoke. Pilots are always pleased to dip their passengers over a school of dolphins frolicking in the Atlantic, circle one of the four lighthouses beaming from these beaches or cruise around the Wright Brothers National Monument where Wilbur and Orville flew the world's first successful heavier-than-air flights. Bring your camera. These treetop adventures provide great photo opportunities of both sea and sound shores of the islands and a true glimpse at these waterlogged wetlands. Trips can be catered to fit any desire and are well worth the reasonable rates to obtain a bird's-eye view of these skinny ribbons of sand.

Reservations are strongly recommended at least a day in advance of takeoff. All flights depend on the wind and the weather. Charter flights to Norfolk and other areas of the Outer Banks also are offered through most of these companies. Several services offer flight instruction to obtain a pilot's license and certification.

Kill Devil Hills

Kitty Hawk Aero Tours
Wright Brothers Airstrip, Kill Devil Hills
• **(252) 441-4460**

Based just behind the Wright Brothers National Monument, off Colington Road, these air tours offer half-hour flights in Cessna aircraft year round. Trips take you soaring south over Oregon Inlet, flying above the waves to see shipwrecks, over Jockey's Ridge and Roanoke Island and back to circle the monu-

ment. It costs $24 per person for parties of two and $19 per person for three- to six-person parties. Tours are offered from 10 AM to 5 PM in the off-season, and from 9 AM to sunset during the summer.

If you're up for more high-flying excitement, try a trip in a 1941 Waco biplane, where the cockpit is open and your head is literally in the clouds. Twenty-minute trips take two passengers around the central Outer Banks for a total of $98. Leather helmets and old-fashioned Red Baron-style goggles are included in the price. Biplane tours are offered from May through September from 9 AM until sunset. Reservations are preferred for both types of flights.

Roanoke Island

OBX Air Tours
408 Airport Rd., Roanoke Island
• **(252) 473-3222, (252) 453-9337,**
(888) 289-8202

OBX Air Tours, an affiliate of SouthEast Air, is at the Dare County Airport, just off U.S. 64. They offer a variety of air tours and great views of the Outer Banks. Well-maintained planes are flown by knowledgeable and professional pilots. Choose from a selection of tours of the northern, central and southern Outer Banks, or customize your own trip. Prices start at $25 per person. Call for more information and reservations (note that walk-ins are accepted as well). OBX Air Tours operates seven days a week from 8 AM to dusk.

Hatteras Island

Island Flying Service
Frisco Shopping Center, N.C. Hwy. 12, Frisco • **(252) 995-6671**

Formerly Burrus Flying Service, Island Flying Service offers sightseeing tours of Hatteras Island. One trip soars over Diamond Shoals and the Cape Hatteras Lighthouse from Rodanthe. Another tour affords aerial views of Ocracoke Island. Additional trips are available,

www.insiders.com
See this and many other
Insiders' Guide® destinations
online — in their entirety.
Visit us today!

including a summer sunset tour. Costs are $75 for two people; it's $90 for three. Tours are offered daily from May 1 through October 31 from 10 AM to 4 PM. Reservations are recommended.

Ocracoke Island

Pelican Airways
Ocracoke Airstrip, Ocracoke
• (252) 928-1661

Half-hour trips above Ocracoke and Portsmouth islands are available any time of year in this Aero-Commander plane. Trips can be tailored to suit individual interests or narrated to explain interesting aspects of the southern Outer Banks area. It costs a total of $55 for two people and $75 for three people. Flight instruction is offered by appointment. Charter service is also available — see the Getting Here, Getting Around chapter.

All-Terrain Vehicles

One of the most exhilarating ways to see the off-road areas of the Outer Banks is on an all-terrain vehicle. Whether you're cruising along the beach or chasing a sunset up the marshy sounds, you get closer to nature on one of these low-to-the-ground, open-air, gasoline-powered dune buggies. But keep in mind you're

limited to 15 mph, and you can't play on the dunes.

Corolla

Corolla Outback Adventures
Wee Winks Shopping Center, N.C. Hwy. 12, Corolla • (252) 453-4484

This outpost on the northernmost area of the Outer Banks has been operating for 17 years and rents ATVs for individual off-road adventures or guided tours. You can ride north of where the pavement ends in protected wildlife refuges, where you might see wild horses, rare waterfowl and even feral hogs in the marshlands. But be cautioned that there are strict off-road rules, including beach riding only between the mean high-water mark and the water's edge. Currituck County has been engaged in discussions about additional changes in beach driving in Corolla and Carova, so ask about updates.

The ATVs seat two people and rent for $55 an hour. Two-hour sunset tours are $85 per vehicle. Additional off-road tours are available in larger vehicles. In 1998 the company will offer a Wild Horse Safari — a two-hour north beach adventure in a four-wheel-drive vehicle. Corolla Outback Adventures also offers four-wheel-drive/kayak expeditions: Finish a tour of beaches, maritime forest and sand trails with a kayak tour in the Currituck Sound. Corolla Outback Adventures is open daily from April through November. Hours may vary in the off-season. All tours and rentals are weather-dependent.

Ocracoke Island

Portsmouth Island ATV Excursions
N.C. Hwy. 12, Ocracoke Village
• (252) 928-4484

In Ocracoke Village at the Jolly Roger Marina, this adventure service is run by Jay Bender, who also owns Corolla Outback Adventures. Up to three ATVs are loaded onto a 24-foot Carolina Skiff, along with the passengers and drivers, for the 20-minute ride to Portsmouth Island.

The isolated land is the only ghost town on the East Coast (see our Daytrippin' and Area Overviews chapters for more details). Besides having the opportunity to explore at least half of the 23-mile long island, four-wheelers will have access to the beaches with some of the best shelling on the coast. Since Portsmouth Island is owned by the National Park Service, shell-gathering is regulated; however, each sheller is allowed to take home the contents of a 1-gallon bucket. ATV Excursions does up to three runs daily to Portsmouth Island in summer. Trips last about three hours. The cost is $125 per vehicle, allowing up to two persons per vehicle. Reservations are required.

Athletic Clubs

Despite all the outdoor activities the Outer Banks has to offer, many locals and visitors still crave vigorous indoor workouts at traditional gyms and health clubs. These fitness centers are open year round and include locker room and shower facilities. They are open to the public for annual, monthly, weekly and walk-in daily membership rates.

Sanderling

Sanderling Inn Resort Health Club
N.C Hwy. 12, Sanderling
• (252) 255-0870, (252) 449-6656

Part of the lovely convention center/restaurant/hotel complex that was a former life-saving station, the Sanderling's health club, 5 miles north of Duck, offers a full line of free weights and weight machines. Stair-steppers, stationary bikes and other aerobic machines are also available in the gym. A Jacuzzi, sauna and a massage therapist (by appointment) are on hand to soothe your tired muscles after your work out. Tennis courts are open on a seasonal basis, with court fees. Sanderling's fitness club is open 7 AM to 8 PM daily. Call for membership rates and walk-in charges.

Escorted eco-tours on kayaks through Pine Island National Audubon Sanctuary are also booked through the health club. Kayaks, canoes, paddleboats and bicycles can be rented here.

Kitty Hawk

Barrier Island Fitness Center
U.S. Hwy. 158, MP 1, Kitty Hawk
• (252) 261-0100

One of the newest health clubs on the Outer Banks, Barrier Island Fitness Center (behind Wal-Mart) has a full weight room with Trotter circuit-training equipment, free weights and a Smith machine. Eight aerobics machines are also available, including treadmills, stair-steppers and stationary bikes. Low-impact through high-impact aerobic classes are offered, as are water aerobics. Call for schedules and membership rates.

Other amenities at the center include a game room with a pool table, video machines and table tennis. Tennis courts are available for play outside. Massage therapy, a sauna, a steam room and indoor and outdoor pools are also available to fitness center customers. The facility is staffed by fitness instructors and two ACSM-certified personal trainers. Hours are Monday through Friday 6 AM to 10 PM; Saturday and Sunday, 9 AM to 10 PM. The weight room closes earlier on the weekends.

Kill Devil Hills

Outer Banks Nautilus & Athletic Club
N.C. Hwy. 12, MP 7, Kill Devil Hills
• (252) 441-7001

Free weights and a full line of Nautilus, Paramount, Icarian, and Hammer Strength

exercise equipment is available here. Exercise bikes, stair machines and treadmills offer other workout options. In business for more than 15 years, this gym offers one of the largest fully certified aerobic programs on the beach. The club offers a small pro shop where vitamin supplements and fitness apparel are sold, and towels are included with your use charge. The cost is $10 per day or $30 a week for aerobics classes and gym privileges. To use the gym only, memberships cost $50 per month, $125 for three months and $299 per year. For aerobics and gym use, memberships cost $65 per month, $150 for three months and $399 annually.

Outer Banks Nautilus is open Monday through Friday from at least 6 AM to 9 PM and Saturdays from 8 AM to 5 PM. This facility is closed Sunday.

Roanoke Island

Nautics Hall Health & Fitness Complex
U.S. Hwy. 64, Manteo • (252) 473-1191

A competition-size, indoor heated pool is the centerpiece of this health club at the Elizabethan Inn, where water aerobics, swimming lessons and lap times are offered throughout the year. There's also a workout room with Nautilus and Paramount equipment, free weights, Stairmasters and an aerobicycle. Low-impact and step aerobics instruction is available daily.

Other amenities include an outdoor pool, a hot tub, a racquetball court, sun decks, a sauna and massage therapy on the premises. Nautics Hall is open from 6:30 AM to 9 PM, Mondays through Fridays, and from 9 AM to 9 PM on summer weekends. Off-season weekend hours are 9 AM to 9 PM on Saturdays and 9 AM to 6 PM on Sundays. Monthly memberships cost $50 per person. Daily passes cost $5 each for 18 years and younger, $7 for 19 years and older and $5 for seniors.

Hatteras Island

Frisco Fitness Works
N.C. Hwy. 12, Frisco • (252) 995-3900

Starting its fourth year in 1998, this athletic club is in the Indiantown Center. It is open year round from 7 AM to 8 PM Monday through Friday and from 8 AM to 4 PM Saturday and Sunday. State-of-the-art Sybex weights, free weights, exercise bikes, treadmills and stair machines are offered here. There's a changing facility on-site, but showers are not available. Call for the aerobics schedule. The cost for aerobics and the gym is $37 per month. Guest fees are $10 daily or $37 a week. Yearly rates are also available.

Biking and Skating

With two lanes of N.C. Hwy. 12 stretching along more than 100 miles of blacktop from Corolla to Ocracoke, and hugging the seaside almost all the way, cyclists and in-line skaters can cruise throughout the Outer Banks and get almost anywhere they want to go. The flat terrain on these barrier islands makes the area perfect even for beginners. Three off-road, paved paths on Roanoke Island and in South Nags Head and Kill Devil Hills provide safer routes for everyone to follow (see the listing in our Getting Here, Getting Around chapter). Also, Wheels of Dare bicycle club schedules sporadic tours and treks throughout the year; call Charles Hardy at (252) 473-3328 daytime or (252) 441-3805 at night.

Kill Devil Hills and Nags Head restrict in-line skating along U.S. Highway 158 and the Beach Road. But there's a wonderful bike path near the Wright Memorial off Colington Road that winds behind the monument and connects up to another path behind First Flight Village in Kill Devil Hills. You're also allowed to use paths in the memorial, where you can ride or skate for miles. It's a good idea to check the rules with each town before putting your wheels on the asphalt.

While there is little crime on the Outer Banks, bicycles do disappear. Lock up carefully, and never leave your bike parked overnight in a front yard or in an easy access spot. If your bike is stolen, call the local police. Sometimes bikes are taken on nocturnal "joy rides" and then picked up by the local police department, so call them before you panic. It's also a good idea to record your bike's serial number for identification purposes.

You might also want to arm yourself with some safety tips. A little bit of prevention goes a long way, and you'd be surprised how many folks don't know the bicycle safety rules.

Remember:

• Use designated bike paths when available (see our Getting Around chapter for path locations)

• Wear safety helmets

• Ride on the right side of the road with the flow of traffic

• Always maintain a single file

• Obey all traffic rules

• Use hand signals for stops and turns

• Don't double up unless the bike is designed for more than one

• Keep your hands on the handlebars

• Observe pedestrian's right of way on walks, paths and streets

• Many Outer Banks areas harbor tire-puncturing cacti

• Look out for soft sand that can cause a wipe out

• Use a front-lighted white lamp and a rear red reflector when riding at night

Corolla

Ocean Atlantic Rentals
Corolla Light Village Shops, N.C. Hwy. 12, Corolla • (252) 453-2440
N.C. Hwy. 12, Duck • (252) 261-4346
N.C. Hwy. 12, MP 10, Nags Head • (252) 441-7823
N.C. Hwy. 12, Avon • (252) 995-5868

Bicycles and Rollerblades of all shapes and sizes can be rented by the day, weekend and week from each location of Ocean Atlantic Rentals. Adult bikes rent for an average of $10 a day or $25 per week in the off-season and $35 per week in the summer. Children's cycles lease for $7 a day, $25 per week. In-line skates rent for $15 a day or $25 for three days. These rental outfits also lease volleyball and croquet sets and other recreational equipment. Most Ocean Atlantic outposts are open seven days a week, year round from 10 AM to 6 PM in the off-season (call ahead for the Avon location) and 10 AM to 9 PM throughout the summer.

Kitty Hawk Kites/Outer Banks Outdoors
N.C. Hwy. 12, Corolla • (252) 453-3685
U.S. Hwy. 158, MP 13, Nags Head • (252) 441-4124
The Waterfront, Manteo • (252) 473-2357
Hatteras Landing, Hatteras • (252) 986-1446, (800) 334-4777

This recreational haven on the Outer Banks sells and rents Rollerblades by the day or week from its Manteo, Nags Head and Corolla locations. In-line skating clinics, lessons and festivals also are held throughout the summers. Skates rent for $10 a day or $25 for three days. Lessons cost $15 and require advance reservations. The Nags Head store is open year round from at least 9 AM to 6 PM, with extended hours in the summer. Other outposts are open seasonally.

Bicycle tours of Roanoke Island and Corolla in which you rent your own cycle or a beach cruiser also are offered by Kitty Hawk Kites. Two-hour tours cost $20 per person and are offered on varied days and times during the summer. Bike rentals are $6 for the first two hours, $2 each additional hour or $12 per day. Child seats are available for an additional $2. Bicycles are available to rent at the Nags Head and Hatteras locations.

Kill Devil Hills

The Bike Barn
Monteray Plaza, N.C. Hwy. 12, Corolla
• (252) 453-0788
1312 Wrightsville Blvd., Kill Devil Hills
• (252) 441-3786
N.C. Hwy. 12, Hatteras • (252) 986-BIKE

For 14 years, The Bike Barn has sold and repaired various makes and models of bikes on the Outer Banks. This shop also rents bikes and sells equipment from brand names such as Giant, Caloi, Jamis, Trek, and Diamond Back. The Kill Devil Hills shop is open year round Monday through Saturday. The Corolla shop opens in late March and operates until Thanksgiving. The Hatteras shop is open March through December. Please call the main store in Kill Devil Hills for more information.

KDH Cycle and Skate
Sea Holly Square, N.C. Hwy 12, MP 8,
Kill Devil Hills • (252) 480-3399

Open year round, this full-service bicycle shop rents excellent equipment at competitive prices. Owner Chip Cowan says his store has the best rental fleet on the beach, offering all types of bikes (including cruisers and mountain bikes) and a full range of in-line skates that can be leased. A 24-speed Cannondale with suspension rents for $15 per day or $50 per week. Cruisers rent for $10 per day or $35 per week. K-2 in-line skates rent for $10 per

day or $30 per week. All safety equipment is included in the rental cost.

KDH Cycle and Skate, celebrating its fifth year in business in 1998, is open daily from 8 AM to 8 PM in summer and 10 AM to 6 PM in the off-season.

Nags Head

Family Life Center
U.S. Hwy. 158, MP 11½, Nags Head
• (252) 441-4941

A recreational facility for the Outer Banks Worship Center, this Christian-affiliated roller-skating rink behind the Ark is open to the public on Friday evenings from 7:30 to 10 PM and on Saturdays from 7 to 9 PM year round. Here, kids can rent regular, old-fashioned roller skates for $2.50 and cruise around the slick floor. Ping-Pong and video games also are available.

Kitty Hawk Sports
U.S. Hwy. 158, MP 13, Nags Head
• (252) 441-6800

Two-hour bicycle tours are given every summer morning and afternoon. The $19 cost includes bikes, helmets, water bottles and the guided tour. Tours depart from Kitty Hawk Woods, Nags Head Woods and Roanoke Island. Call for off-season schedules. Bikes are also available for rent. Call for prices.

Hatteras Island

Island Cycles
N.C. Hwy. 12, Avon • (252) 995-4336,
(800) 229-7810

This all-encompassing bicycle shop is north of the only stoplight in Avon, right next to the Subway sandwich shop. Sales, repairs, advice and bicycle rentals are offered. Mopeds are also available for sale or rent. Cyclists can lease seven-speed beach cruisers for $15 a day or $45 a week; single- speed beach cruisers for $10 a day or $30 per week; mountain bikes and road bikes for $15 a day or $45 a week; or higher-end bikes and tandems for slightly higher prices. Kids' bikes lease for $7 a day or $25 a week. Cycles also can be rented by the hour for $4 or $5, de-

Photo: Courtesy of J. Aaron Trotman

Soar over the fragile barrier islands for a view that's literally tops!

pending on the style. Group and off-season rates are available. Island Cycle is open year round. Summer hours are 9 AM to 6 PM. Off-season hours will vary, so call ahead.

Hatteras Wind & Surf
N.C. Hwy. 12, Avon • (252) 995-6257

Besides catering to your watersports needs, Hatteras Wind & Surf, across from the pier, rents bikes and in-line skates. Bike cruisers rent for $4 an hour, $8 for four hours, $10 per day, $20 for three days or $25 per week. In-line skates rent for $10 for four hours, $15 a day, $25 for three days or $35 per week. Rental fees include pads and helmets. The shop closes during the winter months.

Lee Robinson's General Store
N.C. Hwy. 12, Hatteras Village • (252) 986-2381

Here, bikes can be rented year round,

seven days a week for cycling tours around the southern end of Hatteras Island. Bikes rent for $2 an hour, $10 a day or $35 per week. Lee Robinson's is open until 11 PM in the summer, with abbreviated hours during the off-season.

Ocracoke Island

Slushy Stand
N.C. Hwy. 12, Ocracoke Village • (252) 928-1878

Take a breather and rock a spell in a chair on the wraparound porch before renting a two-wheeler here. You can't miss the bike racks spread out in front of this juniper-sided building just across from Silver Lake Harbor. Traditional coaster and kids' bikes rent by the hour, day or week from April through November. Special tandem bicycles and tricycles also can be leased. Call for rental rates. After a long ride through Ocracoke Island, be sure to sample a hand-dipped ice cream cone or old-fashioned slushy at the snack bar.

Island Rentals
Silver Lake Rd., Ocracoke Village
• (252) 928-5480

Adults' and kids' bikes can be rented by the day, three days or week from this Ocracoke Island outpost, which is at Sharon Miller Realty. Weekly rental rates are $24 for children's cycles and $30 for adult bikes. Reservations can be made in advance for weekly rentals.

Island Rentals also leases volleyball, horseshoe and croquet sets for recreation at your rental cottage. Clam rakes rent for $15 a week.

Beach Outfitters
N.C. Hwy. 12, Ocracoke Village
• (252) 928-6261, (252) 928-7411

Beach Outfitters, in the Ocracoke Island Realty office, is open all year and accepts reservations. You can rent bikes and other items here. See our Cottages and Long-term Rentals chapter for more information.

Bowling

Sometimes even the most dedicated sun-worshippers need an afternoon or evening in air-conditioned comfort. When you've caught too many rays or the weather just won't cooperate, bowling is an alternative way to wile away the hours on the Outer Banks.

Nags Head

Nags Head Bowling
U.S. Hwy. 158, MP 10, Nags Head
• (252) 441-7077

Open for year-round league and recreational excitement, this is the Outer Banks' only bowling center. Here, 24 lanes are available for unlimited members of a party. There is also a pro shop, a video arcade and a cafe serving light meals, sandwiches, wine, beer and hamburgers. Laser light and glow-in-the-dark bowling is offered at 10 PM, and a new

billiards room opened in 1997. Bowling costs $2.85 per game, and shoes rent for $2. Nags Head Bowling is open from noon to midnight Sunday through Friday and from 10 AM to midnight on Saturdays. Call for league information.

Climbing

Sport climbing walls are available at the following locations.

Kitty Hawk Kites/Outer Banks Outdoors
Monteray Plaza, N.C. Hwy. 12, Corolla
• (252) 453-3685
TimBuck II, N.C. Hwy 12, Corolla
• (252) 453-8845
U.S. Hwy 158, MP 13, Nags Head
• (252) 441-4124
Hatteras Landing, N.C. Hwy. 12, Hatteras Village • (252) 986-1446

If you're tired of our flat Outer Banks landscape and are itching for more than scaling lighthouse steps, try one of Kitty Hawk Kites/Outer Banks Outdoors' indoor climbing walls. Three climbs and basic instruction cost $7 per person. Rappelling equipment, climbing shoes and ropes are all part of the package.

At the Nags Head location, an hour training class is available for $19. The cost of the lesson includes equipment and climbs. At TimBuck II, scale the 22-foot high wall with four main routes and an overhang for extra challenges. At Monteray Plaza, there's a 25-foot indoor climbing wall with four main routes and an overhang. Only the Nags Head location is open year round. Call for hours at other locations.

Dolphin Tours, Boat Rides and Pirate Trips

Most Outer Banks boat cruises are included in our Watersports and Fishing chapters. However, a few unusual offerings are worth mentioning here as well. These trips, of course, are weather-dependent and available only during warmer spring and summer months. Reservations are recommended for

Recreation ranges from a dip in the sound to high-flying hang-gliding adventures.

each of these tours. Unlike sailing and more participatory water adventures, you don't have to be able to swim to enjoy these activities and you probably won't even get wet on board these boats that slip along the shallow sounds.

Nags Head

The Waterworks
U.S. Hwy. 158, MP 17, Nags Head
• (252) 441-8875

3pm.
$22/adult

If you'd like to get a glimpse of dolphins up close, take a one-hour cruise through schools of the gentle creatures who will leap and dive alongside your boat. Trips are offered daily throughout the summer. Call for rates.

Waterworks also offers a 40-minute, 15-mile airboat ride through the Bodie Island Wildlife Refuge. Passengers are motored through salt marshes and treated to a wonderful view of Bodie Island Lighthouse. These expeditions on the Roanoke Sound cost $18 for adults, and $9 for children.

Willett's Wetsports
Caribbean Corners, Nags Head/Manteo Cswy., Nags Head • (252) 441-4112, (252) 473-1748

In the bright pink building, Willett's offers

dolphin tours in the Roanoke Sound conducted by marine biologist Rich Mallon-Day four times daily June through September. In 1997 they achieved sightings of the beloved animals on every trip. Customers were so delighted that they applauded, owner Artie Tillett says. Passengers are informed about other regional wildlife during the tour, and they get to be part of the scientist's research team to boot. Tours cost $10 for children and seniors and $20 for adults.

Roanoke Island

The Crystal Dawn
Pirate's Cove Marina, Manteo
• (252) 473-5577

Sunset cruises around Roanoke Island are offered every evening except Sunday throughout the summer on this sturdy, two-story vessel. Trips include commentary about the Outer Banks, while the boat cruises past Andy Griffith's house, the *Elizabeth II*, Jockey's Ridge or the scenic fishing village of Wanchese. The boat departs at 6:30 PM, returning about 90 minutes later. Adult admission is $8 per person, and children 10 and younger pay $4 each. Moonlight trips around Roanoke Island also are available aboard the *Crystal Dawn*, from 8:30

PM to 10 PM on Thursdays and Fridays in May through October. Call in advance. The cost is $8 per person. For additional information see our Fishing chapter.

Captain Johnny
Queen Elizabeth St., Manteo
• **(252) 473-1475**

Manteo's only fast multipurpose pontoon boat, *Captain Johnny* is a great way to cruise around looking for dolphins, something captain Stuart Wescott has a knack for finding. Wescott, owner of *Captain Johnny*, says he had a more than 97 percent success rate finding dolphins in 1997. Dolphin cruises are guaranteed: If you don't see any dolphins, you ride free next time. Two-hour cruises cost $15 each and depart from the entrance to the *Elizabeth II* site at 1:30 PM five days a week. A Sunset Sound Safari cruise, narrated by ninth-generation native Wescott, is available by charter. Call for schedules and rate information.

Downeast Rover
Manteo Waterfront Marina, Manteo
• **(252) 473-4866**

A 55-foot topsail schooner, the *Downeast Rover* tall ship is a modern reproduction in steel of a traditional 19th-century sailing vessel. Two-hour cruises into the Albemarle and Roanoke sounds delight passengers with views of dolphin, osprey, heron and seabirds. A hands-on adventure is also possible on this lovely boat: Passengers can help trim the sails and take a turn at the wheel. Tickets can be purchased on the *Downeast Rover*, which also has a ship's store and rest room on board. Deck seating and a below-deck lounge are available. Daytime cruises are $10 for children age 2 to 12 and $20 for adults. Sunset cruises are $20 per person. Daytime cruises depart at 11 AM and 2 PM daily. Sunset cruises depart at 6:30 PM in the summer. Call for updates and off-season schedules. Reservations are recommended but not required. Private charters are available.

Hatteras Island

Captain Clam
N.C. Hwy. 12, Hatteras Village
• **(252) 986-2460**

Three-hour dolphin tours around Hatteras Inlet are offered each Thursday afternoon at 1 PM throughout the summer aboard this inshore headboat, which leaves from Teach's Lair Marina. Passengers aboard *Captain Clam* are virtually guaranteed to see dolphin because the crew constantly communicates with spotter planes on radios. The cost is $20 per person.

Captain Clam crews, clad in pirate garb, also put on plays about Blackbeard and other Outer Banks renegades from 5 to 7 PM each Thursday in-season. As you cruise around the pirate's haunts wearing complimentary eye patches and swords, you'll be treated to tales of mutiny on the high seas, buried treasure and other local lore. The cost is $15 per person.

Ocracoke

The Windfall
The Community Store, N.C. Hwy. 12, Ocracoke Village • **(252) 928-7245**

You can sail around Blackbeard's former haunts aboard this traditional gaff-rigged schooner that seats up to 30 passengers. One-hour cruises depart from The Community Store several times daily in summer, and it costs $10 per person. Call for the schedule.

Go-carts

If you're looking for a way to race around the Outer Banks without fear of getting a ticket,

---

INSIDERS' TIP

If you really want to understand the forces of nature, take a walk by Oregon Inlet, at the abandoned Coast Guard station south of the Bonner Bridge. There, you can stroll out onto the rock jetty and see and feel the power of wind and current. Notice how sand has covered the adjacent parking lot and roadway.

several go-cart rental outlets offer riders a thrill a minute on exciting, curving tracks. Drivers have to be at least 12 years old to take the wheel at most of these places, but younger children are often allowed to strap themselves in beside adults to experience the fast-paced action.

Corolla

Corolla Raceway
TimBuck II Shopping Village,
N.C. Hwy. 12, Corolla • (252) 453-9100

Entering its second season in 1998, Corolla Raceway is the sister track of Nags Head Raceway. It is in TimBuck II Shopping Center and features one large track with 16 Indy cars. The go-cart raceway is open Easter through November. A five-minute race costs $8 for singles and $10 for doubles. After riders have spun around the track enough, they can engage in "Water Wars," with either a $3 or a $5 bucket of water balloons that are thrown from two stations situated 40 feet apart. There's also a family arcade onsite for those wanting some dryer fun. Summer hours are 10 AM until 11 PM daily.

Kill Devil Hills

Colington Speedway
1064 Colington Rd., Kill Devil Hills
• (252) 480-9144

The Outer Banks' newest go-cart facility, Colington Speedway features three tracks and about 40 Indy-style or NASCAR-style 5.5 horsepower cars. Riders choose between a kiddie track, a family road course or a slick track. The facility has been expanded with a gift shop that features NASCAR items, Outer Banks souvenirs and children's toys. Colington Speedway is open daily from Memorial Day through Labor Day until 10 PM. The track is also open on weekends until 10 PM in the shoulder season. Call for opening hours and more information.

Nags Head

Dowdy's Go-Karts
N.C. Hwy 12, MP 11, Nags Head
• (252) 441-5122

This is one of the area's oldest go-cart tracks, across from the ocean next to Tortuga's Lie Shellfish Bar & Grill. All the cars are only a few years old and can take tight turns around the oval track. Outdoor bleachers provide a perfect place for parents to spectate this noisy sport. These motorized carts can be rented daily throughout the summer from midmorning until 11 PM. Call for prices.

Dowdy's Amusement Park
U.S. Hwy. 158, MP 11, Nags Head
• (252) 441-5122

A second go-cart track, also owned by the Dowdys, awaits riders at the Outer Banks' only amusement park. This long, oval track is open evenings only from May through early September. There's also an indoor video arcade and snack bar here (see our Kidstuff chapter).

Speed-n-Spray Action Park
U.S. Hwy. 158, MP 15, Nags Head
• (252) 480-1900

This racetrack treats drivers to wild rides around quick curves that twist back toward the blacktop just as you think you might slip off into the sound. It's open from early May through September daily. Call for prices.

Nags Head Raceway
U.S. Hwy. 158, MP 16, Nags Head
• (252) 480-4639

Speed demons and thrill seekers will revel in this fun roadway, complete with two-seater carts and slick new racers. A five-minute spin around the track costs $7 in a single cart and

INSIDERS' TIP

Outer Banks weather is kind to outdoor recreation hounds. Because the mighty Gulf Stream bullies away many weather fronts, summers and winters here are never too extreme in temperature.

$8 for a double. Drivers can time themselves trying to beat the clock or sprinting against their friends in hurried heats. Nags Head Raceway is open from April through Thanksgiving. Calmer pursuits can be had at the family arcade on the premises. Summer hours are from 10 AM until 11 PM, seven days a week.

Hatteras Island

Waterfall Park
N.C. Hwy. 12, Rodanthe • (252) 987-2213

This sound-to-sea amusement area offers the biggest selection of go-cart tracks on the Outer Banks — and more recreational opportunities in a single spot than anywhere else on Hatteras Island. Here, kids of all ages will enjoy six separate race car tracks where drivers can test their skills on a different style vehicle at each pit stop. Wet racers are great for hot afternoon sprints against the wind — and other boaters. Bumper boats, two minigolf courses and a snack bar also are open from 11 AM to 10 PM daily from May through October. Each ride costs $6 per person.

Hang Gliding

The closest any human being will ever get to feeling like a bird is by flying beneath the brightly colored wings of a hang glider, with arms and legs outstretched and only the wind all around. Lessons are available for flight of all ages. Just watching these winged creatures soar atop Jockey's Ridge or catching air lifts above breakers along the Atlantic is enough to make bystanders want to test their wings.

Kitty Hawk Kites/Outer Banks Outdoors
U.S. Hwy. 158, MP 13, Nags Head • (252) 441-4124, (800) 334-3777

The country's most popular hang gliding school, this Nags Head training center across from Jockey's Ridge State Park offers a variety of ways to learn to fly — or just enjoy the thrill of being airborne while strapped in with an experienced instructor. Whether you want to soar solo 5 feet above a sand dune or cruise through the clouds after taking off from the shoreline,

teachers here can help you meet your goals. After all, they've taught more than 200,000 people how to fly since first opening their doors on the Outer Banks more than 25 years ago.

Beginning dune training programs probably are the most common methods of learning to hang glide. In these classes, you learn how to launch a rental craft by foot from the undulating sand dune of Jockey's Ridge State Park, and you never have more than 15 feet to fall. These are solo flights, where you and the hang glider are alone in the air. No experience is necessary, and both group and private lessons are offered. Basic instruction and three flights off Jockey's Ridge cost $49 and are available most of the year. Two additional flights can be purchased for $20 more.

Aerotow training programs are based at Maple Airport in Currituck County. With these flights, you're strapped behind an ultralight plane with an instructor who helps you take off after the aircraft tows you to a safe altitude. You never have to go it alone in one of these gigs. Tandem flights are offered up to 2,000 feet — the views are spectacular — and packages are available. Please call for rates.

If you'd rather take off from the water, boat tow training programs are available. Call for the location. Again, you and an instructor are strapped together, but a boat tows you to the proper altitude before you begin to soar off the long line. Tandem flights are available up to 2,000 feet.

Paragliding is the fastest growing form of individual aviation in the world, featuring an elliptical shaped, completely flexible parachute-like wing that operates more as a hang glider. These easy-to-operate crafts are launched by running until the chute fills with wind and air. You control the fate of your own solo flight by using handles that change the shape of the wing. These chutes are slower and easier to maneuver than hang gliders. They are also light enough to stuff into a backpack. Paragliding training takes place at Maple Airport in Currituck County and allows students to fly from 500 to 1,000 feet into the air. Three-hour lessons are offered. Call for rates.

Although most sports enthusiasts seek out these activities during the summer, you can achieve most of these high-flying thrills year-round. Reservations are required for most adventures. Discount packages offer more in-depth instruction and a shot at certification.

Horseback Riding

Our favorite way to experience the Outer Banks is without gasoline or motors — on the back of a gentle horse clopping through the sand. Some folks in Kitty Hawk and Wanchese villages keep their own horses for private rides, and we envy their freedom to roam these barrier islands on the backs of such majestic animals. Even if you don't own your own horse, you can still enjoy riding one. Year-round trips are offered on Hatteras Island, and seasonal sojourns near sea and sound are available on Ocracoke.

Hatteras Island

Buxton Stables
N.C. Hwy. 12, Buxton • (252) 995-4659
Sturdy, reliable horses take riders on unforgettable tours from these wooden stables year round. No experience is necessary for one-hour trail rides through the maritime forest of Buxton Woods, but you have to be an experienced rider who can sit at all gaits to enjoy the three-hour beach ride that winds through the woods onto the wide sand, and into the surf. The horses are ridden with English saddles. Riders must be older than age 10, weigh less than 200 pounds and not be pregnant. One-hour rides through the woods are offered in the afternoons and cost $27 per person. The three-hour trip costs $65 each and departs in the morning. The stables are open every day except Sunday from 7 AM to 8 PM. Call for reservations.

Ocracoke Island

Seaside Stables
N.C. Hwy. 12, Ocracoke • (252) 928-3778
Warm and energetic, owner Karen Lewis leads riders on one-hour beach/sound rides and two-hour sunset rides along the Atlantic. The excursions are offered on a daily and thrice-weekly basis. Since Lewis opened for business in 1991, she has expanded from three to 15 horses, all well-behaved mounts that are mostly cool-blooded Appaloosas and quarter horses. She will choose the right mount to fit your level of expertise, even if you've never before laid eyes on a horse.

Seaside Stables is near Ocracoke Village and is open April through October, depending on the weather. Reservations are required. In 1997, the one-hour rides cost $25, and the two-hour rides cost $40. Call ahead for further information and updates.

Miniature Golf Courses

No beach vacation is complete unless you putt a brightly colored ball through a windmill, under a pirate's sword or across a slightly sloping hill into a small metal cup. On the Outer Banks, more than a dozen minigolf courses await fun-loving families and friends from Corolla through Hatteras Island. Themed fairways featuring African animals, circus clowns and strange obstacles await even the most amateur club-swinging families. Small children will enjoy the ease of some of these holes, and even skilled golfers can get into the new par 3 grass courses that have been growing in numbers over recent years.

You can tee off at most places by 10 AM. Many courses stay open past midnight for night owls to enjoy. Several of these attractions offer play-all-day packages for a single price. Almost all minigolf courses operate seasonally, and, since they are all outside, their openings are weather-dependent.

Corolla

The Grass Course
N.C. Hwy 12, Corolla • (252) 453-4198
Offering the Outer Banks' first natural grass course, these soundside greens are open throughout the summer season. The 18-hole course includes par 3s, 4s and 5s. The undulating hills winding around natural dunes will provide intriguing challenges for beginning and better golfers. It costs $7 for adults, and $5 for kids 6 and younger. The course is open from April to November. Summer hours are 10 AM to midnight daily; it's open weekends only in the off-season.

Kitty Hawk

The Promenade
U.S. Hwy. 158, MP ¼, Kitty Hawk
• (252) 261-4900

This family fun park includes Victorian-style buildings, turn-of-the-century streetlights, waterside recreation, a children's playground and an 18-hole themed minigolf course called Waterfall Greens where the cost is $5 per game. There's also a nine-hole, par 3, natural grass putting course, complete with separate putting greens and a target driving range; the cost is $5 per game. A par 3, chip-and-putt nine-hole course can also be played for $7 a game; the 18-hole costs $12. A snack bar and picnic tables are on-site. The Promenade is open Easter weekend through early October. Summer hours are 8:30 AM to midnight, seven days a week.

Bermuda Greens
U.S. Hwy. 158 and N.C. Hwy. 12, MP 1¼, Kitty Hawk • (252) 261-0101

This lovely, landscaped course is at the intersection of U.S. Highway 158 and N.C. Highway 12. It's straight ahead if you're going east from the Wright Memorial Bridge, between the turnoffs to Duck and Kitty Hawk beaches. Two 18-hole miniature golf courses are open here from Easter through Thanksgiving. The cost for one round, on one course, is $7 for adults and $5 for children 10 and younger. During summer, the greens stay open from 10 AM until midnight daily. There's also a video arcade on site and a Dairy Queen stand for cool, creamy refreshments after a heated game of golf.

The Grass Course
U.S. Hwy. 158, MP 5½, Kitty Hawk
• (252) 441-7626

More challenging than the usual minigolf fairways, this natural grass course includes two 18-hole, par 56 courses. Most holes are 110 feet from the tees. The courses are open from 10 AM until midnight daily during summer. The cost for one 18-hole game is $7 for adults and $5 for children younger than 10. If you play a second round of 18 holes in succession, discounts are offered. JK's Ribs is on-site, offering great lunch and dinner specials in case you work up an appetite (see our Restaurants chapter).

Kill Devil Hills

Lost Treasure Golf
U.S. Hwy. 158, MP 7¼, Kill Devil Hills
• (252) 480-0142

One of the barrier islands newer — and most attention-getting — minigolf parks, Lost Treasure Golf features two 18-hole courses situated among five waterfalls that are illuminated with different colors at night. Kids will love the little train that carts them up to the first hole and through pretend caves and mines. Professor Hacker, a fictional adventurer, tells his story about gold and diamond expeditions that the kids can read about as they play. Lost Treasure Golf is open April through November. Hours are 9 AM to 11 PM daily in the summer and are decreased accordingly in the off-season. Costs are $7 per person and kids age 3 and under are free. Rates vary in the off-season.

Diamond Shoals Family Fun Park
U.S. Hwy. 158, MP 9¾, Kill Devil Hills
• (252) 480-3553

Two 18-hole miniature golf courses await putters here from Easter through October. All the grass is natural. The cost is $7 for one game for adults, and $5 for children. Also, enjoy a video arcade, a batting stadium where you can slam a softball or baseball up to 250 feet, paddleboats, waterslides and a snack bar. Diamond Shoals is open from 10 AM to midnight during the summer.

Nags Head

Pink Elephant Mini Golf
N.C. Hwy. 12, MP 11, Nags Head
• (252) 441-5875

Colorful circus animals in bright cages surround 36 lighted holes of minigolf at this popular Outer Banks course across from the Atlantic. You can't miss this place, because the world's freakiest clown presides over its grassy greens, mocking would-be putters to try to sink one in. Pink Elephant is open on weekends in April, early May, September and October and daily throughout the summer. In-season hours are 9 AM to midnight. You can play all day until 6 PM for $5 per 18 holes. Children younger than 4 with a paying adult play free. The price doesn't change after dark as it does on many minigolf courses.

Blackbeard's Miniature Golf Park
U.S. Hwy. 158, MP 15, Nags Head
• (252) 441-4541

The Outer Banks' most infamous pirate wields his 6-foot sword above these greens. Open daily, summers only, until at least 10 PM, Blackbeard's includes a video arcade if you're tired of putting around.

Jurassic Putt
U.S. Hwy. 158, MP 16, Nags Head
• (252) 441-6841

Formerly King Neptune Golf, this minigolf course revamped its theme and remodeled last season. Life-size models of dinosaurs from the Jurassic period hover over and among the greens, delighting kids and adults alike. Two 18-hole courses wind through caves and streams and around the dinosaur models. Jurassic Putt is open daily from mid-March until November. Hours are 9 AM until midnight. Call or stop by for rates.

Hatteras Island

Avon Golf
N.C. Hwy. 12, Avon • (252) 995-5480

Adjacent to the Avon Pier, this 18-hole, natural grass course is open from noon to 11 PM, seven days a week all summer. You can play as many games as you can squeeze in from noon until 6 PM. The cost is $6 for adults, and $5 for children. After 6 PM, the price goes up a little — $7 for adults, and $6 for children — but it's still play 'til you drop, or the lights

go out, whichever comes first. Avon Golf is open from Easter through the week after Thanksgiving, depending on business.

Cool Wave Ice Cream Shop and Miniature Golf
N.C. Hwy. 12, Buxton • (252) 995-6366

Located in the neighborhood of the Cape Hatteras Lighthouse, this nine-hole course is open from Easter through Thanksgiving. Summer hours are noon until 10 PM, seven days a week. Call for prices. If you play one round of nine holes, the second time around is free. Ice cream, milk shakes and the best banana splits on Hatteras await players after a good game.

Movie Theaters

On some steamy summer afternoons or rainy Saturday nights, there's no better place to be than inside a dark, air-conditioned movie theater catching the latest flick with a friend. First-run movies are offered at most Outer Banks theaters. Popcorn, candy and sodas are, of course, sold at all moviehouses. Note that you can call (252) 441-5630 for recorded feature information on all local theaters except the Pioneer in Manteo.

Corolla

RC Theater
Monteray Plaza, N.C. Hwy. 12, Corolla
• (252) 453-2399

This seasonal establishment in Monteray Plaza includes four wide screens and is open from May through Labor Day. The theater re-opens for shows again from Thanksgiving through New Year's Day. Movies are shown seven days a week from 11 AM to midnight. Tickets cost $7 for adults, and $4.50 for children younger than 11. Matinees cost $4.50 for children and adults.

INSIDERS' TIP

Kitty Hawk Kites, the largest kite store on the East Coast, offers 90-minute stunt kite flying lessons Mondays at 3 PM or by appointment. Cost is $5. The store also sponsors four kite-flying events, complete with kite-making classes, every summer. Call (252) 441-4124 for more information.

Southern Shores

RC Theater
The Marketplace, U.S. Hwy. 158, MP 1, Southern Shores • (252) 261-7866

Two screens feature first-run movies in this theater year round, seven days a week. Matinee prices before 6:30 PM are $4.50 for everyone. Tickets for children and seniors cost $4.50 in evening. Evening-only shows are offered during the off-season weekdays. Movies begin at 11 AM on weekends and throughout the summer. Tickets cost $7 for adults in the evening.

Kitty Hawk

RC Theater
U.S. Hwy. 158, MP 4, Kitty Hawk • (252) 261-7949

Open from Memorial Day weekend through Labor Day, this moviehouse has two screens that show films seven days a week from 11 AM until midnight. Tickets are $7 for adults, and $4.50 for children.

Nags Head

Cineplex
U.S. Hwy. 158, MP 10½, Nags Head • (252) 441-1808

Offering four screens and first-run movies year round, this large moviehouse shows films all day on weekends and throughout the summer, and on evenings only in the off-season. Admission is $7 for adults and $4.50 for children. Matinee shows are $4.50 for everyone.

RC Theater
Outer Banks Mall, U.S. Hwy. 158, MP 14, Nags Head • (252) 441-3900

Two wide screens feature films throughout the year. During the summer and on weekends, they're shown from 11 AM until midnight. On off-season weekdays, the movies only run in the evening. Tickets are $7 for adults and $4.50 for children. Matinees, again, are $4.50 per person.

Roanoke Island

Ye Olde Pioneer Theatre
113 Budleigh St., Manteo • (252) 473-2216

The nation's oldest theater operated continuously by one family, the Pioneer is our favorite place to see films on the Outer Banks. It's filled with nostalgia and smells of just-buttered popcorn. And it's been showing great flicks since 1934. For the $3 admission price — and the feel of the place — it can't be beat. Even the popcorn, sodas and candy are a great deal. The Pioneer is open year round, and all movies start at 8 PM daily. Listings change weekly on Fridays. See the Attractions and Area Overviews chapters for more information.

Parasailing

If you've always wanted to float high above the water, beneath a colorful parachute, opportunities for such peaceful adventures await you at a variety of locations along the Outer Banks. This is one of the most enjoyable experiences we've had during summer. Our only regrets are that the incredible rides don't last longer. We could stay up at these lofty heights, strapped comfortably into a climbing harness, swinging beneath billowing air-filled chutes for hours.

Although a boat pulls you from below, allowing the wind to lift you toward the clouds, you don't get wet on these outdoor adventures over the sounds unless you want to. Riders don't even have to know how to swim to soar with the sea gulls above whitecaps and beach cottages. Anyone of any age, without any athletic ability at all, will enjoy parasailing and find it one of their most memorable pastimes. And it's safe too. Unbreakable ropes are standard.

Corolla

Kitty Hawk Watersports
N.C. Hwy. 12, Corolla • (252) 453-6900

Parasail flights are offered daily throughout the summer at this TimBuck II shop, owned by Kitty Hawk Sports. Rates are set according to the height you choose to soar at — call for rates and schedules.

Photo: Courtesy of Mary Ellen Riddle

Several Outer Banks marinas offer a variety of fishing recreation options.

Duck

Above It All Parasail
1446 Duck Rd., Duck • (252) 261-4200

Stephen Halterman, with six years in the Coast Guard and four as a parasailing boat pilot, claims to be the most experienced parasailing captain in the area. You can fly at 400 feet, 700 feet or 1,000 feet above the Currituck Sound. Rates are subject to change, so call ahead for reservations and charges. Above It All is open year round, by appointment.

North Beach Sailing
N.C. Hwy. 12, Duck • (252) 261-7100

Specializing in tandem flights, North Beach Sailing was one of the original parasailing locations on the Outer Banks. All vessels that give you your ride are Coast Guard inspected and are able to take up to 12 passengers from 400 to 1,200 feet. Parasailing is available at North Beach Sailing, at the Barrier Island pier, from May through October. Call for more information.

The Waterworks
N.C. Hwy. 12, Duck • (252) 261-7245
U.S. Hwy. 158, MP 17, Nags Head
• (252) 441-8875

Whatever height you wish to reach, parasailing captains from The Waterworks can take you there. Uplifting experiences are offered daily from 8 AM to 5 PM in Duck and Nags Head from April through November. These eight- to 15-minute flights allow you to float at 300, 600, 900 or 1,200 feet and cost $38 to $98 per person, depending on how high you want to fly.

Nags Head Watersports
Nags Head/Manteo Cswy., Nags Head
• (252) 480-2236

Owner Artie Tillett says he has had smooth sailing with no problems in the five years he has done parasailing at this central beach location. A 27-foot Precision powerboat will give you the freedom to soar from 300 feet to 2,000 feet over the Roanoke Sound. Piloted by licensed captains certified by the U.S. Coast Guard, Tillett says the boat uses unbreakable line that costs $200 a foot. Parasailors can fly solo or tandem. Rates are based on height of flight, ranging from $35 up to $180. Nags Head Watersports is open 8 AM through 7 PM mid-May through October.

Hatteras Island

Island Parasail
N.C. Hwy. 12, Avon • (252) 995-4970

All summer long, you can soar over the Pamlico Sound beneath a rainbow-colored parachute based at this Avon outpost. Ten-minute flights are offered from 9:30 AM to 6:30 PM daily at heights of 300, 500, 700, 1,000 or 1,200 feet. Costs range from $47 to $75 per person, depending on what lofty level you wish to reach. As long as you're strapped in and sitting on air, go ahead and take it to the top. You'll be glad you saw everything you can see from high above the salty marshes and shallow sound. These soaring adventures are booked by Windsurfing Hatteras.

Tennis

Many cottage rental developments throughout the Outer Banks have private tennis courts for their guests. Outdoor public tennis courts are located near the Kill Devil Hills Fire Station, at the Baum Senior Center in Kill Devil Hills, behind Kelly's Restaurant in Nags Head, at Manteo Middle School, at Manteo High School and next to Cape Hatteras School in Buxton. If you don't own a racquet, or left yours back on the mainland, you can lease one by the day or week from Ocean Atlantic Rentals in Corolla, (252) 453-2440; Duck, (252) 261-4346; Nags Head, (252) 441-7823; or Avon, (252) 995-5868.

Duck

Pine Island Racquet Club
N.C. Hwy. 12, Duck • (252) 453-8525

Offering the Outer Banks' only indoor tennis courts, Pine Island is 2.5 miles north of the Sanderling Inn and is part of that property's athletic package. It is open to the public year round for recreational or competitive play, and several tournaments are held here each season.

Three hard-surface courts are under a vaulted roof for air-conditioned or heated comfort, while two clay courts and two platform tennis courts are outdoors. There are indoor squash and racquetball courts and an upper-level observation deck overlooking all indoor courts. Restroom, locker and shower facilities are included.

Pine Island also recently added two ball machines, a radar gun to time your serves and a videotape analysis machine to help improve your game. U.S. P.T.R. professional Rick Ostlund and his assistant Betty Wright teach clinics for adults and children and offer individualized instruction at any skill levels. The pro shop sells racquets, clothes, tennis accessories and provides stringing services.

Reservations are suggested for indoor and outdoor courts. It costs $14 an hour in the off-season and $18 an hour in the summer months for outdoor facilities. Indoor courts cost $20 an hour September through May and $24 an hour June through August. Racquetball and squash courts cost $12 per hour. Pine Island is open every day except Christmas from at least 9 AM to 6 PM. During the summer, they are open from 8 AM to 9 PM.

Waterslides, Arcades and Other Amusements

On those hot afternoons when you're ready for a break from sand and saltwater, slip on down to a waterslide, and splash into one of their big pools. Most of these parks are open daily during the summer — some well into the evening. Waterslides generally close on rainy days.

Among the recreational outposts, many include video arcades with their offerings, but the Outer Banks' oldest and newest amusement centers also offer bright computerized games and other unusual activities. We can't list everything the owners of these establishments include, so you'll have to experience these places for yourself to discover all the surprises in store.

Photo: Courtesy of Georgia Beach

Parasail and soar with the gulls over the Outer Banks.

Nags Head

Diamond Shoals Family Fun Park
U.S. Hwy. 158, MP 9¾, Kill Devil Hills
• (252) 480-3553

Entering its fourth season, this enormous wet playground includes three twisting, twirling waterslides, complete with tunnels and mats, that drop frolicking bathers into a wide, waist-deep pool. Parents will enjoy splashing afternoons away with their kids here.

Diamond Shoals is open from 10 AM until midnight daily during the season. There's also a kiddie pool for little tykes. All-day passes are available for sliders and spectators or for the kiddie pool only. Season passes are also available. Call for 1998 prices.

Paddleboats, a video arcade, batting stadium, snack bar, sunbathing deck with lounge chairs and minigolf courses also are on the premises.

Surf Slide
U.S. 158, MP 10, Nags Head
• (252) 441-5755

Three 35-foot-high waterslides that twist and turn will keep the kids amused all day long at Surf Slide, and it's a safe, cool diversion for the speed demon in all of us. You'll also find a baby pool, bleachers, a snack bar and a game room, so everyone in the family can have fun or relax. Surf Slide is open daily from Memorial Day through Labor Day from 10 AM till dark. From Monday through Saturday, the entrance charge is $6, and on Sunday the charge is $4 and you can come and go all day.

Village Playhouse
105 Mall Dr., Nags Head
• (252) 441-3277

Village Playhouse is nestled into a small shopping area between U.S. Hwy. 158 and the Beach Road at Milepost 14. This is a great place for kids when the weather acts up or they're beach-worn. See our Kidstuff chapter for details.

Capt. Marty's
U.S Hwy. 158, MP 14½, Nags Head
• (252) 441-3132

State-of-the-art DART archery and firearm target ranges tucked in the back of this hunting and fishing outfitter provide a fun diversion and are one-of-a-kind on the Outer Banks. Target shooting skills can be honed at the facility's unique virtual reality shooting target. Owner Marty Brill provides a special rifle with laser "bullets" for shooters to aim at computerized screens depicting wildlife or arcade-type targets. Guidance is gladly provided for shooters who have never handled firearms before. This is an especially fun activity for teenagers or anyone who enjoys target shooting. Charges depend on how long you shoot.

A 20-yard paper target archery range is available for archers to practice. Seminars on hunting and fishing are also conducted at this barrier island business. Call for dates and times. Capt. Marty's is open 10 AM to 9 PM Monday through Saturday and 10 AM to 6 PM on Sunday year round. Hours are extended in the spring and summer.

Hatteras Island

Waterfall Action Park
N.C. Hwy. 12, Rodanthe • (252) 987-2213

You can't miss this palm tree-lined playground, geared for hours of fun for both adults and kids. Entering its 20th season as an Outer Banks fixture, this amusement park has more than 20 rides and the area's only bungee jumping outlet for those dyed-in-the-wool daredevils. Two waterslides, the Corkscrew and the Cyclone, give heart-thumping, thrill-filled rides.

But this wonderland has a multitude of other offerings: two minigolf courses, scale-model Grand Prix racecars, Winston Cup stock cars, Outlaw sprint cars, NASCAR super trucks and free-fall go-karts — not to mention speedboats. Children have to be at least 12 years old to ride the adult rides. Kiddie Land features rides for the age 3 to 9 set. There's no admission charge to get into the park; individual tickets for rides start at $6. Your best deal can be had with one of the 40 combination tickets, which save you more money the more you ride. Waterfall Action Park is open daily 10 AM to 9 PM from Memorial Day through Labor Day.

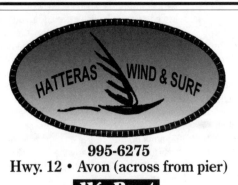

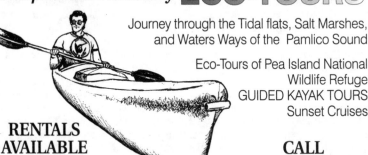

Watersports

If you've ever flown over the Outer Banks, the earth, trees and even sand seem to be overwhelmed by vast amounts of water. Bodies of it, ranging from stagnant ponds to man-made canals to numerous sounds to the unending Atlantic, push into land from every angle. With about 900 square miles of water in Dare County alone, visitors and residents can — and do — take full advantage of the range of opportunities to play in and on the pristine waterways that dominant this unique strand of islands. Even in the off-season months, waters can stay warm enough for bathers to enjoy a quick frolic. In the winter, real devotees can plunge in with a wetsuit. When the weather cooperates, boats and recreational watercraft, like sun-warmed critters who emerge temporarily from their winter hideouts, swarm out onto the sounds and sea.

Surfing and windsurfing are among the area's most popular watersports. Each summer season, thousands of novice to expert athletes arrive at the Outer Banks to whet their appetites for those outdoor adventures. Dozens of other folk move to these barrier islands annually to be closer to the waves and shallow sounds year round.

Personal watercraft, including Jet Skis, Sea Doos and Waverunners, have exploded in popularity, with rental outposts opening all along the sound shores. Kayaking, canoeing and sailing also are more available, as ecotours and sunset cruises become increasingly popular pastimes. For more unusual endeavors, the National Park Service offers occasional snorkeling expeditions for families. Some Outer Banks surf shops have begun leasing skimboards to daredevils who like to skirt the shoreline breakers. A few marinas along the barrier islands are even renting powerboats for near-shore fishing and water-skiing.

Weather plays a big factor in whether a particular watersport is available. Many area sports stores offer surfing hotlines or wave updates, and even when temperatures begin to drop, you can heat things up in the ocean or sound with increasingly warm wetsuits sold just for watersports fans at almost all Outer Banks surf shops.

Some water workouts require special training and equipment, but shops and sports schools in almost every area of the Outer Banks rent and teach whatever you need to know. (Also, see our Beach Information and Safety chapter for information about rip tides and other hazards.)

What makes water activities on these waterlogged barrier islands so attractive is that every person, whether an athletic adventurer or a couch potato, can have exactly what they want. Kayaking, for example, requires neither physical prowess nor extraordinary skill if done properly. On the flip side, scuba diving in these waters is dangerous without proper training and experience. Generally, you'll have fun sharing the wet wonderlands with the fish and birds — and scores of other water lovers who are just as thrilled as you are to be part of the Outer Banks water scene.

Surfing

Warmer than New England waters and wielding more consistent waves than most Florida beaches, the Outer Banks are reputed to have the best surf breaks on the East Coast. Local surfing experts explain that since we are set out farther into the ocean in deeper waters than other coastal regions, our beaches pick up more swells and wind patterns than any place around. Piers, shipwrecks and offshore sandbars also create unusual wave patterns.

The beaches from Duck through Hatteras are some of the only spots left that don't have strict surfing regulations: As long as you keep a leash on your board and stay at least 300 feet away from public piers, you won't get a surfing citation.

Although California's surfing subculture didn't really surface until the late 1950s, Outer Banks historian David Stick said he saw the first local surfboard in the 1930s, when native Tommy Fearing built one after hearing about guys riding waves on big boards in Hawaii. He said it took six men to handle the board, a clumsy 9-foot giant made of juniper. Whether anyone caught waves on this board may be information lost to history, but wouldn't present-day surfers love to get a look at that board!

By the late 1960s, station wagons loaded with teenagers — and their surfboards — began arriving on the sparsely populated Outer Banks. Surfers skirted the soft sands each weekend, traveling from Virginia Beach, Virginia, and Ocean City, Maryland, to hang ten in the Outer Banks' huge waves. Hatteras Island native Johnny Connor Jr., said boys sold their boards when they ran out of money. He bought several. He then turned around and rented those surfboards to local friends and newcomers who also wanted to ride the waves.

Cape Hatteras' black-and-white striped lighthouse, set in the elbow of the barrier islands, had become known as a magnet for East Coast swell seekers by the early 1970s. Jim Vaughn opened one of the Outer Banks' first surf stores at Whalebone Junction in Nags Head in 1975. Today, more than 20 shops can be found up and down the barrier islands.

In the late 1970s, the East Coast Surfing Championships started here. The U.S. Championships were held on the Outer Banks in 1978 and 1982. Each summer, and during winter storms, famous surfers can be seen riding the competition circuit along the Atlantic or just riding waves with hundreds of other "boardheads." The Outer Banks surfing subculture, those surfers who live here year round, is a far cry from the young, sun-bleached stereotype. Lawyers, engineers, middle-aged parents, waiters, doctors, construction workers, architects and restaurateurs all have been known to rearrange busy schedules to catch a few waves.

Surfers at shops along the barrier islands design, shape and sell their own boards, with prices ranging from $100 for used models to $600 for custom styles. Some stores offer lessons for beginning surfers, and many rent boards for as little as $10 a day plus a deposit. Don't forget board wax, or you won't be riding very long!

Surfing is a strenuous sport, and you need to be able to swim well in wicked waves, but with a variety of board lengths — and 90 miles of oceanfront to choose from — there are usually breaks to accommodate almost every surfer's style and stamina.

Since the beaches have been getting increasingly crowded with summer surfers, some folks won't reveal favorite spots to catch waves. We'll share some of the best-known haunts with you here, though: Kitty Hawk Pier and Avalon Pier in Kill Devil Hills each boast ample parking and pretty rideable waves. The public beach access at Barnes Street in Nags Head, with plenty of parking, provides some steady swells. Nags Head Pier also is a favorite spot. If you don't mind hiking across the dunes with a board under your arm, Pea Island and Coquina Beach both have waves worth the walk. Rodanthe has always been a popular destination, with the pier there producing waves even when almost everything else around is flat. Ramp 34, just north of Avon, is another good location, as are the turnout north of Buxton, Ramp 49 in Frisco, Frisco Pier and the public beach access area between Frisco and Hatteras Village.

The best and biggest waves by far, however, roll in around the Cape Hatteras Lighthouse. Here, beaches north and south of Cape Point, which juts closest to the Gulf Stream, face in two directions, doubling the chances for good conditions. Concrete and steel groins jut out into the Atlantic near the beacon's brick base though, so beware of being tossed toward one of these head-bashing barriers.

Waves along the Outer Banks average 2 to 3 feet high in the summer, and winter swells usually double those heights. Many areas along the barrier islands also have strong rip currents and strange sandbars — so always surf with a friend and stay alert of water, weather and beach conditions. You'll need a wetsuit for surfing in the spring, fall and winter. If you can stand the sea's cold shock, winter rides are well worth that frigid first dive.

With hurricanes and other summer storms often skirting off the coast, swells here can usually keep surfers plenty happy. Remember, though: surfing Atlantic waters is far less predictable than West Coast wave riding. Surfers report that one day Mother Ocean will serve up perfectly curled waves and prime conditions for great rides. The very next day, however, the fickle Atlantic may offer only a few ripples lapping meekly at the shoreline. As weather conditions change, along with the waves, you may notice people leaving work early and heading to the beach: Surf's up!

How to Surf

If you've never tried to surf, you might want to begin on a body board or a Boogie Board. Area surf shops also rent these short, light boards that will allow you to get the feel of the waves without worrying about getting whacked on the head. It's pretty difficult to stand up on a Boogie Board, but most first-time wave riders can't stand up on surfboards anyway. Boogie Boards are also cheaper and easier to maneuver than real surfboards.

Strong swimming skills are a prerequisite for any surfer. Like most sports, the younger you start, the easier it is to learn. If you feel confident braving waves 100 yards off the beach and are patient enough to learn to work with, rather than against, the Atlantic, you can learn to ride waves on the Outer Banks.

Start off in small swells that are breaking cleanly and evenly. You'll probably want to work in uncrowded areas at first because it's difficult to maneuver surfboards around other people — and good surfers won't want you getting in their way.

Paddling is the first step. Lie on your stomach, with your chest across the thickest part of the surfboard. Paddle your arms in a freestyle stroke, practicing until you can really control the board and find a good balance spot. Paddle around just beyond shore break, and when you're comfortable, stroke on out into the real waves.

To ride a swell, you have to get slightly

ahead of it and travel at almost the same speed as it's moving. Paddle out past the breaking waves, then turn around until you're facing the beach. Watch your back until you see a swell forming. Waves are cyclical, so once you've watched a few, it will be easier to gauge the timing you'll need to paddle with the wave and let it crest beneath you. You'll know when the wave begins to carry you. Just as in body surfing, you can feel it carry you forward fast.

When you're positioned in the breaking wave, stand up as if you're doing a push-up on the speeding board. Don't try to get to your knees first. Just pop up on your feet and keep your arms outstretched for balance. Place one foot in front of the other, about shoulder-length apart, and enjoy the ride.

Surf only until you've had enough, and don't exhaust yourself. This sport takes incredible stamina and strength and can get the best of you if you've been out in the Atlantic too long. Once you've gotten good enough to hang with other boardheads, respect their space. And try to stay out of others' way — or, at least, share the waves.

Surf Reports

A couple of Outer Banks rock radio stations — WOBR-95.3 FM and WVOD-99.1 FM — offer daily surf reports. The WVOD report is at 8:10 AM; WOBR runs its update at 12:20 PM.

Most surf shops have an even more up-to-the minute pulse on the surf, but not all provide a formal "surf line" service. Following is a list of numbers to call for the daily wave report. Most shops give the scoop only on the portion of the beach in their geographical area.

• Corolla Surf Shop, Corolla,
(252) 453-WAVE
• Wave Riding Vehicles, Kitty Hawk,
(252) 261-3332
• Whalebone Surf Shop, Kitty Hawk,
(252) 255-1234 ext. 2215
• The Pit Surf Hangout, Kill Devil Hills,
(252) 255-1234 ext. 2220
• Rodanthe Surf Shop, Rodanthe,
(252) 987-2435
• Natural Art Surf Shop, Buxton,
(252) 995-4646
• Hatteras Wind & Surf, Avon,
(888) 963-SURF

Surf Shops

Ranging from sublime to specialized to hip, the Outer Banks is inundated with surf shops. And the shops are the hotspots for wave riders of all ages and skill levels. Each summer, surf shop managers post competition schedules for beginners through surfing-circuit riders near the storefronts. Most shops stock gear, and many offer instruction during the season. Following are some favorites of Outer Banks' surfers.

Corolla

Corolla Surf Shop
Corolla Light Village Shops, 110-A Austin Dr., Corolla • (252) 453-WAVE
TimBuck II Shopping Village, N.C. Hwy. 12, Corolla • (252) 453-9273

The only surf shop on the northern Outer Banks is so popular it has two locations in Corolla, now that they've opened a second store in the Timbuck II shopping center — and it has all the goodies of the first store, including a portion of the surfer's museum. This is a full-service surfer-owned business that offers repairs, lessons and rentals. The store also has a full line of new surfboards for sale (more than 80 boards are in stock) including Stewart, Hobie, Rip Curl, Aloha, Tropicglass, Weber, HIC, Price and New Sun. A good stock of used boards is available for purchase, along with new and used skateboards, skimboards and Boogie Boards. The store also carries clothing, shoes, shades and jewelry.

Surf lessons, including all equipment, are $38 for an hour and a half. Call for group rates. Rentals are available on a daily and weekly basis. Call for rates. The shop is also the home of the Nalu Kai Surf Museum, a free exhibit of 15 collectible surfboards and other surfer memorabilia. Corolla Surf Shop is open March 1 through January 1. Winter hours vary. Listen for surf reports by Gary, the Corolla Surf Shop owner, at 8:10 AM on WVOD-99.1 FM and at 12:20 PM on WOBR-95.3 FM.

Kitty Hawk

Wave Riding Vehicles
U.S. Hwy. 158, MP 2, Kitty Hawk
• (252) 261-7952

On the Outer Banks for 18 years, WRV puts its emphasis on what the owner calls "the godfather of watersports" — surfing. Although this year-round shop also sells skateboards and snowboards, it is one of the largest full-service surf shops on the barrier islands. WRV is also the biggest surfboard manufacturing company under one label on the East Coast. The company produces in-house private-label surfwear, which is sold wholesale from Maine to Florida and overseas. Surfboards can be rented for $10 to $20 daily. Body boards rent for $5 a day.

Whalebone Surfshop
U.S Hwy. 158, MP 2, Kitty Hawk
• (252) 261-8737
U.S. Hwy. 158, MP 10, Nags Head
• (252) 441-6747

Surfer-owned and operated, Whalebone boasts that it has been in business longer than any other Outer Banks surf shop. All major brands of surfboards, and the best of the smaller brands, are available at this well-stocked store. Both popular and hard-to-find surfwear and bathing suits can also be found in what is billed as the largest locally owned store of its kind. If you can't find it here, check out the sister store of the same name 8 miles south. The Nags Head store is open year round, but hours vary depending on the weather. The Kitty Hawk shop is open

---

INSIDERS' TIP

If you've never sailed before, try renting a WindRider trimaran. The innovative craft is virtually impossible to capsize and is manageable on all but the windiest days. It's a fearless way to learn the basics of sailing while getting a fast ride. Rentals, along with a short lesson are available at Outer Banks Outdoors' Manteo location.

most of the year — less if the surf is great or the weather is cold.

Kill Devil Hills

Watermans Class Longboards-Surf Boutique
Cooke's Corner, U.S. Hwy. 158, MP 6, Kill Devil Hills • (252) 449-0459

Starting its second season in 1998, the Outer Banks newest surf shop is a specialty store catering to folks who are into surfing collectibles and memorabilia. Watermans' retro focus is reflected in its wide selection of Hawaiian print shirts and tropical decor. An assortment of T-shirts with logos of the original surfboard builders can also be found at this unique shop.

Watermans stocks longboard lines from around the world including Takayama, Town, T & C, Robert August, Michael Price and Driftwood. Dakine accessories, a huge surfboard fin selection and Bodyglove and O'Neil wetsuits also are available here. Surf wear includes HIC, Toes on the Nose, Birdwell, O'Neil and Katin board shorts for men. The expanded women's line features a large assortment of long and short sundresses, board shorts and bathing suits from Soda Blue, Girl Star, Bodyglove, Doll House, Leilani, 8.5 Quake and Toes on the Nose. Sandals and Indonesian jewelry are also available. Watermans is open year round. Hours vary in the winter months.

The Vitamin Sea
U.S. Hwy. 158, MP 6, Kill Devil Hills • (252) 441-7512

A landmark since 1978, Vitamin Sea offers a large variety of every imaginable item a surfer could want. New and used surfboards, Boogie Boards and beach goods are available. They also offer ladies, junior and misses clothing and other surfwear. A great selection of surfing stickers lines the walls and racks of this fascinating store. Sunglasses, T-shirts and swimwear are reasonably priced. Skateboards, gravity boards and accessories can also be purchased at Vitamin Sea. Discounts and special services are offered for locals at this locally owned business.

Look for a new stock of Chinese herbs, vitamins and natural food — the owner figured they might as well fulfill shoppers' expectations inspired by the shop's colorful name. Surfboards can be rented here for $20 a day. The store is closed in January and February.

The Pit Surf Hangout
U.S. Hwy. 158, MP 9, Kill Devil Hills • (252) 480-3128

Check it out! The Pit is a surf shop where you can surf the Net, hang with friends, eat, play games, listen to live music, watch videos and even find all the surfing equipment you'd ever need. As owners Ben Sproul and Steve Pauls — both devout surfers — embark on their fifth season in 1998, the "cybercafe" they opened last season has become the hottest gathering spot in Kill Devil Hills. They decided to move from the Beach Road in Nags Head in 1996 to get more visibility for their new, expanded venture.

Besides a selection of all sizes of surfboards, the shop carries the hard-to-find Harbour long boards. The Pit also features an excellent choice of high-end skim boards and used surfboards and skateboards. Rentals are available. Light food, coffee and juice are available in the cybercafe. A limited selection of microbrews and wine should be available by summer. Internet access is offered for free. A pool table, Foosball table, video screening room, several booths and a small stage are also on the premises. See the Nightlife chapter for more information about The Pit's entertainment offerings.

Nags Head

The Secret Spot
U.S Hwy. 158, MP 11, Nags Head • (252) 441-4030

No secret to surf enthusiasts, The Secret Spot is one of the old-timers of the barrier island's surf scene. Smaller than some but packed with the best of contemporary and classic boards and favorite surfwear, the store prides itself in catering to both younger and older surfers without the corporate or highly commercialized underpinnings. In other words, quality is emphasized over trendiness. The business has been manufacturing its own surfboards since 1977; the shop was opened five years later.

Surfing along the Outer Banks dates back to the 1930s.

Photo: Courtesy of J. Aaron Trotman

Surfboards can be rented for $10 daily. Lessons are available for about $40, including equipment. "Live" surf reports can be given when you call the shop. In 1998 look for an expanded version of The Secret Spot, with more boards, a special women and children's section and new skateboard merchandise. The vibe, however, will remain the same.

Hatteras Island

Rodanthe Surf Shop
N.C. Hwy. 12, Rodanthe • (252) 987-2412

Rodanthe Surf Shop owners Randy Hall and Debbie Bell moved to the southern Outer Banks to surf, and the shop evolved naturally from their lifestyle. A hands-on, no-frills operation, the shop sells only the boards it makes, Hatteras Glass Surfboards, along with surfing equipment and surfer lifestyle clothing. Surfboards and Boogie Boards are available to rent. Call for rates. Surfing lessons are also available upon request. The shop is open March through December.

Hatteras Island Surf Shop
N.C. Hwy. 12, Waves • (252) 987-2296

Veteran surfers Barton and Chris Decker have operated Hatteras Island Surf Shop for 28 years. In recent years, they've expanded their ventures to a windsurfing business, Hatteras Island Sail Shop, which is minutes from the surf shop. The surf shop sells surfboards, balsa boards, long boards, Boogie Boards and some in-line skates. Surfwear, beach clothing and bathing suits are also for sale in this no-nonsense surf shop for the dedicated surfer.

Natural Art Surf Shop
N.C. Hwy. 12, Buxton • (252) 995-5682

Natural Art specializes in both custom-made surfboards and a full line of handmade surfwear for men, women and kids. The shop also carries shoes, wetsuits, skatewear and videos. The surfboards are shaped by owner Scott Busbey in a shop right in the storefront's backyard. After 21 years in the Buxton shop, Busbey has gained a national reputation for his beautiful craftsmanship and reasonably priced boards. Surfboards can be rented for $10 a day or $50 a week, Boogie Boards for $5 day or $25 a week and wetsuits for $10 a day with a board or $5 daily without a board. Videos are also available to rent for $2 daily.

Hatteras Wind & Surf
N.C. Hwy. 12, Avon • (252) 995-6275, (888) 963-SURF

Specializing in rentals and lessons, this fully equipped surf shop keeps 200 surfboards in stock. Boards are available to rent for $10 a day, and weekly rates are also offered. Custom boards can be rented for $25 a day. Daily surf lessons are offered at $39 for 3 hours, including equipment. Body boards can be rented for $5 a day; skim boards for $8 a day. Accessories are also available for rent or sale.

Ocracoke

Ride The Wind Surf Shop
N.C. Hwy. 12, Ocracoke • (252) 928-6311

Owner Tony Sylvester last year moved to new and bigger quarters, his third shop in 12 years of business. Featuring two floors of merchandise ranging from the latest contemporary surf gear to casual comfortable clothing and footwear for men and women non-surfers, the shop has appealing decor and unusual display units, such as draped fish nets, an old trunk of a car and a hollowed boat, all highlighted by a beautiful view of the Pamlico Sound outside the window and great surfer memorabilia inside. Ride The Wind rents surfboards, Boogie Boards and practically all watersports equipment except windsurfing items. Call for prices. The shop is open from Easter through Thanksgiving.

Windsurfing

Since the early 1980s, windsurfing has grown from a relatively obscure sport to one of the most popular activities on the Outer Banks. Each year, especially in autumn, thousands of northern visitors descend on the bar-

rier islands to skim the shallow sounds or surf the sea's whitecaps on brightly colored sailboards. When the wind is whipping just right, hundreds of neon-striped sails soar along the shores of Hatteras Island, silently skirting the salty water like bright butterflies flitting near the beach.

Whether you're an expert athlete or novice who knows nothing about wind and water, windsurfing is not an easy sport. Once you get the hang of it, however, it is one of the most intoxicating experiences imaginable. It's clean and quiet. You can do it alone or with friends. With the proper equipment, sailboarders can control their speeds, sliding slowly into a sunset or cruising more than 40 mph across choppy breaks. On the Outer Banks, sailboarders can usually find some wind to ride year round. Windsurfing is permitted any place you can set your sails, except lifeguarded beaches. This sport truly lets you feel like a part of the natural surroundings — and it's an incredible rush to be able to maneuver with the wind.

Many sailboarders swear by the Outer Banks, calling it the best windsurfing spot on the Atlantic seaboard and one of the top-three locations in the country. International windsurfing magazines say that Hatteras Island's Canadian Hole is one of the continent's best sailboarding spots. Canadians, especially, come in droves, driving as many as 30 hours or more at a clip to catch the warm October breezes in their Mylar sails.

Canadian Hole, on the west side of N.C. 12 between Avon and Buxton, is undoubtedly the most popular windsurfing spot on the Outer Banks and the East Coast. Formed in the early 1960s, it was created after a storm cut an inlet across Hatteras Island, just north of Buxton, and workers dredged sand from the sound to rebuild the roadway. Dredging activities carved troughs just offshore in the Pamlico Sound. The deep depressions, which extend to about 5 feet, help create ideal conditions for sailboarders. Additionally, Canadian Hole flanks one of the skinniest strips of sand on the barrier islands. Windsurfers can sail the sound and then walk their boards across N.C. 12 to cruise in the ocean in fewer than five minutes.

Besides the sound and the Atlantic, Canadian Hole offers other amenities many windsurfers find helpful. There's a 100-space paved lot to park big vans and trailers in, four Porta-Johns, a phone booth and a half-dozen metal trash cans. Even the beach at Canadian Hole is much wider than other soundside stretches of sand — it's about 50 yards wide and able to accommodate sunbathers, coolers and plenty of spectators.

The wide and flat sound here allows sailboarders to sail for miles without turning. Better still, no signs or buildings obstruct the sailors' views of the natural beauty surrounding them. From October through Christmas, scores of Canadians arrive at the Hole, turning Hatteras Island into a temporary French-speaking haven.

Nags Head's soundside beaches also provide great sailboarding. The sounds are more shallow than Canadian Hole, thus safer for beginners. In spring and fall, tourism officials estimate, as many as 500 windsurfers a week arrive at the Outer Banks. Dozens of other visitors try the sport for the first time while vacationing in Dare County.

Learning to Windsurf

From Duck through Ocracoke Island, there are more than a dozen outposts that sell windsurfing gear and sailboards. Many of those shops offer windsurfing lessons for less than $40. We recommend receiving professional instruction if you're just starting out. It's also better to learn whether you like this sport or not on rented equipment, as even beginning rigs cost about $500. Windsurfing is free once you're outfitted, but the equipment can be quite expensive.

Anyone who's patient enough to learn to understand wind and wave patterns can eventually learn to ride a sailboard. People of all ages (except young children) who are in good health can learn to windsurf. With a good instructor, few will fail. Most beginners are able to gain enough skill to at least have fun within two hours; however, even some sailboarders who have been skimming the seas for 20 years say they still haven't mastered all the complexities windsurfing offers.

In a nutshell, windsurfing is based on a system of manipulating a mast, boom and sail with a device that swivels and pivots in every direction while balanced on a board. To sail crosswind, the mast should be up and down. To sail downwind, tip the mast toward the front of the board, which will turn the front of the board downwind. Lean the mast toward the back of the board, and it turns upwind.

Some sailboard instructors let their students start out on land, on specially made boards that let you feel how to balance and move before ever getting wet. Learning how to work with the wind is the toughest part, but you also need some arm and back strength to hold up the sail.

Sailboarders are strapped onto their masts in a sling-like contraption similar to those used in rappelling or rock climbing. You control the board with your feet and the sail with your hands. You have to learn to upright yourself in case you fall, but even standing the sail up again is difficult when it fills with water.

If you're just starting out, don't sail too far from shore at first. If your rig breaks, or the wind dies down, you won't have as far to walk back through the shallow sound with your board. One of the best ways to learn windsurfing maneuvers is to watch the good sailboarders who make this challenging sport seem so effortless.

Along the Outer Banks, several windsurfing competitions and speed trials are held each year, including the Hatteras Wave Classic in October and the Pro-Am each spring. (See our Annual Events chapter for related information).

Windsurfing Shops

Whether you're looking for a lesson, need a sail of a different size or want to ask for advice about sailboarding, more than a dozen shops from Corolla through Ocracoke stock windsurfing supplies, and many provide instructors in season.

Duck

Barrier Island Boats
N.C. Hwy. 12, Duck • (252) 261-7100

Barrier Island Boats, at the Barrier Island Inn pier, is under new ownership in 1998. Formally North Beach Sailing, they are accredited by Windsurfing Instructors of America. Beginner lessons are guaranteed, using special training equipment with professional instructors. A 90-minute demo lesson costs $29 per person; three-hour beginner lessons are $49; beginning lesson packages, which include three hours of instruction and a two-hour rental, cost $64; certification lessons with two three-hour sessions cost $89; and a one-hour private lesson costs $45. Rigs can be rented at $15 an hour for beginning windsurfers, $55 for four hours and $80 for a full day.

Nags Head

Kitty Hawk Watersports
U.S Hwy. 158, MP 16, Nags Head • (252) 441-2756

Dealing foremost in windsurfing on the Outer Banks for more than 15 years, Kitty Hawk Watersports manager Keith Wood says Kitty Hawk Watersports was one of the first windsurfing operations on the barrier islands. At its site on Roanoke Sound, the watersports center is open year round and offers windsurfing instruction spring, summer and fall. Rig rentals start at $20 an hour. Free windsurfing lessons are available in the summer for kids 15 years and younger who are accompanied by a paying adult. Basic lessons cost $44 for three hours, including instruction and rental.

Hatteras Island

Windsurfing Hatteras
N.C. Hwy. 12, Avon • (252) 995-4970

The only shop on Hatteras Island with private access to the Pamlico Sound, Windsurfing Hatteras Kitty Hawk Sports was opened in 1988 by a group of dedicated local windsurfers. The operation offers camps and clinics every year for beginners and advanced windsurfers. The camp is staffed by some of the best windsurfing talent around.

Lessons are taught by trained, qualified personnel with guaranteed success for begin-

ners. Lessons start at $44 for beginners, including all equipment and on-the-water instruction. Private lessons for beginners to advanced are $49 per hour. Complete boards with two sails can be rented for $20 an hour or $45 for four hours at the site. Call for rates on rentals on other equipment.

Hatteras Island Sail Shop
N.C. Hwy 12, Waves • (252) 987-2292

On the soundfront near the former Pescado's Restaurant, this windsurfing shop was opened in 1996 by the owners of Hatteras Island Surf Shop, which is 250 yards north. They offer sales, rentals and lessons. Owner Barton Decker says the sailing site here is the largest on the Outer Banks, with a grassy rigging area and a sandy beach launch. With about 150 new and used boards in stock, the store also has all necessary accessories in its complete inventory. A beginner lesson costs $40 for about 3 hours. Rentals are available for $15 an hour, $25 a half-day and $40 a day.

Hatteras Wind & Surf
N.C. Hwy. 12, Avon • (252) 995-6275

Whether you're a novice or a pro, you'll find something to suit your windsurfing needs at Hatteras Wind & Surf. Qualified staff offer private and special lessons daily for all skill levels. You can take a three-hour beginner lesson, including equipment rental, for $39. Perfect your board handling during a two-hour board speed and handling course for $35. Practice beach starts, pivot jibes and upwind sailing during a one-hour private intermediate class for $45. Advanced lessons are also available at $55 an hour. If you're looking to rent equipment, you can choose from body boards, Boogie Boards, skim boards and windsurfing gear.

Kayaking and Canoeing

The easiest, most adaptable and accessible watersports available on the Outer Banks —

Windsurfing is a favorite pastime for watersports enthusiasts, and boy, do we have wind!

kayaking and canoeing — are activities people of any age or physical ability can enjoy. These lightweight paddlecrafts are extremely maneuverable, can glide almost anywhere along the seas or sounds and afford adventurous activity as well as silent solitude. They're also relatively inexpensive ways to tour uncharted waterways and see sights you'd miss if you stayed on shore.

In recent years, more than a dozen ecotour outlets have opened on the barrier islands. Stores offer everything from rent-your-own kayaks for less than $40 a day to guided, day-long and even overnight tours around abandoned islands. With no fuel to foul the estuaries, no noise to frighten wildlife and little skill needed to chart your own course, kayaks and canoes offer a sport as strenuous or relaxing as you want it to be — an outdoor activity that will make a splash with the entire family.

Unlike the closed-cockpit kayaks used in whitewater river runs, most kayaks on the Outer Banks are a sit-on-top style and stretch from 7 to 10 feet long. They're molded in bright colored plastic, are light enough for even adolescents to carry to a launch site and come in one- and two-seat models. A double-blade paddle and a life jacket are the only other pieces of equipment you'll need, and these are included with all rentals and lessons.

Canoes are heavier and harder to get into

the water but slightly more stable than kayaks. They seat two or three people and include a more sheltered hull to haul gear or picnic lunches inside. Single-blade paddles, usually two per boat, are needed to maneuver these traditional watercraft.

Perhaps the best aspect of kayaking and canoeing is versatility. You can perform these paddle sports in any weather, with or without wind, in calm or rough seas and in shallow sounds and narrow creeks. You can paddle around alone, just communing with nature; or, you can share the sights with a single friend in the same boat or a group along for a guided ride.

Thrill-seekers can splash kayaks through frothy surf in the Atlantic or paddle past the breakers and float alongside schools of dolphin. For more tranquil times, kayakers and canoeists can slip slowly through marshy creeks at the isolated Alligator River National Wildlife Refuge, explore narrow canals that bigger boats can't access or slip alongside an uninhabited island in the middle of the shallow sound. There are historical tours around Roanoke Island, nature tours through maritime forests and self-guided trails with markers winding through a former logging town called Buffalo City on the Dare County mainland. Virtually anywhere there's 2 feet of water or more, you can take a kayak or canoe.

Learning to Paddle

Unlike other watersports, little to no instruction is needed to paddle a kayak or canoe. It helps to know how to swim, in case you capsize, but since most of the sounds are only 4 feet deep, you can walk your way back to shore if you stay in the estuaries — or, at least, jump back in your boat from a standing position.

Different strokes are required for each type of craft. Kayakers' double-blade paddles are designed to be used by one person. The blades are positioned at opposing angles so you can work across your body with a sweeping motion and minimal rotation and still paddle on both sides of the boat. The trick is to get into a rhythm and not dig too deeply beneath the water's surface. Canoeing is done with one person paddling on each side of the boat, if there are two passengers, or a single operator alternating sides with paddle strokes.

Most kayak- and canoe-rental outfits also offer lessons. Even if you prefer to be on your own, rather than with a guided group trip, people renting these watercraft are happy to share advice and expertise with you. If you have any questions, or need directions around the intricate waterways, just ask.

Paddling Places

All the sounds around the Outer Banks are ideal for kayaking and canoeing, because they are shallow, warm and filled with flora and fauna. There are marked trails at Alligator River National Wildlife Refuge; buoys around Wanchese, Manteo and Colington; and plenty of uncharted areas to explore around Pine Island, Pea Island, Kitty Hawk, Corolla and the Cape Hatteras National Seashore. Unlike other types of boats, you don't even need a special launching site to set a kayak or canoe in the water and take off.

Corolla

Corolla Outback Adventures
Wee Winks Shopping Center, N.C Hwy. 12, Corolla • (252) 453-4484

Guided kayak ecotours are offered in the marshes and protected estuaries in Carova, the northernmost area of the Outer Banks, from

April through November. Accessible only by four-wheel-drive vehicles, the excursions are led by expert guide Scott Trabue, who spends the off-season conducting kayak tours in Jamaica. Tours cost $34 per person. A discount is available for children.

Duck

Barrier Island Boats
N.C. Hwy. 12, Duck • (252) 261-7100

Single and tandem kayaks are available for sale or rent at Barrier Island Boats, near Barrier Island Restaurant pier. A two-and-a-half-hour tour of Currituck Sound and the Audubon Wildlife Sanctuary is offered for $39, including equipment.

Nags Head

Outer Banks Outdoors
U.S. Hwy. 158, Nags Head
• (252) 441-4124, (800) 334-4777

With a variety of launch sites from Corolla to Hatteras, Outer Banks Outdoors claims to be one of the largest kayak ecotour operations on the barrier islands, with nine tours offered April through November. Some tours are even tailor-made for children. Tours include all equipment, lessons and guide service. An exclusive retailer of Wilderness Systems kayaks, Outer Banks Outdoors sells and rents a full selection of touring, sit-on-top and surf kayaks. Single and tandem kayaks are available. Call for rates and reservations.

Kitty Hawk Kayaks
U.S Hwy. 158, MP 13, Nags Head
• (252) 441-6800

A division of Kitty Hawk Sports, the kayak service provides two-hour tours of the sounds, the Alligator River and the ocean starting at $29. Launch sites are in Corolla, Kitty Hawk, Nags Head, Manteo and Avon. Sales and rentals are also available. Kayaks rent for $10 an

hour, $24 a half-day, $32 a full day and $79 a week.

Roanoke Island

Wilderness Canoeing Inc.
Melvin T. Twiddy Jr., P.O. Box 789, Manteo, NC 27954 • (252) 473-1960

Twiddy conducts canoeing and kayaking wilderness adventure tours around Alligator River National Wildlife Refuge, through the former frontier town Buffalo City. All equipment is provided. Call for rates and more information.

Hatteras Island

Hatteras Wind & Surf
N.C. Hwy. 12, Avon • (252) 995-6275

A complete kayak outfitter, Hatteras Wind & Surf has a full line of kayaks and paddling gear. Guided three-hour wildlife tours are offered daily from March 15 through December 15 to Hatteras, Pea, Ocracoke, Bird and Portsmouth islands, ranging from $29 to $59. Group discount rates are available. All-day tours from Ocracoke to Portsmouth Islands and sunset tours can also be arranged.

Kayaking Hatteras
N.C. Hwy. 12, Avon • (252) 995-3033

Ecotours of Pea Island National Wildlife Refuge and Bird Island are offered with guides for $39, along with a $29 evening sunset tour. Call for schedules. The Avon Adventures tour, a historical guide from Avon to the Pamlico Sound, is available three times daily. Kayaks are also available for sale or rent.

Ocracoke Island

Ocracoke Adventures
N.C. Hwy. 12 and Silver Lake Rd., Ocracoke Village • (252) 928-7873

Kayak ecotours in the Pamlico Sound and to Portsmouth Island give paddlers the oppor-

---

INSIDERS' TIP

Don't ever be casual about wearing life jackets. Many drownings here result from people accidentally falling from boats when not wearing flotation devices.

tunity to learn about the fragile plant and animal life that inhabits these remote islands. Daily ecotours include Early Bird Catches the Worm, Blackbeard's Domain, Ocean Excursions, Horsepen Point, Sunset Cruise and Full Moon Cruise. The two- and two-and-a-half-hour cruises are often guided by native Michael O'Neal and biologist Shirley Schoelkopf, owners of Ocracoke Adventures.

The owners also oversee several Ocracoke natives who take out paddlers. Fees include the kayak, paddle, back rest, life jacket, dry bag and instructions. Any size group can be accommodated, and customized tours are available. Kayaks can be rented on an hourly, daily or weekly rate, with free delivery on Ocracoke. Call for prices. Reservations are recommended in the summer. Kids 8 years and younger are free, and daily programs for children are available. There is also a rental site located next to the post office on Silver Lake.

Ride The Wind Surf Shop
N.C. Hwy. 12, Ocracoke • (252) 928-6311

Ride The Wind, near Silver Lake, offers four two-and-a-half-hour kayak tours (The Sunrise, The Sunset, The Midday and The Snorkel) of the Pamlico Sound and the surrounding estuarine waters every day, weather permitting.

Naturalist/ecologist Terrilyn West is charged with guiding the tours or overseeing the several ecology interns who take out paddlers. Terns, pelicans, waterfowl, egrets, herons, many species of fish and porpoises are just some of the species that paddlers may see on their tour through the waterways. Any size group can be accommodated with advance notice. The fee includes the kayak, life jackets and a four-page plastic field guide on area fish, shellfish and fauna. Call for prices. Reservations are strongly suggested during the summer.

Scuba Diving

Cloudier and cooler than waters off the Florida Keys and the Caribbean Islands, offshore areas along the Outer Banks offer unique scuba-diving experiences in "The Graveyard of the Atlantic." More than 500 shipwrecks, at least 200 named and identified, are strewn along the sand from Corolla to Ocracoke. Ex-

perienced divers enjoy the challenge of unpredictable currents and always seem to find something new to explore beneath the ocean's surface. From 17th-century schooners to World War II submarines, wreckage lies at a variety of depths, in almost every imaginable condition. After each storm, it seems, a new shipwreck is unearthed somewhere near the barrier island shores. Many of these wrecks haven't been seen since they sank beneath the sea.

Some underwater archaeological shipwreck sites are federally protected and can be visited — but not touched. Others offer incredible souvenirs for deepwater divers: bits of china plates and teacups, old medicine and liquor bottles, even brass-rimmed porthole covers and thick, hand-blown glass that's been buried beneath the ocean for more than a century. If you prefer to leave history as you find it, waterproof cameras are sure to bring back even more memorable treasures from the mostly unexplored underwater world.

Sharks, whales, dolphin and hundreds of varieties of colorful fish also frequent deep waters around these barrier islands. There's even a coral reef off Avon — the northernmost one in the world. Submerged Civil War forts are also scattered along the banks of Roanoke Island in much more shallow sounds.

While dive-boat captains will carry charter parties to places of their choosing, some shipwrecks have become popular with scuba divers and are among the most frequently selected sites. The freighter *Metropolis*, also called the "Horsehead Wreck," lies about 3 miles south of the Currituck Beach Lighthouse off Corolla, 100 yards offshore, in about 15 feet of water. This ship was carrying 500 tons of iron rails and 200 tons of stones when it sank in 1878, taking 85 crewmen with it to a watery grave. Formerly the Federal gunboat *Stars and Stripes* that worked in the Civil War, this is a good wreck to explore in the off-season. If you have a four-wheel-drive vehicle, you can drive up the beach and swim out to this shipwreck site.

Off Kill Devil Hills, an unidentified tugboat rests about 300 yards south of Avalon Pier, about 75 yards off the beach, in 20 feet of water. Two miles south, the Triangle Wrecks, *Josephine*, *Kyzickes* and *Carl Gerhard*, sit

about 100 yards offshore, about 200 yards south of the Sea Ranch motel, in about 20 feet of water. These vessels sank in 1915, 1927 and 1929, respectively. They can also be reached by swimming from the beach.

Nags Head's most famous dive site is the USS *Huron*, a Federal gunship that sank in 1877, bringing 95 crew men to the bottom with it. This wreck is about 200 yards off the beach at MP 11, resting in about 26 feet of water and including many salvageable artifacts. The tugboat *Explorer* is nearby.

Long known as the East Coast's most treacherous inlet, Oregon Inlet between Nags Head and Hatteras Island has claimed hundreds of ships — and scores of lives — through the ages. The liberty ship *Zane Grey* lies about a mile south of this inlet in 80 feet of water. A German sub U-85 sank northeast of the inlet in 100 feet of water in 1942. The *Oriental* has been sitting about 4 miles south of Oregon Inlet since sinking there in 1862; its boiler is visible above the surf. Most of these dive excursions can be accessed only from boats.

About a mile north of Rodanthe Fishing Pier, 100 yards offshore, the LST 471 sits in about 15 feet of water. This ship sank in 1949 and is accessible by swimming out from shore. Nearby off Rodanthe, about 22 miles southeast of Oregon Inlet, the tanker *Marore* is about 12 miles offshore. It sank after being torpedoed in 1942 and lies in about 100 feet of water.

More experienced deepwater divers enjoy the *Empire Gem*, a British carrier that sank in January 1942 after being torpedoed by a German U-boat. This shipwreck sits about 17 miles off Cape Hatteras in 140 feet of water and was one of the first vessels to go down in World War II. It, too, must be reached by boat.

Learning to Dive

Unlike other watersports, scuba diving isn't something you can learn on your own. You have to be certified to do deep dives. This takes special training by certified instructors — and, sometimes, weeks of practice in a pool. Average recreational dives are 80 to 100 feet deep, while extreme divers reach depths of more than 300 feet. There are dangers associated with such deep dives, however. Almost every diver has heard horror stories about people who died during underwater cave dives, friends they've had who were attacked by sharks and days they've spent in hospital recompression chambers, waiting for their bodies to readjust after swimming over the ocean floor. Divers universally agree, however, that the thrill and tranquility of deep wreck diving are well worth the risks.

Several Outer Banks dive shops offer lessons, advanced instruction and all the equipment you'll need to get started. This is a relatively expensive sport. Divers say it takes at least $1,500 just to get the necessary tanks, hoses, wetsuits and other paraphernalia to take that first plunge. Dive boat charters, which all dive shop workers will help arrange, begin at about $550 per day, depending on how far offshore you want to go.

Some dive shops can also recommend shallow dive spots that you don't need a boat to get to as well as near shore or sound areas you can explore with just a face mask and snorkel. Ocean Atlantic Rentals in Corolla, (252) 453-2440, and Avon, (252) 995-5868, rents fins, masks and snorkels. Ride the Wind Surf Shop, on Ocracoke Island, (252) 928-6311, offers an afternoon snorkeling trip daily in season. And the National Park Service also offers sporadic snorkeling adventures along the Cape Hatteras National Seashore in the summer. Call (252) 473-2111 for tour times and information.

Before You Dive

If you're going scuba diving, you might want to jot down these important emergency numbers.

U.S. Coast Guard Stations:

Oregon Inlet
(252) 995-6411, (252) 987-2311, (252) 441-1685

Hatteras Inlet
(252) 986-2175

Ocracoke Inlet
(252) 928-3711

Diver Alert Network
(DAN) 684-8111

Ocean Rescue Squad
(helicopter available)
911

Dive Shops

Nags Head

Nags Head Pro Dive Center
Surfside Plaza, U.S. Hwy. 158, MP 13½,
Nags Head • (252) 441-7594

The oldest dive shop on the Outer Banks, Nags Head Pro Dive Center opened 19 years ago and is now off the bypass, a half-mile south of the former location across from Jockey's Ridge. This full-service facility offers everything you'll need to get started scuba diving, from PADI-certified lessons and advice to equipment sales and rentals. Diving experts can give airfills to 5,000 psi and charter boats for interested parties. Rentals for everything from a mask with a snorkel to full gear are available. Three-day and five-day rental rates are offered. Nags Head Pro Dive Center is open seven days a week in the summer. The center is open five days a week from Easter through Memorial Day and Labor Day through Thanksgiving.

Sea Scan Dive Centre
N.C. Hwy. 12, MP 10, Nags Head
• (252) 480-3467

On the west side of the Beach Road, Sea Scan Dive Centre in Nags Head is a full-service NAUI Pro facility offering scuba equipment sales, rentals, repairs, tank refills, char-

ters and instruction. Sea Scan specializes in charters to the many offshore shipwrecks fringing the Outer Banks. Certification classes offered through Divemaster are also available. Sea Scan is open year round by appointment.

Hatteras Island

Diamond Shoals Diving
52346 N.C. Hwy. 12, Frisco
• (252) 995-4021

The only full-service dive shop on Hatteras Island, Diamond Shoals Diving boasts that their dive boat *Gunsmoke* is the largest and fastest on the island, with an average cruise speed of more than 20 knots. The cabin is heated and air conditioned and can carry up to 20 divers. With many years of experience in the diving and boating industry, *Gunsmoke*'s captain Andrew "Hoss" Overcash is Coast Guard- and PADI-certified. The entire crew has been diving for 10 to 20 years and is trained in safety, first aid and oxygen administration. Crew members also are available as dive buddies, wreck guides or just for general dive guidance. Diamond Shoals works together with other boats on bookings and tank fills, as well as gear rental. Staff will even pick up and deliver gear at the dock. *Gunsmoke* moors and departs from Teach's Lair Marina. Multi-day discounts, group rates and private charters are available.

Sailing

With wide, shallow sounds and more than 90 miles of easily accessible oceanfront, the Outer Banks has been a haven for sailors since Sir Walter Raleigh's explorers first slid along these shores more than four centuries ago. Private sailboat owners have long enjoyed the barrier islands as a stopover en route along the Intracoastal Waterway. Many sailors have also dropped anchor beside Roanoke or Hatteras islands — only to tie up at the docks permanently and make Dare County their year-round home.

INSIDERS' TIP

Always secure your sunglasses well on your head when participating in watersports. You would not believe how many people lose their glasses when the wind turns suddenly, or their speed picks up. Sunglass ties are inexpensive and widely available.

Watersport activities abound on the Outer Banks.

Until recently, you had to have your own sailboat to cruise the area waterways. Now, dozens of shops from Corolla through Ocracoke rent sailboats, Hobie Cats and catamarans to weekend water bugs. Others offer introductory and advanced sailing lessons. Some even take people who have no desire to learn to sail on excursions across the sounds aboard multi-passenger sailing ships. Ecotours, luncheon swim-and-sails and sunset cruises have become increasingly popular with vacationers who want to glide across the waterways but not necessarily steer their own vessels. From 40-passenger catamarans sailed by experienced captains to pirate-like schooners carrying up to six passengers to single-person Sunfish sailboats, you can find almost any type of sailing vessel you desire on these barrier islands.

Unlike motorized craft, which pollute the water with gasoline and cause passengers to shout over the whirr of engines, sailing is a clean, environmentally friendly sport that people of all ages can enjoy. You can sail slowly by marshlands without disturbing the waterfowl or cruise at 15 mph clips in stiff southern breezes. It all depends on your whim — and the wind.

If you've never sailed before, don't rent a boat and try to wing it. Breezes around the Outer Banks are trickier than elsewhere, subject to blow up out of nowhere and shift direction without a moment's notice. If you get caught in a gale, you could end up miles from land if you don't know how to maneuver the vessel. A two-hour introductory lesson is well worth it to learn basic sailing skills such as knot tying, sail rigging and steering.

Sailors with even some on-water experience, however, can usually manage to navigate their way around the shallow sounds. All boats come with life jackets, but it's best to be in one that's comfortable for swimming in case your sailboat capsizes.

Sailboat Cruises, Courses and Rentals

Prices for sailboat cruises depend on the amenities, length of voyage and time of day. Midday trips sometimes include boxed lunches or at least drinks for passengers. Some sunset tours offer parties wine, beer and appetizers. Almost all of the excursions let people bring their own food and drink aboard, and some even accept dogs on leashes aboard the decks. Special arrangements can also be made for handicapped passengers. Prices generally range from $30 to $60 per person. Some captains will also offer their services along with the sailboats, beginning at $50 per hour per vessel, and allowing the renter to fill the craft with its capacity of passengers.

Lesson costs, too, span a range, depending on how in-depth the course is, what type of craft you're learning on and whether you prefer group or individualized instruction. Costs can be from $10 to $50 per person. Call ahead for group rates if you've got more than four people in your party.

If you'd rather rent a craft and sail it yourself, dozens of Outer Banks outfitters lease sailboats by the hour, day or week. Deposits generally are required. Costs range from $25 to $60 per hour and $50 to $110 per day. Most shops accept major credit cards.

Duck

Barrier Island Boats
N.C. Hwy. 12, Duck • (252) 261-7100

In recent years, Duck has become one of the Outer Banks' busiest sailing hubs and is among the easiest places in the Albemarle area to learn to sail or take a calm cruise. Barrier Island Boats is near the Barrier Island Restaurant pier. Formally North Beach Sailing, they rent 19-foot Flying Scots for $39 an hour and $159 a day. A 16-foot Hobie Cat rents for $29 per hour and $109 per day. Daysailers and Sunfish are also available to rent. A two-hour beginner lesson costs $49, and a one-hour private lesson costs $45. Guided cruises and additional lessons and packages are also offered.

Kitty Hawk

Promenade Watersports
U.S Hwy. 158, MP ¼, Kitty Hawk
• (252) 261-4400

At the foot of the Wright Memorial Bridge, the Promenade is the only full-service watersports center in Kitty Hawk. Of its multitude of services, it offers sailboat lessons and rentals. Call for prices. Reservations are recommended.

Nags Head

The Waterworks
U.S. Hwy. 158, MP 16½, Nags Head
• (252) 441-8875

Sailboat rentals and sailing lessons are of-

fered at this complete watersports center from April through November. Other sites are in Duck and at the Manteo-Nags Head Causeway.

Roanoke Island

Outer Banks Outdoors
Queen Elizabeth St., Manteo
• (252) 473-2357, (800) 334-4777
Atlantic Estates, N.C. Hwy. 12, Avon
• (252) 995-6060

The WindRider trimaran, a near foolproof and extraordinarily stable sailing vessel, can be rented here at hourly and full-day rates. The lightweight Escape, a less destructible and more portable version of the Sunfish, is also available for rent or sale. The Escape is equipped with a Windicator, which sets the sail by measuring wind speed and direction. The sailboats are also available at the Avon location. Call for prices.

Island Sail
The Waterfront, Manteo • (252) 473-1213

Zack and Pam Sylvester opened their sailboat rental and sailing lessons business in 1996 at Shallowbag Bay behind The Waterfront Shoppes. Sailors can rent a boat and ply the lovely waters near where the *Elizabeth II* 16th-century representative sailing ship is docked. Sailor wannabes can take a group or solo lesson from Zack, usually on a classic Hampton 18-foot sailboat or a 1953 24-foot Raven. Lessons are $20 per person per hour.

Sailfish can be rented for $10 an hour, $30 a half-day or $50 all day. An O'Day, Designer's Choice or Hobie Cat are available to rent for $20 an hour, $60 a half-day or $100 for a full day. A Barnegat can be rented for $20 an hour, $75 a half-day or $125 a whole day. Island Sail is open daily in the summer, but you should call ahead for conditions and availability. Hours vary in the off-season.

Hatteras Island

Hatteras Island Sail Shop
N.C. Hwy. 12, Waves • (252) 987-2292

Catamarans, daysailors and Hobie Cats are available for rent for $25 an hour at this extension of the respected Hatteras Island Surf Shop. Kayaks are also available to rent. Sound access is onsite. Lessons are also offered. Call for more information. The sail shop is open April through Thanksgiving.

Hatteras Watersports
N.C. Hwy. 12, Salvo • (252) 987-2306

Sailing cruises, rentals and lessons are some of the offerings at this popular watersports center, on the soundside, across from the Salvo Volunteer Fire Department. Two-hour trips aboard a Hobie Cat can accommodate up to three people and cost a total of $69 for the entire party. Sunfish can be rented for $18 per hour or $52 a day. Hobie Cats rent for $29 an hour or $88 a day. Showers for sailors also are provided here, along with picnic areas and volleyball near a small beach. Kayaks rentals and tours are also available.

Avon Watersports
N.C. Hwy. 12, Avon • (252) 995-4970

At Windsurfing Hatteras Kitty Hawk Sports, this watersports center gives sailing lessons, offers cruises aboard catamarans and day sailors and rents Hobie Cats and Sunfish by the hour or day. Call for prices.

Boating

From small skiffs to luxurious pleasure boats, there is dock space for almost every type of boat on the Outer Banks. Most marinas require advance reservations. Space is extremely limited on summer weekends, so call as soon as you make plans to visit the area. Prices vary greatly, depending on the dock location, amenities and type of vessel you're operating.

If you're not lucky enough to own your own boat, you can still access the sounds, inlets and ocean around the Outer Banks by renting powerboats from area outfitters. Most store owners don't require previous boating experience. If you leave a deposit and driver's license, they'll include a brief boating lesson in the rental price. Whether you're looking to lease a craft to catch this evening's fish dinner or just want to take the kids on an afternoon cruise, you can find a vessel to suit your needs at a variety of marinas. Prices range from $15 an hour to more than $100 per day, depending on the type of boat. Some places require a two-hour or more minimum. Most accept major credit cards. See our Fishing chapter for charter information.

Marinas, Dock Space and Public Launch Ramps

If you just need a place to put your boat in the water, you'll find free public launch ramps on the soundside end of Wampum Drive in Duck; on Kitty Hawk Bay in Kitty Hawk; at the end of Soundside Road, behind Jockey's Ridge State Park in Nags Head; below the Washington Baum Bridge between Nags Head and Manteo; near Thicket Lump Lane in Wanchese; at the oceanside end of Lighthouse Road in Buxton; and on the sound in Ocracoke Village.

Roanoke Island

Pirate's Cove Yacht Club
Nags Head-Manteo Cswy., Manteo
• (252) 473-3906, (800) 367-4728

This marina can accommodate pleasure boats up to 65 feet long and includes power, showers, cable and laundry facilities in the slip rental fee. Pirate's Cove offers loaner vehicles to transport boaters to area attractions on land. There are 155 slips available at this full-service marina.

Daily rates are $1.10 per foot; monthly rates are $12 per foot; and annual rates are $90 per foot. There are 155 slips available at this full-service marina. Daily rates are $1.10 per foot; monthly rates are $12 per foot; and annually rates are $90 per foot. Pirate's Cove is open 5 AM through 7 PM in-season. Hours vary in the cooler months.

Manteo Waterfront Marina
207 Queen Elizabeth Ave., Ste. 14,
Manteo • (252) 473-3320,
(888) 473-BOAT

Located within walking distance of restaurants, a movie theater, a bookstore and various retail shops, this full-service marina has 53 slips and can accommodate boats up to 130 feet — and it's close to a beach to boot.

Air-conditioned heads and showers are available here as well as laundry facilities, a

Feel the wind through your hair on a boat in our sounds.

picnic area with gas grills, e-mail access and rental cars. Both 30-amp and 50-amp power is on-site. The marina has a ship's store on the premises, with nautical charts and both block and cube ice for sale.

Rates are $1.10 per foot and are subject to change. During special events like July Fourth weekend, rates will be higher. Ask about weekend packages. Manteo Waterfront Marina is open year round.

Salty Dawg Marina
U.S Hwy. 64, Manteo • (252) 473-3405

Salty Dawg has 55 slips, all with power and water, and an air-conditioned/heated bathhouse. Light repairs can be done on-site. Boats up to 150 feet can be docked at Salty Dawg, which is on Shallowbag Bay near downtown Manteo. Rates are 95¢ per foot per day for transient boats, plus electricity; $6.50 per foot per month; and $46.65 per foot per year, with a minimum of 30 feet. A ship's store and dry storage for boats up to 26 feet are also on the premises. Commercial towing and courtesy cars are available. Salty Dawg monitors Channel 16, the hailing and distress frequency on marine radios. The marina is open year round,

8 AM to 6 PM in-season. It closes at 5 PM November through February.

Thicket Lump Marina
Thicket Lump Rd., Wanchese
• (252) 473-4500

This family owned and operated marina rents dock space to pleasure and fishing vessels up to 45 feet by the day, week or year. A full-service repair center, ships' store and tackle shop are at the marina. Dry storage is available for boats up to 28 feet. Stop upstairs in the marina's yacht club. It's open seven nights a week and features entertainment on weekends. Thicket Lump is open year round.

Hatteras Island

Frisco Cove Marina
N.C. Hwy. 12, Frisco • (252) 995-4242

On the Pamlico Sound about 9 miles from Hatteras Inlet, this full-service marina (formerly the Scotch Bonnet) has 30 slips available to rent for boats up to 35 feet long for $8 a day, $120 a month or $799 a year. The on-site boat ramp costs $5. The facility also has a well-equipped marine store that sells a full line of

Photo: Courtesy of J. Aaron Trotman

You can boogie board, skim board or surf until you drop.

marine parts and supplies including Sea Value products. The marina also sells and services Suzuki outboards and Carolina Skiff boats.

A bathhouse with men's and women's showers and sinks, a convenience store, a large gift shop and fuel island are also located at Frisco Cove. The marina is open year-round. Summer hours are 7 AM to 9 PM; hours vary in the off-season. See our listings under personal watercraft, boat rentals and campgrounds for more information about Frisco Cove's offerings.

Hatteras Harbor Marina
N.C. Hwy. 12 and Gulfstream Way, Hatteras Village • (252) 986-2166

This marina can accommodate boats up to 68 feet for a day, month or year. Rates are 75¢ per foot per day or $12 per foot per month. Call for annual charges. Hatteras Harbor also has four apartments available for customers to rent: one bedroom units with a queen-size bed, three day beds, a living room, a fully fur-

nished kitchen, linens, cable TV, microwaves and coffee makers rent for $80 a night for two people. Each extra person in the room costs $5. A full-service deli and ships' store are located at the marina. Diesel fuel is available. Hatteras Harbor is open year round.

Willis Boat Landing
N.C. Hwy. 12, Hatteras Village
• (252) 986-2208

This marina accepts small craft up to 25 feet for short-term stays. Charges are set on a daily rate only, ranging from $6 to $10 a day. About 20 boats can be accommodated at a time. Boat and motor repairs can be done on-site. Bait and tackle are available for sale. Willis Boat Landing is open year round.

Oden's Dock
N.C. Hwy. 12, Hatteras Village
• (252) 986-2555

Oden's has a deep draft that can accommodate vessels up to 65 feet. Of the 27 slips at the marina, 20 are deep draft. Slips cost $1 per foot per day, $4.50 per foot per week and $10 per foot per month. Rates include water and electric. Reservations are suggested during the peak season.

A seafood market and Breakwater restaurant are also at Oden's Dock. Diesel fuel and gasoline are sold at the ships' store on-site, along with bait, tackle and food and beverages. Showers are available during business hours, and fish-cleaning facilities are also available for anglers. One headboat and a charter fishing fleet dock here. Oden's is open year-round. In-season hours are 5 AM to 7 PM daily. Hours vary off-season.

Teach's Lair Marina
N.C. Hwy. 12, Hatteras Village
• **(252) 986-2460**

This year-round, full-service marina has 87 slips that can accommodate boats up to 65 feet. Call for rates. A launching ramp is also located at the marina. Teach's Lair has a bathhouse, dry storage and a ship's store on-site. Fuel, oil and tackle are all available at the store. A headboat and charter fishing fleet dock here. The marina is open year round from 5 AM to 7 PM.

Ocracoke Island

The National Park Service Dock
Silver Lake, Ocracoke Village
• **(252) 928-5111**

From April through November, dockage here costs 50¢ per foot plus $3 a day for 110-volt electricity hookups, or $5 a day for 220-volt connections. During the rest of the year, the cost is 25¢ per foot, while the electric hookups stay the same price. There's a two-week limit on summer stays, and dock space is assigned on a first-come, first-served basis. No water is available in the winter season. Free anchorage is also allowed year round in Silver Lake itself.

Boat Rentals

If you don't own a powerboat but want to explore the vast waters of this region, you can rent a boat. Lots of places, even marinas or rent-all services, will often rent boats. Follow-

ing are some reliable sources if you're looking for motorboats.

Duck

Barrier Island Boats
N.C. Hwy. 12, Duck • (252) 261-7100

Formerly North Beach Sailing, Barrier Island Boats is on the Currituck Sound at the Barrier Island Restaurant pier. Carolina Skiffs rent for $60 an hour, or $75 for two hours. A 24-foot pontoon boat can be leased for $189 a half-day or $279 for a full day.

Waterworks Too
N.C. Hwy. 12, Duck • (252) 261-7245

With direct access to the Currituck Sound, Waterworks Too is a great place to find the perfect boat to explore the northern waters of the Outer Banks. You can find Waterworks Too at Duck Landing Water Tower at Wee Winks Square.

Jet boats, which hold three to four passengers, rent for $65 a half-hour, $85 for 45 minutes and $99 an hour. Sixteen-passenger, 24-foot-long pontoon boats, including a partial canopy, rent for $99 for two hours, $159 for a half day and $249 for a full-day. Center-console 19-foot outboard motorboats, with 40-horsepower engines, rent for $90 for 2 hours, $115 for half day and $165 for 8 hours. Waterworks Too is open in the summer months Monday through Saturday from 9 AM to 6 PM. Check out Waterworks' other location in Nags Head.

North Duck Watersports
N.C. Hwy. 12, Duck • (252) 261-4200

Entering its fifth season in 1998, North Duck Watersports is right on the Currituck Sound. Sport boats, pontoon boats, cruise boats and party boats are all available to rent here. North Duck is open spring through fall. Call for rate information.

Kitty Hawk

Promenade Watersports
**U.S. Hwy. 158, MP ¼, Kitty Hawk
• (252) 261-4400**

Right across from the Wright Memorial Bridge on the Currituck Sound, Promenade bills itself as the only full-service watersports center in the Southern Shores, Kitty Hawk and the Kill Devil Hills area. If you want to rent a boat, you're likely to find just what you want at this complete fun spot. Sailboats, kayaks, pontoon boats, fishing and crabbing boats and paddleboats are all available for rent here. Call for information and rates. Promenade is open spring through fall.

Nags Head

Nags Head Watersports
**Nags Head/Manteo Cswy., Nags Head
• (252) 480-2236**

Nags Head Watersports offers a myriad of water fun possibilities, including the opportunity to rent a motorboat. Just about midway on the Outer Banks on the Roanoke Sound, this complete center offers rentals of pontoon boats, fishing boats and jet boats. Call for details and prices. Nags Head Watersports is open from spring through fall.

The Waterworks
**U.S Hwy. 158, MP 16½, Nags Head
• (252) 441-8875**

Not only can you rent 19-foot powerboats, pontoons and jet boats at The Waterworks, you can also get any kind of watercraft supplies at this site. This watersports center claims to be the only one in the area that sells and repairs watercraft and boats. See our entry for Waterworks Too in Duck for more details about boat rentals. The Nags Head location is open daily 8 AM to 6 PM April through November.

Hatteras Island

Hatteras Jack Inc.
N.C. Hwy. 12, Rodanthe • (252) 987-2428

Right on the Pamlico Sound, Hatteras Jack is a year-round angler's haven. Six fiberglass, unsinkable Carolina Skiffs can be rented from March through December. Equipped with a 20-horsepower motor, the 14-foot skiff, which can hold 5 passengers, rents for $15 an hour, $65 a half day and $100 for 8 hours. The six-passenger 16-foot skiff with a 25-horsepower motor rents for $16 an hour, $70 a half day and $110 for the full day. The price does not include gas, but it does include a short instruction course. Boats are available from dawn to dusk. A bait and tackle shop with a full-line of custom-built rods is also on-site. You can also charter fishing trips at Hatteras Jack.

Frisco Cove Marina
N.C. Hwy. 12, Frisco • (252) 995-4242

You can rent motorboats at this full-service marina. Four 24-foot Carolina Skiffs are available to rent for $40 an hour, $135 for a half day and $199 a full day. Several 16-foot aluminum boats equipped with outboard motors can be rented for $15 an hour, $69 a half-day or $89 for a full day. Weekly rentals are available on the aluminum boats only. See our listing under marinas for more information on Frisco Cove.

Ocracoke Island

Island Rentals
Silver Lake Rd., Ocracoke Village
• (252) 928-5480

Island Rentals, at Sharon Miller Realty, rents two 16-foot fiberglass flat-bottom boats with 25-horsepower motors. It also rents one 17-foot, 30-horsepower boat and a 19-foot, 60-horsepower boat at half-day, daily, three-day and weekly rates. Prices start at $65 a half-day. Call for more details.

Personal Watercraft

If you feel a need for speed and enjoy the idea of riding a motorcycle across the water, more than a dozen Outer Banks outposts rent personal watercraft by the hour. No experience is necessary to ride these powerful boat-like devices, although a training session is a must if you've never before piloted a personal watercraft. Unlike land-locked go-carts and other speedy road rides, there aren't any lanes to stick to on the open sound or ocean.

Several styles of personal watercraft have developed over the past decade. Waverunners allow drivers to maneuver these crafts sitting down and a second passenger to hold on, also sitting, from behind. Most Jet Skis don't have seats and can accommodate only one person at a time in a standing or kneeling position. Newer Runabouts, also known as blasters, give riders the choice of

standing or sitting. Waverunners are the easiest style craft to balance and control because you don't have to worry as much about tipping over. Jet Skis are, however, more prone to tricks — and spills — and better able to leap ocean waves. Almost all of these motorized vessels can cruise for up to two hours on five gallons of fuel.

Personal watercraft are akin to motorboats with inboard motors that power a water pump. There aren't any propellers or outside engine parts, so fingers and toes generally stay safe. Like other motorized boats, however, personal watercraft are loud and can be dangerous if you don't know what you're doing. Most rental outposts include brief instructions and sometimes even a video on how to handle Waverunners, Jet Skis and Runabouts.

Practicing on Personal Watercraft

Basic operations of a personal watercraft include an ignition and stall button on the left handle; the throttle on the right. Push the start button on the left to take off. Your right hand can control the speed by turning the throttle forward or back. If you fall off, a wrist lanyard that wraps around your hand automatically snaps away from the handle and shuts off the engine. To get aboard again, climb on from the back. Always steer to the right when approaching another personal watercraft — just like you would on the road.

A quick, easy trick on Jet Skis and Waverunners, if you're game, is to throw the throttle open and then turn hard. It's like doing a 360-degree doughnut on the water. As the back of the personal watercraft comes around, the front submerges. Gun the throttle again and you can fly out over your own wake.

While most rental shops are on the sound side of the Outer Banks, where the water's surface is generally slicker and depths are much more shallow, a few personal watercraft outlets will let you take the vessels into the ocean. There, shore break and offshore waves provide great takeoffs and challenges to more experienced Jet Ski drivers. Remember to watch out for surfers, swimmers and other Jet Ski drivers who might not see you coming.

Renting
Personal Watercraft

Jet Skis and Waverunners sell for $5,000 to $10,000 new. Several Outer Banks rental shops also sell used personal watercraft for cheaper prices at the end of the summer season. Remember, you'll probably need a trailer to haul these vessels behind your vehicle.

If you're just here on vacation, or don't think you'd ride one enough for the price to pay off, shops from Corolla to Hatteras Island rent personal watercraft beginning at $30 a half-hour. Price wars occasionally will result in the cost being slashed to rock bottom. Regardless, more powerful models are generally more expensive. Additional charges also sometimes apply for extra riders on the Waverunners. Personal watercraft also can be rented by the hour, day or even week at some spots.

When you're out riding through the waves, keep in mind these personal watercraft "rules of the road":

• Stay in designated buoyed areas at all times.
• Stay at least 50 yards away from other Jet Skiers, swimmers and watercraft.
• Do not excessively flip your vehicle.
• Wear a life jacket.
• Keep the lanyard attached to wrist at all times.
• Be aware that Waverunners and similar vehicles are low profile and often difficult for others to see. Stay a safe distance away.
• Return to shore immediately if gas has turned to "reserve" or if any mechanical problems are apparent.
• Do not wake jump, splash, race or interact in any way with other watercraft.

Corolla

Corolla Watersports at the Inn at Corolla Lighthouse
1066 Ocean Tr., Corolla • (252) 453-8602

A sister store to North Duck Watersports, Waverunner III can be rented here. Call for rates and more information. Corolla Watersports is open May through October.

Kitty Hawk Watersports
N.C. Hwy. 12, Corolla • (252) 453-6900

Kitty Hawk Watersports, behind TimBuck II Shopping Village, and affiliated with Kitty Hawk Sports, runs a complete watersports store in these northern barrier island beaches. You can rent Waverunners at hourly, half-day and daily rates. Waverunner adventure tours are also offered on the Currituck Sound. Call for prices and more information. Kitty Hawk Watersports is open in Corolla from early spring through fall. The Nags Head location at Milepost 16 on U.S. 158 is open longer.

Duck

North Duck Watersports
N.C. Hwy. 12, Duck • (252) 261-4200

Three miles north of the village on the Sanderling border, this watersports center rents Waverunners and Jet Skis to race across the nearby Currituck Sound. Call for information on rates. North Duck Watersports is open May through October. During the peak season, hours are 9 AM to 6 PM daily.

Barrier Island Boats
N.C. Hwy. 12, Duck • (252) 261-7100

Under new ownership for the 1998 season, Barrier Island Boats is near the Barrier Island Restaurant pier. Formally North Beach Sailing, Barrier Island Boats rents Waverunner III, Wave Ventures, Pro Jet by Zodiac, Exciter and Jet Boats by the half-hour and hour. Guided 90-minute Waverunner tours are also available. Call for rates and more information.

Kitty Hawk

Promenade Watersports
U.S Hwy. 158, MP ¼, Kitty Hawk
• (252) 261-4400

Even before you hit the sandy Outer Banks from the Wright Memorial Bridge, you'll see the Promenade on your right. A watersports and kiddie recreational park, Promenade includes enough to keep everybody delighted on land while you're racing around on the Currituck Sound on a personal watercraft. Waverunners and Runabouts can be rented by the hour, half-day or full day. Early-bird specials are offered on Waverunners. Call for price information. Promenade is open only during the warm-weather months.

Nags Head

The Waterworks
U.S. Hwy. 158, MP 16½, Nags Head
• (252) 441-8875

One of the many watersports activities and services Waterworks offers is rental of personal watercraft. Jet Skis, Sea Doos and Waverunners are available at half-hour, 45-minute and hourly rates. Call for prices. Waterworks also sells personal watercraft. This location in Nags Head is open daily April through November.

Nags Head Water Sports
Nags Head/Manteo Cswy, Nags Head
• (252) 480-2236

On the Roanoke Sound, Nags Head Water Sports has a small beach with picnic and swimming areas on the grounds. New one-, two- and three-seater Jet Skis and Waverunners are available for rent. Call for prices. Nags Head Water Sports closes in the winter months.

Willett's Wetsports
Nags Head/Manteo Cswy, Nags Head
• (252) 441-4112

On the south side of the causeway on the Roanoke Sound, at Caribbean Corners, Willett's rents brand new one-, two- and three-seat Waverunners and Jet Skis. Half-hour to one-hour jaunts in the wide open sound will cost between $38 to $68. This bright pink watersports center is open 8 AM to 7 PM daily May through October.

Hatteras Island

Hatteras Watersports
N.C. Hwy. 12, Salvo • (252) 987-2306

Hatteras Watersports rents the Waverunner 500, which seats one or two persons, for $39 per half-hour and $58 per hour. Waverunner III, which seats up to three persons, rents for $49 per half-hour and $69 per hour. Hatteras Watersports is on the soundside, across from the Salvo Volunteer Fire Department.

Frisco Cove Marina
N.C. Hwy. 12, Frisco • (252) 995-4242

Frisco Cove, among its other services, rents personal watercraft to vacationers seeking some speed in the adjacent Pamlico Sound. Waverunners rent for $69 an hour. Drivers must be 14 years or older, and parents must sign for children younger than 18. The watercraft are rented daily between 9 AM and 5 PM in-season.

Chances of a good catch are enhanced by physical conditions existing here that you won't find anywhere else. And that ain't no fish story!

Fishing

If you haven't already heard through the grapevine about our infamous Outer Banks fishing, you're in for a treat. The diversity of fish available in the waters here makes this area a hot spot for anglers from far and wide. Charter boats leave the docks year round for offshore waters teeming with big game fish. The inlets, sounds, rivers and lakes abound with saltwater and freshwater species, and surfcasters and pier anglers have plenty of opportunities to catch a variety of fish from the shell-fringed beaches or wooden planks that hover over the sea and sounds. Whether you're a novice or a pro, angling with heavy or light tackle for food or for sport, the Outer Banks is a world-class fishing center — and we can prove this boast by checking the International Game Fish Association World Record Game Fishes listings.

Many record-breaking fish have been caught here — both offshore and inshore — including the all-tackle record for blue marlin (1,142 pounds) in 1974, and the all-tackle world-record bluefish (31 pounds, 12 ounces), caught off Hatteras in 1972. And then there was that world-record red drum caught off Avon, a record-breaking Spanish mackerel caught in Ocracoke Inlet, a lemon shark caught off Buxton and a scalloped hammerhead shark landed off Cape Point. Let's not leave out an oyster toadfish and a myriad of saltwater fly-rod and saltwater-line class world-record catches.

You might think, "the variety draws expert anglers, hence the great catches." Well, there's more to the story. Chances of a good catch are enhanced by physical conditions existing here that you won't find anywhere else. And that ain't no fish story! Stay tuned. We outline these characteristics in our offshore section below.

Another factor that influences the catch is that the Outer Banks has multiple experienced charter fleets with mates on board to show you the ropes. Getting a job as a mate on a charter boat is no simple matter — the competition to work these famous waters is fierce.

While anyone who's gone fishing knows you can't predict catching fish, they'll be guided by charter boat captains who know what species should be in the area and who will help you make wise choices on the morning of the trip. Charters leave the docks for inshore and offshore fishing every day that the weather permits. When you call to book a boat (see our Marinas listings in this chapter), you may find it hard to know what kind of trip to choose unless you've fished before. Booking agents at each marina will guide you.

In the following sections, we describe offshore and inshore angling, backwater, surf, fly and pier fishing. Offshore trips generally leave the docks at 5:30 AM and return no later than 6 PM. Inshore trips are half-day excursions that leave twice daily, generally at 7 AM and again around noon. Intermediate trips can last all day but generally don't travel as far as the Gulf Stream.

We're certain you'll have a pleasant adventure no matter how far out you venture. If you're taking out your own boat, it's important to get information on size limits, creel limits and season dates. You don't want to risk getting a fine by bringing in too small or too many restricted fish. Check with any tackle shop, or call the North Carolina Division of Marine Fisheries at (800) 682-2632 for this kind of information. For information on freshwater licenses, check the regulations digest published by the North Carolina Wildlife Resources Commission. It's available at sporting-goods stores and tackle shops. Official weigh stations are listed toward the end of this chapter.

Offshore Fishing

The majority of Outer Banks captains who lead you to offshore fishing grounds have been working these waters for years. Many are second- and third-generation watermen. They generally choose the daily fishing spot depending on recent trends, seasons and weather. Occasionally, when there's a slow spell, a captain will move away from the rest of the fleet to play out a hunch. If the maverick meets with success, it's common for him/her to share this find with the rest of the fleet. In other words, our area boasts of a brother- or sisterhood that visiting anglers say they've experienced nowhere else. This camaraderie can't help but enhance the fishing experience, plus, fishing together is safer.

Anglers fishing offshore for big game fish generally troll (drag fishing lines behind the moving boat). If you run into a school of fish, such as dolphin (mahi mahi), the captain will stop the boat so the party can cast into the water that's been primed with chum, or fish bits. Chumming also is used on bluefin tuna trips. All these techniques are explained the day of the trip. Expect to pay about $950 for six people to charter an offshore fishing excursion. Bluefin tuna trips are higher, costing between $1,000 and $12,000. Some offshore charters go as low as $700. You have to shop around.

One offshore area that's frequented with great regularity is called The Point (not to be confused with Cape Hatteras Point). Approximately 37 miles off the Outer Banks, this primary fishing ground for local captains and mates is rich in game fish such as tuna, dolphin, wahoo, billfish and shark. Blue marlin, wahoo and dolphin show up at The Point in April and May. Yellowfin, bigeye and blackfin tuna are the anglers' mainstay year round. A significant population of yellowfin inhabit this area in the winter, providing a tremendous seasonal fishery. You have to be patient to fish in the winter because plenty of bad weather days make traveling offshore a waiting game. If you hold out though, you can fight a deep-diving tuna.

Deep-swimming reef fish, such as grouper, snapper and tilefish, also inhabit The Point. Because of the strong current, however, you

must travel a little bit south of The Point to fish for them effectively.

The Point has unique characteristics that give it a reputation for attracting and harboring a variety and quantity of fish from the minute baitfish to massive billfish (see our Natural Wonders chapter).

What also helps set this spot apart is its proximity to the edge of the Continental Shelf. Where there's a drop-off, you'll find a concentration of baitfish because of the nutrient-rich waters present and currents playing off the edge to stir things up. Anglers don't have to travel far to get to The Point since the Shelf is particularly narrow off Cape Hatteras. And The Point is the last spot where the Gulf Stream appears near the Shelf before it veers off in an east-northeasterly direction. Weather permitting, there are some days when the Gulf Stream entirely covers The Point. Other days, prevailing winds can push it farther offshore.

At about 50 miles wide and a half-mile deep, the Gulf Stream has temperatures that rarely drop below 65 to 70 degrees, providing a comfortable habitat for a variety of sea life. The Gulf Steam flows at an average rate of 2.5 mph, at times quickening to 5 mph. This steadfast flow carries away millions of tons of water per second, continually pushing along sea life in its path, including fish, microscopic plants and animals and gulfweed. Gulfweed lines the edge of the Gulf Stream when the winds are favorable, creating a habitat for baitfish. You can easily pull up a handful of vegetation and find it teeming with minute shrimp and fish. Anglers fish these "grass lines" as well as the warm-water eddies that spin off from the Gulf Stream. These warm pockets, which vary in size from 20 to 100 miles long by a half-mile to a mile wide, are sometimes filled with schools of dolphin (mahi mahi), tuna and mako.

Catch-and-release fishing for bluefin tuna has anglers from across the globe traveling to Hatteras to partake in a bonanza that has really revived winter offshore charter fishing along the Outer Banks. For at least four years, captains have been noticing a massive congregation of bluefin tuna inhabiting the wrecks about 20 miles from Hatteras Inlet. We've seen the action firsthand, and the quantity of bluefin available and the frequency with which they bite are phenomenal.

Fish weighing from 200 to more than 800 pounds have been caught. These giants, which U.S. biologists say comprise an overstressed fishery in most parts of the world, are a federally protected species, so anglers almost always must release them. Restrictions state that during bluefin tuna season anglers may keep one fish from 27 to 73 inches per boat per day. The length of the tuna season is determined annually by the National Marine Fisheries and is contingent on overall poundage caught.

But just reeling in a bluefin of any magnitude will make the blood of an avid angler run hot! The bluefin seem to strike with less provocation on the choppy days — plus there aren't tons of boats flooding the area during rougher weather. On days when the fish are spooked by excessive boat traffic or simply aren't biting for whatever reason, mates will sprinkle the water with chum (chopped-up fish parts, guts and blood that smells strong and draws fish) to increase the chance of a strike. These giants often jump 4 feet out of the ocean just to bite a bloody bait.

Local anglers troll, chum and use live or dead bait. We've seen great success with 130-pound test line. Some folks like to use lighter tackle for the sport of it, but the heavier the line, the better the condition of the fish when it's released. Circle hooks are also recommended for the fish's comfort — they tend to lodge in the mouth cartilage rather than in the fleshy gullet or gills.

Even though most of the fish are caught on heavy tackle, carefully handled and subsequently released, recreational charter boat captains are contemplating a self-imposed quota for catch and release to try to protect the fish even further. When there are large groups of boats present day after day, it's likely the same fish will have to do battle over and over.

Fishing parties enjoy feeding the fish and catching them on hookless lines just to watch the strike. It's like being at a huge aquarium.

You can enjoy offshore fishing year round, but with the bluefin fishing off Hatteras, you should book a trip from January through March. Some fish may show up earlier, and there are bluefin available in early April, but by then, captains begin concentrating on yellowfin again. Bluefin boats leave the dock between 5:30 and 7 AM. You can book charters by calling any of the Outer Banks' marinas listed in this chapter. To avoid the crowds, book a weekday trip.

As the Stomach Turns: Battling and Preventing Seasickness

OK, we know what you've been thinking: "What about seasickness?" Almost everyone who has ever been on the water for any length of time has gotten seasick or at least battled that unmistakable queasy feeling. Seasickness is a one-of-a-kind experience. We've spent plenty of time on the water and know what it's like to want to throw yourself overboard. Here are some do's and don'ts that should help you avoid that feeling. Experiment to find what works best for you.

1. Take an over-the-counter remedy for motion sickness the night before your trip and, again, an hour before departure. This allows time for the medicine to get into your system. Ask your pharmacist about the specifics on these medications. Some will make you more sleepy than others. If you're bringing children along, you'll need to find out whether the medication you are taking is safe for them too.

2. Some folks try medication patches that are now available over the counter. The patch fits behind your ear and administers the medication via absorption through the skin.

3. Eat nongreasy food the night before the trip (and no alcohol!), and always eat a nongreasy breakfast. Pancakes and toast are good choices. Despite what you may think, a full stomach is much better than an empty one.

4. Carry this notion through by bringing a nonspicy, nongreasy lunch with you. It also helps to nibble on saltines or ginger snaps all day. Ginger is an Oriental remedy for motion sickness. Some people actually take ginger capsules, but we like the snaps — and the kids do too.

5. Some folks swear that you should drink a lot of fluids while offshore. This makes sense when it comes to dehydration, but we've seen plenty of folks get even sicker by downing a soda hoping to ward off the oncoming surge. We refrain from drinking anything until the latter part of the trip. Again, this is a highly personal choice, and some folks may need the extra fluid.

6. If you happen to get sick, the worst may be over if you follow this simple rule: Always eat immediately after getting sick (so says Hatteras native, Capt. Spurgeon Stowe, of the *Miss Hatteras*). We've had success following this rule. NO LIE!!

7. If you're feeling queasy, stay out on deck in the fresh air. Don't hole up in the salon, and do not go into the head (bathroom). Throw up overboard if the water is not too rough to keep you away from the edge. This is common and acceptable etiquette. Concentrate on the horizon if possible. Orient yourself with a stable point, and you should feel better. Above all, don't be embarrassed. An old sailor friend of this Insider believes that anyone who brags about never being sick has spent little time on the water.

8. This may sound bizarre, but another little trick may work. If you're out of shape and have weak stomach muscles, wear something tight across your abdomen. By holding tight to the stomach, the queasy feeling subsides somewhat.

Offshore Headboat Fishing

Headboat fishing can give you an offshore experience without the price of chartering a boat (see our "Inshore Fishing" section on headboat fishing). Several large boats take parties — charging "by the head" — offshore all day. While you won't be targeting tuna here, you still have the chance for plentiful catches of a variety of bottom species, fine-tasting fish in their own right, including black sea bass, triggerfish, tilefish, amberjack, tautog, grouper and snapper. The species vary slightly from north to south. Occasionally small shark are hooked over the wrecks, and once in a while you'll run into some bigger game fish, but you're generally dropping a line over the side into the artificial and natural reefs or wrecks, not trolling.

The boats are open from the stern to the bow to hold anglers comfortably, and all the gear is supplied. All you have to bring is a cooler with food and drinks, sunscreen and a jacket in case the weather changes. Anglers don't need fishing licenses.

If you're venturing out in winter months, dress in layers. If you're near the Gulf Stream and the wind is blowing over it in your direction then you may be able to layer down to a T-shirt. Most of the headboats that go offshore have heat in the salon or an area that can be shut off from the cold air.

Many parents want their children to experience an offshore trip, and that's understandable. You not only fish but often get to see whales, turtles and dolphin. Our advice: Think carefully before you take a really young tyke offshore. The day is long, approximately 10 hours, and the captain doesn't turn around except in an emergency, and that does not include seasickness. The boat's deck can be slippery, and the water can be choppy. Life vests are available.

The Country Girl
Pirate's Cove Yacht Club, Nags Head-Manteo Cswy. • (252) 473-3906, (252) 473-5577

The *Country Girl* launches from Pirate's Cove Yacht Club and takes 27 people for an offshore bottom-fishing trip over the wrecks for only $65 per person. Bird-watching excursions also are available (see our Natural Wonders chapter).

Miss Hatteras
Oden's Dock, N.C. Hwy. 12, Hatteras Village • (252) 986-2365

The *Miss Hatteras* ties up at Oden's Dock

INSIDERS' TIP

A word of caution to any angler: Winds can blow a bare hook wayward, so always fasten it to one of the rod guides when it's not in the water.

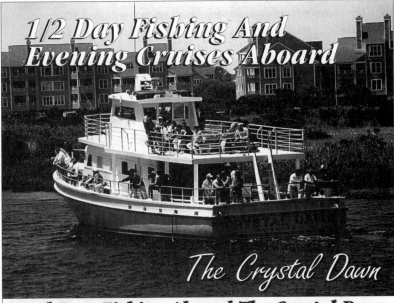

1/2 Day Fishing And Evening Cruises Aboard

The Crystal Dawn

Head Boat Fishing Aboard The Crystal Dawn

Inlet & Sound Bottom Fishing **All Bait, Tackle & Fish Bags Furnished**
Tickets Sold In Advance **Daily Trips Except Sundays**
In Season: (June 1 thru Sept. 1): Departs 7am-Returns 12 Noon;
Departs 12:30pm-Returns 5pm • $20.00/Child $25.00/Adult
Off Season: Departs 8am-Returns 1pm

Evening Cruises

Departs 6:30pm daily (except Sunday) with commentary of the Outer Banks
• $4.00/Child $8.00/Adult

Moonlight Cruises

8:30pm to 10:00pm
Cruise the Manteo Water front (Home of the Elizabeth II) or Wanchese Harbor

Head Boat & Charter Fishing Aboard

**Off Shore
Wreck Fishing**
Tuesday - Friday
Departs: 7:00am
Returns: 5:00pm
$65 per person

**Gulf Stream
Charters
are Available**
Departs: 5:30am
Returns: 5:00pm

The Country Girl

**Located at Pirates Cove Yacht Club
On the Nags Head/Manteo Causeway** **(252) 473-5577**

Office located in the Ship Store: Write 100 Patty Lane, Manteo NC 27954 or call (252) 473-5577

Visually Impaired Anglers Are Truly VIPs

Every October, hundreds of visually impaired persons visit the Outer Banks as part of the annual Lions VIP Fishing Tournament. Entering its 15th year in 1998, the tournament not only provides these VIPs (visually impaired persons) with the chance to  fish, but a three-day program filled with motivating activities and information.

Scheduled around the fishing highlights are seminars that include job training and placement and introduction to new technology designed to make life easier for the visually-challenged. Socializing with peers plays a valuable role in the success of this program that has expanded from a one- to a three-day event. A banquet and dance provide the opportunity to make friends, share personal stories and swap coping skills. Fishing trophies are awarded at the banquet, which is always highlighted by an inspirational speaker. Newly blind folks and those with individual struggles gain hope from such testimonials.

One day is set aside for fishing from a host of local piers and headboats for a

— continued on next page

Photo: Courtesy of The Sportfishing Report

With the help of technology and a little creativity, many disabled anglers can still take to the sea.

variety of species, sometimes giving participants their first-ever fishing experience. A day spent casting lines side-by-side on local piers and headboats provides a hands-on experience that Insiders swear weaves its own magic for the 400 guests enjoying the world-class fishing of the Outer Banks.

Autumn has produced record-breaking fish catches from the surf, boats and piers. Whether the catch makes its way into the International Game Fish Association (IGFA) world-record ranks or not, the sport yields plenty of fun along with tasty and often feisty species such as sea mullet, croaker, flounder and spot. Everything needed to fish is provided, including volunteers to give as much or as little help as anglers desire. It's the perfect sport for the visually impaired because it relies less on sight and more on feel.

Volunteers always play a major role in the program that has grown in attendance over the years; however, the VIP tournament is able to target only a fraction of the 21,000-person visually challenged population in North Carolina. The primary reason for this is the lack of a meeting place to accommodate the large group, but help may arriving soon as plans are underway to construct a for-profit convention center in Dare County by Memorial Day 1998. In the meantime, generous souls (including visually-impaired entertainer Doc Watson, who performed for the group in the past) keep the program afloat. Local businesses and civic organizations underwrite most of the tournament costs that in the past have amounted to over $100,000. Piers, boats, restaurants and motels donate their services, the Lions Club Foundation has made grant money available and the Dare County Tourist Bureau funded the publishing of a twin-vision brochure in print and Braille.

Individuals can get involved through the adopt-a-fisherman program, which is available year round. Each donor contributes $25 to sponsor an angler. In turn, they are invited to fish with the individual, but attendance is not required. Because of the outpouring of help, the only cost to the participants in past tournaments has been $35 for the entry fee and the cost for transportation — a small price to pay for a big experience that yields far more than a fish wriggling at the end of a line.

Applications are sent out through the North Carolina Division of Services for the Blind. State social workers that service the visually-impaired and Lions Clubs distribute them. For donation or entry information call Dare County Lion Gwen White at (919) 441-4966.

in Hatteras Village and also offers offshore headboat excursions. The boats leave the dock by 6:30 AM. Costs are $65 for adults and $40 for children 12 and younger. The *Miss Hatteras* also hosts birdwatching excursions (see our Natural Wonders chapter).

Tideline Charters
Thicket Lump Marina, Thicket Lump Rd., Wanchese • (252) 261-1458

Captains Jay Bender and Clay Hauser take turns as captain and mate running offshore, inshore and intermediate trips off the *Tideline*. Their 27-foot custom takes one to four anglers for half- and full-day fishing trips in search of Spanish mackerel, bluefish, king mackerel and cobia. You can live-bait fish or troll in the sounds, inlet or ocean from March through December. Half-day fishing

for one to four people is $325; full-day trips cost $600. All bait and tackle are provided.

Inshore Fishing

A variety of inshore opportunities abound that will strike the fancy of the novice or expert angler. The offshore gang doesn't corner the market on fun here. Inshore generally refers to inlet, sound, lake, river and some close-range ocean fishing on a boat.

Outer Banks anglers enjoy fishing for rockfish (also called striped bass or stripers) year round. They are fun to catch and make a great tasting dinner. Though it is a regulated species, they've steadily been making a comeback during the last six years. Each year stripers spawn under the dam in Weldon, North Carolina. The young live in estuaries for several years

before joining the Atlantic migratory population. A moratorium initially was placed on the fish in summer 1984, when striper stocks in the Chesapeake Bay started to decline rapidly. This was significant since about 90 percent of the Atlantic migratory stock comes from the Chesapeake Bay. Marine fisheries experts blamed overfishing and water quality for the drop. A widespread East Coast moratorium gave the species a chance to thrive again. There was a partial lifting of the moratorium in 1990, and today, while the species still is closely monitored, they afford Outer Banks anglers a hearty catch-and-release recreational fishery.

The ocean season for stripers is open year round. Anglers can keep two fish (28 inches or larger) per person per day. Though a body of stripers are present in our waters year round, the sound inhabitants are protected by restrictions. Since the sound fishing season fluctuates, the best thing to do is call your favorite tackle shop for up-to-date regulations. If you just want to catch and release, go at it anytime.

When a cold snap hits the Chesapeake Bay area, rockfish migrate down past Corolla into Oregon Inlet. November is one of the best months to fish for them around the Manns Harbor bridge that connects Roanoke Island to the East Lake community. Anglers also fish in the winter for stripers behind Roanoke Island in East and South lakes.

Stripers tend to congregate around bridge pilings. They cluster near these nutrient-covered supports that entice smaller bait fish. You can troll, use spinning tackle with lures, fly-cast or surf fish for them. Stripers are bottom feeders, so a planer can be used to catch them. If you're fishing with double hooks, once you've hooked the first fish, keep it steady in the water. Another should soon grab the second hook. Insiders suggest using a butter bean with a white bucktail on the end. You can catch them on slick calm days and in rougher weather, but a little current seems to help.

Summertime finds Outer Bankers fishing the sounds from Manteo to Ocracoke for speckled trout. Insiders suggest you move to the surf or pier to catch them in fall. The speckled trout fishing is excellent in early fall around Oregon and Hatteras inlets. They are best enjoyed on light tackle with artificial lures or on a fly rod. Light spinning tackle is another good choice. Artificial lures are the norm. Insiders suggest using a lead head jig with a soft plastic twister tail for sound, bridge and inlet fishing. For the beach, try MirrOlures. Currently the fish must be a 12-inch total length minimum to be a keeper. Call your local tackle shop for more information.

Inshore Headboat Fishing

A couple of Outer Banks' headboats ply the sounds and inlets and occasionally go several miles offshore to the wrecks on calm days.

Photo: Courtesy of Mary Ellen Riddle

Day or night, a fishing break always hits the spot.

Photo: Courtesy of Bob Reardon

It's a mad dash for the blues during this blues blitz.

These excursions provide the perfect chance for a youngster to hold a rod, bait a hook, reel in a fish (we hope) and learn respect for wildlife. The inshore headboats are generally between 60 and 75 feet long and accommodate about 50 people. As with the offshore trips, tackle and bait are provided. We suggest you bring your own food; some headboats sell sodas and snacks, and the Miss Hatteras has a full snack bar.

Inshore headboat captains are very accommodating to families, and the mates will give you as much or as little help as you need. They'll tell you if your fish is a keeper or needs to be thrown back (some fish are not of legal size, or big enough to keep). If you're squeamish about baiting a hook or handling a fish, a mate will assist you. They seem to have a sense of when to back off and when to lend a helping hand. Half-day bottom fishing trips generally run $20 for kids and $25 for adults. Expect to bottom fish for croaker, trout, spot,

flounder, sea mullet, blowtoads and pigfish; these pan-size fish are very tasty. The crew usually can identify your fish if you cannot.

Some of these headboats-by-day offer nonfishing pleasure cruises in the evenings. Many captains enjoy talking with passengers about the area's history. Local boats such as the *Miss Oregon Inlet*, *Miss Hatteras* and *Crystal Dawn* offer nonfishing excursions. Prices vary, but the average is $4 for children and $8 for adults.

A quick tip about kids on boats: Watch them carefully, and enforce a no-running code. These boats typically carry a large crowd, and not everyone will have their hooks or rod tips in the right place at the right time.

Remain positive when fishing with kids. Everywhere in the world, there are days when the fish don't bite. If you're having one of those days, let the trip be a lesson in nature, patience and people — and let your imagination roam. The adult sets the tone. A positive attitude will go far in "hooking" your little ones for life.

Small-boat Fishing

Small boats (smaller than the offshore vessels and generally in the 30-foot range) offer sound, inlet, lake, river and ocean trips that are as varied as the weather. Inshore captains generally book half-day trips but also offer intermediate all-day trips to take you farther out. If you're interested in bluefish, Spanish mackerel, cobia, king mackerel, bonito, trout, flounder, croaker and red drum, you can book trips from virtually any marina. Half-day trips are a little easier on the pocketbook.

Spanish mackerel are a mainstay of the area. Ocracoke Island captains begin looking for them in late April and typically enjoy catches through late October. Farther north on the Outer Banks, Spanish mackerel usually arrive the first or second week in May, depending on the water temperature. Casting to them is the most sporting way of catching them. We suggest you use 8-pound test on a medium to medium-light spinning rod with a pink and white Stingsilver. Other colors work well also; if the people next to you are catching fish and you aren't, see what kind of lures they are using.

If it's flounder you're after, you can find these flat fish in both Hatteras and Oregon inlets, in clear water. Anglers drift bottom rigs on medium-light spinning tackle. Croakers are found in the sounds around deep holes, oyster rocks and sloughs.

You can dine on almost all inshore species, but one bony fish with little food value that cannot be overlooked is the tarpon. A release category fish, the tarpon is probably one of the strongest fighting fish available inshore. While the Outer Banks is not a destination spot for tarpon, a handful of locals fish for them around Ocracoke in the Pamlico Sound and south to the mouth of the Neuse River. We recommend fresh-cut bait, such as spot or trout, and very sharp hooks to penetrate the tarpon's hard mouth. Remember, it's one thing to hook up and a whole other to bring a tarpon to the boat. Good luck!

Marinas

The Outer Banks is dotted with more than a half-dozen marinas that can help you book a charter for inshore or offshore fishing. You can call any of these marinas and request a particular captain or boat. If you are new in town, you'll be glad to know that the marinas book reputable captains on a rotating basis. While personalities vary, rarely does dependability.

If you want to ensure that you get to go fishing, especially during the busy holiday periods, it's wise to call at least a month in advance to make sure you get on board. The marinas stay open year round, so you can call well in advance of your trip if you know when you'll be vacationing here. Don't be afraid to ask questions (the marina personnel are very helpful), but if you wish to have a lengthy conversation, reservationists have more time to chat in the off-season.

Makeup parties are available for folks who want to hook up with a group to make six. If everything is booked up, ask to be put on a waiting list. The list below represents some of the choices in marinas on the Outer Banks. We list more in our weigh station listing at the end of the chapter. See our Watersports chapter for marina information for the individual boater.

Manteo

Pirate's Cove Yacht Club
Nags Head/Manteo Cswy., Manteo
• (252) 473-3906, (800) 367-4728

Pirate's Cove is the Outer Banks' most modern marina with 153 wet slips for yachts up to 90 feet long. It's surrounded by upscale, permanent and rental waterfront homes and has a ship's store that can supply almost every maritime need. Reservations are accepted for dock space. A growing number of charter fishing boats run Gulf Stream trips from Pirate's Cove most of the year. Between 4 and 5 PM each day, visitors can watch captains and crews unload more than a dozen vessels filled with fresh dolphin, tuna and wahoo.

Offshore prices average $950 for a full day trip. Intermediate trips at half day run $375

Photo: Courtesy of Aycock Brown/Outer Banks History Center

The Outer Banks is famous for world-record catches, including this bluefish caught by James Hussey in 1972.

and $600 for full day. Inshore trip prices vary but average $300 per half day and $500 per full day trip. The *Country Girl*, (252) 473-5577, is the only offshore headboat that fishes out of here that will accommodate more than six passengers per trip (see their listing).

For inlet and sound bottom fishing, plus an interesting commentary on the Outer Banks, take a trip on the *Crystal Dawn*, (252) 473-5577, daily except Sundays throughout the year. (The Crystal Dawn also offers moonlight cruises along the Manteo waterfront or Wanchese harbor — a nice change of pace.)

On all trips, anglers just have to furnish food and drinks in a small cooler. Coolers for fish can be left in cars back at the dock. While on-board, all fish is either put on ice in a fish box or on stringers, depending on size. Fish-cleaning service is available at the dock. Slip rentals are also available.

If you're interested in learning more about saltwater angling, Pirate's Cove operates a fishing school each March and October (see our Annual Events chapter).

Besides fishing supplies, the Ship's Store

at Pirate's Cove sells sportswear, T-shirts, souvenir hats and drink huggies, groceries and ice. A restaurant above the store, Hurricane Mo's, includes a raw bar and fresh steamed seafood. Boaters can brown-bag liquor at this establishment that sells only beer and wine (see our Restaurants chapter).

Pirate's Cove Marina is scheduled to host the 15th Annual Billfish Tournament in mid-August of 1998 (see our Annual Events chapter). Other tournaments for kids, small boats and women only are held from June through November. For advance notification, write P.O. Box 1997, Manteo, NC 27954. For more information on Pirate's Cove, see our Attractions chapter.

Salty Dawg Marina
U.S. Hwy. 64, Manteo • (252) 473-3405

The Salty Dawg offers more than 50 slips, power, water and a bathhouse. It's open year round seven days a week. Call for reservations on holidays. You can also charter offshore, inshore and intermediate fishing trips here. For parties of six, expect to pay between $875 and $950 for an offshore trip, $300 for a half-day inshore trip and $500 for a full-day inshore trip. Salty Dawg has a convenient location near accommodations, a grocery store, pharmacy and coin-operated laundry.

Wanchese

Thicket Lump Marina
212 Thicket Lump Rd., Wanchese
• (252) 473-4500

Thicket Lump offers wet slips and dry storage, gas and diesel fuel, bait and tackle, ice, beer and soft drinks, plus inshore and offshore charter trips from six charter boats. Prices vary boat to boat; call for specific information. Thicket Lump also sells Suzuki outboard motors, Kencraft and Maycraft boats and Kawasaki Jet Skis and generators. The marina features a full-service maintenance department for boat body and engine repairs. It's open year round.

Bodie Island

Oregon Inlet Fishing Center
N.C. Hwy. 12 • (252) 441-6301

Over 30 well-equipped boats comprise the historic charter fishing fleet at Oregon Inlet Fishing Center, just north of the Herbert C. Bonner Bridge. Most captains leave before sunrise and return by 6 PM. Fish cleaners will fillet your day's catch on the docks. A full day of offshore fishing, which includes a two-hour trip to the Gulf Stream, costs $930 per boat; $900 with cash discount. Most boats carry parties of six anglers., and captains supply rods, reels, tackle, bait, ice, coolers and advice. Charter parties should bring food and drinks. Mates working for the charter fleet usually depend heavily on tips for their wages, and we suggest tipping at least 10 percent of the cost of your trip. There are daily limits per person on tuna and dolphin. Most captains require anglers to release marlin and sailfish alive.

Prices for 1997 ran as follows: intermediate trips, $594 for all day, $575 with a cash discount; $384 for half day and $375 with a cash discount. Inshore fishing costs $540 for a full day or $525 with cash discount. Half-day inshore trips are $312, and $300 if paid in cash.

To make reservations (you'll want to make them early), call the booking desk or contact the charter captains directly. Major credit cards are accepted. This marina is one of the most popular on the Outer Banks. If you don't have six anglers in your party, marina officials may be able to help you find a "makeup" party, or you can try a headboat for a cheaper day of fishing.

The *Miss Oregon Inlet* is a 65-foot headboat docked at Oregon Inlet that offers half-day fishing for $26 per person, and $16 for children younger than 4. Anglers aboard this wide, inshore fishing vessel catch spot, croaker, gray trout, bluefish, mullet and other seasonal species. Bait and tackle are included in the price. In early spring and late fall, the boat makes one trip per day, leaving at 8 AM and returning at 12:30 PM. From Memorial Day through Labor Day there are two trips: 7 to 11:30 AM and noon to 4:30 PM. A nonfishing Twilight Cruise also is offered Tuesday, Thursday, Friday and Saturday at 5:30 PM. Admission is $6 per person, and $3 for children younger than 7.

The marina at Oregon Inlet has a bait and tackle shop that opens at 5 AM, just in time to stock up before the boats leave. The tackle shop carries a complete line of surf and deep-sea fishing equipment, drinks and snacks. A taxidermy service also is on the premises for fish you can't bear to leave behind.

Even if you don't want to catch anything, this marina is an educational and exciting experience. Mates usually unload the day's catch on the docks between 4 and 5 PM each day and will proudly pose for photographs with 4-foot tunas or show you how to slice a thick dolphin steak. Check out the World Record Atlantic Blue Marlin as you exit the parking lot. This 1,142-pound fish, which hangs in a glass case near the marina, was caught off the inlet in 1974 by Jack Herrington and brought in on Capt. Harry Baum's *Jo-Boy*. Baum still launches his charter boat from these docks along with his brother, Billy, on the *Dream Girl*.

Hatteras Island

Frisco Cove Marina
N.C. Hwy. 12, Frisco • (252) 995-4242

Frisco Cove is the former Scotch Bonnet Marina and offers Jet Ski rentals, fish-cleaning

tables and one sound-fishing charter on the *Gratitude* with Capt. Jim Powell (charters cost $195 for half-day trips and $375 for full-day trips) as well as boats slips, regular fuel for boats and an on-site gift shop. Anglers can purchase ice, cold drinks, tackle, frozen bait and lures. The marina is open year round.

Hatteras Harbor Marina
N.C. Hwy. 12, Hatteras Village
• **(252) 986-2166, (800) 676-4939**

You can charter an offshore or inshore excursion here year round, with than 20 vessels depart regularly from this marina. All tackle and bait are supplied, and experienced mates on board will show you the ropes. You don't have to be an expert angler to try tangling with a blue marlin or tuna. A fish-cleaning service is available. Offshore fishing prices change with the season so call for more information. The marina store carries fishing supplies and gifts. Call for reservations.

Hatteras Landing Marina
N.C. Hwy. 12, Hatteras Village
• **(252) 986-2205, (800) 551-8478**

Hatteras Landing offers fully metered slips with cable TV, telephones, 30- and 50-amp service and water. The marina has laundry facilities, bathrooms with showers, fish-cleaning service, freezer storage, inshore ($400 to $550), offshore ($750 to $850) and headboat

charters (call for details). There is a complete ships' store with tackle and fresh and frozen baits and lures, sportswear, diesel and premium fuel and a deli with breakfast and provisions service. Located at Hatteras Landing along with the marina are the Holiday Inn Express and a market with beer, wine and groceries. The marina is open year round except Christmas Eve, Christmas and New Year's Day.

Oden's Dock Marina
N.C. Hwy. 12, Hatteras Village
• **(252) 986-2555**

This family owned and operated marina is one of the oldest businesses in Hatteras Village. They offer inshore and offshore charter boat fishing excursions. Standard offshore charter trip prices can go as low as $700 here, while bluefin trips run around $1200. Both a fish-cleaning service and on-site seafood market add to the summer offerings. Oden's has a full line of supplies and a repair shop, and Texaco marine products are available here. As we stated in an earlier chapter, the headboat *Miss Hatteras* docks at Oden's. This state-of-the-art 72-foot-long vessel is equipped with a snack bar, comfortable booths to sit in and an air-conditioned salon. The *Miss Hatteras* offers offshore and inshore bottom fishing excursions, a seafood cruise that's out of this world, bird-watching trips, a history cruise and evening cruises. Capt. Spurgeon Stowe is one of the most personable chaps you're going to come across.

Teach's Lair Marina
N.C. Hwy. 12, Hatteras Village
• (252) 986-2460

Offshore and inshore trips depart year round every day from this marina. In the winter, Teach's is full of bluefin tuna anglers. Teach's also has a supply store where you can fulfill all your fishing needs, including ice and bait, and don't forget the film! Those bluefin tuna are breathtaking. No one will believe you without picture proof.

Ocracoke Island

Ocracoke Fishing Center and Anchorage Marina
N.C. Hwy. 12, Ocracoke Village
• (252) 928-6661

Owned by the Anchorage Inn, this fishing center at Silver Lake includes three 200-foot piers and a building where customers can book charter-boat trips to the sound, Gulf Stream and inshore areas. Water is at least 6 to 13 feet deep along the piers. Docking costs 85¢ per foot per day and includes a pool, telephones and other services. Gas and diesel fuel are available on-site, and the boat ramp is free for motel and marina guests. Marine supplies and a small tackle shop are nearby. A dockside cafe highlights the marina, serving light fare that includes fresh seafood sandwiches and beer and wine.

Fishing the Backwaters

Journey the backwaters into a world of great beauty, peace and fish. Small boats fish Manns Harbor, the Alligator River or East and South lakes. There are several captains that offer backwater services. Check our list at the end of this section for more information.

You can troll, spin- and bait-cast or flyfish year round on trips to our backwaters. You'll find an interesting mix of freshwater and saltwater species in the backwaters. Depending on the season, you can fish for crappie, rockfish (striped bass), largemouth bass, flounder, bream, sheepshead, drum, perch, croaker, spot, catfish and trout. How about that mix?!

The fishing is so laid-back that you might find the captain occasionally throwing in a line too. In these more protected waters, anglers can fish even when it's blowing offshore. If a storm comes, you can duck in behind an island. The most you can get is wet, and you're usually wading distance from shore.

Bring your camera. Depending on the time of day and season, you might spot deer, bears and even alligators. It's a nice alternative to ocean fishing, and is a good choice for families.

Backwater Charters

If the following options are unavailable, you can always launch your own vessel from any of a number of local ramps (see our Watersports chapter) or contact the nearest marina or tackle shop for more information.

Phideaux Too
P.O. Box 343, Manns Harbor, NC 27953
• (252) 473-3059

Capt. V.P. Brinson uses a 21½-foot twin-engine bateau that he constructed himself. Brinson offers spin-casting, fly rod, bait-casting and trolling charters in lakes, sounds and rivers. You'll fish for rockfish, trout, red drum, flounder, bass, bream, crappie and perch. Trips cost $175 for a half day for two people, and $25 extra for up to four people. Whole-day trips cost $300 for two people and $50 for additional people.

Custom Sound Charters
152 Dogwood Tr., Manteo
• (252) 473-1209

Captain Rick Caton has long been fishing all Outer Banks waters, both inshore and offshore, and he offers a wide variety of trips. Year round, you can charter sound fishing trips with Caton, who specializes in catching striped bass. He'll take you fly fishing or light-tackle fishing for trout, flounder, puppy drum, striped bass and bluefish. Everything you need is furnished.

For a half day of fishing, he charges $200 for two people, and $350 for all day for two people. On half-day trips if you want to add a

You're never too young to enjoy fishing.

person (with a six-person maximum) it costs $25 extra per person and $50 extra per person for full-day trips. Caton also offers shrimping and crabbing trips, inshore half- and all-day Spanish mackerel inlet trolling trips, bluefish and king mackerel fishing trips plus light-tackle bottom fishing over the wrecks for triggerfish and black sea bass; or, you can choose to anchor up and chum for sharks, cobia and king mackerel. These trips are half-day trips for six people, at $330 per trip. Caton fishes the *Free Agent*, a 42-foot charter boat, for most trips and takes out his 18-foot center console, *Iron Will*, when he's fishing the back-waters in spring and fall.

Fly-Fishing

Flat Out
P.O. Box 387, Nags Head, NC 27949
• (252) 449-0562

Fly-fishing is a sport many Outer Banks anglers swear by. Fly-fishing guide and columnist Brian Horsley is a real Insider when it comes to this style of fishing. Horsley, who docks at Oregon Inlet Fishing Center, not only guides fishing parties but also fishes almost daily himself, and ties and sells his own flies. This Nags Head angler has the distinction of

being the first full-time saltwater fly-fishing guide in North Carolina. He's held a saltwater fly-rod world record in the tippet class for a 16-pound, 9-ounce bluefish he caught off Kitty Hawk Beach on 20-pound test. He dreams about someday catching a white marlin and a big drum on a fly.

Horsley says the Outer Banks are a fly-fishing paradise, calling the fly-fishing opportunities here "unlimited." He takes parties out in his North Carolina-built, Jones Brother's Cape Fisherman, and runs nearshore fly-fishing/light-tackle charters from the end of April through November. He fishes the Pamlico, Croatan and Roanoke sounds for speckled trout, bluefish, puppy drum, little tunny, flounder and cobia. A half-day outing for two people costs $250 ($400 for a full day). The cost is $25 for a third person on half-day trips and $50 for all-day trips.

Captain Bryan De Hart's Coastal Adventures Guide Service
141 Brakewood Rd., Manteo
• (252) 473-1575

Captain De Hart books light-tackle and fly-fishing charters. He fishes inshore, brackish and saltwater, and coastal rivers and sounds. He charges $200 for two people to fish a half day, and $350 to take two people fishing all day. On the backwaters, DeHart uses an 18-foot Polar Kraft; in the open sound, he fishes from a 22-foot Javelin. DeHart has been featured on ESPN's *Fly-Fishing America* program.

Outer Banks Waterfowl
67 E. Dogwood Tr., Kitty Hawk
• (252) 441-3732

Captain Vic Berg runs sound and inlet fly- or spinning-tackle fishing trips. Everything you need is included, or you can bring your favorite tackle. Berg also offers instruction on fly- or surf fishing. Family and group rates are available. For full-day fishing for one to three people he charges $175. Half-day trips for the same number of anglers run $125.

Surf Fishing

Surf fishing is a popular Outer Banks pastime for the competitor or amateur alike. While there are miles of beach from which to cast a line, experienced local anglers say a surfcaster's success will vary depending on sloughs, temperature, currents and season. One of the hottest surf-casting spots on the Outer Banks is Cape Point, a sand spit at the tip of Cape Hatteras. Anglers often stand waist-deep in the churning waters, dutifully waiting for red drum to strike.

About nine months out of the year, anglers can fish for red drum on the Outer Banks. The best time to catch big drum is mid-October through mid-November. During this period large schools of drum are feeding on menhaden that migrate down the coastline. Cape Point is the hot spot for drum, but it tends to be a very crowded place to fish. A good second choice is the beach between Salvo and Buxton. But in the fall, you can capture them from Rodanthe down to Hatteras Inlet. From mid-April through about the third week in May, red drum show up around Ocracoke Inlet, both in the ocean and shallow shoal waters at the inlet's mouth and also in the Pamlico Sound.

Serious drum anglers fish after dark for the nocturnal feeders. Insiders prefer a southwesterly wind with an incoming tide and water temperatures in the low 60s. Big drum are known to come close to the surf during rough weather. Puppy drum or juvenile drum are easier to catch than the adult fish. They show in the surf after a northeast blow in late summer or early fall. Anglers use finger mullet with success as well as fresh shrimp (and we do mean fresh). Red drum are a regulated fish, both in size and limit. Call your local tackle shop for more information. If you're interested in learning more about red drum tag and release programs, call (252) 473-5734 or (252) 264-3911.

And speaking of Cape Point, the list of fish caught there is lengthy. Other common species include small, dogfish, Spanish mackerel, bluefish, pompano, striped bass and Spanish mackerel as well as bottom feeders such as croaker, flounder, spot, sea mullet and both gray and speckled trout. More uncommon are tarpon, cobia, amberjack, jack crevalles and shark weighing several hundred pounds.

Shoaling that takes place off Cape Hatteras makes Cape Point a haven for baitfish, and the influence of the nearby Gulf Stream and its warm-water jetties also contribute to the excellent fishing there. The beach accommodates many four-wheel-drive vehicles, and during peak season (spring and fall) is packed with anglers. If you want to try fishing Cape Point, take N.C. Highway 12 to Buxton and turn at the road that leads to the Cape Hatteras Lighthouse; it's well-marked by a sign. Turn right at the "T" in the road by the lighthouse, and then travel straight to the first vehicle access ramp, Ramp 43. (For more information about driving on the beach, see our Beach Information and Safety chapter.)

A section on surf fishing would not be complete without discussing bluefish. For years, we've enjoyed the arrival and subsequent blitzes of big bluefish during the Easter season and again around Thanksgiving. During a blitz, big blues chase baitfish up onto the beach

---

INSIDERS' TIP

If you want the scoop on viable offshore-fishing days, talk with charter boat captains. They can tell you when it's safe to venture out and when to stay put.

in a feeding frenzy. This puts the blues in striking distance of ready surf-casters. It's a phenomenal sight to watch anglers reel in these fat and ferocious fish one after the other. Anglers line up along the shore like soldiers, and many a rod is bent in that telltale C-shape, fighting a bluefish. Some days you can see a sky full of birds feasting on the baitfish that the bluefish run toward the shore.

The last few years, the blues have not blitzed like they used to; however, 1997 did produce decent Thanksgiving weekend fishing for blues. As with most species, population figures (or at least landings) tend to rise and fall in cycles; perhaps they're tending toward a low point in the pattern. Maybe the big bluefin tuna, which feed on bluefish, are taking over these days, but blitz or not, you can usually catch some bluefish in the surf or in greater numbers offshore.

Outer Banks Surf Fishing School
415 Bridge Ln., Nags Head
• **(252) 441-4767**

If you're interested in learning some pointers from an angler who has certainly put his time into the sport, pick up a copy of Joe Malat's *Surf Fishing*. This easy-to-read, illustrated book outlines methods of catching species common to our area. Malat shares tips on the lures, rigs, baits and knots favored by local surf anglers. You can also read about catch-and-release techniques and how to locate and land fish. This comprehensive book also includes useful information about tides, currents, wind and other factors that affect surf fishing.

Malat also leads the Outer Banks Surf Fishing School each spring and fall. This combination classroom and "on the beach" program teaches beginners surf fishing fundamentals. The experienced angler can also pick up tips on how to catch more fish from the beach. One-to-three-day schools are usually held during the spring and fall. Call Joe Malat for more information.

Pier Fishing

Pier fishing is a true Outer Banks institution and has delighted anglers young and old for more than 50 years. The appeal is obvious: low cost and a chance to fish deeper waters without a boat. The variety of fish available also lures anglers. Depending on the time of year, you can catch croakers, spot, sea mullet, red drum, cobia and occasionally a tarpon, king mackerel, sheepshead or amberjack.

Bait and tackle are sold at each pier, or you can rent whatever gear you need. Avid anglers usually come prepared, but newcomers to the sport are always welcome on the pier, and staff are more than willing to outfit you and offer some fishing tips. Pier fishing is a good way to introduce kids to the sport. Many Outer Banks locals spent their youth on the pier soaking in know-how and area fishing lore. For instance, Garry Oliver, who owns the Outer Banks Pier in South Nags Head, spent many a summer day at the Nags Head Fishing Pier when he was a lad. Today, Garry is a member of an award-winning surf-casters team.

Kitty Hawk Fishing Pier
N.C. Hwy. 12, MP 1, Kitty Hawk
• **(252) 261-2772**

After you cross the Wright Memorial Bridge and arrive on the Outer Banks, it's a matter of seconds before you get your first glimpse of the ocean at the Kitty Hawk Fishing Pier. Turn left at the fourth traffic light (by Aycock Brown Visitors Center) on U.S. Highway 158 as if you were traveling to Duck. Make an immediate right onto the Beach Road (N.C. Highway 12) and head south. On your left will be a turn onto a short access road that leads to the pier.

The Outer Banks has no oceanfront boardwalks, but the piers more than make up for it. The smell of salt air and tar-treated lumber greets you as you walk the wide plank up to the barn-like structure built in the mid-'50s. The central feature is the breezeway with a bait and tackle shop on the south end of the building and a diner-style restaurant on the north. From the breezeway, the fishing pier itself extends 714 feet over the ocean.

You don't have to fish to appreciate the Kitty Hawk Fishing Pier. For starters, it's an Insider's best-kept breakfast secret. Nothing beats the ocean view, the omelets or the pitch and roll of the dining room when the surf's up. Next, pay the $2 to walk out to the end of the pier for an eye-opening experience. Peopled with anglers, this structure has endured many powerful storms, and many citation fish have been caught off its weathered railings.

Kitty Hawk Fishing Pier is open April through Thanksgiving from 5 AM until 10 PM. Parking is ample, and daily admission is $5 for adults and $3 for children; a weekly pass is $25; season passes are $125. Handicapped persons are admitted free. Tackle rental is $5.

Avalon Fishing Pier
N.C. Hwy. 12, MP 6, Kill Devil Hills
• **(252) 441-7494**

Avalon Pier was built in the mid '50s and is 705 feet long. The pier has lights for night fishing, a snack bar, bait and tackle shop, ice, video games and rental fishing gear. A busy place in-season, the pier is open 24 hours a day. The pier house is open from 5 AM until 2 AM. The pier is closed December through February. Admission prices have recently been set at about $5 for adults and $2.75 for children younger than 12. A weekly pass should run about $30. A weekend pass will be about $15; ask about their season passes. Handicapped persons are admitted free.

Nags Head Fishing Pier
N.C. Hwy. 12, MP 12, Nags Head
• **(252) 441-5141**

This is one of the most popular fishing piers on the Outer Banks. It is 750 feet long and has its own bait and tackle shop. Enjoy night fishing, game tables for the kids and a restaurant. The Pier House Restaurant features fresh seafood and wonderful views of the ocean. The restaurant serves breakfast, lunch and dinner. (See our Restaurants chapter for more information.) The pier is closed December through March and reopens in April. It is open 24 hours during the season. Admission is $6 per day for adults, $3 per day for kids 12 and younger, $15 for a three-day pass and $40 for an eight-day pass. Season rates are $150 for singles and $240 for couples. Tackle rental is $5. Inquire about cottage rentals near the pier;

weekly and nightly rentals are available for these one- to four-bedroom cottages.

Jennette's Pier
N.C. Hwy. 12, MP 16½, Nags Head
• **(252) 441-6116**

Built in 1932, Jennette's is the oldest pier on the Outer Banks, and friends have been gathering here since the last plank was put in place. The pier's restaurant and lounge remain open until January 1 (see Restaurants). One in a series of fierce nor'easters during the winter of 1997-98 made off with about a 50 foot chunk of the pier, but it shouldn't impact any anxious anglers. The current rates are $6 per day, $15.00 for a three-day pass and $32.50 for a weekly pass. Children 11 and younger gain access for free if accompanied by a paying adult. Adults can walk out on the pier for $1 per person. Tackle rental costs $5.

This pier is usually crawling with anglers. But we're told that the crowds here have not put a damper on the fish being caught. It's in the heart of Whalebone Junction — along a hotbed of big catches and tall stories. Rest assured, the pier, busy almost anytime, will be even more so in late spring and summer. The pier opens April 1 and closes November 30. Hours do vary, but the schedule is 6 AM til 6 PM, April 1 through Memorial Day. The pier is open 24 hours a day, seven days a week from Memorial Day through Labor Day. Snacks are available. Jennette's retail store features items to round out all your fishing and beach needs.

Outer Banks Pier and Fishing Center
N.C. Hwy. 12, MP 18½, South Nags Head
• **(252) 441-5740**

This 650-foot ocean pier was originally built in 1959 and rebuilt in 1962 after the Ash Wednesday storm. Owner Garry Oliver has all you need in the bait and tackle shop for a day of fishing along this somewhat remote stretch of beach. A 300-foot sound fishing and crab-

Headboat fishing with friends is a great way to spend the day.

bing pier is also available. The piers are open 24 hours a day from Memorial Day until mid-October and close during the winter. They re-open in late March. Rates are $6 per day, $15 for three days, $30 per week, $100 per season for one person and $175 per season for a couple. Tackle rental is $5. Drinks and snacks are available. Senior citizen discounts and group rates are available. Snack at the pier's on-site oceanside deli that features sand-wiches, subs, hot dogs, chili and ice cream.

Hatteras Island Fishing Pier
N.C. Hwy. 12, Rodanthe • (252) 987-2323

You can come with your own gear or buy tackle here. The pier sells bait, of course, and drinks and snacks for the hungry an-gler. The pier is open from Easter until Thanksgiving. It's open 24 hours a day in the summer; other times you can fish from 6 AM til 10 PM. The restaurant, Down Under, is on-site (see our Restaurants chapter). The costs to fish at this 36-year-old pier are: adults, $6 per day; $3 for kids 12 and younger; and $1 for sightseeing. A weekly pass is $30; tackle rental is $7.50.

Avon Golf & Fishing Pier
N.C. Hwy. 12, Avon • (252) 995-5480

Avon Golf & Fishing Pier has a reputation for being a hot spot for red drum. The all-tackle world record red drum, weighing in at 94 pounds, 2 ounces, was caught about 200 yards from the pier in 1984. The pier opens at the beginning of April and remains open through Thanksgiving. You can purchase or rent all your fishing supplies here, buy sand-wiches and drinks, and also pick up nautical gifts including T-shirts and sand mirrors. Op-erating hours are 6 AM to 10 PM. They also offer an 18-hole natural grass putting green on the premises. Play is unlimited, and you can come and go as you please for $7. After Memorial Day, the pier remains open 24 hours a day until it closes for the season. In 1997 adults paid $6 to fish all day, and kid's all-day passes were $5. Weekly passes ran $35, and tackle rental was $8. Sightseeing passes were $1. After you work up an appetite fishing or golfing, stop in the on-site Barefoot Pub for lunch or dinner (see our Restaurants chap-ter). Save your fishing ticket for $2 off your meal.

Cape Hatteras Pier
N.C. Hwy. 12, Frisco • (252) 986-2533

The Cape Hatteras Pier, locally called the Frisco Pier, is open mid-March through November. The pier is noted for its great king mackerel fishing during the summer and sells or rents everything you'll need for fishing, including live bait for those big kings! Snacks and soft drinks are available. The pier is open from 6 AM to 11 PM during the week, and 6 AM till 1 AM on Friday and Saturday. The Frisco Pier is on the South Beach, and folks who fish here often boast about the large quantity of fish that frequent the vicinity. In 1997, fishing was $6 daily and $32 weekly. Tackle rented for $5, and for $1 you could go sightseeing on the pier.

Citation Fish

Citation fish are caught in the waters off the Outer Banks every year. The North Carolina Division of Marine Fisheries manages the North Carolina Saltwater Fishing Tournament, which recognizes outstanding angling achievement. The tournament runs yearlong from January 1 through December 31. Except charter boat captains and crew for-hire, everyone is eligible for a citation fish award. Eligible waters include North Carolina sounds, surf, estuaries and the ocean. This tournament is for the hook-and-line angler; use of electric or hydraulic equipment is not allowed. There is one award per angler per species, and all fish must be weighed in at an official weigh station. Anglers receive a certificate after the close of the tournament. There is no registration fee. Following is a list of the area's weigh stations, where you can pick up a species list and receive rules for the tournament at any of these. Citations are also awarded for the catch and release of some species.

Official Weigh Stations

Duck

Bob's Bait & Tackle, Duck Road and N.C. 12, (252) 261-8589

Kitty Hawk

Kitty Hawk Bait & Tackle, U.S. 158, MP 4½, Kitty Hawk, (252) 261-2955
Kitty Hawk Fishing Pier, N.C. 12, MP 1, (252) 261-2772
TW's Bait & Tackle Shop, U.S. 158, MP 4, (252) 261-7848

Kill Devil Hills

Avalon Fishing Pier, N.C. 12, MP 6, (252) 441-7494

Nags Head

Tatem's Tackle Box, U.S. 158, MP 13, (252) 441-7346
Jennette's Pier, N.C. 12, MP 16½, (252) 441-6116
Nags Head Fishing Pier, N.C. 12, MP 12, (252) 441-5141
T.I.'s Bait & Tackle, 100 W. Clark Street, (252) 441-3166
Whalebone Tackle Shop, Nags Head-Manteo Causeway, (252) 441-7413
Outer Banks Pier and Fishing Center, N.C. 12, MP 18½, (252) 441-5740

Manteo

Pirate's Cove, Nags Head-Manteo Causeway, (252) 473-3906
Salty Dawg Marina, U.S. 64, (252) 473-3405

Oregon Inlet

Oregon Inlet Fishing Center, N.C. 12, 8 miles south of Whalebone Junction, (252) 441-6301

Rodanthe

Hatteras Island Fishing Pier, off N.C. 12, (252) 987-2323

Salvo

The Fishin' Hole, 27202 Sand Street, (252) 987-2351

Avon

Frank and Fran's Fisherman's Friend, N.C. 12, 995-4171
Avon Fishing Pier, N.C. 12, (252) 995-5480

Buxton

Dillon's Corner, N.C. 12, (252) 995-5083
The Red Drum Tackle Shop Inc., N.C. 12, (252) 995-5414

Frisco

Cape Hatteras Fishing Pier Inc., 54221 Cape Hatteras Pier Drive, (252) 986-2533 Frisco Rod & Gun, N.C. 12, (252) 995-5366

Hatteras Village

Hatteras Harbor Marina, N.C. 12,
(252) 986-2166
Hatteras Marlin Club, 57174
Saxon Cut Drive, (252) 986-2454
Pelican's Roost, N.C. 12, (252) 986-2213
Teach's Lair Marina, N.C. 12,
(252) 986-2460
Village Marina, N.C. 12, (252) 986-2522
Willis Boat Landing, 57209 Willis Lane,
(252) 986-2208

Ocracoke

Tradewinds Tackle Shop, N.C. 12,
(252) 928-5491
O'Neal's Dockside and Tackle Shop,
N.C. 12, (252) 928-1111

Bait and Tackle Shops

Full-service tackle shops are scattered from Duck to Ocracoke. They are good sources for not only rods and reels, bait and other fishing gear but also for tips on what's biting and where. You'll find bait and tackle at all Outer Banks fishing piers and most marinas too. Just about every department store and general store on the islands carries some sort of fishing gear, and many shops also offer tackle rental. You can ask for guide information at any of the shops listed below.

Duck

Bob's Bait & Tackle
Duck Rd. and N.C. Hwy 12, Duck
• **(252) 261-8589**

Stop in Bob's if you're looking for advice on where to catch the really big one. The old building is left over from Duck's early days, when a soundside dock out back was the distribution point for shiploads of fresh ocean fish. The shop carries a good supply of rods, reels and bait.

Kitty Hawk

Kitty Hawk Bait & Tackle
U.S. Hwy. 158, MP 4½, Kitty Hawk
• **(252) 261-2955**

A great selection of saltwater and freshwa-ter tackle, plus a complete line of fresh bait and live minnows, makes this a good stop for everything you'll need for reelin' in the big ones. While this Insider hasn't used one of their custom rods yet, owner Vince Mascitti says they are their specialty and that he tests them extensively. You can also rent rods and reels, arrange offshore charters and have your equipment repaired here.

TW's Bait & Tackle
U.S. Hwy. 158, MP 4, Kitty Hawk
• **(252) 261-7848**

TW's Bait & Tackle, next to the 7-Eleven in Kitty Hawk, is a great place to find the right stuff for your fishing adventure.. The gear is top-notch and so is the info on what's biting. Owner Terry "T.W." Stewart has been in business for more than 15 years and can sell you what you need, including ice and live bait. There is another location in Corolla, (252) 453-3335, but it's closed in the winter. The Kitty Hawk location stays open year round. TW's has taken over the former Tackle Express in Nags Head at MP 10½, (252) 441-4807. They're not sure if this will remain open year round yet. All three locations are official weigh stations.

Whitney's Bait & Tackle
U.S. Hwy. 158, MP 4½, Kitty Hawk
• **(252) 261-5551**

Whitney's specializes in custom rods made by Whitney Jones, plus offshore and inshore bait and tackle. The shop also offers rod and reel repairs. The walls are lined with Jones' impressive freshwater and salt-water citations and trophies. Call for Whitney's fishing report.

Kill Devil Hills

T.I.'s Bait & Tackle
U.S. Hwy. 158, MP 9, Kill Devil Hills
• **(252) 441-3166**

T.I.'s is an official weigh station and member of the N.C. Beach Buggy Association. The shop offers quality tackle and fresh bait and is an authorized Penn parts distributor and repair station. T.I.'s is also a factory-authorized Daiwa service warranty center. The shop is open year round. Check out their Nags Head

location at N.C. 12, MP 16½, in Nags Head, (252) 441-5242.

Nags Head

Tatem's Tackle Box Inc.
U.S. Hwy. 158, MP 13, Nags Head
• (252) 441-7346

This is the original Outer Banks tackle shop, and it's still going strong. The shop sells fresh and frozen bait, tackle, fishing licenses and more. It repairs reels and rods and makes custom rods. The shop, which is located next to Jockey's Ridge Exxon, is open all year.

Capt. Marty's Fishing and Hunting Tackle Shop
U.S. Hwy. 158, MP 14, Nags Head
• (252) 441-3132

Capt. Marty's is a full service fishing and hunting shop across from the Outer Banks Mall. It's a good place to shop for all kinds of fishing gear and supplies including ice, sunglasses, waders, decoys and more. Stop here or call for fishing lessons or charter referrals. Capt. Marty's offer offshore fishing lessons in conjunction with Pirate's Cove Yacht Club. If you need any kind of fishing information or service and Capt. Marty's doesn't offer it, it's a sure thing they'll know where to find it. These guys are real pros with years of fishing and hunting experience. They are open year round.

Whalebone Tackle
U.S. Hwy. 158 at U.S. Hwy. 64 Jct.,
Whalebone Junction • (252) 441-7413

Whalebone is a full-service tackle shop offering ice, bait, tackle and rod and Penn reel repairs. Summer hours are 6 AM until 9 PM. Call for off-season hours.

Fishing Unlimited
Nags Head/Manteo Cswy., U.S. Hwy. 64
• (252) 441-5028

Fishing Unlimited specializes in fresh bait and is a full service tackle shop. You can purchase custom rigs and lures here as well as crabbing supplies, snacks and drinks. Services include 16-foot outboard and 20-foot pontoon boat rentals. Fish from their 300-foot sound pier. The cost is $2. The shop is open Easter until Thanksgiving.

Salvo

The Fishin' Hole
27202 Sand St., Salvo • (252) 987-2351

The Fishin Hole, in it's 22nd year in 1998, is a general tackle shop that also sells beach supplies, and provides rod and reel repair. They're an official weigh station for the North

Carolina and the North Carolina Beach Buggy Association. The shop is open from April through mid-December.

Avon

Frank and Fran's Fisherman's Friend
N.C. Hwy. 12, Avon • (252) 995-4171

A full-service tackle shop, official weigh station and headquarters for the local Red Drum Tournament held every October, Frank and Fran's is an emporium of fishing gear. This is another official weigh station for the state and the North Carolina Beach Buggy Association.

Buxton

Cape Point Tackle
N.C. Hwy. 12, Buxton • (252) 995-3147

Mike Hostetter offers everything you need to fish and have a fun day at the beach. Look here for tackle, bait, waders, drinks and snacks, beach chairs, T-shirts and sweatshirts and a variety of gifts. Cape Point Tackle is an official weigh station. It's open year round except for a couple of weeks around Christmas.

Dillon's Corner
N.C. Hwy. 12, Buxton • (252) 995-5083

Stop here for an assortment of tackle, including custom rods and bait. The shop also carries a wide selection of gifts, T-shirts and, in the upstairs shop, fine art (see our Shopping chapter). The shop also offers rod repairs and has gas pumps. Dillon's Corner is open all year but has shorter hours in winter.

Red Drum Tackle Shop
N.C. Hwy. 12, Buxton • (252) 995-5414

Get the latest in fishing information and select gear at Red Drum Tackle Shop. It offers everything you need in the way of custom rods, bait and tackle plus reel repairs. They're a Penn warranty center and official weigh station for the state, North Carolina Beach Buggy Association and the Cape Hatteras Anglers Club.

Frisco

Frisco Rod and Gun
N.C. Hwy. 12, Frisco • (252) 995-5366

You'll find everything here you need for a hunting or fishing trip on the Outer Banks, including offshore and inshore fishing equipment, fly-fishing equipment, guns, ice, bait, tackle and one of the best selections of knives we've seen anywhere. They also offer rod and reel repairs and carry camping supplies, name-brand outdoor apparel, Sperry footwear and T-shirts.

Ocracoke

Tradewinds
N.C. Hwy. 12, Ocracoke • (252) 928-5491

Tradewinds is a one-stop tackle shop that can supply all your fishing needs, including fresh and frozen bait, tackle, clothing items and plenty of good advice about fishing. The shop also offers tackle rentals and rod and reel repair. Tradewinds is an official North Carolina weigh station and is open seven days a week from mid-March through mid-December.

O'Neal's Dockside Tackle Shop
N.C. Hwy. 12, Ocracoke • (252) 928-1111

O'Neal's offers fresh and frozen bait, fishing, marine and hunting supplies and can furnish you with any license you need for both sports. They are a full service tackle shop and offer tackle rentals. These folks have been in business for 16 years and are official North Carolina Wildlife and Marine Fisheries agents. If you have any questions on official regulations, stop here.

Fishing Reports

For the latest word on what's biting, check with the following sources:

Kitty Hawk Fishing Pier
(252) 261-2772
Nags Head Fishing Pier
(252) 441-5141
Pirate's Cove Yacht Club
(252) 473-3906

Oregon Inlet Fishing Center
(252) 441-6301
Red Drum Tackle Shop
(252) 995-5414
Frisco Pier
(252) 986-2533
Hatteras Island Fishing Pier
(252) 987-2323
O'Neal's Dockside
(252) 928-1111
Also read *The Virginian-Pilot* daily North Carolina section and *The Carolina Coast* for Damon Tatem's report. Check out Joe Malat's informative column in the weekly *Outer Banks Sentinel*. For more Insiders' information, you can pick up a copy of the *Sportfishing Report*, the Outer Banks first fishing magazine, which has now expanded to cover the entire East Coast. This magazine is available on the newsstands or by calling (252) 480-3133. Subscriptions are available.

Whether choosing to wander a lush soundside course or practice on a putting green, amateurs and pros alike can satisfy their golfing needs.

Golf

Challenge. Variety. Beauty.

If that doesn't hook you on the Outer Banks golf experience you might want to retire your clubs. OK, we admit that most golf courses in general have a certain lushness if they're well-maintained, but how many can boast pristine natural settings including soundside views, dunescapes and teasing glimpses of the ocean? Couple Mother Nature's contributions with the artificial creations and the Outer Banks golfer will experience a peaceful respite with variety in layouts, club atmosphere and prices. Whether choosing to wander a lush soundside course or practice on a putting green, amateurs and pros alike can find something here to satisfy their golfing needs.

Courses are spread from the Currituck County mainland and Corolla south to Hatteras Island. We've included an excellent Hertford course that's only an hour drive from the Outer Banks. It's a good idea to check periodically for any new courses sprouting up because golf on the Outer Banks is spreading like wildfire. Look for a brand new club opening in July 1998 in Grandy. We haven't tested the course, but it is owned by the same folks who own The Pointe Golf Club that we review in this chapter. The Carolina Club will be on U.S. Highway 158, sporting 7000 yards and five sets of tees. A residential area will be developed around the course.

Something you can't overlook when playing ocean and soundside golf is the wind factor, which can turn even the most well-aimed shot wayward. Year-round golf is possible, however, with some adjustments in course choice and playing habits. Some courses offer more natural shelter than others, and you can always shorten your game (that is to say, lay up more often) if necessary. Despite the wind, it's glorious to play golf while breathing salt air under spectacular skyscapes and being surrounded by natural vegetation — and nothing beats a summer round followed by a dip in the salty sea.

Check out our course listings. All the regulation courses are semiprivate (the general public may pay and play), and all welcome beginners and newcomers as well as seasoned low handicappers. Yardage and par figures in the following listings are based on men's/white tees.

Regulation and Executive Courses

Currituck Club
N.C. Hwy. 12, Corolla • (252) 453-9400, (888) 453-9400

Golf magazine places the scenic Currituck Club in their top-10 course list. Comprising 600 acres of pristine wetlands, this golf and resort community features a links-style course designed by prominent golf architect Rees Jones. Previously, visitors to this parcel of land were mostly of the feathered and furred kind. Bearing that in mind, Jones was careful to preserve and protect their habitat while offering golfers a course set amid dunes, wetlands and marsh fringes. Golfers enjoy views of the Atlantic Ocean and Currituck Sound. Within the property lies the historic and private Currituck Shooting Club, an outdoors-lovers' escape since the mid-1800s.

The course features a full driving range. Year-round lessons are offered along with weekly clinics, and Craig Menne is the golf pro here. Golf school is held every Tuesday, Wednesday and Thursday during the summer from 9 AM until 11 AM. These classes cost $30 daily or $75 for all three sessions. Private lessons are available at $45 for 45-minute sessions.

Coming attractions include a clubhouse, lockers, a bar and a restaurant. These should be completed by the spring of 1999. Five miles of biking trails and a private beach access also are available to residents. The natural beauty of this course makes the Currituck Club one of the most peaceful and prettiest golfing spots around.

Duck Woods Country Club
50 Dogwood Tr., Kitty Hawk
• (252) 261-2609

Duck Woods is the club to play on windy days, since it offers more shelter than the soundside clubs. This 18-hole, 6161-yard, par 72 course was built in 1968. Designed by Ellis Maples, Duck Woods features a traditional layout with tree-lined fairways. Shots must be placed with care, especially on the par 5 14th hole, where water dissects the fairway. Water comes into play on 14 holes. You might want to warm up before your round; the course begins with a 481-yard, par 5 and ends with a 506-yard, par 5.

While the club accommodates 900 members, it accepts public play year round. Nonmembers can take advantage of the driving range and putting green on the day of play only. Target greens and a practice bunker are available. Duck Woods offers a pro shop, complemented by the presence of golf pro Tommy Wine, and club rentals. Members enjoy clubhouse and locker room privileges and the bar and restaurant. Beer and wine are sold to nonmembers, but no other alcoholic beverages are available, as the club does not hold a liquor license.

Riding is mandatory for nonmembers. Booking is accepted a week in advance for members and two days in advance for nonmembers. Call for more information. The greens fee, including cart, is $63 year round for nonmembers. Greens fees vary November through February 1. Call for off-season fees schedule.

Goose Creek Golf and Country Club
U.S. Hwy. 158, Grandy • (252) 453-4008, (800) 443-4008

Goose Creek, a 5943-yard, par 72 public course, offers an easygoing track complete with a hospitable atmosphere. The greens and

fairways on this flat course are blanketed with bermudagrass. Greens are relatively small. Trees line the course, with tighter fairways on the first nine but more undulating and open terrain on the back.

Designed by Jerry Turner and built by Jernigan Enterprises, Goose Creek is a player-friendly golf course. Water comes into play on five holes. No. 13 is considered the signature. The hole plays differently according to the wind (it's generally to your back during the summer and in your face in fall and winter).

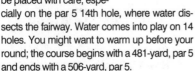

The clubhouse is a former hunting lodge that the owners converted into private locker rooms. Kick back in the pine-paneled lounge for a cool drink or nibble on all sorts of sandwiches and treats from buffalo wings to crab cakes.

A driving range and practice green are available. Walking is allowed for members only. This is a great course for the entire family, and children are both welcome and encouraged; however, it's recommended that young golfers check in after noon.

Goose Creek is also pocket-friendly. Greens fees range from $28 during late afternoon to $45 for prime morning tee times. A three-day golf pass is offered for $110.

Nags Head Golf Links
5615 S. Seachase Dr., Nags Head
• (252) 441-8073, (800) 851-9404

This soundside course is in the Village at Nags Head just off U.S. 158 at Milepost 15. Architect Bob Moore left most of the natural setting intact here, and the 6100-yard, par 71 course is a real beach beauty. Golfers enjoy idyllic views of Roanoke Sound from nearly every hole. With the sound to the west and the ocean to the east, wind plays a constant role here.

If your ball is blown off course (we know you'd never actually hit it astray!), you may need to spend some time searching for it in the dense underbrush that lines the fairways. You really come up against the wind when you reach the 18th hole, which runs very close to the sound. This 583-yard par 5 will test your golfing skills. Think about leaving your woods

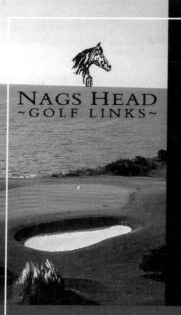
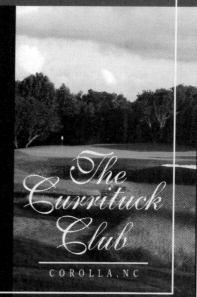

in the bag and playing only with irons on this course.

It doesn't take but one quick gust of wind to blow your ball off-course on the 221-yard 15th, a lengthy par 3. The green is fronted by a pond. Of course, on virtually every barrier island track, you'll have to deal with wetlands. All but four holes are affected by water here.

Danny Agapion, the golf director for this club and the Currituck Club, and Nags Head Golf Links pro Jeff Lewis invite you to try this mercurial course. The environment is so refreshing that we think it's worth a round regardless of what's controlling the shots. As with the Currituck Club, golf school is offered mornings three days a week during the summer. You can enroll for a daily class for $30 or for all sessions for $75. Private lessons are available at $45 for 45 minutes.

Walking is not allowed. Cart and greens vary seasonally and daily: January 1 through March 12, $40; March 13 through May 7, $50; May 8 through June 21, $60; June 22 though August 28, $65 to $85 (depending on the time of day); August 2 through September 24, $65; September 25 through October 25, $55; October 26 through November 29, $5; November 30 though December 31, $40. A nine-hole scramble, played every Sunday, costs $35. Tee times may be booked up to a year in advance.

If you work up an appetite, enjoy good food and excellent views of the Roanoke Sound from the Links Grill, which is open for lunch only. Nags Head Golf Links also has a bar, golf shop, driving range, putting green and rental clubs. The course is open every day, except Christmas, from sunrise to sunset. Call for more information.

Ocean Edge Golf Course
Off N.C. Hwy. 12, Frisco • (252) 995-4100

Ocean Edge is a public, nine-hole executive course that also permits 18-hole play. Look out for the big pond — the first, second, fifth and eighth holes play over the water.

Ocean Edge is open all year. This 1400-

yard, par 30 Hatteras Island course covers 23 acres of dunes. Tee times are required. Golf carts and club rentals are available. Rates, including cart, are $25 for nine holes and $35 for 18. Off-season rates are $15 for nine-hole play and $25 for 18-hole play. On same-day plays, after your first round of 18 holes, your second round is $5 for each additional nine-hole play. Walking is permitted.

The Pointe Golf Club
U.S. Hwy. 158 E., Powells Point
• (252) 491-8388

Golfer's heaven well describes this 5911-yard, par 71, 18-hole championship golf course. Both the recreational golfer and the professional will find a challenge on this verdant course created by Russell Breeden. Breeden's unique design features soundfront views from wooded and links-style holes with gentle mounds and slopes. This was the first course in the country to feature A1 bentgrass greens, a new disease-resistant dense grass. It's no surprise really, because the folks at Pointe are grass experts. Pointe owner Keith Hall is the president of United Turf, and he takes his business seriously (he was responsible for growing the grass that blanketed U.S. soccer fields hosting World Cup play). Expect highly manicured, lush greens and concrete cart paths.

In a rural Carolina setting, The Pointe offers a nice respite from the beach scene. The course sports a traditional design, with water hazards coming into play laterally on 15 holes. The signature hole is No. 6, a 457-yard par 4 with a carry over wetlands, a blind shot to the fairway, water, bunkers and slopes to the right.

You can fine-tune your game on the driving range, in the practice bunker or on the full-size putting green. The Pointe offers a full-service pro shop headed by resident golf pro David A. Donovan III. Other amenities include a clubhouse, carts, lessons, sales and rentals. Enjoy a cool drink or lunch in the bar and grill.

Walking is allowed after noon for greens fee pass-holders from October 1 through May

---

INSIDERS' TIP

Bring lots of golf balls! Don't waste time searching for a wind-blown ball on a busy summer day.

Photo: Courtesy of J. Aaron Trotman

After a round of golf, how about some cool refreshments at one of our eateries?

24. Greens fees vary, so it's a good idea to call for timely information. In peak season, fees average $65; from October 1 through 31, $45; November 1 through January 1, $35; April 1 through 30, $40; May 1 through 24, $45. Fees include carts. Weekday and weekend rates may vary. Call for winter rates. Annual golf packages are offered through Outer Banks Golf Getaways, (800) 916-6244 and Outer Banks Golf Packages, (800) 946- 5383; Accommodations packages are available through area rental companies.

The Pointe Golf Course is 3.5 miles west of the Wright Memorial Bridge. Call for tee times up to a month in advance.

Sea Scape Golf Links
300 Eckner St., Kitty Hawk
• (252) 261-2158

Keep your eye on the ball and not the view here if you don't want to be distracted. You get a real taste of Outer Banks beauty with water vistas from almost every hole, especially from the elevated ninth tee. Sea Scape is cut into Kitty Hawk's maritime forest, just off U.S. 158 E. at Milepost 2½. Designed by Art Wall, the 6052-yard, par 72 course features bentgrass greens and fairways, which are fairly wide.

Opened in 1965, the links-style course was given a face-lift, and now you can expect cart paths on all holes. Wind is a factor here, and you may find yourself puttering around in the sand and brush looking for your ball. Expect a challenge on No. 11. Look to play against the wind on this 410-yard, par 4 hole. Sea Scape will test your ability and patience, with five par 3s and five par 5s.

The Outer Banks Golf Academy offers golf instruction three days a week for beginning as well as advanced players. Sea Scape offers club fitting, rental clubs, a driving range, bar, restaurant and fully stocked pro shop. Longtime Sea Scape pro Bryan

Sullivan is available to discuss your game or the course.

Walking is not allowed. Greens fees range from $40 to $70, including the cart. Call ahead for tee times, especially if you plan to play during the summer (there's no established rule, but we were informed that eight months in advance isn't too soon). The course is open every day except Christmas from 7:30 AM until dark.

The Sound Golf Links
101 Clubhouse Dr., Hertford
• **(252) 426-5555, (800) 535-0704**

Tucked within Albemarle Plantation, The Sound is a 5836-yard, par 72, 18-hole course. It's also a world-class golfing and boating community at the tip of the Albemarle Sound near Hertford. The beautiful 12,000-square-foot clubhouse overlooks the water. You have to be familiar with the really good golf courses in the Carolinas to know about this Dan Maples original. Owner and designer Maples stamped his signature here. As with all Maples-designed courses, you get a break on the par 4s and 5s, but the par 3s are extremely difficult. It's a target golf course with a few similarities to a links course.

Fairways are wide, and marsh must be carried frequently. It's a fair course overall but a tough one from the back tees. On the 7th and 13th holes, the landing areas are extremely small. Both are par 4s.

This course is surrounded by undisturbed wetlands and tall pines. Enjoy the ride from the 16th green to the 17th tee over the wetlands; In fact, you'll probably enjoy all the cart rides over the bridges. The three finishing holes stretch along water and provide breathtaking views.

The golf pro here is Ellsworth Franklin. The clubhouse includes a golf shop and restaurant, The Soundside Grille, which serves lunch and dinner. A driving range and putting green are also available. The marina, available to the public, is the largest in the area.

Greens fees, including the cart, range from $30 to $35. Walking is restricted, so call for details. Tee times may be booked up to nine months in advance. The course is approximately an hour's drive from Kitty Hawk.

Practice Ranges

The Promenade
U.S. Hwy. 158 E., MP¼, Kitty Hawk
• **(252) 261-4900**

Fun for the whole family is a sure bet at The Promenade. On the Currituck Sound at the eastern terminus of the Wright Memorial Bridge, this adventure spot features a 9-hole chip-and-putt course on natural grass. Separate putting green and target driving range facilities are available. Minigolf lovers will appreciate the 18-hole themed Waterfall Greens, and youngsters ages 1 through 12 will have a blast at the Smilin' Island playground (see our Recreation chapter for more information). Prices for 1997 were $7 for 9 holes of chip-and-putt, $12 for 18 holes; 18-hole natural grass play, $5. The Promenade is open March through October.

Golf Equipment and Supplies

Besides course pro shops where you can find quality golf supplies, we suggest the following shops for discount equipment. The folks at these places are especially helpful and patient with golfers who are just starting out.

Teed Off
U.S. Hwy. 158 E., MP 1, Kitty Hawk
• **(252) 261-4653, (888) 829-4653**

Just east of the Wright Memorial Bridge, at Three Winks Shops, Teed Off offers top-quality equipment and apparel at discount prices. Custom-built golf clubs are available. This made all the difference to a particular

---

INSIDERS' TIP

Summer golfers: Schedule a tee time before 9 AM or after 3 PM to avoid the crowds.

Insider who, at just over 5 feet tall, plays a truly "short" game.

Smash Hit
N.C. Hwy. 12, Duck • (252) 261-1138

Smash Hit, in the Scarborough Faire shopping center, offers a variety of top sports fashions. These folks will deck you out just right for a round of golf or game of tennis. We like the mail-order policy: Just give a call and describe what you want; Smash Hit will send you samples. Keep what you like, and return the rest.

New adventures await you just hours from the Outer Banks.

Daytrippin'

Wildlife Adventures

North Carolina Estuarium
223 E. Water St., Washington
• **(252) 948-0000, (888) 737-0437**

Less than two hours from Roanoke Island, this environmental education center offers more than 200 hands-on displays and interactive exhibits about estuarine ecosystems in creative ways kids won't be able to resist. Estuarines — bodies of water with a mixture of fresh and salt water — are vital marine life breeding grounds. The region's Albemarle-Pamlico system, the second largest in the country after Chesapeake Bay, incorporates seven sounds that several river basins drain into. It totals to more than 300,000 square miles. Only Alaska and Louisiana have more square miles of estuarine waters than North Carolina.

The first of several major facilities to be completed by the nonprofit Partnership for the Sounds, the estuarium teaches kids and grownups about the threat of pollution and why marine species couldn't survive without clean estuaries. In addition to the two 130-gallon terrariums and five 130-gallon to 650-gallon aquarium tanks, exhibits include a salinity drip where you can actually sample how salty different types of water bodies can be; an educational game with lighted models of tools that animals mimic; a model of animal skulls that asks you to guess which animals are represented; a working model of wind and tide, where fans are manipulated to move a miniature waterway; and a movie about estuaries that gives an emotional sense of the importance of the system to the coast.

The estuarium also features a nursery area with minnows, shrimp and flounder, plus exhibits with snakes, turtles, lizards and other creatures that live in estuarine areas. A glass-enclosed front room overlooking the Pamlico River is filled with water monitors that measure turbidity, salinity, acidity and dissolved oxygen, and air monitors that measure humidity, wind direction and speed.

The North Carolina Estuarium is open year round Tuesday through Saturday from 10 AM to 4 PM. Hours may be extended in the summer months. Admission is $3 for adults, $2 for schoolage children and free for preschool children.

Merchants Millpond State Park
Access from U.S. Hwy. 158, N.C. Hwy. 32 and N.C. Hwy. 37, Gatesville
• **(252) 357-1191**

Less than a two-hour drive from the Outer Banks, Merchants Millpond is an isolated, undisturbed wonderland like no other place in the world. This scenic backwater swamp boasts family and wilderness campsites, miles of well-marked hiking trails and canoe runs and some of the best largemouth bass fishing in eastern North Carolina.

Between the mid-1800s and early 1920s, the 760-acre millpond was a gathering place for farmers and merchants. A grist and sawmill sat on the edge on the pond. Water controlled by wooden gates in a spillway powered the mill. A general store, a post office and rough-hewn wooden houses also hugged the muddy shores. Today, only fragments of foundations can be found rotting among more than 3,233 acres of surreal state land in the western Albemarle area.

Picnic tables, ranger programs, fishing and at least 201 species of birds still inspire people to flock into these boggy lowlands from early spring through late fall. More than 85,000 visitors tour the site each year. Poisonous snakes, mosquitos and ticks also inhabit the area — so beware.

Merchants Millpond became a state preserve in 1973 after Moyock nature lover A.B. Coleman donated 919 acres to the state of North Carolina. The Nature Conservancy contributed another 925 acres, and additional land has been acquired over the years. The park tries to sponsor at least one activity per weekend throughout three seasons, such as talks, slide programs and moonlit hikes to spot stars or search for screech owls. Most programs are offered in the warmer months.

Campers are welcomed on a first-come, first-served basis at 20 drive-in campsites with drinking water and grills. Three-quarters of a mile from the boat-launching ramp are seven rustic canoe-in sites, and 3.5 miles into the woods are five primitive backpack sites. These sites offer more secluded camping and steel fire rings. The park also has three walk-in and three canoe-in sites 1.25 miles from the launching site for organized groups of up to 50 members. Camping permits are sold at the ranger station for $8 per family. Group permits cost a minimum of $8 per night for up to eight people, with an additional $1 charged for each camper over the eight-person limit. The drive-in area costs $12 per night. Campsites are closed December 1 through March 15, but primitive camping is available year round. North Carolina requires anglers to have freshwater fishing licenses, and these are sold at nearby bait shops.

Even inexperienced boaters can manage to manipulate canoes around these serene, scenic waters. Canoes rent for $3 for the first hour and $1 for each additional hour. Canoes can also be rented overnight at canoe campsites for $15 for 24 hours. Both Merchants Millpond and the adjoining Lassiter Swamp, about a two-hour paddle away, have miles of water trails well-marked by brightly colored buoys. The park is best observed by boat, but it's easy to get lost in this eerie area after dark.

With knobby knees sticking out of the coffee-colored water and long, spiraling Spanish moss beards, the bald cypress in this enchanted forest look like old, wizened wizards wading through the swamp. Some of the ancient trees here are more than 1,000 years old. Their gnarled trunks tower up to 120 feet and grow up to 8 feet in diameter.

Mistletoe has deformed the branches of tupelo gums into zigzags, circles and fantastic spiderwebbing patterns. Pink swamp rose, white water lilies and purple pickerel weed form a floating garden around the edges of this murky millpond. Red and green duckweed weave weird mosaics across the center of the wide, winding waterway.

In canoes, your paddles make thick slurping noises as they drag through this flannel blanket — the only sounds disturbing the silence except for the croaking cricket frogs happily munching on mosquitos.

The deepest fishing spot in the state park is known as the "Polly hole." Here, at the most narrow part of the swamp, a makeshift boardwalk of cypress planks once ran from tree to tree. Legend has it an elderly midwife named Polly drank too much whiskey, stumbled and fell in as she made her way home through the tangled tree trunks.

Beneath the still, dark waters, bluegill, chain pickerel, black crappie, catfish and primitive long-nosed gar lurk between the roots and reeds. Fly-fishing is probably the park's most popular pastime. River otter, beaver and mink also make the millpond their home. Mallards, swans and herons hover overhead, and turtles line up lethargically to sun themselves on logs.

There's plenty of free parking at the canoe, camping and picnic areas. The rangers supply paddles, life jackets and trail maps. You must bring your own food and drinks into the park, although there is a snack and beverage machine on-site if you run out. Don't forget your cameras — the strange sights in this secluded swampland speak thousands of unwhispered words.

Merchants Millpond State Park has a brand new entrance in 1998 that includes a picnic area with a shelter, tables and a bathroom. Large groups can reserve the area for $50. The park is open from 8 AM to 7 PM in March and October. Evening hours extend to 8 PM in April, May and September and to 9 PM June through August. It closes at 6 PM November through February and is closed Christmas Day.

www.insiders.com

See this and many other **Insiders' Guide®** destinations online — in their entirety.

Visit us today!

Alligator River National Wildlife Refuge

U.S. Hwy. 64, near East Lake
• (252) 473-1131

Stands of 6-foot-wide juniper stumps sparkle with the gray-green tentacles of sphagnum moss. Bobcats, wolves, bears, bald eagles and alligators thrive amidst these tangled thickets. Remnants of a century-old railroad track wind 100 miles through the thick forest, rotting tombties of a 19th-century logging town that has long since been swallowed by the swamp.

On the Dare County mainland off U.S. 64 between East Lake, Manns Harbor and Stumpy Point, about a half-hour drive west of Manteo, Alligator River National Wildlife Refuge stretches across the Hyde County line into Alligator River. The U.S. Air Force owns a 46,000-acre Dare County Bombing Range in the center of the refuge, but the rest of this sprawling preserve is federally protected from development.

Endangered species including the peregrine falcon, red-cockaded woodpecker and the American alligator roam freely through the preserve. Dozens of red wolves, extinct in the wild less than two decades ago, have been reintroduced into this region (see our Natural Wonders chapter). The refuge also is reputed to have one of the biggest black bear populations in the mid-Atlantic region.

The U.S Fish and Wildlife Service has called the Alligator River Refuge one of the largest and wildest sections of land left on the East Coast.

The entire 151,000-acre refuge is accessible to four-wheel-drive vehicles, and Jeep trails traverse much of the flat, sandy marshlands. Two half-mile hiking trails and 15 miles of well-marked canoe and kayak trails also are open.

Activities are free, year round and available throughout daylight hours. Parking is available at the well-marked Milltail Road paved lot or at the end of the dirt Buffalo City Road off U.S. Highway 64. Two houses still stand alongside this dusty path leading to Milltail Creek, but only remnants of humans remain. Once the Albemarle's largest logging town, Buffalo City had two hotels, a school, general store, scores of moonshiners, a tavern and more than 3,000 people.

Buffalo City thrived along the sandy banks of Milltail Creek from the late 1870s through the early 1940s. It was built by three men from Buffalo, New York, who bought 168,000 acres to begin a modest logging operation. Shortly after the turn of the century, they sold the remaining white cedars, cypress and juniper to the Dare Lumber Company. Loggers built wooden railroads through the slimy peat bogs and carted their plankings as far as New York and Atlanta. A thriving town grew up around the growing clearing.

When the trees ran out, the lumber company went broke, and townsfolk turned to making moonshine. It was the peak of Prohibition, and the town had an isolated outpost with a built-in rail and water transportation system along the wide Alligator River, so the area became famous for its liquor. By 1936, experts estimate that East Lake had produced 1.5 million quart bottles of liquor, which showed up on the shelves of saloons from Philadelphia to Charleston.

Liquor became legal again, and the government took over small stills. After World War II, residents of what is now Alligator River Refuge returned to farming for a while, but the swamp and snakes reclaimed the land too quickly. The government would not let people drain the marshes, so in 1984 then-owner Prudential Life Insurance donated 118,000 acres to the Nature Conservancy, which later turned that parcel over to the U.S. Fish and Wildlife Service.

Today, there are a variety of ways for visitors to see the refuge. About 4 miles west of the U.S. 64/264 split, travelers can stop at a wooden kiosk and pick up brochures about trails, wildlife and flora. Behind the kiosk there's a paved 15-space parking lot, where the old, dirt Milltail Road ends. Here, a half-mile paved walkway with a boardwalk overlooking the water begins. This Creef Cut Wildlife Trail and Fishing Area is wheelchair-accessible. It opens at a public fishing dock and culminates in a 50-foot boardwalk atop a freshwater marsh.

Interpretive plaques depicting the area's unusual flora and fauna are nailed along freshly plowed pathways. Beaver cuttings, wood duck boxes, rare sundew flowers and warbler nesting areas are among the hidden attractions. Look closely: In some places, the forest is so thick you can't see 20 feet ahead.

Refuge workers estimate there are about 100 alligators in this preserve, which marks the northernmost boundary of the American alligators' habitat. On the Milltail Creek Road, there's a platform winding around the creek. The waters surrounding that platform are supposed to be among the gators' favorite haunts. If you wait quietly, you might catch a glimpse of a scaly, dark green snout.

Sandy Ridge Wildlife Trail is a little more rugged. It starts where Buffalo City Road dead-ends off U.S. 64 about 2 miles south of East Lake. Rough, wooden pallets help hikers traverse swampy spots, but if rain has fallen during the past week, walkers are bound to get wet. Sweet gum, maple and pine trees reach 30 feet high around this path.

Canoe and kayak trails through Sawyer Lake and connecting canals include four main routes marked by colored PVC pipe. Trails range from 1.5 to 5.5 miles, all along a wide waterway that is smooth with no rapids. You can bring your own in and paddle for free. On the Outer Banks, several rental outlets lease canoes and kayaks by the day (see our Watersports chapter). Guided canoe tours are also offered at the refuge. Call Pea Island Visitor Center at (252) 987-2394 for schedule and prices.

If you enjoy nature, isolation and abundant wildlife, there is no better place to spend a day away from the Outer Banks than at Alligator River National Wildlife Refuge.

Lake Mattamuskeet National Wildlife Refuge
Hyde County mainland • (252) 926-4021

About a 90-minute drive southwest of Manteo down lonely U.S. Highway 264, nearly half of the nation's tundra swans swoop into a rare wilderness refuge to feed, nest and wait out the winter.

From December through February, Lake Mattamuskeet National Wildlife Refuge is filled with thousands of the regal white birds. Their black beaks dip into the murky, shallow waters, and their wide wings flap noiselessly through the steely gray sky.

This sprawling marshland spans the largest natural lake in North Carolina that never dips deeper than 5 feet. Foliage and duckweed thrive atop the almost still waters, and swans crane their long, lovely necks through the surface, searching for supper.

Each fall, an estimated 100,000 tundra swans make a cross-continent trek from the wilds of western Canada and Alaska to the warmer waters of North Carolina and the Chesapeake Bay. Biologists estimate that nearly 70 percent of the nation's tundra swans winter in North Carolina. The state's most popular roosting areas are these isolated flatlands surrounded by 400 acres of wheat farms.

An old pumping station near the center of the refuge is being restored with state, federal and private funds. Public hunting opportunities are available in the fall during the regular waterfowl season.

Photographers, bird-watchers and people with only a casual curiosity can drive through the refuge, across the lake on a two-lane causeway, to get a good glimpse of the migration. Swans usually swarm around the water near sunrise and sunset. They spend their days eating in the nearby fields.

Besides the big birds, which can live 20 years or longer, this U.S. Fish and Wildlife Service outpost also is famous for its crabs. The crustaceans creeping around this waterway in the summer are said to be more than twice as big as the Outer Banks variety. Some say that's because the crabs feed off the unusually rich lake bottom, where rich fields of sweet potatoes grew before farmers flooded it.

If you make a trek to the refuge in the summer, be sure to buy some crabs at an area seafood shop and sample them for yourself.

Swan Days, a celebration of the return of the swans, is sponsored annually by the service on the first full weekend in December. The weekend features workshops, tours, and vendors selling food and crafts. If you're a real bird

INSIDERS' TIP

Isolated Portsmouth Island harbors some of the largest and most plentiful shells of any beach around. We've found briefcase-sized conchs, sand dollars, starfish and Scotch Bonnets — the state shell — scattered generously on the sand.

lover, volunteers often are needed to help band the birds for identification projects. The refuge is open sunrise through sunset year round.

Columbia Waterfront and Marina
U.S. Hwy. 64, Columbia • (252) 796-0723

Outer Banks visitors traveling to the beach from Raleigh used to be apt to overlook this isolated outpost in Tyrrell County, but if you're arriving at the beach via U.S. 64, you might want to stop and stretch your legs in this burgeoning new ecotourist attraction. Columbia is about a 30-minute drive west of Manteo on the main highway.

In recent years, local and state officials have raised millions of dollars to revamp this waterfront community. A $1.1-million welcome station, visitors center and rest area opened in fall 1995 along the highway. A few months earlier, work was completed on a winding boardwalk that provides breathtaking views of the Scuppernong River as it slides slowly into Bull Bay. For thousands of feet along the river's edge, tiny electric lights twinkle across the dark water, illuminating the walkway that creeps more about a mile through unspoiled timber wetlands.

Visitors are greeted with sounds from scurrying wildlife, jumping minnows and fat, quacking ducks. Bass bullfrogs clear their throats with resonating croaks. Opossum, raccoon and nutria scuttle for cover beneath the reeds and marsh grasses. A black bear cub ambling along the boardwalk in broad daylight, apparently too lazy to struggle through the swampy underbrush below, astonished one walker on a recent trip.

A fountain, elegant gazebo and wide turnouts to accommodate wheelchair passengers are among the other attractions along this zigzagging boardwalk that twists around towering forest giants and squatty flowering bushes that would have soon disappeared in more chainsaw-oriented communities.

Columbia also houses the Pocosin Art Gallery, an art museum and gallery that sponsors pottery and painting classes. Call the art center at (252) 796-2787 for a schedule of classes and events. And every fall, on the Saturday of Columbus Day weekend, the Scuppernong River Festival features water tours, boat rides, races and vendors and craftspeople displaying their wares.

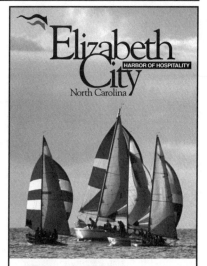

Columbia is a Tyrrell County townlet with a permanent population of about 900. The local folk have helped raise much of their own money for this waterfront revival project, and today Columbia has one of the loveliest little marinas on the East Coast. The river has many miles of easily navigable routes for canoes and small boats, well marked with signposts offering directions and paddling advice. Town leaders hope to enhance the area with additional ecotourism opportunities in an attempt to use — and preserve — their unspoiled wilderness.

One state advisory board recommended that Columbia's development should never include "stores or restaurants that are so fancy or expensive that local people do not feel comfortable in them . . . The architecture should remain of human scale but eclectic, expressing the contradictory ideals and independent eccentricities of the town." So far, work at the waterfront has been extremely successful in meeting those aims. In 1998 the town worked together with the nonprofit Partnership for the Sounds to renovate the Old Columbia Theater. The Columbia Theater Resources Center will highlight the history of farming, forestry and fishing in the area with artifacts and memorabilia. It will also include a gift shop. For information about the center, call (252) 796-1000.

If you'd like to get to know the area by water, you can rent sit-on-top or sit-inside kayaks at Scuppernong Adventures on U.S. 64, (252) 928-7873 or (252) 796-1000. Tours are available. Call for more information and to make reservations.

Edenton National Fish Hatchery
U.S. Hwy. 17 Bus., (W. Queen St. ext.)
• **(252) 482-4118**

Run by the U.S. Fish and Wildlife Service on the grassy banks of the Chowan River, the Edenton National Fish Hatchery includes an expanse of outdoor ponds and a small aquarium. This fascinating hatchery is only about 90 minutes from the Outer Banks.

Officials opened a waterfront walkway and pier at the facility in spring 1995, providing access to Pembroke Creek for people with disabilities. The 15-acre area also gives nature lovers a look at some of the native wildlife

and waterfowl indigenous to the surrounding wetlands.

This $40,000 facility is open to the public. Tours are offered with advance reservations, and many programs are sponsored throughout the year for area school groups. While a $250,000 expansion and renovation of the aquarium is under way in 1998, the aquarium will be closed to the public; however, the remaining attractions at the hatchery will remain open.

The most popular, "Pathway to Fishing," is a 12-station, one-hour tour that teaches youngsters the basics of fishing. Included are brief talks on angler ethics and safety, live baits and lures, ecology, rods and reels, knot-tying, casting and local fish species.

The fish hatchery is open year round 7 AM to 3:30 PM Monday through Friday and 8 AM to 4 PM on weekends. There is no admittance charge.

Cape Lookout National Seashore
Southern barrier islands of N.C.
• **(252) 728-2250**

Low, unpopulated and much less visited than the Outer Banks, the southern stretches of North Carolina's barrier islands extend 55 miles southwest from Ocracoke Inlet and include Portsmouth Island, Core Banks, Cape Lookout and Shackleford Banks.

These remote sand islands are untouched by development and linked to the mainland and other barrier island beaches only by private ferries or private boats. (Call the listed number for ferry schedules and reservations.) In 1976 they came under the control of the National Park Service when a separate national seashore was established south of the Cape Hatteras holdings. Each year, more than 300,000 nature lovers visit these sparse strips of beach.

If you have your own boat, you can get to Cape Lookout by launching from ramps at marinas throughout Carteret County or from Silver Lake on Ocracoke. The easiest access to Cape Point is from Harkers Island. Concession ferries and private boats for hire also are available from Harkers Island to the Cape Lookout Light area, from Davis to Shingle Point, from Atlantic to an area north of Drum Inlet and from Ocracoke to Portsmouth Village. Boats are also available from Beaufort.

There are no roads on these islands, but four-wheel-drive vehicles can cruise on the Core Banks or Portsmouth Island. The beauty of this pristine place can be a deterrent to travelers since there are few facilities along this sparse stretch of sand — however, the islands are perfect for primitive camping year round, four-wheel driving, fishing, bird-watching and photography. Stay alert for sudden storms, because there is little shelter. To help foreshadow bad squalls, call the National Weather Service, (252) 223-5327, before you set out on an excursion. Visitors must supply their own water and food, and pets are not allowed.

Deer ticks, chiggers, deer flies, mosquitoes, gnats and other annoying insects also are abundant around the islands, so bring repellent and wear long sleeves even in the summer months. Water is available from pitcher pumps around Cape Point, but campers are encouraged to bring their own supplies. Primitive camping is allowed throughout the park, but there are no designated sites.

The Cape Lookout grounds include a lighthouse that was first illuminated in 1859, a lighthouse keeper's quarters that has been converted to a visitors center and a Coast Guard station that is no longer active.

Portsmouth Island, the only ghost town on the Eastern Seaboard, is just a 20-minute boat ride south of Ocracoke Island. What was the biggest, most bustling town on the Outer Banks for more than a century is now a remote, uninhabited island, except for two volunteer rangers. Owned by the National Park Service since 1976, the 23-mile-long, 1.5-mile-wide isolated outpost attracts about 10,000 visitors a year. Most come to camp, watch birds, scan for seashells on miles of wide

empty beaches or just hike through the remnants of the historic village and re-enter a long-forgotten world. Two-dozen cottages, a weather-beaten post office and an old church still remain of the former shipping community that was populated by more than 700 people in its prime before the Civil War.

Although about 1,400 ships used to dock at the rough-hewn piers annually, Portsmouth Island was eventually done in by a storm-narrowed Ocracoke Inlet and Civil War evacuations. By 1950 only 14 inhabitants remained on the still-primitive island. The last few holdouts finally abandoned their homes on the island for good in 1971. Although most of the houses remain relatively healthy considering their exposure to the elements and years of being uninhabited, only one is open for public perusal: the turn-of-the-century Salter/Dixon House that now serves as the National Park Service Visitors Center. Beyond the center lies the post office, a cemetery and a cluster of buildings that includes the homes of the most recent residents. A short hike from the village, a visitor will see the Methodist Church, the best preserved structure on the island. Built in 1914, the church has seen quite a few couples take the vow of marriage in recent years. You don't have to get married to see inside, though — like the visitors center, the building is open to the public.

Rudy Austin ferries visitors to Portsmouth Island most of the spring, summer and fall. The boat departs Ocracoke Island at 9:30 AM and costs $15 per person. Call (252) 928-4361 or (252) 928-5431 for reservations and further information. Also, Portsmouth Island ATV Excursions offers tours of the island on all-terrain vehicles. Call (252) 928-4484 for information. Whichever way you visit this remote land,

INSIDERS' TIP

Wanna howl up some wolves? The Alligator River National Wildlife Refuge staff offers a special program on red wolves where you actually go out and, well, howl with the wild ones who do it best. Participants gather at the Creef Cut Trailhead by the intersection of Milltail Rd. and U.S. Hwy. 64 near East Lake. Go dressed for the weather, and bring a flashlight and insect repellent. Howlings are scheduled regularly April through December. Call 473-1131 for times and information.

make sure you bring plenty of bug spray, snacks and drinks.

For more information about Portsmouth Island and Cape Lookout National Seashore, call or write the National Park Service, Cape Lookout National Seashore, 131 Charles Street, Harkers Island, NC 28531. Also, pick up a copy of *The Insiders' Guide® to the North Carolina's Central Coast* from any area bookstore or by using the handy order form in the back of this book. Cape Lookout is closed Christmas and New Year's Day.

Historic Attractions

Museum of the Albemarle
1116 U.S. Hwy. 17 S., Elizabeth City • (252) 335-1453

About 50 miles inland from the Outer Banks, on the west side of Elizabeth City, a state-owned museum preserves the Albemarle area's past with exhibits, photographs and maps.

The Museum of the Albemarle includes permanent interpretive displays depicting Native American tribes and their tools and exhibits on the food, folk tales, crafts and hunting artifacts of early English-speaking colonists. A 19th-century hearth exhibit allows visitors to contrast Colonial living with modern American amenities. Other offerings trace the development of boating, logging and the U.S. Coast Guard in surrounding sites.

With two weeks' notice, the museum can provide guided tours, lectures and audiovisual programs for groups and individuals. A small gift shop sells memorabilia. Admission to the museum is free, and the building is handicapped-accessible with assistance at the front door.

The museum is open Tuesday through Saturday from 9 AM until 5 PM and Sunday from 2 until 5 PM. It is closed Mondays and holidays. Call ahead for program schedules and reservations.

Historic Hertford
Intersection U.S. Hwy. 17 and N.C. Hwy. 1336, Hertford • (252) 426-5657

One of the oldest towns in North Carolina, Hertford was incorporated in 1758 to serve as the Perquimans County seat and commercial center of the surrounding Albemarle area.

About 50 buildings dating from the early 1800s stand as stalwart sentries along the tree-lined lanes of the downtown. These magnificent mansions and well-kept gardens serve as reminders of the early inhabitants who spent their lives fishing, farming and felling trees for lumber. Later, cloth was manufactured in nearby factories.

This tiny town is toured easily by car. We also advise walking around the shady streets to get a closer perspective. Hertford is about an hour's drive from the Outer Banks.

The Newbold-White House
Harvey Point Rd., off U.S. Hwy. 17 S., Hertford • (252) 426-7567

About 60 miles from the Outer Banks in historic Perquimans County, North Carolina's oldest house was built in 1730 and is still open for tours today.

The Newbold-White House is an outstanding example of early American domestic architecture. It's set about a mile off the road across an expansive cotton field. The former plantation home is built entirely of handmade brick molded from the clay that can be found 12 inches below the soil on the grounds surrounding the house.

Joseph Scott, the original landowner, was a magistrate, legislator and Quaker. The original owner of the home was Abraham Sanders, who built this elegant brick abode on a 600-acre tract along the Perquimans River and surrounded it with tobacco fields. Tobacco was frequently used for payments during the 18th century. Later, peanuts and other products also were farmed in these fields.

Numerous other families occupied the house, and Thomas Elbert White bought it in 1903. In 1943, his heirs sold the property to John Henry Newbold, whose heirs in turn sold it to the Perquimans County Restoration Association in 1973. Since then, the house has been beautifully restored to its original condition.

Touring this three-century-old structure is well worth the trip. Sturdy and sophisticated, the dwelling is of English bond construction on the lower portions and Flemish bond-brick construction higher up. Its first floor consists of the traditional great hall and a more intimate parlor, both with cavernous fireplaces, great wooden mantles and superb original pine woodwork.

Winding wooden stairs tucked in the corner of the main first-floor room lead to two dormer-lighted, second-floor rooms. During restoration, leaded window casements with diamond-shaped panes were restored with glass shipped in from Germany. Artisans made these windows by copying a piece of the panes found on the floor of the Newbold-White House before restoration work began.

When you visit the house, be sure to stop at the Perquimans County Restoration Association headquarters on the way. This visitors center of sorts offers an informative audiovisual journey into the house's heyday and inhabitants. Hours are 10 AM to 4:30 PM Monday through Saturday from March 1 through Thanksgiving. The house is closed on Sundays. Special tours can be arranged in advance over the winter. Admission is $2 for adults, and children and students pay 50¢ each.

Albemarle Plantation
1 Plantation Ln., Hertford
• (800) 523-5958 pro shop,
(252) 426-5555, (800) 535-0704

Albemarle Plantation, a golfing and boating community, is just off U.S. Highway 17. Visiting this sprawling complex of recreational and dining facilities along the waters of the Albemarle Sound makes a great daytrip. Albemarle Plantation is part of an upscale residential development that also includes a swimming pool, tennis courts and fitness center. Sound Golf Links, an 18-hole golf course that's open to the public, is one of the most popular venues in the region for dedicated duffers. Call ahead for tee times. After a couple of rounds, you may be ready for lunch or dinner at the Soundside Grille, which has great views of the water.

The 200-slip marina, also open to the public, offers all the amenities and hookups a boater could wish for. The 1,600-acre secured community is designed for 1,000 single-family homes with a few townhomes and condominiums as well. If you're interested in staying for several days, call about the Albemarle Plantation's getaway packages. Follow U.S. 17 from Elizabeth City to Hertford. Drive time from Kitty Hawk is just over an hour. See our Golf chapter for more information.

Historic Edenton
U.S. Hwy. 17, Edenton • (252) 482-2637

Antique stores inhabit iron-gate-sheltered alleys, and bed and breakfasts offer extraordinary escapes in this 18th-century town that has managed to escape the trappings of tourism.

One of the oldest towns in America, Edenton was settled in 1690 along the shallow shores of the Albemarle Sound and Edenton Bay. It was incorporated in 1722. This Colonial community had its own tea party in 1774 when 51 women gathered at Elizabeth King's home and signed a petition protesting British taxes. A journey through town reveals the restored homes of James Iredell, an attorney general during the Revolutionary War who served as U.S. Supreme Court justice from 1790 to 1799; Samuel Johnston, a state governor and post Revolutionary War-era U.S. senator; Dr. Hugh Williamston who signed the U.S. Constitution; Joseph Hewes who put his own John Hancock on the Declaration of Independence; and Thomas Barker, a North Carolina agent to England and husband of Penelope, the reputed leader of the infamous Edenton Tea Party.

Other 18th-century buildings include the Chowan County Courthouse, St. Paul's Episcopal Church, Barker House and Iredell House, all with unsurpassed Colonial architecture. An easy walk along King Street uncovers a remarkable collection of Georgian, Federal and Greek Revival homes nestled among impeccably kept gardens and centuries-old trees. The Historic Edenton Visitor's Center, an East Lake style Victorian built in 1892, is across the street from St. Paul's Episcopal Church at 108 Broad Street. Guided tours of the town begin there, and an audiovisual presentation is given throughout the day.

From 1771 to 1776, Edenton was a prosperous port town. More than 800 ships linked Carolina and Virginia colonists with supplies from Europe and the West Indies. Blackbeard often sailed into Edenton Bay to unload — and pilfer — pirate goods. Sailors continue to cruise into this historic harbor today. Edenton is an easy daytrip from the Outer Banks by boat or automobile.

Everything in this quaint waterfront village is readily accessible by walking. The Lords Proprietors' Inn at 300 N. Broad Street has three restored homes in the heart of the historic district, and 20 guest rooms are available for nightly accommodations. Each home is graced with grand parlors and stately front porches. Guests are served breakfast daily and both breakfast and dinner Tuesdays through Saturdays, except in the month of January, when dinner is not served. Reservations are available year round by calling (252) 482-3641.

Just down the street is the Governor Eden Inn, 304 N. Broad Street. This neoclassical home is fronted by massive, Ionic columns and unusual oval portals of beveled glass. There is a lovely, upper-story front balcony overlooking N. Broad Street. A large wraparound porch is another great place for guests to meet. All rooms have private baths and TVs, and rates are very reasonable. Breakfast is served each morning. To make reservations, call (252) 482-2072.

Granville Queen Themed Inn also offers exquisite accommodations in the historic district. This abode at 108 S. Granville Street features furnishings from around the world. Guest rooms are named for their individual themes, including the Queen of Queen's bedroom and Egyptian Queen bedroom. A five-course gourmet breakfast featuring filet mignon and chicken tarragon is served on the plantation porch. The inn is closed the month of January. For more information, call (252) 482-5296.

At the Captain's Quarters Inn at 202 W. Queen Street, you get more than just a bed and breakfast. Guests are treated to two-night "sail and snooze" specials or golfing trips from March through October that include three-hour sailing excursions on the Albemarle Sound or a golfing expedition. On Saturday nights, dinner is served at this 1907 home in the historic district. Guests also may take a two-hour guided walking tour of the town or help solve a mock murder mystery during Murder Mystery weekends. Reservations can be made by calling (800) 482-8945.

The Trestle House Inn at 632 Soundside Road, is part of a wildlife refuge that is a magnet for migratory birds. Just outside Edenton, the estate was built in 1972. This bed and breakfast inn features five guest rooms and redwood beams that were milled from old railroad trestle timbers. Guests can fish in a small pond that is part of the Albemarle Canoe and Small Boats Trails System or wander the inn's extensive grounds, which are also part of the North Carolina Biking Highway. Canoes can be rented for $10 a half-day or $20 a full day. The inn is open year round. For reservations call (252) 482-2282 or (800) 645-8466.

Edenton can be reached from Roanoke Island via U.S. 64 by driving 40 miles west until you come to N.C. Highway 32, and then turning right and following the signs. A two-hour historic tour is offered at 9:30 AM, 10:30 AM, 1 PM and 2:30 PM every day in the summer; from November 1 through March 31, tours are offered at 10:30 AM and 1 and 2 PM Tuesday through Saturday. The guided walking tour costs $6 for adults and $2.50 per child 18 years or younger. The family rate for two adults and their children is $14. Additional tours may be available. Call (252) 482-2637 for more information.

The Historic Edenton Christmas Candlelight Tour is a favorite annual event held the second weekend in December. Holiday visitors are guided through about a dozen beautifully decorated homes, both historic and contemporary. The cost of the tour is $15 for adults and is free for children 12 and younger with adults.

Somerset Place
Off U.S. Hwy. 64, Creswell
• (252) 797-4560

On the swampy stretch of marshland surrounding Phelps Lake, bordered by hand-dug canals and majestic stands of sycamore, Somerset Place is a historic plantation in Washington County where visitors can learn about antebellum lifestyles of wealthy plantation owners and their slaves.

This state-funded site is 5 miles outside Creswell, near Pettigrew State Park and about an hour's drive from the Outer Banks. Guides offer free tours and special arrangements for school groups. Grounds include isolated walking trails and wooden boardwalks to the water, where nearby fishing is excellent. About 25,000 people visit the site annually.

When a $1 million restoration is complete, this historic place will be the only plantation in the country that documents how both owner and slave populations lived. Planning has begun to rebuild a two-story, four-bedroom house that the field laborers inhabited. Two families shared each small room and helped to wrest the fertile farmland from the ever-encroaching swamp.

Once one of North Carolina's four biggest plantations, Somerset Place used more than 300 slaves to grow corn and rice and work in the expansive wetlands. An incredible collection of the plantation's slave records is open at the house for genealogical research. In August 1996, more than 2,000 descendants of Somerset's slaves gathered for a 10th anniversary homecoming reunion among the twisted cypress tree trunks.

Josiah Collins built the elegant, two-story mansion in 1830 to entertain the cultivated elite of the state's planter aristocracy. Nearby, North Carolina's first Episcopal bishop-elect, Charles Pettigrew, his congressman son and Confederate brigadier general grandson lie buried beneath sprawling limbs of live oak. The plantation home itself has 14 rooms, six original outbuildings and is furnished with period furniture.

When students tour Somerset, they grind corn by hand, haul water from distant streams and make corn bread in a black iron skillet over an open fire. They wash dishes in homemade lye soap, gather broom straw and bind stalks together to clean wood floors. They dip wax and make candles two at a time, clean cotton by hand, weave baskets and sew pin cushions.

The idea, curator Dorothy Redford says, is to simulate experiences of the period slaves and see what it was once like to live on an antebellum plantation.

Somerset Place is open April through October from 9 AM to 5 PM Monday through Saturday and from 1 to 5 PM Sunday. From November through March, it's open Tuesday through Saturday 10 AM to 4 PM, Sunday 1 to 4 PM and closed Monday. To make reservations for large groups, write 2572 Lake Shore Road, Creswell, NC 27928.

Hope Plantation
N.C. Hwy. 308, Windsor • (252) 794-3140

In the 1720s, the Lord Proprietors of the Carolina Colony granted abundant Albemarle-area acreage to the Hobson family. David Stone, a delegate to the North Carolina Constitutional Convention of 1789, began building an impressive plantation home on the site around 1800. About a two-hour drive west of the Outer Banks, this Federal period mansion is included on the National Register of Historic Places and is open to the public for guided tours.

Stone was a judge, representative, senator, trustee of the University of North Carolina and governor of the new state from 1808 until 1810. A contemporary of Thomas Jefferson, he shared many of his Virginia friend's enlightened interests, especially in books. When the Hope Mansion was completed in 1803, it included a 1,400-volume library. Copies of these works are being assembled from an inventory of Stone's belongings at the time of his death. They will be stored in a fireproof room inside the Roanoke-Chowan Heritage Center on the site.

A well-preserved Federal residence furnished with period furniture, Hope Plantation reminds some visitors of Jefferson's Monticello estate and reminds others of Scarlett O'Hara's beloved Tara. The Historic Hope Foundation purchased the home and 18 acres around it in 1966. Now restored, the property includes two smaller structures, the King-Bazemore and Samuel Cox houses. Lovely 18th-century style gardens surround the homesites, and the 16,600-square-foot J.J. Harrington Building nearby includes a museum-like center that promotes the area's history and culture.

To get to Hope Plantation, take U.S. 64 out of Roanoke Island west to its intersection

INSIDERS' TIP

People mean it when they warn you about the necessity of bug spray when you venture out in the woods or swamps of Northeastern North Carolina. Bugs can be vicious and incessant — take heed and bring the insect repellent.

with U.S. 13; go north on U.S. 13 and you'll find the house 4 miles west of U.S. 13 Bypass. From Roanoke Island, it is about a 90-minute drive. It's open January 3 through December 20, Mondays through Saturdays from 10 AM to 4 PM; Sundays 2 to 5 PM. Adult admission is $6.50; seniors age 65 and older pay $6; and students pay $2. Picnic facilities are available.

North Carolina Maritime Museum
U.S. Hwy. 70 south of Cedar Island, Beaufort • (252) 728-7317

If you take the two-hour and 15-minute ferry from Ocracoke to Cedar Island, it's only another hour's drive to the state's maritime museum. In the historic port town of Beaufort, the North Carolina Maritime Museum highlights the history, culture and natural resources of the coast. Free tours are given through a variety of exhibits depicting the history of the state's shipping and water transportation systems, its wildlife and its men and women who have made their living on the sea for centuries.

Visitors can trace the development of the nation's lifesaving stations and lighthouses along the Outer Banks, see old lifesaving artifacts and learn about early rescue techniques. They can marvel at the Watson Shell Collection, an exhibit of about 5,000 shells gathered from the oceans bordering more than 100 countries by Brantley and Maxine Watson. Fish mounts, fossil collections, saltwater aquaria and decoy collections are also displayed. They can learn about boatbuilders, boat types, construction methods and the materials used during the evolution of watercraft in North Carolina.

Field excursions to coastal habitats are provided every year. Marine-life collecting cruises, fossil hunting, canoe trips and coastal bird and plant trips have been some of the museum's regular offerings.

Annual programs include the Summer Science School for Children, which provides hands-on activities and field trips for 1st-through 9th-grade children. The Junior Sailing Program teaches basic through advanced sailing for youths ages 8 to 15 each summer. The Wooden Boat Show is held the first Saturday in May, with demonstrations, workshops, lectures and boat races that are all free.

The museum's Harvey W. Smith Watercraft Center features a small craft collection and a display depicting the construction of wooden boats and ship models. Classes on boatbuilding for novices and experienced woodworkers are given throughout the year.

For a calender of activities and program information write or call North Carolina Maritime Museum, 315 Front Street, Beaufort, NC 28516.

Other artifacts, architectural and historical information are on display at the museum. The North Carolina Maritime Museum is open year round Monday through Friday, 9 AM to 5 PM; Saturday 10 AM to 5 PM; and Sunday, 1 to 5 PM. The museum is closed on major holidays.

Something Different

Currituck County's Produce Stands
Along U.S. Hwy. 158 on the Currituck County mainland

If you're looking for a little lushness near the barren barrier island beaches — or if you're hungering for something sweet to eat on the long, last leg of your drive to the Outer Banks — Currituck County's mainland has the stuff to make your mouth water.

Visitors arriving from Hampton Roads areas travel through fertile farmlands on the last hour of their trip. Like an oasis in a desert of desolation, wooden produce stands pop out of the flatlands. Handpainted signs hawk the homegrown wares: just-ripe melons, cucumbers, corn, blueberries, tomatoes, butter beans and peaches so juicy they should be sold with bibs.

About 20 markets are strewn in sporadic fashion from the Virginia border in Chesapeake to just west of the Wright Memorial Bridge. Each has a personality — and produce — all its own. Many are run by local families who began selling vegetables from the back of pickup trucks parked along the roadside. Some stands include frozen yogurt, dried flowers and even seafood stalls, and almost all sell produce grown within a few miles of the open-air markets.

Decor includes the hospitable deep-green awnings of Grandy Greenhouse and Farm Market, the baby-blue exterior of Tarheel Produce and the pink-and-purple polka dots of S & N Farm Market. Margaret and Alton Newbern have been running the Hilltop Market for more than 42 years. Morris Farm Market is one of the larger outposts along the Currituck stretch. Rufus Jones Farm Market features colorful fruits stacked in tilted wooden troughs and large-wheeled carts. And Soundside Orchard specializes in peach sales beneath a pointy-roofed wooden gazebo.

Whether you know produce or not, local farmers and their families are always glad to give free advice. They can thump a watermelon, peruse a peanut display or just feel a pumpkin and know how long ago it was picked. And they'll load you up with bursting berries, just-jarred apricot preserves and even local lore if you stick around long enough.

The produce of Currituck County is a far cry from the stuff grown amidst the sandy stretches of the Outer Banks, and the wooden markets are only a half-hour jaunt from the barrier island beaches.

Hampton Roads and Williamsburg, Virginia

Although Outer Bankers are constantly going to Chesapeake, Virginia Beach and Norfolk to shop, get supplies or fly somewhere, we sometimes forget there's a multitude of cultural and entertaining gold mines only hours from our doorsteps. Museums, aquariums and a live-music amphitheater are only some of the worthy attractions in the Hampton Roads area. Williamsburg, just 45 minutes from Virginia Beach, is famous not only as an historical attraction but also as the home of Busch Gardens and Water Country USA. Keep in mind that Chesapeake is only a 90-minute drive from Kill Devil Hills; Norfolk and Virginia Beach will take about two hours. If you're in the mood for more citified-fun after days at the beach, check out our the *Insiders' Guide®* to *Williamsburg* and *Insiders' Guide®* to *Virginia's Chesapeake Bay*.

Elizabeth City, N.C.

Our nearby neighbor to the northwest, Elizabeth City, North Carolina, offers more than enough beautiful scenery, historic, architec-

tural and natural attractions, and cultural and culinary options to make for a great daytrip — and it's all just about an hour from the Outer Banks. The area chamber of commerce is your best source for more information.

Elizabeth City Area Chamber of Commerce
502 Ehringhaus St., Elizabeth City
• (888) 258-4832

The chamber offices are jam-packed with information on all there is to see and do in this Pasquotank County jewel of a city, and a friendly staff is on hand to provide assistance. Elizabeth City is steeped in history. The first Grand Assembly of North Carolina met in this county in 1665, the state's first public school opened its doors here 40 years later, and the nation's oldest operational canal — the one snaking through the Dismal Swamp — opened in the early 1800s.

The chamber can get you started on your explorations of these fascinating facts and places, and also is putting the finishing touches on a self-guided walking tour through the city's historic districts. Elizabeth City has five designated districts listed with the National Register of Historic Places. Chamber personnel can also point you toward the Museum of the Albemarle (see previous listing in this chapter), with its collections, exhibits and artifacts that document the history of northeastern North Carolina.

Other great ideas to include on your daytrip or weekend getaway (there are at least a dozen great places to stay in the city; again, ask at the chamber for more information) include the dynamite dirt-track excitement of the Dixieland Motorsports complex, the Elizabeth City State University Planetarium, art galleries and professional theater, and dining from fast-food to four-star finery. And remember, the Pasquotank River rolls right through town, so there are a number of water-related activities available as well.

If you prefer to write for more information, send correspondence to Elizabeth City Area Chamber of Commerce, P.O. Box 426, Elizabeth City, NC 27907.

Whether you're interested in a primary residence, rental income-producing investment or a second home, you can find it on the Outer Banks.

Real Estate

Seaside living is a dream many a land-locked soul envisions when ice glazes car windows, factories pump sooty spirals through black crusted stacks, and traffic is so thick you could read a novel while traveling from your home to office. A trip to the sea has been prescribed in classical literature as a healing tonic for broken hearts, nervous exhaustion and illness. If you were to poll our residents, you'd probably find many who spent their youth frolicking along our wave-licked shores summer after summer.

Seaside living can become more than a summer's swing in an Outer Banks hammock — and you certainly don't have to be ailing to live here. Whether you're interested in a primary residence, rental income-producing investment properties or second homes, there's an avenue for just about everyone to own property on the Outer Banks.

As we predicted, 1997 was a good sales year according to local brokers. Due to even lower interest rates and a dip in inflation, 1998 has a chance to surpass the prior year. Property values have increased, and the scarcity of year-round rental property always helps boost sales. Development on the north beaches continues to grow (Realtors refer to anything north of Duck as the north beaches). But as the north beaches approach a built-up status, the focus is returning to the main beaches, where prices can be lower. A greater concentration of high-dollar homes exists in the north beach area, but resort communities are available anywhere from the Currituck Outer Banks down through Ocracoke.

We touch upon the flavor of individual townships in our Area Overviews chapter. Once you've gotten a feel for the community and what's available in your price range, you can call any of the real estate companies we list in this chapter that specialize in land or homes in the area of your choice.

Here we'll give you a feel for what's available in the resort community venue, including timeshare options. We'll also throw in some special tips for those of you considering building or buying a home here.

One thing to keep in mind when deciding to build or buy is the additional cost of building due to the weather on the Outer Banks. The harsh environment demands stringent building codes, and that shoots the price of your investment up. Local, state and federal agencies and builders are taking a closer look at making structures more storm-resistant. For instance, structures must be able to withstand winds of 110 to 125 mph, depending on proximity to the ocean. The Outer Banks Homebuilders Association can supply you with pertinent information.

Concern for coastal development will partially dictate future building. Water resources and water quality have come under careful scrutiny in recent years. Many developers involved with real estate projects on the north beaches make it a point to balance their vision with a concern for maintaining as much of the integrity of the natural environment as possible.

A World of Possibilities

If you're looking to build, here are some tips that will help make what's usually a stressful project a smoother process. Available property in a variety of sizes is scattered all over the Outer Banks. Even tiny Ocracoke is experiencing growth. Bear in mind most Outer Banks properties are on individual rather than city septic systems. This can influence the size of your house. Many of the newer subdivisions have larger lot sizes and lower density than the more established developments because septic requirements are now more stringent.

Your Realtor can help you choose a building contractor. Realtors usually have certain companies they work with regularly.

North Carolina law requires that building contractors have licenses. Some still get around the laws, so check qualifications and look into reputations before signing on the dotted line. Contact the Outer Banks Homebuilders Association, P.O. Box 398, Kitty Hawk, NC 27949, (252) 255-1733, for information about local builders and building services. Members subscribe to a code of ethics that help protect your interests.

Building a home in a coastal environment exposes you to more than a trifling of codes and restrictions. Regulations set by the North Carolina Coastal Management Authority (CAMA) are in place to protect the environment. A house built by the code is going to be a very sturdy structure, so it behooves you to follow the guidelines. CAMA will become a familiar acronym to you here as you go through the building process.

Local building codes and restrictions vary in each area of the beach. Try to meet with local planning boards. Although the builder obtains permits, it's always good for you to know how it's done and what's required.

Interview several builders, and always ask for references. A single conversation with someone who has used a certain builder's services can be a real eye-opener. Inquire about problems they experienced and changes they would make if they could repeat the process. Walk through a model home when possible. Above all else, examine the home package closely. Three bids that promise you the same features and home size do not mean you are getting three identical products. Quality materials cost more as does quality craftsmanship — point blank. An initial low bid can turn into a higher one as hidden costs come out of the woodwork midway though the project or as repairs down the road boost your initial investment.

Consider your year-round needs before you go bananas over a view. You can get away from beach crowds and revolving-door tenants by purchasing a lot in a neighborhood. Also, many existing homes were designed for vacationers and do not have much storage or closet space.

Obviously, when you design your own home you can include closets galore. While some new construction costs more initially than purchasing an existing home, your costs may be less in the long run when you consider repairs and energy efficiency. New building codes require more insulation, which lowers your cooling and heating costs. Find a builder who understands your needs and will build what you want rather than their own idea of a dream home. Some builders only work from a few plans.

If you're building to rent, make sure you get your brochure printed before the fall rental season begins. Delays can really affect your success in renting. You may want to choose a company to handle your property that is not already overwhelmed with rentals. This way there is less competition to rent within the company, and it can give your rental more attention. You want your property to stand out.

Shop around for financing when considering home loans. There are many plans available that can affect your initial cash outlay and overall payments. Your Realtor should be well-versed in what's available and suitable for your income bracket. New federal loans are always cropping up, but not every Realtor keeps abreast of current options. That's why it's a good idea to do some investigating before you go exclusive.

Before you begin working with any real estate agent, you should know who the agents represent in the transaction. Do they represent the seller, the buyer or are they acting as a dual agents? Ask your agent to supply you with a fact sheet outlining the description of agent duties and relationships. North Carolina law requires the seller to disclose the condition of the property. Ask to review this seller disclosure form before making an offer to purchase. Call the Dare County Board of Realtors, (252) 441-4036, for more information.

Whether you're interested in a single-family home, lot, timeshare or townhouse, here are some of the questions you should consider:

- What type of property do I want?
- How much is affordable?
- Will it be rented?
- Where will the usual services such as water, sewer and electricity come from?
- What area will offer the highest appreciation, lowest taxes, insurance and the best services?
- What types of insurance are available in a coastal community?
- Where are the flood plains?
- What about fire and rescue services?
- Is the proximity of schools and churches a consideration? Medical facilities? Business opportunities?
- What about a nice, quiet, get-away-from-it-all fishing retreat versus a luxury mansion?
- What about a bulkheaded boat dock?
- Do I want to risk erosion if I buy waterfront property?
- Are there restrictive covenants or commercial zoning restrictions? How do these affect the cottage industry?
- How about association fees and amenities?

If you are a potential purchaser, don't forget to inquire about neighborhood homeowner fees. These are costs in addition to your monthly mortgage payments. They can be assessed on a monthly or annual basis.

Fractional ownership, or co-ownership, is very similar to the concept of timesharing. With fractional ownership you share the ownership of a building/house with other parties. Most fractional ownership properties are divided into five-week segments for 10 owners, with two weeks reserved for maintenance each year. The weeks of ownership are spread throughout the year with some weeks in prime time, others in the off-season. At some resorts the weeks rotate through the years, which means everyone is assigned the most favorable season at some point.

Here we provide a rundown of whole own-

ership and timeshare properties. Included in this chapter are some of the brightest and best developments in the area.

Residential Resort Communities

We've listed a combination of newer and more established oceanside and soundside residential communities to give you an idea of what's here on the Outer Banks. We start our journey in Corolla and then move south through the Outer Banks, ending on Ocracoke Island. These communities include resorts that offer recreational amenities and easy access to the ocean and sound, those that provide a mixture of seasonal and year-round living, and neighborhoods with more of a year-round lifestyle.

Most developments have strict architectural guidelines to ensure quality development. It should also be noted that there are many one-road (dead-end streets) subdivisions scattered throughout the Outer Banks. Some of these subdivisions offer private roads and private ocean or sound accesses. These neighborhoods offer great rental opportunities but fewer amenities. Call your local real estate professional for more information about sales or rentals (see the Real Estate Sales section at the end of this chapter).

Carova

North Swan Beach, Swan Beach, Seagull and Penny's Hill Subdivisions
Off the paved road north of N.C. Hwy. 12
• (252) 453-3111, (800) 654-5224

Access to these subdivisions is by four-wheel-drive vehicle only. Enter the beach at the ramp in Corolla's Ocean Hill. (Be sure to read the rules of the road.) You'll be in Fruitville Beach Township. Enjoy the 12-mile

---

INSIDERS' TIP

Carefully check neighborhood restrictive covenants before you buy. Many have minimum square footage requirements for new homes.

ride out to the northernmost subdivision, Carova Beach. You'll be riding on some of the widest beaches anywhere, but it's recommended you drive at low tide. It's debatable whether there will ever be a paved road through these areas. Most of the time it's just you and nature. (Driving into Virginia is no longer permitted from here, and there's a posted area and gate to prevent crossing the border.) Watch for the herds of wild horses!

Virginia's False Cape State Park borders Carova on the north, and North Swan Beach borders Carova on the south. As you continue southward, you'll come to Swan Beach, Seagull and Penny's Hill subdivisions. Development began in Carova Beach in 1967, followed by development in North Swan Beach and Swan Beach. Carova Beach is the largest subdivision off the paved road. There was a planned road through this area when development began, but the road came up from Duck to Ocean Hill in the south instead.

Carova consists of approximately 2,000 lots. Resales are available in most areas. There are approximately 400 improved lots from Ocean Hill to the Virginia line and 2,500 property owners. There are 75 registered voters, indicating a small supply of year-round residents. The Seagull and Penny's Hill subdivisions are much smaller. The Carova subdivision offers lots fronting the canals, sandy trails and open water between Currituck Sound and the Atlantic Ocean. Swan Beach and North Swan Beach are ocean-to-sound developments. Ocean Beach and Penny's Hill do not include sound frontage. Basic amenities are offered, including electricity and telephone service and water/sewer by individual well and septic system. Cable television is not available, but we've been told that television reception from the Hampton Roads network affiliates is excellent. Lots range from $10,000 to $115,000. Houses start at $100,000.

Carova's volunteer fire department was recently enlarged. Riggs Realty knows this area better than most, and employees there are the most active as far as off-road beach sales go. Otherwise, contact your local Corolla agent for more information.

Corolla

The Currituck Club
N.C. Hwy. 12 • (800) 465-3972

This 600-acre golf resort community sports an 18-hole championship golf course (see our Golf chapter) and single family homesites, villas and patio homes ranging from $90,000 up to $398,500. The upscale community features tennis courts, swimming pools, a lighted bike and jogging path and stocked fish ponds. Private ocean access is available with a trolley system. Overall density is just more than one family per acre. Located in a maritime forest environment, on the grounds of the historic Currituck Shooting Club, the scenery can't be beat. Limited oceanfront and oceanside properties remain.

The Villages at Ocean Hill
N.C. Hwy. 12 • (252) 261-8311

On the northern end of the Outer Banks in the village of Corolla, Ocean Hill lies at the northern end of the paved road. This unique resort community covers 153 acres, including lakefront, oceanfront and soundfront lots. There are 300 single-family homesites. Lots start at $60,000; houses are $200,000 and up. This second-home neighborhood-type project is still very much available to the buying public. There are no year-round residents at this time, but many owners plan to retire here. Amenities include oceanfront and lakefront pools, tennis courts and a freshwater lake. Wide, white, sandy beaches are also part of the package. There are strict architectural guidelines to ensure quality development. Call Twiddy & Company for sales information and your local Realtor for resale or rental information.

Corolla Light Resort Village
N.C. Hwy. 12 • (252) 453-2455

More than 200 acres comprise this northern Outer Banks resort. Construction began in 1985, and some very large luxury homes were built here as well as elegant three-bedroom condos and four-bedroom villas. Home sizes range from 1,300 square feet to 3,600 square feet. When it all began, Corolla village was a sleepy, well-hidden oceanside community with a lighthouse, post office and a small general store. The developer, Richard A.

Brindley, and the marketing and sales team at Brindley & Brindley Realty, have created a beautiful ocean-to-sound resort that boasts two oceanfront pool complexes, tennis courts scattered throughout the resort, a soundside pool and an indoor sports center that houses a competition-size indoor pool, tennis courts, racquetball courts and exercise rooms.

Lots sell for $75,000 and up; houses sell for $250,000 or higher. The resort has its own water-treatment facility, and there are strict architectural guidelines to ensure quality development. In 1997 the Board of Directors for the Carolinas Chapter of the National Community Association Institute presented Corolla Light Community Association with the 1997 Association of the Year Award. Contact your local Corolla Realtor for sales and rental information.

Monteray Shores
N.C. Hwy. 12 • (252) 453-3600

Monteray Shores, on the soundside of this northern Outer Banks area, features magnificent homes with a unique Caribbean style. The red tile roofs, arched verandas, spacious decks and an abundance of windows make these homes a popular contrast to the wooden structures found in most Outer Banks residential communities. But if you prefer Outer Banks-style homes, they also are available here. The community features single-

family residences and offers sound or ocean views from every homesite. While there are no oceanfront lots, the full gymnasium, soundside clubhouse, junior Olympic swimming pool, hot tub, four tennis courts, jogging trails, stocked fishing ponds, boat ramps and other recreational amenities provide a dash of sophistication.

Lots start at $45,000, houses at $200,000. The nearby Monteray Shores Shopping Plaza includes a four-screen movie theater, a Food Lion grocery store, specialty shops and eateries. These services provide a tremendous convenience for visitors and residents of the northern Outer Banks. Contact Bob DeGabrielle & Associates at the listed number for sales information; they have an exclusive listing in this resort. For rental or resale information contact your local Realtor.

Buck Island
N.C. Hwy. 12 • (252) 453-3600

In a small section of the northern Outer Banks lies the exclusive community of Buck Island. This development is across from the TimBuck II Shopping Village on Ocean Trail. It is an oceanfront and oceanside development. There are 78 single-family homesites and 41 townhome sites. A limited number of choice homesites are still available to prospective buyers.

Buck Island is reminiscent of the nautical seaside villages of Kiawah and Nantucket and boasts timeless Charlestonian architecture along a promenade of hardwood trees and turn-of-the-century street lights. A guarded entrance, pristine ocean beach, beach cabana, pool and tennis courts complement the commitment to full service and excellence that has become the hallmark of developer Buck Thornton. Lots start at $90,000. Homesites, custom homes and Charlestonian townhomes offer a variety of opportunities if you want to own a retreat on the northern Outer Banks. Contact Bob DeGabrielle & Associates for sales information or your local Realtor for rental or resale information.

Spindrift
Ocean Tr., near the Currituck Club

Spindrift has 40,000-square-foot lots — large in comparison to neighboring developments. The single-family residential development offers no amenities, but the privacy here can't be beat. You can build a dream home and be assured you will not be within an arm's length of your neighbor. Lots start at $115,000, houses at $250,000. Call your local Realtor for more information.

Crown Point
N.C. Hwy. 12 · (252) 453-2105

Crown Point is 1 mile north of Ocean Sands and 10 miles north of Duck. This is a single-family subdivision with oceanfront and oceanside properties. It is completely separate from the Ocean Sands subdivision. There are approximately 90 homes here with a portion of the project remaining for single-family development. Crown Point is a very popular resort for weekly rentals. Amenities include a swimming pool, tennis courts and private beach access. Lots start at $50,000, houses at $250,000. Contact Coastland Realty for sales information and your local Duck or Corolla Realtor for resales and rentals.

Ocean Sands
N.C. Hwy. 12 · (252) 453-2105

Ocean Sands is an oceanside and oceanfront planned unit development, or PUD, considered to be a model of coastal development by land-use planners, government offi-

cials and environmentalists alike. The Ocean Sands concept is centered around clusters of homes that form small colonies buffered by open space. This design eliminates through traffic while increasing privacy and open vistas. Clusters are devoted to single-family dwellings, multifamily dwellings and appropriate commercial usage. Many of the approximately 600 residences at Ocean Sands are placed in rental programs. Amenities include tennis courts, an Olympic-size swimming pool, nature trails and a fishing lake stocked with bass. The development has private roads guarded by a security force.

Ocean Sands is a family-oriented community buffered on the east by the Atlantic Ocean and on the west by the exclusive Currituck Club community (see previous listing). A section consisting of 166 lots is now offered for sale. Lots are priced in the mid-$30,000s; houses sell for $130,000 and up. Contact Coastland Realty for new property sales information and your local Realtor for resales and rentals.

Pine Island
N.C. Hwy. 12 · (252) 453-3600

Pine Island resort is on 385 acres, with 300 single-family homesites and 3 miles of oceanfront. This planned oceanfront and oceanside community is bordered on the west by 1,500 acres of perpetually preserved marsh, islands and uplands that comprise the National Audubon Society Pine Island Sanctuary. Homesites are generous, and there are strict architectural guidelines. Central water and sewer and underground utilities are available.

Owners have access to a tennis court, oceanfront swimming pool, beach club, jogging paths and more. Property owners also have access to a private landing strip. The existing Pine Island design includes the Villa and Beach Club. For those who are familiar with Sanderling, Pine Island will function much like that resort except on a larger scale, and everything will be private. Lots start at $150,000, houses at $300,000. Contact Bob DeGabrielle & Associates at the number listed for new property sales information; they have an exclusive listing in this resort. Contact any local real estate professional for rental or resale information.

Duck

Sea Ridge and Osprey
Duck Rd. (N.C. Hwy. 12)

This area, 1.5 miles north of the village of Duck, claims to have the best views on the Outer Banks and has lots and three- and four-bedroom single-family homes available. No matter how tall you are, you can stand on any lot and see a complete 360-degree panoramic view of the ocean and sound. Natural beauty is this development's calling card! Homes range from $225,000 to $350,000. Call your local Realtor for more information.

Sanderling
Duck Rd. (N.C. Hwy. 12)
• **(252) 261-1794**

This ocean-to-sound community just north of Duck consists of nearly 300 homes and lots and is one of the most desirable residential communities on the Outer Banks. The heavy vegetation, winding lanes and abundant wildlife offer the most seclusion of any resort community on the beach. Developers have taken care to leave as much natural growth as possible, and there are strict building requirements to ensure privacy and value. The Sanderling Inn Resort is just north of the residential area. Homeowners have their own recreational amenities including miles of nature trails, the Soundside Racquet and Swimming Club and sailing and canoeing opportunities. Lots start at around $79,000. Houses are on the market for $190,000 and up. Call your local Realtor for sales and rental information.

Port Trinitie
Duck Rd. (N.C. Hwy. 12)
• **(252) 261-7315**

Port Trinitie, situated on 23 acres of oceanfront/oceanside property, stretches across Duck Road and offers some gorgeous soundfront views. Located 2 miles north of Duck village, amenities include two swimming pools, two tennis courts, a soundside pier and gazebo and an oceanfront sitting area. This development began with condominiums, which are co-ownership properties, but Port Trinitie now offers an even mixture of whole ownership single-family dwellings (cottages and townhomes) and co-owned condos. This family-oriented resort is primarily built out, but resales are available through your local Realtor. Houses start around $250,000. Contact the homeowners' association at the listed number for rental information.

NorthPoint
Duck Rd. (N.C. Hwy. 12)

Fractional ownership is popular at NorthPoint, though some lots remain for individual ownership and development. You'll enjoy an enclosed swimming pool, tennis and basketball courts and a long soundfront pier for fishing, crabbing and small boat dockage. One of the first fractional ownership developments on the northern Outer Banks, NorthPoint has enjoyed good values on resales. Lots start at $89,000, houses at $250,000. Call your local Realtor for more information.

Ships Watch
1251 Duck Rd. (N.C. Hwy. 12)
• **(252) 261-2231, (800) 261-7924**

Mid-Atlantic Country magazine portrayed this community as "the Palm Beach of the Outer Banks." Ships Watch is a community of luxurious seaside homes in the village of Duck. Complete service and maintenance and attention to details are characteristics of this resort. Carefully placed on high rolling dunes, the homes offer spectacular views of either the ocean, the Currituck Sound or both. An Olympic-size pool, tennis courts, jogging trail, soundside pier and boat ramp and weekly socials offer entertainment options for the whole family. Full concierge service includes setting up tee times, dinner reservations and babysitting arrangements. The resort provides rentals, along with fractional and whole ownership. Fractional, one-tenth deeded ownerships range from $40,000 to $120,000. Parlayed as a high-end property, developer Buck Thornton and his associates have experienced great success with this resort. Contact Ships Watch for sales and rental information.

SeaPines
N.C. Hwy. 12 • (252) 261-2131, (800) 488-0738

SeaPines is a 61-lot development tucked away in the heart of Duck. Lot sizes for this oceanside village range from 15,000 to 20,000 square feet. As of presstime, 22 homes have been built in this private community, so there still are plenty of lots to choose from including some with ocean views from upper-level living areas. Amenities include a swimming pool and tennis court. Sales are handled exclusively by Kitty Hawk Land Company. Call for building and protective covenant guidelines. Lot prices begin at $77,000.

Schooner Ridge Beach Club
Duck Rd. (N.C. Hwy. 12)

Schooner Ridge is in the heart of Duck, but its oceanfront/oceanside homes are well-hidden from the hustle and bustle. The high, sandy hills fronting the Atlantic Ocean are perfect for these large single-family homes with ample windows and decks. All lots are sold, but resales are available. The community offers indoor and outdoor recreational amenities. Bike paths wind through the area, and all the shops in the village are within walking distance. Lots start at $75,000, houses in the mid-$200,000s. Call your local Realtor for more information.

Nantucket Village
Duck Rd. (N.C. Hwy. 12)
• **(252) 261-2224**

Nantucket is an upscale private resort consisting of 35 large condominiums with garages and spacious decking. Being built on a high hill overlooking Currituck Sound affords panoramic views and magnificent sunsets. The year-round development offers an indoor pool and tennis court as well as sandy soundfront beaches, a pier with gazebo and boat launch facilities. The sound beach is ideal for wading, children's activities, crabbing, fishing, windsurfing and other watercraft sports.

Two new luxury duplex condominium units have been constructed and are available for preview and sale. Ten additional units will be constructed during 1999. The new luxury units have approximately 1,750 square feet of living space, two-car garages, three bedrooms, two and a half baths, gas fireplaces and panoramic water views. Prices for the new units range from $189,900 to $239,000 for soundfront locations. Existing resale units are priced from $100,000 to $190,000. Call Jim Breit at Duck's Real Es-

tate for more information on new units and re-sales.

Ocean Crest
Duck Rd. (N.C. Hwy. 12)
• **(252) 453-3600**

Near Nantucket Village, Ocean Crest is an ocean-to-sound resort consisting of 54 lots that hit the market in August 1992. Lots are 15,000 square feet or larger and are zoned for single-family dwellings. This is an upscale neighborhood with very strict architectural guidelines. Homes must be 2,000 square feet or larger. Amenities include a swimming pool, tennis courts, private ocean access and good water views. Lots start at $59,000. Contact Bob De Gabrielle & Associates for sales information; they have an exclusive listing in this subdivision.

Southern Shores

Southern Shores is a unique 2,600-acre incorporated town with its own government and police force. Although there is a shopping center on its western boundary, commercial zoning/development is not allowed elsewhere. The town has dense maritime forests along the soundside fringe, wide open sand hills in the middle and beachfront property. The substantial year-round population attests to the popularity of Southern Shores. Development has been carefully paced through the years, and there are still many lots that remain undeveloped. It is considered one of the most desirable places to live on the Outer Banks. Contact your local Realtor for sales and rental information.

Kitty Hawk

Martin's Point
U.S. Hwy. 158, MP 0

Martin's Point is an exclusive waterfront community of magnificent custom homes and homesites. There are stringent building requirements, a guarded entry and some of the most beautiful maritime forests found anywhere. Homes range from 1,200 square feet to 13,000 square feet. This is primarily a year-round neighborhood featuring a marina, dock

and pier on the Currituck Sound. Rentals are available on a very limited basis. Owners here have easy access to the local elementary school, shopping and golf. Lots start at $25,000, houses at $200,000.

When you arrive on the Outer Banks at the eastern terminus of the Wright Memorial Bridge, the entrance to Martin's Point is on your immediate left. The community is closed to drive-through inspections, but if you're considering a permanent move to the Outer Banks, it's an upscale area you'll want to look at. Call your local Realtor for more information.

Kitty Hawk Landing
W. Kitty Hawk Rd.

This is a residential community with mostly year-round homeowners. It's on the far western edges of Kitty Hawk. To get there, turn west off U.S. 158 at MP 4 onto W. Kitty Hawk Road and just keep driving until you see the signs. The community borders Currituck Sound. It has deep canals, tall pines and gorgeous sunsets. Lots start at $25,000, houses at $150,000. Contact your local Realtor for more information.

Sandpiper Cay Condominiums
Sand Dune Dr. • (252) 261-2188

This resort community consists of 280 condominium units and is near Sea Scape Golf Course. About 155 of the units are second homes; some 40 percent of the units are either long-term rentals or primary residences, making this a year-round resort. Five units are

---

INSIDERS' TIP

Look for local writer Chris Kidder's thought-provoking and humanized real estate column for *The Virginian-Pilot's* weekend tabloid *The Coast*.

available for short-term or weekly leases. All the original inventory has been sold, though some resales are available. All units are priced less than $100,000 (with one or two exceptions) including two-story townhouses and single-story garden units. Amenities include a large outdoor pool, clubhouse and tennis court. Homeowner fees apply. Contact Sandpiper Cay for more information.

Kill Devil Hills

First Flight Village
First St.

This is one of the Outer Banks' most popular year-round neighborhoods in the central area of the beach. Generally speaking there aren't too many true year-round areas available on the Outer Banks, and this makes First Flight especially attractive to families. The entrance to First Flight Village is on the west side of U.S. 158 at MP 7½. This is a family-oriented neighborhood, so if you're considering a permanent move to the Outer Banks, you should check out this community. Lots start at $20,000, houses at $80,000. There are quite a few long-term rentals available as well. First Flight Village real estate is considered moderately priced. Contact your local beach real estate professional for sales and rental information.

Colington Island

Colington Harbour
Colington Rd. • (252) 441-5886

Development on Colington Island began more than 20 years ago. To get here, turn off U.S. 158 just south of the Wright Brothers Memorial onto Ocean Bay Boulevard, which eventually turns into Colington Road. Colington Harbour is about 4 miles down the winding road.

The community has some 12 miles of bulkheaded deepwater canals and soundfront lots. Access to Albemarle Sound and the Atlantic Ocean is through Oregon Inlet, which is approximately 25 miles by boat south of Colington

Island. The area has a large number of luxury homes complete with boat docks, but there are also many average-size homes. This community combines a year-round population of more than 2,000 with seasonal and weekly renters. The picnic area, playground, sandy beach on Kitty Hawk Bay, boat ramp, boat slips for rent and fuel dock are available to all residents, including year-round renters. Clubhouse activities, the Olympic-size swimming pool, children's pool and a tennis court are available to club members. What makes Colington Harbour popular is its remoteness, private entry and the many canals that offer waterfront living to most residents. Houses start around $65,000.

Colington Heights
Colington Island • (252) 261-3815

This is the last developable subdivision within Colington Harbour. And it's still possible to enter on the ground level here. There are 23 lots on approximately 35 acres. The inventory includes wooded interior lots, waterview lots and waterfront properties. Lots start at $20,000. Essentially, this is a maritime forest development. Large 3-acre lot sizes contribute to the privacy of the area. Roads are private, and there is private beach access on Albemarle Sound. Architectural controls are in effect, and the developer has paid all of the water-impact fees, making the real estate even more attractive. Contact Beach Realty for more information.

Cliffs of Colington
Schoolhouse Rd. • (252) 441-2450

Cliffs of Colington features 52 acres divided into 29 large wooded lots ranging from 27,000 to 57,000 square feet. The homesites have private road access; some are soundfront. The development has underground utilities, good restrictive covenants and architectural controls. Included is a soundside park and sandy beach, county water and some individual septic systems (soundfront lots have central septic). The location is a plus — it's private, yet near schools and shopping centers. Numerous lots are available, and some homes are for sale here. Lots start at $25,000. Contact Annette Blowe at RE/MAX for more information.

Mariner's Legacy at WatersEdge
Colington Island, off Colington Rd.
• (252) 261-2131, (800) 488-0738

WatersEdge is a gated year-round residential neighborhood on Colington Island. Within WatersEdge is Mariner's Legacy, a 27-site community with homesite packages ranging in price from $129,500 to $149,500. Three home styles are available, measuring from 1,275 to 1,675 square feet. The community has a swimming pool, marina and boat ramp with access to Roanoke Sound, and its own owners' association. Sales are handled exclusively by Kitty Hawk Land Company.

Nags Head

South Ridge
Off U.S. Hwy. 158, MP 13
• (252) 441-2800

This 42-acre parcel is being developed by Sonny Cobb at Nags Head Construction and Development. South Ridge is a no-frills community with 140 homesites on the hill behind the Nags Head Post Office. The development features quarter-acre ocean and soundview lots but no soundfront property. Three models are available for viewing. Square footage for new houses runs between 1,600 and 1,900 for three- and four-bedroom homes. Construction features cathedral or vaulted ceilings, lots of open space and light and bright interiors. Prices range between $130,000 and $150,000. There are no association fees.

The Village at Nags Head
U.S. Hwy. 158, MP 15 • (252) 441-8533 sales, (252) 480-2224 rentals, (800) 548-9688

Development began about a decade at the village, and this community has become one of the best sellers on the Outer Banks. The golf course (with a beautiful clubhouse and popular restaurant) and the oceanfront recreational complex with tennis courts and an outdoor pool make this attractive residential community most desirable. Single-family homes and townhomes provide something for everyone. The Ammons Corporation developed this large community that spans from the ocean to the sound. The oceanfront homes are some of the largest and most luxurious anywhere. There's plenty to do whether you live or vacation here. It's an excellent choice for beach living, vacation rentals or investment. Lots start at $37,000, homes at $130,000.

Seven Sisters
U.S. Hwy. 158, MP 14½ • (252) 441-8533, (800) 441-8533

Seven Sisters is the newest subdivision at The Village at Nags Head, on the northernmost boundary of the village. Developed by George E. Goodrich and Jay Whitehead, this 36-lot development fronts both the Beach Road (N.C. 12) and the Bypass (U.S. 158). Two public ocean accesses are across the street, and the community sports an on-site private pool. Lot sizes average 6,200 to 9,000 square feet, and prices start at $46,500. A model home occasionally is sold here. You can buy a lot and build the home of your choice, or they can put a package together for you. The buyers here lean more toward vacation rental homeowners and second homeowners. Both neighborhood and village covenants apply. Central sewage, private ocean and sound access and two private soundside pier parks are part of the package. Call Marcia Fearing at Village Realty for more information.

Dolphin Run
U.S. Hwy. 158, MP 15 • (252) 441-2800

Dolphin Run is a 42-homesite community developed by Sonny Cobb at Nags Head Construction and Development. It's part of the Village at Nags Head and is between the highways. Lot sizes run a little less than a quarter-acre, approximately 9,000 to 10,000 square feet. Three-, four- and five-bedroom homes can be built here. Two four-bedroom models are available for viewing. Home prices range from $150,000 to $200,000. The Village Beach Club is available to homeowners.

Roanoke Island

Pirate's Cove
Manteo/Nags Head Cswy., Manteo
• (252) 473-1451 sales, (252) 473-6800 rentals, (800) 762-0245

Pirate's Cove is a distinctive residential marina resort community. Hundreds of acres of protected wildlife marshlands border Pirate's Cove on one side, while the peaceful waters of Roanoke Sound are on the other. Deepwater canals provide each owner with a dock at the door, and the centrally located marina is home to many large yachts and fishing boats.

Pirate's Cove offers homesites, homes, condominiums and even "dockominiums" fronting

deepwater canals. There's always activity here. Fishing tournaments seem as important as sleeping to many of the residents, and locals and visitors can get in on the fun. Other recreational amenities include lighted tennis courts, swimming pools, a Jacuzzi, a sauna, fitness center, a restaurant and a beautifully appointed clubhouse. Scheduled recreational activities for all ages are available. One of the prettiest settings on the Outer Banks enhances the Victorian nautical design of these homes. Lots start at $84,000, condos at $98,000.

Roanoak Village
27 Dora Dr., Manteo • (252) 473-1775, (252) 441-7887

Birds already are chirping at Roanoak Village, a brand new development in Manteo. The brainchild of Hudgins Real Estate owner Bobby Harrell, Roanoak Village offers options for building a variety of homes ranging in size from 860 to 2,100 square feet. The development is being built in three phases and encompasses 7.94 acres with a potential of 60 homesites. Interiors range from two-bedroom, one-bath styles to four-bedroom, two-and-a-half-bath homes. Some models even feature hardwood floors.

For the new neighborhood, local architect John Wilson IV designed approximately 10 house plans in keeping with the older building styles still evident in downtown Manteo. It gives the project a homey feel with a historic thrust. Prices range from $89,900 to $170,000. Winstead & Son are the general contractors for the homes. The home and lot are sold in a package. You can visit the model home on Dora Drive from Wednesday through Sunday from 1 to 5 PM. The development is expected to be complete within three years. It's within walking distance of Roanoke Island's bike trails, the public library, local churches, the town hall and the Manteo waterfront.

Heritage Point
Pearce Rd. • (252) 473-1450

This year-round resort community is subdivided into 111 lots off U.S. 64/264 next to Fort Raleigh National Historic Site. Restrictive

covenants are in place. Interior, soundview and soundfront lots overlooking the Croatan and Albemarle sounds are available. Lot sizes range from a half-acre to more than 3.5 acres. Each lot has a boat slip, and there is a fishing pier for homeowners. The community sports two tennis courts, and a parking area and common beach is provided. Homeowner association fees apply. Homes are in the $200,000 range. Contact Ware Realty and Construction Inc. for more information; it has an exclusive sales listing in this development.

The Peninsula
Russell Twiford Rd., Manteo
• (252) 441-1314
This exclusive boating community is possibly the newest Outer Banks realty venture and is scheduled to be completed by midsummer 1998. The Peninsula will include 34 private waterfront homesites with a lighted dock in excess of 2,000 feet, a boat ramp, pump-out station, deepwater canals and three gazebos over the water. A model home should be available for viewing by midsummer as well.

Lot sizes range from 7,500 to 12,000 square feet, and lots cost between $96,000 and $180,000. These homes will be on the Manteo sewage system and feature looped water lines to prevent sediment buildup. Homes have direct access to the sound. Some covenant restrictions apply. Details are still to be finalized, but home sizes will probably be required to be in the 1,800-square-foot range. Construction costs are estimated to be in the $100-per-square-foot range. Development is by Launch N.C. Inc. Call for more information.

Hatteras Island

Rodanthe

Resort Rodanthe
Resort Rodanthe Dr. off N.C. Hwy. 12
• (800) 334-2755
This resort consists of one building featur-

ing 12 two-bed and eight one-bed condominium units. Views of the ocean and sound vary by unit. Lower floor units have sound views. The condos are for sale, but owners also rent them. Amenities include a swimming pool and private ocean access. Condos start at $66,500.

Hatteras High Condominiums
Resort Rodanthe Dr., off N.C. Hwy. 12
• (800) 334-2755

Hatteras High features four oceanfront condominium buildings with 12 units in each. These two-bed, two-bath condos connect to the beach by boarded walkway. A swimming pool is behind the buildings. These units sell for $99,000.

Mirlo Beach
N.C. Hwy. 12 • (252) 987-2350

This sound-to-oceanfront resort community is 12 miles south of the Oregon Inlet Bridge, adjacent to Pea Island National Wildlife Refuge. There are approximately 10 large oceanfront cottages in Mirlo Beach, each of which can comfortably sleep an average of 12. Amenities include tennis courts and private beach and sound accesses. This resort has a solid rental history. Houses start at around $300,000. Contact your local real estate professional for sales and rental information.

Waves

St. Waves
N.C. Hwy. 12

This subdivision, developed during the 1980s, consists of approximately 55 lots and 20 houses. Homes and homesites are available for sale. Properties offer ocean, sound and lake views. The homes are upscale, and architectural controls are in effect. Amenities include a swimming pool, tennis court and a centrally located lake. St. Waves maintains an excellent rental history. Four-bedroom, two-bath houses start at around $180,000. Contact your local real estate professional for more information.

Avon

Kinnakeet Shores
N.C. Hwy. 12

Once a desolate stretch of narrow land between the Atlantic Ocean and Pamlico Sound, Kinnakeet Shores is a residential community that is being carefully developed. It consists of 500 acres next to beautiful marshlands and one of the best windsurfing areas in the world. Recreational amenities include swimming pools and tennis courts. This is the largest development on Hatteras Island, and the homes tend to be big, reminding us of the ones on the northern beaches. This is primarily a second-home development, offering one of the most popular rental programs on the island. A small shopping plaza with a Food Lion grocery store is in Avon, as are a handful of restaurants. The village of Buxton is only 5 miles away. Homes start at around $130,000. Contact your local real estate professional for additional sales and rental information.

Buxton

Hatteras Pines
N.C. Hwy. 12

This 150-acre subdivision is nestled in a maritime forest in the heart of Buxton. Consisting of 114 lots rolling along the dunes and ridges, it may be one of the safest places on the island to build a year-round home because of the shelter of the woods. The roads for this development are intact, along with protective covenants. A pool and tennis court are part of the package. Lots start at $39,500. Contact your local real estate professional for more information.

Hatteras Village

Hatteras Landing
N.C. Hwy. 12 • (252) 986-2841

This development features a potential 41 homesites, a restaurant, clothing stores, gift shop, bookstore, deli, convenience store, coffee shop and other retail opportunities. Homeowners have access to the on-site Holi-

Photo: Courtesy of Mary Ellen Riddle

The Dare County Tourist Bureau in Manteo is a great stop for vacation information.

day Inn Express pool. Oceanfront and soundfront lots are available. Homeowners build the homes of their choice. Prices for lots range from $269,000 to $329,000.

Hatteras By The Sea
N.C. Hwy. 12 • (252) 986-2570

This rather small community of 36 lots on 25 acres is one of the last oceanfront areas available for residential living. There's not much land on the southern end of the Outer Banks, and a good portion is preserved by the National Seashore designation. A large pool and some carefully designed nature paths are included. Sunrise and sunset views are unobstructed here. Lots start at $150,000; upscale homes begin in the neighborhood of $319,000.

Ocracoke Island

Ocracoke Horizon Condominiums
Silver Lake Rd. • (252) 928-5711

These five soundfront condominiums were developed by Midgett Realty in Hatteras but are handled by Sharon Miller Realty on Ocracoke Island. Features include two two-bedroom and three three-bedroom units with either two or two-and-a-half baths and Jacuzzi-jet tubs. The units overlook Pamlico

Sound and Portsmouth Island. Sales and rentals are available. Prices start at $279,000.

Timesharing

Timesharing is a deeded transaction under the jurisdiction of the North Carolina Real Estate Commission. A deeded share is 1/52 of the unit property being purchased. This deed grants the right to use the property in perpetuity. Always ask if the property you're inspecting is a deeded timeshare because there is such a thing as undeeded timeshare — these give the right to use a property, but the property reverts to the developer in the end.

What you are buying in a timeshare is the right to use a specific piece of real estate for a week per share. The weeks are either fixed at the time of sale or they rotate yearly. Members trade their weeks to get different time slots at a variety of locations around the world. Qualifying for the purchase of a timeshare unit can be no more difficult than qualifying for a credit card, but be aware of financing charges that are higher than regular mortgages.

Most timeshare resorts on the Outer Banks are multifamily constructions with recreational amenities that vary from minimal to luxurious and sometimes include the services of a recreational director. Timeshare units usually come furnished and carry a monthly maintenance fee. Tax advantages for ownership and financing are not available to the purchaser of a timeshare, so investigate this angle.

Many timeshare ventures offer "free weekends" — you agree to a sales pitch and tour of the facilities in exchange for accommodations. Listen, ask questions and stay in control of your money and your particular situation. If you get swept away, you'll only have five days to change your mind, according to the North Carolina Time Share Act that governs the sale of timeshares.

If you can afford the relatively small amount of money to cover your vacation lodgings for years to come, along with the option of trading for another location, timesharing is a rather hassle-free and attractive option for many people. It is best to keep the purchase of timeshares in proper perspective; your deeded share only enables you to vacation in that property during a designated time period each year for as long as you own that share. This makes timeshare very different from other potential investments.

All real estate investment decisions require thorough research and planning, and timeshare is no exception. The rental of timeshare units should not really be of any special concern to you because a rental in any case is a onetime deal, just like renting a motel room or a cottage for a week, and you're not being asked to buy anything. Timeshare salespeople are licensed (to everyone's advantage), and they earn commissions. Some great arrangements are out there, some not so good. Check thoroughly before you buy. Several Outer Banks companies specialize in timesharing. The following list includes some of these.

Barrier Island Ocean Pines
N.C. Hwy. 12, Duck • (252) 261-3525

Ocean Pines offers timesharing opportunities featuring oceanfront one- and two-bedroom condominiums. Amenities include an indoor pool, tennis courts, Jacuzzis and, of course, the beach.

Barrier Island Station
N.C. Hwy. 12, Duck • (252) 261-3525

Barrier Island, one of the largest timeshare resorts on the Outer Banks, is on a high dune area of ocean-to-sound property. These are

multifamily units of wood construction. There is an attractive, full-service restaurant and bar with a soundside sailing center, in addition to the beach. A full-time recreation director is on board here for a variety of planned activities and events. Indoor swimming, tennis courts and other recreational facilities round out a full amenities package. This is a popular resort in a just as popular seaside village.

Barrier Island Station at Kitty Hawk
1 Cypress Knee Tr., Kitty Hawk
• (252) 261-4610

Barrier Island Station at Kitty Hawk is a brand-new multifamily vacation ownership resort. It's setting in a maritime forest is incredible. The 100 acres of private land sport a million-dollar sports complex featuring an indoor pool, Jacuzzi and aerobic and Nautilus workout facilities. You can also shoot pool or play table tennis in the game room. Condominiums are one, two or three bedrooms. The privacy can't be beat. The community is near two shopping centers.

Bodie Island Realty
N.C. Hwy. 12., MP 17, Nags Head
• (252) 441-2558
N.C. Hwy. 12, MP 7, Kill Devil Hills
• (252) 441-9443

This company manages timeshares in the Bodie Island Beach Club in Nags Head. The Beach Club features two pools, an oceanfront sundeck, a game room, miniature golf and a playground. The units are two-bedroom, two-bath condos with full kitchens, dining rooms, living rooms, wood-burning fireplaces, Jacuzzis and private decks. The company also handles resales of timeshare units in complexes up and down the Outer Banks.

Dunes South Beach and Racquet Club
N.C. Hwy. 12, MP 18, Nags Head
• (252) 441-4090

Townhome timesharing at this resort features two- and three-bedroom units with fireplaces, washers and dryers and Jacuzzis. There are 20 units, and most are oceanfront; the remainder of the units are oceanside. A pool, tennis court, putting green and playground make up the recreational amenities.

Outer Banks Beach Club
N.C. Hwy. 12, MP 9, Kill Devil Hills
• (252) 441-7036

The round, wooden buildings of the Outer Banks Beach Club were the first timesharing opportunities built and sold on the Outer Banks. The 160 units include oceanfront, oceanside and clubhouse units across the street, near the clubhouse and its indoor pool. There are two outdoor pools in great oceanfront locations. One-, two- and three-bedroom units have access to whirlpools, tennis courts and a playground. There is a full-time recreation director offering a variety of activities and games.

Outer Banks Resort Rentals
Pirates Quay Shopping Center, U.S. Hwy.
158, MP 11, Nags Head • (252) 441-2134

This company deals exclusively with timeshares, handling rentals and resales at all the timeshare complexes on the Outer Banks. All the units this company represents are furnished and self-contained, and all have swimming pools.

Sea Scape Beach and Golf Villas
U.S. Hwy. 158, MP 2½, Kitty Hawk
• (252) 261-3837

There are plenty of recreational opportunities here: tennis courts, three swimming pools, an indoor recreation facility, exercise room and game room. The Villas are next to the Sea Scape golf course. The two-bed, two-bath units are of wood construction, and they are on the west side of U.S. 158. Sea Scape offers a unique opportunity for timeshare ownership and an active rental program.

Real Estate Sales

Visitors to the Outer Banks may stumble upon their dream home, but your best bet is to contact a local real estate professional. Remember, real estate agents and brokers are not necessarily Realtors. Brokers and their agents must join the Board of Realtors to become members, but Realtors subscribe to a strict code of ethics that helps protect buyers and sellers. They help to ensure fair treatment for both parties involved in the deal. Realtors can offer information such as property values, appreciation, history of sales, resales and neighborhood analyses. They can tell you whether a neighborhood is composed of year-round or seasonal residents, and they can render an opinion as to whether you'll be satisfied with the area you are considering.

Boards of Realtors are your best resource for answers about major developments and fair market prices. They supervise the Multiple Listing Service (MLS), an organization that makes all properties for sale available to all real estate agents. Only brokers and their agents who are Realtors have access to MLS information. For real estate-related questions, we've included the addresses and telephone numbers for the state and county Board of Realtors.

• North Carolina Association of Realtors (NCAR), 2901 Seawell Road, P.O. Box 7918, Greensboro, NC 27417, (910) 294-1415.

• Dare County Board of Realtors, P.O. Drawer G, 110 W. Oregon Avenue, Kill Devil Hills, NC 27948, (252) 441-4036.

Following are some Outer Banks real estate sales companies, their locations and contact information. While this list is not all-inclusive, it is representative of reputable real estate sales companies on the Outer Banks. Most, if not all, of these companies are members of the Board of Realtors. Call the Dare County Board of Realtors to be sure.

20/20 Realty
516 U.S. Hwy. 64, Manteo
• (252) 473-2020

Roanoke Island and the Outer Banks are the focus for 20/20 Realty.

Beach Realty & Construction/ Kitty Hawk Rentals
790-B Ocean Tr. (N.C. Hwy. 12), Corolla
• (252) 453-3131
1450 Duck Rd. (N.C. Hwy. 12), Duck
• (252) 261-6600
U.S. Hwy. 158, MP 2, Kitty Hawk
• (252) 261-3815, (800) 849-9888
U.S. Hwy. 158, Kill Devil Hills
• (252) 441-1106

Beach Realty handles real estate sales, rentals and construction. Offices are in Corolla, Duck, Kitty Hawk and Kill Devil Hills. It represents properties from Carova to South Nags Head. The rental offices offer vacation rental properties from Ocean Hill to South Nags Head. For rentals call toll-free at (800) 635-1559.

Bodie Island Realty
N.C. Hwy. 12, MP 7, Kill Devil Hills
• (252) 441-9443, (800) 839-5116
N.C. Hwy. 12, MP 17, Nags Head
• (252) 441-2558, (800) 862-1785

Bodie Island Realty offers general real estate, timeshare and timeshare resales. It covers Corolla to north Hatteras. (See the timeshare listing in this chapter.)

Brindley & Brindley Real Estate
Brindley Bldg., N.C. Hwy. 12, Corolla Light • (252) 453-3000

Brindley & Brindley represents property from Corolla to Southern Shores.

Britt Real Estate
N.C. Hwy. 12, north of Duck
• (252) 261-3566 or (800) 334-6315

Britt represents property from Corolla to Southern Shores.

Cape Escape
N.C. Hwy. 12, Salvo • (252) 987-2336, (800) 996-2336

Cape Escape, across from the local post office, handles sales and rentals in Rodanthe, Waves and Salvo.

Century 21 at the Beach
The Dunes Shops, U.S. Hwy. 158, MP 3½, Kitty Hawk • (252) 261-2855, (800) 245-0021

Century 21 represents property from Carova Beach to South Nags Head.

Coastland Realty
N.C. Hwy. 12, Corolla • (252) 453-2105

Coastland offers real estate sales only. It represents the northern Outer Banks — specifically, Ocean Sands and Crown Point.

Colington Realty
2141 Colington Rd. • (252) 441-3863

Colington Realty specializes in Colington Harbour properties.

Cove Realty
Between N.C. Hwy. 12 and U.S. Hwy. 158, MP 14, Nags Head • (252) 441-6391, (800) 635-7007

Cove represents Nags Head and South Nags Head and specializes in Old Nags Head Cove.

INSIDERS' TIP

Watch out for unexpected fees when building. Water tap fees can vary by as much as $1,000.

Duck's Real Estate

**N.C. Hwy. 12, Duck • (252) 261-2224,
(800) 986-5595**

Duck's Real Estate, in its 50th year in 1998, represents property from Corolla to Nags Head.

Hatteras Realty

N.C. Hwy. 12, Avon • (252) 995-5466

Hatteras Realty has three agents and covers residential and commercial lots and homes on Hatteras Island. They offer property management services.

Hudgins Real Estate

**U.S. Hwy. 158, MP 7, Kill Devil Hills
• (252) 441-7887**

Hudgins specializes in property throughout Dare County including commercial and residential possibilities and lots of condominiums. Three agents work at Hudgins.

Island Realty of Nags Head

**U.S. Hwy. 158, MP 16½ at Whalebone Junction, Nags Head • (252) 441-1314,
(800) 448-0277**

Island Realty, owned by Gail and Jim Jackson, opened in September 1997. Six licensed agents work for the new realty, selling property along the Outer Banks and in Tyrrell County. Island Realty is promoting The Peninsula on Roanoke Island, which is listed in this chapter.

Karichele Realty

**66 Sunset Blvd., Corolla
• (252) 453-2377
TimBuck II, N.C. Hwy. 12, Corolla
• (252) 453-4400**

Karichele covers the entire Outer Banks for sales and the northern beaches including Duck and Corolla for rentals. The company manages more than 30 properties in the Penny's Hill/Carova Beach area.

Kitty Dunes Realty

**U.S. Hwy. 158, MP 5, Kitty Hawk
• (252) 261-2173
Corolla Light Village Shops, Unit 1110,
Corolla • (252) 453-DUNE**

Kitty Dunes represents Corolla to South Nags Head. This company also owns Colington Realty. Residents of Canada should contact the Canadian representative at (514) 252-9566. For a free vacation guide call (800) 511-DUNE.

Kitty Hawk Land Company

**U.S. Hwy. 158, Kitty Hawk
• (252) 261-2131, (800) 488-0738**

Kitty Hawk Land Company has been in the real estate business for more than 50 years. Lee Whitley is the company's sole agent. KHL is credited with developing Southern Shores, Spindrift on the Currituck Outer Banks, WatersEdge on Colington Island, Seapines and Oceancrest in Duck and The Currituck Club in Corolla. They offer properties within these developments as well as select listings of outside properties on the Outer Banks.

Joe Lamb Jr. & Associates, Realtors
U.S. Hwy. 158, MP 2, Kitty Hawk
• **(252) 261-4444, (800) 552-6257**

Joe Lamb represents properties from northern Duck to South Nags Head. The staff is experienced in land use and coastal development regulations.

Frank Mangum Realty
U.S. Hwy. 158, MP 10½, Nags Head
• **(252) 441-3600, (800) 279-5552**

Frank Mangum handles sales covering the entire Outer Banks.

Midgett Realty
N.C. Hwy 12, Rodanthe • (252) 987-2350
N.C. Hwy. 12, Avon • (252) 995-5333
N.C. Hwy. 12, Hatteras Village
• **(252) 986-2841, (800) 527-2903**

Midgett Realty represents properties on the southern end of the Outer Banks.

Sharon Miller Realty
N.C. Hwy. 12, Ocracoke Village
• **(252) 928-5711, (252) 928-5731**

Sharon Miller Realty represents Ocracoke Island properties.

Nags Head Realty
U.S. Hwy. 158, MP 10½, Nags Head
• **(252) 441-4311, (800) 222-1531**

Nags Head Realty represents property from Corolla to Oregon Inlet.

Ocean Breeze Realty
100 E. Third St., Kill Devil Hills
• **(252) 480-0093**

Ocean Breeze is a newly formed business, but owner Brantley Twiford has been in real estate on the Outer Banks for 15 years. As the sole agent at Ocean Breeze, he specializes in both rental and sales of improved and unimproved property from Southern Shores to Nags Head.

Ocracoke Island Realty
N.C. Hwy. 12, Ocracoke
• **(252) 928-6261, (252) 928-7411**

Ocracoke Island Realty represents Ocracoke Island properties.

Outer Banks Ltd.
U.S. Hwy. 158, MP 10, Nags Head
• **(252) 441-7156**

Outer Banks Ltd. represents property from Corolla to Nags Head and Roanoke Island.

Outer Banks Resort Rentals
Pirates Quay, U.S. Hwy. 158, MP 11,
Nags Head • (252) 441-2134

Marvin Beard represents the sales and rentals of timeshares only; he offers options from Duck to South Nags Head as well as a few in Hatteras.

Jim Perry & Company
Executive Center, U.S. Hwy. 158, MP 5½,
Kill Devil Hills • (252) 441-3051,
(800) 222-6135

Jim Perry represents properties in all areas of the Outer Banks.

Pirate's Cove
Manteo/Nags Head Cswy.
• **(252) 473-1451, (800) 762-0245**

The realty arm of Pirate's Cove Yacht Club represents properties in this boating paradise. The development offers condominium owners convenient on-site docking and a variety of festive events within an active community.

RE/MAX Ocean Realty
U.S. Hwy. 158, MP 6½, Kill Devil Hills
• **(252) 441-2450**

RE/MAX represents properties from Corolla to Hatteras Village. This company is planning a new north beach office for 1999.

INSIDERS' TIP

When purchasing a lot, make sure the sale is contingent on a health department evaluation of a septic system.

Riggs Realty
Austin Bldg., N.C. Hwy. 12, Corolla
• (252) 453-3111
Riggs specializes in northern beaches properties.

Sea Oats Realty
Pirates Quay, U.S. Hwy. 158, MP 11½,
Nags Head • (252) 480-2325
Sea Oats handles real estate sales from Duck to South Nags Head.

Southern Shores Realty
N.C. Hwy. 12, Southern Shores
• (252) 261-2000, (800) 334-1000
Southern Shores Realty represents properties from Corolla to Nags Head.

Sun Realty
U.S. Hwy. 158, MP 9, Kill Devil Hills
• (252) 441-8011
N.C. Hwy. 12, Corolla • (252) 453-8811
N.C. Hwy. 12, Duck • (252) 261-4183
U.S. Hwy. 158, Kitty Hawk
• (252) 261-3892
N.C. Hwy. 12, Salvo • (252) 967-2755
N.C. Hwy. 12, Avon • (252) 995-5821
This realty represents properties anywhere on the Outer Banks.

Stan White Realty & Construction
U.S. Hwy. 158, MP 10½, Nags Head
• (252) 441-1515, (800) 338-3233
Stan White represents properties from Corolla to Hatteras Village.

Surf or Sound Realty
N.C. Hwy. 12, Rodanthe
• (252) 987-1444, (800) 237-1138
N.C. Hwy. 12, Avon • (252) 995-6052
Surf or Sound represents properties from Rodanthe to Hatteras Village. See our Weekly and Long-term Cottage Rentals chapter for more information.

Mercedes Tabano Realty
N.C. Hwy. 12, Rodanthe • (252) 987-2711
Mercedes Tabano represents properties on Hatteras Island.

Twiddy & Company Realty
1181 Duck Rd., Duck • (252) 261-8311
Ocean Tr. and Second St., Corolla
• (252) 453-3325
Twiddy represents properties from Corolla through Southern Shores.

The Outer Banks offer a little bit of everything for seniors looking to retire by the sea.

Retirement

If you love the beach, have a sense of adventure or just want to lead a quiet life scouting the shore for shells, the Outer Banks could be the retirement paradise you're looking for. Ninety miles of beach from Corolla to Ocracoke as well as Roanoke Island's Manteo and Wanchese offer a little bit of everything for seniors looking to retire by the sea.

Services for seniors are provided by two county facilities: the Thomas A. Baum Center in Kill Devil Hills and the Fessenden Center in Buxton. A Dare County senior or property owner 55 or older can receive and participate in a bevy of free services through these centers, from rides to medical facilities and hot lunches to trips to out-of-town cultural events and hot bridge games. (A stroll through either of these facilities will instantly prove that our retirement community is anything but retiring.) And homebound seniors never go hungry here thanks to our county and volunteer-based programs.

Though the Outer Banks doesn't have a county retirement housing community, we've shared some information in this chapter about federal-subsidized housing that may be helpful to people on a fixed income. If you are looking for property, check out our Real Estate chapter and read our Area Overviews chapter to get a feel for what each township or island community offers its residents. Options range from a seaside bungalow to a traditional three-bedroom home to a seaside mansion.

Read on for descriptions of these complexes and the services and programs they offer. Also, check out our Annual Events chapter for information on the Outer Banks Senior Games, held every April.

Senior Centers

Thomas A. Baum Center
300 Mustian St., Kill Devil Hills
• (252) 441-1181; (252) 995-4461, ext. 227 from Hatteras Island

The Thomas A. Baum Center is celebrating its 11th year in 1998, but it still sparkles like a brand-new penny. The center is named after a Dare County native who was a pioneer in ferry transportation. His daughter, Diane Baum St. Clair, arranged for the town of Kill Devil Hills to purchase the land, known locally as the Baum Tract, on very generous terms. Dare County bought a section of the land, which today is home to the senior center, a water plant, library, two public schools, the local chamber of commerce and the town's administration and water departments.

The senior center was built and then dedicated on December 7, 1987, and cost more than $600,000 to construct. The more-than-10,000-square-foot building houses the senior center and the county's older adult services. A handful of paid staff and countless senior volunteers operate the center, which is the hub for senior activity north of Hatteras Island. Dare County residents or property owners who are 55 or older, may use the center for free; if you are younger than 55 but your spouse meets the age requirement, you also may use the center.

The facility includes a multipurpose room with a stage where the center's drama group, Center Front, performs various productions annually. Past plays include *Li'l Abner*, which sold out all four evenings. The Outer Banks Senior Chorus, which performs two concerts per year, also uses this room for practice sessions. The Baum Center is home to the Wright Tappers, a seniors tap dancing group, and the Dare Devils, the official cheerleaders for the Outer Banks Senior Games. Line- and square-dance groups round out the foot-tapping activities. And going hand in hand with it's name, the multipurpose room does double-duty for aerobic classes three days a week.

A full-service kitchen is used for social functions and fund-raisers such as the popular annual eat-in or take-out spaghetti supper. The center does not cook daily lunches on the premises.

Seniors can head to the lounge to chat, relax or read a book borrowed from the center's honor-system library that is filled with a variety of paperbacks. Adjacent to the lounge is the game room where seniors play bridge weekly, work puzzles, play cribbage or canasta or sit in on seminars in history, tax aid or health education, just to name a few. The center also hosts support group meetings for such organizations as the Outer Banks Cancer Support Group and the Amputee Coalition of Coastal Carolina. Twice a month seniors gather at the center for an afternoon movie and popcorn.

Outdoor lovers move to the deck to eat lunch or watch for resident deer and foxes. Five picnic tables and various chairs encourage relaxation or conversation. The nearby yard is host to a football target to test your throwing accuracy, horseshoe pits and spincasting targets. Outer Banks Senior Games contenders practice discus and shot put as well as archery using bales of hay for targets. Sore muscles are soothed in the health suite complete with a whirlpool and first-come-first-serve lockers. All seniors have to do is bring a towel and let someone at the front desk know they're using the whirlpool.

The recreation room comes alive as athletes play a leisurely game of billiards, table tennis or shuffleboard. There's plenty of elbow room in this spacious area complete with three pool tables, two Ping-Pong tables and several huge, floor-painted shuffled board games. Coffee is available in the kitchenette just off the recreation room. Cups are in the cabinet. Donations are welcome. Feel free to bring your lunch and store it in the refrigerator or heat it in the microwave.

Off the rec room is a craft room complete with two sinks, projector, storage space, seven tables with four chairs each and a sewing machine. Check the center's newsletter, *Senior Soundings*, for special activities that take place in this room as well as craft courses. The newsletter comes out by the 15th of the month and is available at both county senior centers and the three public libraries.

The center has an information and referral room where you can sign up for programs with topics such as preparing healthy food, birds, growing perennials and acrylic painting. Some activities have a small supplies fee; scholarships are available. There's a wall of pamphlets that cover taxes, health and fire safety. County-wide information is available via the computerized Senior Connection information and referral system. Questions on Alzheimer's disease, in-home services, marriage licenses and the like can be answered by using this program that is manned by trained volunteers.

A small computer room is set up with a Packard Bell unit and a Canon copier. An exercise suite features a treadmill, rowing machine and four stationary bicycles, and a staff exercise specialist offers regular exercise programs.

Seniors also can take advantage of the center's 20-seat conference room complete with a telephone and white marker board. Community groups also use this space from time to time.

The senior center plays a vital role in pro-

---

www.insiders.com

See this and many other **Insiders' Guide®** destinations online — in their entirety.

Visit us today!

viding transportation for elderly handicapped and disabled Dare County residents. A paid staff member is on hand at the center to schedule free rides to doctors appointments and hospitals in Chesapeake and Norfolk, Virginia, as well as Greenville, North Carolina. The transportation volunteer needs 24-hour notice.

Rides also are available for shopping trips, getting to and from the center to attend activities and to lunch at the nutrition site at Mount Olivet United Methodist Church in Manteo. Lunch is served Monday through Friday. Seniors are asked to make a 75¢ donation, but it's not mandatory. Menu selections may include herb-baked chicken with a mixed vegetable and rice pilaf or spaghetti with a tossed salad. Two-percent milk and dessert top off the meal. The meals are prepared off the premises by Best Steaks of Elizabeth City. Twenty-six seniors may participate per day. A day's notice is all they need to make sure the food count is correct. If you can't make it to the luncheon, home delivery is available.

The Baum Center is open Monday through Friday from 8:30 AM until 5:30 PM and for special functions. Grandchildren are welcome at the center as long as they are accompanied and monitored by an adult. But members of the younger set must be at least 15 years old to play pool.

Fessenden Center
N.C. Hwy. 12, Buxton • (252) 995-3888

The Fessenden Center offers services and programs for county residents and property owners of all ages. Seniors must be 55 or older to participate in the older adult activities for free. However, the center schedules activities, such as aerobic classes, for adults of all ages for various fees. The 2-year-old building has a gym with a basketball court. The center operates as a senior center and a site for youth athletic activities. Open gym time is held from 3 to 5 PM Monday through Friday. Seniors enjoy basketball and volleyball at the center as well as fishing, believe it or not. Throw a line in the creek off the back deck — chances are you'll snag a puppy drum (small channel bass).

The full service kitchen/conference room is available for preparing meals. Every second and fourth Thursday of the month, seniors can attend a lunch there. The second Thursday lunch is prepared at the center by seniors; the fourth Thursday lunch is a covered-dish affair. Funds for the lunches are covered by Fesstivities, a volunteer senior group that raises money by running the center's concession stand at athletic functions. Seniors contribute a $1 donation if they are able. The kitchen/conference does double-duty as a county meeting facility.

Seniors at the Fessenden Center are luckier than their counterparts farther up the beach at the Baum Center. The Hatteras Islanders have an on-site pool. (Baum Center seniors must go off-site to swim.) The center also sports an activity room, sitting room and library. Seniors are invited to hone their skills at the outdoor tennis courts or play with grandchildren at the on-site playground. The soccer and baseball fields give them plenty of room to stretch or jog.

Adults can participate in classes such as step aerobics, toning and stretching, abdominal exercise, tae kwon do, tai chi, walking, basketball and dance. They can take Spanish or sign language classes, attend seminars, workshops and classes on fire safety, cardiac rehabilitation, credit fraud, nutrition, home decorating, quilting and painting or take cultural arts trips to shows and parks outside the area. Minimum fees are attached for supplies in the $5 to $10 range.

Transportation is available through the center's coordinator by calling the previously listed number. Shopping trips are scheduled for seniors and physically challenged adults who have transportation problems. Rides are available to medical appointments and out-of-town hospitals and doctors' offices in Norfolk and Chesapeake, Virginia, as well as Elizabeth City, Nags Head and Greenville, North Carolina.

The Fessenden Center is open Monday through Friday from 8:30 AM until 5:30 PM and weekends for youth and special activities.

Senior Services

SCORE
Outer Banks Chamber of Commerce, off Colington Rd., Kill Devil Hills
• (252) 441-8144

SCORE's retired executives offer free counseling on business matters such as putting together a marketing plan, starting a business, compiling financial statements, computerizing an office, obtaining small business loans and expanding business plans. Sessions are held every Tuesday from 11 AM to 2 PM at the Outer Banks Chamber of Commerce. If you can't attend these sessions, you can call the Chamber to schedule an appointment.

Helping Hand
Manteo Police Department, 109 Exeter St., Manteo • (252) 473-2069

Working from a list of voluntary participants, Manteo officers check on more than 70 elderly or disabled citizens twice a week in person or by phone to make sure they are healthy and that their needs are being met. The town list is divided among the officers, who prefer to go in person but will telephone from time to time. Participants include seniors, challenged individuals and persons who live alone. This program is particularly useful in a community like the Outer Banks where storms occasionally threaten the coast and require residents to evacuate. The officers are in such close contact with the community they are able to alert the homebound or needy individuals in the event of a weather emergency. If you're interested in being on the Helping Hands list, call the police department. Anyone there will be glad to assist you with more information. This is a free service.

Hatteras Island Adult Care
(252) 995-5208, (252) 995-4890

In its 11th year, this meals-on-wheels program offers lunch to needy seniors and disabled individuals on Hatteras Island. The year-round program serves meals Monday through Friday, including holidays. Meals are prepared by several local restaurants and markets.

Little Grove United Methodist Church Monthly Luncheon
N.C. Hwy. 12, Frisco • (252) 986-2149

Little Grove usually has a luncheon the third Thursday of the month for anyone interested in food and fellowship. The luncheon includes singing and storytelling that begins at 11:30 AM. You need to call the above number on the Monday before the third Thursday of the month to reserve your space. The luncheon costs $2.

Senior Housing

Bay Tree Apartments
10 Bay Tree Dr., Manteo
• (252) 473-5332

Bay Tree is a subsidized housing community designed for seniors and handicapped citizens 62 or older. The fee to live here is figured according to annual income. Once the rent is established, an additional utility payment is deducted from the fee. Primarily Social Security-dependant citizens occupy these apartments.

Each of Bay Tree's 40 units can accommodate one or two individuals. Small pets are welcome. Each living space has one bedroom and one bathroom with a kitchen/dining area and a storage room. The floor space measures 580 square feet and includes wall-to-wall carpet, range and refrigerator, heat pump and air conditioning. Each home has two emergency chords set up so seniors can alert neighbors if they have an emergency. A bell rings and a light flashes outside the home. Four Bay Tree units are fully handicapped-accessible. Doorways are wide, counters are low, and the units feature walk-in showers and ramps. A separate laundry facility is available with two washers and two dryers.

Bay Tree has a community room with a kitchen that can be used for fellowship or other activities. The community also has a resident manager. The complex has sidewalks, a small front yard that can be cultivated by the resident and a few benches scattered among the units. The complex is minutes from a grocery store, two pharmacies, restaurants and a video and camera store as well as a commercial laundry, dry cleaners, movie theater and various gift shops. Transportation is available to the Mount Olivet nutrition site by calling the Thomas A. Baum Center phone number. This housing community operates under the United States Department of Agriculture's HUD program. If seniors don't qualify for Bay Tree housing, they can ask the resident manager about other options at Harbourtowne Apartments next door. Income can be higher and the age restrictions do not apply in order to rent here.

Information and Help Lines

American Cancer Society, (252) 261-4686

Dare County Department of Social Services (Independent Living Information/ Medicaid), (252) 473-1471

Dare Voluntary Action Center, (252) 480-0500

Food Stamps, (252) 473-5857

Meal Delivery, Hatteras Island, (252) 995-5208, (252) 995-4890

Medicare — U.S. Department of Social Security, Elizabeth City, (252) 338-1155

Mount Olivet Congregate Nutritional Site, (252) 473-2089

Transportation and Meal Delivery, Northern Beaches and Roanoke Island (252) 441-1181

Transportation, Hatteras Island, (252) 995-3888

Senior Connection, (information and referral), (252) 480-1100

Even in a real-life paradise, accidents happen, and illnesses crop up when you least expect them.

Healthcare

We call the Outer Banks a paradise because there are few accessible places left in the world where the beaches are so beautiful and the air so clean. Unfortunately, even in a real-life paradise, accidents happen, and illnesses crop up when you least expect them. Even though we are a vacation resort environment, and we have no hospital, healthcare professionals here are fully prepared to assist visitors with anything from a scraped knee to a major medical challenge. Note that when necessary, emergencies are flown out to nearby North Carolina and Virginia hospitals. (See our Dare Medflight listing below.)

A growing number of alternative medical services are also available. Massage, chiropractic and acupressure therapies, nutritional counseling, stress management and fitness training are now common on the Outer Banks. Our medical community expands every year, so here's some updated information we hope will make your stay on the Outer Banks a safe and smooth one.

Medical Centers and Clinics

Chesapeake Medical Specialists
The Marketplace, U.S. Hwy. 158, MP 1, Southern Shores • (252) 261-5800

Physician specialists form the framework for this affiliate of Virginia's Chesapeake General Hospital. Services include urology, endocrinology, audiology, pediatrics, rheumatology, dermatology, allergy care and ear, nose and throat care. Minor office surgery is performed on the premises, and surgeons specializing in colon/rectal, plastic, vascular and general surgery see patients at this complex. This is not an emergency-care facility. No referrals are necessary. Call for insurance information. The facility serves patients by appointment Monday through Friday from 9 AM to 5 PM and is open year round.

Regional Medical Center
U.S. Hwy. 158, MP 1½, Kitty Hawk • (252) 261-9000

The communities of the Outer Banks rely on this medical center for convenient, high-quality healthcare. The facility offers the widest range of services on the Outer Banks and strives to provide quick and easy access to the appropriate diagnostic and healthcare departments for those in need. Preventive and educational programs are also offered here. MRI and CT scans are provided on-site.

Beach Medical Care and The Surgery Center (see subsequent listings) are in the Regional Medical complex, along with a rotation of about three dozen medical specialists. This group provides care for a wide range of needs. A directory of physicians and specialties can be obtained by calling (252) 261-9000. A diagnostic laboratory is on-site, and blood tests are handled quickly for in-house diagnosis. Outer Banks Radiology, (252) 261-4311, provides routine as well as diagnostic services such as mammograms, ultrasounds and fluoroscopy.

Beach Medical Care
Regional Medical Center, U.S. Hwy. 158, MP 1½, Kitty Hawk • (252) 261-9000

This center provides 24-hour urgent care and family medicine for both scheduled and walk-in patients seven days a week.

The Surgery Center
Regional Medical Center, U.S. Hwy. 158, MP 1½, Kitty Hawk • (252) 261-9009

This is an outpatient surgery center. Procedures such as breast biopsy, hernia repair, laparoscopy, tonsillectomy, adenoidectomy, oral surgery, cosmetic plastic surgery and tendon repair are performed here.

Virginia Dare Women's Center
U.S. Hwy. 158, MP 10½, Nags Head
• (252) 441-2144

Appointments are available for female-related medical needs. Patty Johnson is the center's certified nurse-midwife and family nurse practitioner. Baby and youth care and pap smears are offered along with generalized care. The center is open Monday, Tuesday and Thursday from 9 AM to 1 PM and from 2 to 5 PM.

www.insiders.com

See this and many other **Insiders' Guide®** destinations online — in their entirety.

Visit us today!

Health East Family Care of the Outer Banks
U.S. Hwy. 158, MP 11, Nags Head
• (252) 441-3177

Dr. Charles Davidson, Dr. Mitchell Jenkins and physician assistant Trudy Gardner provide general medical care Monday through Friday from 8 AM to 5 PM. X-ray services are available. Appointments can be made during office hours. Walk-in service was expected to be available by spring 1998.

Outer Banks Medical Center
425 W. Health Center Dr., Nags Head
• (252) 441-7111

To find this healthcare center turn off U.S. Highway 158 at Milepost 11 onto W. Barnes Street by the Ace Hardware, then drive up the hill to the medical center. Chesapeake General Hospital manages this 24-hour medical facility that provides emergency, urgent and family medical care. Physicians are available around the clock, and the medical team is prepared to provide basic trauma, advanced cardiac and pediatric life support as well as preparation for transport to a hospital. X-ray and lab facilities are on the premises. Walk-ins are welcome, and appointments for family medical care are accepted. Mammography services are available by appointment at the Outer Banks Center for Women, (252) 449-4141.

Manteo Family Clinic
U.S. Hwy. 64, Manteo • (252) 473-2500

Dr. Johnny Farrow provides complete family medical care at this office. X-ray services are available, and some lab work is done on the premises. Call for an appointment. The center's general hours are 8:30 AM to 5 PM Monday, Tuesday, Thursday and Friday and 8:30 AM to 12:30 PM on Wednesday.

Dare Medical Associates
U.S. Hwy. 64, Manteo • (252) 473-3478

Dr. Walter Holton provides family service and acute care from this office. X-ray services are available. Hours are 8 AM to 5 PM Monday through Friday.

Hatteras Medical Center
N.C. Hwy. 12, Hatteras Village
• (252) 986-2756

Dr. Seaborn Blair III, Dr. J. Al Hodges Jr. and Carey Le Sieur, family nurse practitioner (FNP), help staff this board-certified family practice on the southern end of Hatteras Island. X-ray services are available. The facility maintains 24-hour emergency call coverage and office hours on weekdays from 8:30 AM to 5 PM. Saturday hours are 9 AM to 1 PM.

Buxton Medical Care
N.C. Hwy. 12, Buxton • (252) 995-4455

Dr. J. Al Hodges and Carey Le Sieur, FNP, offer comprehensive family medical care and operate a 24-hour emergency referral service. The center's hours are Monday, Wednesday and Friday from 1:30 to 5:30 PM.

Ocracoke Health Center
N.C. Hwy. 12, Ocracoke Island
• (252) 928-1511

James Seal, PA-C, provides general medical care for all ages in this small island clinic, which is just past the firehouse. Off-season

---

INSIDERS' TIP

Read our tips in the Fishing chapter to avoid being punctured with hooks. If it happens, don't panic. Outer Banks medical professionals have plenty of experience in removing them.

FACT:

6 children are reported abused or neglected in America every minute!

If you or someone you know has been a victim of a sexual assault, call Hotline at **473-3366**. We provide services to victims and to their families and friends: Medical Center and Court Advocacy/Information, Referral and Counseling/Education and prevention programs available upon request.

All services are free and confidential.

"Against her will is against the law."

hotline

hours are Monday, Tuesday, Wednesday and Friday from 8:30 AM to noon and 1 to 5 PM, and on Thursday from 8:30 AM until noon. Call for summer hours. For emergencies on Ocracoke, call the rescue squad at 911.

Emergency Helicopter Transport

Dare Medflight
Emergency 911
This service is run by the Dare County Emergency Medical Service. It offers advanced life support air ambulance service for flying major trauma and emergency cases to Albemarle Hospital in Elizabeth City; Chesa-

peake General Hospital in Chesapeake, Virginia; Norfolk General Hospital in Norfolk; and Virginia Beach General Hospital in Virginia Beach. The helicopter flies from Outer Banks clinics or from the trauma scene. There is no charge for this service.

Alternative Healthcare

Chiropractic Care

Wellness Center of the Outer Banks
The Marketplace, U.S. Hwy. 158, MP 1, Southern Shores • (252) 261-5424
Daniel Goldberg, DC, offers a full range of

chiropractic services and nutrition management. The office is in The Marketplace shopping center. Office hours are Monday, Wednesday and Friday, 8:30 AM to noon and 3 PM to 6 PM.; Tuesdays and Thursdays, 3 PM to 6 PM.

Dare Chiropractic
U.S. Hwy. 158, MP 5, Kitty Hawk
• (252) 261-8885

Burt Rubin, DC, and Allan Kroland, DC, have the largest full-service chiropractic clinic on the beach. Nutritional counseling and stress management support are available. Call for an appointment.

Outer Banks Chiropractic Clinic
U.S. Hwy. 158, MP 10, Nags Head
• (252) 441-1585

Craig Gibson, DC, offers all chiropractic services. Office hours are Monday, Wednesday and Friday from 8 AM until noon and from 2 to 6 PM. On Tuesdays and Thursdays office hours are from 2 to 6 PM, on Saturday from 9 AM until noon.

Massage Therapy

Massage therapy is available on the Outer Banks in a variety of forms. Swedish massage, shiatsu and reflexology are just a few of the selections. A conference with the masseuse will help clarify what's offered and what your needs are. Folks use these services to help recover from physical trauma or simply to relax. We've listed a smattering of services available. Check the local phone book for a complete list.

Dianna Carter, CMT
208 W. Ocean Acres Dr., Nags Head
• (252) 441-0698

Swedish and therapeutic massage, shiatsu, reflexology and neuromuscular trigger point therapy are offered here. Herbal wraps and body scrubs are also offered. Carter

also has locations in Kitty Hawk and Corolla. Call the Nags Head number for information on services at all three sites and to make an appointment.

Healing Hands Massage Therapy
108 E. Fresh Pond Rd., Kill Devil Hills
• (252) 480-0524

Martha E. David, CMT, offers stress and pain relief and injury rehabilitation through massage. Services are offered Tuesday through Saturday, 10 AM to 6 PM.

Dhanyo Merillat-Bowers, CMT
N.C. Hwy. 12, Buxton • (252) 995-4067

Dhanyo Merillat-Bowers' massage techniques center around neuromuscular work, deep tissue massage, relief from pain and injury and relaxation and stress reduction. Merillat-Bowers is nationally certified in therapeutic massage and body work and is a member of the American Massage Therapy Association. Call for an appointment.

Related Services

Ask-A-Nurse
(800) 832-8836

This number, a free service provided by Albemarle Hospital, gives you access to 24-hour phone consultations with specially trained nurses. A comforting and knowledgeable staff helps direct callers to the appropriate facility, agency or specialist that may best serve their needs.

Outer Banks Hotline
U.S. Hwy. 64, Manteo • (252) 473-3366

Hotline is a 24-hour crisis counseling service that also provides shelter to victims of abuse. This agency operates thrift shops on U.S. 64 in Manteo and at MP 8 on U.S. 158 in Kill Devil Hills. Hotline conducts regular public-awareness seminars and trainings. For crisis counseling, call the number listed.

INSIDERS' TIP

Expect to wait during the height of the season for non-emergency walk-in medical care. Bring something to read and coloring books for the kids.

Dare Home Health & Hospice
106 Sir Walter Raleigh St., Manteo
• **(252) 473-5828**

DCHH offers skilled nursing, physical and occupational therapy and home health aid. This group is Medicare-certified and accredited by the Accreditation Commission for Home Care. The services are available for Dare County citizens who are homebound. Fees are set on a sliding scale depending on income.

Helpful Phone Numbers

AIDS Hotline:
(800) 342-AIDS

Al-Anon/Al-Ateen:
(252) 441-5963
(252) 441-3890
(252) 441-4262

Alcoholics Anonymous:
(252) 261-1681, Kitty Hawk
(252) 480-3837, Kill Devil Hills
(252) 995-4240, Hatteras Island

Albemarle Mental Health Center:
(252) 473-1135, Manteo
(252) 441-9400, Nags Head
(252) 995-4951, Avon

Ask-A-Nurse:
(800) 832-8836

Dare County Health Department:
(252) 473-1101 ext. 220
(252) 995-4404, Buxton

Dare Home Health and Hospice:
(252) 473-5828

Dare County Social Services:
(252) 473-1471

Dare County Older Adult Services:
(252) 441-1181

Health Department Clinic:
(252) 473-1101 ext. 136

HIV Support Group:
(252) 473-5121

Hotline Crisis Intervention:
(252) 473-3366

Mental Health Services
(after hours):
(252) 261-1490, north of Oregon Inlet
(252) 995-4010, Hatteras Island

Narcotics Anonymous:
(252) 261-1681
(888) 332-6362

N.C. Community Child Abuse Educator:
(800) 982-4041

Outer Banks Crisis Pregnancy
(pro-life counseling):
(252) 480-4646

Poison Control Center:
(800) 848-6946

More than 4,000 students from Corolla to Hatteras Island attend one of the nine schools in Dare County.

Education and Child Care

Education on the Outer Banks may have been one of the biggest benefactors of tourism. As property, occupancy and meal tax revenues poured into county coffers at an unprecedented rate in the 1980s, governments found the funds to meet the demands of a rapidly growing population. But now that growth has leveled somewhat, schools are struggling for more funds. In 1998 the Dare County Board of Education purchased land on Hatteras Island and in Kill Devil Hills with state grant funds. With all schools at or over capacity — about 25 students per teacher — more classroom space is needed. The goal is to build a new elementary school in Buxton, and a new high school near the First Flight schools in Kill Devil Hills.

For children who are not school-age or who need care after school, Outer Banks parents depend on a patchwork of day-care providers ranging from grandparents, teenagers and the neighborhood retiree who care for one or several children in the home; to licensed home providers who care for a number of children in their homes; to after-school care service at their child's school; to day-care centers that watch dozens of children in a more controlled and regulated setting. We could not provide listings for grandparents, teenagers and neighborhood retirees here, but we have provided information about area preschools, day-care facilities and babysitting services.

Education

Public Schools

Education has evolved a lot since the days when some Outer Banks kids paddled in their boats to the one-room schoolhouse. Today, more than 4,000 elementary and secondary students from Corolla to Hatteras Island attend one of the nine schools in Dare County. However, the area does have some rather unusual situations. An agreement formalized about 10 years ago requires Dare County to transport students from the Currituck Outer Banks to its schools. There's no school in Corolla, so some kids are on the bus for several hours a day. And on tiny Ocracoke Island in Hyde County, about 80 children from kindergarten through 12th grade attend one school.

Despite the area's remoteness and distance from cultural and educational hubs, schools here have measured up exceedingly well. Dare County schools have consistently ranked in the top 5 on student achievement among school systems statewide. The district, one of the first to connect to the state's Information Highway in 1994, provides computers in every classroom, Internet access for students and a commitment to technological advancement. Cape Hatteras and Manteo high schools are linked through a computer network that allows each school to transmit and share information. Each school has an interactive room with audio and visual equipment. Students are encouraged to produce multimedia shows for their school projects in 8th grade, and graduating seniors are required to do a multimedia presentation as part of their final research project.

The Ocracoke School, built in 1931, was designated in 1996-97 as a School of Excellence, a new state honor awarded to schools where more than 90 percent of students are performing at or above their grade level. One of the smallest schools in the state, the school was also honored that year as an exemplary school (academic growth exceeded expectations by more than 10 percent). And in overall academic growth in one year, The Ocracoke School ranked second among all the schools in the state. Graduation requirements are more stringent, with more emphasis on math and science skills, than at most other schools statewide. Every year Math and Science Week and Arts Week are devoted to hands-on learning through the lessons and examples of guest scientists and artists. Each classroom is equipped with computers that are linked to the rest of the state through the North Carolina Information Highway.

Schools in the area typically open in late August and close in early June. All elementary schools have after-school day care available on-site until 6 PM and includes half-days. (See the Child Care section for more information.)

For more information about these nine Dare County schools, contact the Dare County Board of Education at (252) 473-1151.

Kitty Hawk Elementary (K-5), U.S. Hwy. 158, MP ½, Kitty Hawk, (252) 261-2313

First Flight Elementary School (K-5), Run Hill Rd. off Colington Rd., Kill Devil Hills, (252) 441-1111

First Flight Middle School (6-8), Run Hill Rd. off Colington Rd., Kill Devil Hills, (252) 441-8888

Manteo Elementary School (K-5), N.C. Hwy. 64/264, Manteo, (252) 473-2743

Manteo Middle School (6-8), N.C. Hwy. 64/264, Manteo, (252) 473-5549

Manteo High School (9-12), Wingina Ave., Manteo, (252) 473-5841

Dare County Alternative School (9-12), N.C. Hwy. 64/264, Manteo, (252) 473-3141

Cape Hatteras Elementary School (K-5), N.C. Hwy. 12 Buxton, (252) 995-5730

Cape Hatteras Secondary School (6-12), N.C. Hwy. 12 Buxton, (252) 995-5730

The Ocracoke School is part of the Hyde County school district. For further information about the school, call the Hyde County Board of Education at (252) 926-3251.

The Ocracoke School (K-12), 1 Schoolhouse Rd., Ocracoke, (252) 928-3251

Private Schools

The Wanchese Christian Academy
39 The Lane, Wanchese • (252) 473-5797

The oldest private school on the Outer Banks, this K-12 facility was founded in 1978 by members of the Wanchese Assembly of God church who wanted to be able to teach their children moral values and Bible studies. This Christian school, however, is open to members of any religion. About 75 students from Currituck to Avon attend. (Transportation is not provided.) The Wanchese Christian Academy meets North Carolina private-school requirements.

Higher Education

College of The Albemarle, Dare Campus
132 Russell Twiford Rd., Manteo • (252) 473-2264

The Manteo campus of Elizabeth City's College of The Albemarle is the only community college on the Outer Banks. The college is one of 59 members of the North Carolina System of Community Colleges. Certificate, diploma and associate's degree programs are offered in numerous areas, including air-conditioning, heating and refrigeration technology; practical nursing; cosmetology; real estate; paralegal technology; criminal justice; electronics; and computer engineering. Students at the Dare branch can also apply credits earned at COA toward degrees at other state colleges or universities. Day, evening and weekend classes are offered during the school year; some classes are also available in the summer. Federal financial aid and other student assistance is available.

The college's Small Business Center loans

books, videos, audio tapes and CD-ROM disks. A list of publications is available. Call (252) 335-0821, ext. 223 or 231. Noncredit continuing education courses are also offered through COA at various Outer Banks locations.

Child Care

North Carolina law mandates child/staff ratios at licensed day-care centers and home providers that are different for each age group and type of facility. The state also requires that all teachers meet certain criteria for health and continued education. Anyone who watches more than two children (who are not related to them) for more than four hours a day must be licensed. Home-care providers can care for a maximum of eight children with no more than five preschoolers in the group, including the provider's own kids. But if the provider has school-age children, they are not counted as one of the eight children. Regulators inspect facilities and teacher records on an annual basis. For information on ratios and license requirements, call the state Division of Child Development at (800) 859-0829.

Recently, some centers have stretched their hours to accommodate parents who work nights in one of the slew of restaurants across the barrier islands. Others have put out the welcome mat for tourists who need child-free time during their vacations. A running list of registered and licensed providers is available from the Dare County Department of Social Services. Contact the office at (252) 473-5857 to request the current list of day-care providers.

Dare County schools offer the After School Enrichment Program to serve working parents of K-5 students. Children are cared for in the same building where they attend school, but their after-hours time is spent in free play inside or out on the playground. Crafts and games are on hand for kids to play with one another and the staff. Help with homework is also available, and an optional homework period is set aside every day. Call the Dare County Board of Education, (252) 473-1151, for more information.

The North Carolina Cooperative Extension 4-H provides summer camp programs for elementary and middle school youth, rolling child care and supervised fun activities into one service. And 4-H also offers day care at the schools during spring and winter breaks. Contact the Cooperative Extension office in Manteo at (252) 473-1101, ext. 243.

Additional day-care options are also available through a Head Start program run by the Economic Improvement Council, (252) 473-5246.

Preschool/Day-Care Facilities

First Assembly of God Preschool and Daycare
812 Wingina Ave., Manteo
• (252) 473-5646
Founded as a "Christ-centered" facility, children here are given Bible lessons daily, but attendees do not have to be Christian. Children age 3 through kindergarten are taught preschool three times weekly, including phonics and numbers. The kids are also taken on regular field trips to educational attractions, such as the aquarium or the Norfolk Zoo. The school invites members of the community, such as firefighters or police officers, to give on-site presentations to the children.

The school is conducted Tuesday, Wednesday and Thursday from 8:30 AM to noon. Full-time day care, which includes preschool, is available. Sessions include lunch and two snacks daily. A transitional class for children not quite ready for kindergarten is also offered. The day care is state-certified. Hours are 7:30 AM to 6 PM Monday through Friday. Drop-off service is not available.

Heron Pond Montessori School
3910 Poor Ridge Rd., Kitty Hawk
• (252) 261-6077
Based on the philosophies of Italian physician/educator Maria Montessori, Heron Pond offers half-day programs for 3-to-4-year-olds and an extended day program and kindergarten for children age 4½ to 5. The school is housed in a homey building among trees, tucked at the end of a country road in historic Kitty Hawk Village. A big fenced-in playground is in a side yard adjacent to the school. Teachers Sallie Ackley and Dianna Liverman, both

mothers of teenaged boys, have extensive child-care and educational experience and are trained in the Montessori method. The Montessori spirit of education is rooted in the belief that children are naturally eager to learn, and all the teaching tools at Heron Pond are centered on encouragement of the child's ability to teach him or herself. The school follows the public school calender and is not open in the summer months.

Munchkin Academy
N.C. Hwy. 12, across from Cape Hatteras School, Buxton • (252) 995-6118

This state-certified facility offers parents preschool, prekindergarten, after-school care, full-time day care and drop-in babysitting service. The only A-licensed child-care facility on Hatteras Island, Munchkin Academy also offers 4-H summer camp programs for school-age youth. A homey center with an unusually large playground, the academy provides care for children ages birth through 12 years. All teachers are certified in first aid and CPR and have state child-care credentials. According to director Kyle Williams, the facility far exceeds state standards for teacher-child ratio. A registered nurse is also on-site. Preschool and preK is held Monday through Friday from 7:45 AM to 12:30 PM. Two-, three- and four-day schedules are also available. Call ahead to reserve a drop-in space. Munchkin Academy is open Monday through Friday year round from 7:45 AM to 5:15 PM.

Child-Care Centers and Babysitting Services

At Your Service
(252) 261-5286, (800) 259-0229

The oldest babysitting service on the Outer Banks, At Your Service offers bonded adult babysitters who drive themselves to your home. Sitters are screened thoroughly, and all references are checked. Owner Pamela Price, a state-certified teacher, attracts most of her business from referrals and repeat business from happy clients. At Your Service is the only business of its kind recommended by the Outer Banks Chamber of Commerce. Rates are based on the number of children and number of hours (there is a four-hour minimum). Parents must also pay the travel expenses of the sitter. The 11-year-old service was expanded in 1995 to also provide linen, maid, housekeeping, delivery and grocery shopping services. At Your Service is available year-round. Call for rates and off-season information.

(Also see the listing in the Weekly and Long-Term Cottage Rentals chapter.)

Better Beginnings, Inc.
108 W. Sibbern Dr., off U.S Hwy. 158, Kitty Hawk • (252) 261-2833

This child-care center has been in business on the Outer Banks for 16 years. State-licensed, Better Beginnings provides full-time or after-school care in a safe, educational environment for children ages 6 weeks to 12 years. Director Charlotte Walterhouse hires well-trained professionals who are dedicated to the development of children. The daily schedule is geared to provide structure but allows for flexibility, establishing a rhythm of active play between quiet periods. In addition to the regular curriculum, the center also has a music program, an after-school program, a preschool class and a full-time summer program for school-age children. Nutritional snacks and meals are provided. Call for a complete rate schedule. Better Beginnings is open 8 AM to 6 PM Monday through Friday year round.

INSIDERS' TIP

The North Carolina Sea Grant Extension Program, the aquatic equivalent of Cooperative Extension, offers classes on a broad range of water-related skills, especially for anglers. Most seminars are free and include instruction on crab shedding, shrimping and net making. The Nags Head office at Caribbean Corners is also a resource for environmental information about water. Call (252) 441-3663 for more information.

Ferris Wheel Day Care and Preschool

109 1st St., off U.S. Hwy. 158, Kill Devil Hills • (252) 441-3808

Ferris Wheel staff pride themselves on providing a warm, stable environment that encourages learning. Licensed by North Carolina, the center offers full-day child care for infants, toddlers and preschoolers and after-school care for school-age children. An early education program is held for toddlers and preschoolers. Field trips are also part of the curriculum here. Healthy snacks and lunches are provided, and part-time and drop-in rates are available. Ferris Wheel is open from 7:30 AM to 6 PM year round.

Rocker Room Child Care Center

U.S. Hwy. 158, MP 10½, Nags Head • (252) 480-0241

Family-oriented and state-licensed, Rocker Room provides full developmental play programs with inside and outside activities for infants through 5-year-olds. According to director Sallye Hardy, the facility meets the National Association for the Education of Young Children ratio standards, the highest in the country. Rocker Room's motto is "Care that works for working families," a philosophy that's reflected in the center's flexible approach to child care. For instance, rather than having set hours, the facility tries to work around the needs and schedules of its customers. In the summer the center is open seven days a week from 6:30 AM until midnight. Drop-ins are welcome year round, if there's room. Vacationers are provided with their own beeper, so the staff can find them if they're needed — a real worry reducer and relaxation enhancer.

In the slower season, Rocker Room is usually operating between 7 AM and 6 PM daily. Reservations for drop-ins must be made by noon the day before.

Sandcastle Child Care Center

117 W. Sea Chase Dr., The Village at Nags Head, Nags Head • (252) 480-3388

One of the newer licensed day-care centers on the barrier islands, Sandcastle caters to both residents and tourists. A large center with a capacity for 137 children, the center offers full-time, part-time and drop-in rates for children ages birth through 5 years. All employees are screened and certified in CPR and first aid. Hot meals and snacks are included for full-time attendees. Drop-in care requires 24-hour advance notice. Sandcastle Child Care Center is open daily from 7:30 AM to 5:45 PM year round. In the summer the facility is open until 11:15 PM on Monday and Wednesday through Saturday. Winter hours are extended until 10 PM on those same days.

Ocracoke Child Care, Inc.

Horse Pen Rd., Ocracoke • (252) 928-4131

The only licensed center on Ocracoke Island, this 5-year-old child-care facility moved to a new location in 1998. What's unique about Ocracoke Child Care is that it is owned by its members. For an annual fee, participants are entitled to attend membership meetings and receive the quarterly newsletter. The center, which has a capacity of 40 children, is overseen by a six-member Board of Directors that sets rules and policies. Children ages 6 weeks to 12 years are cared for by a fully trained staff who prefer to think of themselves as teachers rather than babysitters. The new facility has a special infant-toddler room and an age-3-and-older preschool room. Based on the motto "Peace begins in the playground," Ocracoke Child Care has structured playtime as well as indoor and outdoor play areas and revolves activities around a different theme each week. Tourists are welcome to come in the same day they need child care to fill out a form if there is room available. Immunization records are not necessary for out-of-towners. Ocracoke Child Care is open from 7:40 AM to 5:15 PM Monday through Friday year round.

The Outer Banks boasts of being the site from which the first wireless telegraph signal was sent by Reginald Fessenden in 1902.

Media

If you want to know what's happening on the Outer Banks, your options to find out are pretty basic. You can do like Insiders do and burn up the telephone wires or chat at the post office (we revel in word-of-mouth deliveries), or you can access a variety of sources: newspapers, magazines, radio stations, telephone information lines, Internet sites and, of course, the TV. This chapter highlights those sources.

To keep an eye on national and world news while vacationing here, you can pick up a copy of *The Virginian-Pilot*, *The Washington Post*, *The New York Times*, *The Wall Street Journal*, the *Richmond Times-Dispatch*, the *Raleigh News & Observer* and other major metro newspapers at Nags Head News, (252) 480-6397, at the Food Lion Shopping Center, U.S. 158, MP 10. Slightly smaller but still solid selections of daily papers can be found at the Stop 'n' Shop convenience market on N.C. 12 at MP 8½, Kill Devil Hills, (252) 441-6105, and in Duck at Wee Winks Market, 213 Duck Rd. (N.C. Hwy. 12), (252) 261-2937. Costs may be inflated for some papers as the Outer Banks is considered a remote distribution area.

Before we turn you on to what's available, we'd like to share a little bit of radio history. Despite being an Atlantic Ocean outpost of sorts, the Outer Banks boasts of being the site from which the first wireless telegraph signal was sent by Reginald Fessenden in 1902 (see our History chapter). While Guglielmo Marconi has been credited with developing wireless telegraphy, Fessenden was experimenting on the Outer Banks during the same time period with transmitting sound using an entirely different system that's credited as the true basis for radio broadcasting. Read our section in this chapter on radio stations to see how it's progressed on the Outer Banks since Fessenden's day. As you become acquainted with the news sources outlined in these pages, remember that you already hold in your hand the most comprehensive guide for this area: *The Insiders' Guide® to the Outer Banks*.

Newspapers

We have a variety of newspapers that range from a daily Virginia paper with a North Carolina section where Outer Banks news appears coupled with coastal Virginia news, to weekly, triweekly and quarterly periodicals with Outer Banks-only coverage. The writing styles vary in these publications, ranging from highly editorialized and a more laid-back approach to a tighter, stricter journalistic structure.

Some of the smaller papers take some ribbing from locals and visitors for their homespun style and occasional departure from standardized rules of grammar. If you can get beyond the frequent disregard of *The Associated Press Stylebook* rules, you'll find that the pages are loaded with community news — educational, political, environmental and civic happenings that you won't find anywhere else. It's important to note that the work of many past and present reporters and photographers, who since have moved on to bigger, daily venues, first appeared in the pages of these community publications before the *Virginian-Pilot* took a more aggressive role in covering Outer Banks news.

The Virginian-Pilot
Nags Head Bureau, U.S. Hwy. 158, MP 10, Nags Head • (252) 441-1620

This Norfolk, Virginia-based daily broadsheet combines "big-city paper" experience with local knowledge to cover national news and regional news from northeastern and coastal North Carolina and Virginia. *Pilot* circulation is 235,000 total, with about 15,000 of that number going to the Outer Banks and northeastern North Carolina.

A separate North Carolina section is published daily, with articles and photographs composed by an Outer Banks-based news staff, but this section also includes lots of coastal Virginia news due to our proximity to the state line and the small amount of hard news the Outer Banks generate. These writers/reporters/photographers produce well-written, well-researched stories with an emphasis on current and late-breaking news. Center stage in this section is a daily photo by staff photographer Drew Wilson that usually depicts Outer Banks scenes at their finest. The award-winning photojournalist wows us with unbelievable shots of wave-riding surfers, hurtling comets, lush flora or people pics from the high-climbing lineman to powerful politicos.

If you're looking for lighthearted community news such as wedding coverage, civic club updates, job promotions and social stuff, you'll want to pick up one of the weekly or triweekly publications listed subsequently in this chapter. *The Virginian-Pilot* is available at area newsstands and convenience stores for 35¢ Monday through Friday, 50¢ on Saturday paper and $1.25 for the Sunday edition. You can get it at your doorstep each morning by subscription.

The Coast, a free, weekly entertainment and news publication produced by *The Virginian-Pilot*, is available each weekend at grocery and general stores and other locations throughout the Outer Banks from March through December. It is published monthly in January and February. *The Coast* also is delivered as part of the Sunday edition of *The Virginian-Pilot* to North Carolina newsstands and subscribers.

It features regular columns on entertainment, art, real estate and fishing. The award-winning former managing editor of the *Pilot*'s Nags Head bureau, Ronald Speer, muses on things local in his "Song of a Sailor" column. If you want to boogie to the beat of the Outer Banks music scene, John Harper's "After Dark" column is a fine source for happenings of the rhythmic kind.

Cover stories range from profiles of natural habitats such as Jockey's Ridge and the Gulf Stream to lighthearted looks into ghostly legends and pirate haunts. They also publish lists where you can glean gallery, restaurant and nightclub information.

The Coastland Times
501 Budleigh St., Manteo
• **(252) 473-2105**
U.S. Hwy. 158, MP 7½, Kill Devil Hills
• **(252) 441-2223**

The Coastland Times, a local paper, is published on Sundays, Tuesdays and Thursdays. It's available at area newsstands and convenience stores for 50¢; mail delivery is available by calling the above numbers.

Reporters cover Dare, Hyde and Tyrrell counties. You'll find the most extensive local classifieds here including yard sale ads that mostly appear in Thursday's issue. Pick up this paper for wedding, birth, obituary, reunion, community and civic club information. They're famous for their "big fish," public school and other grip-and-grin photographs that give locals and visitors, young and old, a brief step into the limelight. They do offer hard news coverage, but the style is more casual than what's offered in *The Virginian-Pilot*.

www.insiders.com

See this and many other
Insiders' Guide® destinations
online — in their entirety.

Visit us today!

The Outer Banks Sentinel
Central Square, U.S. Hwy. 158, MP 11,
Nags Head • (252) 480-2234

The Outer Banks Sentinel is a weekly broadsheet paper owned by Sentinel Publishing that has been operating since March 1996. Weekly circulation is 10,000, covering news occurring from Corolla to Ocracoke and on Roanoke Island and the Dare County mainland. This industrious paper makes an effort to include everything from hard news to poetry.

The Sentinel provides features on area personalities, editorials and columns about the Outer Banks. Insiders laugh themselves silly while reading local humorist Jack Sandberg's satiric column "Uncle Jack," while others zone in on Ruth Ambrosius' Erma Bombeck-style column "Medium Low." Special calendars and listings include information on weather, fishing, tides, surf conditions, live music and community events.

The Sentinel is published every Thursday

and is sold for 25¢ at area newsstands and bookstores. Mail delivery is available.

Island Breeze
N.C. Hwy. 12 and Dunes Dr., Hatteras Village • (252) 986-2421

The Island Breeze, a Hatteras and Ocracoke tabloid, comes out monthly except during winter. This publication features a variety of articles on local personalities, businesses, the natural environment and community-related news. It is free and available at area shops and restaurants.

North Beach Sun
N.C. Hwy. 12 at Calvin St. and Airstrip Rd., MP 7, Kill Devil Hills • (252) 449-2222

Another newspaper with local appeal is the *North Beach Sun*, with a circulation of 120,000. This popular quarterly tabloid, which began in 1987, is filled with personal and local news from the Northern Outer Banks. Reporters and regular columnists step out in this paper sharing philosophical insights, dining experiences, retail, art and sports information presented in an informal style. The tab also features a separate real estate section. It's published quarterly just prior to Easter, Memorial Day, Labor Day and Thanksgiving and is distributed to post office boxholders, convenience stores, real estate offices and other businesses stretching from Carova to Kitty Hawk. The paper sponsors the annual North Beach Sun Trash Festival & Big Sweep the third Saturday of September (see our Annual Events chapter).

North Banks Beach Baby
U.S. Hwy. 158, MP 4, Kitty Hawk • (252) 255-BABY, (252) 261-2208

The *North Banks Beach Baby* is a modest tabloid published six times a year from May through September by Beach Baby Publishing, a division of Outer Banks Printing Company. It includes features on the local art scene

and Outer Banks history plus dining, fishing, shopping, sports, real estate and entertainment articles.

Magazines and Miscellaneous Publications

There are only a few magazines published on the Outer Banks, and these appeal mostly to mainstream tastes. They focus on either the specific — fishing — or the general — Outer Banks living. We include several free guides in this section that contain lots of restaurant and shopping coupons to help you stretch your vacation dollars, as well as a fun newsletter from our favorite bookstore.

Sportfishing Report
Central Square, U.S. 158, MP 11, Nags Head • (252) 480-3133

Sportfishing Report is the first sportfishing magazine on the Outer Banks. It published its first issue in the winter of 1991 and has gradually expanded from an Outer Banks-only magazine to include East Coast coverage. Readers of this bimonthly publication will find informative saltwater fishing tips, profiles and history that includes surf, sound and sea venues. Gorgeous color photography brings the fishing experience into your living room. The magazine is available at most local news and magazine stands, marinas and tackle shops for $2.95 per copy or by subscription for $14.95 per year.

Outer Banks Magazine
305 Essex Square, Sir Walter Raleigh St., Manteo • (252) 473-3590, (800) 526-7323

In its 16th year in 1998, this annual four-color feature magazine captures the culture, history and flavor of life on the Outer Banks. It recently changed hands and is no longer under the guidance of its creator and editor An-

---

INSIDERS' TIP

Outer Banks radio stations are good sources for up-to-date weather information. Call them to find out if the red flags are flying, which prevents ocean access.

gel Khoury — though she still contributes — but the contents are similar and the cover art and interior photography alone make it worth picking up. Past issues have featured a regular section on Outer Banks crafters that's fun and informative.

The magazine is published in June. Mail subscriptions are available. You can buy the publication on newsstands and at gift and specialty shops for $3.95 per issue.

Hatteras Monitor
18 Baccus Ct., Frisco • (252) 995-5378

The *Hatteras Monitor* is published 11 times a year, February through December, and is filled with historical stories and photographs, real estate planning, fishing reports, poetry, environmental news, a telephone guide, visitors' guide and map, community news and want ads for Hatteras and Ocracoke islands.

You can pick up a free copy at area shops and restaurants or order a subscription for $15 a year.

Outer Banks Visitors Guide
Caribbean Corners, Nags Head/Manteo Cswy., Nags Head • (252) 480-1768

The *Outer Banks Visitors Guide* is in its eighth year and has a circulation of 400,000. It is a free publication that comes out each May and is available at 350 sites from Corolla to Hatteras Island including real estate cottages, hotels, motels, visitor centers and retail businesses. This full-color magazine is loaded with coupons and features on Outer Banks living, history and recreation hotspots. Other highlights include a cable guide plus golf, nightlife, fishing, shopping, restaurant, gallery and real estate listings and information. Special listings include a Dare County Arts Council events calendar.

Sunny Day Guide
Virginia Beach, Va. • (757) 468-0606, (800) SUNNY-DA

Sunny Day is a handy, free guidebook that features articles on Outer Banks living plus area maps, dining and shopping guides and listings for a 24-hour info line that features business specials, sales, events and entertainment information. There are scads of money-saving coupons, an activities guide,

ferry schedules, maps, area services and colorful advertisements. *Sunny Day* is widely circulated and available at most Outer Banks businesses.

The Beach Book
Central Square, U.S. Hwy. 158, MP 11, Nags Head • (252) 480-2787, (800) 844-3128

Don't overlook our first "local" phone book for useful information. The owners of *The Beach Book*, Tom Chisholm and Jeff Graham, who are celebrating their sixth year in 1998, are dedicated to supporting the arts by sponsoring an annual cover art contest each fall featuring the work of a local artist with an accompanying biography within. The phone book includes a vacation guide and restaurant menu section, articles on fishing, art, the National Park Service, area overviews, golf, four-wheel driving, maps and a calendar of events. Business and residential phone numbers are listed including Coinjock, Mamie, Corolla, Duck, Kitty Hawk, Southern Shores, Kill Devil Hills, Nags Head, Manteo, Hatteras Island and Ocracoke Island.

Big Game Tournaments Magazine
Pirate's Cove Yacht Club, Nags Head/ Manteo Cswy., Manteo • (252) 473-3906, (800) 537-7245

This free magazine covers offshore Gulf Stream fishing from a tournament angle. It features Pirate's Cove Yacht Club-sponsored and North Carolina Governor's Cup tournament schedules, rules and guidelines and their histories. The tournaments are nonprofit, charitable functions. You can pick up a copy of *Big Game* at the Pirate's Cove Yacht Club's Ship's Store.

Manteo Booksellers Newsletter
105 Sir Walter Raleigh St., Manteo • (252) 473-1221

This newsletter is published between six and eight times a year and is available free at Manteo Booksellers, or you can subscribe for just $3.50 a year by calling the above number or writing P.O. Box 1520, Manteo, NC 27954. It is created by local writer Chris Kidder and features gift ideas, information on signed books that are available, book reviews, book club news, best buys for kids and a calendar of events, which includes book signings by local and national bestselling authors.

Television

Falcon Cable Television
N.C. Hwy. 12, MP 10½, Kill Devil Hills
• (252) 441-2881

This company supplies cable connection service for most of the Outer Banks, except Ocracoke Island. Most motels, hotels and cottages have cable connections. Some add special features such as HBO, Showtime, Cinemax, The Movie Channel or Disney Channel. Falcon also offers pay-per-view movies, sporting events and concerts. You need a Tocom converter from the cable office to access these special events. Channel 19 is the popular Prevue Channel, providing a continuous update on all programming carried on channels 2 through 61. Tune in to The Weather Channel on 25.

Beach Channel 12, produced by Falcon Television Advertising, is owned by FCT and presents in-depth information on restaurants, real estate and recreational opportunities on the Outer Banks in a fast-paced style.

Radio Stations

As we stated earlier, Outer Banks radio began when Fessenden sent the first transmissions between two 50-foot towers, one near Cape Hatteras and the other on Roanoke Island, in the early 1900s. Sixty-eight years later, the first Outer Banks radio station, WOBR-1530 AM, went on the air, joined three years later by WOBR-95.3 FM. We now have eight local stations featuring country, gospel, album and alternative rock, adult contemporary and oldies formats. One company owns four of these stations. Since

the FCC opened up new frequencies in the mid-'80s, radio stations have multiplied, creating a highly competitive field when it comes to maintaining listeners and achieving advertising dollars. That's a whole lot of radio in one little seasonal area.

Several local stations have informative talk shows once a week that share information on community events such as upcoming symphonies, art shows, entertainment, plays and more. We have one Christian station on the AM frequency, and two stations that religiously cover live local high school basketball. Formats often shift annually as stations try to capture listeners and as the music world evolves on a national level, but the primary listening target is the adult population ranging from age 25 to 54.

The Outer Banks is scheduled to have public radio within the next two years. A frequency has already been assigned, and the programming will be a mix of National Public Radio programming and original, local programming. Stay tuned!

WOBR-95.3 FM
2046 N.C. Hwy. 345, Wanchese
• (252) 473-3434, (252) 473-2444
request line

Broadcasting since 1973, the Outer Banks' first FM radio station, WOBR FM, The Wave, underwent a change in 1998. The format switched from heavy alternative rock to an eclectic album rock mix. Wave announcers — including Lee Lovingood in the morning, Doug Dino in the afternoon, Kari Delacruz in the evening and the notorious E.J. — are pretty passionate about new rock, but they sprinkle plenty of classics along the way that you might not hear on other rock stations. After 7 PM, the station flexes a little more alternative muscle.

Many of the DJs are musicians themselves, and they sometimes bring groups or solo artists into the studio to perform on weekends. The music is speckled with frequent weather reports, public service announcements and morning surf reports. They have a terrific Sunday morning jazz show. WOBR is owned by East Carolina Radio.

WOBR-1530 AM
2046 N.C. Hwy. 345, Wanchese
• (252) 473-9376

This was the first station on either band to hit the Outer Banks. Today, WOBR airs Christian music and programming plus USA Network news, weather, tide info and local obituaries.

WRSF-105.7 FM
U.S. Hwy. 158, MP 10½, Nags Head
• (252) 441-1024, (800) 553-4494

Dixie 105.7 plays "today's hottest country" and also airs local and world news and weather broadcasts. The contest line number is (800) 422-3494. Randy Gill is the program director.

WVOD-99.1 FM
Manteo waterfront, Queen Elizabeth Ave., Manteo • (252) 473-1993, (252) 473-5863 request line

This station, known as The Sound, broadcasts from a studio on the Manteo waterfront. Announcers play a varied format centering around adult rock. Tune in Sunday from 6 AM to 1 PM for a morning of classical music, then at 1:10 PM, listen to the lively Shelley Mills host "Dateline Carolina." Mills talks with a variety of guests concerning upcoming theater productions, art shows and a wide variety of community happenings. Groove to the blues with Margie the Blues Babe from 6 to 8 PM Sunday; from 8 until 10 PM its time for reggae.

The Sound features a Coastal Calender airing area events. They also supply fishing, surf, weather and hourly national news reports. Local news is broadcast a couple of times a day. This community-minded station also offers air time for public service announcements and personnel for charitable causes. The Sound is a great source for information on local school closings and road conditions. And listen carefully to the commercials: These guys employ the infamous Jack Stone, who's the hottest production

man around. Some Insiders tune in just to hear the ads. The Sound is owned by Orbit Communications.

WNHW-92.5 FM
Wrightsville Ave., Nags Head
• (252) 441-9292

Carolina 92.5 plays a variety of country music, including traditional and new artists. CNN and the North Carolina News Network air daily as do local news and fishing reports. The station reaches Dare, Currituck, Hyde and Tyrrell counties. Owner Ken Mann is a true country music fan who's also a musician. He's an Outer Banks native and is at home interviewing folks from all walks of life on his morning talk show, "The Morning Show," which airs from 6 to 9 AM daily. He simulcasts WNHW on another frequency, WYND 97.1, for Hatteras listeners, (252) 995-5055.

We always know what's going on in high school basketball, as Mann is forever faithful in broadcasting the games no matter how far away they are held. He also publishes the *Country Times*, a quarterly tabloid that can be picked up at The Coastland Times offices (see above addresses) or at local businesses. The tab features local and national country artist stories and other country features.

WCXL-104.1 FM
U.S. Hwy. 158, Ste. 104, MP 9½, Kill Devil Hills • (252) 480-0440

This 100,000-watt boomer of a station, Beach XL 104, covers the Outer Banks and Hampton Roads with an adult contemporary and beach music mix that makes for great listening during a day by the ocean. One minute you'll be grooving to a pop diva like Mariah Carey, Whitney Houston or Celine Dion, the next you'll be flashing back with the Beach Boys. WCXL also offers regional and national news and fishing reports.

WERX-102.5 FM
U.S. Hwy. 158, MP 10½, Nags Head
• (252) 441-1025, (888) 75-SHARK

If you like oldies, The Shark supplies plenty of tunes to accompany you on your trip down memory lane. Couple this with their "Charlie Byrd Beach Blast" on Sundays from 4 until 8 PM, and you'll never want to come back. Killer classics air right after Byrd's segment right on up until midnight. ABC, regional and local news air daily, and you can also get your daily dose of Paul Harvey here. Traffic updates and seasonal fishing reports round out their Good Times-Killer Oldies format. The Shark is owned by East Carolina Radio.

Beach Access
Bulletin Board Service
• **(252) 480-4636 modem information, (252) 441-1521 voice line**

Using this local computer bulletin board service, you can obtain beach information — including a local calendar of events — access local and international e-mail and the Internet, chat with locals and view beach and historic photography.

Scattered from Corolla
to Ocracoke and west to
Manns Harbor are
established houses of
worship representing
virtually every
belief system.

Worship

Over the years, people have migrated to the Outer Banks from the world over, bringing with them their personal convictions. Much has changed since Dare County hosted the first recorded Protestant religious ceremony in this hemisphere with the baptism of the Algonquian Native American, Manteo, on August 13, 1587, on Roanoke Island.

Written documentation of the existence of church buildings, however, did not come until the Civil War. Early churches included mostly Baptist, Methodist and Pentecostal. On the Outer Banks, church buildings acted as gathering places for civic functions since the area lacked secular meeting halls and auditoriums where large groups could congregate. Today, our church buildings range from simple wooden structures to more elaborate church complexes with meeting and day-care rooms, kitchens and even a gymnasium.

Some church buildings in the area have exquisite stained-glass windows, including Mount Olivet United Methodist Church in Manteo, which is especially beautiful when the sun pours into the chapel in the late afternoon. Also of note is the Duck United Methodist Church, which was designed by local architect Greg Frucci. Behind the altar is a huge bay window showing off a woody soundside landscape. Frucci had a hard time convincing the powers-that-be to forego conventional stained glass for the natural view. Why not have a perpetually changing view fashioned by the Maker himself, he argued. The church gave the go-ahead, and now worshipers admire the landscape year round.

When we first published *The Insiders' Guide® to North Carolina's Outer Banks* 19 years ago, our church listings were sparse. Today, though our land still appears simple and finite by most standards, especially when you view it from a tall dune or balcony, our people form a diverse community of worshippers whose church listings definitely fill more than one yellow page.

Scattered from Corolla to Ocracoke and west to Manns Harbor are established churches including: Baptist, Catholic, Christian Scientist, Assembly of God, Church of Christ, Mormon, Episcopal, Full Gospel, Jehovah's Witnesses, Lutheran, Methodist, Presbyterian, Unitarian Universalist and Community United. Still, there are some missing links. Folks who wish to attend Jewish synagogue services must drive to Norfolk or Virginia Beach as do those of the Greek Orthodox faith, among others further from the conventional track. Most Outer Banks churches have full time pastors with visiting preachers who fill in during the summer months when the congregation more than doubles. Hatteras Island has a host of United Methodist parishes and often one minister travels to two or more communities on Sunday to hold services.

The Outer Banks offers churches some special site options when the skies are clear. It's not unusual for a service to be held oceanfront and there have been occasions when the Lost Colony outdoor amphitheater has been used for this purpose. Easter sunrise services have awakened Jockey's Ridge year after year.

Some religious sects are branching out beyond Sunday services by offering Christian counseling, athletic opportunities, thrift stores and even entertainment. The Outer Banks Worship Center Ark in Nags Head has developed the Dream Center, 441-1155, which includes a coffee house and theatre called Cafe Agape. The theater and music performances run during the summer season and have mostly a Christian theme in a nonsmoking, nonalcoholic atmosphere. There's also a small Christian gift shop on the premises where you can purchase books, bibles, tapes and gifts. See our Shopping chapter for more Christian gift store information.

Since the number of worship centers now make such a lengthy list we advise you to pick up a current copy of the Sunday edition of *The Coastland Times* for a comprehensive list of churches and services available here.

Index of Advertisers

Index